Entrepreneurship, Collaboration, and Innovation in the Modern Business Era

Mehdi Khosrow-Pour, D.B.A.
Information Resources Management Association, USA

A volume in the Advances in Logistics,
Operations, and Management Science (ALOMS)
Book Series

IGI Global
DISSEMINATOR OF KNOWLEDGE

Published in the United States of America by
    IGI Global
    Business Science Reference (an imprint of IGI Global)
    701 E. Chocolate Avenue
    Hershey PA, USA 17033
    Tel: 717-533-8845
    Fax: 717-533-8661
    E-mail: cust@igi-global.com
    Web site: http://www.igi-global.com

Library of Congress Cataloging-in-Publication Data

Names: Khosrow-Pour, Mehdi, 1951- editor.
Title: Entrepreneurship, collaboration, and innovation in the modern business
  era / Mehdi Khosrow-Pour, editor.
Description: Hershey : Business Science Reference, [2018]
Identifiers: LCCN 2017033735I ISBN 9781522550143 (hardcover) I ISBN
  9781522550150 (ebook)
Subjects: LCSH: Electronic commerce. I Entrepreneurship. I Technological
  innovations--Economic aspects.
Classification: LCC HF5548.32 .E18666 2018 I DDC 658.8/72--dc23 LC record available at https://lccn.loc.
gov/2017033735

This book is published in the IGI Global book series Advances in Logistics, Operations, and Management Science (ALOMS) (ISSN: 2327-350X; eISSN: 2327-3518)

British Cataloguing in Publication Data
A Cataloguing in Publication record for this book is available from the British Library.

All work contributed to this book is new, previously-unpublished material. The views expressed in this book are those of the authors, but not necessarily of the publisher.

For electronic access to this publication, please contact: eresources@igi-global.com.

Advances in Logistics, Operations, and Management Science (ALOMS) Book Series

John Wang

Montclair State University, USA

ISSN:2327-350X
EISSN:2327-3518

MISSION

Operations research and management science continue to influence business processes, administration, and management information systems, particularly in covering the application methods for decision-making processes. New case studies and applications on management science, operations management, social sciences, and other behavioral sciences have been incorporated into business and organizations real-world objectives.

The **Advances in Logistics, Operations, and Management Science** (ALOMS) Book Series provides a collection of reference publications on the current trends, applications, theories, and practices in the management science field. Providing relevant and current research, this series and its individual publications would be useful for academics, researchers, scholars, and practitioners interested in improving decision making models and business functions.

COVERAGE

- Marketing engineering
- Services management
- Finance
- Networks
- Organizational behavior
- Risk Management
- Decision analysis and decision support
- Operations management
- Computing and information technologies
- Information management

IGI Global is currently accepting manuscripts for publication within this series. To submit a proposal for a volume in this series, please contact our Acquisition Editors at Acquisitions@igi-global.com or visit: http://www.igi-global.com/publish/.

Titles in this Series

For a list of additional titles in this series, please visit: www.igi-global.com/book-series

Handbook of Research on Promoting Business Process Improvement Through Inventory Control Techniques
Nita H. Shah (Gujarat University, India) and Mandeep Mittal (Amity School of Engineering and Technology, India)
Business Science Reference • copyright 2018 • 450pp • H/C (ISBN: 9781522532323) • US $345.00 (our price)

Supply Chain Management Strategies and Risk Assessment in Retail Environments
Akhilesh Kumar (Indian Institute of Technology Kharagpur, India) and Swapnil Saurav (JDA Software, India)
Business Science Reference • copyright 2018 • 351pp • H/C (ISBN: 9781522530565) • US $225.00 (our price)

Management Control Systems in Complex Settings Emerging Research and Opportunities
Filippo Zanin (University of Udine, Italy) Eugenio Comuzzi (University of Udine, Italy) and Antonio Costantini (University of Udine, Italy)
Business Science Reference • copyright 2018 • 190pp • H/C (ISBN: 9781522539872) • US $145.00 (our price)

Handbook of Research on Applied Optimization Methodologies in Manufacturing Systems
Ömer Faruk Yılmaz (Istanbul Technical University, Turkey & Yalova University, Turkey) and Süleyman Tüfekçí (University of Florida, USA)
Business Science Reference • copyright 2018 • 449pp • H/C (ISBN: 9781522529446) • US $275.00 (our price)

Grassroots Sustainability Innovations in Sports Management Emerging Research and Opportunities
Marco Tortora (University of Florence, Italy)
Business Science Reference • copyright 2018 • 130pp • H/C (ISBN: 9781522535003) • US $145.00 (our price)

Motivationally Intelligent Leadership Emerging Research and Opportunities
Michael A. Brown Sr. (Florida International University, USA)
Business Science Reference • copyright 2018 • 139pp • H/C (ISBN: 9781522537465) • US $155.00 (our price)

Novel Six Sigma Approaches to Risk Assessment and Management
Vojo Bubevski (Independent Researcher, UK)
Business Science Reference • copyright 2018 • 251pp • H/C (ISBN: 9781522527039) • US $200.00 (our price)

Enterprise Resiliency in the Continuum of Change Emerging Research and Opportunities
Raj Kumar Bhattarai (Tribhuvan University, Nepal)
Business Science Reference • copyright 2018 • 186pp • H/C (ISBN: 9781522526278) • US $150.00 (our price)

IGI Global
DISSEMINATOR of KNOWLEDGE

701 East Chocolate Avenue, Hershey, PA 17033, USA
Tel: 717-533-8845 x100 • Fax: 717-533-8661
E-Mail: cust@igi-global.com • www.igi-global.com

Table of Contents

Detailed Table of Contents

Chapter 1

 Martin Hannibal, University of Southern Denmark, Denmark
 Erik S. Rasmussen, University of Southern Denmark, Denmark

Through a longitudinal case study, this chapter explores the repercussions from introducing a mobile commerce platform as just another instrument in the marketing toolbox in a traditional sales-oriented firm. Findings suggest that the implementation of the m-platform in addition to its intended purpose—establish a marketing channel to key customers—spawns a digital business model that allows the company to change its relations to distributors, retailers, and customers enabling access to direct communication with end-users. However, the emerging new business model has the potential to change the organization essentially. The authors argue that although the emerging digital business model was indeed a success seen from a sales-, marketing-, innovative-, and relational perspective, it was perceived as a disaster from an organizational perspective. Consequently, top management abandoned the new digital platform. The chapter highlights the importance of not underestimating resistance in an organization when implementing a new marketing instrument such as m-commerce platforms.

Chapter 2

 Erastus Ndinguri, Framingham State University, USA
 Krisanna Machtmes, Ohio University, USA
 Ryan J. Machtmes, University of Minnesota, USA
 Jessica I. Hill, Holyoke Community College, USA

Technology disruption as well as changing economies have brought new opportunities and threats to the global entrepreneurial models and transformed societies all over the world. Entrepreneurship as a dynamic phenomenon is being analyzed as a tool for bearing the risk of market uncertainty, innovation, competition, and restructuring, and generating new knowledge. Despite continued analysis of the entrepreneur phenomena, how emerging technologies influence generation of business ideas and business formation is still unexplored. The aim of this chapter is to explore this relationship by analyzing women entrepreneurs. Specifically, the authors ask the question, Does the use and access of emerging technology trigger generation of business ideas which leads to business formation? Also, do demographic characteristics of entrepreneurs play a role in knowing and using emerging technology?

A five-factor e-shopping adoption model grounded upon TAM and an additional dimension of "trust" have been tested through confirmatory factor analysis (CFA). A structured instrument has been administered as part of survey to 600 eligible respondents comprising of online shoppers. A total of 539 shoppers spread across national zones, age, and gender groups constituted the final sample. Perceived usefulness (PU), perceived ease of use (PEOU), trust, intention to use (ITU), and attitude towards use (ATU) are reliable and valid factors predicting e-shopping adoption. PU and PEOU along with trust bear significant causation towards ATU. ATU serves as strong predictor of ITU, while PEOU determines PU as well. Further, ATU partially mediates PU and ITU relationship. This chapter highlights the applicability of modified TAM framework in predicting the inclination of emerging market consumers to embrace online shopping mediums scantly represented in extant literature.

In this chapter, the authors propose a secure payment framework in mobile ad hoc network for disaster areas. In order to enable transactions in a disaster area using existing payment systems, we need infrastructure to communicate such as wired networks and base stations for cellular networks which are damaged by natural disasters. The authors propose to use mobile agent technology and digital signature with message recovery (DSMR) mechanism based on ECDSA mechanism to enable transactions in a disaster area using ad hoc networks.

This chapter has built on research on today's modern organizations to lay the foundations for a comprehensive and systematic theorization of enterprise social systems. Theorizing virtuality marks a fundamental transformation in space-time parameters in communications. This is especially so in the context of rapid current advancements in IT such as cloud computing, as well as numerous other technological fronts. Current IT trends show that increased spatio-temporal plasticity heightens the effectiveness and the efficiency of modern enterprise social systems. In particular, subject-oriented asynchronous communications experience greater inferred plasticity and event-oriented synchronous communications experience greater referred plasticity. Finally, enterprise social systems vary in their degree of virtuality based on the perspective of the relevant stakeholder group considered.

The success of an organization's website is determined by the user's experience (UX). Yet many organizations continue to struggle to find tools to strategically analyze the UX's satisfaction with their websites and overall online presence. While there have been numerous studies offering "best practices" for website design, most of these are dated and do not take into consideration UX's experience and social media tools that come into the market. In this chapter, over 900 surveys were conducted on Inc. Magazine's Top 500 list (2011-13) of fastest growing companies in the United States. The analysis of these surveys resulted in a list of shared elements (best practices) common to the websites surveyed. Through the use of the analytic hierarchy process (AHP) multi-attribute decision model, the authors developed a measure by which companies can assess their customer's experience and compare it to these best practices model. This model provides an internally consistent, robust model against which to measure an organization's website based on the user's experience (UX).

This chapter explores how one company leveraged motorsports to build brand credibility, establish powerful marketing relationships, and connect with distinctly different consumer groups via virtual brand communities. Companies with strong virtual communities may benefit from the case study suggestions that are provided and discussed based on the theoretical perspective of brand equity. Marketing scholars and practitioners alike may find this case study of interest due to the growing desire by companies to develop strong bonds with consumers and their interest in effectively leveraging virtual brand communities as a tool. Several practice recommendations for leveraging virtual communities to enhance brand equity are discussed.

Presently, mobile health (m-health) services is a dynamic example of the integration of information technology into healthcare service provisions. However, citizens are often concerned about the use of this medium. Their apprehensions mostly encircle the quality of such services and extent of their own healthcare knowledge. This chapter thus aims to investigate adoption drivers of m-health services in Bangladesh by employing the UTAUT model. Results reveal service qualities like reliability, privacy, responsiveness, empathy, and information quality along with facilitating conditions, effort expectancy, performance expectancy, and social influence as significant drivers in m-health service adoption. In addition, this chapter suggests a new research agenda wherein perceived risks can act as an additional construct. Several factors that are known to exacerbate perceived risk were identified from literature and thereafter shown as part of a proposed framework. Implications for practice and research are also discussed for better planning and implementation of m-health services.

Collaboration has become a part of our everyday life – including our everyday work life. In addition, our work colleagues are often not in close physical proximity, making face-to-face interactions rare. As a result, we have come to rely on information and communication technologies to connect – in particular, social networking technologies or social media. While traditional technologies are well suited for sharing explicit knowledge that has been articulated and documented as text or other media, tacit knowledge is more challenging. Tacit knowledge is typically experiential knowledge that is very difficult to put into words or document in any way. This chapter investigates the benefits and barriers to using social media with respect to professional communication and collaboration. Recommendations are proposed to help select the best knowledge sharing medium for tacit knowledge.

This chapter investigates effects and issues associated with social media and recruitment and whether it is effective as an innovative e-entrepreneurship method of attracting the right employees for enterprises from a multi stakeholder perspective. Human resources management professionals have been using different methods of social media in their recruitment strategies with varying degrees of success. By examining social media and its effect, this can support the development of a more effective human resources recruitment strategy. Additionally, increased communication channels might enable the development of a more positive internal enterprise culture. The study was conducted using both primary and secondary data. Professionals, recruiters, and employees have been questioned on their views of Social Media from a personal and a professional perspective through a variety of methods including focus groups and questionnaires. This chapter provides a framework that can be used by enterprises in order to create their own social media recruitment cycle.

Recent trends in the world economy, including globalization and advances in ICTs and social media, have enabled networking as a business model. As a result, distributed teams have emerged. This chapter provides a basis for discussion and analysis of knowledge sharing between distributed team members working in a global context in different organizational and national cultures. Cultural dynamics influencing knowledge sharing in different cultural settings is examined by investigating the different cultural values and perceptions related to knowledge sharing. The aims are to make the human and cultural dynamics that bear on knowledge sharing and knowledge management success more explicit. The use of the cultural and organizational diversity evaluation (CODE) model is proposed for assessing the fit between national and organizational culture. The objective of using the CODE model is to raise awareness of the cultural values and attitudes in distributed teams and to help ensure an effective quality management process, and foster a knowledge sharing culture within distributed teams.

Chapter 12

Mukta Mani, Jaypee Institute of Information Technology, India

Entrepreneurship education programs are commonly offered in business schools, but recently, the educationists have started recognizing the need for such programs in engineering education. This chapter is targeted to empirically explore the suitability of entrepreneurship education in engineering curriculum from the perspective of students. The study attempts to unearth the levels of willingness of engineering students to take entrepreneurial activities and investigate the factors that motivate them and the factors that deter them to go for entrepreneurship. The analysis revealed that the students are highly interested in taking entrepreneurship as a career option because of some intrinsic motivating factors such as being their own boss, chasing their dreams. They consider decision-making skills, risk-taking capacity, creativity, communication skills, and ability to prepare business plan are the most important skills. However, lack of experience and funds deter them. The right kind of entrepreneurship education programs can promote more entrepreneurial activities among the engineering students.

Chapter 13

Despo Ktoridou, University of Nicosia, Cyprus
Epaminondas Epaminonda, University of Nicosia, Cyprus
Achilleas Karayiannis, Kes College, Cyprus

Technological, economic, and social developments represent dynamic changes for businesses across industries, creating opportunities for young entrepreneurs to build profitable companies. A key consideration relates to the need to recognize market opportunities and understand when and how to capitalize on them, whether starting a new type of business or growing on existing ideas; entrepreneurial thinking is a central attribute in cultivating an answer to this consideration. This chapter examines the impact of case-based learning introduced in a multidisciplinary undergraduate course, "Management of Innovation and Technology," at the University of Nicosia. A core element in this process are the students' and lecturers' experiences, benefits, and challenges of cultivating entrepreneurial thinking. The findings can be useful for academics teaching entrepreneurship-related topics and seeking ways to incorporate innovative approaches in their teaching and learning processes in order to motivate students towards the development of entrepreneurial thinking in their professional engagements.

This chapter further considers the tax aspect of the internet commerce transaction, which found that the Chinese government imposes a value-added tax at a rate of 17%. The system to impose value-added is extremely complicated. The first buyer pays tax. The tax is transferred to the second buyer, so on and so forth until the last buyer. It requires detailed records. It makes the tax administration highly burdensome. On the contrary, in the United States, the sales tax rate is only 7% and is imposed only on the final consumer. There are no sales between the first buyer and the last buyer. The taxing system is much simpler than its counterpart in China.

Understanding the importance of innovation and entrepreneurship to economic growth and stability, the European Union has implemented policies and programs to create a more uniform context for cross-border business activities within the EU. While initial efforts led to a more unified European region, they did not lead to a more uniform one. Over the past five years, dramatic changes in Europe resulting from the financial crisis, the Eurosceptic movement, and the Syrian refuge crisis have incented nations to create their own national innovation and entrepreneurship efforts. This chapter explores the results of those diverging national programs on entrepreneurial outcomes. Specifically, the research explores national landscapes created as a result of differing endowments, regulatory regimes, tax systems, and venture funding levels. Results indicate that differences in these factors create significantly different entrepreneurial outcomes as measured by patent applications and new business registrations.

Preface

The constant changing landscape of business practices in entrepreneurship in the modern digital era creates a need for knowledge resources that will empower professionals, academic researchers, managers, and organizations all over the world. *Entrepreneurship, Collaboration, and Innovation in the Modern Business Era* is a vital reference source that will meet these needs by exploring the latest coverage on all aspects of online business, e-commerce, and digital marketing, covering topics such as enterprise social systems, online recruitment, entrepreneurship education, and strategic innovation.

This reference source is organized into 15 chapters contributed by global experts, drawing on their experiences, observations, and research findings. A brief description of each of the chapters can be found in the following paragraphs.

In Chapter 1, the authors explore the effects of organizational ethos in business strategies and innovation. While emerging digital business models may appear as a success from multiple perspectives, a lack of acceptance from an organizational viewpoint can lead to a platform's removal. This chapter highlights the importance of not underestimating resistance in an organization when implementing a new marketing instrument such as m-commerce platforms.

In Chapter 2, the authors study the relationship between emerging technologies and the generation of business ideas and business formation by analyzing women entrepreneurs. They specifically focus on the use of and access to emerging technology to trigger the generation of ideas, resulting in business formation. The question of demographic characteristics of entrepreneurs in knowing and using technology is discussed.

In Chapter 3, the authors observe the use of Perceived Usefulness (PU), Perceived Ease of Use (PEOU), Trust, Intention to Use (ITU) and Attitude towards Use (ATU) as reliable and valid factors in predicting e-shopping adoption. The study highlights the applicability of modified TAM framework in predicting the inclination of emerging market consumers to embrace online shopping mediums scantly represented in extant literature.

In Chapter 4, the authors propose a secure payment framework in mobile ad hoc networks for disaster areas. By developing infrastructures to communicate, such as wired networks and base stations for cellular networks, areas damaged by natural disasters can allow transactions using existing payment systems.

In Chapter 5, the authors lay the foundation for a comprehensive and systematic theorization of Enterprise Social Systems. A focus on subject-oriented asynchronous communications show greater inferred plasticity, and event-oriented synchronous communications reveal greater referred plasticity. Additionally, the authors discuss how enterprise social systems vary in their degree of virtuality based on the perspective of the relevant stakeholder group considered.

In Chapter 6, the authors evaluate the success of an organization's website as determined by the User's Experience (UX). The analysis of surveys resulted in a list of shared elements, or best practices, common to the websites surveyed. Through the use of the Analytic Hierarchy Process (AHP) Multi-attribute Decision Model, the authors developed a measure by which companies can assess their Customer's Experience and compare it to the best practices model. The model provides an internally consistent, robust model against which to measure an organization's website based on the User's Experience (UX).

In Chapter 7, the authors present a case study that highlights the methods and theories towards building brand credibility in order to establish powerful marketing relationships and connect with distinctly different consumer groups via virtual brand communities. Several practice recommendations for leveraging virtual communities to enhance brand equity are discussed.

In Chapter 8, the authors investigate the adoption drivers of m-Health services in Bangladesh by employing the Unified Theory of Acceptance and Use of Technology (UTAUT) model. Results reveal service qualities like reliability, privacy, responsiveness, empathy and information quality along with facilitating conditions, effort expectancy, performance expectancy and social influence as significant drivers in m-Health service adoption. Implications for practice and research are also discussed for better planning and implementation of m-health services.

In Chapter 9, the author discusses the reliance on information and communication technologies in order to effectively share knowledge within social media. The chapter investigates the benefits and barriers to using social media with respect to professional communication and collaboration. Recommendations are proposed to help select the best knowledge sharing medium for tacit knowledge.

In Chapter 10, the authors explore the effects and issues associated with social media and recruitment and whether it is effective as an innovative e-entrepreneurship method of attracting the right employees for enterprises from a multi stakeholder perspective. Professionals, recruiters and employees have been questioned on their views of social media from a personal and a professional perspective through a variety of methods including focus groups and questionnaires. This chapter provides a framework that can be used by enterprises to create their own Social Media recruitment cycle.

In Chapter 11, the authors present a method for discussion and analysis in knowledge sharing between distributed team members working in a global context in different organizational and national cultures. The use of the Cultural and Organizational Diversity Evaluation (CODE) model is proposed for assessing the fit between national and organizational culture. The objective of using the CODE model is to raise awareness of the cultural values and attitudes in distributed teams and to help ensure an effective quality management process, as well as foster a knowledge sharing culture within distributed teams.

In Chapter 12, the author presents a study targeted to unearth the levels of willingness of engineering students to take entrepreneurial activities and investigate the factors that motivate them and the factors that deter them from going for entrepreneurship. The analysis revealed that the students are highly interested in taking entrepreneurship as a career option because of some intrinsic motivating factors such as being their own boss and chasing their dreams. However, lack of experience and funds deter them. The right kinds of entrepreneurship education programs can promote more entrepreneurial activities among the engineering students.

In Chapter 13, the authors consider the impact of case-based learning introduced in a multidisciplinary management of innovation and technology undergraduate course. The students' and lecturer's experiences, benefits, and challenges in cultivating entrepreneurial thinking are core elements in the process of business development. The findings seek ways to incorporate innovative approaches in teaching and learning processes to motivate students towards the development of entrepreneurial thinking in their professional engagements.

In Chapter 14, the authors evaluate the development of sales tax on e-business. The chapter examines the problems rooted in the seller's requirement to collect and remit the tax to the buyer's state government. Additionally, it discusses court cases and how the legislation could potentially end or simplify all controversies in e-business taxation. This chapter further notes that the concept of "economic nexus" may be extended to the arena of state income tax.

In Chapter 15, the authors debate the importance of innovation and entrepreneurship to economic growth and stability. The chapter's research explores national landscapes created as a result of differing endowments, regulatory regimes, tax systems, and venture funding levels. Results indicate that differences in these factors create significantly different entrepreneurial outcomes as measured by patent applications and new business registrations.

The comprehensive coverage this publication offers is sure to contribute to an enhanced understanding of all topics, research, and discoveries pertaining to business and entrepreneurship in the modern era. Furthermore, the contributions included in this publication will be instrumental in the expansion of knowledge offerings in this area and will inspire its readers to further contribute to the current discoveries in this immense field, creating possibilities for further research and discovery into the future of innovation.

Chapter 1

Digital Entrepreneurship:
A Longitudinal Case Study in a Traditional Firm

Martin Hannibal
University of Southern Denmark, Denmark

Erik S. Rasmussen
University of Southern Denmark, Denmark

ABSTRACT

Through a longitudinal case study, this chapter explores the repercussions from introducing a mobile commerce platform as just another instrument in the marketing toolbox in a traditional sales-oriented firm. Findings suggest that the implementation of the m-platform in addition to its intended purpose—establish a marketing channel to key customers—spawns a digital business model that allows the company to change its relations to distributors, retailers, and customers enabling access to direct communication with end-users. However, the emerging new business model has the potential to change the organization essentially. The authors argue that although the emerging digital business model was indeed a success seen from a sales-, marketing-, innovative-, and relational perspective, it was perceived as a disaster from an organizational perspective. Consequently, top management abandoned the new digital platform. The chapter highlights the importance of not underestimating resistance in an organization when implementing a new marketing instrument such as m-commerce platforms.

INTRODUCTION

Organizational change or the willingness to change has become an intrinsic good to most companies and is currently an imperative element in management rhetoric (Balogun, Bartunek, & Do, 2015; Christensen, 2002). In relation to this, authors have frequently argued that innovativeness, proactiveness, and competitive aggressiveness have become key ingredients to firm survival and success (Lumpkin & Dess, 1996; Lyon, Lumpkin, & Dess, 2000; Wales, 2016). Other authors have observed this imperative or story being acted upon by managers and leaders of organizations (March, 1995). Consequently, employees often act

DOI: 10.4018/978-1-5225-5014-3.ch001

or are forced to act upon this story – true or not – of being embedded in a turbulent environment; markets and technologies are changing at an increasing tempo, a context that needs to be addressed via innovativeness, proactivity, and competitive aggressiveness (March, 2006). One strategy which has frequently been applied by management to tackle the dilemmas generated by a turbulent environment is to employ new communication technologies on an organizational level. The ambition is to increase the ability to monitor activities, accelerate information flows, and facilitate new ways of collaboration across space and time (Rao, 2001; Sambamurthy, Bharadwaj, & Grover, 2003). This process is also seen as an alley to generate a supportive environment and greater participation by both the employees (Kiesler & Sproull, 1992) and customers (Antorini, Muniz, & Askildsen, 2012). Accordingly, incentive regimes aiming to nurture already existing creativeness, innovativeness, and entrepreneurial behavior amongst employees are often exercised in concurrency to implementing new communication technologies to support the intended increase in organizational responsiveness and flexibility (Lau et al., 2006).

M-commerce technologies have proved an alluring marketing tool to companies that strive for a close(r) contact to a large number of customers, sales staff, and dealers. As they did with E-commerce, organizations have embraced M-commerce platforms in anticipation of improved customer relations and increases in sales, etc. (Frolick & Chen, 2004). In many cases, these expectations have been fulfilled. Nevertheless, it has been observed that unwanted and unintended effects spanning from a counterintuitive tendency to increased work pressure (Sproull & Kiesler, 1992) follow in the wake of a new communication technology's launch. In addition to this, authors have reported more tacitly embedded complications such as organizational ambiguity stemming from both intended and unintended repercussions when new communication technologies are implemented in an existing organization (Levina & Orlikowski, 2009).

Building on concurrent tendencies, this paper contributes to extant studies by addressing the seldom studied case of entrepreneurial failure (Shepherd, 2003). More specifically, the paper focuses on a case in which entrepreneurial behavior has been disregarded, casting the entrepreneurs as the villains of the organization. The case stands in stark contrast to how entrepreneurs are commonly viewed as heroic individuals (Farny, Hannibal, Frederiksen, & Jones, 2016). The case study explores an implementing process of new communication technology: an M-commerce marketing tool. We illustrate how aspirations by the general management of a production firm to remain competitive by expanding the monitoring capabilities of end-customers via an M-commerce tool led to a clash between the extant organizational ethos (Merton, 1968) and the managers responsible for the M-commerce platform. The case illustrates how ambiguity surrounding the M-platform's implementation process led to dramatic discrepancies between the established ethos in the firm that embraced adaptive behavior and "good salesmanship" and the new approach pushed by the implementation process of the M-platform. In turn, this led to a principled discredit of the entrepreneurial or proactive behavior displayed by the M-platform's managers. The conflict culminated in the shutdown of the M-platform.

The case exhibits that managers should consider new communication technologies in a broad perspective involving a duality of scope and role (Orlikowski, 1992; Orlikowski, 2000). The scope of technology is described through what comprises the technology. However, this paper contributes to existing research by providing further insights into the role of new communication technologies. Thus, the paper contributes to the insight into the complex and – in this case – profound social processes involved in adopting new (communication) technologies in existing firms. The study indicates that the role played by technologies is to be considered the more important issue when adopting them. This role describes the interaction between technology and organization (Levina & Orlikowski, 2009) and can be seen as part of the organizational sensemaking (Weick, 1995; Weick, Sutcliffe, & Obstfeld, 2005).

The chapter outlines the theoretical background of the study in section one. The subsequent section sketches the research methodology. The third section presents the longitudinal case findings are presented in four subsections following the time line of the study depicted in Figure 2. Findings are reflected upon in the subsequent discussion section bringing the foundation to the concluding remarks implications for further research.

THEORETICAL BACKGROUND

The concept of organizational culture (Merton, 1968) is used to highlight how the extant organizational culture affects the organizational sensemaking (Weick, 1995). Following the thoughts of (Cyert & March, 1992), firm behavior is to be seen as a result of political goals, bounded rationality, and adaptive behavior. However, recent development in this literature (Dew, Read, Sarasvathy, & Wiltbank, 2008) has shown that firms embedded in volatile industries enacted entrepreneurial behavior based on effectual logics that differs essentially from the firm behavior described by (Cyert & March, 1992). Merton's (1968) structural approach to organizational culture provides a foundation to understand how organizational sensemaking (Weick, 1995) is constructed and thereby how actual behavior is a result of underlying cultural elements. In doing so, we aim to highlight how change related or entrepreneurial behavior differs in ethos from the case firm's established ethos and the subsequent strategizing. This discrepancy is to be considered the main impetus to the closing of an otherwise successful M-commerce platform.

Change and Change Willingness in a Traditional Organization

In a time in which markets and industries are perceived as ever changing, organizational culture has become an important aspect of organizational management practices (Hatch & Schultz, 1997). Consequently, the subject has frequently been discussed in management literature since the early 1970s as in e.g. (Schein, 2010). In his extensive work on organizational culture, Schein argues that culture ascribes the ethos of an organization, thereby embedding the norms to which judgment on organizational member's behavior is passed (Schein, 2010). In earlier work on the subject, Robert Merton (1968) argues that cultures or sub-cultures are differentiated in their fundamental aspects. Merton elegantly illustrates his point by comparing business ethos and academic ethos. The displayed differences in ethos compounds – it is argued – to deviations at three different levels which are norms, processes, and outputs embedded in academic organizations and their commercial counterparts.

As such, organizational ethos circumscribes the (invisible) foundation for the division of right and wrong in an organization (Merton, 1968). This refers to the normative element of the ethos (see Figure 1). The double arrows in Figure 1 indicate that, although the organizational norms (triangle top) are collectively shared it is only to be understood through the emergent interactivities in the organization (Louis, 1980). Hence, the norms only make sense through processes and outputs (Figure 1 mid and bottom) and the resulting interaction with the organizational surroundings. Accordingly, an established ethos on the organizational level will act as an imperative guide to and judgmental tool on behavior and choices enacted by employees in the organizational context. As a consequence of this, Louis (1980) argues that new organizational member socializes to learn the ropes to sufficiently match how members enact the organizational landscape. It is argued that newcomers' prime concern is to clarify their situational identity through their work roles, subsequently securing the approval of others in the process of

Figure 1. Organizational Ethos (adapted from Merton, 1968)

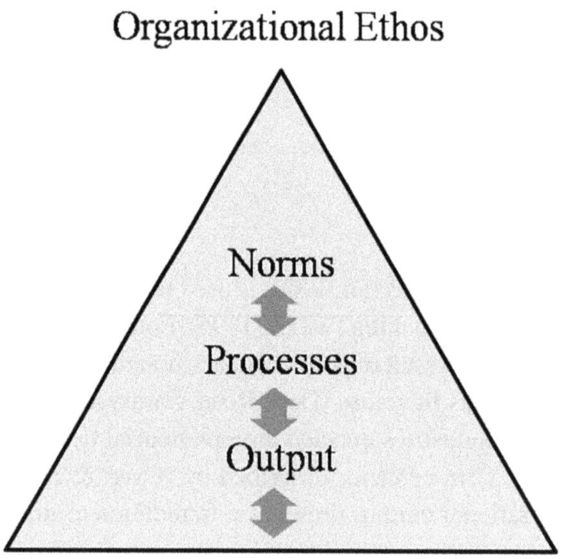

Organizational Ethos

Norms

Processes

Output

doing so (Ibarra, 1999). Accordingly, newcomers search for clues that allow them to elucidate and make sense of the expectations of others.

Most organizations today embrace horizontal management structures in an attempt to nurture creativity and individual innovativeness to survive in a rapidly changing environment (Aoki, 1986). However, on the backdrop of this fluctuating context, management scholars and practitioners have argued that having and withholding an organizational ethos is of utmost importance (Hatch & Schultz, 1997). The aim of the ethos is to create a sense of identity internally (Olins, 2003), to endorse a lasting image externally (Aaker, 1996), and to connect these entities to stage one corporate body and soul (Christensen, 2002). However, although an ethos facilitates a common ground to evaluate problems, strategic decision making, etc. guiding organization members, it is not to be considered a fix-all remedy provided by the management toolbox. In a study by the New York City Port Authorities (PA), Dutton & Dürkerich (1991) provide evidence on how the organizational sensemaking (Weick, 1995) is anchored to the organization's set self-image and how the established ethos guides this. The study focuses on how issues related to bums, winos, and bag ladies in New York has been transformed from a police and security issue into a social issue called homelessness. Dutton & Dürkerich (1991) suggest that the PA struggles to get a foothold on these changes which occur in the organization's immediate surroundings as a consequence of the established ethos. Indeed, the case study is to be considered a special case since the market in which the PA is operating embodies a unique mix of public and private relations. However, Dutton & Dürkerich (1991) illustrates how the ethos, although sought after to establish an image and organizational identity, concurrently circumscribes both restrictions and endorsements on how problems and new market possibilities are to be enacted in the organizational context.

Organizations seek to solve, evaluate problems, and attack new possibilities – in other words: behave – in accordance with a known and relatively stable set of norms and beliefs which describe the ethos concept (Dutton & Dürkerich, 1991; Merton, 1968). Consequently, when met by ambiguity, this established ethos will guide what is to be discarded as non-desirable to achieve (Louis, 1980).

Organizational Behavior and Entrepreneurial Behavior

In their seminal work, Cyert and March (1963) present a clutch of ideas for explaining the behavior of established firms within an environment of well-defined markets, stakeholder relationships, technologies, and so on. Central to the behavioral theory of the firm is the idea that decision-making consists in finding a satisfactory solution (satisficing) rather than in evaluating the best possible alternative (optimization). Cyert and March (1963) introduce a perspective in which strategic decision-making is seen as a consequence of political goals, bounded rationality, and adaptive behavior. Behaviorally speaking, management is thus the art of effectively dealing with the reality of bounded rationality in a changing environment. Accordingly, and using the Mertonian conceptualization from the above (Merton, 1968), the ethos of an organization embedded in a relatively stable and well-defined market would circumscribe the behavior described by Cyert and March (1963).

Recent research has questioned whether the organizational behavior prescribed by Cyert & March (1963) is always the case (Dew et al., 2008). Sarasvathy (2001) argues that managing expectations are tightly coupled to causal logics, which again are connected to the traditional strategic management of the firm as described by Cyert and March (1963). However, firms embedded in volatile markets – defined as knowledge intensive or new technology based markets – have been shown to display divergent behavioral patterns. Consequently, Dew et al. (2008) have put forth an outline of the behavior enacted by these firms dubbing the behavior they enact 'entrepreneurial behavior'.

Contrasting the decision process described by Cyert and March (1963) involving a given – although bounded – well-structured and specific goal to be achieved, the entrepreneurial behavior may be described as being effectual (Sarasvathy, 2001). Instead of well-structured goals, entrepreneurial actions evolve around designing and producing novelty of some kind; a new firm, a new market, new technology, etc. (Sarasvathy, 2003). Design procedures involve a given set of means with associated constraints coupled with a set of the possible operationalization of tentative goals (Sarasvathy, 2001). The means are set in a dynamic and interactive environment that continuously imposes constraints on the possible effects. Accordingly, effectuation predicts behavior which is defined as usages of a given technology, structure, etc. in a way that may very well diverge from its intended (ex-ante) use (Read, Dew, Sarasvathy, Song, & Wiltbank, 2009). The point of departure for this theoretical approach is the entrepreneur's self-perception (who am I), his prior knowledge of the field (what I know), and his immediate network (whom do I know) (Sarasvathy, 2008). These considerations give rise to a specific yet broadly defined way of making sense of the context in which the entrepreneur is embedded. The effectual sensemaking process contrasts the predictive logics observed by Cyert and March (1963) as the latter initiates the decision process from a predetermined goal (Dew et al., 2008).

Connecting to this while shifting focus to the individual dynamics, Ibarra (1999) has studied how new members of an organization struggle to conform to the existing organizational ethos. According to her studies of a private US banking firm, new employees will adapt to identity roles through experimenting with 'provisional selves' (Ibarra, 1999). These continuously serve as possible but not yet fully incorporated professional identities. However, they do so to display 'sensible behavior' in the organizational context or in other words try to enact the organizational ethos. This suggests that sensemaking of any organizational member is over time inclined to re-enact the ethos which has already been established as the truth. However, Ibarra's study is conducted in a well-established firm which is set within an environment of well-defined markets, stakeholder relationships, and technologies compromising the very firm (and its behavior) discussed by Cyert and March (1963). Hence, Ibarra (1999) does not bring any insight to the effects from the introduction of e.g. new communication technologies to an existing organization. Also, the study fails to elucidate to which degree the emergence of new markets impacts the dynamic of the organizational ethos in a well-established firm.

We address this gap as we frame the creation of the mobile commerce platform as the enactment of an entrepreneurial opportunity. Accordingly, we have analyzed the implementation process of the platform through a sensemaking perspective (Weick, 1995). The grounds for this stems from comparing the interviews with the managers of the mobile platform to the interviews conducted on employees at the marketing and sales department of the case firm 'K'. These interviews facilitated the condensation of two essentially different rationales for strategy and behavior. The employees in the sales and marketing department displayed behavioral patterns related closely to means-end causation logics described by Cyert & March (1963). Contrary to this, the strategic processes and behavioral patterns brought to life in the team surrounding the new mobile marketing platform resembled that of the effectual logics since the main focus evoked by these managers was on possible effects created with the set of means given (Sarasvathy, 2001). The two patterns each circumscribe a distinct ethos, which is only accessible via the analysis of the emergent interactivity in the organization. Accordingly, the below research design has been set up on this specific intent.

METHODOLOGY

Approach and Case

As stated in the introductory paragraph, the case study brings a longitudinal description and analysis of the process of implementing a mobile marketing tool in an existing organization 'K' (see Figure 2). 'K' is a traditional producer of blue collar uniforms for carpenters, masons, etc. 'K' has for 30 years been considered the point of reference amongst the competitors because of the firm's large market share and strong brand. For the last 20 or 30 years, 'K' has been going through major changes. First of all, the entire production has been outsourced to low-wage countries leaving only designs, sales, and marketing in Denmark. However, the headquarter remains in Denmark. Secondly, the traditional design has been changed considerably aiming at appealing to younger customers. Thirdly, 'K' has acquired a large number of smaller competing brands operating in the European market. When the case study was initiated, the company was selling its products directly to retail stores in Denmark through personal salespeople. This had been the dominant strategy for about 30 years inspired by a classical push strategy to get access to the end-users on the market (see Figure 3 for illustration). Consequently, the sales department has grown and was at the initiation of the case study positioned as by far the most important, occupying a central position in the organization. It consists of a large number of salespeople who via portfolio management visit each retail store several times a year. Contrasting this, the responsibility of the marketing department had primarily been to produce catalogs aimed at retail shops.

Research Design

Figure 2 provides a timeline of the events that transpired during the longitudinal case study of the company. It also brings an account of the data collected; the different sources included the time of the interviews conducted and the interviewees represented in the data material.

Figure 2. Overview of the case study

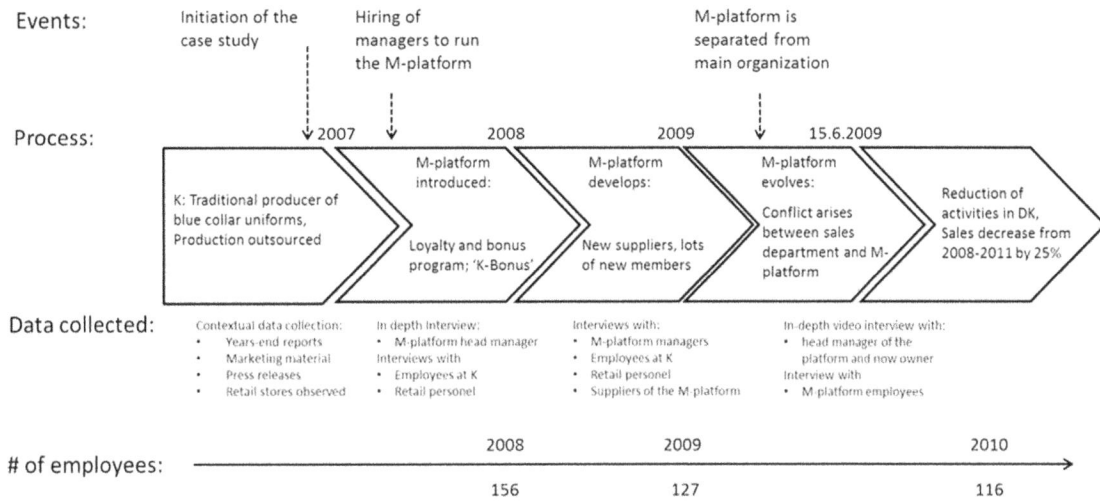

The single case study approach is informed by both the theory applied and the explicit research subject; our aim is to maintain the subject's holistic perspective on the transpiring events to bring accounts on how the events were experienced by the managers involved (Yin, 2013). The transpiring events of the implementation process have been treated as factual events, which all respondents have agreed upon. However, the perception of both the events and their impact on the main organization are the focus of attention of the interpretations presented in the findings. Hence, our research design focuses on a single setting – the introduction of a mobile marketing tool – the M-platform – which is embedded in a spatial and temporal context. The case study facilitates a study of change as it focuses on this unit in its context. The actual processes – the implementation, the judgment, and the termination of the platform – and the dynamics of the relations – extant ethos and the associated (displayed) behavior – are in focus. Thus, the case study is the most appropriate choice of research design (Yin, 2013). The purpose of the study has been to reach an in-depth understanding of the single case contrasting a pattern searching approach as described in (Eisenhardt, 1989; Eisenhardt & Graebner, 2007).

The data upon which the case has been built involves transcripts from in-depth interviews with the managers responsible for the establishment of the mobile marketing tool (the M-platform in the following). Two interviews – each lasting approximately an hour and a half – were conducted with the lead manager (see Figure 2 for the distinct time of data retrieval) while we administered five interviews with the platform's employees lasting approximately 30 minutes. Thus, this material compounds around five and a half hours of in-depth interviews that have been recorded on video and transcribed during late 2008 and 2009. The interviewees have performed draft reviews of the case before finalizing the transcription to strengthen the internal validity by decreasing the likelihood of false reporting in the study through providing the interviewees an opportunity to influence final valuations. The focus of the interviews was to develop a framework on which the interviewees were allowed to stipulate their perspective on the gestational process of M-platform up until its termination.

In addition to these four short semi-structured interviews lasting from 30 minutes to an hour with staff from the 'K's marketing and sales department have been recorded and transcribed, and three short semi-structured interviews have been conducted with suppliers to the mobile platform. Furthermore, three informal interviews of approximately half an hour with front desk staff at the retail shops selling 'K's products have been conducted. Archival data such as newspaper articles, business reports, year-end accounts, etc. have contributed to a general description of the company and its history. Also, the many documents acquired have brought insights into the strategic behavior of the case firm over the last two decades.

The aim of our study has been to follow the implementation, the development, and in the end the termination of the M-platform. In this type of longitudinal study, the research data collection has been developed along with the evolution of the project in the firm (Ven & Poole, 2002). This enables the researchers to set up a 'thick description' of the transpiring events instead of relying on short, well-polished statements by the firm.

Using constant comparison analysis (Glaser, 1992; Glaser & Strauss, 1967), raw interview content was grouped into themes according to the model inspired by Merton (1968) describing the organizational ethos. The constant comparative method uses joint coding and analysis to the purpose of generating theory more systematically than allowed in traditional grounded approach by using the explicit coding and analytic procedures known from analytic induction. It follows that the technique does not completely forestall the development of theory by remaining dedicated to the inductive approach as it still tolerates some of the vagueness and flexibility necessary for (disciplined) creative generation of theory. Thus, the approach leaves the data to speak for itself, and in this specific setup, it lets the data speak in a realm demarked (a priori) by the theory construct encompassing the sensemaking of organizational members displayed through their causal/effectual behavior and the associated ethos (Merton, 1968). Following a narrative approach (Flick, 2009), the case description has an explicit focus on what the managers identified as prominent events and activities unfolding throughout the implementation of the mobile platform to its subsequent termination. To describe the context in which the creation of the mobile platform took place, we have adapted Merton's model (1968) to illustrate the cultural setting in which the employees at 'K' are immersed. Following this line of thoughts, we argue through the case that the organizational ethos of 'K' contains essential differences to the behavior displayed in the management of the mobile platform. Our approach to the implementation process incorporates technologies as "enacted environment" (Weick, 1979) in the sense that the role of communication technologies are constructed by the sensemaking of them (Levina & Orlikowski, 2009). In other words: the signification, domination, and legitimization of a technology are defined by the organization culture. Concurrently, it impacts the very same structures through the ongoing sensemaking processes. To retrieve insights on the ongoing sensemaking processes and to follow the theory constructs described in the above, we have focused on the behavior of organizational members since this circumscribes the sensemaking of these. Following this line of thoughts, we argue through our case that the organizational ethos of 'K' contains essential differences to the behavior displayed in the management of the mobile platform. In the below section, the case findings are presented in a longitudinal approach that matches the events, processes, and data collection point depicted in Figure 2.

CASE FINDINGS

Phase 1: The Traditional Producer Considers a Change in Strategy

Already at the end of the 1990s, 'K' was experiencing difficulties in decreasing customer loyalty. This difficulty had via customer surveys been traced back to the insignificant difference between 'K's products and the other competing brands. Market research showed that 'K' was perceived as carrying a line of good quality products, which was expensive compared to the competitors. As mentioned in the above, 'K' had for some decades opted for a classical salesman driven push-strategy. This strategy had created a privileged status of the sales department as it along with the classical push-strategy was considered essential to the competitiveness of 'K'. The sales department was by far the largest single department of the firm accounting for around three-quarters of the employees at the Danish headquarters. Figure 2 illustrates this situation in which the sales department is established as the sole contact to the retail stores, which again had almost all contact to the end-users. In this respect, the other departments had become subordinates guided by the norms of the sales department (see Figure 3 below).

At the initiation of the case study, the sales department's influence was well defined in the behavior of the employees. The individual salesmen were the only actual contact the firm had with what they perceived to be their customers: the retail stores. Accordingly, the sales force and their interaction with and perception of the customers' needs were considered pivotal to strategizing by all departments. Over the years, this dominance of the sales department had among other things created a norm of (good) salesmanship in the organization. Furthermore, the near-sovereignty had evoked a strong departmental tribalism stemming from the sharp division of the distinct procedures put into the end product. Hence, a norm of rigidity in the strategic tools applied had through the years created a processual perspective in which a causal logic was omnipresent.

Figure 3. The initial distribution and marketing system of 'K'

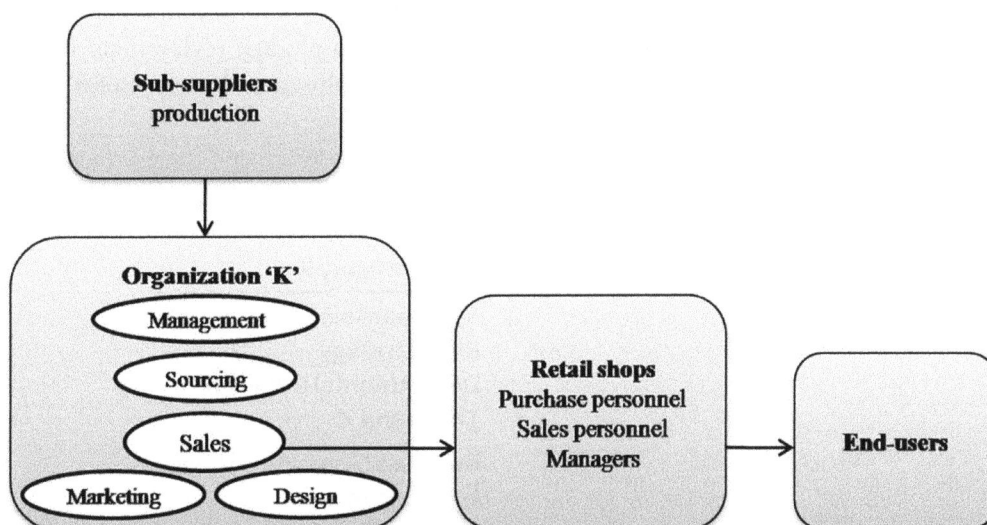

Everything in K was about selling – but not to the end-user. The focus was the retail shops, and the incentives for the salesmen were the bonuses they get from an order when they visit the shop ... and it still is; not the actual sale of the clothes to the end-user [...] Everything in K was focused on this sale – and not on user interaction, design etc...(Platform head manager)

Table 1 summarizes the findings from the initial phase of the case study and illustrates the ethos of 'K' at the time when the organization was considering implementing a mobile marketing application. Findings suggest that this ethos had been left relatively uncontested for at least 20 years.

Phase 2: Introduction of a New Marketing Tool

Market research in the early 2000s had revealed that end-users (craftsmen) found 'K's product line to be very old-fashioned. This brought an incentive to the head management team to get access to the end-users to retrieve insight into how this perception could be countered. The initial idea was to adapt a strategy that introduced a Mobile marketing application (the later M-platform) that enabled access to the otherwise difficult to contact blue-collar workers since market research had revealed that these were not accessible via traditional advertisements through e.g. television and radio. The idea was conceived at 'K's marketing department, and the plan was to shortcut the communication to the end-users, thereby getting feedback on product development. Figure 4 captures the expressed intention of employing the new mobile marketing application as curved arrows illustrating the communication going to and the feedback from end-users. Additionally, it was perceived that the introduction of a modern supplement to the firms marketing tool-box by itself symbolized that 'K' was not old-fashioned at all.

Subsequently, a new sub-department of the marketing department was established with a handful of managers brought in from outside. The head manager of the sub-department had ten years of experience in IT-marketing from her prior work at a news organization, and her educational background was in business management. In agreement with the managers of the other departments it was decided that the M-platform should introduce a loyalty program, 'K-bonus', in which end-users could earn bonus point from purchasing goods from both 'K' and other suppliers relevant for the end-user. The platform furthermore enabled the end-users to reply to advertisements via product reviews and feedback etc. The underlying strategy was to counter the decreasing brand loyalty of end-users. Before the launch,

Table 1. The ethos of 'K'

	The company K
Norms	Salesmanship
	Rigid strategy
	Departmental tribalism
	The brand K
Processes	Business (/causation) logics
	Focus on retail
Output	Products
	Profit

Figure 4. The intention of the new marketing tool – feedback from end-users

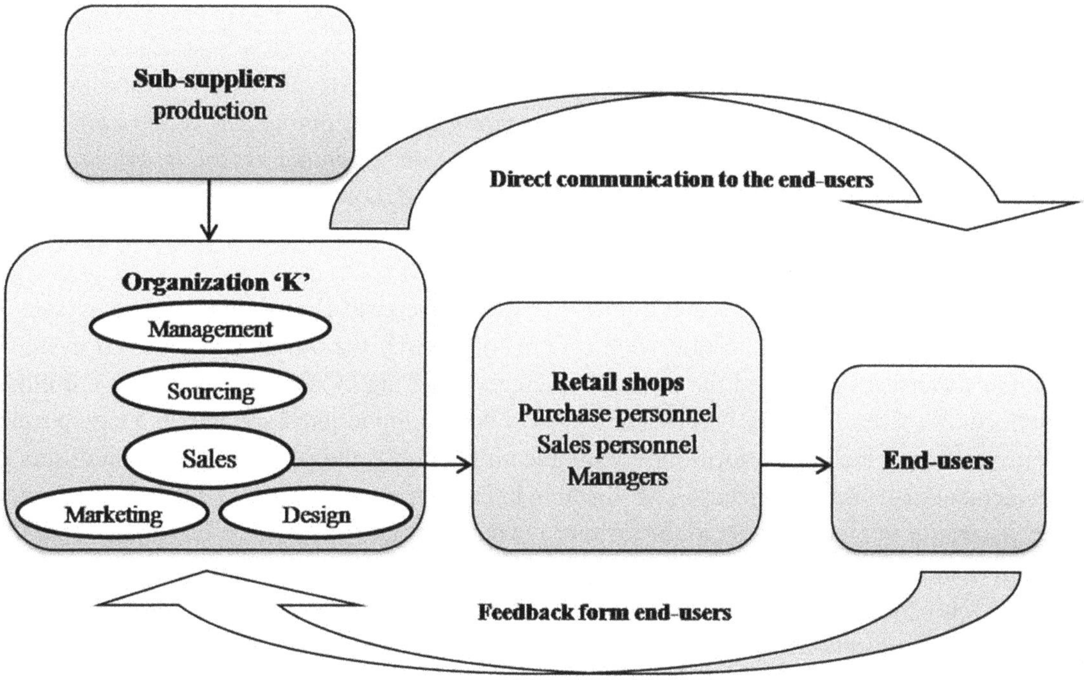

a number of companies were asked to supply prizes and discounts to members of the loyalty program. These suppliers also perceived the platform as an opportunity to get into contact with – and sell their products to – a group of customers – the craftsmen – with whom it was otherwise difficult to establish a dialogue. Accordingly, the platform became an advertisement vehicle and a way of communicating to the customers for the local bakery, power drill sub-suppliers, building material retail stores, truck retail store, etc. In return for getting access to the advertised discounts, end-users were asked to provide the platform managers their data. Within a few months of implementation of the new marketing tool, the firm had received information on 7000 users' age, type of work, where they worked, interests, etc. This extremely valuable information could be combined with the data of each person's purchase. As one platform manager remarked:

A lot of information was collected about the users when they registered, and within the first year we had a large database with information about the customers ... We didn't have that before. It was now possible to segment the messages to the users of 'K-bonus'. (Platform employee)

Through this analysis, the company was ideally in the position to bring important and direct feedback to the design and sales department.

Phase 3: Unintended Evolution of the Platform

The loyalty program evolved during the following months into much more than the managers of both the specific platform and the company 'K' had initially had in mind. "[...] suddenly, it [the platform] just took off! It was really a surprise to me how quickly everything just evolved... it was not anticipated ..." (platform manager). The M-platform seemed a potent communication tool, which brought huge incentives to pay high prices to be visible on the portal.

We were looking for suppliers for bonus items for the program in the beginning, and it was a bit difficult, but when we reached several thousand users, the suppliers began to contact us. It could be a company selling cars for building companies; they gave us a car to be used as a bonus just to get in contact with potential customers (Platform head manager)

As the platform evolved, it facilitated a new and alternative cash flow to the traditional sales of blue-collar workwear. In addition to these bonus items offered by the advertisers enrolled in the M-platform, new advertisers contacted the platform managers offering money to secure their enrollment on the platform. As a result of this, 'K's management suddenly found itself situated in a new business model dominated by a mobile platform for communicating directly and personally with end-users. At first, management explained the success – i.e. the high interest from end users – as a consequence of the end-users' aspirations to receive gifts in the form of the bonus point system. This reasoning fitted their ethos well in as much as the set strategy had succeeded in increasing the sales numbers and strengthening the brand. However, soon it became clear that another powerful incentive also was hidden behind this conspicuous argument. Hence, many customers would like to be a part of the marketing, product development, etc. of 'K'.

[...] to use the mobile phone brings an obligation – the user expect an immediate answer: 'I bought a new pair of K trousers and my smartphone is too big for the mobile pocket – please change that'. You will expect an answer in a very short time (Sales support employee at K)

The development came as a surprise to the management of 'K' who were used to operating on a classical arms-length principle with almost no direct contact with customers due to the established salesman tradition. However, the managers responsible for the M-platform was willing to enter into a dialogue and answered the questions related to the platform but had no competencies to answer questions from customers concerning the products advertised on it. Consequently, they began to forward the questions to the sales department or other relevant departments in the firm with the expectancy that the relevant parties answered the customers' questions. From the initial stage and onwards, the sales department did not see it as their responsibility to communicate with end-users. Similarly, marketing was very reluctant to add another dimension to their classical one-way communications. Also, the design department did not see any use in discussing anything with any end-user. The M-platform managers tried to convince the departments and their respective managers to join this new communication.

[The] immediate response to suggestions and complaints <my mobile does not fit into the pocket> from the customers was not our responsibility. We tried to forward it to design and sales, but typically we didn't receive any answer. The typical answer was that complaints should be handled by the shop where you had bought your clothes. In my previous job, I was used to having a complaint or a question from a customer at 11.00 and replies were sent back the same day at 11.15! (Platform employee)

In the end, the different attitudes to customer service, complaints, and communication, in general, resulted in several tough clashes between the 'old' group of managers and the so-called 'newcomers' in the platform's management team.

Phase 4: Separation and Shut-down

In early 2009, 'K's top management 'outsourced' the new M-platform to a new firm that consisted of the handful of individuals already responsible for the mobile platform (see Figure 3). After the outsourcing, it was evident that the managers responsible for the portal still found themselves situated in a central position in the main organization as they upheld both contacts to end-users, retail stores, and the advertisers to the platform. Thus, the sales staff was no longer at the center of the organization with the sole connection to the main (and only) customers the retail store, and the retailers were accepting and incorporating the platform into their routines.

The retail stores are clearly a part of the K-bonus. It is not the intention to sell directly as we initially feared. We use the program, too (Retailer)

The new roles fell contrary to the traditions of 'K' in which the sales department had held a favored position that over the years had evoked a norm of good salesmanship in the organization. Also apparent from viewing Figure 5 is the lack of sharp divisions that promoted a departmental tribalism. The

Figure 5. The consequence of the new marketing tool

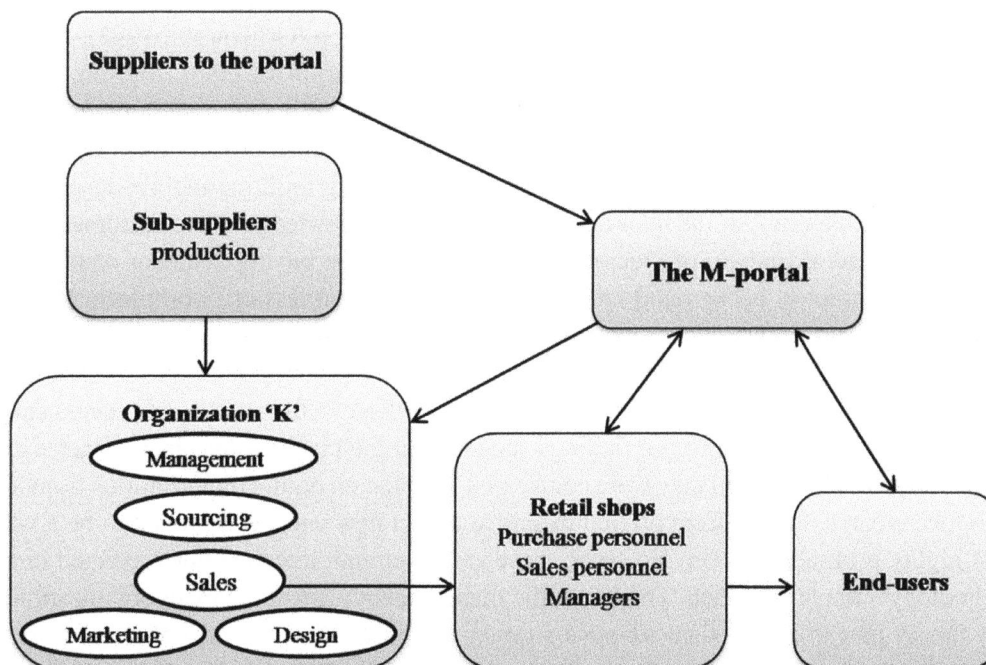

M-platform's managers continued to contact the relevant departments in their quest of answering to the end-users' feedback. Furthermore, the near-sovereignty had evoked a strong departmental tribalism stemming from the sharp division of the distinct procedures put into the end product.

As of June 15th, 2009 (see Figure 2), the management team at 'K' decided to shut down the loyalty program established via the M-platform. Officially, this action was due to the general financial crisis and questionable market tendencies. However, the findings section suggests an alternative argument in which its success strangled the program. From a marketing and sales point of view, the program had been a huge success. However, at the same time, it had been extremely difficult to handle the organizational changes – especially with respect to the norms and processes through which 'K' was operating but also the changes that it meant to the output of the entire organization.

DISCUSSION

The implementation process of the M-platform has been troublesome for the firm with several deep-rooted conflicts between departments, persons, and ideas/strategies. This section conducts an analysis of the case findings. Through adapting Merton (1968), the analysis is summarized in Table 2 below. In this table, we have focused on distinguishing the ethos displayed by the 'old' management of our case firm and the 'new' managers managing the M-platform. Throughout this paper, it has been argued that technology is not just a question of finding the right hardware (or software). Following Orlikowski (1992), technology can be seen as "enacted environment" to borrow a term from (Weick, 1979). Accordingly, the use and design of a communication technology are conditioned by the organization's structures of signification, domination, and legitimization. These organizational structures define the technology in use, but at the same time, it has an impact on these. Typically, this happens without the awareness of the users of the technology or other members of the organization (Orlikowski, 1992). Accordingly, implementation of a new technology can thus either reaffirm or disrupt the ethos (Merton, 1968) of the organization without the members of the organization being aware of it. Our case findings suggest that this was what happened in 'K' as the new technology enabled the organization to collect information about the customers (see section 'Introduction of a new marketing tool: the mobile application'). Instead of favoring the expertise of the sales department and their knowledge of the customers (retailers), the company now had a database of precise information about the buying behavior of the customers (the end-users) and a lot of background knowledge such as age, profession, workplace, interests, etc. The employees at the sales department were thus no longer the customer experts, and in this way, the institutional status quo was disrupted without any of the actors having this as an (ex-ante) objective. However, the ambiguity brought by this disruption led to a change in the norms in a process enacted by the platform managers. Hence, the case findings suggest that the platform managers enacted effectual behavior (Dew et al., 2008) when they were confronted with the emerging opportunities from a mobile platform. Once created, the platform offered means to attract new ends as it proved to be a vehicle to a new and highly profitable market. However, these ends were not intended nor predicted in advance of the technology's implementation. Therefore, the management team at the main organization did not recognize this as part of the original adaptive strategy (Cyert & March, 1963) of (just) getting more information about the users.

The case findings summarized in Table 2 illustrates that the conflict runs deeper. The social interaction in organizations – including the use of technology – can be described in three fundamental elements:

Table 2. Comparison of Ethos in 'K' and the M platform

	The company K	The mobil platform
Norms	Salesmanship Rigid strategy Departmental tribalism The brand of 'K'	Interactive strategy Collaboration across departments The Brand K
Processes	Business (/causation) logics Focus on Retail	Entrepreneurial (/Effectual) logics Focus on end-user
Output	Products Profit	Customer service Profit

meaning, power, and norms (Orlikowski, 1992). Human interaction involves the creation of shared meaning across the organization – the sensemaking processes which establish interpretive schemes (Louis, 1980). Following Merton (1968), these inform the organizational rules of conduct that guide interactions and incorporate a regime – the ethos – that legitimize specific norms, processes, and output while others are discarded. Norms embedded in this ethos are organizational conventions or rules that lead to the appropriate conduct through normative sanctions expressed in the culture of the organization.

In the case of 'K', the sanctioned output was products (clothes for blue-collar craftsmen) and to create profits from (expected) increased sales in retail shops. However, during a relatively short period, an alternative interpretation emerged as a shared meaning amongst the managers of the M-platform as they began to enact the new business opportunity of being an intermediate to a large number of firms and 'K's customers (see Figure 5). The M-platform managers, on the other hand, designed their way through the new possibilities emerging in the interplay between the new M-platform and the market. This effectual behavior stands in sharp contrast to a priori strategizing (Dew et al., 2008) embraced by the financial and the sales departments in concurrency to the organizational ethos.

Accordingly, the case findings suggest that the effectual behavior which is to be seen as a manifestation of the sensemaking processes of the M-platform managers is disqualified on the grounds of the extant ethos (see Table 2) as it will threaten the salesman tradition by weakening the department's position in the organization. This resistance is mounted as a response to the enactment of effectual behavior displayed by the managers designated to the M-platform.

The ethos of the salesperson tradition and the classic organization of 'K' were challenged when the (initially thought to be) new marketing tool evolves into an independent entity. The evolutionary path of the M-application was carefully managed, nurtured, and partially controlled throughout the process by the designated platform managers. Each time a new problem, possibility or surprise surfaced, the management team of the platform attended to it and weighed its potential. However, it was in the very essence of this way of thinking that the M-platform's manager's behavior was perceived as contradictory or even hostile to the existing ethos. As one of the managers of the platform puts it:

[...] the funny thing was that when we stopped trying to predict how the application would be used [...] and focused on how it was actually being used, we started having even greater success in respect to the number of users (platform head manager)

This quote shows a clear shift away from a focus on trying to select the right means to create a specific effect, i.e. a causational perspective. The logics applied by the managers of the mobile platform, on the other hand, describe a perspective in which the given set of means is enacted to create a selected possible effect, i.e. an effectual perspective. This contrast the observation made by Ibarra (1999) that predicts that the managers of the M-platform would have tried to align their enactment processes towards what is established as 'sensible' behavior. However observing the case findings, we see that the M-platform managers feel an obligation towards enacting a high level of customer service through attending to and interactively incorporating the feedback yielded from the M-application in new strategic thinking. Thus, the M-platform's managers do try to make sense of their behavior, but they follow the path opened by the emerging market and enact the perceived customer demands. Accordingly, their aim is not to conform to the existing ethos of good salesmanship.

MANAGERIAL IMPLICATIONS

In comparing the interaction illustrated in Figure 4 and Figure 5, the differences from an outsider's perspective does not seem profound. However, from the perspective of a manager in 'K', the differences were fundamental. This line of research suggests that perhaps the premises for entrepreneurial behavior are slack of some kind (Dew et al., 2008). Following these thoughts, it has been put forth that organizations without slack will not allow for entrepreneurial behavior to be displayed by employees. As seen in the above case, the organization in focus has over a sustained period established an ethos circumscribing key values, norms, and beliefs that contribute to a sense of 'we' in the company. Once challenged, immediate resistance is prompted. Accordingly, the managerial implications drawn from this case suggests that managers are confronted with a dilemma between establishing a persuasive organizational identity and making it too strict and thereby leaving no room for some entrepreneurial fooling around with the opportunities offered by new communication technologies. To keep a sense of 'we' while leaving room for 'out-of-the-box' creative thinking will continue to be of paramount importance to managers in the future. We argue that managers and leaders should aim for an organizational identity that either incorporates entrepreneurial logics (effectuation) or encourage creative clearances to sanction entrepreneurial behavior. That said, tackling with an established organizational ethos is not just something that can be done by tomorrow as it may take years. However, in an ever-changing environment, it seems vital not just to enact adaptive strategizing but also encourage effectual behavior to reap the unexpected benefits from emerging markets, technologies, and structures.

CONCLUSION AND FURTHER RESEARCH

Initially, the M-commerce platform at 'K' was conceived to increase customer loyalty. However, over the course of three months, the platform evolved to change marketing, sales, and in the end innovation processes at 'K'. The platform could have changed the business model of 'K' in the long run by shifting away from a traditional producer of clothing to being the owner of a platform for contacting and marketing to a large group of customers that have been very difficult and expensive to reach via traditional marketing tools. Objectively and seen from a marketing perspective and sales perspective, the M-commerce platform was a huge success that enabled the contact to the customers at a very low price. Within a short period, the platform generated revenue to 'K' as other firms were willing to pay for access to the users. However, as the case findings suggest, the M-platform was closed down because the 'K' ethos did not allow for alternative sensemaking enacted by the newly employed managers of the platform. In other words, there was no tradition at 'K' for direct contact to the end-users. Consequently, the platform's managers were superseded by the organization and the general management in existing departments as no department in specific felt that the contact the platform facilitated was needed.

To conclude, the case illustrates that implementing a new communication technology is not just the new technology. A new technology – in this case, an M-commerce application – being as it is new in its truest sense often implies organizational change as a consequence of new markets opening in the wake of its implementation. However as it has been observed with Web pages, E-business, etc., M-business technologies are very often seen as just a technological 'fix' to some managerial problems. New communication technology will typically have large repercussions on the way a company sets up its business, and it will, if allowed, change the organizational structure of the firm.

The paper contributes to the insight on the complex and in this present case profound social processes involved in adopting new (communication) technologies in existing firms. A fundamental dilemma emerges from the findings. On the one hand, it seems necessary to adopt new (communication) technologies to adapt to a changing environment or industry. On the other hand, this brings broader organizational repercussions, as the role of the new technology needs to be negotiated and made sense of. This is also evident for current state-of-the-art technologies such as additive manufacturing. The implementation process of these technologies may indeed be paved with difficult organizational processes and resistance to adoption may result in new approaches to management, methods of production, access to markets, and essentially new products (Lipson & Kurman, 2013).

Seen from a more theoretical point of view, the case study shows two distinct types of ethos circumscribing different norms, processes, outputs, and their associated behavioral pattern. A longitudinal case study like this suggests that they are not able to co-exist. To the extent that a firm is organized and understood by its members as a traditional organization set in a relatively stable market, incorporating clear communications flows, etc. as discussed by Cyert and March (1963), it seems that there is little room for entrepreneurial behavior (Dew et al., 2008). As observed in the case findings, opportunity-seeking behavior – which is the core in any entrepreneurship and effectuation (Dew et al., 2008) – is not perceived as the way this organization sees itself. The entrepreneurial part of the organization is ostracized: isolated through "outsourcing" and then cut off. The problem is that 'K' is in need of renewal of ideas and effectual behavior. Removing what the organization perceives as annoying intruders is no solution in the long run. In the case of 'K', sales have been receding at a very high rate for the last three years. The profit of the firm has followed the receding sales. From the consumers' point of view, 'K' is looked upon as an old-fashioned brand for elderly men, which is not desirable for a company that targets the segment of young craftsmen. The tentative solution was to redesign the product line by bringing in younger designers. However, management has neglected to revise the distribution channels, the sales strategy, and the communication strategy, which by any standard is not aligned to a new style. The new owners of 'K' (an investment fund) have several other brands similar to 'K' in their portfolio, and if the firm does not deliver a decent return on their investment within a couple of years 'K' will be closed.

For a short period – less than a year – a window of opportunity was opened for the management of 'K'. Nonetheless, this window was abruptly shut when the M-platform was terminated. It could be questioned if this opportunity is ever to be recovered again. In this way, many organizations can be said to be their own worst enemies. The inertia in the organization is so high that organizational members prefer to be slowly suffocated while employing the usual adaptive strategizing guided by predetermined goals (Cyert & March, 1963) rather than experiencing rapid organizational development involving effectuation using the means at hand to embrace a turbulent unpredictable future (Dew et al., 2008). The new future could involve a new business model and new technological means like E-commerce, M-commerce, applications, or web-based services.

Further research should focus on retrieving insight on both successful and failed implementation processes of new technologies. There is a need for insights on the complex social processes involved in employing new (communication) technologies in coping with the increased volatility of both markets and industries. It is increasingly important to adapt to and gain the benefits of the many key enabling technologies, such as additive manufacturing, which has emerged over the last decade, as these will provide the basis for current and new business activities in the coming years (Rayna & Striukova, 2014). By comparing cases of successes and failures, research could guide managers on the underlying social variables involved in successful incorporation of new technologies and what to avoid. However, firms are often very reluctant to share information from failed projects although it has been argued that there is a larger potential of learning from failures compared to studying successful entrepreneurial projects (Shepherd, 2004). In the light of this paper, there is a need for more studies into how to promote the necessary climate for entrepreneurship from within existing firms often labeled intrapreneurship (Hisrich, 1990). The present paper focuses on how top management disregards newly employed managers that enact an entrepreneurial behavior due to an embedded ethos. However, had this been the case of current employees with a long history in the company that pursued entrepreneurial endeavors, the chance of success would have been higher. These 'embedded' entrepreneurs would have a proven (and successful?) track record in the company that offered the basis of legitimacy to their behavior. Accordingly, it seems important to research how managers could promote an ethos that offers room for intrapreneurship: entrepreneurship from within the firm.

REFERENCES

Aaker, D. (1996). *Building Strong Brands*. New York, NY: Free Press Business.

Antorini, Y. M., Muniz, A. M., & Askildsen, T. (2012). Collaborating With Customer Communities: Lessons from the Lego Group. *MIT Sloan Management Review*, *53*(3), 73.

Aoki, M. (1986). Horizontal vs. vertical information structure of the firm. *The American Economic Review*, 971–983.

Balogun, J., Bartunek, J. M., & Do, B. (2015). Senior Managers' Sensemaking and Responses to Strategic Change. *Organization Science*, *26*(4), 960–979. doi:10.1287/orsc.2015.0985

Christensen, L. T. (2002). Corporate communication: The challenge of transparency. *Corporate Communications*, *7*(3), 162–168. doi:10.1108/13563280210436772

Cyert, R. M., & March, J. G. (1963). *A Behavioral Theory of the Firm*. Englewood Cliffs, NJ: Prentice-Hall.

Cyert, R. M., & March, J. G. (1992). *Behavioral Theory of the Firm*. Blackwell Publishing.

Dew, N., Read, S., Sarasvathy, S. D., & Wiltbank, R. (2008). Outlines of a behavioral theory of the entrepreneurial firm. *Journal of Economic Behavior & Organization, 66*(1), 37–59. doi:10.1016/j.jebo.2006.10.008

Dutton, J. E., & Dürkerich, J. M. (1991). Keeping an Eye in the Mirror: Image and Identity in Organizational Adaption. *Academy of Management Journal, 34*(3), 517–554. doi:10.2307/256405

Eisenhardt, K. M. (1989). Making Fast Strategic Decisions In High-Velocity Environments. *Academy of Management Journal, 32*(3), 543–576. doi:10.2307/256434

Eisenhardt, K. M., & Graebner, M. E. (2007). Theory building from cases: Opportunities and challenges. *Academy of Management Journal, 50*(1), 25–32. doi:10.5465/AMJ.2007.24160888

Farny, S., Hannibal, M., Frederiksen, S., & Jones, S. (2016). A CULTure of Entrepreneurship Education. *Entrepreneurship and Regional Development, 28*(7-8), 514–535. doi:10.1080/08985626.2016.1221228

Flick, U. (2009). *An introduction to qualitative research.* Sage Pubns Ltd.

Frolick, M. N., & Chen, L.-D. (2004). Assessing M-Commerce Opportunities. *Information Systems Management, 21*(2), 53–61. doi:10.1201/1078/44118.21.2.20040301/80422.8

Glaser, B. G. (1992). *Basics of Grounded Theory Analysis.* Mill Valley, CA: Sociology Press.

Glaser, B. G., & Strauss, A. (1967). *The Discovery of Grounded Theory.* Chicago: Aldine.

Hatch, M. J., & Schultz, M. (1997). Relations between organizational culture, identity and image. *European Journal of Marketing, 31*(5/6), 356–365. doi:10.1108/eb060636

Hisrich, R. D. (1990). Entrepreneurship/intrapreneurship. *The American Psychologist, 45*(2), 209–222. doi:10.1037/0003-066X.45.2.209

Ibarra, H. (1999). Provisional Selves: Experimenting with Image and Identity in Professional Adaptation. *Administrative Science Quarterly, 44*(4), 764–791. doi:10.2307/2667055

Kiesler, S., & Sproull, L. (1992). Group decision making and communication technology. *Organizational Behavior and Human Decision Processes, 52*(1), 96–123. doi:10.1016/0749-5978(92)90047-B

Lau, H. C. W., Lee, C. K. M., Ho, G. T. S., Ip, W. H., Chan, F. T. S., & Ip, R. W. L. (2006). M-commerce to support the implementation of a responsive supply chain network. *Supply Chain Management, 11*(2), 169–178. doi:10.1108/13598540610652564

Levina, N., & Orlikowski, W. J. (2009). Understanding Shifting Power Relations within and across Organizations: A Critical Genre Analysis. *Academy of Management Journal, 52*(4), 672–703. doi:10.5465/AMJ.2009.43669902

Lipson, H., & Kurman, M. (2013). *Fabricated: The new world of 3D printing.* John Wiley & Sons.

Louis, M. R. (1980). Surprise and Sense Making: What Newcomers Experience in Entering Unfamiliar Organizational Settings. *Administrative Science Quarterly, 25*(2), 226–251. doi:10.2307/2392453 PMID:10247029

Lumpkin, G. T., & Dess, G. G. (1996). Clarifying the entrepreneurial orientation construct and linking it to performance. *Academy of Management Review*, *21*(1), 135–172. doi:10.2307/258632

Lyon, D. W., Lumpkin, G. T., & Dess, G. G. (2000). Enhancing Entrepreneurial Orientation Research: Operationalizing and Measuring a Key Strategic Decision Making Process. *Journal of Management*, *26*(5), 1055–1085. doi:10.1177/014920630002600503

March, J. G. (1995). The Future, Disposable Organizations and the Rigidities of Imagination. *Organization*, *2*(3-4), 427–440. doi:10.1177/135050849523009

March, J. G. (2006). Rationality, foolishness, and adaptive intelligence. *Strategic Management Journal*, *27*(3), 201–214. doi:10.1002/smj.515

Merton, R. K. (1968). *Social theory and social structure*. Free press.

Olins, W. (2003). *On B®and*. London: Thames & Hudson Ltd.

Orlikowski, W. J. (1992). The duality of technology: Rethinking the concept of technology in organizations. *Organization Science*, *3*(3), 398–427. doi:10.1287/orsc.3.3.398

Orlikowski, W. J. (2000). Using technology and constituting structures: A practice lens for studying technology in organizations. *Organization Science*, *11*(4), 404–428. doi:10.1287/orsc.11.4.404.14600

Rao, P. M. (2001). The ICT revolution, internationalization of technological activity, and the emerging economies: Implications for global marketing. *International Business Review*, *10*(5), 571–596. doi:10.1016/S0969-5931(01)00033-6

Rayna, T., & Striukova, L. (2014). The Impact of 3D Printing Technologies on Business Model Innovation. In P. J. Benghozi, D. Krob, A. Lonjon, & H. Panetto (Eds.), *Digital Enterprise Design & Management* (Vol. 261, pp. 119–132). Springer International Publishing. doi:10.1007/978-3-319-04313-5_11

Read, S., Dew, N., Sarasvathy, S. D., Song, M., & Wiltbank, R. (2009). Marketing Under Uncertainty: The Logic of an Effectual Approach. *Journal of Marketing*, *73*(3), 1–18. doi:10.1509/jmkg.73.3.1

Sambamurthy, V., Bharadwaj, A., & Grover, V. (2003). Shaping Agility through Digital Options: Reconceptualizing the Role of Information Technology in Contemporary Firms. *Management Information Systems Quarterly*, *27*(2), 237–263.

Sarasvathy, S. D. (2001). Causation and Effectuation: Toward a Theoretical Shift from Economic Inevitability to Entrepreneurial Contingency. *Academy of Management Review*, *26*(2), 243–263. doi:10.2307/259121

Sarasvathy, S. D. (2003). Entrepreneurship as a science of the artificial. *Journal of Economic Psychology*, *24*(2), 203–220. doi:10.1016/S0167-4870(02)00203-9

Sarasvathy, S. D. (2008). *Effectuation: elements of entrepreneurial expertise*. Cheltenham, UK: Edward Elgar Publishing. doi:10.4337/9781848440197

Schein, E. H. (2010). *Organizational culture and leadership* (4th ed.). Jossey-Bass.

Shepherd, D. A. (2003). Learning from Business Failure: Propositions of Grief Recovery for the Self-Employed. *Academy of Management Review*, *28*(2), 318–328. doi:10.2307/30040715

Shepherd, D. A. (2004). Educating entrepreneurship students about emotion and learning from failure. *Academy of Management Learning & Education*, *3*(3), 274–287. doi:10.5465/AMLE.2004.14242217

Sproull, L., & Kiesler, S. (1992). *Connections: New ways of working in the networked organization*. MIT press.

Ven, A. H. V. d., & Poole, M. S. (2002). Field research methods. In J. A. C. Baum (Ed.), *The Blackwell Companion to Organizations* (pp. 867–888). New York, NY: Oxford University Press.

Wales, W. J. (2016). Entrepreneurial orientation: A review and synthesis of promising research directions. *International Small Business Journal*, *34*(1), 3–15. doi:10.1177/0266242615613840

Weick, K. E. (1979). *The Social Psychology of Organizing* (2nd ed.). Reading, MA: Addison-Wesley.

Weick, K. E. (1995). *Sensemaking in Organizations*. Thousand Oaks, CA: Sage.

Weick, K. E., Sutcliffe, K. M., & Obstfeld, D. (2005). Organizing and the Process of Sensemaking. *Organization Science*, *16*(4), 409–421. doi:10.1287/orsc.1050.0133

Yin, R. K. (2013). *Case study research: Design and methods*. Sage Publications.

KEY TERMS AND DEFINITIONS

Digital Business Model: A business model based on computers and telecommunication that typically use the internet as the main channel of communication.

Effectuation: Effectuation is the way entrepreneurs act in the processes of opportunity identification and new venture creation.

Entrepreneurship: The process of designing, launching, and running a new business. Entrepreneurial behavior can be seen in large and established firms, too.

Ethos: In a modern sense, ethos is the fundamental values associated with a specific person, firm, or organization.

K: The case firm in focus in the article.

M-Commerce: Mobile commerce is parallel to electronic commerce but with the use of handheld devices, typically a smartphone.

Sensemaking: The process by which people give meaning to experience. In organization studies, sensemaking has been used to describe the cognitive activity of framing experienced situations as meaningful.

Chapter 2
Entrepreneurs and Technology:
Use and Access of Technology for Idea Generation

Erastus Ndinguri
Framingham State University, USA

Krisanna Machtmes
Ohio University, USA

Ryan J. Machtmes
University of Minnesota, USA

Jessica I. Hill
Holyoke Community College, USA

ABSTRACT

Technology disruption as well as changing economies have brought new opportunities and threats to the global entrepreneurial models and transformed societies all over the world. Entrepreneurship as a dynamic phenomenon is being analyzed as a tool for bearing the risk of market uncertainty, innovation, competition, and restructuring, and generating new knowledge. Despite continued analysis of the entrepreneur phenomena, how emerging technologies influence generation of business ideas and business formation is still unexplored. The aim of this chapter is to explore this relationship by analyzing women entrepreneurs. Specifically, the authors ask the question, Does the use and access of emerging technology trigger generation of business ideas which leads to business formation? Also, do demographic characteristics of entrepreneurs play a role in knowing and using emerging technology?

INTRODUCTION

Entrepreneurship has been for many years identified as a significant part of the United States' economy (Carland, Boulton, & Carland, 1984; Lamoreaux, 2010; Kritikos, 2014). A call for increased research in entrepreneurship dates to the Schumpeter's era where he urged collaborative effort between historians and economic theorists in providing empirical research on how entrepreneurship has shaped the different

DOI: 10.4018/978-1-5225-5014-3.ch002

economic sectors like firms, industries and the notion of modern capitalism (Jones & Wadhwani, 2006; Schumpeter, 1954). Today research has shown that entrepreneurship is important in building family wealth (Quadrini, 1999), building competitive advantage for firms in technologically intensive industries (Newbert, Gopalakrishnan & Kirchhoff, 2008), as well as development of educational programs that foster entrepreneurial ideas (Solomon, Duffy & Tarabishy, 2002). Variables critical for the success of new entrepreneurial ventures have also been studied including: market and product strategy, entrepreneur characteristics, financial aspects, human capital, origin of the start-up, technology and production aspects, and prevailing social and environmental variables (Serarols-Tarrés, Padilla-Meléndez, & Aguila-Obra, 2006). It is estimated that 20 to 40 percent of the overall labor productivity growth in the eight major industrialized countries can be directly attributed to entrepreneurship (Berglann, Moen, Roed, & Skogstrom, 2011). Research also indicates that starting new ventures leads, after some lag, to higher levels of productivity, a relationship reminiscent of Schumpeterian creative destruction models (Holtz-Eakin & Kao, 2003). Today, technology, innovation and entrepreneurship are crucial to the nation's economic revival and competitiveness in the global marketplace (Sargeant & Moutray, 2010). In the global stage, entrepreneurs perform different functions such as bearing the risk of market uncertainty, innovation, competition and restructuring, and generating new knowledge for the economy (Sternberg &Wennekers, 2005). Additionally, economic development and entrepreneurship is becoming intertwined with both positive and negative influences (Toma, Grigore, & Marinescu, 2014). Because of these contributions to economies, most governments around the world are creating policies that govern and boost entrepreneurship at all levels (Gilbert, Audretsch, & McDougall, 2004). As the area of entrepreneurship has grown the number of women entrepreneurs has increased as well. In the United States, the number of women entrepreneurs increased over 50% by 2012 which is twice the national average (20%) (Womenable, 2015). This increase has not waned as shown by data between 2007 and 2016; the number of women-owned firms increased by 45%, compared to just a 9% increase among all businesses. (Womenable, 2016). On the global scale, higher Total Entrepreneurial Activity (TEA) levels can be seen among women (Kelley, Brush, Greene & Litovsky, 2013). In Sub-Saharan Africa and Latin America/Caribbean, Total Entrepreneurial Activity for women entrepreneurship is 27% and 15%, respectively; while Asia and Europe shows a 4% and 5% rise, respectively (Kelley et al., 2013). As the number of women entrepreneurs has significantly increased it is necessary to understand their participation in the field of entrepreneurship. Growth in entrepreneurship has coincided with the growth in the use of technology. For an entrepreneur to be competitive in this new technology driven economy, they have to be in a position to exploit new technologies that will form the basis of tomorrow's global information networks and ideas built on *e-commerce* (Kowalczyk, Ulieru & Unland, 2003). The first contact in business ideas and motivation to start a business may begin with the use of technologies such as the internet, social media and/or smartphones. By 2012, there were 74.4% American households that had internet, today 84% of American adults use the internet (File & Ryan, 2014; Perrin & Duggan, 2015). As the use of technology grows globally, coupled with the ever increasing role of women entrepreneurs, (Ndubisi, 2007) research on how technology use and entrepreneurial activity interact is necessary. Previous studies have explored both the influence that the external environment has on motivating women entrepreneurial startup businesses and reasons why a business fails or succeeds (Aldrich, 1999; Sandberg, 1986). However, research on how environmental factors such as emerging technology shape the decisions of women entrepreneurs before the business starts remain unknown. To explore this, the study looks at the use of emerging technology as one of the external environmental factors that influences the decision to start a business. Emerging technologies in this study refers to high performance computing platforms such as the World Wide Web, virtual reality, social media, and communication gadgets such as smartphones (Dede, 1996). The purpose of this study is to explore if the use of emerging technology by women entrepreneurs influences a generation of business ideas and business formation.

LITERATURE REVIEW

Over the past decade, there has been considerable growth in women entrepreneurship. According to the American Express OPEN published report, the number of women entrepreneurs in the United States has increased by 45% from 2007 to 2016; this resulted in an estimated 11.3 million women-owned businesses, generating nearly $1.6 trillion in revenues and creating employment for 8% of the private sector workforce (Womenable, 2016). Women entrepreneurs in the U.S. are also known to have greater levels of involvement in business services compared to women in other countries (Kelley et al., 2013). However, the growth in women entrepreneurship is not unique to the United States. Global research indicates that one-third of women are more likely to start businesses out of necessity than men. In six economies (Vietnam, Philippines, Thailand, Malaysia, Peru and Indonesia), women show equal or higher entrepreneurship rates than men (Kelley, Singer & Herrington, 2016). Despite these great strides made by women entrepreneurs, more progress is required for sustainable entrepreneurial growth.

There is limited recognition of women entrepreneurs as major contributors to economic growth, as well as limited research on their businesses. This signals the need for more comprehensive studies of women entrepreneurship (Delmar & Holmquist, 2004). Eleanor Schwartz was among the few pioneers in the seventies that published an article discussing some of the characteristics and would be motivations of women to start a business (Greene et al., 2003). The study concluded that the key motivators for women entrepreneurs were job satisfaction, economic payoffs, and independence (Schwartz, 1976). However, subsequent researchers have offered more insight in to what motivates women to become entrepreneurs. Buttner and Moore (1997) highlighted the pull and push factors and how they contribute to the motivation of women entrepreneurs. The push factors come out of necessity such as insufficient family income, dissatisfaction with a salaried profession, difficulty in finding employment, and the need for flexibility due to family responsibility. The pull factors included the entrepreneurial desire, society status, personal independence, self-fulfillment and power (Buttner & Moore, 1997). In the technology literature, researchers have looked at the role of information and communication technologies in providing tacit knowledge and how this can be used to develop ideas in businesses (Dalkir, 2016); the technology based explanation for innovation research has also led to conclusions that use of technology at an advanced level leads to innovative design processes that helps innovative users become product producers hence entrepreneurs (Baldwin & von Hippel, 2010; Von Krogh & von Hippel, 2006; Lakhani & von Hippel, 2003; Shah & Tripsas, 2007). Entrepreneurial innovation today is also characterized by development and adoption of technology (Doganova & Eyquem-Renault, 2009). Entrepreneurs play a key role in introducing new ventures into the market that are technologically innovative therefore, stimulating the growth of new entrepreneurs and businesses ideas (Miller & Garnsey, 2000). Examples are evident by the development of small startup businesses that are developing inventions and technology with significant potential commercial applications (Gans & Stern, 2003). Given the multiple motivating factors studied, no research has investigated technology as a factor for women entrepreneurs in generating ideas as well as forming businesses. With the growing number of women entrepreneurs and the increasingly present role of technology in fostering innovation, women use of technology must be encouraged (and studied) in order to increase investment (Pascall, 2010). Women also undertake multiple roles in their life. Technology is an important tool that can be used to aid these roles as well as entrepreneurial responsibilities (Jome et al., 2006). Technologies such as social networks, where women tend to be more socially active than men (Lewis et al, 2008), create personal and professional networks that provide opportunity for women to counterbalance and overcome the challenges that they may face in real-life interactions (Herring, 2001). This creates new network-based opportunities which in turn can create a ripe ground for generating business ideas. The upward trend in technology use also affects how businesses operate and how women make their entrepreneurial decisions to start new business ventures (Smith, 2010). Using emerging technologies that are interconnected, different websites have been developed by various organizations (i.e., Women Business Enterprise National Council, National Association of Women Business Owners, Women Business Owners South) to help support and act as virtual professional mentors for women entrepreneurs. As women continue using these emerging technologies for entrepreneurial interactions and as technology continues to evolve, there is a positive influence in the rate of entrepreneurship (Shane, 1996). In addition, certain characteristics of women entrepreneurs such as risk taking and being proactive strongly relate to knowledge acquisition and technological innovation (Nasution, Mavondo, Matanda, & Ndubisi, 2011). The current literature available shows the importance of technology in an innovative economy and how women are using this technology to aid them in the daily activities. However, a significant gap seems to be present in the research on how the use of emerging technology by women entrepreneurs influences generation of business ideas and business formation. This gap needs further exploration as women entrepreneurs continue to look for ways to exchange and transfer knowledge as well as innovate and improve.

THEORETICAL FRAMEWORK

To frame the study, Davis's (1985) theorization of Technology Acceptance Model (TAM) was used. TAM was adapted from the theory of reasoned action. It states that if individuals perceive a technology as easy to use they are more likely to use the system. TAM further creates a connection between the perceived use and perceived usefulness. It highlights the notion that the initial interface that people use in a technology is an important determinant in communicating ease of use (Davis 1985). TAM further suggests that two specific philosophies, perceived ease of use and perceived usefulness, determine one's behavioral intention to use a technology which links to subsequent behavior in this case; idea generation and business formation (Sheppard et al., 1988; Taylor & Todd, 1995). TAM suggests that the effect of external variables (e.g. the design characteristic of emerging technology) on intention mediates through key beliefs (i.e., perceived ease of use and perceived usefulness) (Davis, 1989). In the study, external variables such as emerging technology design characteristics (for example the physical appearance of an I-phone or I-pad) and computer user's self-efficacy are theorized to influence behavioral intention to use, and ultimately usage, indirectly via the influence on the perceived usefulness and perceived ease of use (Davis & Venkatesh, 1996). Further using Davis's (1989) analogy, perceived usefulness is the degree to which a person believes that using emerging technology would enhance his or her productivity. Perceived ease of use is the degree to which a person believes that using emerging technology would be free of effort.

Using TAM as a validating theoretical concept, Ndubisi, Jantan and Richardson's (2001) study looked at the relationship between perceived usefulness, perceived ease of use and usage behavior of information technology among Malaysian entrepreneurs. The study focused on whether any significant relationship existed between given entrepreneurial variables including prior computer use, data intensity use, staff support, computer training and technical support, and the entrepreneurs' information technology perceived usefulness and ease of use. The study revealed that perceived usefulness had a direct positive relationship with information technology use while perceived ease of use had an indirect positive relationship with usage. The results, therefore, provides a starting point for our study's argument that women entrepreneurs perceived useful- ness of emerging technology is directly related to its use. Using the principle of TAM research, the study conceptualizes that the perceived ease of use of technology by women entrepreneurs results into added use of emerging technology which in turn influences generation of business ideas and business formation. Measures of perceived usefulness in this study are perceptions that using emerging technology provides business ideas that are useful in business formation.

To conceptualize this, emerging technology use is measured in terms of the usage behavior of women entrepreneurs. In line with TAM logic of system use the study looks at; 1) Behavioral usage of emerging technologies, 2) The frequency of use of emerging technology, and 3) Usefulness of the emerging technology. For the perceived usefulness, the study uses Davis's (1989) TAM analogy as the degree to which a person believes that using emerging technology would enhance his or her productivity. Research further shows that perceived usefulness and perceived ease of use are determinants of usage (Davis, 1989; Ndubisi et al., 2001). Measures of perceived usefulness in this study are perceptions that using emerging technology provides start up business ideas that are useful in business formation.

METHOD

The target population was women who were aiming to start their own business and/or women who had started a business within the past 5 years. The accessible population was 283 women living in the United States with viable emails. Of the 283 women surveyed, 40 responded for a 14.13% response rate. This study was considered a census (100% sample) of all women who participated in Women in Business (WIB) seminar and provided valid emails. These women were either interested in starting their own business or already owned own a business from the year 2006-2010.

A comprehensive review of the literature revealed that no existing instrument satisfactorily demonstrated the impact of emerging technology on idea generation and business formation among women entrepreneurs. Emerging technology triggers of business ventures have been conceptualized in this study as incorporating women entrepreneurs' knowledge, use, and perceived importance of emerging technology in starting businesses and/or generating business ideas, as well as perceived behavioral attributes of technology use. The survey instrument included questions separated into four sections: 1) User knowledge and use of emerging technologies, 2) Importance of emerging technology in starting or generating a business idea, 3) Behavioral perceptions on the use of emerging technologies, and 4) Demographics. Sections 1 and 2 of the questionnaire were created based on an extensive literature review; section 3 consisted of edited items drawn from an existing instrument on attitude towards online banking scale developed by Kuek and Lai (2006). Several research questions were asked including: Do demographic characteristics play a role in knowing and using emerging technology?; Are there differences between the extent of use of emerging technologies and different entrepreneur women characteristics?; and Is there a possible predictive model of idea generation and business formation, as measured by use of technology overall item mean score?

To measure user knowledge and extent of use of emerging technologies, a total of five items which represent the knowledge and use of emerging technologies were developed for the first section. Respondents were asked to identify the technologies they were familiar with and the average amount of time they used emerging technologies per day. Respondents were required to indicate usage frequency of emerging technology to complete different tasks described in the study and how they use social media To capture the importance of emerging technology in starting a business/generating a business idea, two five-point scales were used in the second section. The first scale assessed the importance of emerging technologies in generating the idea that started the business while the second assessed the importance of emerging technologies in growing the business idea. The third section assessed perceptions towards emerging technology. The items for this section were adapted from attitudes towards online banking scale developed by Kuek and Lai (2006) which reflect the behavioral perceptions and attitudes on online banking. Items, which had online banking emphasis, were either rephrased or deleted and additional items related to our study were added. The instrument used is included in the Appendix.

To measure reliability, George and Malley's (2003) Cronbach's alpha interpretation levels were used. The Cronbach's alpha measurement is interpreted by George & Malley's (2003) as follow: Cronbach's alpha measurements _ > .9 – Excellent, _ > .8 – Good, _ > .7 – Acceptable, _ > .6 – Questionable, _ > .5 – Poor, and _ < .5 – Unacceptable. Section one of the survey had a Cronbach's alpha of 0.70. Section two Cronbach's alpha was measured for the two scales, where the first one had a Cronbach's alpha of 0.75 and the second 0.84. The third section's Cronbach's alpha of items in the scale was 0.93. Based on George and Malley's (2003) analysis all the Cronbach alpha results were above acceptable levels of interpretation therefore the survey instrument tested as reliable.

To establish content validity, four subject-matter experts (SME's) reviewed the instrument. The SMEs' areas of expertise were in the following areas: women entrepreneurship, distance learning and evaluation, social science research, and management. Suggested revisions were made to the instrument based on the input of the experts with regard to the presentation, content and overall structure of the survey. A pre-test was conducted on women entrepreneurs with diverse educational and business backgrounds. They offered feedback as to the necessity, relevance, structure, and clarity of each of the questions and instructions. They also offered feedback on the length and overall ease in completing the questionnaire. Most of the subject-matter experts were administrators in higher education. The feedback of the subject-matter experts was useful because they were all involved in small startup businesses and had a keen understanding of entrepreneurial concepts.

FINDINGS

Demographics

Demographics included ethnicity, highest level of education, age and type of previous business experience. The majority of the respondents had a bachelor's degree or higher and indicated that they had access to some form of technology. Seventy-three percent of the respondents were Caucasian, 19% were African American and 9% were other. Twenty-nine percent of the respondents were between the ages 26-35. Those between the ages of 56-65 and 46-55 represented 21% of the respondents, respectively. Over a third (36%) of the women entrepreneurs were involved in retail business. The demographic makeup of the respondents was similar to other to studies involving women entrepreneurs. Similar women studies by Carter et al., (2003) and Morris et al. (2006) found that a majority of women respondents over the age of 25, Caucasian, and earned a College or higher level of education. In addition, the studies showed that most businesses they owned had been operational for 0-5 years (52% of them).

Use of Emerging Technology

The variable, use of emerging technology, was created by aggregating the sub score from the section that comprises how women entrepreneurs used the emerging technology. Respondents indicated how many hours per day they used emerging technologies and how often they used it to: communicate, search for entrepreneurial ideas, establish business connections, conduct business activities, seek business mentors, create or work on an online business, to socialize and for leisure/entertainment. The variable use of emerging technology was assessed through One-way Analysis of Variance.

Marginally significant differences were observed in the overall use of technology score based on the highest level of education completed (F, 37= 2.52, p = .049; Table 1). The Levene Test ((F, 37 = .54, p = .74) of Homogeneity of Variance revealed the presence of equal variance between the different groups based on the highest level of education. Tukey's statistical results also show that the respondents were likely to use technology more frequently if they had a bachelor's degree versus a professional degree. Respondents that were employed part-time used technology more frequently than those unemployed. The results on increased technology use based upon education level of the respondents are similar to research conducted by Czaja et al. (2006). With the aim of understanding the use of technology among community-dwelling adults, Czaja et al. (2006) found that younger people with higher levels of fluid intelligence and education had lower levels of anxiety about technology and therefore, more likely to use it.

Predictive Model of Idea Generation and Business Formation

The variable, idea generation, was determined by dichotomous response in which respondents indicated whether or not they had a business idea. Respondents that indicated that they had a business idea were asked if they had implemented the business idea. Due to the question's dichotomous nature the variable was analyzed using the binary logistic regression. No statistically significant binary logistic regression model was found to predict the variables, idea generation and use of technology (Table 2). However, the researchers suspect this to be an artificial result due to the low sample size available for testing. Based upon the results from the analysis, use of technology was found to be statistically non-significant at the 0.05 significance level to the binary logistic response of idea generation (Wald = 3.26, p = 0.07). Based on the estimated model parameter β (B = -2.615), the log odds (logit) of generating a business

Table 1. Differences in overall use of emerging technology by highest level of education

	df	SS	MS	F[a]	P[b]
Between Groups	5	4.99	.99	2.52	.049
Within Groups	32	12.65	.39		
Total	*37*	*17.64*			

[a]One Way Analysis of Variance
[b].05 Alpha Level for the Two-Tailed Test of Significance

Table 2. Binary logistic regression illustrating prediction of idea generation based on the variable use of technology

	B	**S.E.**	**Wald**	**Sig.**	*Exp(B)*
Useoftech	-2.61	1.44	3.26	.07	.07
Constant	*8.72*	*5.03*	*3.00*	*.08*	*6123.48*

ᵃVariable(s) entered on step 1: useoftech

idea is indicated to decrease by -2.615, holding all other factors constant. This corresponds to an odds ratio (a ratio of the estimated probability of the occurrence of an event versus the probability the event does not occur) of OR = 0.07, indicating that the model-predicted probability of generating a business idea decreases by approximately ten percent per unit increase in use of technology. This finding, while contradictory to research hypotheses, likely is a byproduct of limited inferential power and possible sampling bias resulting from the low survey response rate.

No statistically significant binary logistic regression model was found to predict the variables, business formation and use of technology (Table 3). However, the researchers suspect this to be an artificial result to the limited survey response rate. Based upon analysis results, use of technology was found to be statistically insignificant at the 0.05 significance level to the binary logistic response of business formation (Wald = 0.050, p = 0.82). Based on the estimated model parameter β (B = 0.109), the log odds (logit) of generating a business idea is indicated to increase by 0.109, controlling for all other factors. This corresponds to an odds ratio (a ratio of the estimated probability of the occurrence of an event versus the probability the event does not occur) of OR = 1.115, indicating that the model-predicted probability of forming a business increases by approximately ten percent per unit increase in use of technology.

DISCUSSIONS AND CONCLUSION

This study contributes to the body of research on women entrepreneurs by evaluating how the use of emerging technology can support the formation of businesses. This is a novel study on women entrepreneurs that lays the groundwork for future research despite the lack of statistical significance in the model in this study. This contributes to the sparse literature on women entrepreneurs (Delmar & Holmquist, 2004; Mitchell, 2011) and provides research opportunities for scholars to further test variables related to entrepreneurship and emerging technology.

As an initial framework that focuses on women entrepreneurs and emerging technology this study has both a practical and theoretical contribution. Theories in academic fields are accounts of social processes

Table 3. Binary logistic regression illustrating prediction business formation based on the variable use of technology

	B	**S.E.**	**Wald**	**Sig.**	*Exp(B)*
Useoftech	.109	.486	.050	.82	1.115
Constant	*-.896*	*1.749*	*.263*	*.60*	*.408*

ᵃVariable(s) entered on step 1: useoftech

that emphasize empirical tests of the likelihood of the narrative and pay attention to the scope or condition of the account (DiMaggio, 1995; Randall, 1981). This study contributes to the holistic research of entrepreneurial theory by introducing a quantitative model that utilizes Technology Acceptance Model and Dynamic capabilities in relating the use of emerging technologies to business formation. Conversely, with the underlying positive odds of forming business coming from the data the study lays groundwork by identifying the positive role that technology can play in 'pushing' or 'pulling' women into starting their own business.

Entrepreneurship affects the growth of an economy in many ways such as job creation, economic growth, new business formation and talent and innovation (Berglann, Moen, Roed, & Skogstrom, 2011). Therefore, different practitioners take part in the entrepreneurship process both directly and indirectly. This study expands knowledge on ways emerging technology affects idea generation and business formation among women entrepreneurs thus, creating new areas of research for scholars and enhancing critical thinking skills for students or clients in the field of entrepreneurship.

LIMITATIONS AND FUTURE RESEARCH

To expand this research, future studies should examine the antecedents of technology use. Use of emerging technology according to the study differs from one device to another. Therefore, understanding the issues leading up to higher frequency use of some emerging technologies and not others is an area of research interest. In addition, the model was limited by testing only women entrepreneurs. Future studies should possibly explore both genders and highlight any statistical differences in the use of technology in generating business ideas. Further work should also build on the framework by exploring differences in business idea generation between respondents that had high emerging technology use and those that had low use of emerging technology. Finally, given the limited response rate future studies should explore a similar study with use of a larger data set.

REFERENCES

Aldrich, H. (1999). *Organizations evolving*. Beverly Hills, CA: Sage Publications Limited.

Alfonso, R. M. (2011). *The American express OPEN state of women-owned business report: A summary of important trends 1997-2011*. Fort Lauderdale, FL: The American Express OPEN.

Berglann, H., Moen, E. R., Røed, K., & Skogstrøm, J. F. (2011). Entrepreneurship: Origins and returns. *Labour Economics*, *18*(2), 180–193. doi:10.1016/j.labeco.2010.10.002

Baldwin, C., & von Hippel, E. (2010). *Modeling a paradigm shift: From producer innovation to user and open collaborative innovation*. Working Paper No. 4764-09. MIT Sloan School of Management.

Bird, B. J. (1989). *Entrepreneurial behavior*. Glenview, IL: Scott Foresman and Co.

Brush, C., Carter, N., Gatewood, E., Greene, P., & Hart, M. (2001). *The Diana project: Women business owners and equity capital: The myths dispelled*. Kansas City, MO: Kauffman Center for Entrepreneurial Leadership.

Buttner, E. H., & Moore, D. P. (1997). Women's Organizational Exodus to Entrepreneurship: Self-Reported Motivations and Correlates with Success. *Journal of Small Business Management, 35*(1), 34–46.

Carland, J. W., Boulton, F. H. W., & Carland, J. C. (1984). Differentiating entrepreneurs from small busi- ness owners: A conceptualization. *Academy of Management Review, 9*(2), 354–359.

Carter, N. M., Brush, C. G., Greene, P. G., Gatewood, E., & Hart, M. M. (2003). Women entrepreneurs who break through to equity financing: The influence of human, social and financial capital. *Venture Capital, 5*(1), 1–28. doi:10.1080/1369106032000082586

Center for Women's Business Research. (2009). *The economic impact of women-owned businesses in the United States (Report No. 1)*. McLean, VA: Author.

Colky, D. L., Colky, M., & Young, W. H. (2006). Mentoring in the virtual organization: Keys to building successful schools and businesses. *Mentoring & Tutoring, 14*(4), 433–447. doi:10.1080/13611260500493683

Collins, R. (1981). On the Microfoundations of Macrosociology. *American Journal of Sociology, 86*(5), 984–1014. doi:10.1086/227351

Cook, S. G. (2012). Women Lead in Adopting New Technologies. *Women in Higher Education, 21*(2), 24–25. doi:10.1002/whe.10296

Creed, A., & Zutshi, A. (2008). The wellhouse of knowledge globalization: IT and virtual communities. *Journal of Knowledge Globalization, 1*(1), 29–42.

Czaja, S. J., Fisk, A. D., Hertzog, C., Rogers, W. A., Charness, N., Nair, S. N., & Sharit, J. (2006). Factors Predicting the Use of Technology: Findings From the Center for Research and Education on Aging and Technology Enhancement (CREATE). *Psychology and Aging, 21*(2), 333–353. doi:10.1037/0882-7974.21.2.333 PMID:16768579

Dalkir, K. (2016). The Role of Technology and Social Media in Tacit Knowledge Sharing. *International Journal of E-Entrepreneurship and Innovation, 6*(2), 40–56. doi:10.4018/IJEEI.2016070103

Doganova, L., & Eyquem-Renault, M. (2009). What do business models do? Innovation devices in technology entrepreneurship. *Research Policy, 38*(10), 1559–1570. doi:10.1016/j.respol.2009.08.002

Davis, F. D. (1985). *A technology acceptance model for empirically testing new end-user information systems: Theory and results* (Doctoral dissertation).

Davis, F. D. (1989). Perceived usefulness, perceived ease of use, and user acceptance of information tech- nology. *Management Information Systems Quarterly, 13*(3), 319–339. doi:10.2307/249008

Dede, C. (1996). Emerging technologies and distributed learning. *American Journal of Distance Education, 10*(2), 4–36. doi:10.1080/08923649609526919

Delmar, F., & Holmquist, C. (2004). *Promoting entrepreneurship and innovative smes in a global economy: Towards a more responsible and inclusive globalization*. Istanbul, Turkey: Organisation for Economic Co-operation and Development.

DiMaggio, P. J. (1995). Comments on "What Theory is Not". *Administrative Science Quarterly, 40*(3), 391–397. doi:10.2307/2393790

Eastin, M. S. (2002). Diffusion of e-commerce: An analysis of the adoption of four emerging activities. *Telematics and Informatics, 19*(3), 251–267. doi:10.1016/S0736-5853(01)00005-3

Farber, H. S. (1999). Alternative and part-time employment arrangements as a response to job loss. *Journal of Labor Economics, 17*(4), 1–12.

File, T., & Ryan, C. (2014). *Computer and Internet Use in the United States: 2013. American Community Survey Reports.* U.S. Department of Commerce. Retrieved from https://www.census.gov/history/pdf/2013computeruse.pdf

Fishbein, M., & Ajzen, I. (1975). *Belief, attitude, intention, and behavior: An introduction to theory and research.* Reading, MA: Addison-Wesley Pub. Co.

George, D., & Mallery, P. (2003). *SPSS for windows step by step: A simple guide and reference. 11.0 update* (4th ed.). Boston: Allyn & Bacon.

Gilbert, B. A., Audretsch, D. B., & McDougall, P. P. (2004). The emergence of entrepreneurship policy. *Small Business Economics, 22*(3), 313–323. doi:10.1023/B:SBEJ.0000022235.10739.a8

Gans, J. S., & Stern, S. (2003). The product market and the market for "ideas": Commercialization strategies for technology entrepreneurs. *Research Policy, 32*(2), 333–350. doi:10.1016/S0048-7333(02)00103-8

Greene, P. G., Hart, M., Gatewood, E., Brush, C., & Carter, N. (2003). *Women Entrepreneurs: Moving Front and Center: An Overview of Research and Theory* (white paper).

Hampton, K. N., Goulet, L. S., Rainie, L., & Purcell, K. (2010). *Social networking sites and our lives.* Washington, DC: Pew Research Centre.

Holtz-Eakin, D., & Kao, C. (2003). *Entrepreneurship and Economic Growth: the Proof is in the Productivity (February 1, 2003).* Syracuse University Center for Policy Research Working Paper No. 50. Available at SSRN: https://ssrn.com/abstract=1809885

Herring, S. C. (2001). *Gender and Power in Online Communication.* Bloomington, IN: Center for Social Informatics, Indiana University.

Jome, L. M., Donahue, M. P., & Siegel, L. A. (2006). Working in the uncharted technology frontier: Char- acteristics of women web entrepreneurs. *Journal of Business and Psychology, 21*(1), 127–147. doi:10.1007/s10869-005-9019-9

Jones, G., & Wadhwani, R. D. (2006). *Entrepreneurship and Business History: Renewing the Research Agenda* (working paper, No 07-007). Harvard Business School.

Kelley, D., Singer, S., & Herrington, M. (2016). *2015/16 global report.* Global Entrepreneurship Monitor. Retrieved from http://www.gemconsortium.org/

Kritikos, A. S. (2014). *Entrepreneurs and their impact on jobs and economic growth.* IZA World of Labor. Retrieved http://wol.iza.org/articles/entrepreneurs-and-their-impact-on-jobs-and-economic-growth/long

Kelley, D. J., Brush, C. G., Greene, P. G., & Litovsky, Y. (2013). *Global Entrepreneurship monitor: 2012 Women's Report.* Boston, MA: Global Entrepreneurship Monitor. Retrieved from www.gemconsortium.org

Kowalczyk, R., Ulieru, M., & Unland, R. (2003). *Integrating mobile and intelligent agents in advanced e-commerce: A survey.* South Clayton, Australia: CSIRO Mathematical and Information Sciences. doi:10.1007/3-540-36559-1_22

Kuek, T., & Lai, M. (2006). An exploratory study on online banking in Malaysia. *The Journal of Business*, *6*(2), 65–84.

Lamoreaux, N. R. (2010). Entrepreneurship in the United States, 1865-1920. In *D.S. Landes, J. Mokyr, & W. J. Baumol (Eds.), The invention of enterprise: Entrepreneurship from ancient Mesopotamia to modern times* (pp. 367–399). Princeton, NJ: Princeton University Press. doi:10.1515/9781400833580-017

Lewis, K., Kaufman, J., Gonzalez, M., Wimmer, A., & Christakis, N. (2008). Tastes, ties, and time: A new social network dataset using Facebook.com. *Social Networks*, *30*(4), 330–342. doi:10.1016/j.socnet.2008.07.002

Lakhani, K. R., & von Hippel, E. (2003). How open source software works: "Free" user-to-user assistance. *Research Policy*, *32*(6), 923–943. doi:10.1016/S0048-7333(02)00095-1

Mattis, M. C. (2004). Women entrepreneurs: Out from under the glass ceiling. *Women in Management Review*, *19*(3), 154–163. doi:10.1108/09649420410529861

Minniti, M., & Arenius, P. (2003, April). *Women in Entrepreneurship.* Paper presented at the Entrepreneurial Advantage of Nations: First Annual Global Entrepreneurship Symposium, New York, NY.

Mitchel, L. (2011). *Overcoming the gender gap: women entrepreneurs as economic drivers.* Ewing Marion Kauffman Foundation.

Morris, M. H., Miyasaki, N. N., Watters, C. E., & Coombes, S. M. (2006). The dilemma of growth: Un- derstanding venture size choices of women entrepreneurs. *Journal of Small Business Management*, *44*(2), 221–244. doi:10.1111/j.1540-627X.2006.00165.x

Miller, D., & Garnsey, E. (2000). Entrepreneurs and technology diffusion: How diffusion research can benefit from a greater understanding of entrepreneurship. *Technology in Society*, *22*(4), 445–465. doi:10.1016/S0160-791X(00)00021-X

Nasution, H. N., Mavondo, F. T., Matanda, M. J., & Ndubisi, N. O. (2011). Entrepreneurship: Its relation- ship with market orientation and learning orientation and as antecedents to innovation and customer value. *Industrial Marketing Management*, *40*(3), 336–345. doi:10.1016/j.indmarman.2010.08.002

Newbert, S. L., Gopalakrishnan, S., & Kirchhoff, B. A. (2008). Looking beyond resources: Exploring the importance of entrepreneurship to firm-level competitive advantage in technologically intensive industries. *Technovation*, *28*(1-2), 6–19. doi:10.1016/j.technovation.2007.07.002

Perrin, A., & Duggan, M. (2015). *Americans' Internet Access: 2000-2015.* Pew Research Center. Retrieved from http://www.pewinternet.org/2015/06/26/americans-internet-access-2000-2015/

Pascall, N. (2010). Women and ICT status report 2009: Women in ICT. Lisbon: European Commission Information Society and Media.

PewResearchCenter. (2015). *Demographics of Key Social Networking Platforms*. Retrieved from http://www.pewinternet.org/files/2015/01/PI_SocialMediaUpdate20144.pdf

Quadrini, V. (1999). The importance of entrepreneurship for wealth concentration and mobility. *Review of Income and Wealth, 45*(1), 1–19. doi:10.1111/j.1475-4991.1999.tb00309.x

Renzulli, L., Aldrich, H., & Moody, J. (2000). Family matters: Gender, networks and entrepreneurial out- comes. *Social Forces, 79*(2), 523–546. doi:10.1093/sf/79.2.523

Sandberg, W. R. (1986). *New venture performance: The role of strategy and industry structure*. Lexington, MA: Lexington Books.

Sargeant, W., & Moutray, C. (2010). *The small business economy (SBR publication No. 375)*. Washington, DC: Small Business Administration. Retrieved from http://www.sba.gov/sites/default/files/sb_econ2010.pdf

Shah, S. K., & Tripsas, M. (2007). The accidental entrepreneur: The emergent and collective process of user entrepreneurship. *Strategic Entrepreneurship Journal, 1*(1-2), 123–140. doi:10.1002/sej.15

Serarols-Tarrés, C., Padilla-Meléndez, A., & Aguila-Obra, A. R. (2006). The influence of entrepreneur characteristics on the success of pure dot.com firms. *International Journal of Technology Management, 33*(4), 373–388. doi:10.1504/IJTM.2006.009250

Solomon, G. T., Duffy, S., & Tarabishy, A. (2002). The state of entrepreneurship education in the United States: A nationwide survey and analysis. *International Journal of Entrepreneurship Education, 1*(1), 65–86.

Schwartz, E. (1976). Entrepreneurship: A new female frontier. *Journal of Contemporary Business, 5*(1), 47–76.

Shane, S. (1996). Explaining variation in rates of entrepreneurship in the United States: 1899-1988. *Journal of Management, 22*(5), 747–781.

Sheppard, B. H., Hartwick, J., & Warshaw, P. R. (1988). The theory of reasoned action: A meta-analysis of past research with recommendation for modification and future research. *The Journal of Consumer Research, 15*(3), 325–343. doi:10.1086/209170

Smith, A. (2010). *Americans and their gadgets*. Washington, DC: Pew Research Center's Internet & American Life Project.

Spanos, Y. E., Prastacos, G. P., & Poulymenakou, A. (2002). The relationship between information and communication technologies adoption and management. *Information & Management, 39*(8), 659–675. doi:10.1016/S0378-7206(01)00141-0

Sternberg, R., & Wennekers, S. (2005). Determinants and effects of new business creation using global entrepreneurship monitor data. *Small Business Economics, 24*(3), 193–203. doi:10.1007/s11187-005-1974-z

Schumpeter, J. A. (1954). *History of Economic Analysis*. New York, NY: Oxford University Press Inc.

Toma, S., Grigore, A., & Marinescu, P. (2014). Economic Development and Entrepreneurship. *Procedia Economics and Finance, 8*, 436–443. doi:10.1016/S2212-5671(14)00111-7

Taylor, S., & Todd, P. A. (1995). Understanding information technology usage: A test of competing models. *Information Systems Research, 6*(2), 144–176. doi:10.1287/isre.6.2.144

Teece, D. J. (1993). The dynamics of industrial capitalism: Perspectives on Alfred Chandler's Scale and Scope (1990). *Journal of Economic Literature, 31*(1), 199–225.

Teece, D. J., Pisano, G., & Shuen, A. (1997). Dynamic capabilities and strategic management. *Strategic Management Journal, 18*(7), 509–533. doi:<509::AID-SMJ882>3.0.CO;2-Z10.1002/(SICI)1097-0266(199708)18:7

Von Krogh, G., & von Hippel, E. (2006). The promise of research on open source software. *Management Science, 52*(7), 975–983. doi:10.1287/mnsc.1060.0560

Womenable. (2015). *The Growth and Development of Women-Owned Enterprise in the United States, 2002– 2012. An Analysis of Trends From the U.S. Census Bureau's Survey of Business Owners*. Author. Retrieved from https://www.nwbc.gov/sites/default/files/Growth%20of%20WOBs%202002-2012%20for%20NWBC%20FINAL.pdf

Womenable. (2016). *The state of women-owned businesses in 2016: summary of key trends*. Author. Retrieved from http://www.womenable.com/content/userfiles/2016_State_of_Women Owned_Businesses_Executive_Report.pdf

APPENDIX: EMERGING TECHNOLOGY ENTREPRENEUR SURVEY

Section 1: User Knowledge and Use of Emerging Technologies

1. Which of the following emerging technologies do you own or have access to? (Response: Y/N)
    a. Smart phones (for example iPhones)
    b. Tablet computers (for example iPads)
    c. Desktop computers
    d. Laptop computers
    e. Internet connected game console (for example Xbox)
    f. Mp3 players (for example IPods)
    g. E- book readers (i.e. Kindle)
    h. Social networking sites (i.e. Facebook and Twitter)
    i. Others
2. Approximately how many hours per day do you use the following emerging technologies? (Response: No. of hours)
    a. Smart phones (for example iPhones)
    b. Tablet computers (for example iPads)
    c. Desktop computers
    d. Laptop computers
    e. Internet connected game console (for example Xbox)
    f. Mp3 players (for example iPods)
    g. E- book readers (i.e. Kindle)
    h. Social networking sites (i.e. Facebook and Twitter)
    i. Others
3. Please indicate how often you use the emerging technologies in performing the following tasks (Response: Very Rarely, Rarely, Occasionally, Frequently and Very Frequently)
    a. To communicate
    b. To search for entrepreneurial ideas
    c. To establish business connections
    d. To conduct business activities
    e. To seek business mentors
    f. For leisure/entertainment
    g. Create or work on an online business
    h. To socialize

Section 2: Importance of Emerging Technology in Starting a Business or Generating a Business Idea

4. Have you Started a Business? (Response: Y/N)

If you have Started a Business;

5. Please describe the type of business venture you have started (Response: statement)
6. How many years has your business been in operation? (Response: statement)
7. Which year did you start your business? (Response: statement)

If you have not started a business;

8. Do you have a business idea or/and intend to start a business in the future? (Response Y/N) If Yes;
9. Please describe the area of business you aspire to venture into (Response: statement)

For respondent with an established business:

10. Please indicate the importance of the following emerging technologies in generating the idea that started your business (Response: Unimportant, Of Little Importance, Moderately Important, Important and Very Important)
    a. Smart phones (for example iPhones)
    b. Tablet computers (for example iPads)
    c. Desktop computers
    d. Laptop computers
    e. Internet connected game console (for example Xbox)
    f. Mp3 players (for example IPods)
    g. E- book readers (i.e. Kindle)
    h. Social networking sites (i.e. Facebook and Twitter)
    i. Others

For respondents with a business idea:

11. Please indicate the importance of the following emerging technologies in developing your business idea (Response: Unimportant, Of Little Importance, Moderately Important, Important and Very Important)
    a. Smart phones (for example iPhones)
    b. Tablet computers (for example iPads)
    c. Desktop computers
    d. Laptop computers
    e. Internet connected game console (for example Xbox)
    f. Mp3 players (for example IPods)
    g. E- book readers (i.e. Kindle)
    h. Social networking sites (i.e. Facebook and Twitter)
    i. Others

Section 3: Behavioral Perceptions on Use of Emerging Technologies

12. Please indicate your agreement with each of the statements (Response: Strongly Disagree, Disagree, Agree and Strongly Agree)

a. I will use emerging technology in generating business venture ideas.

b. I have used emerging technology to generate business venture ideas.

c. Emerging technology is useful in triggering new business ideas.

d. I receive useful entrepreneurial ideas from emerging technologies.

e. Emerging technology is an easy way to trigger new business ideas.

f. Emerging technologies are enjoyable to use.

g. Incentives to use emerging technologies are necessary for me to use it to develop business ideas.

h. I would recommend use of emerging technologies for developing business ideas.

Section 4: Demographics

Please provide the following information. This information is intended to help the researcher understand how these factors are related to women entrepreneurs' efforts to start businesses. The information you provide is completely CONFIDENTIAL.

Your Ethnicity:

African American
American Indian or Alaska Native Asian
Caucasian
Hispanic
Native Hawaiian or other pacific islanders
Other (specify:)

Highest education level achieved:

Less than High School Diploma
High school diploma/GED
1 or 2 years Certificate or Associate degree
Bachelor's Degree (BA/BS)
Master's Degree (MA/MS/ MBA)
Professional Degree (J.D./M.D./D.V.M.)
Doctoral Degree (Ph.D./Ed.D.)

Your current marital status:

Single
Never Married
Married
Living with significant other
Separated Divorced Widowed
Other (specify:)

Current employment status (if any) other than your entrepreneurial business venture:

Unemployed
Employed Full Time
Employed on a Contract Basis
Employed Part Time
Retired

If employed (Full Time, On Contract and Part Time) please indicate your position.
Please indicate your age.

Chapter 3
E–Retail Adoption in Emerging Markets:
A Perspective on Predictive Constructs

Amresh Kumar
Symbiosis International University, India

Pallab Sikdar
Bharatiya Vidya Bhavan's Usha and Lakshmi Mittal Institute of Management, India

Md. Moddassir Alam
Birla Institute of Technology Mesra - Noida, India

ABSTRACT

A five-factor e-shopping adoption model grounded upon TAM and an additional dimension of "trust" have been tested through confirmatory factor analysis (CFA). A structured instrument has been administered as part of survey to 600 eligible respondents comprising of online shoppers. A total of 539 shoppers spread across national zones, age, and gender groups constituted the final sample. Perceived usefulness (PU), perceived ease of use (PEOU), trust, intention to use (ITU), and attitude towards use (ATU) are reliable and valid factors predicting e-shopping adoption. PU and PEOU along with trust bear significant causation towards ATU. ATU serves as strong predictor of ITU, while PEOU determines PU as well. Further, ATU partially mediates PU and ITU relationship. This chapter highlights the applicability of modified TAM framework in predicting the inclination of emerging market consumers to embrace online shopping mediums scantly represented in extant literature.

INTRODUCTION

Recent decade has witnessed exponential growth of e-commerce and internet enabled services (Agarwal & Wu, 2015; Ramcharran, H., 2013). This growth has been a result of several benefits derived by the early adopters of e-commerce practices such as reduced cost, enhanced business opportunities, facilitation of personalized service provisions and reduced lead time. In present times, the significance of the

DOI: 10.4018/978-1-5225-5014-3.ch003

application of web and network based technologies assumes all the more prominence (Turban *et al.*, 2008). Electronic retailing (e-retailing) or online shopping is an e-commerce variant enabling consumers to directly purchase goods or services from a seller over the internet using a web browser. An e-shop is the virtual equivalent of buying products or services at a brick and mortar retail store.

According to the Global Retail E-Commerce Index (2015) released by AT Kearney, USA (100), China (100), United Kingdom (87.9) and Japan (77.6) are the top four countries in terms of online market size; comparatively smaller markets like Venezuela, Saudi Arabia, Belgium, Mexico and Chile recorded high scores in terms of growth potential. The index highlights that global e-retail sales stood at $694.8 billion in 2013, and forecasts that the figure would touch $1,506 billion by 2018. Further, statistics portal Statista reveals that 41 percent of global internet users purchased products online during the year 2013.

In recent years, developing and emerging economies previously viewed as unattractive markets have witnessed an unprecedented rise in domestic e-shopping habits. In fact, the 2013 edition of IT major Google's Online Shopping Festival (GOSF) saw 16 million Indians shopping online within a span of four days. According to a research report released by Internet and Mobile Association of India (IMAI) in the year 2013, online shopping has grown by a CAGR of 35 per cent between 2009 ($3.8 billion) and 2013 ($12.6 billion). Projections by IMAI and Price waterhouse Coopers (PwC) forecast that the CAGR may reach the 50 per cent mark by the year 2020 in context of Indian e-shopping. These statistics demonstrate the existence of huge untapped opportunities waiting to be exploited by retailers in India and other emerging markets.

While the growth and future scope of e-commerce has been generally established, the dramatic development of commerce through the Internet has also brought forth its own set of risks (Forouhandeh *et al.*, 2011), such as: risk pertaining to financial loss (due to reliance on electronic information, exposure to incomplete, inaccurate or distorted information given by Web vendors and third parties; risk arising from providing private information (willingly or involuntarily) to Web traders; uncertainty regarding quality of service/product delivery; and lack of control in the transaction (Luhmann, 1979). As a result, on-line transactions seem to be shrouded in uncertainty and customer trust in on-line interactions remains shaky. According to Stewart, Pavlou, and Ward (2002), trust is probably the most significant element in consumer-marketer transactions.

Pastore (2000) revealed that despite the significant increase of online shopping in the past, fewer consumers than anticipated actually purchased electronically; they increasingly used the medium to obtain information, but not for purchasing products. Authors such as (Luhmann, 1989; Wicks *et al.*, 1999) argue that exercising trust and pursuit of information are substitute instruments to cope with uncertainty. In other words, more trust in any given circumstance would result in lesser search for information, and vice-versa. According to Tomkins (2001), perceived uncertainty levels and probable negative outcomes of an act affect the equilibrium between information and trust which is required for dealing with uncertainty. Several scholars have emphasized trust as essential for understanding interpersonal behavior and economic exchanges (Hoffman *et al.*, 1999; Tan & Thoen, 2004). Further, it has been viewed as a catalyst in buyer-vendor transactions that provides customers greater expectations of fulfilling exchange relationships. While many studies (Luhmann, 1982; Mcknight & Chervany, 2001) have examined trust, trust as an influencer of initial use has received relatively less research attention. An understanding of trust as initial use influencer is critical for e-retailers to enhance customer attitude and usage intention towards their offerings.

In light of the above, the present study attempts to validate an integrated TAM and Trust model of e-retailing adoption. It determines empirical significance of adoption factors in terms of causality towards future usage intention. An extended TAM has been used on account of its high explanatory power in technological behavior in general and e-commerce in particular (Ahn *et al.*, 2004; Shih, 2004; Shang *et al.*, 2005; Barkhi & Wallace, 2007). Following sections of the paper report a theoretical background leading to conceptualized model, review of extant studies on e-retailing adoption in diversified settings, methodology adopted for research execution, data analysis procedures employed and key findings extracted, and discussion of the research findings along with implications for retailers and other practitioners.

THEORETICAL BACKGROUND: TECHNOLOGY ADOPTION THEORIES

Several models have been developed to investigate and understand the factors affecting the acceptance of computer technology. The theoretical models employed to study user acceptance, adoption, and usage behavior include the Theory of Reasoned Action (TRA) (Ajzen & Fishbein, 1980), Theory of Planned Behavior (TPB) (Ajzen, 1991; Mathieson, 1991), Technology Acceptance Model (TAM) (Davis, 1989; Davis, Bagozzi & Warshaw, 1989), the Decomposed TPB (Taylor & Todd, 1995), and Innovation Diffusion Theory (IDT) (Agarwal & Prasad, 1997, 1999; Brancheau & Wetherbe, 1990).

Individual attitude towards using a computer system is affected by twin perceptions of usefulness and ease of use. Explaining general determinants of computer acceptance constitutes the main aim of TAM. An additional utility of TAM has been exploring user perceptions of system usage and probability of online system adoption (Wang *et al.*, 2010). TAM has also been used to predict user acceptance (Lederer *et al.*, 2000). The model provides an insight into the factors of technology adoption affecting user acceptance and why people resist using computers (Chung & Tan, 2004). Studies have augmented TAM with other theories towards improving its specificity and explanatory power (Wang *et al.*, 2010; Legris *et al.*, 2003; Hu *et al.*, 1999).

TRA explicitly incorporates attitudes towards behavior and subjective norm as two independent variables. TRA unambiguously describes the mechanisms through which individual differences influence behavior, suggesting that attitudes are impacted by people's beliefs about whether others think they should perform the action. Its usage in predicting cognitive and affective behavior using the belief-attitude relationship in social psychology have been well demonstrated by (Shih, 2004) and similar line of studies.

TPB, forwarded by (Ajzen, 1985), was designed to predict behavior across many settings, and can be applied to information systems use. TPB proposes that behavior is determined by the intention to perform the behavior. Intention is predicted by three factors - attitude towards the behavior, subjective norms and perceived behavioral control. Subjective norm is the individual's perception of his or her control over performance of behavior. Beliefs are antecedent to attitude, subjective norms and perceived behavioral control. Attitude is a function of the products of behavioral beliefs and outcome evaluations. A behavioral belief is the subjective probability that the behavior will lead to a particular outcome. Outcomes are fairly specific, utilitarian results, such as 'using the system will save time compared to current methods.' An outcome evaluation is a rating of the desirability of the outcome.

Research on diffusion of innovation has been widely applied in disciplines such as education, sociology, communication, agriculture, marketing and information technology, etc. (Rogers, 1995; Karahanna *et al.*, 1999; Agarwal *et al.*, 2000). An innovation is "an idea, practice, or object that is perceived as new by an individual or another unit of adoption" (Rogers, 1995 pp. 11). On the other hand, diffusion refers to "the process by which an innovation is communicated through certain channels over time among the members of a social system" (Rogers, 1995 pp. 5). Thus, IDT argues that "potential users make decisions to adopt or reject an innovation based on beliefs that they form about the innovation" (Agarwal, 2000 pp. 90).

IDT includes five significant and innovation characteristics: relative advantage, compatibility, complexity, trialability and observability. Relative advantage is defined as the degree to which an innovation is considered better than the idea it replaced. This construct has been found to be one of the best predictors of the adoption of an innovation. Compatibility refers to the degree to which innovation is regarded consistent with existing values, prior experiences and needs of potential end users. Complexity is the end-users' perceived level of difficulty in understanding innovations and their ease of use. Trialability implies the extent to which innovations can be tested over a small time window. Observability is the degree to which the results of innovations can be visible to other people. The aforementioned characteristics are used to explain end user adoption of innovations and their decision making process.

TAM has been forwarded as good predictor of information technology based system usage by Davis, (1989). Grounded on the theory of reasoned action (Ajzen & Fishbein, 1980), the TAM framework demonstrates that beliefs influence attitudes which lead to intentions and consequently generate behaviors. Such belief-attitude-intention-behavior relationship can effectively forecast user acceptance of an Information Technology (IT) system.

Beliefs leading to acceptance of IT systems are determined by perceived usefulness and ease of use. Perceived Usefulness (PU) refers to "the degree to which a person believes that using a particular information system would enhance his or her job performance" (Davis, 1989, pp. 320). Such an enhancement can result in a reduction in time taken to accomplish a task or provision of timely information. On the other hand, Perceived Ease of Use (PEOU) represents "the degree to which a person believes that using a particular system would be free of effort" (Davis, 1989, pp. 320).

In addition to initial perceptions, two other constructs included within TAM are 'Attitude towards Use' (ATU) and 'Behavioral Intention to Use' (ITU). Attitude towards use can be viewed as "the user's evaluation of the desirability of employing a particular information system based application" (Lederer *et al.*, 2000, pp. 270). Behavioral intention to use can be considered as the likelihood that a person will employ the IT based application (Ajzen & Fishbein, 1980).

Prior research has emphasized 'Website Quality' and 'Trust' as key dimensions influencing consumer purchase in an e-retailing environment (Gefen *et al.*, 2003). Regarding websites as a popular form of IT, past studies have investigated purchase behavior modeled upon TAM. Existing IT literature establishes logical ties between trust and TAM (Chen & Barnes, 2007; Koufaris & Hampton-Sosa, 2004; Lee, 2009; Suh & Han, 2002). Trust in the context of technology usage can be defined as "the extent to which one believes that the new technology usage will be reliable and credible" (McKnight & Chervany, 2001, pp. 566). Ongoing trust being an underlying theme of several studies, affords an implication that trust is essentially a post-acceptance variable which is formed after an initial purchase is made. Thus, researchers have attempted to exhibit the determinants of initial usage and continued usage together in a unified model.

While many studies have examined trust, initial trust as an influencer of initial use has received relatively less research attention. Further, trust as a pre-acceptance criterion to initial use has not been acknowledged by literature. According to (Kim, 2012) "first purchase intention from unknown e-retailers is mainly dependent on their abilities to build initial trust in potential consumers" (p. 126). Thus, it's both pertinent and critical for existing as well as aspiring e-retailers to gain an understanding as to how initial trust as a pre-acceptance variable influences attitude and in turn, usage intention.

TAM framework has been upheld by contemporary theories like self-efficacy theory, cost-benefit research, expectancy theory, innovation and channel disposition.

The present research has considered TAM as base framework because it seeks to understand the relationship between perceptions (such as perceived usefulness and perceived ease of use of technologies) and usage behavior. Backdrop of the study being emerging markets where technology adoption in retailing perspective has been less refined and prolonged as compared to developed markets, thus testing adoption antecedents required a baseline model.

REVIEW OF LITERATURE AND DEVELOPMENT OF HYPOTHESES

Perceived Ease of Use and Usefulness-Led Attitude Towards Use

Perceived usefulness from an e-retailing perspective could be viewed as the degree to which a person believes that using a particular website would enhance his or her shopping performance and efficiency. It constitutes a major determinant of attitude towards online shopping (Davis *et al.*, 1989) as majority of internet-based shopping problems like issues of access, connection, complexity and Internet familiarity are related to this dimension. A system high in perceived usefulness on the other hand, is one in which a user believes exists a positive use-performance relationship (Davis, 1989).

PEOU and PU act as active initiators of positive attitude towards usage of an online information system. Such causality links have been evidenced in the context of e-commerce as well (Winter *et al.*, 1998; Chen & Tan, 2004; Moon & Kim, 2001; O'Cass & Fenech, 2003; Lee *et al.*, 2006; Kim & Forsythe, 2007).

According to McCloskey (2004), the capacity to enhance shopping performance and shopping efficiency, and achieving shopping objectives were substantial determinants of what made customers' shopping activity a success. If online shopping sites are perceived to be useful, then consumers form positive attitudes and strong intentions to shop online. In such a scenario, they will find online shopping very useful as it would enhance their shopping effectiveness (Lim & Ting, 2012).

Several studies (Ahn *et al.*, 2007; Ha & Stoel, 2009; Klopping & McKinney, 2004; Bisdee, 2007) confirm that an online shopping site is useful if it helps consumers in making better decisions and creates favorable attitudes towards the shopping site. This is in accordance with the findings of (Barkhi *et al.*, 2008) which indicate that shoppers will create positive attitudes towards products and/or services they believe provide sufficient benefits or solutions to problems. Contrarily, negative attitudes would be formed towards products or services that are considered inadequate or seen as not providing solutions to problems.

Similar causalities have been endorsed by studies (Lim & Ting, 2012; McKechnie *et al.*, 2006; Shroff *et al.*, 2011) which propose that customers believe retailers to be useful if they improve their productivity, effectiveness and ability of shopping. Such customers usually form a favorable attitude towards online shopping and exhibit intentions to use it out-rightly.

There are however, a few studies that contradict the causality structure of TAM in terms of PU and consumer attitude towards use based on insignificant effects revealed in e-shopping context (Van der Heijden & Verhagen, 2004; Liu *et al.*, 2003). Such contradictions may be attributed to the dominant effects of extraneous variables and weaker controls factored in towards these. To provide a better clarification of these mixed findings from previous literature and applicability of cited causations in emerging markets, we propose:

- **Hypothesis 1 (H1):** Perceived usefulness of an e-retailing website will have a significant positive effect on user attitudes towards the portal.
- **Hypothesis 3 (H3):** Perceived ease of use of e-retailing web portal will have a significant positive effect on user attitudes towards the portal.

Perceived Usefulness and Behavioral Intention to Use

The TAM framework incorporates both an indirect link (mediated through usage attitude) and a direct causation link between PU and intention to use an online facility. The direct link is based on the theoretical and empirical support that, irrespective of any positive or negative affect towards a particular behavior, an individual's cognitive assessment of the outcome of engaging in the behavior (i.e. usefulness) can have a direct bearing on his/her behavioral intention. (Vijayasarathy, 2004, p.752). Such direct effects between PU and usage intentions have also been upheld by (Bagozzi, 1982; Brinberg, 1979). Thus, we propose:

- **Hypothesis 2 (H2):** Perceived usefulness of an e-shopping facility bears a significant positive effect in terms of behavioral intention to use the facility.

Perceived Ease of Use and Usefulness

Adoption of a device or system by a prospective user fundamentally depends on the extent to which the same is perceived as easy to handle, comprehend and use by the user, other factors remaining constant. A system characterized by complex user interface requiring extraneous aids such as user manual, demonstration tutorials etc. leads to an initial repulsion from user. This in turn proves detrimental towards creation of a positive attitude in terms of usage and negates any possible future usage intention.

Perceived Usefulness occupies major significance as part of the TAM framework and an outcome of the above cited ease of usage perception. Users' perception of ease has a determining effect towards forming perception of usefulness as indicated by (Davis *et al.*, 1992; Mathieson, 1991). However, this holds true when the task performed by the system in use is considered sufficiently important by the user (Davis *et al.*, 1992). Causality between ease of use and usefulness has been well supported by prior researches (Radner & Rothschild, 1975; Goodwin, 1987; Davis, 1989; Taylor & Todd, 1995; Davis & Venkatesh, 1996; Gefen & Straub, 2003; Cyr *et al.*, 2007; Lee & Chang, 2011).

Previous research has found effective search engines, transparent navigational structures, and user-friendly interfaces conducive to usage in context of online retailing good layout have (Shim *et al.,* 2001; Devaraj *et al.,* 2002; Agarwal & Venkatesh, 2002; Vijayasarathy, 2004). In light of these observations, we propose:

- **Hypothesis 4 (H4):** Perceived ease of use of an e-retailing website significantly explains the extent of usefulness perceived by website users.

Trust Led Perceived Usefulness and Attitude Towards Usage

Trust is the most important attribute of e-vendors which consumers respond to (Grabner-Kräuter & Kaluscha, 2003; Gregg & Walczak, 2010; Kracher *et al.,* 2005; Reichheid & Schefter, 2000; Salo & Karjaluoto, 2007). Trust has been considered an important and insightful integrative dimension in TAM studies (Tung *et al.,* 2008). Trust reduces risk and uncertainty (Pavlou, 2003; Suh & Han, 2002) and generates a sense of safety. Therefore, consumer trust in e-tailers and internet technology is believed to play a pivotal role in consumers' e-shopping behavior.

A unique characteristic of the virtual shopping environment is that the prospective buyer cannot directly see and touch a product; the absence of face-to-face interaction results in the buyer remaining uncertain and at risk while making online buying decisions (Ha & Stoel, 2009). It is clear that in context of online shopping, trust assumes more importance as compared to brick-and-mortar stores (Grewal *et al.*, 2004; Reichheld & Schefter, 2000).

Safety issues are major apprehensions that prevent buyers from buying online (Gefen & Straub, 2003). Consumers' trust of e-tailers and internet technology is a key factor that influences beliefs about safety. Trust as a construct incorporates critical aspects like privacy and security as highlighted by existing literature (Flavian & Guinalíu, 2006; Campbell *et al.,* 2003; Jaruwachirathanakul & Fink, 2005). Studies (Pavlou, 2001) have also viewed privacy and security as antecedents of generic trust dimension.

Previous empirical research has integrated Trust into TAM in different ways. Dahlberg *et al.,* (2003) integrated trust into the TAM model with a view to enhance its usefulness in explaining consumer technology adoption. They found that the integrated model provided a better explanation of consumer technology adoption than the basic TAM. Prior studies have highlighted significant causation effect of trust on perception of usefulness (Dahlberg *et al.*, 2003; Pavlou, 2003) and favorable attitude towards usage.

The relationship between trust in e-vendor and perceived usefulness (PU) has been greatly explored. If consumers trust an e-vendor, they are more likely to perceive the usefulness of the online shopping system (Wu & Chen, 2005). Such a relationship between trust and PU has been established, both conceptually and empirically, in previous studies of ongoing trust (Lee, 2009; Gefen *et al.*, 2003; Ortega Egea & Roman Gonalez, 2011; Tung *et al.*, 2008; Wu & Chen, 2005).

While some researchers have determined that perceived usefulness influences trust (Suh & Han, 2002), others have demonstrated trust based influences on usefulness (Gefen, 2004). In a study of e-shopping behavior, Pavlou (2003) reported that trust influenced usefulness as well as ease of use. Towards lending clarity to past observations, we propose:

- **Hypothesis 5 (H5):** Trust bears a significant positive effect towards perceived usefulness

Research supports trust as an antecedent of attitude (Chen & Tan, 2004; Suh & Han, 2002). Kim (2012) empirically established a significant association between consumer trust and attitude towards usage in the context of an e-commerce facility. Based on such evidence we propose:

- **Hypothesis 6 (H6):** Trust has a significant influence on attitude of use in context of e- retailing websites.

Attitude Towards Use and Behavioral Intention to Use

Attitude towards Usage (ATU) has been widely considered in literature concerning technology acceptance. It finds a pivotal space both in the initial version of TAM (Davis *et al.*, 1989) and subsequent adaptations (Chen & Tan, 2004; Schneberger *et al.*, 2007/2008). It has been firmly established as an intermediating link between initial user perceptions and final behavior in terms of intention to use (Ahn *et al.*, 2004; Yu *et al.*, 2005; Vijayasarathy, 2004).

The original version of TAM along with numerous subsequent studies concerning intention-based theories have conceptualized usage attitude as mediator between initial twin perceptions and ultimate usage intentions. However, theoretical and empirical evidence exists that establishes a direct effective linkage between attitude and intentions (Bajaj & Nidumolu, 1998; Swanson, 1982). Based on these observations, we propose:

- **Hypothesis 7 (H7):** Attitude towards usage of an e-shopping website has significant association with ultimate usage intentions towards such website.

The conceptual model proposed as part of the study has been depicted in Figure 1.

METHODOLOGY OF RESEARCH

Data Collection

The current study employed a survey research in order to understand how consumers form their attitudes and make online shopping intentions. In terms of data collection, self-administered questionnaires that consist of 5 socio-demographic questions and 30 questions using a 5-point Likert scale measuring the research constructs were administered to 600 consumers. The respondents (above 18 years) were selected on convenience basis from shopping malls within National capital region and through online shopping

Figure 1. Conceptual model

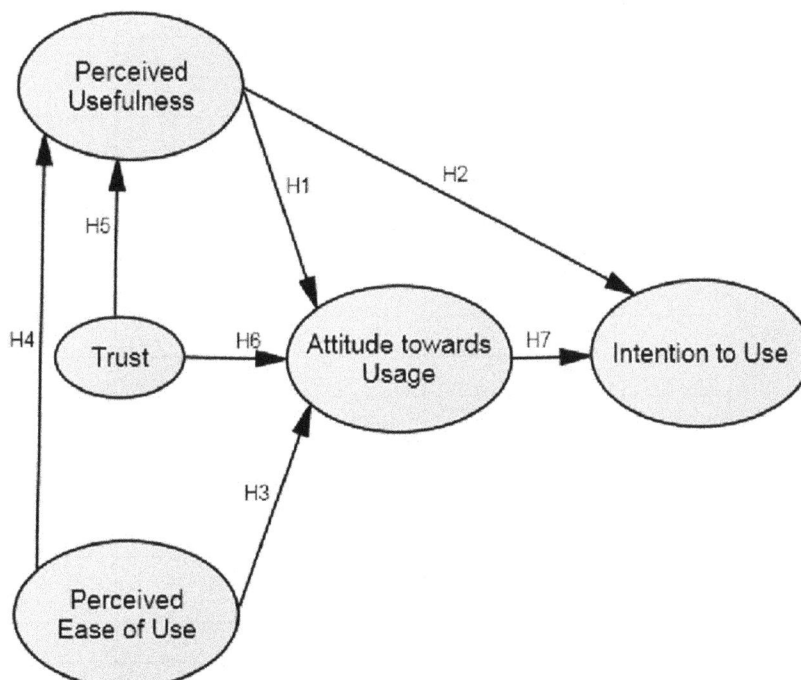

websites/social networking cite across India (all zone). A total of 539 valid responses after data screening were selected for the study. Majority of the responses were collected online across country, thus enhances the generalization of results to all Indians. On the basis of responses received, Exploratory Factor Analysis (EFA), Confirmatory Factor Analysis (CFA) and Structural Equation Modeling (SEM) based path analysis has been conducted.

Demographic Analysis

Table 1 presents the frequencies and percentages of the 539 respondents/customers divided according to Gender, Age Group, Occupation, Geographic Zone and Education. The sample consisted of 277 males (51.4 per cent) and 262 females (48.6 per cent). The respondents have been categorized into four age ranges. All the age categories present a relatively balanced distribution except 46 & above category. Majority of the sample constituents are from salaried class (58.6 per cent) and relative to the educational level, more than half of the sample comprises of graduates or postgraduates (62.7 per cent).

Table 1. Summary of respondent socio-demographics profile

Demographic Characteristics	Measures	Frequency	Valid Percentage
Gender (*n*=539)	Male	277	51.4
	Female	262	48.6
	Total	**539**	**100**
Age Group (in Years) (*n*=539)	15-25	123	22.8
	26-35	172	31.9
	36-45	162	30.1
	46 & Above	82	15.2
	Total	**539**	**100**
Occupation (*n*=539)	Self-employed/Business	223	41.4
	Salaried	316	58.6
	Total	**539**	**100**
Geographic Zone (*n*=539)	North	242	44.9
	West	144	26.7
	East	72	13.4
	South	81	15.0
	Total	**539**	**100**
Education (*n*=539)	High School	114	21.2
	Graduate	228	42.3
	Post Graduate & Above	110	20.4
	Professional Qualification (CA, CS, ICWA etc.)	87	16.1
	Total	**539**	**100**

Source: Compiled from SPSS output

Development of the Instrument

The measurement scales of respective constructs in this study are adapted from previous studies that have been validated to be reliable. Modifications were made in the wording of the items/questions in order to meet the consistency among constructs. Additional items/questions were added in a few constructs in order to reflect the local retail-shopping context. Our research TAM integrated Trust model consisted of 30 items that measured "perceived usefulness" (7 items), "perceived ease-of use" (6 items), "attitude towards usage" (6 items), "behavioral intention to use e-retailing websites" (6 items) and "trust" (5 items). The response scale for all items was a five-point likert scale coded as, 5: Strongly agree; 4: Slightly agree; 3: Neutral; 2: Slightly disagree; 1: Strongly disagree. The summary of the measurement scales and their reliability are shown in Table 2.

Before testing the hypotheses, the scales were tested for Reliability using Cronbach's Alpha statistic and Validity.

The present study is characterized by the following objectives:

- Determining the reliability and validity of individual constructs forming part of the proposed conceptual model of e-shopping adoption.
- Explaining the extent of relational significance of the hypotheses considered.
- Ascertaining the cumulative prediction of variance in intermediate and final outcome constructs.

DATA ANALYSIS AND FINDINGS

Exploratory Factor Analysis and Reliability

The factor-item composition considered as part of our study was further verified by undertaking Exploratory Factor Analysis (EFA). Kaiser-Meyer-Olkin (KMO) statistic of sampling adequacy was found to be 0.91 evidencing the suitability of the study sample for undertaking EFA. A KMO statistic greater than 0.60 can be considered as ideal (Kaiser & Rice, 1974). Further, the Bartlett's Test of Sphericity was recorded as significant indicating the presence of multi-collinearity amongst variables, a pre-requisite for EFA procedure. Principal Component Analysis (PCA) based factor extraction coupled with Varimax Rotation supported the factor-item composition adapted from the extant literature. All the variables

Table 2. Summary of items and sources

Construct	Sources	No. of Items	Scale
Perceived Usefulness (PU)	Bruner and Kumar (2005) Ramayah *et al.* (2009)	7	5-point Likert
Perceived Ease of Use (PEOU)	Chen (1999) Buton-Jones &Hubona (2005)	6	5-point Likert
Trust	Shroff *et al.* (2011) Vijayasarathy (2004)	5	5-point Likert
Attitude towards Use (ATU)	Ramayah *et al.* (2009) Kim & Forsythe (2010)	6	5-point Likert
Intention to Use (ITU)	Shroff *et al.* (2011) Vijayasarathy (2004)	6	5-point Likert

achieved factor loadings above the floor criteria of 0.50 (Guadagnoli & Velicer, 1988) (Table 3). Further, all factors achieved a cumulative variance explanation of 76 percent, much above the minimum recommended explanation based on Variable-Factor ratio (Costello & Osborne, 2005) (Appendix-1). All constructs were found to be reliable as their individual Composite Reliability (CR) values are greater than the floor estimate of 0.7 (Nunnally & Bernstein, 1978) (Table 3).

Table 3. Summary of Exploratory Factor Analysis and Cronbach's Alpha test

Factors	Variables	Variable Labels	Factor Loadings	Alpha
PU	PU1	I am able to accomplish my shopping goals more quickly when I shop online.	.899	0.951
	PU2	I am able to improve my shopping performance when I shop online (e.g. save time or money).	.898	
	PU3	I am able to increase my shopping productivity when I shop online (e.g. make purchase decisions or find product information within the shortest time frame).	.879	
	PU4	I am able to increase my shopping effectiveness when I shop online (e.g. get the best deal or find the most information about a product).	.851	
	PU5	I find the website of online retailers useful in aiding my purchase decisions.	.841	
	PU6	Shopping from online retailers improves my purchase decisions.	.825	
	PU7	Shopping from online retailers makes it easier for me to satisfy my needs.	.692	
PEOU	PEOU1	I find most online shopping portals easy to use.	.928	0.962
	PEOU2	I find it easy learning to use most online shopping portals.	.888	
	PEOU3	I find it easy to use most online shopping websites to find what I want.	.887	
	PEOU4	I find it easy to become skillful at using most online shopping websites.	.881	
	PEOU5	I find it easier to compare products when shopping at online retailers.	.880	
	PEOU6	I feel that most online shopping sites are flexible to interact with.	.864	
TRUST	Trust1	I feel like my privacy is protected at this site.	.855	0.875
	Trust2	I feel safe in my transactions with this web site.	.818	
	Trust3	I believe no money will be lost in unauthorized electronic fund transfers.	.770	
	Trust4	If possible, I don't avoid using new technologies to purchase products and services.	.750	
	Trust5	I believe that online sellers provide detailed information about the purchase process.	.674	
ATU	ATU1	I am comfortable to shop from online shopping websites.	.891	0.921
	ATU2	I like to purchase what I need from online shopping portals.	.844	
	ATU3	I like to seek for product information from online shopping websites.	.835	
	ATU4	I feel happy when I do my shopping online.	.820	
	ATU5	I feel shopping online is a wise choice.	.820	
	ATU6	I hold a positive evaluation of shopping online.	.770	
ITU	ITU1	I intend to use e-shopping website in the coming times.	.833	0.929
	ITU2	I intend to frequently use e-vendors for my shopping needs.	.826	
	ITU3	I intend to use online shopping portal as often as possible.	.811	
	ITU4	I plan to use the e-retailing website in future.	.788	
	ITU5	I expect continuance of my e-shopping portal usage in future as well.	.787	
	ITU6	I intend to use the internet whenever appropriate to do my shopping.	.746	

Source: Compiled from SPSS output

Validity Analysis

Towards establishing validity of independent constructs and over all measurement model Confirmatory Factor Analysis (CFA) has been carried out. Validity measures are mainly of three types viz. Content Validity, Convergent Validity and Discriminant Validity.

Content Validity

The content validity of a construct can be defined as the degree to which the measure spans the domain of the construct's theoretical definition (Rungtusanatham *et al.*, 1998). For the purpose of this study content validity of the instrument was established in consultation with academicians and professional domain experts.

Convergent Validity

Convergent validity refers to the degree to which multiple methods of measuring a variable provide the same results (O'Leary-Kelly and Vokurka, 1998). Convergent validity can be established with the help of Construct Reliability (CR) based on Cronbach Alpha and Average Variance Explained (AVE). Following criteria must be satisfied towards ensuring convergent validity: CR > 0.7, CR > AVE and AVE > 0.5 (Hair *et al.*, 2011). The Alpha value of all the constructs is higher than 0.7. AVE of all individual constructs were found to be greater than 0.5. Further, in case of all individual constructs, the CR (Alpha) statistic is significantly greater than their respective AVE statistic (Table 4). Thus, all individual constructs, with the satisfied all pre-requisites of convergent validity.

Discriminant Validity

Discriminant validity is the degree to which the measures of different latent variables are unique. Discriminant validity is ensured if a measure does not correlate very highly with other measures from which it is supposed to differ (O'Leary-Kelly and Vokurka, 1998). Discriminant validity is established on the basis of AVE and Maximum Shared Variance (MSV). Criteria for ensuring discriminant validity are MSV < AVE and ASV < AVE (Hair *et al.*, 2011). Within the present study, MSV and ASV for each of the individual constructs have been determined (Table 4). The discriminant validity statistics

Table 4. Validity estimates

Construct	(CR)	(AVE)	(MSV)	(ASV)	Convergent Validity	Discriminant Validity
PU	0.951	0.738	0.274	0.117	Yes	yes
PEOU	0.962	0.809	0.232	0.060	Yes	yes
TRUST	0.875	0.586	0.223	0.103	Yes	yes
ATU	0.921	0.660	0.274	0.126	Yes	yes
ITU	0.929	0.686	0.232	0.064	Yes	yes

Source: Compiled from Validity concerns tool-kit output

for the individual constructs were determined using Microsoft Excel based Validity Concerns Toolkit developed by Prof. Gakingston.

Model Fit Estimation: Measurement Model

Figure 2 shows the overall Measurement model of the proposed research framework. Model fit of the framework is assessed on the basis of CMIN/*df*, *P*-value, Comparative Fit Index (CFI), Goodness of Fit Index (GFI), Adjusted Goodness of Fit Index (AGFI), Root Mean Square Error of Approximation (RMSEA) and *P* close. Model fit indices for the measurement model were found to be acceptable and the results have been indicated in Table 5. Further, all the individual constructs i.e. perceived usefulness, perceived ease-of use, attitude towards usage, behavioral intention to use e-retailing websites and trust generated good results with respect to all the specified indices hence were deemed fit.

Figure 2. Measurement model

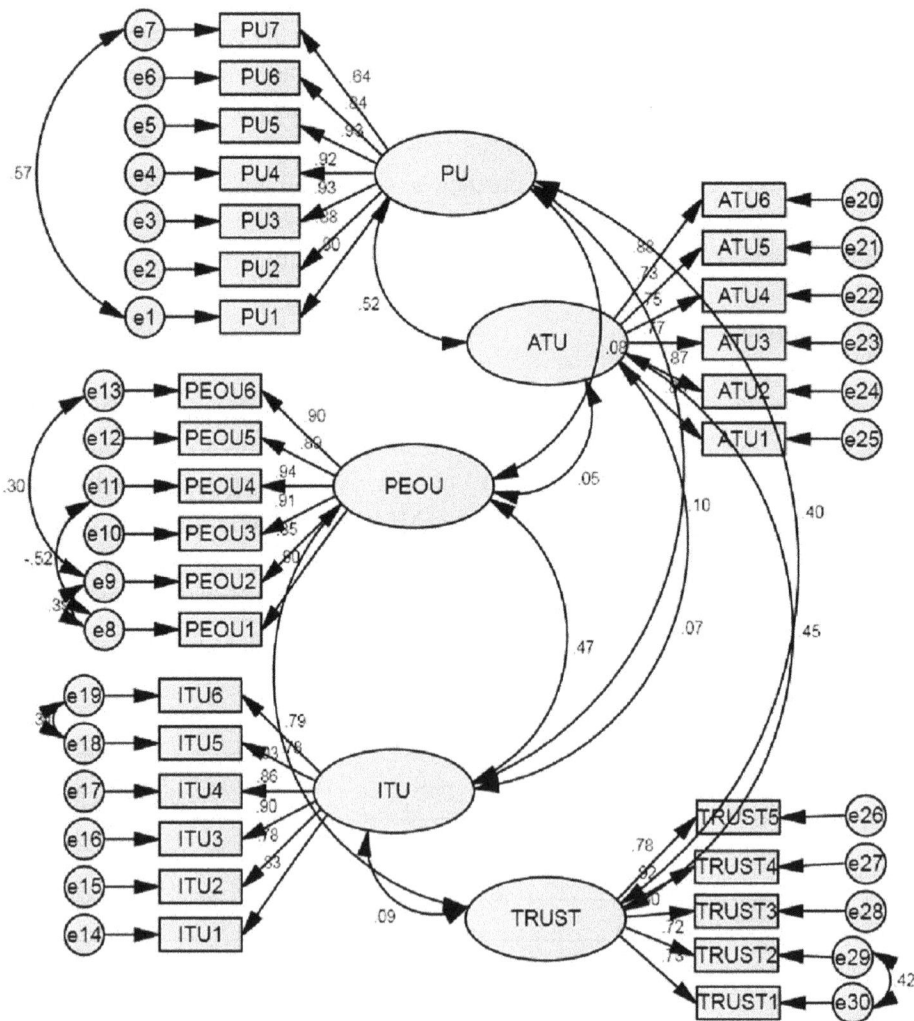

Table 5. Model fit indices (Measurement model)

Indices	Recommended Value	Model Fit Indices
P-value	≥ 0.05	.894
CFI	≥ 0.95	.967
GFI	≥ 0.95	.838
CMIN/df	< 3	1.387
AGFI	≥ 0.80	.806
RMSEA	≤ 0.05	.047
P close	≥ 0.05	.667

Source: Compiled from AMOS output

Structural Model

Figure 3 shows the overall explanatory power, the standardized path regression coefficients that indicate the direct influences of the predictor upon the predicted latent constructs for the model and associated sig. values of the paths of the research model. All the links including TAM model are positive and significant. The variance explained (R^2) for perceived usefulness is 0.29, the variance for attitude towards usage is 0.45, and the variance for behavioral purchase intention is 0.55.

Figure 3. Structural model

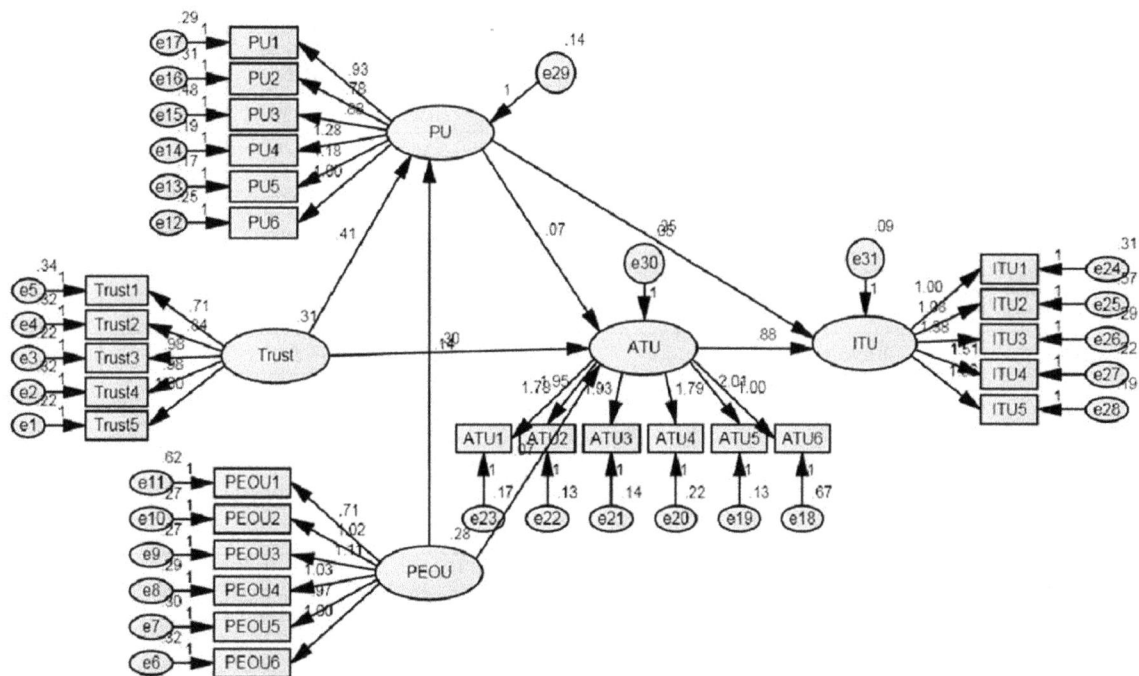

Hypotheses Testing

Direct Effects

On the basis of structural model (Figure 3), the hypotheses testing (Direct effect) are conducted. The standardized regression weights from the respective direct pathways that related to hypotheses, derived from the results of the revised model, are shown in Table 6.

The results in Table 6 indicate that the pathways from Perceived Usefulness to Attitude towards Usage (β=0.102, CR=2.380, p=0.017) (H1), Perceived Usefulness to Intention to Use (β=0.253, CR=5.369, p<0.001) (H2), Perceived Ease of Use to Attitude towards Use (β=0.127, CR=2.832, p=0.005) (H3), Perceived Ease of Use to Perceived Usefulness (β=0.166, CR=3.493, p<0.01) (H4), Trust to Perceived Usefulness (β=0.519, CR=9.197, p<0.01) (H5), Trust to Attitude towards use (β=0.745, CR=6.528, p<0.01) (H6), and Attitude towards usage to Intention to Use (β=0.594, CR=6.611, p<0.01) (H7) are significant and positively related. Therefore, the hypotheses 1, 2, 3, 4, 5, 6 and 7 are supported.

Indirect Effect (PU - ATU - ITU) and Mediation Analysis

The standardized regression weights for the indirect path (PU - ATU - ITU), derived from the results of the structural model, are included in (Table 7). The results in (Table 7) indicate that there exists only a partial mediation cum no indirect effect of ATU on the relation hypothesized between PU and ITU (Baron & Kenny, 1986). The standardized beta values for the direct effect i.e. PU-ITU (in presence/

Table 6. Summary of support for hypothesis based on results of SEM in conceptual model

Hypothesis: Path Proposed (Construct Relationship)	Stdzd. Reg. Weight	Critical Ratio	p-value	Status
H1: Perceived Usefulness →Attitude towards Usage	.102	2.380	.017	Sig[a]
H2: Perceived Usefulness →Intention to Use	.253	5.369	***	Sig
H3: Perceived Ease of Use → Attitude towards use	.127	2.832	.005	Sig
H4: Perceived Ease of Use → Perceived Usefulness	.166	3.493	***	Sig
H5: Trust → Perceived Usefulness	.519	9.197	***	Sig
H6: Trust → Attitude towards Use	.574	6.528	***	Sig
H7: Attitude towards Usage → Intention to Use	.594	6.611	***	Sig

[a]Significant
Source: Compiled from AMOS output

Table 7. Mediation analysis results (PU - ATU - ITU)

Hypothesis	Direct Effect without Mediator	Direct Effect with Mediator	Indirect Effect	Outcome
PU - ATU – ITU	0.122[a] (***)[b]	0.123 (***)	0.063 (0.183)	Partial Mediation, No Indirect Effect

a: Standardized Beta, b: P-value, ***: p-value < 0.01
Source: Compiled from AMOS output

absence of mediating variable) is greater than the standardized beta value for the ATU mediated indirect effect. Further, direct effect in both the scenarios remains statistically significant; while indirect effect recorded a p-value > 0.05 deemed to be insignificant.

DISCUSSIONS, IMPLICATIONS AND CONCLUSION

The proposed model includes a safety/security based dimension (Trust) and four usage oriented dimensions, namely Perceived Ease of Use, Perceived Usefulness, Attitude towards Usage and Intention to Use. On the basis of Average Variance Extracted (AVE), PEOU was found to be the most significant and valid dimension (0.808) explaining online shopping adoption followed by PU (0.731), ITU (0.684), ATU (0.656) and Trust (0.576). This indicates a substantial departure from findings in developed economies where the element of Trust has been established as a key predictor of e-commerce habits (McKnight & Chervany, 2002; Lee & Turban, 2001).

The endogenous items under latent constructs recording weaker standardized beta values can render major implications for e-retailers towards plugging service delivery gaps and ensuring online shopping adoption. The succeeding sections lay down construct wise items which were found to offer scope for strategic improvements based on the study outcomes.

Discussions and Implications of Model Constructs

Trust

From the interactions with, and feedback received from online shopping customers, concerns towards privacy of information while transacting through an online medium became clear. Such privacy concerns led to lower levels of Trust in online platforms. Further, the quality of output offered by e-retailing websites emerged to have failed to align with general customer expectations. Customers explicitly reported that websites lacked sufficient clarity in terms of the purchase process and the steps involved therein. E-retailers must strive towards keeping customers well informed right from the point of initial access to the completion of transaction.

Avoidance of usage of new technological offerings by customers serves as key indicator of extent of trust and reliance reposed on them. E-retailing in present times has moved beyond conventional access points like PCs and laptops towards portable gadgets like smart-phones and tablets. Such gadgets necessitate the use of e-retailer applications (Apps) which create an inhibition in the minds of customers. Traditional brick and mortar retailers who have off-late forayed into the e-commerce landscape can draw fruitful implications from the above findings, and strive towards removing young e-tailer linked inhibitions from customers' perspective.

In an electronic retailing environment quality and variety of post-purchase payment options are the key trust influencers from customer's perspective. Conventional economic environments witness a sizeable volume of cash-on-delivery based orders along with usage of credit/debit cards and Net Banking option towards payment settlements. In an economy marked with liquidity crunch and currency deficit such as demonetization, buyers tend to show greater reliance towards electronic wallets enabling payment settlements on the move and facilitating currency conservation. Thus, it can be argued that economic circumstances have the power to enhance or undermine the level of trust reposed on specific modes of e-retailing based payments by the customers.

Perceived Ease of Use

The e-retailers, in a bid to continually provide easy to use facilities, can take regular customer feedback and inputs regarding their individual service experiences. To minimize the time required to spend on online buying, the e-retailer should strive towards improving website navigation and interactivity. Items such as 'I find it easier to compare products when shopping with online retailers' and 'I feel that most online shopping sites are flexible to interact with' gave a relatively weaker explanation of the PEOU. Such weaker explanations can be attributed to the lack of product variants offered by the concerned web based retailers along with inadequacy of fruitful product specifications. Moreover, the complexities involved in the process of operating the websites can also be a major barrier causing consumers to shy away from online shopping.

The major implication for e – retailers is that they must provide customers with sufficient options in terms of product categories and clear product specifications so that buying decisions become easier. Further, e- retailers must try to ensure that the operating interface offered by the websites remains flexible in terms of all time accessibility, convenient navigational options, query resolution via help menus, etc.

Perceived Usefulness

A customer essentially perceives an online shopping system to be useful if the same caters to his or her specific buying needs. Its usefulness declines substantially if a customer has to move on to another e-retailing website due to paucity of merchandise categories or intra-category variants satisfying his/her specific product requirements. Our survey outcomes reveal that existing e-retailers are yet to satisfy the needs of customers in India. Further, availability of accurate and comprehensive product information facilitates customers in taking informed and superior purchase decisions. Retailers should strive towards leveraging informational adequacy as tool for enhancing perceived usefulness of their online selling mediums and attracting buyers into the e-shopping ambit.

A parallel view of the usefulness of an e-shopping platform can stem from the fact that it affords a non-cash means of purchasing to the buyers. It eliminates the need of currency handling and maintenance abhorred by large segments of population, more so in a currency-strapped economy. Thus, predictive relevance of usefulness in the context of e-retail adoption can't be generalized across diverse economic environments and remains open for further exploration by researchers.

Attitude Towards Usage

Online shopping must provide pleasing experience to consumers to ensure future association of customers with the e-retailer. Retailers must strive towards providing an interface which leads shoppers to believe that shopping online is the wiser alternative to physical stores. The trust element and perceived beliefs of customers, as discussed in the above segments, go a long way in shaping customer attitudes towards usage of e-retailing websites.

The present study finds that customers' evaluation of existing online shopping websites is not quite positive. Retailers must consider the same as a priority implication and realign the features of their e-selling websites to suit customer expectations.

Intention to Use

E-retailers derive true long-term patronage exclusively from the customer's behavioral intention to use their retailing websites. If the favorable usage led attitudes are not transformed into sustained future usage, it amounts to an opportunity lost by the retailers. Buyers should ideally be made to view an e-shopping website as their preferred point of purchase whenever a purchase proposition arises. This will then serve as a testament to retailers' efficient and seamless service delivery.

Findings reveal concerns amongst customers in terms of both the aspects specified above, i.e. future usage of e-retailing website and embracing such portals as a preferred purchasing medium. Retailers, by taking a cue from such observations, could ensure repeat website usage by introducing incentives in the form of discount codes, cash-backs on high frequency purchases, privileged customer categories eligible for special service offerings, etc.

Usage intentions towards a technology can be formed by social influences. The effect of social influence on acceptance decisions is more significant in mandatory settings, where the mechanism of compliance with social pressure and expectations comes into play (Venkatesh & Davis, 2000; Venkatesh *et al.*, 2003). Under the conventional economic circumstances marked by economic stability and adequate levels of disposable currency with the households, intention to use e-shopping mediums will be markedly lower amongst general populace compared to times when currency demonetization prevails within the economy. This stems from the fact that disposable cash in hand can be spent at the physical stores to acquire similar set of products which are being offered by an e-shopping platform. The direct effect of social influence on behavioral intention has been suggested in technology acceptance studies (Karahanna, Straub, & Chervany, 1999; Venkatesh & Davis, 2000; Venkatesh *et al.*, 2003). Thus, social influence can act as an extraneous factor influencing usage intentions in e-shopping context and offers a scope of examining its moderating effects under monetized and demonetized economic settings.

Discussions and Implications of Structural Model

The relationship between PU and ATU (H1) was found significant which is consistent with the findings of Davis *et al.*, (1989). However, few studies like that of Shroff *et al.*, (2011) have found this causality to be insignificant. One possible explanation of this relationship may be that PU leads to positive attitude towards use of e-retailers' web facility among prospective customers.

Perceived usefulness was also found to positively influence Intention to Use (H2). In addition, the indirect relationship between PU and ITU mediated by usage attitude was also found to be significant (H1 and H7.) Similar relationship was portrayed as significant in a number of previous studies (Lee, 2009; Liaw & Huang, 2003; Tung *et al.*, 2008). There are a few studies however, that have contradicted such causation (Wu & Chen, 2005; Yu *et al.*, 2005).

Consistent with prior research (Davis, 1989; Hu *et al.*, 1999), perceived ease of use (PEOU) was found to have a significant effect on attitude toward using (H3). A possible explanation can be that when the customer perceives an e-retailing website as easy to use and nearly free of mental effort (in terms of easy navigation and lesser complexities involved in operating the websites), he/she may develop a favorable attitude towards the usefulness of the system. The relationship between PEOU and PU (H4) was also found significant. This positive relationship could be attributed to the fact that customers are willing to adopt the online system based on felt ease of use. Such customers ultimately tend to identify usefulness of the technology itself.

The causality between Trust and Perceived Usefulness (H5) was found to be positive and significant. The result confirmed findings of previous studies (Lee, 2009; Egea & González, 2011; Tung *et al.*, 2008; Wu and Chen, 2005) that trust and belief are significant determinants of PU. This proves that consumers perceive the usefulness of online shopping systems when they trust the website. It implies that establishing initial trust and belief is an antecedent to the adoption of online shopping systems. Thus, to enhance the online shopping attractiveness, it is imperative that e- retailers build trust amongst online shoppers.

The hypothesized link between Trust and Attitude towards Use (H6) was found to be statistically significant and strong, having path coefficient and p-value of 0.564 and 0.000 respectively. It can be concluded that usage attitude towards an online shopping system is influenced by the trust in the online shopping system. This significant relationship signifies the crucial role of Trust in shaping usage attitude towards e-shopping portals and ensuring purchase intention.

The relationship between Attitude towards Usage and Intention to Use (H7) portrayed highest causal strength amongst all the hypothesized relations, with a path co-efficient of 0.594. At the same time, significance of the relationship was established by a p-value <0.05. Such observation is similar to the findings by Cases *et al.,* (2010).

SCOPE FOR FUTURE RESEARCH

The present study offers a reliable and valid modified TAM in the context of e-retail adoption in India. Further the presented modified TAM model can be tested into mobile wallet market in India in a demonetized economy which is growing exponentially in the recent months. According to an ASSOCHAM study titled 'Indian M-wallet market: Forecast 2022', mobile payment transaction value in India is projected to achieve a Compound Annual Growth Rate (CAGR) of 150 percent and cross Rs. 2,000 trillion by FY 2021-22 from just over Rs. 8 trillion as of FY 2015-16. This highlights the extent of expansion possibilities in store for the current and prospective e-wallet promoters and service providers. Further, within a demonetized macro-economic environment as prevalent in India during the few months immediately following November 2016, the e-wallet service providers leveraged upon the acute household cash deficits resulting from severely reduced levels of currency notes circulation in economy. Paytm one of the major e-wallet platforms in India, experienced roaring success in a span of 12 days after the announcement of demonetization. The firm experienced over 7 million transactions worth Rs.120 crores a day. Paytm consistently recorded more transactions than the combined average daily usage of credit and debit cards for several months following demonetization.

Thus, influence of macro-economic and environmental forces (*viz.* demonetization) on adoption behavior can been gauged as part of future study. Researchers can probe whether significant predictors of adoption are varying in a demonetized environment as compared to those found as key adoption drivers by past studies under the conventional circumstances.

REFERENCES

Agarwal, J., & Wu, T. (2015). Factors influencing growth potential of e-commerce in emerging economies: An institution based N-OLI framework and research propositions. *Thunderbird International Business Review, 57*(3), 197–215. doi:10.1002/tie.21694

Agarwal, R. (2000). Individual acceptance of information technologies. In *Framing the Domains of IT Management: Projecting the Future through the Past* (pp. 85–104). Academic Press. Retrieved July 2015 from http://www.c4ads.seas.gwu.edu/classes/CSci285_Fall_2004/readings/9/required/Agarwal_02.pdf

Agarwal, R., & Prasad, J. (1997). The role of innovation characteristics and perceived voluntariness in the acceptance of information technologies. *Decision Sciences, 28*(3), 557–582. doi:10.1111/j.1540-5915.1997. tb01322.x

Agarwal, R., & Prasad, J. (1999). Are individual differences germane to the acceptance of new information technologies? *Decision Sciences, 30*(2), 361–391. doi:10.1111/j.1540-5915.1999.tb01614.x

Agarwal, R., Sambamurthy, V., & Stair, R. M. (2000). Research report: The evolving relationship between general and specific computer self-efficacy - An empirical assessment. *Information Systems Research, 11*(4), 418–430. doi:10.1287/isre.11.4.418.11876

Agarwal, R., & Venkatesh, V. (2002). Assessing a firm's web presence: A heuristic evaluation procedure for the measurement of usability. *Information Systems Research, 13*(2), 168–186. doi:10.1287/ isre.13.2.168.84

Ahn, T., Ryu, S., & Han, I. (2004). The impact of the online and offline features on the user acceptance of internet shopping malls. *Electronic Commerce Research and Applications, 3*(4), 405–420. doi:10.1016/j. elerap.2004.05.001

Ahn, T., Ryu, S., & Han, I. (2007). The impact of web quality and playfulness on user acceptance of online retailing. *Information & Management, 44*(3), 263–275. doi:10.1016/j.im.2006.12.008

Ajzen, I. (1985). *From intentions to actions: A theory of planned behavior. In Action Control* (pp. 11–39). Berlin: Springer Berlin Heidelberg; doi:10.1007/978-3-642-69746-3

Ajzen, I. (1991). The theory of planned behavior. *Organizational Behavior and Human Decision Processes, 50*(2), 179–211. doi:10.1016/0749-5978(91)90020-T

Ajzen, I., & Fishbein, M. (1980). *Understanding attitudes and predicting social behavior.* Englewood Cliffs, NJ: Prentice Hall.

Amoroso, D. L., & Ogawa, M. (2013). Comparing mobile and internet adoption factors of loyalty and satisfaction with online shopping consumers. *International Journal of E-Business Research, 9*(2), 24–45. doi:10.4018/jebr.2013040103

Bagozzi, R. P. (1982). A field investigation of causal relations among cognitions, affect, intentions, and behavior. *JMR, Journal of Marketing Research, 19*(4), 562–583. doi:10.2307/3151727

Bajaj, A., & Nidumolu, S. R. (1998). A feedback model to understand information system usage. *Information & Management, 33*(4), 213–224. doi:10.1016/S0378-7206(98)00026-3

Barkhi, R., Belanger, F., & Hicks, J. (2008). A model of the determinants of purchasing from virtual stores. *Journal of Organizational Computing and Electronic Commerce, 18*(3), 177–196. doi:10.1080/10919390802198840

Barkhi, R., & Wallace, L. (2007). The impact of personality type on purchasing decisions in virtual stores. *Information Technology Management, 8*(4), 313–330. doi:10.1007/s10799-007-0021-y

Ben-Shabat, H., Nilforoushan, P., Yuen, C., & Moriarty, M. (2015). *Global retail e-commerce keeps on clicking: The 2015 global retail e-commerce index.* Retrieved on July, 2015, from https://www.atkearney.com/consumer-products-retail/e-commerce-index/full-report/-/asset_publisher/87xbENNHPZ3D/content/global-retail-e-commerce-keeps-on-clicking/10192?_101_INSTANCE_87xbENNHPZ3D_redirect=%2Fconsumer-products-retail%2Fe-commerce-index

Bisdee, D. (2007). *Consumer attitudes review.* Office of Fair Trading. Retrieved on June 2015 from http://citeseerx.ist.psu.edu/viewdoc/download?doi=10.1.1.106.2145&rep=rep1&type=pdf

Brancheau, J. C., & Wetherbe, J. C. (1990). The adoption of spreadsheet software: Testing innovation diffusion theory in the context of end-user computing. *Information Systems Research, 1*(1), 115–143. Retrieved onJuly2015. doi:10.1287/isre.1.2.115

Brinberg, D. (1979). An examination of the determinants of intention and behavior: A comparison of two models. *Journal of Applied Social Psychology, 9*(6), 560–575. doi:10.1111/j.1559-1816.1979.tb00816.x

Bruner, G. C. II, & Kumar, A. (2005). Explaining consumer acceptance of handheld Internet devices. *Journal of Business Research, 58*(5), 553–558. doi:10.1016/j.jbusres.2003.08.002

Bryant, J., & Zillmann, D. (2002). Media influences on marketing communications. In *Media Effects: Advances in Theory and Research* (pp. 353–396). Taylor & Francis. Retrieved on June 2015 from https://books.google.com/books?hl=en&lr=&id=KnQXQOP5uoMC&pgis=1

Burton-Jones, A., & Hubona, G. S. (2005). Individual differences and usage behavior. *ACM SIGMIS Database, 36*(2), 58–77. doi:10.1145/1066149.1066155

Campbell, R., Muhtadi-Al, J., Naldurg, P., Sampemane, G., & Mickunas, M. D. (2003). Towards security and privacy for pervasive computing. In M. Okada, B. C. Pierce, A. Scedrov, H. Tokuda, & A. Yonezawa (Eds.), *Software Security - Theories and Systems* (Vol. 2609, pp. 1–15). Berlin: Springer Berlin Heidelberg. doi:10.1007/3-540-36532-X_1

Casaló, L. V., Flavián, C., & Guinalíu, M. (2007). The role of security, privacy, usability and reputation in the development of online banking. *Online Information Review, 31*(5), 583–603. doi:10.1108/14684520710832315

Cases, A.-S., Fournier, C., Dubois, P.-L., & Tanner, J. F. Jr. (2010). Web Site spill over to email campaigns: The role of privacy, trust and shoppers' attitudes. *Journal of Business Research, 63*(9-10), 993–999. doi:10.1016/j.jbusres.2009.02.028

Chen, L.-D., & Tan, J. (2004). Technology adaptation in e-commerce: Key determinants of virtual stores acceptance. *European Management Journal, 22*(1), 74–86. doi:10.1016/j.emj.2003.11.014

Chen, Q. (1999). Attitude toward the site. *Journal of Advertising Research, 39*(5), 27–37. Retrieved from http://dialnet.unirioja.es/servlet/articulo?codigo=474770

Chen, S.-C., Li, S.-H., & Li, C.-Y. (2011). Recent related research in technology acceptance model: A literature review. *Australian Journal of Business and Management Research, 1*(9), 124–127. Retrieved from http://search.proquest.com/openview/3b8f1978447af91117b06bf44adf319b/1?pq-origsite=gscholar

Chen, Y., & Barnes, S. (2007). Initial trust and online buyer behaviour. *Industrial Management & Data Systems, 107*(1), 21–36. doi:10.1108/02635570710719034

Childers, T. L., Carr, C. L., Peck, J., & Carson, S. (2001). Hedonic and utilitarian motivations for online retail shopping behavior. *Journal of Retailing, 77*(4), 511–535. doi:10.1016/S0022-4359(01)00056-2

Costello, A. B., & Osborne, J. W. (2005). Best practices in exploratory factor analysis: Four recommendations for getting the most from your analysis. *Practical Assessment, Research & Evaluation, 10*(7). Retrieved from http://pareonline.net/pdf/v10n7a.pdf

Cyr, D., Hassanein, K., Head, M., & Ivanov, A. (2007). The role of social presence in establishing loyalty in e-Service environments. *Interacting with Computers, 19*(1), 43–56. doi:10.1016/j.intcom.2006.07.010

Dahlberg, T., Mallat, N., & Öörni, A. (2003). Trust enhanced technology acceptable model: Consumer acceptance of mobile payment solutions. In *Stockholm Mobility Roundtable* (pp. 22–23). Academic Press.

Davis, F. D. (1989). Perceived usefulness, perceived ease of use, and user acceptance of information technology. *Management Information Systems Quarterly, 13*(3), 319–340. doi:10.2307/249008

Davis, F. D., Bagozzi, R. P., & Warshaw, P. R. (1989). User acceptance of computer technology: A comparison of two theoretical models. *Management Science, 35*(8), 982–1003. doi:10.1287/mnsc.35.8.982

Davis, F. D., Bagozzi, R. P., & Warshaw, P. R. (1992). Extrinsic and intrinsic motivation to use computers in the workplace. *Journal of Applied Social Psychology, 22*(14), 1111–1132. doi:10.1111/j.1559-1816.1992.tb00945.x

Davis, F. D., & Venkatesh, V. (1996). A critical assessment of potential measurement biases in the technology acceptance model: Three experiments. *International Journal of Human-Computer Studies, 45*(1), 19–45. doi:10.1006/ijhc.1996.0040

Devaraj, S., Fan, M., & Kohli, R. (2002). Antecedents of B2C channel satisfaction and preference: Validating e-commerce metrics. *Information Systems Research, 13*(3), 316–333. doi:10.1287/isre.13.3.316.77

Flavián, C., & Guinalíu, M. (2006). Consumer trust, perceived security and privacy policy. *Industrial Management & Data Systems, 106*(5), 601–620. doi:10.1108/02635570610666403

Forouhandeh, B., Nejatian, H., & Ramanathan, K. (2011). The online shopping adoption: Barriers and advantages. In *2nd International Conference on Business and Economic Research (2nd ICBER 2011) Proceeding* (pp. 2149–2171). Academic Press. Retrieved on June 2015 from http://www.internationalconference.com.my/proceeding/icber2011_proceeding/390-2nd ICBER 2011 PG 2149-2171 Online Shopping Adption.pdf

Gefen, D., Karahanna, E., & Straub, D. W. (2003). Trust and TAM in online shopping: An integrated model. *Management Information Systems Quarterly*, *27*(1), 51–90. Retrieved from http://dl.acm.org/citation.cfm?id=2017181.2017185

Gefen, D., & Straub, D. W. (1997). Gender differences in the perception and use of e-mail: An extension to the technology acceptance model. *Management Information Systems Quarterly*, *21*(4), 389–400. doi:10.2307/249720

Gefen, D., & Straub, D. W. (2003). Managing user trust in B2C e-services. *e-Service Journal*, *2*(2), 7–24. doi:10.2979/esj.2003.2.2.7

Grabner-Kräuter, S., & Kaluscha, E. A. (2003). Empirical research in on-line trust: A review and critical assessment. *International Journal of Human-Computer Studies*, *58*(6), 783–812. doi:10.1016/S1071-5819(03)00043-0

Gregg, D. G., & Walczak, S. (2010). The relationship between website quality, trust and price premiums at online auctions. *Electronic Commerce Research*, *10*(1), 1–25. doi:10.1007/s10660-010-9044-2

Grewal, D., Lindsey-Mullikin, J., & Munger, J. (2004). Loyalty in e-Tailing. *Journal of Relationship Marketing*, *2*(3-4), 31–49. doi:10.1300/J366v02n03_03

Guadagnoli, E., & Velicer, W. F. (1988). Relation to sample size to the stability of component patterns. *Psychological Bulletin*, *103*(2), 265–275. doi:10.1037/0033-2909.103.2.265 PMID:3363047

Ha, S., & Stoel, L. (2009). Consumer e-shopping acceptance: Antecedents in a technology acceptance model. *Journal of Business Research*, *62*(5), 565–571. doi:10.1016/j.jbusres.2008.06.016

Hair, J. F., Ringle, C. M., & Sarstedt, M. (2011). PLS-SEM: Indeed a silver bullet. *Journal of Marketing Theory and Practice*, *19*(2), 139–152. doi:10.2753/MTP1069-6679190202

Hoffman, D. L., Novak, T. P., & Peralta, M. (1999). Building consumer trust online. *Communications of the ACM*, *42*(4), 80–85. doi:10.1145/299157.299175

Hu, P. J., Chau, P. Y. K., Sheng, O. R. L., & Tam, K. Y. (1999). Examining the Technology Acceptance Model using physician acceptance of telemedicine technology. *Journal of Management Information Systems*, *16*(2), 91–112. doi:10.1080/07421222.1999.11518247

Hu, P. J., Chau, P. Y. K., Sheng-Liu, O. R., & Tam, K. Y. (1999). Examining the technology acceptance model using physician acceptance of telemedicine technology. *Journal of Management Information Systems*, *16*(2), 91–112. doi:10.1080/07421222.1999.11518247

Igbaria, M., Guimaraes, T., & Davis, G. B. (1995). Testing the determinants of microcomputer usage via a structural equation model. *Journal of Management Information Systems*, *11*(4), 87–114. doi:10.1080/07421222.1995.11518061

Jaruwachirathanakul, B., & Fink, D. (2005). Internet banking adoption strategies for a developing country: The case of Thailand. *Internet Research*, *15*(3), 295–311. doi:10.1108/10662240510602708

Joshi, P., & Upadhyay, H. (2014, January). e-Retailing in India: Despite issues, customers satisfied with top retailers. *Consumer Voice*, 35–40. Retrieved on May 2015 from http://consumeraffairs.nic.in/consumer/writereaddata/e-Retailingindia.pdf

Kaiser, H. F., & Rice, J. (1974). Little Jiffy, Mark IV. *Educational and Psychological Measurement*, *34*(1), 111–117. doi:10.1177/001316447403400115

Karahanna, E., Straub, D. W., & Chervany, N. L. (1999). Information technology adoption across time: A cross-sectional comparison of pre-adoption and post-adoption beliefs. *Management Information Systems Quarterly*, *23*(2), 183–213. doi:10.2307/249751

Kim, J., & Forsythe, S. (2007). Hedonic usage of product virtualization technologies in online apparel shopping. *International Journal of Retail & Distribution Management*, *35*(6), 502–514. doi:10.1108/09590550710750368

Kim, J., & Forsythe, S. (2010). Factors affecting adoption of product virtualization technology for online consumer electronics shopping. *International Journal of Retail & Distribution Management*, *38*(3), 190–204. doi:10.1108/09590551011027122

Kim, J. B. (2012). An empirical study on consumer first purchase intention in online shopping: Integrating initial trust and TAM. *Electronic Commerce Research*, *12*(2), 125–150. doi:10.1007/s10660-012-9089-5

Klopping, I. M., & Eark, M. (2004). Extending the Technology Acceptance Model and the task-technology fit model to consumer e-commerce. *Information Technology, Learning and Performance Journal*, *22*(1), 35–48.

Koufaris, M., & Hampton-Sosa, W. (2004). The development of initial trust in an online company by new customers. *Information & Management*, *41*(3), 377–397. doi:10.1016/j.im.2003.08.004

Kracher, B., Corritore, C. L., & Wiedenbeck, S. (2005). A foundation for understanding online trust in electronic commerce. *Journal of Information. Communication and Ethics in Society*, *3*(3), 131–141. doi:10.1108/14779960580000267

Lederer, A. L., Maupin, D. J., Sena, M. P., & Zhuang, Y. (2000). The technology acceptance model and the World Wide Web. *Decision Support Systems*, *29*(3), 269–282. doi:10.1016/S0167-9236(00)00076-2

Lee, H., Fiore, A. M., & Kim, J. (2006). The role of the technology acceptance model in explaining effects of image interactivity technology on consumer responses. *International Journal of Retail & Distribution Management*, *34*(8), 621–644. doi:10.1108/09590550610675949

Lee, H.-H., & Chang, E. (2011). Consumer attitudes toward online mass customization: An application of extended technology acceptance model. *Journal of Computer-Mediated Communication*, *16*(2), 171–200. doi:10.1111/j.1083-6101.2010.01530.x

Lee, K. O. M., & Turban, E. (2001). A trust model for consumer internet shopping. *International Journal of Electronic Commerce*, *6*(1), 75–91. doi:10.1080/10864415.2001.11044227

Lee, M.-C. (2009). Predicting and explaining the adoption of online trading: An empirical study in Taiwan. *Decision Support Systems*, *47*(2), 133–142. doi:10.1016/j.dss.2009.02.003

Legris, P., Ingham, J., & Collerette, P. (2003). Why do people use information technology? A critical review of the technology acceptance model. *Information & Management, 40*(3), 191–204. doi:10.1016/S0378-7206(01)00143-4

Liaw, S.-S., & Huang, H.-M. (2003). An investigation of user attitudes toward search engines as an information retrieval tool. *Computers in Human Behavior, 19*(6), 751–765. doi:10.1016/S0747-5632(03)00009-8

Lim, W. M., & Ting, D. H. (2012). E-shopping: An analysis of the Technology Acceptance Model. *Modern Applied Science, 6*(4), 49. doi:10.5539/mas.v6n4p49

Liu, S., Tucker, D., Koh, C. E., & Kappelman, L. (2003). Standard user interface in e-commerce sites. *Industrial Management & Data Systems, 103*(8), 600–610. doi:10.1108/02635570310497648

Luhmann, N. (1982). Trust and power. *Studies in Soviet Thought, 23*(3), 266–270. Retrieved from http://philpapers.org/rec/LUHTAP-2

Mathieson, K. (1991). Predicting user intentions: Comparing the technology acceptance model with the theory of planned behavior. *Information Systems Research, 2*(3), 173–191. doi:10.1287/isre.2.3.173

McCloskey, D. (2004). Evaluating electronic commerce acceptance with the technology acceptance model. *Journal of Computer Information Systems, 44*(22), 49–57.

McKechnie, S., Winklhofer, H., & Ennew, C. (2013). Applying the technology acceptance model to the online retailing of financial services. *International Journal of Retail & Distribution Management, 34*(4), 388–410. doi:10.1108/09590550610660297

McKnight, D. H., & Chervany, N. L. (2001). What trust means in e-commerce customer relationships: An interdisciplinary conceptual typology. *International Journal of Electronic Commerce, 6*(2), 35–59. doi:10.1080/10864415.2001.11044235

Moon, J.-W., & Kim, Y.-G. (2001). Extending the TAM for a World-Wide-Web context. *Information & Management, 38*(4), 217–230. doi:10.1016/S0378-7206(00)00061-6

Novak, T. P., Hoffman, D. L., & Yung, Y.-F. (2000). Measuring the customer experience in online environments: A structural modeling approach. *Marketing Science, 19*(1), 22–42. doi:10.1287/mksc.19.1.22.15184

Nunnally, J. C., & Bernstein, I. H. (1978). *Psychometric Theory* (3rd ed.). New York: McGraw Hill.

O'Cass, A., & Fenech, T. (2003). Web retailing adoption: Exploring the nature of internet users Web retailing behaviour. *Journal of Retailing and Consumer Services, 10*(2), 81–94. doi:10.1016/S0969-6989(02)00004-8

O'Leary-Kelly, S. W., & Vokurka, R. J. (1998). The empirical assessment of construct validity. *Journal of Operations Management, 16*(4), 387–405. doi:10.1016/S0272-6963(98)00020-5

Ortega Egea, J. M., & Román González, M. V. (2011). Explaining physicians' acceptance of EHCR systems: An extension of TAM with trust and risk factors. *Computers in Human Behavior, 27*(1), 319–332. doi:10.1016/j.chb.2010.08.010

Pantano, E., & Di Pietro, L. (2012). Understanding consumer's acceptance of technology-based innovations in retailing. *Journal of Technology Management & Innovation*, 7(4), 1–19. doi:10.4067/S0718-27242012000400001

Pastore, M. (2000). *Young consumers shy away from e-commerce*. Retrieved on July 2015, from http://www.clickz.com/clickz/news/1708147/young-consumers-shy-away-e-commerce

Pavlou, P. (2001). Integrating trust in electronic commerce with the technology acceptance model: Model development and validation. In *Americas Conference on Information Systems (AMCIS) Proceedings* (pp. 816–822). Academic Press. Retrieved on May 2015 from http://aisel.aisnet.org/cgi/viewcontent.cgi?article=1598&context=amcis2001

Pavlou, P. A. (2003). Consumer acceptance of electronic commerce: Integrating trust and risk with the Technology Acceptance Model. *International Journal of Electronic Commerce*, 7(3), 101–134. doi:10.1080/10864415.2003.11044275

Pricewaterhouse Coopers (PwC) PLC. (2014). *Evolution of e-commerce in India: Creating the bricks behind the clicks*. Retrieved on July 2015 from http://www.pwc.in/assets/pdfs/publications/2014/evolution-of-e-commerce-in-india.pdf

Ramayah, T., Rouibah, K., Gopi, M., & Rangel, G. J. (2009). A decomposed theory of reasoned action to explain intention to use Internet stock trading among Malaysian investors. *Computers in Human Behavior*, 25(6), 1222–1230. doi:10.1016/j.chb.2009.06.007

Ramcharran, H. (2013). E-commerce growth and the changing structure of the retail sales industry. *International Journal of E-Business Research*, 9(2), 46–60. doi:10.4018/jebr.2013040104

Reichheld, F. F., & Schefter, P. (2000). E-Loyalty. *Harvard Business Review*, 78(4), 105–113. Retrieved from http://academy.clevelandclinic.org/Portals/40/SamsonParticipants/E-Loyalty.pdf

Rogers, E. M. (1995). *Diffusion of Innovations* (3rd ed.). New York: Free Press. Retrieved on May 2015 from http://www.nehudlit.ru/books/detail8765.html

Rungtusanatham, M. J. (1998). Let's not overlook content validity. *Decision Line*, 29(4), 10–13.

Salo, J., & Karjaluoto, H. (2007). A conceptual model of trust in the online environment. *Online Information Review*, 31(5), 604–621. doi:10.1108/14684520710832324

Schneberger, S., Amoroso, D. L., & Durfee, A. (2007). Factors that influence the performance of computer-based assessments: an extension of the technology acceptance model. *The Journal of Computer Information Systems, 48*(2), 74–90. Retrieved on June 2015-from-http://search.proquest.com/openview/6db431e40f310a511b62e7c85b3c47f3/1?pq-origsite=gscholar

Shang, R.-A., Chen, Y.-C., & Shen, L. (2005). Extrinsic versus intrinsic motivations for consumers to shop on-line. *Information & Management*, 42(3), 401–413. doi:10.1016/j.im.2004.01.009

Shih, H.-P. (2004). An empirical study on predicting user acceptance of e-shopping on the Web. *Information & Management*, 41(3), 351–368. doi:10.1016/S0378-7206(03)00079-X

Shim, S., Eastlick, M. A., Lotz, S. L., & Warrington, P. (2001). An online prepurchase intentions model: The role of intention to search: Best overall paper award - The sixth triennial AMS/ACRA retailing conference, 2000. *Journal of Retailing, 77*(3), 397–416. doi:10.1016/S0022-4359(01)00051-3

Shroff, R. H., Deneen, C. C., & Ng, E. M. W. (2011). Analysis of the technology acceptance model in examining students' behavioural intention to use an e-portfolio system. *Australasian Journal of Educational Technology, 27*(4), 600–618. doi:10.14742/ajet.940

Suh, B., & Han, I. (2002). Effect of trust on customer acceptance of internet banking. *Electronic Commerce Research and Applications, 1*(3-4), 247–263. doi:10.1016/S1567-4223(02)00017-0

Swanson, E. B. (1982). Measuring user attitudes in MIS research: A review. *Omega, 10*(2), 157–165. doi:10.1016/0305-0483(82)90050-0

Szajna, B. (1996). Empirical evaluation of the revised Technology Acceptance Model. *Management Science, 42*(1), 85–92. doi:10.1287/mnsc.42.1.85

Tao, D. (2009). Intention to use and actual use of electronic information resources: further exploring Technology Acceptance Model (TAM). In *AMIA Annual Symposium Proceedings* (Vol. 2009, pp. 629–633). AMIA. Retrieved on May 2015 from http://www.pubmedcentral.nih.gov/articlerender.fcgi?artid=2815463&tool=pmcentrez&rendertype=abstract

Taylor, S., & Todd, P. (1995a). Assessing IT usage: The role of prior experience. *Management Information Systems Quarterly, 19*(4), 561–570. doi:10.2307/249633

Taylor, S., & Todd, P. A. (1995b). Understanding information technology usage: A test of competing models. *Information Systems Research, 6*(2), 144–176. doi:10.1287/isre.6.2.144

Teo, T. S. H., Lim, V. K. G., & Lai, R. Y. C. (1999). Intrinsic and extrinsic motivation in internet usage. *Omega, 27*(1), 25–37. doi:10.1016/S0305-0483(98)00028-0

Tomkins, C. (2001). Interdependencies, trust and information in relationships, alliances and networks. *Accounting, Organizations and Society, 26*(2), 161–191. doi:10.1016/S0361-3682(00)00018-0

Tung, F.-C., Chang, S.-C., & Chou, C.-M. (2008). An extension of trust and TAM model with IDT in the adoption of the electronic logistics information system in HIS in the medical industry. *International Journal of Medical Informatics, 77*(5), 324–335. doi:10.1016/j.ijmedinf.2007.06.006 PMID:17644029

Turban, E., David, K., Lee, J., Warkentin, M., & Chung, M. H. (2008). *E-Commerce: A Managerial Perspective*. Prentice Hall Inc.

Van der Heijden, H., & Verhagen, T. (2004). Online store image: Conceptual foundations and empirical measurement. *Information & Management, 41*(5), 609–617. doi:10.1016/j.im.2003.07.001

Venaketsh, V., Morris, M., Davis, G., & Davis, F. (2003). User acceptance of information technology: Toward a unified view. *Management Information Systems Quarterly, 27*(3), 425–478.

Venkatesh, V., & Davis, F. D. (2000). A theoretical extension of the Technology Acceptance Model: Four longitudinal field studies. *Management Science, 46*(2), 186–204. doi:10.1287/mnsc.46.2.186.11926

Venkatesh, V., Speier, C., & Morris, M. G. (2002). User acceptance enablers in individual decision making about technology: Toward an integrated model. *Decision Sciences*, *33*(2), 297–316. doi:10.1111/j.1540-5915.2002.tb01646.x

Vijayasarathy, L. R. (2004). Predicting consumer intentions to use on-line shopping: The case for an augmented technology acceptance model. *Information & Management*, *41*(6), 747–762. doi:10.1016/j.im.2003.08.011

Wang, J., Gu, L., & Aiken, M. (2010). A study of the impact of individual differences on online shopping. *International Journal of E-Business Research*, *6*(1), 52–67. doi:10.4018/jebr.2010100904

Winter, S. J. M., Chudoba, K., & Gutek, B. A. (1998). Attitudes toward computers: When do they predict computer use? *Information & Management*, *34*(5), 275–284. doi:10.1016/S0378-7206(98)00065-2

Wu, I. L., & Chen, J. L. (2005). An extension of Trust and TAM model with TPB in the initial adoption of on-line tax: An empirical study. *International Journal of Human-Computer Studies*, *62*(6), 784–808. doi:10.1016/j.ijhcs.2005.03.003

Yao-Hua Tan, W. T. (2014). Toward a generic model of trust for electronic commerce. *International Journal of Electronic Commerce*, *5*(2), 61–74. doi:10.1080/10864415.2000.11044201

Yu, J., Ha, I., Choi, M., & Rho, J. (2005). Extending the TAM for a t-commerce. *Information & Management*, *42*(7), 965–976. doi:10.1016/j.im.2004.11.001

Chapter 4
Formal Verification of Secure Payment Framework in MANET for Disaster Areas

Shaik Shakeel Ahamad
Majmaah University, Saudi Arabia

V. N. Sastry
Institute for Development and Research in Banking Technology, India

Siba K. Udgata
University of Hyderabad, India

ABSTRACT

In this chapter, the authors propose a secure payment framework in mobile ad hoc network for disaster areas. In order to enable transactions in a disaster area using existing payment systems, we need infrastructure to communicate such as wired networks and base stations for cellular networks which are damaged by natural disasters. The authors propose to use mobile agent technology and digital signature with message recovery (DSMR) mechanism based on ECDSA mechanism to enable transactions in a disaster area using ad hoc networks.

INTRODUCTION

The unprecedented growth of mobile communication technology stimulated by the ever increasing demand for personal mobility in communications has led researchers to develop new technologies. One such recent development is Multi hop Cellular Networks (MCN) which is an integration of Single hop Cellular Networks (SCN) and ad hoc networks. Single hop cellular networks (SCN) is one where a mobile station (MS) communicates with base station (BS) and ad hoc networks are dynamic, decentralized, infrastructure less, self-organizing and easily deployable without any planning. Both the technologies have their own merits and demerits. SCN's performance is reliable and has strong and mature technol-

DOI: 10.4018/978-1-5225-5014-3.ch004

ogy support but the infrastructure is very costly. On the other hand ad hoc networks are very cheap, easily deployable mainly due to the use of unlicensed spectrum of IEEE 802.11. Integration of these two technologies has led to the development of a new technology called Multi hop Cellular Networks (MCN) which provides the merits of both the technologies. The integration of cellular networks with mobile ad hoc networks offers lot of promising applications. Using Multi hop Cellular Networks mobile devices can communicate and access information at any time and everywhere. For any secure electronic payment system to be successful two conditions need to be satisfied a) Need of Public Key Infrastructure (PKI) to provide trust services for the engaging entities (i.e. engaging entities need to prove their credentials with the help of PKI) and b) Need of an online connection with the Bank in order to commit transaction and prevent fraud (double spending and overspending). Satisfying these two conditions is a challenging task in Multi hop Cellular Network environment so we propose to use Digital Signature with Message Recovery (DSMR) based on ECDSA mechanism for satisfying the first condition and Mobile Agent technology in order to satisfy the second condition. DSMR eliminates the need of certificates and removes the hurdle of PKI thereby reducing the consumption of resources. In addition to this DSMR requires smaller band width for data communications in order to achieve confidentiality, integrity, authentication and non-repudiation properties. The authentication of public keys is implicitly being accomplished with DSMR verification. On the other hand Mobile Agent technology has many benefits such as bandwidth conservation, reduction of latency, reduction of completion time, Asynchronous (disconnected) communications. Mobile agent overcomes low bandwidth and disrupted network which is very common in Multi-hop Cellular-Networks. Using mobile agent the client need not be connected during the entire session thereby reducing the consumption of resources which are very scarce in mobile devices. This is achieved by sending an agent to the Issuer's server carrying all the data necessary for the transaction. So by adopting DSMR mechanism and Mobile Agent technology provides an optimal solution for Mobile Payments in Multi hop Cellular Network environment. For reducing the size of messages and for greater efficiency in terms of key sizes and bandwidth we have used DSMR mechanism based on ECDSA. So ECDSA is suitable for resource constrained devices.

A typical scenario applying mobile agents for Mobile Payment framework in Multi hop Cellular Networks (MCN) environment would operate as follows. A Client tries to buy goods/services from merchant through a communication network i.e. internet and the client's platform is mobile phone equipped with UICC (Universal Integrated Circuit Card) as secure element which is tamper resistant. Client cannot tamper the inner working of UICC because of tamper resistant nature of the UICC, the communication channel between UICC and mobile phone is secure and reliable. Mobile agents are created from the tamper resistant UICC which can be used as a communication bridge between the host and the agent so that a malicious host is unable to access the agent directly. UICC launches a smart mobile agent containing all the necessary negotiation and shopping logics to the Internet. The agent shops around and makes decisions based on the contained logics and finally returns the best quote to the UICC. As a result, during the shopping phase, once the agent has been launched only one message must be received and responded to by the UICC. Another advantage of using mobile agent technology is that agent's real-time interaction capability. For many time-critical applications, the mobile agent can make decisions on the spot, without interactively asking for its owner's confirmation. After the agent brings back a Order Information (OI), the UICC verifies the Order Information (OI) and performs the final purchase transaction.

The rest of the paper is organized as follows in section 2 we present Background, in section 3 we present our proposed a Secure Mobile Payment Framework in Multi hop Cellular Network environment (SMMP). In section 4 we present Security analysis of SMMP, In section 5 we present Formal Verification of the Proposed Protocol's Security using BAN logic' AVISPA and SCYTHER TOOLs, Section 6 presents Performance Analysis of our proposed framework with Related Works, and Section 7 concludes our work.

BACKGROUND

This section introduces entities involved in the proposed framework (SMMP), introduction to Wireless Public Key Infrastructure (WPKI), Mobile agents, Digital Signature with Message Recovery (DSMR), Proxy certificate, Trusted Processing Environment (TPE) and Mobile Agents in MANET Environment.

BASIC STRUCTURE FOR MOBILE PAYMENTS

Mobile Payment framework in MCN is composed of the following entities: a Client (C) represented UICC, Merchant, Issuer, Acquirer and Payment Gateway (PG). These entities are also issued certificates by Certification Authority (CA) within this WPKI. UICC (Universal Integrated Circuit Card) stores client's credentials and payment information. UICC is capable of generating and verifying digital signatures.

WIRELESS PUBLIC KEY INFRASTRUCTURE (WPKI):

Wireless Public Key Infrastructure (WPKI) is the core cryptographic mechanism for non-repudiation protocol; it consists of two parts, one is the operation; the other is the entity. UICC (Universal Integrated Circuit Card) is personalized by the client. UICC personalization involves the following steps

1. Generation of Private Keys (one for Authentication and the other for Signing) using On Board Key Generation (OBKG) procedure.
2. Two PINs and One PUK code are used protecting Private Keys.

There are two major WPKI operations in our non-repudiation protocol, one is the PKI encryption and decryption, the other is the digital signature-based evidence generation and verification. The entities involved are

Mobile Network Service Provider (MNSP)/ Mobile Network Operator (MNO)

Mobile Network Service Provider (MNSP) is the crucial stakeholders of this ecosystem as they control connectivity and enable the entire over-the-air (OTA) transaction system and services. MNSPs provide UICC which can be used as a Secure Element with some modification so they can potentially be an issuer of SE.

Certificate Authority (CA)

There is only one CA in this WPKI (Wireless Public Key Infrastructure). CA issues certificates to clients, banks, merchants and trusted third party (TTP). These entities can authenticate each other by verifying digital signatures and transmit encrypted information if necessary. A CA needs to provide certificate management service to ensure the validity of certificates. CA also supports Digital Signature with Message Recovery (DSMR) mechanism.

Banks (Issuer, Acquirer)

Issuer and Acquirer are the Key Stakeholders in this ecosystem. The Issuer (I) holds the client's money, and whenever a transaction is made it provides the payment ability to that client for purchasing goods and services. In addition banks play a bigger role by acting Application Issuer (AI)/ Service Providers (SP) providing secure services to consumers through their application implemented on a UICC. In our proposed mobile payment framework Issuer (I) installs and personalizes the mobile payment application on the UICC. Once the payment application is installed and provisioned, it is updated by the Issuer (I) server.

Universal Integrated Circuit Card (UICC)

UICC is the Secure Element used in this framework which is a generic platform for smart card applications. It has been standardized by ETSI EP SCP (ETSI Project Smart Card Platform). The UICC can host a number of different applications, either from the UICC issuer or from other parties, each defining and controlling its own application(s).

Payment Gateway (PG) Acting as a Trusted Third Party (TTP)

PG acts as a trusted third party which acts as a medium between Issuer (I) and Acquirer (A) and acts as an arbitrator. It generates necessary evidences for clients, merchants, Issuer (I) and Acquirer (A).

MOBILE AGENTS

Mobile agents are considered to be an alternative to client-server systems, in particular for mobile commerce where mobile devices and communications have limited computing resource. A mobile agent of the host is a set of code and data which can execute the code with the data as parameter in some trusted processing environment (TPE). End users are able to virtually install new software in targeted foreign hosts by creating and launching a personalized mobile agent onto the Internet, thereby automatically accomplishing the assigned mission without the need for interactive guidance from the user. The advantage of adopting this mobile agent architecture is the following: the client needs only to send the Order Information (OI) while its device connects to the mobile base station; once such order is sent to the Broker, mobile devices may be disconnected from this base station. Once the transaction is complete, this mobile agent can carry the message of payment and transaction completion and returns to its host (client). This is an ideal transaction model for mobile commerce. Mobile agents play an important role in future mobile commerce due to their flexibility for information gathering on prices and goods available from varied merchant servers, in addition to aspects of the electronic transactions from price settlement to paying and delivery of the purchased goods. For three basic stages of mobile payment systems, namely, information gathering, negotiation and payment & delivery, mobile agents may play active role in every stage according to the involvement of these agents. In particular, for payment & delivery, mobile agents can be used to pay for purchased goods and help collect an evidence of payment transaction. In many applications, one essential security requirement is that all participant parties reach their goals of fairness. Undeniability of exchange data for commercial transaction is also essential. A mobile agent consists of the following components: agent owner, identifier, goal/result, life time and states. Each agent carries items which are intended to be exchanged. These items include Order Information (OI) and payment information (PI).

DIGITAL SIGNATURE WITH MESSAGE RECOVERY (DSMR)

Secure Electronic Payments in MCN can revolutionize the way payments are being done. For secure payments PKI should be used as it provides trust to the parties engaged in the transaction. PKI uses Digital signatures and a digital signature can be re-presented as a secure base because it provides authentication, data integrity, and non-reputation cryptography services. However, the traditional digital signature schemes are based on asymmetric techniques which make signature computations very expensive and are not suitable for resource constrained devices like Mobile Phones operating in MCN environment. Moreover, these schemes suffer from the well-known authentication problem (i.e. an imposter may impersonate any innocent user with a valid but incorrect public Key) which requires the usage of certificates to avoid it (A. Menezes, P. Van Oorschot, S. Vanstone (1997)). The public-key certificate must be verified by a Certificate Authority (CA), and that verification causes an additional information exchange during a transaction which adds communication cost for mobile phones. So in this paper we propose a protocol where the clients do not have direct communication between client and Merchant/ Issuer. So traditional digital signatures cannot be used because of connectivity restrictions therefore communication with other engaged parties (such as Certification Authority for verifying a certificate, merchant, issuer, acquirer and PG) is not possible during payment transaction. The solution is to use non-traditional digital signature scheme to satisfy the requirements of the proposed protocol in this research. Digital Signature with message recovery using self-certified public keys (Shiang-Feng Tzenga, Min-Shiang (2004), Zuhua Shao (2004), Y. Chang, C. Chang, H. Huang (2005) and Y. Tseng, J. Jan, H. Chien (2003)), provides an authenticated encryption scheme that integrates the mechanisms of signature and encryption, which enable only the specified receiver to verify and recover the original message. The authentication of the public key can implicitly be accomplished with signature verification. We use DSMR mechanism proposed in (Zuhua Shao (2004)) in this work.

PROXY CERTIFICATES

[5] Proposed secure mobile agent digital signatures with proxy certificates. The proxy certificate basically follows standard certificate format (X.509) with minor change. The major difference is the subject identifier (SID), which is the certificate field, recorded the owner of this certificate. In proxy certificate,

its subject identifier is equal to the certificate issuer. A proxy certificate (PC) of a mobile agent is issued and digitally signed by its owner. Beside standard certificate fields, this certificate contains a set of constraints which specifies valid operations that the agent is allowed to perform while using this certificate.

$Cert\_Ver(PC\{C, K_{Ag}[D]\}_{K_c^{-1}})$ is successful if and only if

$Sign\_Ver(PC\{C, K_{Ag}[D]\}_{K_c^{-1}})$ is successful namely

$$K_c(PC\{C, K_{Ag}[D]\}_{K_c^{-1}}) = H(PC\{C, K_{Ag}[D]\}_{K_c^{-1}})$$

We use the notation $PC\{C, K_{Ag}[D]\}_{K_c^{-1}}$ to represent the proxy certificate of the Mobile Agent (Ag) belonging to its owner Client (C) with data 'D'. This PC is carried by this Mobile Agent (Ag) along with the message in the DSMR. The receiver receives DSMR verifies and gets the message from the received DSMR. The received message also contains PC of the Mobile Agent (Ag) which can be verified by the receiver using the public key of the client.

TRUSTED PROCESSING ENVIRONMENT (TPE)

A TPE in a mobile agent system provides a safe environment for the execution of any alien program; these include Software-based fault isolation and safe-code interpretation. In our proposed framework TPE is provided by Issuer (I) (which is trusted by Client (C)), Acquirer (A) (which is trusted by Merchant (M)), and Payment Gateway (PG) (which is trusted by Client (C) & Merchant (M).

MOBILE AGENTS IN MANET ENVIRONMENT

The Internet Engineering Task Force's mobile Internet protocol is a widely accepted standard that uses mobile agents to support seamless handoffs, making it possible for mobile hosts to roam from subnet to subnet without changing IP addresses. Another emerging wireless architecture, mobile ad hoc networks, can be flexibly deployed in most environments without the need for infrastructure base stations. In most cases, MANET's use IEEE 802.11 network interface cards. MANET's applications include situations in which a network infrastructure is not available but immediate deployment of a network is required, such as a battlefield, outdoor assembly, or emergency rescue. Integrating these two architectures will facilitate the current trend of moving to an all-IP wireless environment (Yu-Chee Tseng, Chia-Ching Shen and Wen-Tsuen Chen (2003)). (Yu-Chee Tseng, Chia-Ching Shen and Wen-Tsuen Chen (2003)) Proposes an architecture that extends the typical wireless access points to multiple MANET's, each as a subnet of the Internet, to create an integrated environment that supports both macro and micro IP mobility. From the mobile IP perspective, foreign agents' service ranges are no longer limited to hosts within a single wireless hop; the use of MANET's lets mobile hosts immediately utilize available Internet services without concern about disconnection. In this work Mobile Agents use the architecture proposed in (Yu-Chee Tseng, Chia-Ching Shen and Wen-Tsuen Chen (2003)) for communicating with the base station.

RELATED WORK

As per our knowledge mobile payment protocols were not proposed in MCN environment. Mobile payment protocols proposed by Téllez et al. (Téllez, J., & Sierra, J. (2007a), Téllez, J., & Sierra, J. (2007b), Téllez, J., Sierra, J., Izquierdo, A., & Torres, J (2006) & Téllez, J., Sierra, J., Zeadally, S., & Torres, J. (2008)) are the examples of mobile payment protocols suitable for scenarios with communication restrictions. W. Li *et al.* (2012) introduced an electronic payment mechanism that permits a payment transaction between a vehicle and a merchant when there is a limited connection, however, this mechanism needs a constant link from the merchant to the bank to complete the transaction, and cannot be used, therefore, to provide the needed services for people in a disaster area. Dai *et al.* (2006) proposed an offline payment mechanism that is used to buy digital goods. Their proposed mobile payment system adopts mechanisms from Dai's previous works, which introduced a debit-based payment protocol. Patil and Shyamasundar (2004) introduced an offline electronic coupon micro-payment system. Their scheme is based on credit and allows users to delegate their ability to pay for an item to another person device. The electronic coupon scheme delegation protocol is based on multiseed payword chains. Their scheme focuses on minimizing the computational cost of mobile devices with limited resources. Mobile Ad hoc networks also has communication restrictions such as low bandwidth and disrupted network which is very common in these networks. In order to overcome these drawbacks we adopt mobile agent because mobile agents overcome low bandwidth and disrupted network, using mobile agents the client need not be connected during the entire session thereby reducing the consumption of resources which are very scarce in mobile devices. This is achieved by sending an agent to the Issuer's server carrying all the data necessary for the transaction. We have adopted DSMR because it eliminates the need of certificates and removes the hurdle of PKI thereby reducing the consumption of resources. In addition to this DSMR requires smaller band width for data communications in order to achieve confidentiality, integrity, authentication and non-repudiation properties. The authentication of public keys is implicitly being accomplished with DSMR verification thereby reducing the number of communication passes of the client.

GAPS FOUND IN RELATED WORK

1. Protocols proposed by Tellez et.al (Téllez, J., & Sierra, J. (2007a), Téllez, J., & Sierra, J. (2007b), Téllez, J., Sierra, J., Izquierdo, A., & Torres, J (2006) & Téllez, J., Sierra, J., Zeadally, S., & Torres, J. (2008)) employs symmetric-key operations and Digital Signature with Message Recovery using Self-Certified public keys schemes based on RSA (which consumes more computational and communication cost compared with ECC).
2. The number of Client interactions with other engaged parties are more.
3. Protocols proposed by Tellez et.al (Téllez, J., & Sierra, J. (2007a), Téllez, J., & Sierra, J. (2007b), Téllez, J., Sierra, J., Izquierdo, A., & Torres, J (2006) & Téllez, J., Sierra, J., Zeadally, S., & Torres, J. (2008)) do not ensure forward secrecy.

4. In protocols proposed by Tellez et.al (Téllez, J., & Sierra, J. (2007a), Téllez, J., & Sierra, J. (2007b), Téllez, J., Sierra, J., Izquierdo, A., & Torres, J (2006) & Téllez, J., Sierra, J., Zeadally, S., & Torres, J. (2008)) every Client C needs to register itself with merchant in merchant registration protocol thereby consuming lot of resources.

5. This paper differs from related work given by Dai *et al.* (2006), W. Li *et al.* (2012) and Patil and Shyamasundar (2004) as our proposed secure payment system that utilizes infrastructure less mobile ad-hoc networks (MANETs) to permit users to buy recovery goods in disaster areas.

6. Protocol proposed in (Téllez, J., & Sierra, J. (2007a)) does not ensure non repudiation.

7. Protocols proposed by Tellez et.al (al (Téllez, J., & Sierra, J. (2007a), Téllez, J., & Sierra, J. (2007b) & Téllez, J., Sierra, J., Izquierdo, A.) cannot withstand Replay attack, Impersonation attack, and MITM attack.

8. Security protocols are error prone and are not easy to identify errors and prove their correctness. Mobile Payment Protocols proposed by Tellez et.al. were not verified using Manual Formal verification methods (like BAN Logic, SVO Logic) or using Automated Formal verification Tools like AVISPA, Scyther and CryptoVerif.

CONTRIBUTIONS

1. We have proposed a Secure Mobile Payment Framework in Multi hop Cellular network environment using Mobile Agents and Digital Signature with Message Recovery (DSMR) based on ECC. Mobile Agent technology has many benefits such as bandwidth conservation, reduction of latency, reduction of completion time, Asynchronous (disconnected) communications. Digital Signature with Message Recovery based on ECC eliminates the need of adopting PKI cryptosystems.

2. Our protocol is proposed in the UICC of Mobile Device which is considered to be a tamper resistant device so UICC is a Secure Signature Creation Device (SSCD) because the signature processes are performed in the UICC and the private key never leaves the Wireless Identity Module (WIM). So non repudiation is ensured in devices where private key is stored in Wireless Identity Module (WIM).

3. The transaction flow in our proposed Secure Mobile based Merchant Payment (SMMP) Protocol is from client to Issuer decreasing the risk of reusing client's Payment Information (PI) for the later transactions and issuer is a trusted entity of the client. So client can trust Trusted Processing Environment (TPE) provided by the Issuer.

4. In our proposed Secure Mobile based Merchant Payment (SMMP) client need not register itself with merchant in merchant registration protocol thereby reducing the consumption of resources.

PRELIMINARIES

1. Our proposed Secure Mobile Payment Protocol ensures Authentication, Integrity, Confidentiality and Non Repudiation, achieves Identity protection from merchant and Eavesdropper, achieves Transaction privacy from Eavesdropper and Payment Gateway, achieves Payment Secrecy, Order Secrecy, forward secrecy, and prevents Double Spending, Overspending and Money laundering.

2. In addition to these our proposed SMMP withstands Replay, Man in the Middle and Impersonation attacks.

3. Our proposed SMMP was successfully verified using BAN Logic, the code and the results using BAN Logic are given in section 5.1.

4. Our proposed SMMP is modeled using the High Level Protocol Specification Language (HLPSL) and was verified successfully using AVISPA (Automated Validation of Internet Security Protocols and Applications) tool, the results using this tool are given in section 5.2.

5. Our proposed SMMP is modeled using the high-level formal language SPDL (Security Protocol Description Language) and was verified successfully using Scyther tool, the code and the results using this tool are given in section 5.3.

OUR PROPOSED MOBILE PAYMENT FRAMEWORK

Assumptions

1. Client (C) is considered to have a mobile device with UICC Mobile Payment Application is installed in the UICC by the Bank (B) and private key is stored in the tamper resistant UICC

2. Client personalizes UICC (Generation of private key and public key using On-Board Key Generation procedure). Installation and Personalization (Authentication and Key-Agreement protocol) of Mobile Payment Application (which is on UICC) is done by the remote bank server Over The Air.

3. Issuer (I) is the Client (C's) financial institution and is trusted by the Client. It provides the payment instrument to the Client (C) and manages Client's accounts including funds transfer. Acquirer (A) is the Merchant's (M) financial institution and is trusted by the Merchant. It manages M's account.

4. In our proposed framework, Trusted Processing Environment (TPE) is provided by Issuer (I) and this TPE is trusted by Client (C), Acquirer (A) provides Trusted Processing Environment (TPE) and this TPE is trusted by Merchant (M) and Payment Gateway (PG) provides Trusted Processing Environment (TPE) for Client (C) & Merchant (M)) and is trusted by both Client (C) & Merchant (M).

5. Payment Gateway (PG) is an entity that acts as a medium between A and I at Private banking network whose function is to clear and settle funds and acts as an arbitrator. PG is trusted by all the engaging parties. Payment Gateway (PG) also acts as a Trusted Third Party.

6. A secure private banking network connecting (I, A and PG) ensures security of the messages exchanged among them.

7. Issuer Installs and Personalizes (Authentication and Key-Agreement protocol) Mobile Payment Application (on UICC) i.e. a symmetric secret key is shared between Issuer (I) and Client (C) (Kci).

8. Payment Instruction (PI) contains sensitive information such as credit/debit card account number and is encrypted using shared secret key between C and I i.e. Shared secret key is known only to Client (C) and Issuer (I).

9. Single CA is used in our model which issues certificates and is trusted by all the engaged parties. All the engaged parties/actors/entities have their own digital certificates. CA supports DSMR mechanism.

10. We have modified system initialization phase from i.e. when a client C wants to join the system, he has to prove his credentials and requests for anonymous identity $anonid_C$ then CA allocates anonymous identity to the client so instead of C, CA issues $anonid_C$ as client's identity thereby achieving anonymity.

SECURE MOBILE BASED MERCHANT PAYMENT PROTOCOL IN MCN (SMMP)

Entities involved in SMMP protocol: Client (C), Merchant (M), Issuer (I), Acquirer (A) and Payment Gateway (PG). Client (C) and Merchant (M) have accounts in Issuer (I), Acquirer (A) and both (i.e. C & M) trust their banks. Payment Gateway (PG) acts as an arbiter; Issuer (I) authorizes Payment Information (PI) and Merchant (M) authorizes Order Information (OI). Client (C) initiates the payment transaction for purchasing goods from the merchant (M).

There are four phases in SMMP protocol they are

1. Registration Phase
2. Negotiation Phase
3. Payment Phase and
4. Deposit Phase

Figure 1. Entities involved in SMMP Framework

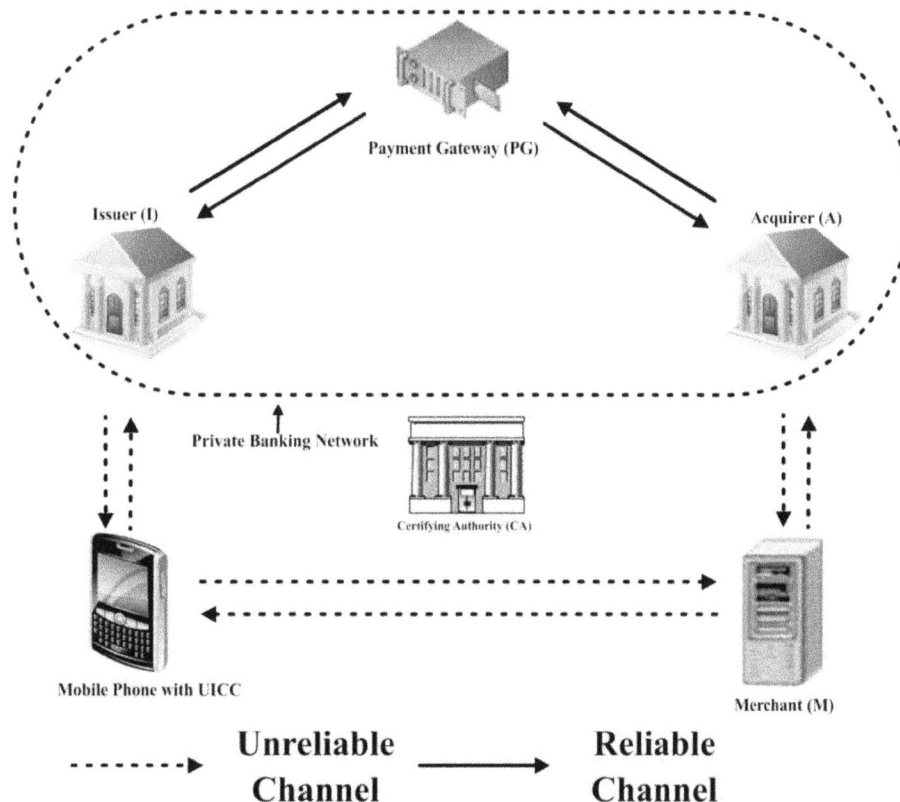

Registration Phase (This Is Done When There Is Network Connectivity)

- **Step 1:** Client delegates the validation of Issuer's (I) certificate to OCSP using the Algorithm 1.
- **Step 2:** If the response from OCSP is positive go to Step 3
- **Step 3:** Client sends its certificate to the Issuer (I)
- **Step 4:** Issuer (I) validates client's certificate.
- **Step 5:** Client downloads Mobile Payment Application from Issuer (I) and sends the following message to the Issuer (I)

$$C \rightarrow I : \{M1, SIG_I^C(M1)\}_{k_I}, cert_C \text{ Where } M1 = \{PI, phno, NRP, T_c, N_c\}$$

UICC initiates the process to negotiate shared symmetric key with the Bank and sends $SIG_I^C(M1)\}_{k_I}, cert_C$ where $M1 = \{PI, phno, NRP, T_c, N_c\}$. Issuer (I) decrypts the received message from UICC using his private key and checks the authenticity of $SIG_I^C(M1)\}_{k_I}$, checks the timestamps and nonce if all the checks are successful then it generates a shared symmetric key K_{ci} between the I and C. Issuer (I) sends $\{M2, SIG_C^I(M2)\}_{k_c}, cert_I$ to C containing $M2 = \{AI, phno, K_{ci}, N_I, T_I, N_c\}$ session keys are generated using hashing algorithms with one bit cyclic shift of a master secret each time a session key is generated as shown in (Supakorn Kungpisdan, Bala Srinivasan, and Phu Dung Le (2003)). The key set K_{ci} (with $\{1, 2, 3, .n\}$) is generated from the secret key K_{ci} and is stored in Mobile Payment Application of the UICC at the client end and in the bank server.

- **Step 6:** Issuer (I) personalizes Mobile Payment Application on the client's UICC

$$I \rightarrow C : \{M2, SIG_C^I(M2)\}_{k_c}, cert_I \text{ Where } M2 = \{AI, phno, K_{ci}, N_I, T_I, N_c\}$$

Figure 2. Registration Phase of SMMP

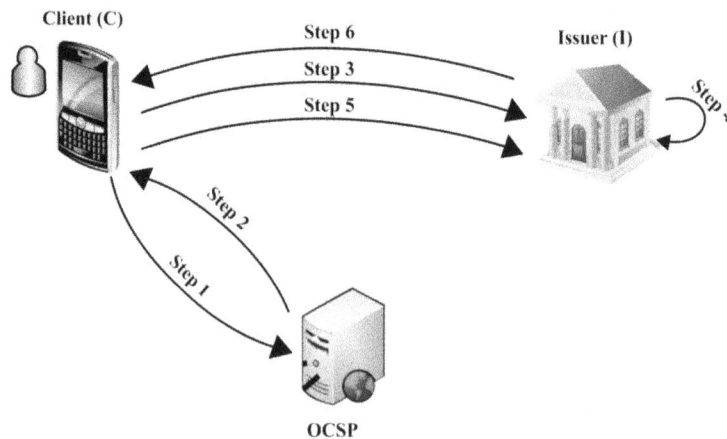

Upon receiving the message client checks the authenticity of the message, if the check is successful then it accepts K_{ci} as a shared symmetric key between Issuer and Client. Session keys are generated using hashing algorithms with one bit cyclic shift of a master secret each time a session key is generated as shown in (Supakorn Kungpisdan, Bala Srinivasan, and Phu Dung Le (2003)). The key set K_{ci} (with {1, 2, 3, .n}) is generated from the secret key K_{ci} and is stored in Mobile Payment Application of the UICC card at the client end and in the Issuer server.

Negotiation Phase

In our proposed framework we employ three mobile agents performing three different tasks: (i) Information gathering and Negotiation Agent (INAg) for brokering and negotiating, which is used in Negotiation phase as shown in figure 2 and (ii) Payment Agent (PAg1 and PAg2) for making payments used in Payment and Deposit phase. INAg is sent to collect the information about goods and the corresponding merchant information and return to client. PAg1 and PAg2 perform payment operations at the Issuer (I) and Payment Gateway (PG). Before starting the Negotiation phase of the protocol the client needs to get authenticated by the mobile payment application in the UICC. Client establishes the requirements about the goods and affordable price to INA. INA then travels to merchants' sites to search for such information as given in step 1 of figure 3. Upon receiving this request, the merchant generates a unique transaction identifier (TID) and sends Order Information (OI), TID, HOI(Hashed OI), MID (Merchant's Identity) and Amt as given in step 2 of figure 3. Once merchant creates a quote and sends it to a client the merchant cannot repudiate it because no one except the merchant can generate a DSMR using his/her private key on the message.

$Step1 : C \rightarrow M : SIG_{C_M}(MS1), WSLC_C$ (Remote Mobile Payments)

Table 1. Notations

Notation	Meaning	Notation	Meaning
C,M,I,A, PG,CA,In	Client, Merchant, Issuer, Acquirer, Payment Gateway, Certifying Authority, Intruder	NRP	Non-Repudiation PIN
$SIG_{X_Y}(MS)$	DSMR generated by entity 'X' intended to be verified by 'Y' and MS is the message received by 'Y'	$Anonid_c$	Anonymous Identity of C
TID_X	Transaction Identity generated by entity 'X'	HPI_X	Hashed Payment Information generated by entity 'X'
Kci	Symmetric Key shared between entities Client & Issuer	Amt_X	Amount generated by entity 'X'
N_x	Nonce generated by entity 'X'	DSMR	Digital Signature with Message Recovery
T_x	Timestamp generated by entity 'X'	$Success$	Success of Transaction
HOI_X	Hashed Order Information of entity 'X'	UICC	Universal Integrated Circuit Card

Figure 3. Negotiation Phase in SMMP Framework

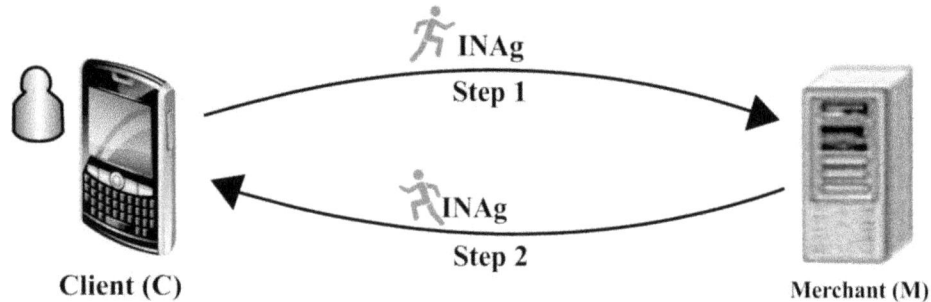

$$MS1 = \{PO, nc, Tc\}$$

$$Step2 : M \rightarrow C : SIG_{M_A}(MS2), WSLC_M$$

$$MS2 = \{MQ, TID, nc, nm, Tm, Tc, Amt\}$$

Client's Purchase Order: =SEQUENCE {

client's Anonymous Identity Client's Anonymous Identity
client's Public key Alphanumeric (SIZE(163))
merchant's Public key Alphanumeric (SIZE(163))
merchandise item code Numeric String (SIZE(16))
quantity Numeric String (SIZE(12))
unit price Numeric String (SIZE(16))
}

Upon receiving this request, the merchant generates a unique transaction identifier (TID) and generates a Merchant Quote (MQ) containing merchant's identity, merchant's Public key, client's Anonymous Identity, client's Public key, merchandise item code, quantity, unit price, amount, order identity
Merchant's Quote(MQ): =SEQUENCE {

merchant's identity Alphanumeric (SIZE(163))
merchant's Public key Alphanumeric (SIZE(163))
client's Anonymous Identity Client's Anonymous Identity
client's Public key Alphanumeric (SIZE(163))
merchandise item code Numeric String (SIZE(16))
quantity Numeric String (SIZE(13))
unit price Numeric String (SIZE(16))
amount Numeric String (SIZE(24))
order identity Alphanumeric (SIZE(163))
}

Note: The size of all the attributes in data structures are given in bits.

Payment and Deposit Phase

$$Step1 : C \to_{\{PAg1\}} I : SIG_{C_I}(MS1), Pubkey_c$$

$$MS1 = PC_{PA1}, (PI)_{K_{ci}}, HOI_C, TID_C, MID, SIG_{C_M}(MS2), N_c, T_c, Amt_C$$

$$MS2 = OI, HOI_M, TID_M, MID, N_c, T_c, Amt_M$$

/* $C \to_{\{PAg1\}} I : MS$ means client (C) generates a Payment Agent 1 (PAg1) and sends message with the generated Payment Agent */

Client (C) generates a Payment Agent 1 (PAg1) for sending message $MS1$ to Issuer (I) PAg1carries this information to Issuer (I). Issuer (I) verifies the digital signature, validates the authenticity of the public key and recovers message $MS1$ from $SIG_{C_I}(MS1)$.

The transaction flow in our proposed Secure Mobile based Merchant Payment (SMMP) Protocol is from client to Issuer which decreases the risk of reusing client's Payment Information (PI) for the later transactions and issuer is a trusted entity of the client. So client (i.e. PAg1) can use Trusted Processing Environment (TPE) provided by the Issuer.

$$Step2 : C \to_{\{PAg2\}} PG : SIG_{C_{PG}}(MS3), Pubkey_c$$

$$MS3 = PC_{PA2}, HPI_C, HOI_C, TID_C, MID, N_c, T_c, Amt_C$$

Client (C) generates a Payment Agent 2 (PAg2) for sending message $MS3$ to Payment Gateway (PG) PAg2 carries this information to Payment Gateway (PG). Payment Gateway (PG) verifies the digital signature, validates the authenticity of the public key and recovers message $MS3$ from $SIG_{C_{PG}}(MS3)$.

$$Step3 : I \to PG : HOI_C, HPI_I, TID_C, MID, SIG_{C_M}(MS2), N_c, T_c, Amt_C$$

The issuer (I) decrypts the message $SIG_{C_I}(MS1)$ using $Pubkey_c$ using the Algorithm 2 and gets $PC_A, (PI)_{K_{ci}}, HOI, TID, MID, SIG_{C_M}(MS2), N_c, T_c, Amt$,decrypts the PI using the shared symmetric key between the Client and the Bank, checks the PI if found successful it authorizes the PI (Payment Information) and proceeds with the protocol else it aborts the protocol. If the checks are successful it sends $HOI, TID, MID, SIG_{C_M}(MS2), N_c, T_c, Amt$ to Payment Gateway (PG).

$$Step4 : PG \to A : TID_C, MID, SIG_{C_M}(MS2), Amt_C$$

The Payment Gateway (PG) receives $SIG_{C_{PG}}(MS3), Pubkey_c$ from Client (C), decrypts the message $SIG_{C_{PG}}(MS3)$ using $Pubkey_c$ using the Algorithm 1 and gets $PC_{PA2}, HPI_c, HOI_c, TID, MID, N_c, T_c, Amt$

Payment Gateway (PG) also receives $HOI_c, HPI_i, TID, MID, SIG_{C_M}(MS2), N_c, T_c, Amt$ from issuer (I) through Private Banking Network which is very secure.

Payment Gateway (PG) will do the following verifications as given in using the Algorithm 2 from the data it received from Issuer (I) and Client (C)

Checks $HOI_c = HOI_i$

Checks $HPI_c = HPI_i$

Checks N_c, T_c

If all the verifications are found successful then it keeps a copy of the received messages from Issuer (I) and Payment Gateway (PG) and forwards $TID, MID, SIG_{C_M}(MS2), N_c, T_c, Amt$ to the Acquirer (A) through Private Banking Network which is very secure.

Algorithm 1: Verification of Message

```
Algorithm 1 VerfMS {
/* Verification of DSMR SIG_{S_R}(MS) */
```

Figure 4. Payment and Deposit Phase in SMMP Framework

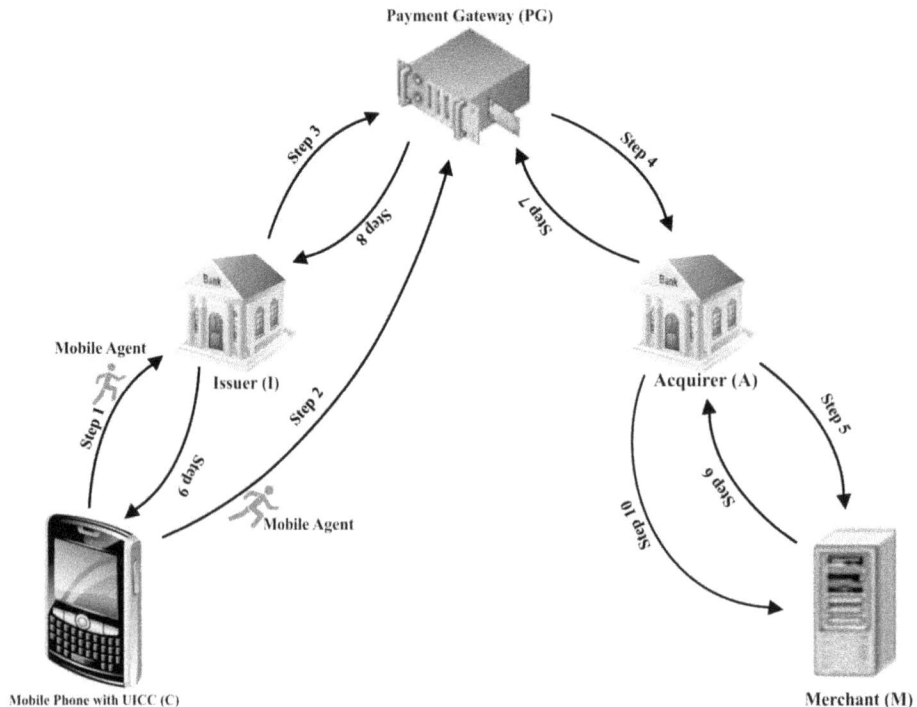

```
   IF Verification of SIG_{S_R}(MS) =TRUE    {
Authentication, Confidentiality, Integrity & Non repudiation properties are
ensured,
Authentication Senders Public Key is accomplished &
Receiver recovers message MS
}
   ELSE   {
Authentication, Confidentiality, Integrity & Non repudiation properties are
not ensured,
Authentication Senders Public Key is not accomplished &
Receiver will not recover message MS
   }
  IF Verification of (Nonce and Timestamps) =TRUE   {
Freshness and Timeliness of the message are ensured
}
   ELSE   {
Freshness and Timeliness of the message are not ensured
  }
/* IF Verification of SIG_{S_R}(MS) =TRUE & Verification of (Nonce and Timestamps)
=TRUE   */
{
   Verification of message MS is successful
}
ELSE {
     Verification of message MS is Unsuccessful
} }
```

Algorithm 2: Authorization of Transaction by Payment Gateway

```
Algorithm AuthPG {
  IF HOI_C = HOI_I = HOI_M =TRUE    {
    So HOI_C sent by C, HOI_I sent by I and HOI_M sent by M are same then
    PG Authorizes Order Information (OI)
}
   ELSE   {
    So HOI_C sent by C, HOI_I sent by I and HOI_M sent by M are not same then
    PG will not Authorize Order Information (OI)
   }
IF TID_C = TID_I = TID_M =TRUE    {
    So TID_C sent by C, TID_I sent by I and TID_M sent by M are same then
    PG Authorizes Transaction Identity (TID)
}
```

```
    ELSE   {
      So TID_C sent by C,  TID_I sent by I and  TID_M sent by M are not same then
      PG will not Authorize Transaction Identity (TID)
    }
IF  HPI_C = HPI_I =TRUE    {
      So HPI_C sent by C &  HPI_I sent by I are same then
      PG Authorizes Payment Information (PI)
}
    ELSE   {
      So HPI_C sent by C &  HPI_I sent by I are not same then
      PG will not Authorize Payment Information (PI)
    }
/*  IF  HOI_C = HOI_I = HOI_M =TRUE,  TID_C = TID_I = TID_M =TRUE &  HPI_C = HPI_I =TRUE
*/
{
    PG authorizes the transaction
}
ELSE {
      PG will not authorize the transaction it aborts the Transaction}      }
```

$Step 5: A \rightarrow M : SIG_{A_M}(HOI_C, TID_C, MID, SIG_{C_M}(MS2), Amt_C)$

A receives $TID_C, MID, SIG_{C_M}(MS2), N_c, T_c, Amt_C$ from Payment Gateway (PG) and forwards it to M in the form of $SIG_{A_M}(TID_C, MID, SIG_{C_M}(MS2), Amt_C)$

$Step 6: M \rightarrow A : SIG_{M_A}(HOI_c, TID, MID, Authorizes OI, HOI_m, Amt)$

M receives $SIG_{A_M}(HOI_C, TID_C, MID, SIG_{C_M}(MS2), Amt_C)$ from A and decrypts it using his private key and gets $HOI_C, TID_C, MID, SIG_{C_M}(MS2), Amt_C$ using the Algorithm 2. Merchant (M) will do the following verifications from the data it received from Acquirer (A).

Checks $HOI_C = HOI_M$
Checks $Amt_C = Amt_M$

If the verifications of the message are successful M authorizes Order Information and sends $SIG_{M_A}(HOI_M, TID_M, MID, Authorizes OI, HOI_M, Amt_M)$ authorization of Order Information to the Acquirer.

$Step7 : A \rightarrow PG : HOI_c, HOI_m, TID, MID, AuthorizesOI, Amt$

A receives $SIG_{M_A}(HOI_M, TID_M, MID, AuthorizesOI, HOI_M, Amt_M)$ from M and decrypts it using his private key and gets $HOI_M, TID_M, MID, AuthorizesOI, HOI_M, Amt_M$ using the Algorithm 2. Acquirer (A) forwards $HOI_M, TID_M, MID, AuthorizesOI, HOI_M, Amt_M$ message to PG.

$Step8 : PG \rightarrow I : TID, MID, AuthorizesOI, Amt$

PG receives $HOI_M, TID_M, MID, AuthorizesOI, HOI_M, Amt_M$ from Acquirer (A) and Checks Payment Gateway (PG) will do all the verifications as given in Algorithm 3 ($HOI_c = HOI_m$ $TID_C = TID_M$ and $Amt_C = Amt_M$) if the checks are successful it forwards $TID, MID, AuthorizesOI, Amt$ message to Issuer (I).

$Step9 : I \rightarrow C : TID, Success / Failure, Amt$

Issuer(I) receives $TID, MID, AuthorizesOI, Amt$ from PG and sends forwards $TID, Success / Failure$ to Client (C).

$Step10 : A \rightarrow M : TID, Success / Failure, Amt$

Acquirer (A) sends $TID, Success / Failure$ to Merchant (M).

Note: The data exchanges among the Issuer (I), Acquirer (A) and Payment Gateway (PG) are exchanged through the private banking network which is secure so we have not encrypted the data exchanges among these entities.

SECURITY ANALYSIS OF SMMP

To analyze our proposed Secure Mobile based Merchant Payment protocol (SMMP) a generic set of security goals are defined in subsequent subsections. The security goals are categorized into four sections namely Data security, Client Security, Bank (Issuer, Acquirer and PG) security and Merchant security. We present our analysis of the protocols with respect to each security goal.

DATA SECURITY

Third Party

- **Goal:** Mobile Payment system consisting of registration, Negotiation, payment and deposit protocols, any party not involved in the payment system should not obtain access to participant's transactional data or their secret keys that will lead to a successful execution of a payment (or deposit) protocol and the Mobile Payment system should withstand attacks.

All the entities involved in the SMMP protocol store their credentials (Private Keys, NRP and Certificates) in tamper resistant hardware tokens so their credentials cannot be compromised. All the entities involved in the SMMP protocol will transmit data using DSMR mechanism (Mobile Agent carries data in the form of DSMR, MA will not carry client's private key to Issuer's/PG TPE) which is a combination of encryption and digital signature so any third entity will not be able to gain access to participant's transactional data thereby achieving Data confidentiality, Entity Authentication, Data Integrity and Non-Repudiation. Our proposed Mobile Payment protocol (SMMP) withstands the following attacks

Replay Attacks

If an Intruder (In) wants to impersonate a legitimate client by replaying the client's transmitted message, then the timestamps included in the messages exchanged ensures the timeliness and nonce (n_c) ensures the freshness of the message thereby avoiding replay attacks. Thus, our proposed protocol is secure against Replay attacks.

Impersonating Attack

An intruder (In) tries to impersonate a client C to CA, which results in CA being cheated. Since In does not have C's private key he fails in doing so. As a result, impersonating attacks fail in our protocol.

Man in the Middle Attack

Man in the Middle Attack is a common attack of intercepting communications in banking protocols the attacker is able to read, insert, and modify messages in the intercepted communication. The attack targets the integrity of the protocol. Our proposed protocol SMMP withstands this attack because the intruder (In) does not have receiver's private key.

SECRECY

- **Goal:** In a Mobile Payment system, from the view of the client, the merchant, PG and A should not have access to client's Payment Information (PI) i.e. Payment Secrecy should be achieved and the bank (I, A, PG) should not have access to client's Order Information (OI) i.e. Order Secrecy should be achieved. In addition to this transaction privacy is achieved from PG and Eavesdropper.

In our proposed Mobile Payment Protocol (SMMP) Payment Secrecy is achieved by encrypting the Payment Information (PI) using secret symmetric key which is shared between Client (C) and Issuer (I). Merchant will not be able to decrypt Payment Information (PI) and Order Secrecy is achieved by hashing OI (HOI_C) (done by both the Client (C) and Merchant (M)). PG will not know about OI and PI thereby achieving Transaction privacy from PG. Eavesdropper cannot get OI and PI because the messages are sent using DSMR mechanism thereby achieving Transaction privacy from Eavesdropper.

claim_C2(C,Secret,PI);
claim_C3(C,Secret,OI);
claim_I2 (I,Secret,PI);
claim_M2 (M,Secret,OI);

UNIQUENESS

- **Goal:** In a Mobile Payment system, every transaction processed should be unique

In our proposed Mobile Payment Protocol (SMMP) every transaction is unique. The uniqueness is obtained is due to the fresh generation of Transaction id by the merchant, and its verification by the PG. PG checks TID_C (sent by Client), TID_I (sent by Issuer) and TID_M (sent by Merchant). If all the TID's are same then only PG authorizes TID. Every the transaction is also linked to TID, Timestamps and Nonce.

claim_C4(C,Secret,nm);
claim_C5(C,Secret,nc);
claim_M1 (M,Secret,nm);

CLIENT SECURITY

Authentication

- **Goal:** In a Mobile Payment system, the client should obtain un forgeable proof of other participant's Authenticity before it engages in a protocol with that participant.

Our proposed Mobile Payment Protocol (SMMP) uses certification authority, to certify the authenticity of public keys held by the Client, Merchant, Issuer, Acquirer and PG. SMMP protocol uses Digital Signature with Message Recovery (DSMR) based on ECDSA mechanism. DSMR eliminates the need of certificates and removes the hurdle of PKI thereby reducing the consumption of resources. The authentication of public keys is implicitly accomplished with DSMR verification. In addition to this DSMR requires smaller band width for data communications in order to achieve confidentiality, integrity, authentication and non repudiation properties. Client and Issuer share a symmetric key between them.

claim_M3(M,Niagree);
claim_I3(I,Niagree);
claim_C1(C,Secret,Kci);
claim_I1(I,Secret,Kci);

Identity Protection From Merchant and Eavesdropper

- **Goal:** In a Mobile Payment system, the client should be able to achieve Identity Protection from merchant and eavesdropper

In order to achieve Identity Protection from merchant and eavesdropper we have modified the initialization phase of (Zuhua Shao (2004)). The client will be issued an anonymous identity $anonid_C$ by the CA after successful verification of client's credentials.

BANK SECURITY (ISSUER, ACQUIRER AND PG)

Authentication

- **Goal:** In a Mobile Payment system, the Issuer (I) should be presented with an un forgeable proof, certifying the authenticity of the other participants.

Our proposed Payment Protocol (SMMP) uses certification authorities, to certify the authenticity of public keys held by the Client, Merchant and Payment Gateway. The authenticity of all the entities involved in the framework is proved by verifying their certificates when they are online. In addition to this client and Issuer shares a symmetric key between them. DSMR mechanism can be used to authenticate the public keys when they are offline. SMMP protocol uses Digital Signature with Message Recovery (DSMR) based on ECDSA mechanism. DSMR eliminates the need of certificates and removes the hurdle of PKI thereby reducing the consumption of resources. The authentication of public keys is implicitly accomplished with DSMR verification. Issuer, Acquirer and Payment Gateway communicate with each other using private banking network.

claim_M3 (M,Niagree);
claim_C6(C,Niagree);
claim_PG1 (PG,Niagree);
claim_C1(C,Secret,Kci);
claim_I1 (I,Secret,Kci);

Authorization by the Issuer (I)

- **Goal:** In a Mobile Payment system, the Issuer (I) before it authorizes a transaction should obtain un forgeable proof from the Client certifying that the Client has agreed to the transaction details and authorized to proceed with the transaction.

The Issuer obtains an authorization proof for transaction from the client in the form of DSMR and PI (Payment Information) encrypted with the shared symmetric key between Client and Issuer which contains payment details, merchant identity and hashed OI.

claim_C2 (C,Secret,PI);
claim_I2 (I,Secret,PI);

Authorization of Transaction by the Payment Gateway (PG)

- **Goal:** In a Mobile Payment system, the Payment Gateway (PG) acts as a TTP and as an arbitrator. It obtains un forgeable proof from all the entities involved in the transaction. In case of disputes among the entities it uses these un forgeable proofs

PG receives messages from Client, Issuer and Acquirer it verifies the message received in the form of DSMR form using Algorithm 2 and authorizes the transaction using Algorithm 3.

Prevents Double Spending, Overspending and Money Laundering

- **Goal:** In a Mobile Payment system, the bank should be able to prevent Double Spending, Overspending and money laundering

Issuer (I) keeps $(PI)K_{ci}, TID, nc, nm, Tm, Tc$ in its archives. If the client or merchant tries to double spend the PI, Issuer can detect this from the TID, timestamp and nonce. So double spending is avoided in SMMP by Issuer. If the client or merchant tries to overspend, I avoids them in doing so since it checks Client's funds for every transaction, if the check is successful it authorizes the payment else it aborts the transaction thereby preventing overspending. Banks are always involved in every transaction which prevents money laundering.

Issuer, Acquirer and PG Turning Malicious

If any one or all the entities in the private banking network (Issuer, Acquirer and PG) turns malicious then also they will not succeed in performing transaction on behalf of Client (C) because they have no knowledge about the private key of the Client (C).

MERCHANT SECURITY

Authentication

- **Goal:** In a Mobile Payment system, the Merchant should be presented with a un forgeable proof, certifying the authenticity of the other participants.

Our proposed Payment Protocol (SMMP) uses certification authorities, to certify the authenticity of public keys held by the Client, Merchant and Payment Gateway. The authenticity of all the entities involved in the framework is proved by verifying their certificates when they are online. In addition to this client and Issuer shares a symmetric key between them. DSMR mechanism can be used to authenticate the public keys when they are offline. SMMP protocol uses Digital Signature with Message Recovery

(DSMR) based on ECDSA mechanism. DSMR eliminates the need of certificates and removes the hurdle of PKI thereby reducing the consumption of resources. The authentication of public keys is implicitly accomplished with DSMR verification. Issuer, Acquirer and Payment Gateway communicate with each other using private banking network.

claim_C6(C,Niagree);
claim_A1(A,Niagree);

Authorization

- **Goal:** In a Mobile Payment system, the Merchant before it authorizes a transaction should obtain un forgeable proof from the Client

Merchant checks the authenticity and integrity of the message received from A, validates, DSMR, checks $OI, TID, nc, nm, Tm, Tc, Amt$. If the Merchant is convinced about TID, OI, Amt then only M authorizes the OI thereby achieving order secrecy OI is not known to any of the engaging entities other than C and M. So Merchant authorizes the transaction after obtaining un forgeable proof from the Client.

claim_C3(C, Secret,OI);
claim_M2 (M,Secret,OI);

FORMAL VERIFICATION OF SMMP

Need of Formal Verification

A protocol is a set of rules that followed the defined conventions to establish semantically correct communications between the participating entities. A security protocol is an ordinary communication protocol in which the message exchanged is often encrypted using the defined

cryptographic mechanisms. However, merely using cryptographic mechanisms, does not guarantee security-wise semantically secure operation of the protocol, even if it is correct. There indeed have been reported breaches in the security protocols, after being published and accepted as a safe protocol (C. J. F. Cremers (2006)). Therefore the design of security protocol is an intuitive process which is severely error-prone so a more rigid framework is required within which we can safely design secure protocols.

The network is assumed to be hostile as it contains intruders with the capabilities to encrypt, decrypt, copy, forward, delete, and so forth. Considering an active intruder with such powerful capabilities, it becomes extremely difficult to guarantee proper working of a security protocol. Several examples show how carefully designed protocols were later found out to have security breaches (Muhammad, S., Furqan, Z. and Guha, R.K (2006), Muhammad, S., Furqan, Z. and Guha, R.K (2007)). So Formal verification of cryptographic protocols is essential as it can detect flaws that have lead to protocol failure. Formal methods are classified as Manual Verification and Automated Verifications (A. Armando et al (2005) & Nalin V. Subramanian and Josh Dehlinger). Such successful use of the formal methods for verification has led to the upsurge in devising similar tools for verifying the security properties of a cryptographic protocol, too. In order to gain confidence in the cryptographic protocol employed, it has been found desirable that the protocol be subjected to an exhaustive analysis that verifies its security properties. Some of the tools developed for the purpose are Scyther (C. J. F. Cremers (2006)) and AVISPA (A. Armando et al (2005)), to name a few. These tools differ in their input language and also in the way they verify the protocols and provide the output. Though these tools eliminate the possibility of human error, but still the selection of these automated tools is very important in verifying the correctness of security protocols. Only very few automated tools explore all the possible behaviors', whereas others explore strict subsets. Most of the Mobile payment protocols proposed in the literature were verified using only manual verification but were not verified with Automated Tools. We have successfully verified SMMP using BAN logic (Abadi,M., Burrows,M., Kaufman,C. and Lampson,B (1993) & Burrows,M., Abadi,M. and Needham,R (1990)), AVISPA Tool and Scyther Tool.

FORMAL VERIFICATION OF SMMP USING AVISPA TOOL

Need of Automated Tools

- The number and scale of new security protocols under development is out-pacing the human ability to rigorously analyze and validate them.
- To Speed up the development of new security protocols and to improve their security it is important to have tools that support the rigorous analysis of security protocols, by either finding flaws (or) establishing their correctness.
- Good in finding attacks.
- Optimally, these tools should be completely Automated, Robust, Expressive and easily usable, so that they can be integrated into the protocol development and Standardization process.

In order to gain confidence in the cryptographic protocol employed, it has been found desirable that the protocol be subjected to an exhaustive analysis that verifies its security properties. Some of the tools developed for the purpose are Scyther (C. J. F. Cremers (2006)) and AVISPA (A. Armando et al (2005)) to name a few. These tools differ in their input language and also in the way they verify the protocols and provide the output. We have chosen the model checker AVISPA tool because it is powerful, easy to use and open source. It is a project sponsored by the European Union to validate the security goals of different protocols. Already 85% of the IETF protocols were proven by this tool.

To prove the efficiency of our security design by AVISPA, we implement our proposed protocol in HLPSL (High level Protocol Specification Language) code that can be processed by the tool. AVISPA uses also the channel (dy) as communication channel ruled by the Dolev and Yao attack model. This model supposes that the intruder can intercept every message in the channel and can build any message from the intercepted messages using for that infinite memory and processing capabilities. However, this model is based on the perfect cryptography which means that the intruder cannot decrypt a message M ciphered with a key K with another key K' different from K. This model is very challenging because it gives advantage to the intruder.

Though Scyther and AVISPA (C. J. F. Cremers (2006)) and AVISPA (A. Armando et al (2005)) tools eliminates the possibility of human error, but still the selection of these automated tool is very important in verifying the correctness of security protocols. Only very few automated tools explore all the possible behaviors, whereas others explore strict subsets. Ignoring these kinds of differences will lead to completely wrong interpretations of the output of a tool. Cas Cremers and Pascal Lafourcade's applied study of state space relations in performance comparison of several well-known automatic tools for security protocol verification, After the analysis of performances of tools over comparable state spaces,

Figure 5. Result using "OFMC" backend in AVISPA

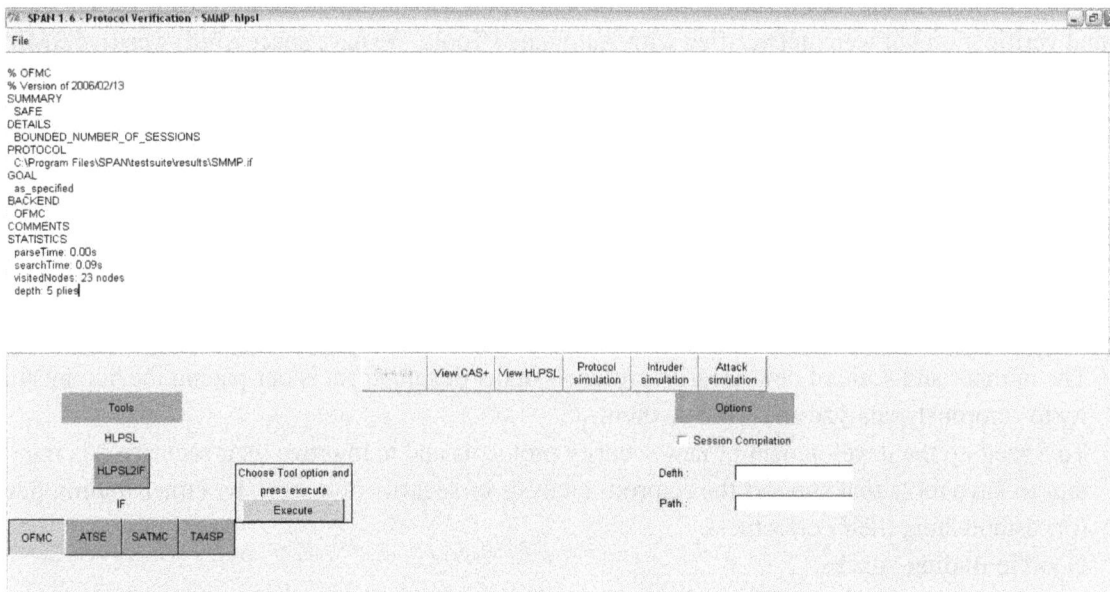

Figure 6. Result using "ATSE" backend in AVISPA

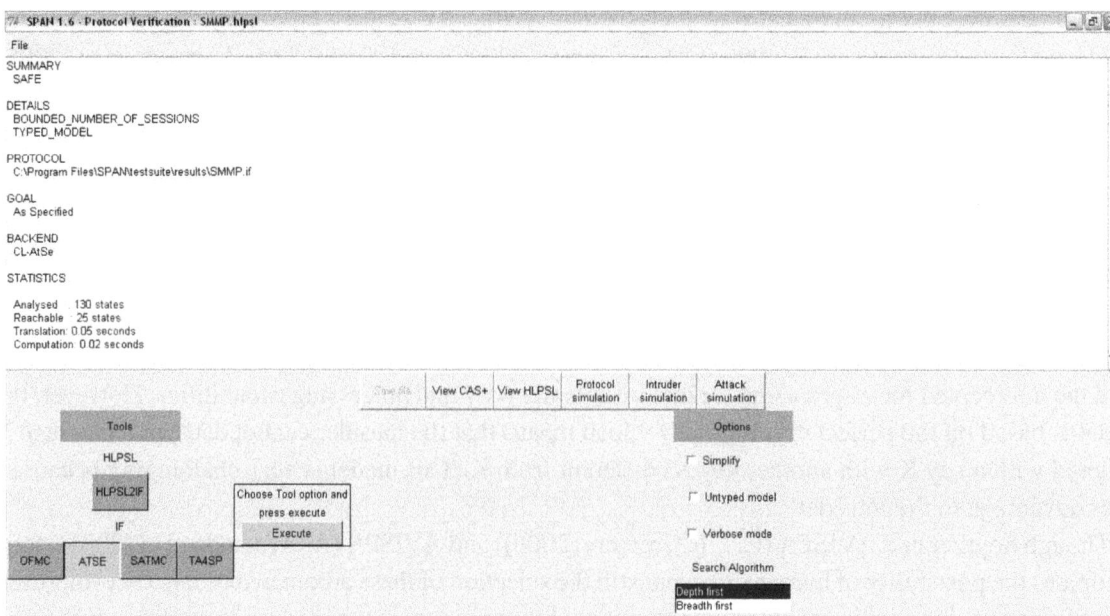

they found in their conclusion about the efficiency of the tools that Scyther and ProVerif are the fastest, their approximation techniques are effective, and both can handle unbounded verification. Scyther tool has the advantage of not using approximations.

FORMAL VERIFICATION OF SMMP USING SCYTHER TOOL

Traditionally, verification methods for security protocols typically assume that the protocols are used in isolation of other protocols (i.e., there is only a single protocol using a network at a given time). However, in practice it is unrealistic to assume that a security protocol runs in isolation in an insecure network. A multi-protocol attack is an attack in which more than one protocol is involved. The verification methods for security protocols that assume a single protocol on a network will fail to verify a protocol's resistance/ vulnerability to multi-protocol attacks. Scyther is a tool used for security protocol verification, where it is assumed that all the cryptographic functions are perfect. The tool can be used to find problems that arise from the way the protocol is constructed. It can also be used to generate all the possible trace patterns. The verification here can be done using a bounded or an unbounded number of sessions. The language used to write protocols in Scyther is SPDL (Security Protocol Description Language) (C. J. F. Cremers (2006)) . We have evaluated our proposed SMMP using the Scyther model checking security protocol verification tool. SMMP protocol is written using the SPDL (Security Protocol Description Language) and then validated using "Automatic claim" and "Verification claim" procedures in the Scyther tool.

```
const pk: Function;
secret sk: Function;
inversekeys (pk,sk);
usertype Timestamp;
usertype success;
usertype PI,amt,Ack,Tc,Ti;
// Protocol description
protocol REG(C,I)
{
role C
{
const nc: Nonce;
var ni: Nonce;
const Kci:SessionKey;
/* Authentication and Key Agreement Protocol */
send_1 (C,I, { nc,PI,Tc }pk(I));
read_2 (I,C, { nc,ni,PI,Kci,Ti,Tc}pk(C));
send_3 (C,I, { Tc,Ti,nc,ni,Ack}Kci);
claim_C1 (C, Secret, Kci);
claim_C2 (C, Secret, nc);
claim_C3 (C, Secret, PI);
claim_C4 (C, Secret, ni);
claim_C5 (C, Niagree);
```

```
claim_C6 (C, Nisynch);
}
role I
{
const ni: Nonce;
var nc: Nonce;
const Kci:SessionKey;
/* Authentication and Key Agreement Protocol */
read_1 (C,I, { nc,PI,Tc }pk(I));
send_2 (I,C, { nc,ni,PI,Kci,Ti,Tc}pk(C));
read_3 (C,I, { Tc,Ti,nc,ni,Ack}Kci);
claim_I1 (I, Secret, Kci);
claim_I2 (I, Secret, nc);
claim_I3 (I, Secret, PI);
claim_I4 (I, Secret, ni);
claim_I5 (I, Niagree);
claim_I6 (I, Nisynch);
}
}
// An untrusted agent, with compromised key
const e: Agent;
untrusted e;
compromised sk(e);
```

The result of this code (for Registration Phase of the Protocol) using "Verification Claim" Procedure in Scyther Tool is shown in Figure 7.

The result of this code (for Registration Phase of the Protocol) using the "Automatic Claim" Procedure in Scyther Tool is shown in Figure 8.

```
const pk: Function;
secret sk: Function;
inversekeys(pk,sk);
usertype Timestamp,Authorize;
usertype PCa,MID,HPO,PI,TID,OI,Amt,MQ,Tc,Tm;
usertype success;
usertype Sessionkey;
protocol SMMP(C,M,A,PG,I)
{
    role C
    {
        const nc: Nonce;
        var nm,ni,na: Nonce;
        const kci: SessionKey;
        send_1(C,I,{{PCa,MQ,Tc,Amt,nc,HPO,TID,MID,{{OI,MID,Amt}sk(C)}pk(M),{PI}
```

Figure 7. Shows the secrecy of Kci, PI, MQ, nm, nc and the claim for Niagree and Nisynch of all the entities involved are successfully verified in Authentication and Key Agreement Protocol using the "Verification Claim" Procedure in Scyther Tool

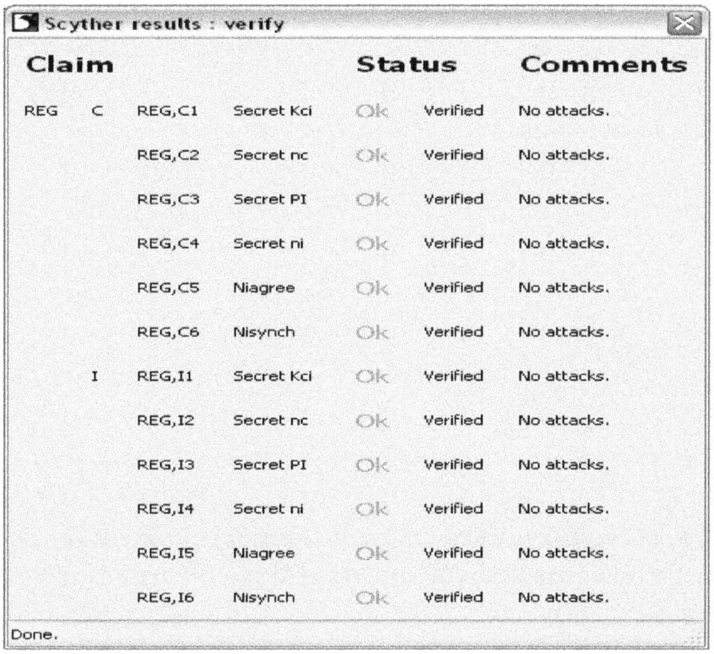

Figure 8. Shows the secrecy of Kci, PI, MQ, nm, nc and the claim for non-injective Agreement and non-injective synchronization of all the entities involved are successfully verified using the "Automatic Claim" Procedure in Scyther Tool

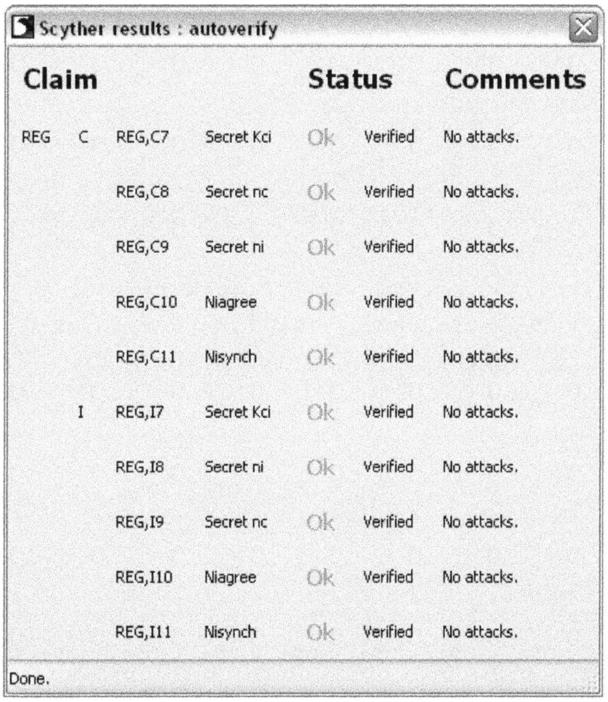

```
kci}sk(C)}pk(I));
        read_8(I,C,{{success,Amt,TID,MID}sk(I)}pk(C));
        claim_C1(C,Secret,kci);
        claim_C2(C,Secret,PI);
        claim_C3(C,Secret,MQ);
        claim_C4(C,Secret,nm);
        claim_C5(C,Secret,nc);
        claim_C6 (C,Niagree);
        claim_C7(C,Nisynch);
    }
    role M
    {
        const  nm: Nonce;
        var  nc,ni: Nonce;
        const kci: SessionKey;
        read_4(A,M,{{Tc,Amt,nc,HPO,TID,MID,{{OI,MID,Amt}sk(C)}pk(M)}sk(PG)}
pk(A));
        send_5(M,A,{{Tc,Amt,nc,HPO,TID,MID,Authorize}sk(M)}pk(A));
        read_9(A,M,{{success,Amt,TID,MID}sk(A)}pk(M));
        claim_M1(M,Secret,nm);
        claim_M2(M,Secret,MQ);
        claim_M3(M,Niagree);
        claim_M4(M,Nisynch);
    }
    role A
    {
        const na: Nonce;
        var nc,nm: Nonce;
        const kci: SessionKey;
        read_3(PG,A,{{Tc,Amt,nc,HPO,TID,MID,{{OI,MID,Amt}sk(C)}pk(M)}sk(PG)}
pk(A));
        send_4(A,M,{{Tc,Amt,nc,HPO,TID,MID,{{OI,MID,Amt}sk(C)}pk(M)}sk(PG)}
pk(A));
        read_5(M,A,{{Tc,Amt,nc,HPO,TID,MID,Authorize}sk(M)}pk(A));
        send_6(A,PG,{{Tc,Amt,nc,HPO,TID,MID,Authorize}sk(M)}pk(A));
        send_9(A,M,{{success,Amt,TID,MID}sk(A)}pk(M));
        claim_A1(A,Niagree);
    claim_A2(A,Nisynch);
    }
    role PG
    {
        const npg: Nonce;
        var nc,nm: Nonce;
        const kci: SessionKey;
```

```
        read_2(I,PG,{{Tc,Amt,nc,HPO,TID,MID,{{OI,MID,Amt}sk(C)}pk(M)}sk(I)}
pk(PG));
        send_3(PG,A,{{Tc,Amt,nc,HPO,TID,MID,{{OI,MID,Amt}sk(C)}pk(M)}sk(PG)}
pk(A));
        read_6(A,PG,{{Tc,Amt,nc,HPO,TID,MID,Authorize}sk(M)}pk(A));
        send_7(PG,I,{{Tc,Amt,nc,HPO,TID,MID,Authorize}sk(PG)}pk(I));
        claim_PG1(PG,Niagree);
       claim_PG2(PG,Nisynch);
        }
    role I
      {
        const ni: Nonce;
        var nc,nm: Nonce;
        const kci: SessionKey;
        read_1(C,I,{{PCa,MQ,Tc,Amt,nc,HPO,TID,MID,{{OI,MID,Amt}sk(C)}pk(M),{PI}
kci}sk(C)}pk(I));
        send_2(I,PG,{{Tc,Amt,nc,HPO,TID,MID,{{OI,MID,Amt}sk(C)}pk(M)}sk(I)}
pk(PG));
        read_7(PG,I,{{Tc,Amt,nc,HPO,TID,MID,Authorize}sk(PG)}pk(I));
        send_8(I,C,{{success,Amt,TID,MID}sk(I)}pk(C));
        claim_I1 (I,Secret,kci);
          claim_I2(I,Secret,PI);
        claim_I3 (I,Niagree);
       claim_I4 (I,Nisynch);
        }
}
const C,M,A,PG,I,E: Agent;
untrusted E;
const ne: Nonce;
const te: Timestamp;
compromised sk(E);
```

The result of this code (for Payment and Deposit Phase of the Protocol) is shown in Figure 9.

PERFORMANCE ANALYSIS OF SMMP

Shown in Tables 2 and 3.

Figure 9. Shows that the secrecy of Kci, PI, MQ, nm, nc and the claim for non-injective Agreement and non-injective synchronization of all the entities involved are successfully verified Payment and Deposit Phase of the Protocol using the "Verification Claim" Procedure in Scyther Tool

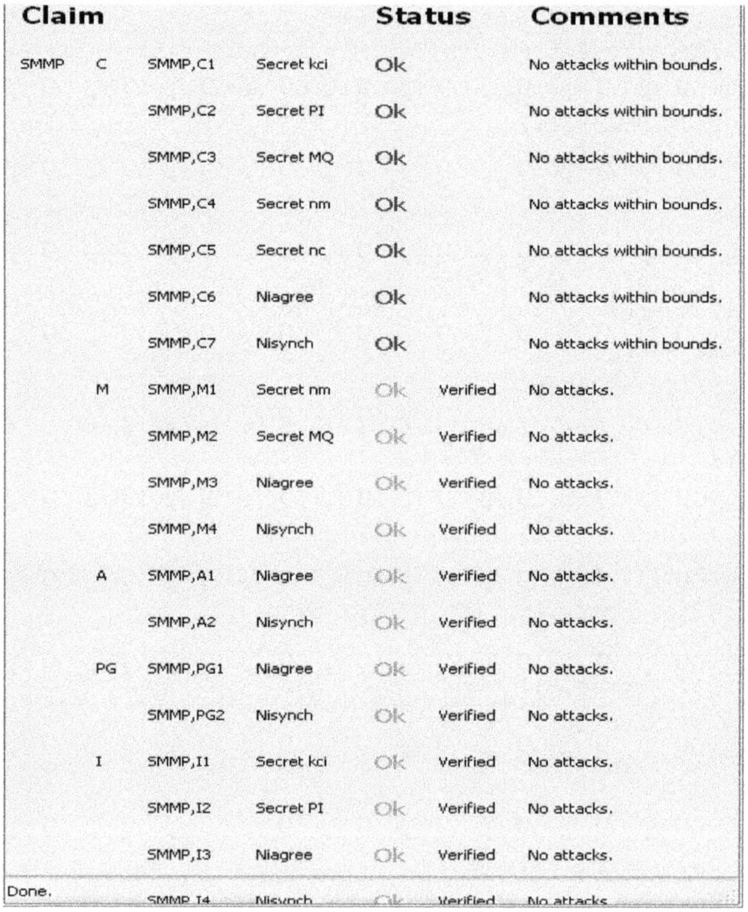

Claim				Status		Comments
SMMP	C	SMMP,C1	Secret kci	Ok		No attacks within bounds.
		SMMP,C2	Secret PI	Ok		No attacks within bounds.
		SMMP,C3	Secret MQ	Ok		No attacks within bounds.
		SMMP,C4	Secret nm	Ok		No attacks within bounds.
		SMMP,C5	Secret nc	Ok		No attacks within bounds.
		SMMP,C6	Niagree	Ok		No attacks within bounds.
		SMMP,C7	Nisynch	Ok		No attacks within bounds.
	M	SMMP,M1	Secret nm	Ok	Verified	No attacks.
		SMMP,M2	Secret MQ	Ok	Verified	No attacks.
		SMMP,M3	Niagree	Ok	Verified	No attacks.
		SMMP,M4	Nisynch	Ok	Verified	No attacks.
	A	SMMP,A1	Niagree	Ok	Verified	No attacks.
		SMMP,A2	Nisynch	Ok	Verified	No attacks.
	PG	SMMP,PG1	Niagree	Ok	Verified	No attacks.
		SMMP,PG2	Nisynch	Ok	Verified	No attacks.
	I	SMMP,I1	Secret kci	Ok	Verified	No attacks.
		SMMP,I2	Secret PI	Ok	Verified	No attacks.
		SMMP,I3	Niagree	Ok	Verified	No attacks.
		SMMP,I4	Nisynch	Ok	Verified	No attacks.

Done.

Table 2. Information with the engaged entities

Entities involved in the Protocol	PI	OI	Kci
Client	Yes	Yes	Yes
Agent	No	No	No
Issuer	Yes	No	Yes
Merchant	No	Yes	No
Acquirer	No	No	No
Payment Gateway	No	No	No

Table 3. Comparative Analysis of SMMP Protocol with related works

Protocols Features	Téllez, J., & Sierra, J. (2007a)	Téllez, J., & Sierra, J. (2007b)	Téllez, J., Sierra, J., Izquierdo, A., & Torres, J (2006)	Tellez, J., Sierra, J., Zeadally, S., & Torres, J. (2008)	SMMP
Authentication	YES	YES	YES	YES	YES
Confidentiality	YES	YES	YES	YES	YES
Integrity	YES	YES	YES	YES	YES
Non- Repudiation	NO	YES	YES	YES	YES
Agent based Protocol	NO	NO	NO	NO	YES
Agent and Host binding	NO	NO	NO	NO	YES
Protocol is proposed in Tamper resistant device	NO	NO	NO	NO	YES
Key pairs are generated and stored in Tamper resistant device	NO	NO	NO	NO	YES
Forward Secrecy	NR	NR	NR	NR	YES
Order Secrecy	YES	YES	YES	YES	YES
Payment Secrecy	YES	YES	YES	YES	YES
Identity Protection from Merchant	YES	YES	YES	YES	YES
Identity Protection from Eavesdropper	NR	NR	NR	NR	YES
Transaction Privacy Protection from Eavesdropper	NR	NR	NR	NR	YES
Transaction Privacy Protection from PG	NR	NR	NR	NR	YES
Symmetric key generation is required in merchant registration protocol	YES	YES	YES	No	No
Certificate Validation is needed	NO	NO	NO	NO	NO
Prevents Double Spending	NR	NR	NR	NR	YES
Prevents Over spending	NR	NR	NR	NR	YES
Prevents Money Laundering	NR	NR	NR	NR	YES
Uses ECDSA for Signcryption / Digital signature with message recovery	NO	NO	NO	NO	YES
Withstands Replay Attack	NO	NO	NO	YES	YES
Withstands Impersonation Attack	NO	NO	NO	YES	YES
Withstands MITM Attack	NO	NO	NO	YES	YES
Number of Client interactions with engaging entities	2+4=6	2 + 4=6	2 + 2=4	2	2
Prone to Attacks	YES	YES	YES	YES	No
Formal Analysis using BAN Logic, SVO Logic	NO	NO	NO	NO	YES
Formal Analysis using AVISPA and SCYTHER TOOL	NO	NO	NO	NO	YES

NR= Not Referred

CONCLUSION

Authors propose a Secure Payment Framework in Mobile Ad hoc Network for disaster areas. In order to enable transactions in a disaster area using existing payment we use Mobile Agent technology and Digital Signature with Message Recovery (DSMR) based on ECDSA mechanism. Mobile Agent technology and Digital Signature with Message Recovery based on ECDSA mechanism provides secure mobile payments in Multi hop Cellular Networks. Our proposed protocol ensures Authentication, Integrity, Confidentiality and Non Repudiation, achieves Identity protection from merchant and Eavesdropper, achieves Transaction privacy from Eavesdropper and Payment Gateway, achieves Payment Secrecy, Order Secrecy, forward secrecy, prevents Double Spending, Overspending and Money laundering. In addition to these our proposed protocol withstands Replay, Man in the Middle and Impersonation attacks. The security properties of the proposed protocol have been verified successfully using BAN Logic, AVISPA and Scyther Tools.

REFERENCES

Abadi, M., Burrows, M., Kaufman, C., & Lampson, B. (1993). Authentication and delegation with smart-cards'. *Science of Computer Programming*, *21*(2), 93–113. doi:10.1016/0167-6423(93)90002-7

Armando, A. (2005). The AVISPA Tool for the Automated Validation of Internet Security Protocols and Applications. In Lecture Notes in Computer Science: Vol. 3576. Proceedings of Computer Aided Verification'05 (pp. 281-285). Springer. doi:10.1007/11513988_27

Burrows, M., Abadi, M., & Needham, R. (1990). A logic of authentication. *ACM Transactions on Computer Systems*, *8*(1), 18–36. doi:10.1145/77648.77649

Chang, Y., Chang, C., & Huang, H. (2005). Digital signature with message recovery using self-certified public keys without trustworthy system authority. *Applied Mathematics and Computation*, *161*(1), 211–227. doi:10.1016/j.amc.2003.12.020

Cremers, C. J. F. (2006). *Scyther-Semantics and Verification of Security Protocols* (Ph.D. Thesis). Eindhoven University of Technology.

Dai, X., Ayoade, O., & Grundy, J. (2006). Off-line micro-payment protocol for multiple vendors in mobile commerce. *Proc. 7th Int. Conf. Parallel Distrib. Comput. Appl. Technol. (PDCAT)*, 197–202. doi:10.1109/PDCAT.2006.83

Kungpisdan, S., Srinivasan, B., & Le, P. D. (2003). *Lightweight Mobile Credit-Card Payment Protocol. In LNCS 2904* (pp. 295–308). INDOCRYPT.

Li, W., Wen, Q., Su, Q., & Jin, Z. (2012). An efficient and secure mobile payment protocol for restricted connectivity scenarios in vehicular ad hoc network. *Computer Communications*, *35*(2), 188–195. doi:10.1016/j.comcom.2011.09.003

Menezes, A., & Van Oorschot, P. S. (1997). *Handbook of Applied Cryptography*. CRC Press.

Muhammad, S., Furqan, Z., & Guha, R. K. (2006). Understanding the intruder through attacks on cryptographic protocols. *Proceedings of the 44th ACM Southeast Conference ACMSE*, 667–672. doi:10.1145/1185448.1185594

Muhammad, S., Furqan, Z., & Guha, R. K. (2007). A logic-based verification framework for authentication protocols. *Int. J. Internet Technology and Secured Transactions*, *1*(1/2), 49–80. doi:10.1504/IJITST.2007.014834

Nalin, V. (2004). *Multi-Protocol Attacks: A Survey of Current Research*. Academic Press.

Patil, V., & Shyamasundar, R. K. (2004). An efficient, secure and delegable micro-payment system. *Proc. IEEE Int. Conf. e-Technol. e-Commerce e-Service (EEE)*, 394–404.

Romao & da Silva. (2001). Secure mobile agent digital signatures with proxy certificates. *LANI*, *2033*, 206–220.

Shao, Z. (2004). Improvement of digital signature with message recovery and its variants based on elliptic curve discrete logarithm problem. *Computer Standards & Interfaces*, *27*(1), 61–69. doi:10.1016/j.csi.2004.03.011

Téllez, J., & Sierra, J. (2007). Anonymous payment in a client centric model for digital ecosystems. In IEEE international conference on digital ecosystems and technologies (IEEE-DEST 2007) (pp. 422–427). IEEE.

Téllez, J., & Sierra, J. (2007). *A secure payment protocol for restricted connectivity scenarios in M-commerce*. EC-Web.

Téllez, J., Sierra, J., Izquierdo, A., & Torres, J. (2006). Anonymous payment in a Kiosk centric model using digital signature scheme with message recovery and low computational power devices. *Journal of Theoretical and Applied Electronic Commerce Research*, *1*(2), 1–11.

Téllez, J., Sierra, J., Zeadally, S., & Torres, J. (2008). A secure vehicle-to-roadside communication payment protocol in vehicular ad hoc networks. *Computer Communications*, *31*(10), 2478–2484. doi:10.1016/j.comcom.2008.03.012

Tseng, Y., Jan, J., & Chien, H. (2003). Digital signature with message recovery using self-certified public keys and its variants. *Applied Mathematics and Computation*, *136*(2–3), 203–214. doi:10.1016/S0096-3003(02)00010-3

Tseng, Y.-C., Shen, C.-C., & Chen, W.-T. (2003, May). Integrating Mobile IP with Ad Hoc Networks. *Computer, Volume*, *36*(5), 48–55.

Tzenga & Hwang. (2004). Digital signature with message recovery and its variants based on elliptic curve discrete logarithm problem. *Computer Standards & Interfaces*, *26*(2), 61–71. doi:10.1016/S0920-5489(03)00069-2

Chapter 5
Theorizing Virtuality in Enterprise Social Systems

James J. Lee
Seattle University, USA

Jessica L. Imanaka
Seattle University, USA

ABSTRACT

This chapter has built on research on today's modern organizations to lay the foundations for a comprehensive and systematic theorization of enterprise social systems. Theorizing virtuality marks a fundamental transformation in space-time parameters in communications. This is especially so in the context of rapid current advancements in IT such as cloud computing, as well as numerous other technological fronts. Current IT trends show that increased spatio-temporal plasticity heightens the effectiveness and the efficiency of modern enterprise social systems. In particular, subject-oriented asynchronous communications experience greater inferred plasticity and event-oriented synchronous communications experience greater referred plasticity. Finally, enterprise social systems vary in their degree of virtuality based on the perspective of the relevant stakeholder group considered.

INTRODUCTION

Due to fast evolving information techonologies (IT), organizations are always faced with a rapid changing environment that requires flexible and dynamic responses to frequently changing business needs. Many organizations have responded by adopting decentralized, team-based, and distributed structures thanks to the communications through IT today. Advances in communication technologies have enabled organizations to acquire and retain such distributed structures by supporting coordination among people working from different locations (Ahuja, Carley 1998). Yet, IT implementations in cloud computing platform provide another dimension in enterprise social systems.

Since the early 2000, Web 2.0 has emphasized relationships using the Web technologies. With this social restructuration, companies are reaping the benefits of Web 2.0 as Enterprise 2.0 (McAfee, 2006). Enterprise social systems will use the communication benefits from Web 2.0 by emphasizing relation-

DOI: 10.4018/978-1-5225-5014-3.ch005

ship management in the Enterprise's internal social networking. As Web 2.0 and Enterprise 2.0 in this context are now absorbed by the advancement of cloud computing (Wided Guedria, 2014), it is imperative to investigate what drives this virtualized environment in the form of cloud computing platform.

Ontologically, Cloud Computing has been empowered by the advancements in networking, providing three service models; Software as a Service (SaaS), Platform as a service (PaaS), and Infrastructure as a Service (IaaS). With the implementations in organizations' IT, cloud computing can builds an "emptying of organization" by separating the content and process of organizations. Cloud Computing today has many predecessors. Heavy use of relational database management systems made Business Process Reengineering (BPR) practically possible in the early 1990s, indicating the separation of data from its organizational practice. In the late 1990s, use of many process integration tools, such as ERP and EAI, achieved the separation of process from business organizations. A major concern is how to manage human agents. The Internet creates e-business markets as well as the e-management of organizational resources remotely, emphasizing relationship management.

Back in the 1990's companies like SAP AG, Oracle, Baan, PeopleSoft and J. D. Edwards created multi-billion dollar businesses with ERP technology that automated and connected what had once been disparate parts of corporations – human resources, manufacturing processes, inventory supply and financial planning. These companies rode the wave of the corporate BPR (business process re-engineering) trend that gained steam in the middle of the decade. Along the way, the ERP industry began to be saturated and experience its growth struggle due to its focus on internalization. The main reasons for this were the Internet revolution and the surprising speed with which e-business began to change the way business was done, i.e., externalization of enterprise. Almost immediately, businesses had started to become Web centric. In the 90's ERP was too inward looking and not global centric (internalization of enterprise integration). However, this does not mean that the internal efficiencies that can be achieved by ERP systems are no longer crucial. Many practitioners claimed that a well-implemented ERP system is more critical today than it has ever been because it provides a solid start to an externalization of enterprise.

Enterprise integration has been a great focus in the 1990s with its internalization slogan. With the big boom of e-business, companies now have moved their directions to the Internet, thus focusing on externalization. E-business revolutionized the market both in customers and business partners. Naturally, it leads business organizations to a global focus and to manage their own resources, creating the concept of Enterprise Social Systems.

Figure 1 summarizes the history of organization structure with the development of information systems (IS) and information communication technologies (ICT). It is obvious that advanced information technologies these days drive the structure of organizations. Modern organization structure formed in the 1920s with the demolition of feudalism. Along with systematic management from the military, the bureaucratic organization structure dominated through the middle of the 1900s. With help from IS, business process reengineering was adopted, which revolutionized the traditional business concept, introducing flat organizations. With ICT and a global network (internet), almost every part of an organization is interconnected, regardless of its location and time, transforming into network organizations, and now Enterprise Social Systems these days. A major difference between network organizations and Enterprise Social Systems is the use of information technologies in terms of relationships among resources. Enterprise Social Systems, interestingly, create unique images of business, freeing limitations on human activities, but maintaining the same or higher levels of relationship management. As Figure 1 shows, collaborative systems and current web technologies are the main justifications for Enterprise Social Systems today.

Figure 1. Chronicle of IS Organizations

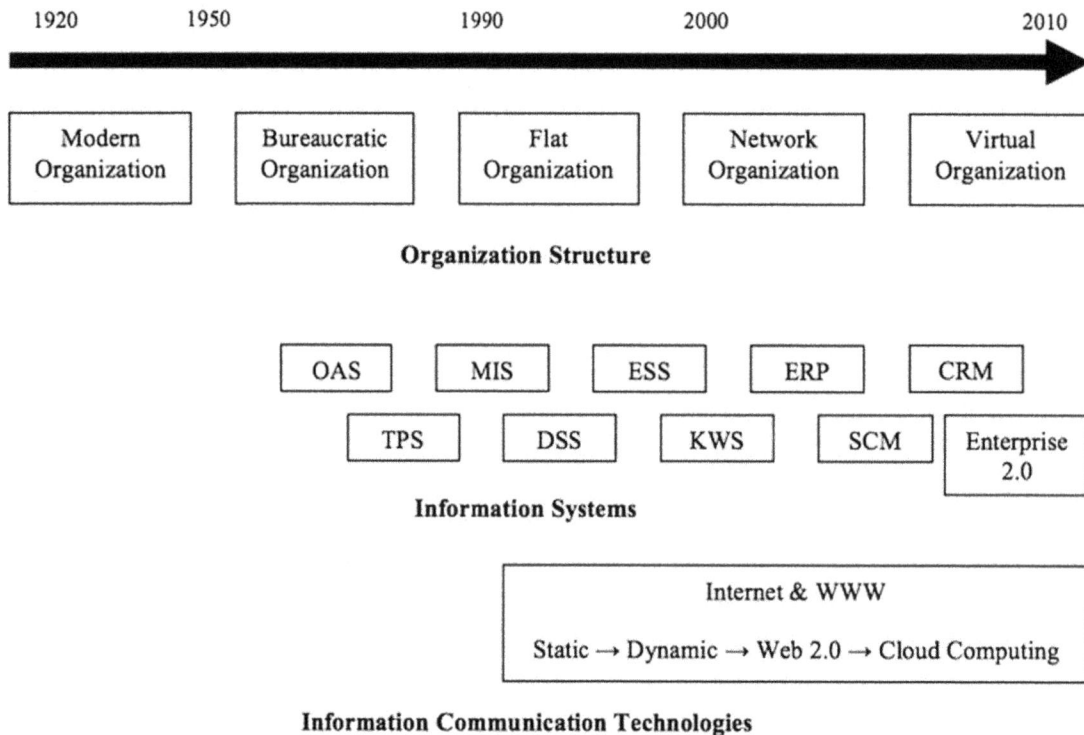

Managing Virtuality

A few decades ago, the concept of a virtual organization captivated the attention of researchers. Many companies hadn't realized the importance, processes or functionality of virtuality, and subsequently went bankrupt - .com bubble, Borders, etc. Today, as multifarious aspects of virtuality have come to prevail in many dimensions of social life, some of the buzz around virtual organizations has faded. Yet, this widespread acceptance of virtuality is precisely a reason to deepen studies of the phenomena that characterize it. More businesses than ever before have come to rely upon virtual communications, from email to teleconferencing to social media, so much so that the virtuality of organizations is taken for granted. Indeed, pioneers like Amazon.com have expanded virtuality into marketspace, expanding even further the scope of virtual processes in business and markets. Most of functionalities in organizations now are virtual. Yet, the meaning and parameters of the concept of virtuality remain insufficiently understood.

This research extends the theoretical scope of virtuality in organization studies (Schultze and Orlikowski, 2001) to Enterprise Social Systems, by analyzing the experience of individuals with collective memberships in virtual space. Because Enterprise Social Systems inherit the attributes of virtual space, they do not have the same physical properties as an organization tied exclusively to material reality. For this reason, metaphors of consciousness are more useful in understanding Enterprise Social Systems than metaphors of physicality. A key contrast between a virtual and a traditional organization lies in the degree to which the former depends on mental construction whereas the latter depends on physical construction. The analysis of virtual organizations in this study applies to Enterprise Social Systems, although Enterprise Social Systems broaden the meaning of virtuality further than previous analyses of virtual organizations.

The main goal of Enterprise Social Systems remains the same as in a traditional organization, which is to serve the interests of its members. As a major component of any organization, human members historically have contributed the majority of the roles to prolong an organization (without the need for a virtual environment). However, the roles of members have now evolved as organizational practices come to depend upon advanced information technologies (IT) and forms of managed virtually, such as information systems (IS), information and communication technologies (ICT), networking, cloud computing, etc. (Lee, 2011). This phenomenon frees the traditional roles of members and the scope of actions they can perform. Along with this freedom, modern organizations now require knowledge workers who have the capabilities to utilize these new technologies responsibly. Ultimately, the rise of Enterprise Social Systems issue in new meanings in virtuality among their human members.

The prevalence of the trend toward virtuality in organizations can be most simply noted in the rise of 'Cloud Computing', a phenomenon lauded by the field of IT. Because of the separation of organizational processes from their previous physical bindings (such as office work practices in traditional organizational settings) and the advancement of IT (such as business processes in IS via networks), accessing and manipulating organizational activities can be achieved purely virtually. Indeed, virtualization is now happening all around us today. The term 'Cloud Computing' may be a buzz word for many academics, but it is not frequently known by the average person who makes use of it on a daily basis. The typical knowledge worker in a modern organization enjoys the world of cloud computing (Venters and Shitley, 2012) every day in the most basic business processes, such as free web mail services (Google email, Yahoo email, etc.). The trend toward 'Cloud Computing' turns a web browser into a new form of computing platform. The traditional meaning of a platform in computing implies operating system software such as Microsoft Windows or Mac OS. Now, most companies' websites run as web applications on web browsers (such as Firefox, Safari, Chrome, or Internet Explorer). Because we have achieved a technological state where any information system can be viewed as an interface on a website, web browsers play a key role in communications today and have become a new platform for the future of computing.

One of the values of cloud computing for organizations is the possibility of real-time communications between members and extended access to the organization's information systems. Members now have perpetual access as long as they possess computers with web browsers and an Internet connection. Cloud computing makes organizational management more cost effective. In addition to this efficiency implication and its financial ramifications, this trend toward virtuality impacts the experience of an organization's human members. As Enterprise Social Systems can be established in the clouds (via networks), the roles and work practices of their members have transformed. One of the most significant indications of this transformation can be identified in the nature of the dynamic, spatial, and temporal characteristics of a virtual organization. It is not just efficiency, but the mobility of work practices that has changed as workers can work with each other from different locations at the same time (synchronous collaboration) and at different times of the day (asynchronous collaboration). The spatio-temporal shift in human relations brought on by the liberation of the organization from traditional physical boundaries and extension into virtual reality is highly dynamic and continually evolving (Breu and Hemingway, 2004). Along with the evolved role of the knowledge worker due to the separation of practice from physical locations to virtual organizations (Giddens, 1990), human members can manage multiple memberships effectively in the virtual organization settings. Without the limitations of face to face interaction between people in physical reality, workers can more easily control and manipulate the kinds of information they share about themselves and craft or even fabricate appearances online. Facebook and other forms of social media are notorious for the presentation of online persona that alter, amplify, and at times distort the identity of the person as they appear in physical reality (Venkataraman and Das, 2013). With an extension of spatio-temporal parameters, workers are freer to assume and manage diverse roles with different people and groups both within and outside of their organizations. In other words, a person can have virtual multiplicity of human identities and effectively manage multiple memberships in multiple groups, organizations, communities, and societies.

In the realm of business, we have experienced many of the 20th century's great discoveries through Google search engines and online stores like Amazon.com and eBay. These companies are almost pure e-businesses due to the introduction of the Internet, especially World Wide Web technology. Amazon. com started as a small e-store but the trend it helped spur became the *de facto* evolved form of business models in coming years of Internet technology. A major impetus for this research arises from this root planted and cultivated by Amazon.com. Regarding electronic communications as evolved business models enables us to envision the foundations of virtuality in human thinking and conceptualization. There has been extensive research in virtuality and virtual organizations (Maznevski, M. L. and Chudoba, K. M. (2000), Knights, D., Noble, F., Vurdubakis, T., and Willmott, H. (2001), Schultze, U., & Orlikowski, W. (2001), Orlikowski, W. and Yates, J. (2002), Verona, G., Prandelli, E., and Sawhney, M. (2006), McAfee, A. P. (2006), Linstead, S. and Thanem, T. (2007), Miller, R. (2007), Kolb, D. (2008), Lyytinen, & K., Newman, M. (2008), Wilson, J., O'Leary, M., Metiu, A., and Jett, Q. (2008), Overby, E. (2008), Kouyoumjian, V. (2010), Armbrust, M., *et. al.* (2010), Bailey, D., Leonardi, P., and Barley, S. (2012), Wilson, J., Crisp, C.B., and Mortensen, M. (2013), Child, J., Ihrig, M., and Merali, Y. (2014), Kamoche, K., Kannan, S., and Qixun Siebers, L. (2014). However, none of these studies has theorized these e-business models in terms of an encompassing conceptual framework, as we do in this paper with a theory of virtuality in organizations.

The purpose of this paper is to lay the foundations for a comprehensive and systematic theorization of Enterprise Social Systems by focusing on how virtuality figures in e-business companies. We explain the methodology generating this study, provide an overview of the virtuality phenomenon, detail communications evolutions in space and time, develop a new apply virtuality characteristics to Enterprise Social Systems, build a rubric for Enterprise Social System considering how virtuality is experienced across multiple stakeholder groups, discuss implications of this study, and conclude with recommendations for future directions in research and practice.

Methodology: Grounded Theory

Schultze and Orlikowski (2001) proposed the metaphors of virtuality with the stance of interpretive study. The study showed the insights of metaphors and identified how we treat virtuality. We adopted the approach of the above work and extended it with grounded theory methodology that would allow us to derive a generic set of metaphors that could explain the essence of the virtual organization.

There are six steps to analyze metaphors in their study based on Beer's method (Beer, 1984). Beer's scientific modeling (Beer 1984, Tsoukas 1991) explains the transformation of concepts when researchers conduct and build theories. Since this procedure discusses the role of metaphors, it is important to map Beer's method with the main strategy of this study, grounded theory (Glaser and Strauss, 1967). Grounded theory constitutes a series of theory building processes (Charmaz, 2000). Since both methods start from insights and end at scientific theory (grounded theory) and model (Beer's method), it is important to identify the gaps between the corresponding steps in each methodology due to different directions in their logics, induction vs. deduction. These gaps were further analyzed and used in metaphorical analysis as shown as 'Activities' in Table 1.

We also adopted the now of the data collection of Grounded Theory, *theoretical sampling* (Glaser, 1978; Glaser and Strauss, 1967). Authors decide which data will be analyzed and where they find interesting phenomenon. After initial data are collected, analyzing data is followed with iterative process of what additional data directed to be collected. The main focus is to collect selective data that are important for conducting research. In this way, researchers can enhance understanding and build theories. A data collection stage will be ended when researchers reach the point where no more new data is needed – theoretical saturation (Glaser, 1978).

By following the steps 1 – 3, we initially generated 555 terms from 59 articles in IS journals, spanning from the mid-1990s to mid-2000s. After a reevaluation of all the terms, we eliminated irrelevant terms. Final categorization resulted in 16 metaphors. Based on the above 16 metaphors derived from the aforementioned literature, seven groups emerged shown in the next section.

DATA DISCUSSION: VIRTUALITY PHENOMENON

IT- Information Technology is a crucial component of contemporary virtuality. Without advances in technology, many of the realities of today's virtual companies would be merely science fiction. These components include the Internet, LAN and WAN networks for business, email, online chat/bulletin boards, video conferencing, instant messaging, etc. The rapid innovations with handheld devices such

Table 1. Methodological overview

Step	Beer's Method (1984)	Schultz and Orlikowski (2001) Activities	Grounded Theory
1		Find metaphoric content in the articles. Identify all of the metaphoric expressions contained in the articles, whether they appeared to be directly relevant to a virtual organization or not.	Data Collection
2	Insight	Each instance of a metaphoric expression was captured in a list together with the page number on which the trope was located, terms of source domain used for metaphorical expressions, and a short comment explaining the meaning or significance that the researcher had attributed to it at the time of reading.	Open Coding
3	Perception	From multiple analyses, eliminate from initial lists those metaphoric expressions that are unrelated to virtual organizations and refine the terms of metaphorical expressions.	Open Coding
4	Analogy	Review the terms of metaphorical expressions and create categories to put similar attributes together. Focus attention on the strategy in the texts – where authors contrast the "real" organization with the "virtual" one in order to construct a definition of virtual organizations.	Open Coding
5	Homomorphism	Analyze categories from the previous stage and discover the connections between each category using Meaning of Metaphors, Entailment, Affordance, and Challenge.	Axial Coding
6	Isomorphism	Establish a set of defining metaphors, using the concepts of Opposition, Meaning of Metaphors, Source, Entailment, Affordance, and Challenge.	Selective Coding

as smartphones, tablets, ultra-light laptops, and now Google glass and commercial drones cannot be underestimated for an understanding of contemporary virtuality. With advanced IT, we have access to a tremendous amount of information at the right time and the right place. Information systems we built on the basis of today's IT have become the backbone of our communications and activities. For example, information systems backed by cloud computing (IT) can virtualize an e-commerce site such as Amazon. com. By building such an information system, humans are experiencing the fastest progress in history by adding a most efficient and effective communication scheme (both manual and automatic) on top of the fastest and most accurate processing power (computer H/W and S/W). Contemporary virtuality may be characterized by the following seven features.

1. **Independence:** These technologies allow smaller workgroups as part of a larger company to operate independently of each other, across a room or the globe. This independence creates new forms of collaborative endeavor. The technologies also permit greater independence and convergence of interests for consumers, social and political groups.

2. **Flexibility:** Flexibility constitutes an essential characteristic of virtuality. Virtual organizations are, by their nature, flexible. Traditional organizational structures are rooted in the physical world and rely on structures, unalterable networks and specific locations to function properly. Consequently, when it becomes necessary to introduce change into a specific organization, a barrier is reached where further alteration requires costly, physical modifications. A virtual organization remains unhindered by these problems. These structures are designed so that they can operate regardless of time or place, independent of existing physical realities.

3. **Permeability:** Virtual worlds are defined by vague/fluid/permeable boundaries. As a continuation of flexibility, the virtual organization is characterized by vague boundaries as to the extent of its use and purpose. Since small tweaks can easily and largely affect the overall organization, it is quite possible to extend the boundaries of an organization so that they encompass new purposes, people or controls.

4. **Geographic Dispersion:** Geographical dispersion of individual workers/consumers/players/members characterizes virtual activities. The combination of a virtual organization with IT allows groups of employees to make progress on one project while working in tandem with another group in a distant physical location. The same geographic dispersion pertains to online stores, social events, and political action. Because information can be shared and meetings can be held with the use of high-speed networks and computers, tasks can be carried out in the location that is most appropriate and germane to that function. Hence, the geographic place where work occurs may change depending on the requirements of the job. Geographic dispersion is hence accompanied by malleability of geographic activity.

5. **Location Freedom:** Along with geographic dispersion, virtuality also enables us to overcome other spatial barriers. Since two members can theoretically connect to a virtual organization from any location around the globe (via network connections, the Internet or a private intranet), work can continue or be observed without regard to that location. If a business trip is necessary to meet with a supplier or provider, a virtual organization may establish virtual private networking (VPN) for its users so that they can log-on to the company's intranet as if they are work inside of company by checking emails, chatting with other members on the progress of the meetings and uploading work that has been completed in their absence.

6. **Temporary Interactions:** Virtuality also engenders more temporary interactions. Virtual organizations are often formed to fill temporary needs, only extending to the end of the specific project that is charged to them. In a manufacturing project, a virtual organization may be formed between the engineers who design the project, suppliers who provide the raw materials and the factory that processes those into finished goods. At the end of that particular project, those alliances are dissolved, as they are no longer necessary to benefit the three independent groups. We see similar effects with consumers, social and political action groups.

7. **Time Freedom:** Just as virtuality enables us to overcome spatial barriers, so does it also enable us to overcome temporal barriers. Much like the limited barrier presented from spatial location, work in a virtual organization can theoretically take place twenty-four hours a day, regardless of time zone changes across the world. Members can constantly update their work at any time of day or night and have that information be instantly visible to a member who may be twelve hours apart.

In sum, independence, flexibility, permeability, geographic dispersion, temporary interactions, and the overcoming of spatial/temporal barriers (location and time freedom) make for greater plasticity in virtual domains. In what follows we engage in further concept clarification and build new rubrics for theorizing virtuality and Enterprise Social Systems.

FINDINGS: COMMUNICATION EVOLUTION IN SPACE AND TIME

Table 2 summarizes the characteristics of reality and virtuality. We differentiate the *place embedded reality* we use regularly and the *space embedded virtuality* from which we increasingly benefit.

The benefits of the Internet revolution include the convergence of data and devices. This means we can use any device or media, and still communicate effectively. With today's networking, there are two important categories in computer-mediated communication modes: asynchronous and synchronous.

Asynchronous communications allow for *greater plasticity in time*. Asynchronous communications tend to be topic, material, or *subject oriented* and apply to interactions at different times between parties that may be at the same or distant places. It has been represented by the use of email, but with the revolution of the Internet and web technologies we now communicate not only through email, but through online postings, online shopping, online discussions, and even blogging, etc. These Internet communications contrast greatly with letters, "snail mail", and the postal service in that there was a longer time delay for asynchronous communications in pre-computer eras. With networking today, asynchronous com-

Table 2. Place Embedded Reality vs. Space Embedded Virtuality

Reality	Virtuality
Body	Mind
Physical	Mental
Bounded	Permeable / Fluid
Rigid	Flexible
Fixed / Solid	Malleable / Plastic
Singular	Multiple

munications' travel time reaches virtually **zero** seconds. The major issue now involves the management of communications. For example, even in the same place of work, people do not have to respond right away to email they receive. They can wait for a time when it is more convenient to respond. Business communications across time zones have also become more convenient. All these changes in asynchronous communications reveal that time provides less of a restraint on connectivity. Time lags have grown shorter and people enjoy much more freedom in how to use time between correspondences. These effects lead to a perception of greater plasticity in time.

Perpendicularly, synchronous communications allow for *greater plasticity in space*. Synchronous communications have to be *event oriented* and apply to interactions that occur at the same time. Skype, teleconference, and the telephone are examples of this type of communication in different places. People across the globe can now enjoy near instantaneous communications, which is unprecedented in world history and another example of zero travel time. Contrast our present business practices to a time when merchants traveled for months or years at sea with often but a guess about what would be needed by the consumers of the goods to be acquired.

Greater plasticity in time and space has significant impacts on organizational performance in both efficiency and effectiveness. It is important to address that time and space are not two independent variables. Instead, time and space are woven together to create synergy effects. Efficiency is increased by sharing resources and core competences. The flexible and communicative nature of a virtual organization facilitates the sharing of resources amongst independent groups that are part of the same organizational structure. Each unit is expected to assist others by making their most important facilities and information easily available to others who may benefit from their use. The various technological components installed in the organization make this possible with ease.

One way that effectiveness is increased by virtuality is through the ease of switching. The switching principle offers a fundamental advantage that a virtual organization has over a traditional one. Because the links between organizational functions are largely electronic and non-physical, it is easy to replace a weak component with a stronger one. Where this activity could be considerably expensive if the item in question was a physical supply chain, it may only be a change of suppliers for the virtual organization and can be made with a phone call and database edit, as opposed to a building project.

In sum, asynchronous communications provide greater plasticity in time in that they engender a perceived minimization in spatial parameters, so that people far away are much more accessible in the subject they work on, as synchronous communications have similar effects in terms of space. Virtual time speeds up processes and enables better management of communications, making work and activities more efficient. Virtual space ends up feeling closer than real space, making ones job more productive, *effective*. This plasticity leads to greater efficiencies and effectiveness.

To be sure, the development of mobile devices like the iPhone, Blackberry, and Android, tablets, along with the good "old-fashioned" computer provides platforms for myriad forms of synchronous and asynchronous communications, labeled as social computers (Wareham, Busquets, and Austin, 2009). Social media like Facebook also blur the lines between synchronous and asynchronous as posting, chats, and messages can occur simultaneously, and with variable differences in time. While social media is mostly communication oriented, the above devices provide other forms of virtual interface with the environment, such as through mapping and search tools that help the user identify their directionality in space and plan trips with greater immediacy. In a sense, the ease of photo and video-documentation also provides an intriguing upgrade in the virtual relationship to one's surroundings. These media promote

Figure 2. Place and Time Dimensions (co-located and synchronous)

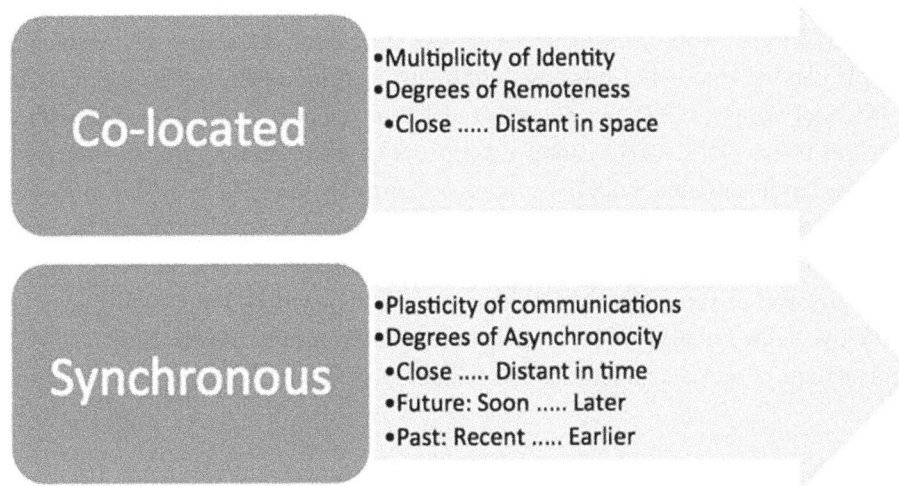

virtual connectivity with the environment that parallel the virtual communications discussed above. This is another indication of "communications convergence".

Together, the shifts in asynchronous and synchronous communications that constitute the virtual world mark a fundamental transformation in space-time parameters. Greater space plasticity reduces the time needed to accomplish tasks with both reference (co-located) and inference (remote) modes of communications. For example, if someone works two jobs virtually, they save time in not having to commute or physically move their body around to interact with people. Yet, time restraints do not entirely disappear. People are still tethered to physical bodies that must make the communications, i.e., type the inputs. In addition, there is only so much work and activity someone can do in a single day. Finally, pure virtual communications remain undesirable to many people. Even given these restraints, there is a net shift in the perception that distance across space is shrinking, which results in a reduction in the time needed to accomplish tasks (zero travel time, efficiency).

Virtual Organization Characteristics in Enterprise Social Systems

From an organizational perspective, we are now coming to see that there is a spectrum of possibilities between the two polar opposites of a virtual organization and a real organization. On one extreme you might have a location-less organization managed entirely through networks and online communication. On the other extreme, you might have an organization strictly defined by its physical premises. Yet, even structuration theory suggests that there is really no such thing as a purely non-virtual organization. Likewise, there may be no such thing as a completely virtual organization. It is interesting to note that previously the concept of a virtual organization was a hot topic. Now virtuality is so prevalent in organizations that the term has become defunct as nearly all organizations have virtual dimensions. The views on virtuality we have delineated and developed serve to problematize the meaning of virtuality and its use in modeling organizations.

From an employee perspective, a virtual organization often implied a great degree of freedom in where and how to work. They enjoy the benefits of a Virtual office, remote work, meaning they can work from home, other locations, or on their own schedules. Therefore, it is clear that the difference between a virtual organization and structuration is where we work. In human history, many people worked at work sites, such as farmers' work in farms or fields. As we invented 'money' for exchange, trade, and commerce, people can manage better business, contracts, or relationships. These supporting activities (value chain, Michael Porter, 1998) can be analyzed for better competition. And this phenomenon is mainly classified as office work. This systemized concept of business with the introduction of military strategy philosophy has formulated modern business organizations as offices in buildings, and a physical organization. With advanced computing and networking, people can work from anywhere, like virtual offices, virtual teams, and now even Enterprise Social Systems. Obviously, the work site determines if your job is more physical or virtual. In addition, employees experience the possibilities of multiplicity in human identity, with the benefits of expanded choices and multiple memberships.

Below we articulate a set of characteristics of Enterprise Social Systems that derive from virtual organizations..

- **Boundary Crossing:** An Enterprise Social System transgresses different boundaries, both physical and virtual. Traditional corporations can be constrained by the traditional boundaries of countries and continents, while a virtual one can move beyond those. In addition, there are certain virtual boundaries that are crossed with computer networks and telecommunications.
- **Network of Independent Organizations:** Many Enterprise Social Systems are comprised of independent companies who ally themselves under one central name in order to provide a comprehensive schedule of services in points across the globe. Therefore, many Enterprise Social Systems, while appearing to be one large corporation, are really many single entities that derive part (or all) of their business from this alliance with a larger entity.
- **Reconfigurable Structures:** The transience of an Enterprise Social System allows for components to be regularly switched in and out of use, altering the overall structure of the organization. Because this can be done with relatively little impact, the frequency with which components are switched is high and allows each organization to quickly adapt itself to a changing environment.
- **Modularized:** Since the components and functions of an Enterprise Social System can be changed with such ease, Enterprise Social Systems are categorized by a high level of modularity. Frequent changes are easily implemented and commonplace among Enterprise Social Systems.
- **Separability:** While each member of an Enterprise Social System is indeed linked to a much larger corporate structure that oversees them all, they each remain a separate and often self-sustaining entity. They rely very little on outside help from the larger organization and work independently of the majority of other members.
- **Division of Labor:** Each member of the Enterprise Social System exists to fulfill a specific need of the larger organization. Since assignments are divided up specifically, there is little overlap in job function.
- **Explicit Goals:** Similar to meta-management, each member of the organization is charged with an explicit task to complete as it relates to the overall function of the organization. Often times, after this single goal is completed, the link between the organization and the entity is dissolved until a further need for it is realized. At that point, the link is re-established.
- **Complementary Core Competencies/the Pooling of Resources:** The ease with which two members of an Enterprise Social System can communicate allows them to pool their resources, even

with members not directly involved in a specific project. Separate entities can quickly be called upon to provide secondary service or consult on a project via virtual channels.

- **Sharing of Knowledge:** Members of an Enterprise Social System collaborate to share their knowledge gained from individual activities performed. Since collaboration is facilitated through the communications channels that are afforded through virtuality, it is common to find "knowledge bases" or other database systems that contain information and documents pertaining to past experience.
- **Geographical Dispersion:** The nature of an Enterprise Social System lends itself to being spread across the globe; this is its primary reason for functioning. Enterprise Social Systems allow for members to be located at a distance apart.
- **Changing Participants:** Members of an Enterprise Social System, no matter their level of commitment, can be easily switched with new or other existing members if the project lends itself to that change. Since temporary alliances can be formed merely through the addition of a network node or the reconfiguration of an external network, a project participant can be added as changing conditions necessitate.
- **Electronic Communication:** A vital concept to the Enterprise Social System is the ability to communicate through purely electronic means, eliminating the need for physical contact and allowing the geographical dispersion of organization members. Online collaboration via email, discussion boards, chat and other methods, as well as telephone and facsimile communications are primary contributors to the removal of time and space in this new organizational concept.

Stakeholder Virtuality in Enterprise Social Systems

A virtual organization is regarded as virtual on the basis of stakeholder perspective. Enterprise Social Systems have extended beyond employees to consumers, and arguably to all other stakeholders. The table below articulates this broader view of a virtual organization, by showing how its meaning and techniques change depending on which stakeholders assume the virtual role. Examples are given for each category. Of course, it is possible for an organization to be virtual across multiple stakeholder dimensions. In that case, the meaning and techniques may be more than mere aggregations of each category, as the virtualization of multiple groups creates manifold virtual relationships between them (Riemer and Klein, 2008).

Table 3. Work Practices in Real and Enterprise Social Systems

Real Organization	Virtual Organization
Geographic concentration	Geographic dispersion Boundary crossing
Semi-permanent needs	Separable units Modularized Changing participants Reconfigurable structures
Less cross standards	Sharing of knowledge Electronic communication
Weak co-operability	Networked independence Pooling of resources
Ambiguous value proposition	Division of Labor Explicit goals

Table 4. Types of Enterprise Social Systems

Stakeholders	Meaning	Techniques	Examples
Traditional Stakeholders			
Employees	Remote Work	Meta-managed	Expedia
Shareholders	Absentee Ownership	E-trading	All publicly traded co.
Managers	Remote Management	Meta-management	
Customers	Internet Retailing	Online shopping	Amazon, E-bay
Suppliers	Remote businesses	Remote transactions	All global supply chains
Community	Remote Users of Products / Services	Social media	FB, Linked-in, Skype, Ventrilio
Expanded Stakeholders			
Government	Absentee voting; Great distance between politicians and constituencies Security State; Intelligence community	Electronic polling; E-communications, sometimes media mediated Surveillance	Amazon.com-CIA
Competitors	Internet rivalry	e-espionage; social media and advertising wars on internet	Amazon: Book Publishers, Grocery Stores, Netflix, Apple itunes
Industry	Remote membership	E-conferences	IT, retail,
Society	Remote relationships	Media-mediated	Seattle-Bellevue, Silicon Valley
Technological Environment Natural Environment – Places constraints on all of The above.	Global scope; cross-sector partnerships (especially Academia)	Moore's Law impacts all of the above	Google Glass, commercial drones

IMPLICATIONS

Virtuality carries social idenities, imposing the social, ethical, and political dimensions of organizational life. Ultimately, it is human beings who constitute and are constituted by these structures. Furthermore the cloud computing platform today forms virtuality in these structures and as such experience benefits and harms. Further research should assess the value-laden import for human players in virtual spaces. Below we identify implications to be considered for such future work.

- **Customer Based/Customized Products:** An Enterprise Social System provides the unique opportunity to provide their customers with highly specialized products as per their specific needs. This can be accomplished through outsourcing work to a separate organization or through the use of a virtually connected inter-organizational node located closer to the customer. Either way, it becomes simple to add a function based on the customer's request and seamlessly integrate that function into the existing framework.
- **Participant Equality:** Since the ideal and practically achievable situation in an Enterprise Social System is that all members have equal access to the overall network, it is assumed that each member is able to and will participate equally to the work in progress. Each individual facet of an Enterprise Social System is expected to contribute an equal amount of work towards a given goal,

if appropriate. While the equality may not be measured best in quantity, it can be restated as effort and the successful completion of all tasks assigned to it, be they large or small. Since every task is considered to be essential as a part of the project, the equality comes in the addition of that piece to a larger puzzle.

- **Open Communication:** The foundation of an Enterprise Social System is its communications components that exist in the absence of face-to-face exchanges. An Enterprise Social System can only survive if its members communicate freely through the provided channels between them, be they based on the Internet or more traditional telephone technologies. The organization cannot continue to function unless it is aware of what all its members are currently completing and often times, when communication is more closed, work that is being completed in tandem by more than one member can be hindered or brought to a halt.

- **Semi-Stable Relations:** While a stable relationship between entities can be expected during the course of normal progress on a project, the relationship between them becomes less stable once that work is completed. With no reason to remain aligned virtually, the relationship is expected to dissolve and, obviously, become less stable.

- **Trust:** The lack of physical interaction places a higher regard to the trust that exists between each entity involved in the organization. Since fewer "checks and balances" can be placed on appropriate departments, management and other entities trust that they will complete the appropriate work on time or be straightforward about delays or problems. If two entities working on a project together separated by thousands of miles are unwilling to trust each other, the work slows and suffers to a critical point.

- **Functionally or Culturally Diverse:** The nature of global diversity and the ability to locate organizational functions across the globe creates a diverse environment for the entire organization. Since members are all in different locations and charged with different tasks, diversity exists that is only found in the very largest multi-national corporations.

- **Cohesion:** An extension of the independent network, this component represents the coming together of separate entities to form an organization on a large scale and to provide one service on a smaller one.

- **One Identity:** Though comprised of separate entities that may be in themselves independent corporations, an Enterprise Social System takes on a single identity. This identity if most often how the public refers to the company, unaware of the complexities that lie beyond.

- **Focus on the Individual:** Though not always accurate in every Enterprise Social System, members can operate completely independently of each other within the organization.

- **Laterally Connected:** This model of an Enterprise Social System involves a group of members working together to complete one project with each member contributing equally but not assigned to a specific duty.

- **Vertically Integrated:** While a group of members remain assigned to the same project, they do their work independently of each other yet the work is not performed simultaneously. Each member has one task, which they complete before passing the sum of completed work to the member who is assigned to the next step.

- **Hierarchical Framework:** An Enterprise Social System that bases the completion of its work on vertically integrated members is said to have a hierarchical framework. The separation of members into a path puts them on different levels of the framework.

- **Collaborative Culture:** By their nature, Enterprise Social Systems foster camaraderie between members even in the absence of face-to-face communications. Since the built-in communications tools are so easy to access and use, relationships form between members who haven't even met. A corporate culture forms out of friendship that produces a highly collaborative nature unlike traditional organizations where such extensive communicating is not required.

CONCLUSION

This study has built on research on today's modern organizations with cloud computing platform to lay the foundations for a comprehensive and systematic theorization of Enterprise Social Systems. The trend toward virtuality marks a fundamental transformation in space-time parameters in communications. This is especially so in the context of rapid current advancements in IT from cloud computing service providers as they open their internal IT engines to business organizations as cloud computing service models (Boukhedouma et. al., 2017).

Current IT trends show that increased spatio-temporal plasticity heightens the effectiveness and the efficiency of predominantly Enterprise Social Systems in the cloud computing platform. In particular, subject oriented asynchronous communications experience *greater inferred plasticity* and event oriented synchronous communications experience *greater referred plasticity*.

Finally, Enterprise Social Systems vary in their degree of virtuality based on the perspective of the relevant stakeholder group considered. Future research should study these effects on the value-laden experience of human players in virtual space.

REFERENCES

Ahuja, M., & Carley, K. (1999). Network Structure in Virtual Organization. *Organization Science, 10*(6), 741–757. doi:10.1287/orsc.10.6.741

Allcorn, S. (1997). Parallel Enterprise Social Systems: Managing and working in the virtual workplace. *Administration & Society, 29*(4), 412–439. doi:10.1177/009539979702900402

Armbrust, M., Fox, A., Griffith, R., Joseph, A. D., Katz, R., Konwinski, A., ... Zaharia, M. (2010). A View of Cloud Computing. *Communications of the ACM, 53*(4), 50–58. doi:10.1145/1721654.1721672

Bailey, D. E., Barley, S. R., & Leonardi, P. M. (2012). The Lure of the Virtual. *Organization Science, 23*(5), 1485–1504. doi:10.1287/orsc.1110.0703

Barley, S., & Tolbert, P. (1997). Institutionalization and Structuration: Studying the Links between Action and Institution. *Organization Studies, 18*.

Baron, R. A., & Nambisan, S. (2010). Different Roles, Different Strokes: Organizing Virtual Customer Environments to Promote Two Types of Customer Contributions. *Organization Science, 21*(2), 554–572. doi:10.1287/orsc.1090.0460

Bartel, C. A., Wiesenfeld, B. M., & Wrzesniewski, A. (2012). Knowing Where You Stand: Physical Isolation, Perceived Respect, and Organizational Identification Among Virtual Employees. *Organization Science*, *23*(3), 743–757. doi:10.1287/orsc.1110.0661

Beer, S. (1984). The viable system model: Its prvenance, development, methodology and pathology. *The Journal of the Operational Research Society*, *35*(1), 7–25. doi:10.1057/jors.1984.2

Boukhedouma, S., Alimazighi, Z., & Oussalah, M. (2017). Adaptation and Evolution Frameworks for Service Based Inter-Organizational Workflows. *International Journal of E-Business Research*, *13*(2), 28–57. doi:10.4018/IJEBR.2017040103

Breu, K., & Hemingway, C. (2004). Making organisations virtual: The hidden cost of distributed teams. *Journal of Information Technology*, *19*(3), 191–202. doi:10.1057/palgrave.jit.2000018

Brown, J. S., & Duguid, P. (1991). Organizational Learning and Communities of Practice: Toward a Unified View of Working, Learning, and Innovation. *Organization Science*, *2*(1), 40-57.

Charmaz, K. (2000). Grounded Theory: Objectivist and Constructivist Methods. In *Handbook of qualitative research*. Sage Publications.

Child, J., Ihrig, M., & Merali, Y. (2014). Organization as Information – a Space Odyssey. *Organization Studies*, *35*(6), 801–824. doi:10.1177/0170840613515472

Chudoba, K. M., & Maznevski, M. L. (2000). Bridging Space Over Time: Global Virtual Team Dynamics And Effectiveness. *Organization Science*, *11*(5), 473–492. doi:10.1287/orsc.11.5.473.15200

Cohen, S. G., Gibbs, J. L., Gibson, C. B., Stanko, T. L., & Tesluk, P. (2011). Including the "I" in Virtuality and Modern Job Design: Extending the Job Characteristics Model to Include the Moderating Effect of Individual Experiences of Electronic Dependence and Copresence. *Organization Science*, *22*(6), 1481–1499. doi:10.1287/orsc.1100.0586

Crisp, C. B., Mortensen, M., & Wilson, J. (2013). Extending Construal-Level Theory to Distributed Groups: Understanding the Effects of Virtuality. *Organization Science*, *24*(2), 629–644. doi:10.1287/orsc.1120.0750

Dodgson, M., Gann, D. M., & Phillips, N. (2013). Organizational Learning and the Technology of Foolishness: The Case of Virtual Worlds at IBM. *Organization Science*, *24*(5), 1358–1376. doi:10.1287/orsc.1120.0807

Fiol, C. M., & O'Connor, E. J. (2005). Identification In Face-to-Face, Hybrid, And Pure Virtual Teams: Untangling The Contradictions. *Organization Science*, *16*(1), 19–32. doi:10.1287/orsc.1040.0101

Flake, G. W., Pennock, D. M., & Fain, D. C. (2003, July). *The self-organized web: the Yin to the semantic web's Yang. IEEE Intelligent Systems*, 72–86.

Giddens, A. (1984). *The Constitution of Society*. Berkeley, CA: University of California Press.

Giddens, A. (1990). *The Consequences of Modernity*. Stanford, CA: Stanford University Press.

Glaser, B. G. (1978). *Theoretic Sensitivity*. Mill Valley, CA: The Sociology Press.

Glaser, B. G., & Strauss, A. L. (1967). *The discovery of grounded theory: strategies for qualitative research.* New York, NY: Aldine Publishing Company.

Goodall, K., & Roberts, J. (2003). Repairing Managerial Knowledge-Ability Over Distance. *Organization Studies, 24*(7), 1153–1175. doi:10.1177/01708406030247007

Guedria, W. (2014). A Conceptual Framework for Enterprise Interoperability. *International Journal of E-Business Research, 10*(3), 54–64. doi:10.4018/ijebr.2014070104

Harrington, J. (1991). *Organizational structure and information technology.* Hertfordshire, UK: Prentice Hall International.

Hinchcliffe, D. (2007). The state of Enterprise 2.0. *ZDNet.* Retrieved from http://www.zdnet.com/blog/hinchcliffe/the-state-of-enterprise-2-0/143

IBM Smart Business. (2010). *Dispelling the vapor around cloud computing.* Thought Leadership White Paper. Retrieved from ftp://public.dhe.ibm.com/common/ssi/ecm/en/ciw03062usen/CIW03062USEN.PDF

Jett, Q. R., Metiu, A., O'Leary, M. B., & Wilson, J. M. (2008). Perceived Proximity in Virtual Work: Explaining the Paradox of Far-but-Close. *Organization Studies, 29*(7), 979–1002. doi:10.1177/0170840607083105

Kamoche, K., Kannan, S., & Siebers, L. Q. (2014). Knowledge-Sharing, Control, Compliance and Symbolic Violence. *Organization Studies, 35*(7), 989–1012. doi:10.1177/0170840614525325

Knights, D., Noble, F., Vurdubakis, T., & Willmott, H. (2001). Chasing Shadows: Control, Virtuality and the Production of Trust. *Organization Studies, 22*(2), 311–336. doi:10.1177/0170840601222006

Kolb, D. G. (2008). Exploring the Metaphor of Connectivity: Attributes, Dimensions and Duality. *Organization Studies, 29*(1), 127–144. doi:10.1177/0170840607084574

Kouyoumjian, V. (2010). The New Age of Cloud Computing and GIS, ArchWatch. *ESRI.* Retrieved from http://www.esri.com/news/arcwatch/0110/feature.html

Lai, L. S. L., & Turban, E. (2008). Groups Formation and Operations in the Web 2.0 Environment and Social Networks. *Group Decision and Negotiation, 17*(5), 387–402. doi:10.1007/s10726-008-9113-2

Lakoff, G., & Johnson, M. (1980). *Metaphors we live by.* Chicago, IL: University of Chicago Press.

Lee, I. (2011). Overview of emrging web 2.0-based business models and web 2.0 applications in business: An ecological perspective. *International Journal of E-Business Research, 7*(4), 1–16. doi:10.4018/jebr.2011100101

Linstead, S., & Thanem, T. (2007). Multiplicity, Virtuality and Organization: The Contribution of Gilles Deleuze. *Organization Studies, 28*(10), 1483–1501. doi:10.1177/0170840607075675

Lyytinen, K., & Newman, M. (2008). Explaining information systems change: a punctuated socio-technical change model. *European Journal of Information Systems, 17*, 589-613. Retrieved from www.palgrave-journals.com/ejis/

Maznevski, M. L., & Chudoba, K. M. (2000). Bridging Space Over Time: Global Virtual Team Dynamics and Effectiveness. *Organization Science*, *11*(5), 473–492. doi:10.1287/orsc.11.5.473.15200

McAfee, A. P. (2006). Enterprise 2.0: The Dawn of Emergent Collaboration. *MIT Sloan Management Review*, *47*(3), 21–28.

McKinney, V. R., & Whiteside, M. M. (2006). Maintaining Distributed Relationships. *Communications of the ACM*, *49*(3), 82–86. doi:10.1145/1118178.1118180

Miller, R. (2007). Enterprise 2.0 Definition and Solutions. *CIO*. Retrieved from http://www.cio.com/article/print/123550

Morgan, G. (2006). *Images of organization*. Sage.

Nevo, S., Nevo, D., & Kim, H. (2012). From recreational applications to workplace technologies: An empirical study of cross-context IS continuance in the case of virtual worlds. *Journal of Information Technology*, *27*(1), 74–86. doi:10.1057/jit.2011.18

O'Reilly, T. (2005). *What is web 2.0: design patterns and business models for the next generation of software*. Retrieved from http://www.oreillynet.com/lpt/a/6228

O'Reilly, T. (2005). *What is Web 2.0*. Retrieved from http://oreilly.com/lpt/a/6228

Orlikowski, W. (1992). The Duality of Technology: Rethinking the Concept of Technology in Organizations. *Organization Science*, *3*(3), 398–427. doi:10.1287/orsc.3.3.398

Orlikowski, W. (1996). Improvising organizational transformation over time: A situated change perspective. *Information Systems Research*, *7*(1), 63–92. doi:10.1287/isre.7.1.63

Orlikowski, W. (2002). Knowing in Practice: Enacting a Collective Capability in Distributed Organizing. *Organization Science*, *13*(3), 249–273. doi:10.1287/orsc.13.3.249.2776

Orlikowski, W., & Yates, J. (2002). It's About Time: Temporal Structuring in Organizations. *Organization Science*, *13*(6), 684–700. doi:10.1287/orsc.13.6.684.501

Orlikowski, W. J., & Robey, D. (1991). Information technology and the structuring of organizations. *Information Systems Research*, *2*(2), 143–169. doi:10.1287/isre.2.2.143

Overby, E. (2008). Process Virtualization Theory and the Impact of Information Technology. *Organization Science*, *19*(2), 277–291. doi:10.1287/orsc.1070.0316

Palmer, J. W., & Speier, C. (1997). *A Typology of Enterprise Social Systems: An Empirical Study*. Retrieved from http://hsb.baylor.edu/ramsower/ais.ac.97/papers/palm_spe.htm

Porter, M. (1998). *Competitive Advantage: Creating and Sustaining Superior Performance* (1st ed.). Free Press. doi:10.1007/978-1-349-14865-3

Prandelli, E., Sawhney, M., & Verona, G. (2006). Innovation and Virtual Environments: Towards Virtual Knowledge Brokers. *Organization Studies*, *27*(6), 765–788. doi:10.1177/0170840606061073

Riemer, K., & Klein, S. (2008). Is the V-form the next generation organization? An analysis of challenges, pitfalls and remedies of ICT-enabled virtual organisations based on social capital theory. *Journal of Information Technology*, *23*(3), 147–162. doi:10.1057/palgrave.jit.2000120

Robey, D., & Orlikowski, W. (1991). *Information Technology and the Structuring of Organizations*. The Institute of Management Sciences.

Sachs, P. (1995). Transforming Work: Collaboration, Learning and Design. *Communications of the ACM*, *38*(9), 36–45. doi:10.1145/223248.223258

Salesforce.com. (2012). *Software as a Service*. Retrieved from http://www.salesforce.com/saas/

Schultze, U., & Orlikowski, W. (2001). Metaphors of Virtuality: Shaping and Emergent Reality. *Information and Organization*, *11*(1), 45–77. doi:10.1016/S1471-7727(00)00003-8

Tsoukas, H. (1991). The missing link: A transformational view of metaphors in organizational science. *Academy of Management Review*, *16*(3), 566–585.

Venkatarman, S., & Das, R. (2013). The influence of corporate social media on firm level strategic decision making: A preliminary exploration. *International Journal of E-Business Research*, *9*(1), 1–20. doi:10.4018/jebr.2013010101

Venters, W., & Whitley, E. (2012). A critical review of cloud computing: Researching desires and realities. *Journal of Information Technology*, *27*(3), 179–197. doi:10.1057/jit.2012.17

Wareham, J., Busquets, X., & Austin, R. (2009). Creative, convergent, and social: Prospects for mobile computing. *Journal of Information Technology*, *24*(2), 139–143. doi:10.1057/jit.2009.1

Zander, U., & Kogut, B. (1995). Knowledge and Speed of the Transfer and Imitation of Organizational Capabilities: An Empirical Test. *Organization Science*, *6*(1), 76–92. doi:10.1287/orsc.6.1.76

Chapter 6
UX (User Experience)–Driven Website Design Utilizing Analytic Hierarchy Process (AHP) Multi–Attribute Decision Modeling

Ron Cheek
University of Louisiana at Lafayette, USA

Martha Sale
Texas State University, USA

Colleen Carraher Wolverton
University of Louisiana at Lafayette, USA

ABSTRACT

The success of an organization's website is determined by the user's experience (UX). Yet many organizations continue to struggle to find tools to strategically analyze the UX's satisfaction with their websites and overall online presence. While there have been numerous studies offering "best practices" for website design, most of these are dated and do not take into consideration UX's experience and social media tools that come into the market. In this chapter, over 900 surveys were conducted on Inc. Magazine's Top 500 list (2011-13) of fastest growing companies in the United States. The analysis of these surveys resulted in a list of shared elements (best practices) common to the websites surveyed. Through the use of the analytic hierarchy process (AHP) multi-attribute decision model, the authors developed a measure by which companies can assess their customer's experience and compare it to these best practices model. This model provides an internally consistent, robust model against which to measure an organization's website based on the user's experience (UX).

DOI: 10.4018/978-1-5225-5014-3.ch006

INTRODUCTION

Organizations are continually challenged to develop websites that successfully meet the expectations of the User's Experience (UX). Wikipedia.org explains

"User Experience (UX) refers to a person's emotions and attitudes about using a particular product, system, or service. It includes the practical, experiential, affective, meaningful and valuable aspects of human-computer interaction. User experience is dynamic as it is constantly modified over time due to changing usage circumstances and changes to individual systems as well as the wider usage context in which they can be found."

Through the use of the Analytic Hierarchy Process (AHP) Multi-attribute Decision Model, we developed a measure by which companies can assess the UX of their web presence in comparison to this best practices model. This model provides an internally consistent, robust model against which to measure the UX of an organization's website. Author Steve Krug in his book "Don't Make Me Think" offers a guide to help web designers understand the principles of intuitive navigation and information design. As a usability consultant for Apple, AOL, Lexus and others he explains the problems occur when organizations build websites based on technical components rather than being focused on the UX.

The impact and importance of website design on organizations of all sizes continues to dramatically increase. In 2001, Michal Porter rationalized that the World Wide Web (WWW or W3) would have a dramatic impact on organizational business practices and strategies. Indeed, websites provide a way for customers, potential customers, employees, and other visitors to interact with the organization without time barriers and across geographic distances. The question for many organizations is, "How do they measure their websites compared to others both inside and outside their industries? What are the 'good components' in the design of a website?" Perhaps most importantly what do Users desire in the design of a website.

Limited academic research has been done in the area of strategic website design specifically focused on UX (Wani et al 2017; Frederick et al 2015). The purpose of this research was the development of a measurement instrument that could be used by organizations to produce an internally consistent, robust measure of their website design that takes into consideration the UX. In our research, 900 surveys were conducted from Inc. Magazine's Top 500 list (2011-13) of fastest growing companies in the United States. The analysis of these surveys resulted in a list of shared elements (best practices) common to the websites surveyed. Through the use of the Analytic Hierarchy Process (AHP) Multi-attribute Decision Model, we developed a measure by which companies can assess their web presence in comparison to this best practices model. This model provides an internally consistent, robust model against which to measure an organization's website.

Although much work has been done on the individual components of websites design, little work has looked at the overall look and functional design of a website from the User's perspective. These are in fact the components exerting a direct impact on the public's perception of the organization's brand. Newman and Landay (2000) proposed that the areas of navigation, information, and visual design should also be considered. Fan and Tsai (2010) suggest that visual components may indeed be the most important and valuable components of a website.

Websites provide a valuable opportunity to interact with existing and potential customers as well as other interested parties on a one-on-one basis. Organizations of all types provide virtual addresses for customers, potential customers, employees, and other visitors. An organization's website is often the first point of contact for visitors (Schmidt and Ralph, 2013). Despite the increased importance of organizational websites, limited research has been conducted to develop an internally consistent, robust measure for website design not on functionality, but rather on the UX. In our research, we conducted 900 surveys of Inc. Magazine's Top 500 fastest growing companies in the United States. These surveys were utilized to develop a "best practices" approach for the measurement of effective organizational websites from the User's perspective, through the use of the Analytic Hierarchy Process (AHP) Multi-attribute Decision Model. The model offers an internally consistent, robust measure against which an organization's website can be compared.

This paper provides a contribution to the literature through the development of a measure that allows for a systematic process to evaluate web presence using the results from an Analytic Hierarchy Process (AHP) model using the UX as the primary objective.

LITERATURE REVIEW

We conducted a literature review based on peer-reviewed journal articles for UX website design. Wani et al (2017) examined travel websites to study the hedonic effectiveness of the experience of the user. By adding the construct of User Experience to the DeLone and McLean model of IS Success, the study indicates that both hedonic and utility based measures are important factors for customer IS evaluation (Wani et al 2017).

Hsu et al (2017) employ a gamification context to examine the role of user experience on perceived value and attitude of a website. Through the use of a structural equation model, their findings indicate that hedonic features and utilitarian features impact a user's experience, which in turn impacts their perception of value and attitude (Hsu et al 2017).

We also found this topic to be highly dynamic. New applications and social media tools having high impact on internet traffic and websites are being continually created. These social media tools demand continuous change and adaptations by organizational websites. Top-level peer-reviewed journals may take anywhere from 2-3 years for an article to be published. By that time, the standards for websites have gone through several iterations.

For example Pinterest, an application that offers visual discovery, collection, sharing, and storage tools was started in 2010. It already has over 300 million active users. Hootsuite was founded in 2008, but only after a $200 million investment in 2012 did it actually gain wide acceptance. It is a tool used by most websites to do manage their brands. These are only two examples of recent "must have" social media tools for organizational websites.

In their book "Absolute Value," Stanford Professor Itamar Simonson and Emanuel Rosen (2014) offer unique insight on the value of an organization's website and its role in consumer behavior. From their perspectives, an organization's website plays a significant role in customer relations. They found that organizational websites exert an impact on customer segmentation, positioning, and overall brand value. The design and function of an organization's website enhances its brand value. Additionally, many organizations fail to recognize the importance of the organization's online presence and its impact on consumer perceptions and behaviors.

Tang and Jang (2014) explain that few studies have actually been done examining the information, communication, and strategies for organizational websites. They posit that with the increasing importance of websites on overall organizational performance, additional research and studies is needed. Blom et al. (2014) found that the deliberative process to respond to commenters, which was long used by newspapers, was no longer sufficient. The value of forums attached to opinion articles on the websites of 15 major U.S. newspapers supported the needs of their readers. Fry (2014) explains that with the 25th anniversary of the World Wide Web (www), the importance of an organization's online presence (website) has never had greater significance.

DeVries and Carlson (2014) found with the dramatic rise of social media, a website presence was a determining factor in an organization's brand value. An effective website could positively impact the consumer's perception of overall organizational brand value. The enhancement of an organization's website has the potential to improve customer involvement and increase return on investment. By adding experiential benefits, organizations were able to increase aesthetics, service excellence, and increase customers' interaction with organizations (Saeed et al, 2014).

CHALLENGES IN ORGANIZATIONAL WEBSITE DESIGN

The "digital revolution" entered its second decade in the 21st century. Organizations now recognize the importance of providing a well-designed web presence, with some organizations investing in site redesign after recognizing the impact of the website. Effective website design begins with a framework that is consistent with an organization's overall goals (Simeon, 2010) and meets the requirements of the UX. However, many organizations continue to struggle with a strategic analysis of their websites and online presence. There are studies offering "best practices" for website standardized technologies and practices (Aladwani and Palvia, 2002; Ranganathan and Ganapathy, 2002). These "best practices" may address structural issues, but they do not address the current expectations of the wired community and their UX.

Traditional website design has been focused on the online B2B (Business-to-Business) and B2C (Business-to-Consumer) organizations. Luo and Duan's (2013) research emphasizes the importance of the organization's online presence and explains that both positive and negative social media has the potential to impact overall firm value. Zavyalova et al. (2012) explains the value of handling social media via an organization's website during times of crisis. In Basdeo's et al's (2006) research they found that effective organizational websites could mitigate the impact of market actions on firm reputations. A company's website may even impact the perceived difference between actual organizational legitimacy and reputation (Deephouse and Carter, 2005).

Social media has been found to impact markets as it cascades between the media and investors (Rindova and Maggitti, 2008). The contagion effect of social media can occur across business suppliers, retailers, and consumers (Rapp et al, 2013). This interaction between organizations and visitors is referred to as Social Media. As Morgan et al (2012) explains "Social media differentiates from traditional/industrial media in many aspects such as quality, reach, frequency, usability, immediacy, and permanence." Initially, organizations considered Social Media as a domain for the younger generation. Curran and Lennon (2013) in their examination of social media users found that Social Media has significant value for all generations.

Both public and private organizations are impacted by their website design. While the contribution of a webmaster to a public organization's website is important, research indicates that the real perception of quality comes from the UX of the site (Sorum et al, 2013). Initial self-congruity and flow have been found to affect the way consumers make an initial evaluation of a website. This initial evaluation is important as it is forms the basis of one's behavioral intention to stay on a site or abandon it. The design of a website is key to its success (Cho and Youn-Kyung, 2013). Wakefield, Stocks, and Wilder (2004) further explained that overall success was determined by their initial positive UX on how it would achieve their goals for coming to the website.

Traditional bricks and mortar sites continually fine tune their locations to encourage visitors to "come in, stay awhile or even go away" (Clark et al, 2009). In their opinion, organizational websites are fast becoming the primary way both existing customers and prospective customers will interact with an organization. They also agree that "one size" does not fit all. Others such as Li, Guang, and Thatcher (2009) in their research found that the development of "swift trust" would successfully encourage customers and visitors to spend additional time on a website. While they explained that "appearance and functionality" were important, they also acknowledged their study was limited to "swift trust" and there are many other variables that should be considered. Ignored by many organizations in their design and redesign of their websites is the UX. In 2006 Brown, Rahman, and Hacker compared the website designs of the fastest growing companies in the United States to the largest companies in the USA. They benchmarked the designs of these companies against "best practices" as defined by a leading consultant. Utilizing this consultant's best practices, they found most of the high growth organizations were not employing a systematic process to evaluate their homepages.

This paper reports the results of using the Analytic Hierarchy Process (AHP) to develop a measure that would allow for a systematic process to evaluate web presence. Companies from which to develop a best practices measure could have been chosen in a number of ways. Inc. Magazine's Top 500 list of fastest growing companies was chosen because these companies have evinced the ability to excel in a challenging economic environment. Through their continued growth, they have demonstrated that they have achieved higher than average performance.

THE ANALYTIC HIERARCHY PROCESS

Managing conflicting goals constitutes one of the most difficult aspects of many decision processes. The Analytic Hierarchy Process (AHP) is one of the most frequently used and best established methods for solving the issue of balancing conflicting goals (Bernasconi et al, 2014; Saaty, 1996, 1994, 1990; Zahedei, 1986). Careful evaluation of the web presence of numerous corporations indicates that there is a need to consider keeping a web page complete yet simple, informative yet readable, and consistent yet interesting (Kraft, 2012). Krug emphasizes the importance of "don't make the User think". Renowned online guru Seth Godin in his book "The Big Red Fex" takes it a step further and explains "a web site visitor is a lot like a monkey looking for one than: a banana. If that banana isn't easy to see and easy to get, your visitor is gone with a quick click on the 'Back' button". AHP provides a method for balancing the goals to achieve an efficient website design focused on the UX.

With AHP, the problem is modeled as a hierarchy of criteria and decision alternatives with the importance of each element at each level of the hierarchy assessed utilizing a matrix of pairwise comparisons that weighs each element along with the others. For each pairwise comparison matrix, the process uses the eigenvector of the matrix to provide relative weights of the elements at each level of the hierarchy. Using hierarchic composition, the aggregate of weights across various levels of the hierarchy are then aggregated to provide a final weight for each alternative. AHP organizes various factors in a systematic way and provides a simple structured solution to complex decision-making problems (Utkin and Simanova, 2012).

AHP was developed in the 1970s to aid in solving complex problems (Triantaphyllou and Mann, 1995). Using the judgment of individuals with a common understanding of the situation, it provides the theory and methodology for the modeling of unstructured problems (Saaty, 1980). The decision problem is broken down into small easily understandable elements, organized into a hierarchy of levels. AHP provides a mechanism for evaluating the interrelationships among the components of the hierarchy (Saaty, 1994). Use of AHP requires only pair-wise comparisons allowing inclusion of criteria that are difficult or impossible to quantify except by expressing that one is preferred to another. AHP also allows comparison of factors which interact with other factors. AHP is a process designed to facilitate the formalization of multi-criteria decision-making. It enables the decision maker to incorporate both "hard data" and less quantifiable elements such as judgments, feelings, and experiences. AHP has been widely used in a variety of decision-making applications (Saaty 1996).

Using AHP, the decision problem is structured hierarchically into a value tree from higher level criteria to lower level sub-criteria. If the criteria being compared are objective, the numeric values for the criteria are compared in a series of pair-wise comparisons. If, however, the criteria are wholly or partially subjective, then the comparisons are made on the basis of relative preference between the two. Once these comparisons have been established for each criterion, an n x n matrix of comparisons is constructed, where n equals the number of criteria. In this matrix, the elements are arrayed where the Aij element is always the reciprocal of the Aji element. That is, if the first criterion is preferred over the second criterion by a factor of four then the A12 element of the matrix is four and the A21 element is 0.25. The principle eigenvector of the matrix is then calculated and normalized. This eigenvector represents the complete set of the relative importance of the criteria. This method results in a dependable, mathematically rigorous, quantitative approach that overcomes the complexities and difficulties inherent in measuring unlike elements and delivers a system that can be trusted and relied upon by managers (Saaty, 1996). For a more complete discussion of the mathematical process and theory underlying AHP see Saaty (1994). Furthermore, Harker and Vargas (1987) provide a discussion of the inherent theoretical strengths and weaknesses of AHP.

AHP has been utilized successfully in a wide variety of decision support applications including assessment of the financial strength of publicly traded companies (Seyed et al, 2013), the choice of an advertising strategy (Zolfani et al, 2012), and maintenance strategy (Fouladgar, 2012). It lends itself to use in a variety of situations where the attributes are difficult to measure because it is based on pairwise comparisons that require only the assignment of relative importance of the two elements under consideration. By using a mathematically rigorous process it offers a measure of internal consistency (Saaty, 1996). AHP has become one of the most popular aids to decision-making and is now widely accessible through commercially available software programs (Expert Choice, Inc, 2000; Forman et al, 1983). This paper presents a format for using AHP to produce an internally consistent, robust measure of an organizational website's overall effectiveness.

PROCEDURE

Inc. magazine publishes an annual list of the 500 "fastest growing companies" in the United States. We took the top 40 companies over a three-year period (2011-2013) and conducted 900 surveys. Companies were chosen from Inc. magazines top 500 companies because these were considered by the authors to be the most innovative, fastest growing, innovative organizations in the United States. The website analysis surveys were completed by approximately 180 senior-level business students. The web analysis assignment was given at the end of an Electronic Management course. Each student was randomly assigned seven websites to analyse based on a survey provided by the first author.

The survey instrument was developed by the first author based on his eight years of experience in the UX website design industry. The survey provides an overview of shared elements (best practices) common to the websites surveyed. We posit that by identifying the design elements included in the websites of fastest growing organizations, we can employ this information to develop a measure of website effectiveness utilizing AHP. Students were provided links to the websites being surveyed and used Survey Monkey as the survey instrument. Individual students completed seven surveys of different companies. The surveyed websites were selected randomly for students. The surveys comprised forty-four items concerning the key components of effective websites and included both qualitative and quantitative items.

This resulted in a list of shared elements (best practices) common to the websites (Table 1). We then developed a concept map of those elements which facilitated the identification of the predominant relationships between the individual web elements (Figure 1). This facilitated the grouping of the elements into four categories: Look, User Interface, Content, and Memorability. Look includes the visual aspects of the website. User Interface refers to the clarity and readability of the language used and the ease of user navigation. Content includes all aspects of the information content about the company and its products or services. The elements that comprise Content are subdivided into those that are related to information about the company and those that are related to establishing and maintaining a relationship with users termed About and Relations. Memorability captures those qualities that make the website easy to remember and share with others. This category was subdivided into two categories that are termed Presentation and Repetition. Presentation captures those elements that represent how easy the name and URL are to remember and share, while Repetition captures the degree to which graphics, trademarks and other identifying marks are repeated. Once data from this analysis was aggregated, it provided a benchmark by which an AHP measurement instrument was developed.

UTILIZING AHP TO ESTABLISH A BENCHMARK WEBSITE SCORE

Use of a formal multi-attribute decision analysis process makes it possible to incorporate the numerous elements of a well-developed website into a decision process that is capable of handling the complexity of the interaction between the elements and provides the degree of internal validity required to assure that the measurement of website quality is consistent from one evaluation to the next and from one subject to the next.

Using the AHP to structure a benchmark website measure first requires the decision maker to structure the problem as a hierarchy. Then, the elements of the hierarchy are prioritized by responses to questions about the dominance, or importance, of each element compared to the others (Liberatore and Miller, 1998).

The first, and perhaps most creative, step in the AHP process involves structuring the problem as a hierarchy. A useful approach is to start with the goal and decompose it into the most general and easily controlled factors at the simplest or most basic level possible. The decision maker then works back up through the hierarchy starting with the simplest sub-criteria that must be met and combining the sub-

Table 1. Best Practices Elements of a Website

Design Elements	Description
Blog/Newsletter	The website includes up-to-date blogs or newsletters?
Brand/Logo Consistency	The organization's brands (colors, logo, contact information) are consistent on different pages of the website?
Consistent Page Image	The overall image of the website is consistent.
Design Consistency	There is a consistent design profile across all pages of the website.
Easy Name	The website has a short easy-to-remember/share title.
First Impression	There is a professional is the look and feel of the website
Navigation/ Tabs	It is easy to navigate the website
Niche	The "About" section clearly describe the niche of the organization.
Product Service	The "About" section clearly describes the organization's products and services.
Reading	Information available on the website is clear and easy to follow
Social Media	The website includes easy-to-access social media tools.
URL - Name	The website's URL includes the organization's name.
URL - Prod/Serv	The website's name reflects the products/services of the organization.
Vision/Mission	The "About" section describes the vision/mission of the organization.
Visual Appeal	The website is visually appealing.
Blog/Newsletter	The website includes up-to-date blogs or newsletters?
Brand/Logo Consistency	The organization's brands (colors, logo, contact information) are consistent on different pages of the website?
Consistent Page Image	The overall image of the website is consistent.
Design Consistency	There is a consistent design profile across all pages of the website.
Easy Name	The website has a short easy-to-remember/share title.
First Impression	There is a professional is the look and feel of the website
Navigation/ Tabs	It is easy to navigate the website

criteria into generic higher level criteria until the various measurements are linked in such a way that comparisons between unlike elements are possible (Liberatore and Miller, 1998).

At this point, several words of caution are in order. As the number of objects to be compared increase, the number of pair-wise comparisons necessary to rank them rapidly becomes unwieldy. In addition, the method necessities that the comparisons rate one of each pair of choices as more important than the other; a determination must be made as to which element is more important and to what degree it is more important. This may be accomplished a number of ways, including calculation with a hand-held calculator, spreadsheet software, or math software. However, AHP software is available to facilitate the comparison and ranking operations of the AHP as well as providing the numeric solution. These software packages make it possible to easily manipulate a large number of variables, keeping track of comparisons, rankings, and weights. They also provide measures of the consistency of the judgments and allow complete sensitivity analysis. Calculations for this example were done using Web-HIPRE, a publicly available Web based software package provided by the Systems Analysis Laboratory of Helsinki University of Technology (Web-HIPRE, 1998).

Figure 1. Hierarchical Relationships

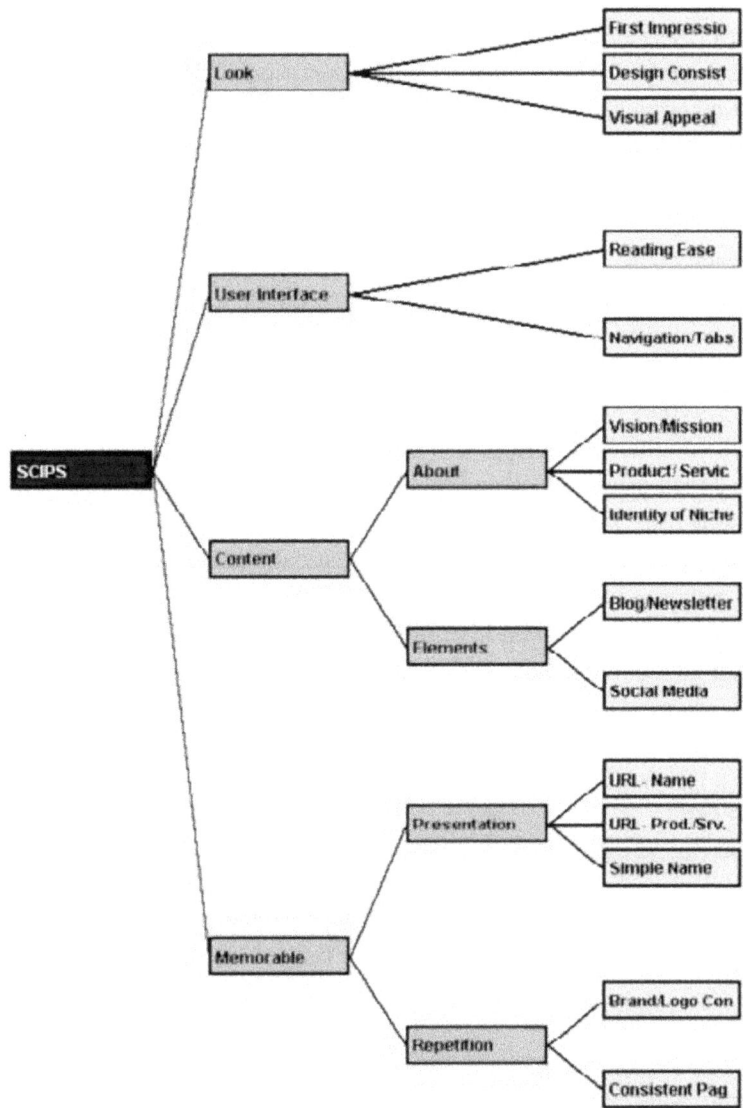

The balance of this paper describes the development of a benchmark measure for websites using AHP as is available through Web-HIPRE (1998).

MECHANICS OF THE AHP

The first step in using AHP for a decision process is to construct a hierarchy for the process. In this example, the first level of the hierarchy is the goal of the AHP (developing a benchmark measure of website quality) and is followed by the second level (four distinct categories of website elements), and the third consisting of the individual web site elements themselves.

Once the elements are identified in the software program, they must be connected to depict their relationships (Figure 1). In the first column the goal of the analysis is listed. In this case it is designated SCIPS (S-C Internet Presence Score). Feeding into this score are the four categories of elements previously identified and discussed. These categories are identified with the elements with which they are associated as identified previously.

Once these relationships are established, the weighting procedure is performed to compare the importance of each of the element to the other elements to which it is attached. Through a series of questions concerning "how much more important" one element is compared to another, Web-HIPRE requires the user to either rank each of the elements on a scale of one to ten or express their relative relationship as how many times one is more preferred over the other, as in, "A is 1.23 more prevalent than B." To determine the relative weights of the elements for inclusion in the AHP the percentage of the websites analyzed that included each element was tabulated. These percentage scores were normalized by conversion to z-scores. The z-scores which ranged from less than three to greater than negative three were then converted to all positive numbers so they could be used in AHP. To accomplish this, each was added to three which preserved their original rank and relative magnitude, but made it possible to easily calculate their relative magnitude (See Table 2).

When this process is complete, the program automatically generates the matrices and eigenvector utilized in AHP and returns a weighing factor for each of the lowest level elements. The weighting factors for each of the elements is displayed in Table 3.

These weights can now be utilized in scoring the Internet presence of an organization's website as described next.

Table 2. Normalized Data

Element	Score
Reading	3.694
Consistent Page Image	3.229
First Impression	2.707
Navigation-Tabs	2.707
Brand-Logo Consistency	2.707
Visual Appeal	2.247
Product Service	2.247
Niche	2.000
Easy Name	1.836
URL - Name	1.668
Design Consistency	1.489
Vision-Mission	1.293
Blog-Newsletter	0.929
Social Media	0.929
URL – Includes Produce or Service	0.298

Table 3. Element Weighting Factors

Element Name	Weight
First Impression	0.13
Design Consistency	0.07
Visual Appeal	0.11
Reading Ease	0.15
Navigation/Tabs	0.11
Vision/Mission	0.05
Product/Service	0.01
Identity of Niche	0.04
Blog/Newsletter	0.03
Social Media	0.03
URL – Name	0.05
URL – Product/Service	0.01
Simple Name	0.05
Brand/Logo Consistency	0.08
Consistent Pages	0.09
Total	**1.00**

USING THE RESULTS

The weights for each of the individual elements are displayed in Table 3. To evaluate a website, indicate the degree to which it meets each criterion using a consistent scale, multiply the score on each criterion by the appropriate weight from Table 3 and sum the scores. Note that the score of the benchmark totals one. Therefore, if a consistent scale of one to ten were used to evaluate a website, a score of less than ten would indicate the degree to which the website's design met the benchmark.

IMPLICATIONS FOR PRACTICE

The results from this study provide UX guidance to practitioners in the development of their website. When designing and developing a website, website developers typically experience budgeting and time constraints. Our findings provide direction for organizations about the importance the primary focus on the UX in the design of their websites. This enables designers to focus their limited time and budget on the elements that are most important to the UX.

Moreover, the findings provide an analytical tool that organizations can utilize to assess their Internet presence. Companies that have already built a website can easily evaluate the effectiveness of their website to UX by calculating the degree to which the website's design met the benchmark.

It has been found that website design influences an individual's intention to visit a physical location (Pallud and Straub, 2014). Therefore, if organizations would like customers to visit their location, then they must first start with a well-designed website. This study specifies those parameters and reinforces the importance of the UX.

Therefore, this study provides direction for our collegues-in-practice.

IMPLICATIONS FOR RESEARCH

This study also contributes to the UX-based website design research stream.

Effective UX-based website design is critical to the success of organizations today. Therefore, this topic has been widely studied in the literature. However, most of these studies are dated and do not take into consideration new applications and social media tools that have come onto the market. Thus, this study provides an updated view of website quality.

Moreover, it also provides a new method focusing on UX rather than on its technical components. While website quality has been assessed with experiments (Coursaris and Kripintris, 2012), structural models (Al-Qeisi et al, 2014) and other modelling techniques (Cebi, 2013), it is the first study to apply the Analytic Hierarchy Process (AHP) Multi-attribute Decision Modeling technique to the website design research stream. Therefore, this study contributes to the body of knowledge by providing a new lens through which to assess website quality.

CONCLUSION

As organizational UX website design increases in importance, we continue to increase our knowledge of what constitutes an effective organizational website. In this study, we performed 900 surveys of organizations identified in the Inc. Magazine's Top 500 lists of the fastest growing companies in the United States (2011-13). Utilizing these organizational websites as benchmarks of effective UX website design, we were able to develop a measurement tool that can be used by organizations to produce an internally consistent, robust measure of their website design. In the future, we urge other researchers to build upon our study and continue the quest to develop tools that facilitate the development of effectively UX designed organizational websites.

REFERENCES

Al-Qeisi, K., Dennis, C., Alamanos, E., & Jayawardhena, C. (2014). Website design quality and usage behavior: Unified theory of acceptance and use of technology. *Journal of Business Research*, *67*(11), 2282–2290. doi:10.1016/j.jbusres.2014.06.016

Aladwani, A. M., & Palvia, P. C. (2002). Developing and validating an instrument for measuring user perceived web quality. *Information & Management*, *39*(6), 467–476. doi:10.1016/S0378-7206(01)00113-6

Basdeo, D., Smith, K. G., Grimm, C., Rindova, V. P., & Derfus, P. (2006). The impact of market actions on firm reputation. *Strategic Management Journal*, *27*(12), 1183–1204. doi:10.1002/smj.556

Blom, R., Carpenter, S., Bowe, B. J., & Lange, R. (2014). Frequent contributors within U.S. newspaper comment forums: An examination of their civility and information value. *The American Behavioral Scientist*, *58*(10), 1314–1328. doi:10.1177/0002764214527094

Brown, W., Rahman, M., & Hacker, T. (2006). Home page usability and credibility. *Information Management & Computer Security*, *14*(3), 252–269. doi:10.1108/09685220610670404

Cebi, S. (2013). Determining importance degrees of website design parameters based on interactions and types of websites. *Decision Support Systems*, *54*(2), 1030–1043. doi:10.1016/j.dss.2012.10.036

Cho, E. C., & Youn-Kyung, K. (2012). The effects of website designs, self-congruity, and flow on behavioral intention. *International Journal of Design*, *6*(2), 31–39.

Clark, W. R., Ezell, J., Clark, J., & Sheffield, D. N. (2009). Stay or leave: Applying approach-avoidance theory to virtual environments. *Journal of Database Marketing & Customer Strategy Management*, *16*(4), 231–240. doi:10.1057/dbm.2009.25

Coursaris, C., & Kripintris, K. (2012). Web Aesthetics and Usability: An Empirical Study of the effects of white space. *International Journal of E-Business Research*, *8*(1), 35–53. doi:10.4018/jebr.2012010103

Curran, J. M., & Lennon, R. (2013). Comparing younger and older social network users: An examination of attitudes and intentions. *The Journal of American Academy of Business, Cambridge*, *19*(1), 28–37.

De Vries, N., & Carlson, J. (2014). Examining the drivers and brand performance implications of customer engagement with brands in the social media environment. *Journal of Brand Management, 21*(6), 495–515. doi:10.1057/bm.2014.18

Deephouse, D. L., & Carter, S. M. (2005). An examination of differences between organizational legitimacy and organizational reputation. *Journal of Management Studies, 42*(2), 329–360. doi:10.1111/j.1467-6486.2005.00499.x

Expert Choice, Inc. (2000). Retrieved from http://www.expertchoice.com

Fan, W.-S., & Tsai, M.-C. (2010). Factors driving website success: The key role of internet customization and the influence of website design quality and internet marketing strategy. *Total Quality Management & Business Excellence, 21*(11), 1141–1159. doi:10.1080/14783363.2010.529335

Forman, E., Saaty, T., Selly, M., & Waldron, R. (1983). *Expert Choice.* McLean, VA: Decision Support Software, Inc.

Fouladgar, M., Yazdani-Chamzini, A., Lashgari, A., Zavadskas, E., & Turskis, Z. (2012). Maintenance strategy selection using AHP and COPRAS under fuzzy environment. *International Journal of Strategic Property, 16*(1), 85–104. doi:10.3846/1648715X.2012.666657

Frederick, D., Mohler, J., Vorvoreanu, M., & Clotzbach, R. (2015). The Effects of parallax scrolling on User Experience on Web Design. *Journal of Usability Studies, 10*(2), 87–95.

Fry, A. (2014). Helping the public see the value of social research using social media. *International Journal of Market Research, 56*(4), 421–423. doi:10.2501/IJMR-2014-030

Godin, S. (2002). *The big red fez: How to make any web site better.* Simon & Schuster.

Harker, P., & Vargas, L. (1987). The theory of ratio scale estimation: Saaty's analytic hierarchy process. *Management Science, 33*(11), 1383–1403. doi:10.1287/mnsc.33.11.1383

Hosseini, S., Ezazi, M., Heshmati, M., Moghadam, S., & Moghadam, H. (2013). Top companies ranking based on financial ratio with AHP-TOPSIS combined approach and indices of Tehran stock exchange. *International Journal of Economics and Finance, 5*(3), 126–133. doi:10.5539/ijef.v5n3p126

Hsu, C., Chen, Y., Yang, T., & Lin, W. (2017). Do website features matter in an online gamification context? Focusing on the mediating roles of user experience and attitude. *Telematics and Informatics, 34*(4), 196–205. doi:10.1016/j.tele.2017.01.009

Kraft, C. (2012). *User Experience Innovation, User Centered Design That Works.* New York: Apress Media.

Krug, S. (2014). *Don't make me think, revisited: A common sense approach to web usability* (3rd ed.). New Riders.

Li, X., Rong, G., & Thatcher, J. B. (2009). Swift trust in web vendors: The role of appearance and functionality. *Journal of Organizational and End User Computing, 21*(1), 88–108. doi:10.4018/joeuc.2009092205

Liberatore, M., & Miller, T. (1998). A framework for integrating activity-based costing and the balanced scorecard into the logistics strategy development and monitoring process. *Journal of Business Logistics*, *19*(2), 131–155.

Luo, X., Zhang, J., & Duan, W. (2013). Social media and firm equity value. *Information Systems Research*, *24*(1), 146–VI. doi:10.1287/isre.1120.0462

Newman, M., & Landay, J. (2000). *Sitemaps, storyboards, and specifications: A sketch of website design practice.* ACM. doi:10.1145/347642.347758

Pallud, J., & Straub, D. (2014). Effective website design for experience-influenced environments: The case of high culture museums. *Information & Management*, *51*(3), 359–373. doi:10.1016/j.im.2014.02.010

Porter, M. (2001). Strategy and the internet. *Harvard Business Review*, *89*(3), 63–78. PMID:11246925

Ranganathan, C., & Ganapathy, S. (2002). Key dimensions of business-to-consumer websites. *Information & Management*, *39*(6), 457–465. doi:10.1016/S0378-7206(01)00112-4

Rapp, A., Beitelspacher, L. S., Grewal, D., & Hughes, D. E. (2013). Understanding social media effects across seller, retailer, and consumer interactions. *Academy of Marketing Science Journal*, *41*(5), 547–566. doi:10.1007/s11747-013-0326-9

Saaty, T. L. (1980). *Analytic Hierarchy Process: Planning, Priority Setting, Resource Allocation.* New York: McGraw-Hill International Book Company.

Saaty, T. L. (1994). How to make a decision: The analytic hierarchy process. *Interfaces*, *24*(6), 19–43. doi:10.1287/inte.24.6.19

Saaty, T. L. (1996). *The analytic hierarchy process.* Pittsburg, PA: RWS Publications.

Schmidt, S. M. P., & Ralph, D. L. (2013). Marketing using your website. *The Business Review, Cambridge*, *21*(1), 52–58.

Shobeiri, S., Mazaheri, E., & Laroche, M. (2014). Improving customer website involvement through experiential marketing. *Service Industries Journal*, *34*(11), 885–900. doi:10.1080/02642069.2014.915953

Simonson, I., & Emanuel, R. (2014). *Absolute value: What really influences customers in the age of (nearly) perfect information.* HarperCollins Publishers.

Tang, L., & Jang, S. (2014). Information Value and Destination Image: Investigating the Moderating Role of Processing Fluency. *Journal of Hospitality Marketing & Management*, *23*(7), 790–814. doi:10.1080/19368623.2014.883585

Triantaphyllou, E., & Mann, S. (1995). Using the analytic hierarchy process for decision making in engineering applications: Some challenges. *International Journal of Industrial Engineering: Applications and Practice*, *2*(1), 35–44.

Tsiaousis, A. S., & Giaglis, G. M. (2014). Mobile websites: Usability evaluation and design. *International Journal of Mobile Communications*, *12*(1), 29–55. doi:10.1504/IJMC.2014.059241

Utkin, L. V., & Simanova, N. V. (2012). The DS/AHP method under partial information about criteria and alternatives by several levels of criteria. *International Journal of Information Technology & Decision Making, 11*(2), 307–326. doi:10.1142/S0219622012400044

Wakefield, R. J., Stocks, M. H., & Wilder, W. M. (2004). The role of website characteristics in initial trust formation. *Journal of Computer Information Systems, 45*(1), 94–103.

Wani, M., Raghavan, V., Abraham, D., & Kleist, V. (2017). Beyond utilitarian factors: User Experience and travel company website successes. *Information Systems Frontiers, 19*(4), 769–785. doi:10.1007/s10796-017-9747-1

Web-HIPRE. (1998). Retrieved from http://www.hipre.hut.fi/

Wikipedia.org. (2009) Retrieved from https://en.wikipedia.org/wiki/User_experience

Zavyalova, A., Pfarrer, M., Reger, R., & Shapiro, D. (2012). The effects of firm actions and industry spillovers on media coverage following wrongdoing. *Academy of Management Journal, 55*(5), 1079–1101. doi:10.5465/amj.2010.0608

Chapter 7
Leveraging Virtual Communities to Enhance Brand Equity:
A Case Study

Kelley A. O'Reilly
Western Michigan University, USA

Brett M. Kelley
Western Michigan University, USA

Karen M. Lancendorfer
Western Michigan University, USA

ABSTRACT

This chapter explores how one company leveraged motorsports to build brand credibility, establish powerful marketing relationships, and connect with distinctly different consumer groups via virtual brand communities. Companies with strong virtual communities may benefit from the case study suggestions that are provided and discussed based on the theoretical perspective of brand equity. Marketing scholars and practitioners alike may find this case study of interest due to the growing desire by companies to develop strong bonds with consumers and their interest in effectively leveraging virtual brand communities as a tool. Several practice recommendations for leveraging virtual communities to enhance brand equity are discussed.

INTRODUCTION

Integrated marketing communications (IMC) began generating interest in the early 1990s and has since been accepted by marketers as "…a natural evolution of traditional mass-media advertising, which has been changed, adjusted and refined as a result of new technology" (Schultz 1999, p. 337). IMC can be understood as a broader marketplace view that is sensitive to the impacts and effects of new technologies and communication channels. In this way, IMC extends beyond traditional mass marketing communication which historically put the emphasis on mass media techniques for brand building efforts (Keller, 2009).

DOI: 10.4018/978-1-5225-5014-3.ch007

Typically driven by either strategy or efficiency, IMC planning focuses on various media mix elements as instrumental for branding efforts (Gabrielli and Balboni, 2010). Along these lines, marketers evaluate different communication options from a perspective of horizontal and vertical coordination, that is, both across and within media with particular focus on the coordination of consumer messaging. This highlights the essence of IMC planning which is a method for coordinating company communications in such a way as to *send* a clear and singular message regarding the company's unique value proposition. This viewpoint is still fairly traditional, with the company sending communications, and the consumer receiving the communication. However, Keller notes that these traditional techniques may be suboptimal in "...a marketplace where customers have access to massive amounts of information about brands, products and companies... (2009, p. 139). There is no doubt that technology, the Internet, and social networking sites have put consumers more in control than ever before as integrators and co-creators of brand meaning.

Considering this perspective, we consider a unique application of IMC that is consumer, rather than company, lead. Necessitated by a high degree of competition and lack of resources for more traditional market spending, the case company explored here focused on a little known motorsport in an attempt to build brand awareness. Consumer fans of the sport then guided the company to new alternative online environments which resulted in consumers, rather than the company, acting as integrators of promotional elements within the communication mix.

The case study explored here, as well as the phenomenon occurring, highlights the power that engaged current fans in virtual fan communities provide. It also furthers the idea that brand control and communication may be well-placed in the hands of online fans. Done properly, virtual communities can act as a conduit to new consumers (e.g. the network of friends and followers of fans). As demonstrated by the case company, tapping into the power of consumer-driven virtual communities resulted in brand "likes" driving as much brand equity as did brand "buys." Marketing scholars and practitioners alike may find this case study of interest due to the growing desire by companies to develop strong bonds with consumers and their interest in effectively using social media as a marketing tool.

BACKGROUND LITERATURE

Key Literature on Brand Equity

In simple terms, brand equity is the value that originates from the brand's customers, rather than from the product or service the brand represents. Brand equity is of interest to marketers due to the financial implications of value, but also because brand equity is positively correlated to favorable responses from consumers to an element of the marketing mix (Keller, 1993). Understanding how to build brand equity is of practical value to managers since it aids in refining the marketing mix elements. Defined as, "the differential effect of brand knowledge on consumer response to the marketing of the brand" (p. 8), it is desirable to establish strong connections and involvement between the consumer and the brand. These connections often start at consumer engagement whereby marketers attempt to influence and encourage consumers to interact with and about the brand (Schultz & Peltier, 2013), with often positive results. A number of brands have shown an improvement in business performance as a result of consumer engagement. According to the ENGAGEMENTdb Study by Wetpaint/Altimeter Group (Li, 2009), "the most valuable brands in the world are experiencing a direct correlation between top financial performance and deep social media engagement" (p. 1). In this way, we can view consumer engagement as the first step towards building brand equity. It should be noted that consumer loyalty and retention are often positively correlated with increased levels of consumer engagement (Vivek, Beatty, & Morgan, 2012).

To create and build brand equity requires brand familiarity and brand strength that yields positive unique brand associations in the minds of consumers (Keller, 1993). Considering that many marketing programs have been traditionally crafted to drive consumer purchases of the product or service, managing brands more holistically is particularly salient against the backdrop of the social media landscape and phenomenon of virtual brand communities. As means of example, Facebook is currently the dominant social-networking site, with an audience of over 200 million users (Statista, n.d). Facebook leads all other social networking sites when it comes to time spent, with 53 percent of Facebook users logging in multiple times a day (Morning Consult, n.d.). To remain successful in these virtual communities, marketers must acknowledge the role of the consumer as a co-creator of brand meaning if they hope to establish strong associations between the consumer and brand (Brown, Kozinets, & Sherry, 2003; Fournier & Avery, 2011). Brand communities give consumers a place to share content, and ultimately express their identity (Wang, Ma & Li, 2015). Chou suggests that, "establishing an online brand community is an effective way to enhance a company's brand equity as long as customer relationships are strengthened" (Chou, 2014, p. 137).

However, this cannot be done with a traditional marketing mindset of "capturing, driving, and convincing" consumers to take a certain action (O'Reilly & Lancendorfer, 2013). Authenticity is a vital ingredient in building and maintaining a successful brand because it forms a unique brand identity and provides a strong, favorable association (Gundlach & Neville, 2012)., Algesheimer, Dholakia, and Herman (2005) suggest that brand community members various behavioral intentions translate into actual behaviors – empirical support for advocates favoring the building of brand communities.

Key Literature on Social Media

Social media is best understood as a digital platform for creating content, sharing ideas, and connecting with companies and other customers. Its importance to marketers is fast-outstripping that of traditional media since it is relatively inexpensive and can quickly get marketing messages to prospects through interactive discussions and rapid word-of-mouth (Owyang, 2009). Social media tools are moving into a golden time as more and more consumers, born into the "Internet generation" reach their 20s, 30s and beyond. Research tells us that this generation enjoys using social media to socialize with friends, stay in touch with family, connect with old acquaintances, connect with people via shared interests, make new friends, follow celebrity posts, and find romance (Pew Internet, 2011). Indeed, it seems this is "…a generation [that] is growing up in an era where digital media are part of the taken-for-granted social and cultural fabric of learning, play, and social communication" (Ito, Davidson, Jenkins, Lee, Eisenberg & Weiss, 2008, p. vii).

"In the social media environment, every time a person uses an application designed by or about the company, the company gains increased exposure to its brand, often in highly relevant contexts" (Hoffman & Fodor, 2010, p. 46). This creates a distinct shift in control of brands across contexts whereby, "Consumers are now the individuals broadcasting personal or second-hand stories to their social networks and the world. They are a brand's storytellers and the new brand ambassadors" (Booth & Matic, 2011, p. 185). Menachem et al. suggest that managers should actively empower customers to become brand advocates, and thus be a voice for the company (Menachem, Sujata, Padman, Bishnoi, & Upadhye, 2016).

Interestingly, a consumer's relationship with a specific brand has been shown to be an "antecedent to his or her identification with the brand community" (Algesheimer et al., 2005, p. 30).

Companies who take a proactive stance to social media commonly empower employees to talk, listen, and respond to what consumers post on social media (Smith, Fischer, & Yongjian, 2012). Because marketer created content may encourage more sharing online, user-generated content can be indicative of brand engagement and word-of-mouth. Therefore, these co-created brand environments (Fournier & Avery, 2011) reward social media marketing strategies that "put the brand to work for the customers by satisfying their needs to create, consume, connect and control in the social Web" (Hoffman & Fodor, 2010, p. 49, italics in original). New technologies have made this very easy as, "… new low-cost digital production tools mean that amateur and casual media creators can author, edit, and distribute video and other rich media forms that were once prohibitively expensive to produce and share with others" (Ito et al., 2008, p. viii).

Key Literature on Virtual Communities

Brand communities can best be described as a "group of ardent consumers organized around the lifestyle, activities, and ethos of the brand" (Fournier & Avery, 2011, p. 133). In the online environment, the communication between members is virtual with groups coalescing through self-selection. Typically formed around a specific brand, members share values, practices, feedback, and have a strong sense of member identity with each other (Fournier & Lee, 2009).

Virtual brand communities are of interest to academics and practitioners alike since they have the ability to influence community members, speed up communications between members, provide robust access to member opinions and evaluations, and provide opportunities for interaction (Algesheimer et al., 2005). Virtual brand communities attract millions of users daily, so once consumers are aware and engaged with a brand they are in a position to communicate their opinions to other consumers (Habibi, Laroche, & Richard, 2014). In the age of social media marketing, it is common to determine the strength of these brand associations by quantifying the number of reviews, "likes", new member sign-ups, and the number of comments and quantity of user-generated content. Therefore, highly engaging social media campaigns involving user-generated content [will] likely generate commitment on the part of the consumer, reinforcing loyalty to the brand and making the customer more likely to commit additional effort to support the brand in the future (Hoffman & Fodor, 2010, p. 46).

This suggests that the traditional top-down approach to marketing should be abandoned in favor of more participatory and interactive cooperation between marketer and consumer (Christodoulides, Jevons, & Bonhomme, 2012). When marketers encourage online community participation, this strengthens relationship quality which in turn generates brand loyalty (Hajli, Shanmumgam, Papagiannidis, Zahay, & Richard, 2016). This will then create stronger brand associations, thereby improving consumer-based brand equity. In addition, consumers' experiences with brands can be shared and communicated more effectively through interactive environments than through traditional media outlets (Kim & Yu, 2016). Therefore, it seems that we are now faced with a new truth that "…corporate marketing never had control of the brand" (Booth & Matic, 2011, p. 185).

BACKGROUND ON CASE COMPANY

In 1983, Falken Tire Corporation (FTC), a subsidiary of Sumitomo Rubber Industries, launched the Falken brand in its native country of Japan. Two years later the brand was introduced in the North American market. The Falken brand was originally perceived in the U.S. market as a niche tire within the ultra-high performance replacement market. During its first two decades in the U.S., FTC's market share remained stagnant at less than 1%, with first tier brands such as Goodyear, Michelin, and Bridgestone controlling the market as shown in Table 1.

Positioned as a mid-range second tier tire, FTC sells through the wholesale and retail aftermarket channels. Most of FTC's marketing focus is business-to-business with promotional support and trade incentives targeted at the retail channel in the hope that retail salespeople will recommend the Falken brand during their interactions with customers. Over the years, this strategy had proven limited and FTC struggled to make head-way against larger competitors who had substantial budgets for marketing and advertising directed at both the business-to-business and business-to-consumer channels. One of the reasons was that most of FTC's top competitors had control over retail outlets giving them a competitive advantage and better control over the "retail sales floor." For example, Goodyear owned its own chain of retail stores and other competitors exerted influence in the retail aftermarket by offering associate dealer contracts providing signage, merchandising, and other incentives for retailers. In these cases, the tire manufacturer exerts some control over which brands a retailer carries, promotes, and ultimately recommends to customers.

In 2003, in an effort to improve their market share, FTC's President challenged the management team to deliver more exposure to the Falken brand in the performance market. From this challenge, one of FTC's managers suggested the motorsport of Drifting as a way to showcase the company's products. From a technical perspective, Drifting is a driving technique where the driver intentionally over steers, causing loss of traction in the rear wheels, while maintaining control through tight corners on small racetracks. Often the front wheels are pointing in the opposite direction of the turn (e.g., car is turning left, wheels are pointed right or vice versa) when Drifting. Drifting is best known today from Hollywood releases such as "The Fast and the Furious: Tokyo Drift", but at the time, the sport was relatively obscure, affordable, and exciting.

Table 1. 2016 US Performance Replacement Market Brands by Tier (Listed in order of market share)

Tier One	Tier Two	Tier Three
1 Goodyear	6 Toyo	11 Firestone
2 Michelin	7 BF Goodrich	12 Nexen
3 Bridgestone	8 Continental	13 Cooper
4 Yokohama	**9 Falken**	14 Pirelli
5 Hankook	10 Kuhmo	15 Dunlop

Source: Modern Tire Dealer

http://www.moderntiredealer.com/uploads/stats/MTD-Hi-Perf-chart.jpg

Using Motorsports to Establish Brand Credibility

Drift brought several elements to bear that were not true for other motorsports. First, Drifting uses relatively inexpensive street-legal vehicles that are within the reach of enthusiasts. Second, the tires and automotive components on the cars are the same that consumers can purchase at tire retailers or online. And third, it put the fans next to the track and up close to the action. To test whether this new sport would have broad enough appeal, FTC decided to host the first-ever Drift Show-off in southern California[1]. Massive positive fan response from this first event fueled FTC's desire to use the sport to build the credibility of its ultra-high performance tires. Although FTC had no experience managing a motorsports racing team, the opportunity seemed like a good strategic fit for the company – the sport was affordable and no other tire brand was dominant. Likewise, FTC was open to following their racing fans online in a move that would later create unexpected opportunity and benefit.

Developing Consumer-Based Brand Equity at the Track

When FTC first entered motorsports, the sales and marketing groups were not performing optimally. Interestingly, the track proved to be fertile ground for recruiting. This grassroots building of the management team proved to be a key element of the company's culture and passion for sport and more importantly, the fans of the sport. This motivation to "stay connected, approachable, and authentic" is evident throughout marketing decisions that FTC made in regard to racing and non-racing activities at the track and online. Reflecting on FTC's choice to be an active sponsor and participate in Drift, the VP of Marketing compared that decision to competitor moves into more formal sports such as Major League Baseball and explained, "…just because your brand is in the outfield doesn't mean they [consumers] are going to understand what you do or what you're about… but because we're out there in the dirt with enthusiasts, we became relevant." Adding to this "relevance" is the fan community that began to gather online to disseminate videos, blogs, and other brand-related information to an even broader audience. FTC noticed and began "follow" their fans online to learn what worked, and what didn't.

Following Online Brand Communities to New Media

While brand equity was being built through FTC's sponsorship efforts at the track, it was secondary to the impact of FTC's growing online virtual brand community. From the first Drifting event, photos, videos, and comments popped up online. In the early days, this was typically youtube.com videos posted by fans that attended the event. As FTC's success at the track continued, the company invested in personnel and equipment to document events making them a pioneer in "consistent video messaging" of their events and results. What is perhaps most interesting, is that the majority of racing fans and brand fans online were not active purchasers of the company's brand. This finding contradicts the linear cycle we expect from customer-based brand equity (Keller, 1993). From that theory we expect that customers will form some memory of the brand, the memory will hopefully build a positive and strong association, and that this association leads to brand loyalty as measured by sales turnover of the product or service. In this case study, loyalty seems to exist as evidenced by the willingness of customers to actively promote the brand, yet this is occurring before their first purchase. This suggests that consumer activation (rather than turnover) may be an alternative measure of loyalty, making the power of "likes" online a valuable metric of success and worthy of securing.

Leveraging Online Relationships

Perhaps recognizing that the most loyal are not active brand purchasers, the management team focused more on driving fan engagement and "likes" on social media sites. As part of this strategy, FTC used a combination of tools and techniques such as online video messaging, QR promo codes, promotional giveaways, and online marketing tactics to solicit user-generated content and engagement in the company's web assets. In essence, they created a culture of encouragement for the brand's fans to create the brand's stories online. As more participation evolved in the virtual brand community, FTC began to fine-tune messages, graphics, and imagery based upon the feedback they secured through their online presence. From this early online success, the company experienced collateral benefits of their strong online presence when new opportunities were created for additional online exposure among a new consumer segment: gamers.

One of the earliest marketing relationships that FTC established was with the digital gaming company, EA Games. The EA relationship gave the Falken brand a unique consumer branding opportunity with customers at a very early age. This relationship also helped to solidify the viability of the brand in the minds of B2B retail personnel and customers. Understanding the power of the retailer and crafting programs to best serve this unique market segment continues to be a focus of FTC; extending their success in Drift into other motorsports events such as Super Cross and American Le Mans Racing.

BEST PRACTICES FOR LEVERAGING VIRTUAL COMMUNITIES

This case study has shown how FTC engaged fans online, at motorsports events, and at retail. However, it is the virtual fan communities online that helped steer them to additional online venues, into new relationships, and into new consumer segments. It is this same online community that comprises one of the best and relatively untapped opportunities for many companies today.

It's important to remember that in the deployment of any virtual brand community strategy, a combination of both strategic actions and organizational capabilities must be considered. According to the consulting firm, Aberdeen Group (2008), a virtual brand community strategy requires "not only the need to create new cross-functional, enterprise-wide business processes to collect, manage, and share information with relevant stakeholders, as well as to measure success, but also the need to educate employees about the value …and why it should matter to them in the context of their specific areas of accountability" (p. 9). Accordingly, to aid companies and help them identify their firms' likelihood of success in leveraging virtual communities to enhance brand equity, the following suggestions are offered.

Tip 1: Be a Good Follower

Companies ensconced in traditional marketing mindsets tend to use online social media like advertising; focusing on creating compelling messages that draw interested potential buyers to the brand. In this way, the media is used as a draw to the brand. Interestingly, the results from the case company and academic research suggests that the reverse may be more effective in expanding online brand communities – that is, follow consumers to their choice of media. The tools (e.g. Facebook, Twitter, Snapchat, etc.) are dynamic while the practice recommendation is constant: the decision is not what tool to use, but rather where fans of our brand are having conversations, and what is being said. Secondarily, companies can then look to fans to help them improve the environment so that consumers loyal to the brand can draw others to the online medium of choice. As highlighted in previous research, "Enroll existing, long tenured customers who already have an affirmative relationship with the brand" (Algesheimer et al., 2005, p. 30), and then drive them to the online experience. In the instance of this case study, FTC used the motorsport event to create the desire for customers to use online channels for further interaction. Then FTC followed their customers to where the conversations were taking place online.

Tip 2: Community First, Brand Second

Increased brand exposure is a top benefit of social media (Social Media Examiner, 2013). From the same report, other benefits include increasing traffic, providing marketplace insight, and developing loyal fans - in fact, most marketers now recognize that developing loyal brand fans ranks higher in importance that generating leads. In fact, "when a brand focuses on acquiring and engaging fans, it can benefit from a significant secondary effect – exposure among friends of fans that often surpasses reach among fans" (Lipsman, Mudd, Rich, & Bruich, 2012). Because one of the primary benefits of social media is increasing exposure, virtual communities can have a significant positive effect on driving fan exposure → engagement → loyalty → influence → equity. In the case of FTC, the company found that many of their most avid brand fans were "virtually loyal." Meaning, they had a high degree of engagement on FTC's web assets, explicitly "liked" the brand, but had not yet purchased the product. These fans are the easiest to reach, and may indeed be the most valuable online asset of the company since recent research has shown that "Friends of fans typically represent a much larger set of consumers (34 times larger, on average, for the top 100 brand pages) and can receive social-media brand impressions by way of their friends" (Lipsman et al., 2012, p. 40). So for each "like" on FTC's brand pages, 34 additional potential customers are waiting in the wings to be enticed, motivated, or incentivized to communicate and interact with the company. For FTC, this was a central idea moving forward – driving the friends of fans since it appears that "like" may in fact be as good as buy. To drive "likes" research suggests including vivid and interactive posts such as videos or contests and avoiding the posting of questions or unrelated entertainment content (de Vries, Gensler, & Leeflang, 2012). Additionally, the creation of materials that encourage member embeddedness and engagement are recommended (Porter & Donthu, 2008; Porter, Donthu, MacElroy, & Wydra, 2011).

Tip 3: Get Comfortable With Conflict

The strength of a brand's virtual community is often borne from the ashes of conflict (Fournier & Lee, 2009). Because these groups are formed around their common shared commitment to the brand and what it stands for, strong opinions are often the norm. Combine this strength of conviction with the "keyboard courage" that accompanies online communication and incendiary conditions may prevail. This is good. In order for a group of like-minded folks to coalesce around the brand online, there must be a group who does not share the same view. This creation of an "in-group" versus an "out-group" is vital for the health and sustainability of the community. Think Ford vs. Chevy, i-Phone vs. Samsung, or Coke vs. Pepsi. Without battle-lines being drawn, your virtual community is more likely to be weak and fragmented. But, a virtual community that fans the flames of why their brand is better than the other brand, signals a stronger, more entrenched avid group of followers and shows that the brand's strength and loyalty is building brand equity. The key is not to feel as though conflicts should be regulated, monitored, or smoothed over. In fact, companies should consider reinforcing rivalries head-on and/or encouraging others to fan the flames.

Tip 4: Follow Aspirant Brands

Because of the velocity of trends and proliferation of virtual communities, marketers may be leery of their own ability to interact effectively with virtual communities of brand fans. One way to help companies leverage their presence in virtual brand communities is for companies to identify a group of peer companies outside of their own industry. In this way, marketing managers can identify with peer-companies who are targeting similar customers and positioning their brands in a complementary manner to their own brand. By watching these peer-companies, marketing managers can observe, learn, and expand their own approaches to virtual community interactions that might help further brand-building within their own firms. By selecting and "following/liking" a peer-group of firms and paying attention to their iterative marketing efforts both offline and online, companies can more easily monitor marketplace changes and develop new ideas to improve their own efforts. This strategy can be particularly helpful for companies that have traditionally only followed their own industry closely, but have not looked beyond their core industry. We recommend that marketers expand their view in order to recognize broader marketplace changes, virtual community trends, and audience preferences.

Tip 5: Fund It

As mentioned, virtual community trends, platforms, and audience preferences are changing at an amazing pace. With this rate of change it can be difficult to stay on top of virtual communities. While it was suggested earlier in this chapter to follow aspirant peer companies that you identify with and that are doing a good job targeting the same customer groups as your firm; likewise, you must take action to keep your own firm abreast of new online developments. This can sound daunting and expensive, but remember: online efforts are quickly outstripping that of traditional media. As such, online efforts, data collection and analysis, and strategic initiatives need to be funded with the same commitment of the company's more "mainstream" media. No longer can companies rely on the summer intern or recent grad to simply pump out Google Analytics and make some basic recommendations. Instead, consider the online data as valuable to the firm as any consultant's research report. Therefore, hiring analysts who can connect the dots between the raw consumer data and the behaviors that accompany each data point is vital.

Tip 6: Create a Web Policy

As soon as your company ventures into virtual communities, you will notice a curious thing – you will begin to hear the chatter of your customers more clearly, more loudly, and often more critically. The Internet is the great liaison between companies and the customers they serve, and therefore, virtual communities will activate customer feedback that is typically faster, harsher, and less private. Because it is recommended that you have a team of marketers monitoring all of your web assets as they relate to the brand's virtual presence, it is vital that these individuals know how to handle critical feedback and what actions they should take when they come across an inaccuracy in an online customer review of your product/service (Bastone, 2010, Brogan & Bastone, 2014). When a customer publicly posts a story about a gross-injustice experienced at the hands of your firm or brand, should you react? If misinformation is posted about your firm or brand, should you reply? These questions and dozens more like it must be contemplated in advance and captured via a web policy for your employees so they know how to monitor user-generated content on your site and across related social media sites. Don't assume your employees will know how to handle customer inquiries, complaints, and viral misinformation on the web. Ensure that your employees know what is expected, what they should do, and who they should contact if something pops up that they do not know how to handle.

Tip 7: Understand Your Own Bias for Control

Commonly senior management determines strategic corporate direction. While this is not inherently problematic, consideration must be given to the decision-makers own characteristics and biases. For instance, managers in their 40s or 50s may not appreciate the value of mobile marketing or a virtual brand community strategy which gives full control to the customers online. Therefore, leaders should understand their own biases and invite the views of customers and/or employees into the dialogue so that a wide range of feedback is received regarding how best to interact with customers online. To truly build brand value for the firm and equity from customers, requires a give-and-take that will likely reward balanced approaches to how and where these interactions take place.

Tip 8: Determine If the Organizational Culture Is Open to Honest Feedback

Because virtual brand communities typically involves open dialogue with customers, organizations will quickly begin to harvest both positive and negative input from the marketplace. For some organizations this will be received positively and viewed as a means to develop improvement strategies that focus on the cares and concerns of its current customers. For other firms, negative feedback may be met with a less open culture. Make sure your firm is ready for 'honest' feedback from consumers. Consider the current processes and procedures that are in place to receive, respond, and act on suggestions from customers. Research tells us that the quickest way to shut down customer feedback is to do nothing or worse yet, delete feedback from your own forums or threaded discussion boards that don't meet your own version of the brand's strengths. Firms should be ready for the good, the bad, and the ugly of online communications since for many customers, the Internet provides a large dose of "keyboard courage" which may be a jagged pill for some marketing managers to swallow. If you are not ready for negative feedback, you are not ready for a virtual brand community strategy.

FUTURE RESEARCH DIRECTIONS

The nature of e-Business applications, like virtual brand communities, will continue to hold great promise as well as challenge for practitioners in regard to creating stronger connections with consumers and enhancing brand-building efforts. Understanding the role that people, business processes, and technology play as a conduit between firm and customer, and customer to customer, is key. Therefore, we suggest that future research on virtual brand communities should be viewed from a cross-disciplinary lens that considers research from information systems, marketing, management, and psychology to name but a few. To effectively bridge this research divide requires a holistic look at the combination of people, processes, and technology as key drivers of online innovation and change.

CONCLUSION

Overall, this case has demonstrated that brands can be positively affected through virtual fan communities. From this view, companies may stand to experience positive market share gains by refining their online social media efforts to improve fan engagement online. By doing so, companies may broaden their appeal through the unique strategy of driving "likes" and leveraging 'friends of fans'. In this way, "likes" are indeed as good as "buys." The advent of social media requires practitioners today to shift their thinking; away from a one-way, push model, to a scenario where consumers are actively involved with companies and increasingly connected to other consumers through a variety of channels. The locus of control has now shifted to the consumer, and firms must both actively listen to consumers and agree to engage in open, two-way conversations to succeed (Stone & Woodcock, 2013). In order to utilize the opportunities provided by new media, managers must thoroughly understand the tools available to them.

This chapter has highlighted an approach for enhancing brand equity via virtual brand communities. Virtual communities offer companies the opportunity to become a more active partner "in the conversation" with empowered consumers through social media exposure, the engagement of loyal fan and brand advocate networks, and tapping into valuable market intelligence via social listening and crowdsourcing. With only 20% of U.S. companies focusing marketing efforts on consumer-centric social media strategies (Forrester, 2011), the time is right for insightful practitioners to commit to the deeper interactions with consumers through virtual communities that correlate with increased brand equity and better financial performance.

REFERENCES

Aberdeen Group. (2008). *Social media monitoring and analysis: Generating consumer insights from online conversation.* Retrieved September 1, 2013 from: http://robertoigarza.files.wordpress.com/2008/10/rep-social-media-monitoring-and-analysis-aberdeen-group-2008.pdf

Algesheimer, R., Dholakia, U. M., & Herrmann, A. (2005). The social influence of brand community: Evidence from European car clubs. *Journal of Marketing, 69*(3), 19–34. doi:10.1509/jmkg.69.3.19.66363

Bastone, J. (2010). Evaluate social media by listening, leveraging and engaging. *Direct: Magazine of Direct Marketing.* Retrieved February 12, 2014 from http://www.chiefmarketer.com/web-marketing/evaluate-social-media-by-listening-leveraging-and-engaging-17082010

Booth, N., & Matic, J. A. (2011). Mapping and leveraging influencers in social media to shape corporate brand perceptions. *Corporate Communications, 16*(3), 184–191. doi:10.1108/13563281111156853

Brogan, C., & Bastone, J. (2014). Acting on customer intelligence from social media. *AMA Marketing Effectiveness Online Seminar Series.* Retrieved February 12, 2014 from https://www.sas.com/offices/NA/canada/en/resources/whitepaper/wp_21122.pdf

Brown, S., Kozinets, R. V., & Sherry, J. F. Jr. (2003). Teaching old brands new tricks: Retro branding and the revival of brand meaning. *Journal of Marketing, 67*(3), 19–33. doi:10.1509/jmkg.67.3.19.18657

Chou, C. (2014). Social media characteristics, customer relationship and brand equity. *The Journal of Applied Business and Economics, 16*(1), 128–139.

Christodoulides, G., Jevons, C., & Bonhomme, J. (2012). Memo to marketers: Quantitative evidence for change. How user-generated content really affects brands. *Journal of Advertising Research, 52*(1), 53–64. doi:10.2501/JAR-52-1-053-064

de Vries, L., Gensler, S., & Leeflang, P. S. H. (2012). Popularity of brand posts on brand fan pages: An investigation of the effects of social media. *Journal of Interactive Marketing, 26*(2), 83–91. doi:10.1016/j. intmar.2012.01.003

Forrester Research, Inc. (2011). *Listening and engaging in the digital marketing age*. Retrieved August 31, 2013 from: http://i.dell.com/sites/content/corporate/secure/en/Documents/listening-and-engaging-in-the-digital-marketing-age.pdf

Fournier, S., & Avery, J. (2011). The uninvited brand. *Business Horizons, 54*(3), 193–207. doi:10.1016/j. bushor.2011.01.001

Fournier, S., & Lee, L. (2009, April). Getting brand communities right. Harvard Business Review, 1-10.

Gabrielli, V., & Balboni, B. (2010). SME practice towards integrated marketing communications. *Marketing Intelligence & Planning, 28*(3), 275–290. doi:10.1108/02634501011041426

Habibi, M. R., Laroche, M., & Richard, M. (2014). The roles of brand community and community engagement in building brand trust on social media. *Computers in Human Behavior, 37*, 152–161. doi:10.1016/j.chb.2014.04.016

Hajli, N., Shanmugam, M., Papagiannidis, S., Zahay, D., & Richard, M. (2016). Branding co- creation with members of online communities. *Journal of Business Research, 70*, 136–144. doi:10.1016/j. jbusres.2016.08.026

Hennig-Thurau, T., Malthouse, E., Friege, C., Gensler, S., Lobschat, L., Rangaswamy, A., & Skiera, B. (2010). The impact of new media on customer relationships. *Journal of Service Research, 13*(3), 311–330. doi:10.1177/1094670510375460

Hoffman, D. L., & Fodor, M. (2010). Can you measure the ROI of your social media marketing? *MIT Sloan Management Review, 52*(1), 41–49.

Ito, M., Davidson, C., Jenkins, H., Lee, C., Eisenberg, M., & Weiss, J. (2008). Youth online authorship. In D. Buckingham (Ed.), *Youth, identity, and digital media. The John D. and Catherine T. MacArthur Foundation Series on Digital Media and Learning (pp. vii-ix)*. Cambridge, MA: The MIT Press.

Keller, K. L. (1993). Conceptualizing, measuring, and managing customer-based brand equity. *Journal of Marketing, 57*(1), 1–22. doi:10.2307/1252054

Keller, K. L. (2009). Building strong brands in a modern marketing communications environment. *Journal of Marketing Communications, 15*(2), 139–155. doi:10.1080/13527260902757530

Kim, J., & Yu, E. (2016). The holistic brand experience of branded mobile applications affects brand loyalty. *Social Behavior and Personality, 44*(1), 77–87. doi:10.2224/sbp.2016.44.1.77

Li, C. (2009). *The world's most valuable brands. Who's most engaged? ENGAGEMENTdb: Ranking the top 100 global brands.* Retrieved February 9, 2014 from: http://www.altimetergroup.com/2009/07/engagementdb.html

Lipsman, A., Mudd, G., Rich, M., & Bruich, S. (2012). The power of "like": How brands reach (and influence) fans through social media. *Journal of Advertising Research, 52,* 40–52. doi:10.2501/JAR-52-1-040-052

Menachem, D., Sujata, J., Padman, A., Bishnoi, K., & Upadhye, R. (2016). Online Brand Communities and Their Impact on Brand Equity of Indian Telecommunication Industry. *International Conference on Qualitative and Quantitative Economics Research. Global Science and Technology Forum,* 16–24.

Morning Consult. (n.d.). Frequency of Facebook use in the United States as of October 2017. *Statista - The Statistics Portal.* Retrieved October 22, 2017, from https://www.statista.com/statistics/199266/frequency-of-use-among-facebook-users-in the-united-states/

O'Reilly, K., & Lancendorfer, K. M. (2013). Consumers as "integrators" of marketing communications: When "like" is as good as "buy". *International Journal of E-Business Research, 9*(4), 1–15. doi:10.4018/ijebr.2013100101

Owyang, J. (2009). *The future of the social web: In five eras.* Retrieved April 24, 2012 from: http://www.web-strategist.com/blog/2009/04/27/future-of-the-social-web/

Pew Internet. (2011). Why Americans use social media. *Pew Research Center.* Retrieved October 25, 2017, from http://www.pewinternet.org/2011/11/15/why-americans-use-social-media/

Porter, C. E., & Donthu, N. (2008). Cultivating trust and harvesting value in virtual communities. *Management Science, 54*(1), 113–128. doi:10.1287/mnsc.1070.0765

Porter, C. E., Donthu, N., MacElroy, W. H., & Wydra, D. (2011). How to foster and sustain engagement in virtual communities. *California Management Review, 53*(4), 59–73. doi:10.1525/cmr.2011.53.4.80

Schultz, D. E. (1999). Integrated marketing communications and how it relates to traditional media advertising. In J.P. Jones (Ed.), The Advertising Business: Operations, Creativity, Media Planning, Integrated Communications (pp. 325-338). London, UK: Sage. doi:10.4135/9781452231440.n34

Schultz, D. E., & Peltier, J. (2013). Social media's slippery slope: Challenges, opportunities and future research directions. *Journal of Research in Interactive Marketing, 7*(2), 86–99. doi:10.1108/JRIM-12-2012-0054

Smith, A. N., Fischer, E., & Yongjian, C. (2012). How does brand-related user-generated content differ across YouTube, Facebook, and Twitter? *Journal of Interactive Marketing, 26*(2), 102–113. doi:10.1016/j.intmar.2012.01.002

Social Media Examiner. (2013). Retrieved January 3, 2014 from: http://www.socialmediaexaminer.com/social-media-marketing-industry-report-2013/

Statista. (n.d.). Number of Facebook users in the United States from 2015 to 2022 (in millions). *Statista - The Statistics Portal.* Retrieved October 20, 2017, from https://www.statista.com/statistics/408971/number-of-us-facebook-users/

Stone, M., & Woodcock, N. (2013). Social intelligence in customer engagement. *Journal of Strategic Marketing, 21*(5), 394–401. doi:10.1080/0965254X.2013.801613

Vivek, S. D., Beatty, S. E., & Morgan, R. M. (2012). Customer engagement: Exploring customer relationships beyond purchase. *Journal of Marketing Theory and Practice, 20*(2), 127–145. doi:10.2753/MTP1069-6679200201

Wang, Y., Ma, S., & Li, D. (2015). Customer participation in virtual brand communities: The self-construal perspective. *Information & Management, 52*(5), 577–587. doi:10.1016/j.im.2015.04.003

ADDITIONAL READING

Castronovo, C., & Huang, L. (2012). Social media in an alternative marketing communication model. *Journal of Marketing Development and Competitiveness, 6*(1), 117–134.

Grimes, S. (2013). The rise and stall of social media listening. *Information Week, 1361* (March 25), 5-6.

Hennig-Thurau, T., Malthouse, E., Friege, C., Gensler, S., Lobschat, L., Rangaswamy, A., & Skiera, B. (2010). The impact of new media on customer relationships. *Journal of Service Research, 13*(3), 311–330. doi:10.1177/1094670510375460

Kaplan, A. M., & Haenlein, M. (2010). Users of the world, unite! The challenges and opportunities of social media. *Business Horizons, 53*(1), 59–68. doi:10.1016/j.bushor.2009.09.003

LaPointe, P. (2011). The rock in the pond: How online buzz and offline WOM can make a strong message even more powerful. *Journal of Advertising Research, 51*(3), 456–457. doi:10.2501/JAR-51-3-456-457

LaPointe, P. (2012). Measuring Facebook's impact on marketing: The proverbial hits the fan. *Journal of Advertising Research, 52*(3), 286–287. doi:10.2501/JAR-52-3-286-287

McAlexander, J. H., Schouten, J. W., & Koenig, H. F. (2002). Building brand community. *Journal of Marketing, 66*(January), 38–54. doi:10.1509/jmkg.66.1.38.18451

Morgan, R. M., & Hunt, S. D. (1994). The commitment-trust theory of relationship marketing. *Journal of Marketing, 58*(July), 20–38. doi:10.2307/1252308

Naylor, R. W., Lamberton, C. P., & West, P. M. (2012). Beyond the "like" button: The impact of mere virtual presence on brand evaluations and purchase intentions in social media settings. *Journal of Marketing, 76*(6), 105–120. doi:10.1509/jm.11.0105

Nelson-Field, K., Riebe, E., & Sharp, B. (2012). What's not to "like?" Can a Facebook fan base give a brand the advertising reach it needs? *Journal of Advertising Research, 52*(2), 262–269. doi:10.2501/JAR-52-2-262-269

Pomirleanu, N., Schibrowsky, J. E., Peltier, J. W., & Nill, A. (2013). Internet marketing research: A review of the literature. *Journal of Research in Interactive Marketing, 7*(3), 166–181. doi:10.1108/JRIM-01-2013-0006

Quinton, S., & Harridge-March, S. (2010). Relationships in online communities: The potential for marketers. *Journal of Research in Interactive Marketing, 4*(1), 59–73. doi:10.1108/17505931011033560

Trueman, M., Cornelius, N., & Wallace, J. (2012). Building brand value online: Exploring relationships between company and city brands. *European Journal of Marketing, 46*(7/8), 1013–1031. doi:10.1108/03090561211230179

Weiss, A. M., Lurie, N. H., & MacInnis, D. J. (2008). Listening to strangers: Whose responses are valuable, how valuable are they, and why? *JMR, Journal of Marketing Research, 45*(August), 425–436. doi:10.1509/jmkr.45.4.425

KEY TERMS AND DEFINITIONS

Brand Ambassador: A person recruited by an organization to advocate its products or services.

Brand Equity: Is the idea that having a well-known and well-received brand creates more monetary value for an organization than a lesser known brand.

Social Media Marketing: Refers to the practice of using social media sites to draw attention to a brand. The emphasis in social media marketing is to create interesting content that will attract readers and encourage them to share content on their own social media pages.

Top-Down Marketing: Is a traditional advertising structure where an idea is generated by an organization then broadcasted to the consumer.

User-Generated Content: Any online content such as photos, videos, tweets, pages, and other forms of media that is created by users of online services and generally shared through social media.

Virtual Communities: A group that forms online, typically on social media websites, where community members join on the basis of loyalty to a particular brand.

Word-of-Mouth: Is defined as the oral communication of brand or product information from one consumer to another that is encouraged by the organization selling the product.

ENDNOTE

[1] A fan-filmed video from this first event is available online at: http://www.youtube.com/watch?v=zwQk4YzRH90.

Chapter 8

Service Quality and Knowledge as Determinants of Mobile Health Services:
Empirical Investigation and Further Considerations

Nabila Nisha
North South University, Bangladesh

Mehree Iqbal
North South University, Bangladesh

Afrin Rifat
North South University, Bangladesh

ABSTRACT

Presently, mobile health (m-health) services is a dynamic example of the integration of information technology into healthcare service provisions. However, citizens are often concerned about the use of this medium. Their apprehensions mostly encircle the quality of such services and extent of their own healthcare knowledge. This chapter thus aims to investigate adoption drivers of m-health services in Bangladesh by employing the UTAUT model. Results reveal service qualities like reliability, privacy, responsiveness, empathy, and information quality along with facilitating conditions, effort expectancy, performance expectancy, and social influence as significant drivers in m-health service adoption. In addition, this chapter suggests a new research agenda wherein perceived risks can act as an additional construct. Several factors that are known to exacerbate perceived risk were identified from literature and thereafter shown as part of a proposed framework. Implications for practice and research are also discussed for better planning and implementation of m-health services.

DOI: 10.4018/978-1-5225-5014-3.ch008

INTRODUCTION

Information and communication technology (ICT) offers great potential for improving the quality of services provided along with the efficiency and effectiveness in health care sectors. In recent times, electronic health (e-Health) services truly serves as a tool with a huge potential for health care organizations to deliver quality and cost-effective care to geographically dispersed populations through the Internet (Jung, 2008). However, a branch of e-Health services - mobile health (m-Health) has been constantly expanding over the last decade.

The m-Health services can be broadly defined as the use of mobile computing and communication technologies in health care and public health. This service application generally provides patient monitoring, sends text messages reminding patients to take needed medications and offers suggestions for maintaining health while pregnant, even in war-ravaged places (Idrish et al., 2017). Current evidence suggests that the use of mobile technology can improve diagnosis and compliance with treatment guidelines, as well as patient information and can increase administrative efficiency (Rashidee, 2013). In a broader sense, m-Health is not just improving health status rather it is the use of mobile technology to address health care challenges such as access, quality, affordability, behavioral norms, skill development in communication, supply management, information management and financial transactions through the exchange of information (Sultana, 2014). The m-Health services are a great initiative in health care sectors, since there are a number of patients who possess less knowledge and understanding of personal health problems but cannot afford time or money to visit doctors or medical centres on a regular basis (Nisha et al., 2015). However, the benefits of m-Health services are often outweighed by the fact that many users are still skeptical of the quality of services that can be provided through such mediums. As such, it becomes imperative to examine the role of service quality and knowledge among other factors that can influence the acceptance, use, future prospect and necessity of m-Health services from the perspective of a developing country.

In the context of developing countries, technology may be well-perceived but when the content is sensitive like healthcare provisions, acceptance of the technology often depends upon the quality of the services and individual knowledge related to the service, among other factors. Therefore, the unified theory of acceptance and use of technology (UTAUT) model has been used for this chapter. This study employed proposed constructs of system quality (system reliability, system efficiency, system privacy), information quality, interaction quality (responsiveness, assurance, empathy) and healthcare knowledge, to examine the factors that can influence users' intention to use m-Health services in Bangladesh. Moreover, this study has both theoretical and managerial implications. Theoretically, drawing upon relevant literature, this study aims to provide a model that is capable of understanding the determinants behind the future adoption of m-Health services among the people of Bangladesh. From a managerial perspective, the findings of this research should provide further insights into understanding and managing potential m-Health users, particularly hailing from the developing countries. This study can also assist various public and private hospitals and various telecommunication networks to consider the idea of providing m-Health services to the people of Bangladesh.

BACKGROUND

Bangladesh is experiencing significant advances and development in health care sectors in recent years, since the government has started a new era in the health sector by introducing ICT for health service delivery. The government has developed a Health Management Information System (MIS) department under the Directorate General of Health Services (DGHS). The purpose of this department is to ensure the best use of ICT to build and maintain nationwide health information system of Bangladesh (DGHS, 2014). This works as the backbone of the e-Health service network of Bangladesh and m-Health service is rendered using the national wide mobile phone network. The health professionals provide basic health advices and initial diagnosis when the service recipients' contacts through specialized 24/7 call centers. It has established free tele-consultation with government doctors, free SMS services for patient management and communication with staff, particularly for the needy people of the country. These cell phone numbers are circulated among the surrounding community. As such, people residing in the rural areas can contact with the health professionals through this network.

Additionally, web-camera has been installed in each sub-district, district, medical college and post-graduate institute hospitals in Bangladesh for providing telemedicine services using video conferencing platform. In recent times, there are few m-Health programmes that are operational in Bangladesh like m-Care, Aponjon and such others. These provide information and advice to pregnant mothers regarding health and nutrition related matters (Sultana, 2014). In addition, the Mobile Alliance for Maternal Action (MAMA) Bangladesh program from D.Net with assistance from USAID and Johnson & Johnson provides voice messages to pregnant women to support the antennal, natal and post-natal information in Bengali (the native language of Bangladesh) (Reza, 2012). Many mobile phone companies are also providing medical advice and prescriptions to millions of callers in their networks at nominal fees, alleviating some of the access and timeliness related challenges in the provision of healthcare services in Bangladesh (Rashidee, 2013).

However, m-health service does not yet have a wide usage rate in Bangladesh. Across the entire country, m-Health services are being extensively adopted in the rural side of the country, which shows that the capital city of Dhaka is yet to adopt the use of such services. This chapter, therefore, argues that factors like the service quality and necessary health care knowledge may influence the adoption and use of m-Health services among the dwellers of Dhaka city in Bangladesh.

ISSUES, PROBLEMS AND CONTROVERSIES

Previous studies on adoption behaviors of technologies have seen the inclusion of the most influential variables like information technology factors, psychological factors, and sociological factors relating to consumer behavior and consumer perceptions. In particular, a large number of researchers have empirically studied user adoption in the context of health information systems. Recent researches by Putzer and Park (2012) and Jackson et al. (2013) revealed that consumers with more positive beliefs about the relative advantage of m-Health services form a favorable attitude, while those who find m-Health easy to use are more willing to use them for their healthcare needs. Evans et al. (2012), Burner et al. (2013) and Maddison et al. (2014) provided empirical evidence that perceived self-efficacy is a determinant in influencing consumer intention towards m-Health adoption. However, some studies like Holtz and Lauckner (2012) and Free et al. (2013) argued that self-efficacy is not a direct determinant that can affect individual intention to adopt m-Health initiatives. On the other hand, empirical evidence by Sieverdes et al. (2013) supported the existence of a causal relationship between perceived self-efficacy and behavioral intention of consumers towards m-Health services.

Some more important driving factors towards the adoption of m-Health services have been identified in literature related to the use of such services and its providers. Huili and Zhong (2011) provided empirical evidence that economic factors like service fees play an essential role in the adoption of any technology-based services, particularly those related to the mobile platform. Even researchers like Deglise et al. (2012), Tamrat and Kachnowski (2012) and Kumar et al. (2013) argued that the construct of perceived financial cost has a negative impact upon the behavioral intention of consumers to use m-Health services. A recent study by de la Torre-Diez et al. (2015) also claimed that if consumers need to spend considerable money to pay for the m-Health services, they may be unlikely to use the technology, indicating a negative relationship between its cost effectiveness and adoption intention. Trust has also been found to have a direct, positive effect on usage intentions in various technology-based studies. Researchers like Akter et al. (2013) and Vedder et al. (2014) investigated trust and revealed a positive relationship between the level of trust in systems of care and their care provider and consumers' use of healthcare services. Along the same line, findings of Boudreaux et al. (2014), Agarwal et al. (2015) and Nisha et al. (2015) relates credibility to the process of generating trust in mobile based technological services like m-Health – thereby, stating that the credibility of the healthcare service provider can create trust among consumers and have an indirect influence upon consumers' use of technology-based health services.

Personal consumer factors like innovativeness and anxiety have been part of m-Health past studies too. In particular, West (2012) claimed that consumers with innovativeness in their nature generally showcase a positive behavior towards the adoption of new technology-based services. While, findings of Brian and Ben-Zeev (2014), Cairney et al. (2014) and Deng et al. (2014) claimed that a certain level of technology anxiety among users can act as a resistance towards m-Health services, forming an unfavorable attitude and less willingness to use such a technology for their healthcare needs. Even moderators like demographical characteristics or other situational variables have a profound impact on user adoption of m-Health services (Jung, 2008). Along this line, Xue et al. (2012) adopted aging-specific constructs, including perceived user resource, technology anxiety, and perceived physical condition, and revealed that perceived user resource and technology anxiety were the antecedents for perceived usefulness, whereas perceived physical condition significantly affected perceived ease of use. Guo et al. (2013) studied the negative aspect of elderly acceptance of mobile health services in China, highlighting that resistance to change and technology anxiety influenced the perception of users regarding enablers and inhibitors, which in turn, affected the intention of users to adopt m-Health services. Lee and Rho (2013) also argued that middle-aged people display more enthusiasm towards adopting m-Health technology than the younger people.

An impressive body of academic research further adapted various forms of quality dimensions in order to investigate users' quality perceptions regarding a technology-based product/service. Some recent studies like Sunyaev et al. (2014) and Hoque et al. (2015) argued that reliability, efficiency and privacy are the major dimensions of system quality that should be inspected in the context of sensitive mobile-based technologies like healthcare services. According to Hoque and Sorwar (2015), users' perception of system reliability can be a major factor in capturing users' perceptions towards m-Health services in countries like Bangladesh, where mobile-based services are relatively new today. System efficiency, on the other hand, is the technical availability of the system, wherein accessibility, flexibility and response time are three major attributes. James et al. (2015) claimed that users with more positive impressions about accessibility, flexibility and response time are more willing to use m-Health services. The third dimension of system quality that has been explored in many studies is privacy. In the context of the adoption of technology-based services, privacy has always been considered as an important factor to gain reliance on the service platform as it protects personal information of the user (Guo et al., 2016). Particularly, if it is customized mobile health services, these three factors of reliability, efficiency and privacy play a more significant role since health information requires confidentiality and maintenance of anonymity (Ren et al., 2010). Hence, it has been considered as a construct of the current study.

Information quality is another additional construct that has been included in the proposed model of this study. This variable generally plays a critical role in building user satisfaction and customer loyalty for mobile healthcare services (Kumar et al., 2013). According to Kahn et al. (2010), information that is provided to the patients over the mobile platform is mostly considered to be significant in such contexts. Therefore, it is very important that whatever information about healthcare services is provided should be complete, accurate and up-to-date (Fox, 2011). Free et al. (2013) stated that more complete, accurate and up-to-date healthcare information will ultimately result into the enhancement of information quality. As such, this construct is deemed to be a crucial service quality that can influence the consumers to adapt the facilities of m-Health services and taken as part of the current study.

Responsiveness, assurance and empathy are three other elements considered in this study and perceived under interaction quality of m-Health services. According to Yin et al. (2015), interaction quality in the form of responsiveness, assurance and empathy affects user's loyalty indirectly and directly towards the use of mobile technology. Interaction quality is often vital in m-Health services, as people seek for customized attention with prompt consultancy in such matters (Nambisan, 2011). Usually, the consumers seeking such services lack contextual emotional stability and hence timely responsiveness, accurate consultancy with emotional support and care tend to ease the conditional mind set at that context. Washington et al. (2015) claimed that relationship marketing has always played an important role in any service sector and so, empathy can lead to a strong relationship developed with the consumer base for such providers. Moreover, Xue et al. (2012) argued that by mentioning the name of the consultant providing the service in the delivered information and taking the accountability of credible consultancy, assurance can also be provided to the consumers. Even while delivering the service promptly over mobile devices, Huang et al. (2015) stated having the providers address the consumer with name and showing care with follow-up interactions, along with assurance and empathy the variable of responsiveness can be ensured as well.

Healthcare knowledge has been considered as an important factor in this study since healthcare is an area of which people are mostly sensitive. The probability of consumers seeking m-Health services is dependent on their prior knowledge on such. Gagnon et al. (2015) claimed that users lacking confidence about their relative knowledge related to healthcare are more likely to adopt this service. Townsend et al. (2015) further stated when knowledge is handy by other means, instead of seeking the service elsewhere consumers prefer using healthcare services over the mobile platform. On the other hand, Domínguez-Mayo et al. (2015) claimed that ensuring a basic healthcare knowledge among the citizen should be one of the major priorities of government for any developing economy. This is because such knowledge can facilitate the execution of m-Health services provided and ensures relatively quick relief, since consumers can relate their healthcare problems in a more proper way (Hasanain et al., 2015).

Overall, the existing literature states that among other factors, service quality and knowledge play significant roles in influencing future usage intentions for m-Health services. Moreover, very few studies have focused on these two dimensions in particular from the perspective of a developing economy. This chapter thus taps into this opportunity and attempts to significantly contribute to the literature by conceptualizing a proposed research model to investigate the influencing factors for m-Health services in the context of Bangladesh.

RESEARCH MODEL AND HYPOTHESES

The purpose of this chapter is to examine the role of service quality and knowledge in order to determine the factors that can explain and predict users' intention to use m-Health services significantly in the context of Bangladesh. Here, both the original UTAUT and UTAUT2 model has been used as a theoretical foundation to develop a proposed research model for the domain of healthcare from the consumers' perspective. Venkatesh et al. (2003) developed the unified theory of acceptance and use of technology (UTAUT) model and the factors (performance expectancy, effort expectancy, social influence and facilitating conditions) has been primarily used to predict the behavioral intention to use a technology in organizational contexts, moderated by individual difference variables like age, gender, experience and voluntariness. However, given the number of technology devices, applications, and services that are targeted at consumers in recent times, Venkatesh et al. (2012) introduced a revised UTAUT2 model to identify factors that can influence consumer adoption of technologies (Stofega and Llamas, 2009). Venkatesh et al. (2012) claimed that the addition of new constructs in a consumer context can contribute to the expansion of the theoretical horizons of the UTAUT model. Following the suit, four additional constructs, drawn from previous literature of m-Health services, has been incorporated to make a significant theoretical contribution to the user context of the UTAUT model. The proposed research model used to address the influencing factors for healthcare technologies has been presented in Figure 1. In addition, all the variables hypothesized in this study and their likely relationships towards consumer acceptance and use of m-Health services in Bangladesh has been discussed next.

Figure 1. The Proposed Research Structure

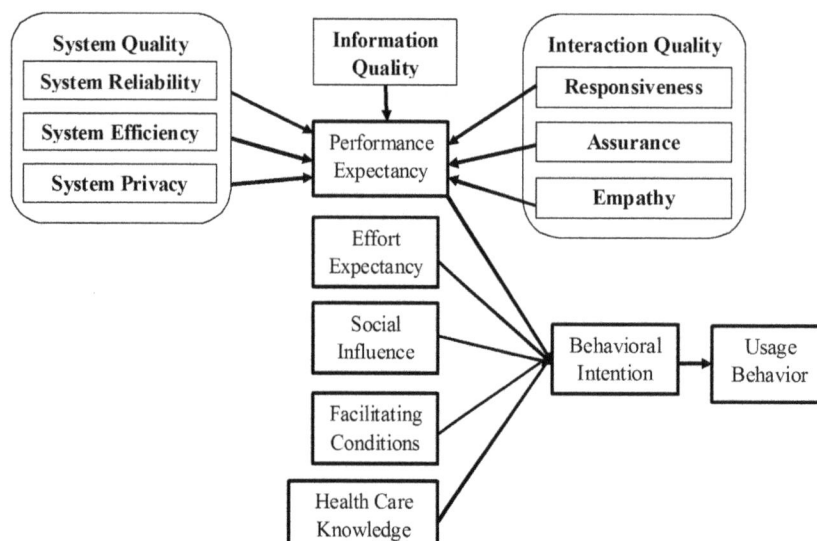

System Quality

System quality is an overall measure of the information processing system itself. Even though system quality is sometimes perceived to be overlapped with factors that are closely related to service quality and ease of use, it has its own unique dimensions (Nelson et al., 2005). The three most significant dimension of system quality are discussed below.

System Reliability

System reliability explains the accuracy of the technical functioning of the system and the truthfulness of service promises (Parasuraman et al., 2005). According to Nelson et al. (2005), it can be defined objectively as the technical availability of the system or the ability of the system to provide error free services. Thus, often consumers' perception of system reliability plays a vital role in defining consumers' adoption of m-Health services (Akter et al., 2010). Particularly, for countries like Bangladesh where the concept of m-Health is relatively new, consumers' perception of reliability regarding m-Health is really questionable.

System Efficiency

From a consumer perspective, an efficient system is the one that is simple to use, structured properly, and requires minimum information to be input by individual (Parasuraman et al., 2005). Therefore, how quickly consumers can reach the system when needed, how fast the system can be acclimatized to a variety of user needs and changing conditions and how quickly or timely the system responds to requests for information or action – all define system efficiency (Nelson et al., 2005). This attribute usually has a strong influence on performance expectancy of m-Health services as they guide the perceptions of system quality and ultimately affect the usage intention of people.

System Privacy

Perceived privacy of consumer can be defined as the users' perception of protection against security threats and control of their personal health care information in an online environment (Lallmahmood, 2007). It measures the degree to which the user believes the system is safe from intrusion and personal information is protected (Akter et al., 2010). According to Angst and Agarwal (2009), concern over privacy and security of personal health information is one of the reasons that held consumers from using m-Health services in developing countries like Bangladesh.

Hence, this study proposes the following hypotheses from the three characteristics of system quality:

- **H1A:** System reliability positively influences performance expectancy of m-Health services.
- **H1B:** System efficiency positively influences performance expectancy of m-Health services.
- **H1C:** System privacy positively influences performance expectancy of m-Health services.

Information Quality

Lee and Chung (2009) suggest that information quality can significantly predict users' perception regarding the use of mobile based technology in sensitive areas like m-Health. Generally, the three most important indicators of information quality are completeness, accuracy and currency (Masrek et al., 2012). Accuracy has been defined as the extent to which the information is correct, unambiguous, objective and meaningful or believable (Wand and Wang, 1996). On the other hand, completeness refers to the extent to which all possible states relevant to the user population are available in the stored information, while currency can be defined as the degree to which the available information is up-to-date (Nelson et al., 2005). As such, information quality can have a significantly positive effect on performance expectancy, which in turn can impact the behavioral intention of consumers towards m-Health. Thus, the study hypothesizes that:

- **H2:** Information quality positively influences performance expectancy of m-Health services.

Interaction Quality

In this study, interaction quality has been perceived as a combination of three elements - responsiveness, assurance and empathy. Lin (2011b) claims that interaction quality in the form of responsiveness, assurance and empathy affects users' loyalty indirectly and directly toward mobile internet technology. All these three factors are therefore discussed below.

Responsiveness

Responsiveness is the most important indicator of interaction quality (Lau et al., 2013). It can be defined as the willingness to help users and to provide prompt services (Akter et al., 2010). It can further be explained by the providers' ability to understand the users' problems and to provide precise services. Lau et al. (2013) found positive relationship between responsiveness and consumer loyalty. Based on this evidence, this study used responsiveness as a factor that will guide consumers regarding m-Health service adoption.

Assurance

Assurance measures knowledge, competency and courtesy of the provider that generate users' trust and confidence in the system (Akter et al., 2010). It is the second most important factor of interaction quality that inspires consumer loyalty (Lau et al., 2013). The service provider's ability to provide their promised and accurate healthcare services and their tendency of keeping commitments can only assure users regarding the adoption of mobile based technology. As past evidences from Lin (2011a) and Lau et al. (2013) found positive relationship between assurance and consumers' acceptance of mobile technology, it has been perceived as an influencing factor for m-Health in this study.

Empathy

The final dimension of interaction quality is empathy that refers to the understanding ability of the users' needs and ability to provide personalized attention (Akter et al., 2010). Consumers always appreciate a friendly and considerate environment. Hence, if the service provider shows genuine interest, enthusiasm and seriousness toward the users' healthcare needs, it will automatically lead consumers towards usage of m-Health services. In fact, Lau et al. (2013) found the highest correlation between empathy and customer satisfaction. This study thus proposes that empathy can positively influence performance expectancy, which can lead to the behavioral intention of consumers towards m-Health.

This study hypothesizes the following from the three characteristics of interaction quality:

- **H3A:** Responsiveness positively influences performance expectancy of m-Health services.
- **H3B:** Assurance positively influences performance expectancy of m-Health services.
- **H3C:** Empathy positively influences performance expectancy of m-Health services.

Performance Expectancy

Burgess and Sargent (2007), Wu et al. (2007) and Nisha (2016) argue that the effect of performance expectancy is the most relevant factor for the adoption of internet-based technology. Performance expectancy generally depicts a users' view of the usefulness of adopting a technology (Venkatesh et al., 2003). Sun et al. (2013) claim that in the context of m-Health services, the usefulness can only be captured by the extent to which it can help users to solve their health-related issues. If users believe that using m-Health services can help them to solve their problems, they are more likely to adopt this technology. Hence, the hypothesis is:

- **H4:** Performance expectancy significantly affects individual intention to use m-Health services.

Effort Expectancy

Effort expectancy is considered to be directly related with the ease of using a particular technology (Phichitchaisopa and Naenna, 2013). According to Venkatesh (1999), all of these effort-oriented constructs act as more significant factors during the early stages of adopting a new technology. Several studies like Park et al. (2007), Moores (2012) and Sun et al. (2013) claims that perceived ease of use or effort expectancy has considerable impacts on attitude towards the adoption of m-Health or any other healthcare related technology. As a result, the following hypothesis has been proposed:

- **H5:** Effort expectancy significantly affects individual intention to use m-Health services.

Social Influence

Social influence refers to the degree to which an individual perceives that important others believe he or she should use the new system or technology (Venkatesh et al., 2003). The idea behind social influence is that even though an individual may not be in favour of adopting a new technology, they intend to use it as he/she believes it will enhance his/her image among his/her family and peers (Venkatesh and Davis, 2000). Researchers like Jung (2008) and Sun et al. (2013) empirically showed that there is a significant positive relationship between social influence and adoption of m-Health technology. Thus, the proposed hypothesis is:

- **H6:** Social influence significantly affects individual intention to use m-Health services.

Facilitating Conditions

According to Venkatesh et al. (2003), facilitating conditions refer to the resources and technical infrastructure that a user believes exists to support the adoption of a particular technology. In other words, facilitating conditions indicates the prospective conditions that may restrain or facilitate adopting a technology (Nisha et al., 2016b). Venkatesh et al. (2012) claims that a consumer with a lower level of facilitating conditions can have a lower intention to use a particular technology. Moreover, Boontarig et al. (2012), Phichitchaisopa and Naenna (2013) and Sun et al. (2013) showed that there is a positive significant relationship between facilitating conditions and healthcare technologies. Based on these findings, this study hypothesizes that:

- **H7:** Facilitating conditions significantly affects individual intention to use m-Health services.

HealthCare Knowledge

Users' knowledge regarding healthcare can act as an important predictor of m-Health adoption. This is relatively a less investigated construct and was developed to measure the users' extent of knowledge and understanding of personal health problems (Wilson and Lankton, 2004). Given all the resources and necessary infrastructure, people may tend to use internet-based health technologies to gain information regarding a health issue and increase their knowledge. This indicates that users who feel that they have relatively little knowledge about healthcare are more likely to adopt healthcare technologies. However, when Wilson and Lankton (2004) investigated this construct against the backdrop of e-Health technology they found it insignificant as a predictor of behavioral intention. To focus on this relationship further, this study hypothesizes that:

- **H8:** Health care knowledge significantly affects individual intention to use m-Health services.

Behavioral Intention

Behavioural intention, which refers to the intention to use a system, is the major determinant of the actual behaviour. Researchers like Venkatesh and Zhang (2010), Yu (2012) and Nisha et al. (2016a) have repeatedly emphasized the strength of the construct of behavioural intention on usage behaviour. These past studies claim that individual behavior is predictable and can be influenced by individual intention that, in turn, can have a significant influence on technology usage. In the context of m-Health services, Jung (2008) and Sun et al. (2013) investigated and empirically proved that behavioural or adoption intention of the technology positively affects its usage. Following the lead, this study next hypothesizes that:

- **H9:** Behavioral intention significantly affects individual behavior of using m-Health services.

DATA ANALYSIS AND DISCUSSION

The predominant existence of mobile health services in the rural areas has inadvertently raised the question as to why urban people still avoid the use of such services. In addition, the absence of city hospitals as the provider of m-Health services has made it imperative to examine the acceptance and use of m-Health services among the city dwellers of Bangladesh. As such, the population selected for this study only represented urban people who are currently exposed to the use of mobile phones and can thereby avail mobile health services in the future. Data for this study was thus collected by conducting a survey through paper-based questionnaires on a sample of 1000 respondents in the capital city of Bangladesh – Dhaka. By using probability sampling and a stratified random sampling method, respondents were then selected for the sample. The use of this particular sampling method allowed us to avoid biasness in data and provided equal opportunity for all city dwellers who can be the potential users of mobile health services in Bangladesh. Respondents were mostly educated and had English proficiency and so they were asked to self-administer the English version of the questionnaire. In other cases, the participants self-administered the Bengali version of the questionnaire or the research assistants themselves filled in the questionnaire based on the respondents' verbal responses. After a four-week survey, 927 completed and usable responses were obtained from the structured questionnaires. Table 1 represents the demographic information of respondents in terms of gender and age.

All the items used to measure the research variables of the survey were adapted from previous studies on information and technological advancements, e-Health services and m-Health services - with minor changes in wording to tailor them to the context of Bangladesh. This ensured the content validity of the questionnaire used to assess each constructs depicted in Figure 1. The quantitative survey contained 42 statements in order to evaluate the original constructs of the UTAUT model and the eight new constructs proposed for the model, as listed in Table 2. The scales for the UTAUT constructs (performance expectancy, effort expectancy, social influence, facilitating conditions and behavioral intention) were adapted from Jung (2008), Venkatesh and Zhang (2010) and Sun et al. (2013). The scales for system quality (reliability, efficiency and privacy), information quality and interaction quality (responsiveness, assurance and empathy) were drawn from Nelson et al. (2005), Lallmahamood (2007), Jung (2008) and Lau et al. (2013). On the other hand, the items used to assess health care knowledge were solely based

Table 1. Demographic Profile of Respondents

Demographics	Frequency	Percentage (%)
Gender		
Male	546	58.9
Female	381	41.1
Age		
20 or below	158	17.0
21 – 30	476	51.3
31 – 40	145	15.6
41 – 50	94	10.1
Above 50	54	5.8

Table 2. Constructs and Corresponding Items

Constructs	Corresponding Items	Items Sources
System Reliability	(SR1) I believe m-Health services operate reliably (SR2) I believe m-Health services perform reliably (SR3) I believe the operation of m-Health services is dependable	Nelson et al. (2005)
System Efficiency	(SE1) I feel m-Health services make health information easy to access (SE2) I feel m-Health services provide health information in a timely fashion (SE3) I feel m-Health takes too long to respond to my healthcare problems	Nelson et al. (2005)
System Privacy	(SP1) I trust the ability of m-Health services to protect my privacy (SP2) I feel safe when I release health information to m-Health services (SP3) I feel matters on security has no influence in using m-Health services	Lallmahamood (2007)
Information Quality	(IQ1) I believe m-Health services provide complete information (IQ2) I believe m-Health services provide up-to-date information (IQ3) I believe m-Health services provide relevant information	Jung (2008)
Responsiveness	(R1) I think m-Health provides precise healthcare services (R2) I think m-Health has the ability to understand my healthcare needs (R3) I think m-Health services are helpful	Lau et al. (2013)
Assurance	(As1) I think m-Health provides healthcare services as promised (As2) I think m-Health provides accurate healthcare services (As3) I think m-Health services will keep their commitments	Lau et al. (2013)
Empathy	(E1) I think m-Health has the knowledge to solve my healthcare problems (E2) I think m-Health has the enthusiasm to understand my healthcare needs (E3) I think m-Health services will put my healthcare needs in the first place	Lau et al. (2013)
Performance Expectancy	(PE1) Using m-Health services will improve my life quality (PE2) Using m-Health services will make my life more convenient (PE3) Using m-Health services will make me more effective in my life (PE4) Overall, I find m-Health services to be useful in my life	Sun et al. (2013)
Effort Expectancy	(EE1) Learning to use m-Health services is easy for me (EE2) Becoming skillful at using m-Health services is easy for me (EE3) Interaction with m-Health services is easy for me (EE4) Overall, I think m-Health services are easy to use	Sun et al. (2013)
Social Influence	(SI1) People who are important to me think that I should use m-Health services (SI2) People who are familiar with me think that I should use m-Health services (SI3) People who influence me think that I should use m-Health services (SI4) Most people surrounding me use m-Health services	Jung (2008), Sun et al. (2013),
Facilitating Conditions	(FC1) Using m-Health services suits my living environment (FC2) Using m-Health services fits into my working style (FC3) Using m-Health services is compatible with my life (FC4) Help is available if I have problems in using m-Health services	Venkatesh & Zhang (2010)
Health Care Knowledge	(HCK1) I am very knowledgeable regarding care for my health problems (HCK2) I understand my health problems and how to care for them	Wilson & Lankton (2004)
Behavioral Intention	(BI1) I prefer to use m-Health services (BI2) I intend to use m-Health services (BI3) I plan to use m-Health services	Sun et al. (2013)

on Wilson and Lankton (2004). All these items were measured using a five-point Likert scale, ranging from "strongly disagree" to "strongly agree".

The conceptual research model was then tested using the structural equation modeling (SEM) facilitates of SmartPLS (version 2.0). The method of partial least squares (PLS) was mainly chosen to conduct this analysis since a number of interaction terms have been included in the research model and PLS is capable of testing these effects (Chin et al., 2003). As such, the measurement model was examined first to assess the reliability and validity of the variables and then, the structural model was analyzed to examine the relationships hypothesized in the research model.

MEASUREMENT MODEL ANALYSIS

Table 3 and Table 4 present the measurement results regarding the reliability, validity, correlations and factor loadings. The composite reliabilities of the constructs ranged between 0.731 and 1.000, which exceeds the 0.7 cut-off value as recommended by Nunnally and Bernstein (1994). The average variance extracted (AVE) was greater than 0.5 in all cases and greater than each square correlation, which indicates that the model has both convergent validity and discriminant validity (Fornell and Larcker, 1981). Moreover, the internal consistency reliabilities (ICRs) of multi-item scales modeled with reflective indicators was 0.75 or greater, suggesting adequate reliability. The pattern of loadings and cross-loadings also supported internal consistency and discriminant validity, with some exceptions: one item from each construct of information quality, empathy (interaction quality), social influence, facilitating conditions, healthcare knowledge, and two items from system reliability (system quality) and system efficiency (system quality) were deleted due to their low loadings and high cross-loadings.

STRUCTURAL MODEL ANALYSIS

Figure 2 presents the path coefficients and significance levels in the structural model of the present study. Among the three constructs of system quality, system reliability (0.240, p<0.05) and system privacy (0.120, p<0.05) showed significant and positive path towards performance expectancy, while system efficiency (0.084, p>0.05) reported an insignificant path. The factor of information quality (0.100, p<0.05) also displayed a significant and positive path towards performance expectancy. On the other hand, responsiveness (0.135, p<0.05) and empathy (0.072, p<0.05) under interaction quality had a significant and positive path towards performance expectancy, but assurance (0.070, p>0.05) showed an insignificant path.

Among other factors, facilitating conditions (0.235, p<0.05), effort expectancy (0.169, p<0.05), performance expectancy (0.155, p<0.05) and social influence (0.134, p<0.05) showed significant and positive paths to the behavioral intention of using mobile health services, in their order of influencing strength. However, the construct of healthcare knowledge (-0.024, p>0.05) reported an insignificant path towards the individual behavior of using mobile health services. Therefore, all hypotheses (except H1B, H3B and H8) dealing with behavioral intention to use mobile health services are supported. Subsequently, the hypothesized relationship between behavioral intention and usage (0.251, p<0.05) is found to be statistically significant, thereby supporting hypothesis H9.

FINDINGS AND IMPLICATIONS

This study has revealed quite a few understandings on the back stage possibilities of the potential usage of mobile health services among the urban population of Bangladesh. Facilitating conditions is found

Table 3. Factor Loadings, Composite Reliability and AVEs

Constructs	Items	Factor Loadings	Composite Reliability	AVE
System Reliability	SR1	1.000	1.000	1.000
System Efficiency	SE1	1.000	1.000	1.000
System Privacy	SP1	0.755	0.789	0.555
	SP2	0.731		
	SP3	0.749		
Information Quality	IQ1	0.908	0.887	0.797
	IQ2	0.876		
Responsiveness	R1	0.801	0.844	0.643
	R2	0.858		
	R3	0.743		
Assurance	As1	0.825	0.881	0.711
	As2	0.849		
	As3	0.855		
Empathy	E2	0.833	0.875	0.778
	E3	0.928		
Performance Expectancy	PE1	0.807	0.889	0.668
	PE2	0.847		
	PE3	0.850		
	PE4	0.761		
Effort Expectancy	EE1	0.822	0.895	0.680
	EE2	0.834		
	EE3	0.840		
	EE4	0.802		
Social Influence	SI1	0.867	0.891	0.732
	SI2	0.876		
	SI3	0.823		
Facilitating Conditions	FC1	0.776	0.864	0.680
	FC2	0.877		
	FC3	0.818		
Health Care Knowledge	HCK2	1.000	1.000	1.000
Behavioral Intention	BI1	0.868	0.891	0.731
	BI2	0.873		
	BI3	0.823		

as the strongest direct determinant in influencing respondents' behavioral intention of m-Health services. This finding is consistent to Boontarig et al. (2012), Phichitchaisopa and Naenna (2013), Sun et al. (2013) and Nisha et al. (2015). The penetration of mobile phones is a comparatively new concept in Bangladesh and particularly, when such devices are being used as a platform of commuting other errands

Table 4. Measurement Model Estimations

	ICRs	As	BI	E	EE	FC	HCK	IQ	PE	R	SE	SI	SP	SR
As	0.8	**0.8**												
BI	0.8	0.3	**0.9**											
E	0.8	0.1	0.0	**0.9**										
EE	0.8	0.3	0.5	0.0	**0.8**									
FC	0.8	0.3	0.5	0.0	0.4	**0.8**								
HCK	1.0	0.0	0.1	0.0	0.1	0.1	**Single-Item Construct**							
IQ	0.8	0.3	0.5	0.0	0.4	0.8	0.1	**0.9**						
PE	0.8	0.3	0.4	0.0	0.6	0.4	0.1	0.4	**0.8**					
R	0.8	0.2	0.4	0.1	0.3	0.3	0.1	0.3	0.3	**0.8**				
SE	1.0	0.8	0.2	0.1	0.3	0.3	0.1	0.3	0.3	0.2	**Single-Item Construct**			
SI	0.8	0.3	0.4	0.1	0.4	0.3	0.2	0.3	0.3	0.2	0.2	**0.9**		
SP	0.8	0.3	0.5	0.1	0.4	0.7	0.2	0.7	0.4	0.3	0.3	0.7	**0.7**	
SR	1.0	0.2	0.4	0.0	0.4	0.3	0.1	0.3	0.4	0.3	0.2	0.2	0.3	**Single-Item Construct**

Notes:

1. As (Assurance); BI (Behavioral Intention); E (Empathy); EE (Effort Expectancy); FC (Facilitating Conditions); HCK (Health Care Knowledge); IQ (Information Quality); PE (Performance Expectancy); R (Responsiveness); SE (System Efficiency); SI (Social Influence); SP (System Privacy); SR (System Reliability).

2. Diagonal elements represent the AVEs, while off-diagonal elements represent the square correlations.

Figure 2. Results of Structural Equation Modeling

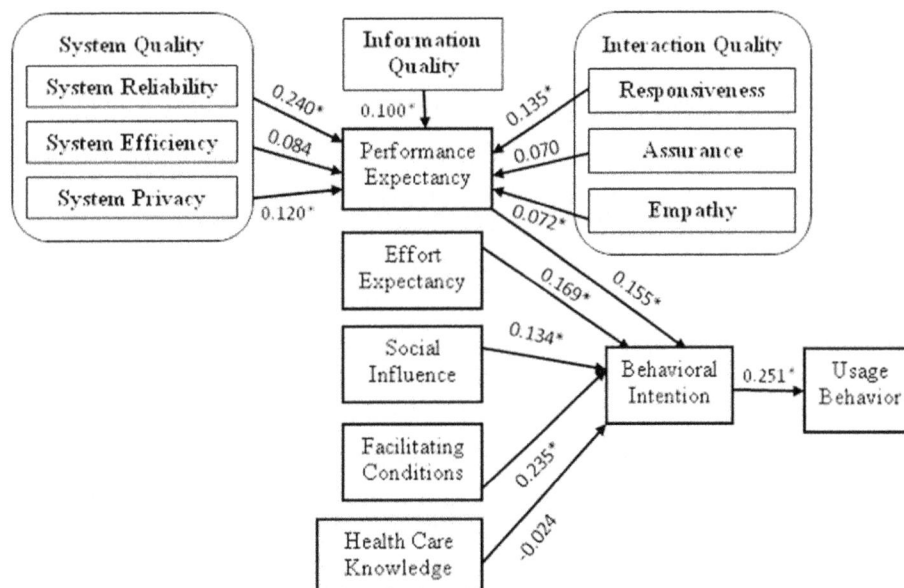

such as receiving instant health care advices, ensuring facilitating conditions has a strong role to play. In perspective of Bangladesh, facilitating conditions generally tend to be wide availability of computers, strong mobile networks and fast internet services. Therefore, the first business implication is that, beyond offering ease-of-use and useful m-Health services, providers might emphasize on the compatibility between the offered services and the working/living styles of their target customers. That is, putting efforts in designing suitable services and infrastructures to meet specific needs of different customer segments. Both government and private sector hospitals and clinics have already started showing a lot of interests and concerns in this regard. As a matter of fact, entities like Medinova Telemedicine, eClinic24 (Chakaria Project), AMCARE and health services for expatriates in Singapore by TRCL, Breast Cancer Finding via mobile by Amader Gram, JBFH Telemedicine, all leading telecom companies of Bangladesh and many others have already set their foot targeting the rural segments and working on developing the infrastructure challenges. However, city hospitals need to work more towards the development of such conditions for the city dwellers. Strong and correct comprehension on available facilitating conditions is important to ensure to build the right perception in the mind of the target market by showing repeatedly that all they need is a mobile phone of any type and a mobile connection mainly to take the benefits of mobile health care services.

The study drills that most of the current and potential users of m-Health services tend to judge the importance of the service based on the required effort expectancy for it. Respondents who expect less effort input in the service consuming process, especially at the adoption stage like that of m-Health services in Bangladesh, are more likely to show positive attitude in embracing the service. This finding is consistent with the evidence provided by Moores (2012), Sun et al. (2013) and Nisha et al. (2015). By making sure that the target market perceives the efforts needed to avail these services as an ease, companies can net a positive attitude towards these services. Communications of the providers, particularly of the city hospitals, should focus more on the actual handiness of such services. To do this, the software platform of the m-Health service applications should be made more compatible and user-friendly for the ease of use of the urban population of Bangladesh.

Performance expectancy is the next most important construct according to the research findings of this study. Sustainable qualities of m-Health service such as saving time, receiving immediate and accurate healthcare advices, etc. play an important role in shaping behavior in terms of adopting such new technologies. Jimison and Sher (2008), Holden and Karsh (2010) and Sun et al. (2013) have also found such similar results in their studies. The underlying cause behind such result is the novelty of such technology in the culture of Bangladesh, where most of the errands are preferred to be served in a traditional manner from physical locations. Take away for marketers from this finding is to ensure a lot of confidence among the users by highlighting the value propositions of such service with their importance in their daily life through the marketing mix of the companies. Clinching benefits such as the quality of system and of information, high responsiveness with empathy, ease of using m-Health services and the relative conveniences (outcomes) that are attached with such usages should be used as the major selling ideas of their communication campaigns to build a strong positive comprehension in the response process of the target market. The providers must also ensure a lot of empathy and a high level of responsiveness while providing the accurate information through the call center personnel to the users. They must keep in mind that one negative case in terms of accurate and quick response with empathy may lead to decreasing brand equity and hence, hospitals and clinics should train the front liners accordingly. Developing a sustainable system which ensures privacy and efficiency to support the clinching benefits of m-Health services is additionally important to encourage the consumption of such services among the city dwellers of Bangladesh.

Since the culture of Bangladesh is mainly based on collectivism, this is the root cause behind the impact of the factor of social influence on behavioral intention towards m-Health services. Being consistent with the findings of Jung (2008) and Sun et al. (2013), which argued that subjective norm was the most influential factor for technologically related services, this study identified social influence as a powerful factor that can affect the intention to use m-Health services in Bangladesh. Further analysis revealed that respondents are significantly influenced by peer groups and interpersonal world-of-mouth, which is also consistent to the findings of Venkatesh and Davis (2000). Taking the above together, the business implication for the m-Health service providers is to create a buzz to get the benefit of social capita. Semiotics such as catchy jingle and slogans with positive testimonials might also help the providers to bag a positive viral response from the market. Creative publicity and sales promotional activities using a lot of support media, particularly targeting the city dwellers may lead to a viral word of mouth. Social media such as Facebook and You Tube may also be exploited to get the viral going in urban markets.

Alternatively, the construct of healthcare knowledge has been noted to have an insignificant role to play in terms of shaping behavioral intention for m-Health services in Bangladesh. As per the Human Development Report by UNDP (United Nations Development Programme), the HDI (Human Development Index) of Bangladesh is 0.558 with a positive growth. This indicates that the healthcare knowledge of general citizens is below the line and most of the people, particularly in rural areas, are unaware of basic healthcare processes which make Bangladesh a potential for m-Health service providers. Take away for marketers will be to capitalize this dependency and to develop better ways to provide m-Health services in order to support the growth of the HDI index of Bangladesh. Also, the busy lifestyle of the city dwellers in Bangladesh often adds to this dependency of people on online or mobile health care services, which is why city hospitals should think about introducing such services in the urban areas as well.

Once city hospitals manage to introduce such services for the urban population, they can even think of establishing criterions like experience and original certifications of doctors before including them in the panel of the medical team that involves in the provision of m-Health services. This will be instrumental in reducing the concerns of the urban population regarding whether to take advice from unknown hospital doctors. Furthermore, it can accelerate the acceptance and use of m-Health services in Bangladesh if the urban population can trust the quality of the doctors and therefore, the quality of m-Health services in turn.

FURTHER CONSIDERATIONS

By embarking upon essential factors like service quality and knowledge related to m-Health services in Bangladesh, this chapter has particularly emphasized how challenging it is for the developing nations to make healthcare services easily available and accessible over the electronic network to their citizens. However, there are other very real concerns about turning over personal health information to unknown health service providers like various levels of perceived risks. According to Featherman and Pavlou (2003), perceived risk is defined as the potential for loss (financial, psychological, physical or social) in the pursuit of a desired outcome of using an electronic service. For m-Health services, perceived risk thus represents all uncertainties regarding possible negative consequences of using such services.

Although this chapter did not examine the influence of perceived risk, we suggest that it is a new concept that should be employed in order to explain behavioural intention and usage behavior of m-Health services. We firmly believe that timely initiatives on emerging m-Health concepts may help explain how risk perceptions might affect the eventual dispersion of innovative technologies. This notion is further motivated by recent researches like Alalwan et al. (2016), Park and Tussyadiah (2016), Khalilzadeh et al. (2017), and Hubert et al. (2017) that suggests manifold dimensionalities for risk and highlights risk as one of the major factors behind the lack of willingness of adopting an e-service like m-Health. Based on the frameworks of the risk literature, this chapter proposes a new research agenda wherein we introduce the construct of perceived risk to address the adoption of m-Health services.

Alalwan et al. (2016) empirically examined the impact of usefulness, ease of use, self-efficacy and perceived risk on the adoption of mobile technology and found a significant negative relationship between perceived risk and behavioral intention. In a similar but extended study by Park and Tussyadiah (2016), multidimensional aspects of risk like time risk, financial risk, performance risk, privacy/security risk, psychological risk, physical risk, and device risk have been investigated. Findings of the study provided evidence in favor of the significant negative influence of perceived risk over perceived usefulness, attitude, and behavioral intention in the context of technology adoption. Lately, Khalilzadeh et al. (2017) provided strong evidence of the effect of risk on users' intention to use mobile-based technology and identified performance risk, financial risk and privacy risk as hindrance to adoption. Hubert et al. (2017) too empirically proved the dominating effect of different facets of risk i.e. performance risk, financial risk and security risk on technology acceptance.

A review of the above literature reveals that different risk components compose the overall perceived risk which has the capacity to affect users' intention to adopt m-Health services negatively. To assure citizens, the fact that their personal health information will be treated in an extremely secure environment and will not be subject to any levels of risk needs to be ensured by the health service providers and the government, alike. This means that the health information they have listed with the government or service providers cannot make them the victims of reprisals by disaffected individuals or institutions. It can therefore be expected that the less averse the users will be towards the risk concerns, the more they are likely to adopt m-Health services. On this note, this chapter suggests the use of the following risk components to further the study of the adoption of m-Health services. Figure 3 shows the proposed research framework for the integration of risk components to examine the factors that can influence future use intentions for m-Health services. The constructs have been primarily identified from the past studies highlighted above, as depicted in Table 5.

Table 5. Proposed Risk Constructs

Constructs	Explanations	Items Sources
Information Technology (IT) Risk	Includes virus attacks, worms, Trojans, backdoors, and other malwares, hardware failures due to power loss or data corruption due to software failures.	Hubert et al. (2017)
Individual Risk	Defined as the risks that occur because of human errors like careless data disposition by the user. Also termed as time risk which is defined as the risk of wasting time due to inaccurate data submissions, website downtime or the risk of missing deadlines.	Park and Tussyadiah (2016)
Cyber Risk	Relates to an individual's reluctance to use an online system due to the likelihood of being a victim of cybercrimes i.e. hacking, fraud or password theft.	Khalilzadeh et al. (2017)

Figure 3. New Research Framework

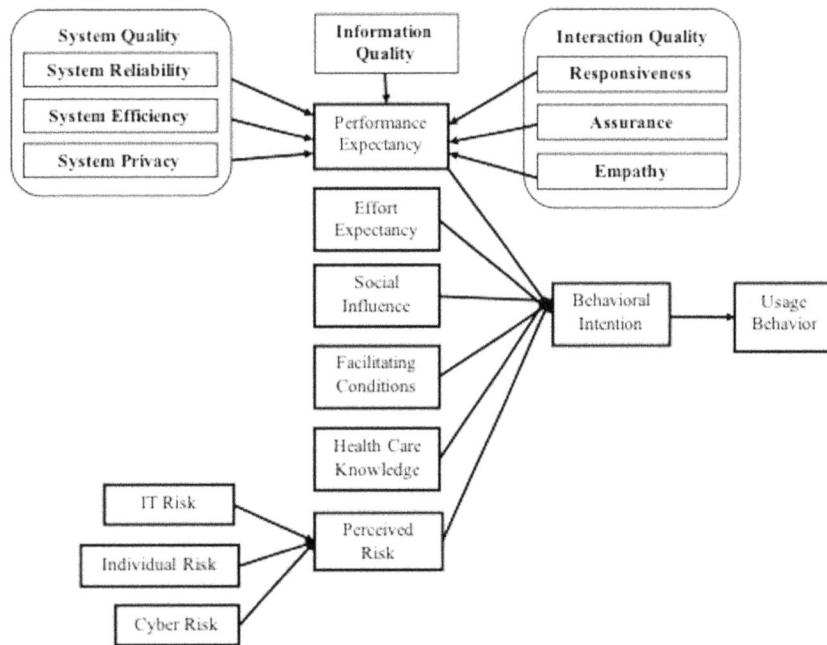

FUTURE RESEARCH DIRECTIONS

An emerging trend today is to provide electronic services and using mobile applications for such service provisions is quite a challenge for the service providers. This is particularly true if the service providers are dealing with sensitive services like healthcare. Currently, the government of Bangladesh is attempting to provide healthcare services to its citizens through both an electronic and mobile platform. The objective is to make healthcare delivery more accessible and affordable for the rural as well as the urban crowd. Although the current study tried to capture the perceptions of a moderate sample size of the urban population, people of other major cities or even the rural areas of the country are not considered for analysis. Future research could examine a wider respondent base in order to provide a better insight into the perceptions of potential m-Health service users in Bangladesh. The research model used in this study has been generalized and is only tested in a very specific condition of healthcare mobile services in a single country. The application of a similar conceptual model to study the context of other developing countries in South Asia like India and Pakistan can add further value. Also, panel data can be gathered regarding m-Health services from different developing countries and compared to do a more constructive analysis. Additional constructs like perceived self-efficacy, innovativeness, anxiety, and riskiness of the m-Health services can be added in the research model to enhance the understanding of individuals' intention to adopt m-Health services in Bangladesh. Besides, a very important characteristic for the optimization of such services in developing countries is a careful research of the target market and their service requirements. With the continued rapid expansion of the number, variety and sophistication of internet and mobile devices on the market, the need for effective, user-friendly, and high performance service applications is likely to increase substantially. This is especially true for health-based services. Therefore, aspects like graphical user interface, data network and database requirement, image optimization, code compression, responsive frameworks, clear-focused content, simple menu navigation and consistent coverage are some of the areas where focus of m-Health services should be emphasized. This, in turn, can improve the viability and success of implementation of such services in developing countries like Bangladesh.

CONCLUSION

The primary objective of this chapter is to investigate the adoption drivers of m-Health services in Bangladesh, emphasizing upon the role of service quality and healthcare knowledge. Findings claim that service qualities like reliability, privacy, responsiveness, empathy and information quality along with facilitating conditions, effort expectancy, performance expectancy and social influence play an important role in capturing individuals' overall perceptions of m-Health services. Furthermore, the study proposes to incorporate perceived risk into the conceptual model as a new research agenda, directing the focus to Information Technology risk, Individual risk, and Cyber risk factors. Inclusion of perceived risk is expected to make a significant contribution to the emerging literature on m-Health service adoption. Moreover, the research model with perceived risk can be used as a reference for studies to cater to m-Health service adoption across various country contexts.

REFERENCES

Agarwal, S., Perry, H. B., Long, L. A., & Labrique, A. B. (2015). Evidence on feasibility and effective use of mHealth strategies by frontline health workers in developing countries: Systematic review. *Tropical Medicine & International Health*, 20(8), 1003–1014. doi:10.1111/tmi.12525 PMID:25881735

Akter, S., D'Ambra, J., & Ray, P. (2010). *18th European Conference on Information Systems: conference proceedings*. University of Pretoria. Retrieved from http://ro.uow.edu.au/cgi/viewcontent.cgi?article=4188&context=commpapers

Akter, S., D'Ambra, J., & Ray, P. (2013). Development and validation of an instrument to measure user perceived service quality of mHealth. *Information & Management*, 50(4), 181–195. doi:10.1016/j.im.2013.03.001

Angst, M. C., & Agarwal, R. (2009). Adoption of electronic health records in the presence of privacy concerns: The Elaborate Likelihood Model and individual persuasion. *Management Information Systems Quarterly*, 33(2), 339–370.

Boontarig, W., Chutimaskul, W., Chongsuphajaisiddhi, W., & Papasratorn, B. (2012). Factors influencing the Thai elderly intention to use smartphone for e-Health services. *IEEE Symposium on Humanities, Science and Engineering Research*, p242-246. doi:10.1109/SHUSER.2012.6268881

Boudreaux, E. D., Waring, M. E., Hayes, R. B., Sadasivam, R. S., Mullen, S., & Pagoto, S. (2014). Evaluating and selecting mobile health apps: Strategies for healthcare providers and healthcare organizations. *Translational Behavioral Medicine*, 4(4), 363–371. doi:10.1007/s13142-014-0293-9 PMID:25584085

Brian, R. M., & Ben-Zeev, D. (2014). Mobile health (mHealth) for mental health in Asia: Objectives, strategies, and limitations. *Asian Journal of Psychiatry*, *10*, 96–100. doi:10.1016/j.ajp.2014.04.006 PMID:25042960

Burgess, L., & Sargent, J. (2007). Enhancing user acceptance of mandated mobile health information systems: The ePOC (electronic point-of-care project) experience. *Studies in Health Technology and Informatics*, *129*(2), 1088–1092. PMID:17911883

Burner, E., Menchine, M., Taylor, E., & Arora, S. (2013). Gender differences in diabetes self-management: A mixed-methods analysis of a mobile health intervention for inner-city Latino patients. *Journal of Diabetes Science and Technology*, *7*(1), 111–118. doi:10.1177/193229681300700113 PMID:23439166

Cairney, J., Veldhuizen, S., Vigod, S., Streiner, D. L., Wade, T. J., & Kurdyak, P. (2013). Exploring the social determinants of mental health service use using intersectionality theory and CART analysis. *Journal of Epidemiology and Community Health*, *68*(2), 145–150. doi:10.1136/jech-2013-203120 PMID:24098046

Chin, W. W., Marcolin, B. L., & Newsted, P. R. (2003). A partial least squares latent variable modeling approach for measuring interaction effects: Results from a Monte Carlo Simulation study and an Electronic-Mail Emotion/Adoption study. *Information Systems Research*, *14*(2), 189–217. doi:10.1287/isre.14.2.189.16018

de la Torre-Diez, I., López-Coronado, M., Vaca, C., Aguado, J. S., & de Castro, C. (2015). Cost-utility and cost-effectiveness studies of telemedicine, electronic and mobile health systems in the literature: A systematic review. *Telemedicine Journal and e-Health*, *21*(2), 81–85. doi:10.1089/tmj.2014.0053 PMID:25474190

Deglise, C., Suggs, L. S., & Odermatt, P. (2012). SMS for disease control in developing countries: A systematic review of mobile health applications. *Journal of Telemedicine and Telecare*, *18*(5), 273–281. doi:10.1258/jtt.2012.110810 PMID:22826375

Deng, Z., Mo, X., & Liu, S. (2014). Comparison of the middle-aged and older users adoption of mobile health services in China. *International Journal of Medical Informatics*, *83*(3), 210–224. doi:10.1016/j.ijmedinf.2013.12.002 PMID:24388129

Directorate General of Health Services (DGHS). (2014). *Health information system & e-Health*. Retrieved from http://www.dghs.gov.bd/index.php/en/ehealth/our-ehealth-eservices/84-englishroot/ehealth-eservice/97-telimedicine-services-in-comunity-clinics

Domínguez-Mayo, F. J., Escalona, M. J., Mejías, M., Aragón, G., García-García, J. A., Torres, J., & Enríquez, J. G. (2015). A Strategic Study about Quality Characteristics in e-Health Systems Based on a Systematic Literature Review. *The Scientific World Journal*, *2015*, 1–11. doi:10.1155/2015/863591 PMID:26146656

Evans, W. D., Abroms, L. C., Poropatich, R., Nielsen, P. E., & Wallace, J. L. (2012). Mobile health evaluation methods: The Text4baby case study. *Journal of Health Communication*, *17*(1), 22–29. doi:10.1080/10810730.2011.649157 PMID:22548595

Featherman, M. S., & Pavlou, P. A. (2003). Predicting e-services adoption: A perceived risk facets perspective. *International Journal of Human-Computer Studies*, *59*(4), 451–474. doi:10.1016/S1071-5819(03)00111-3

Fornell, C., & Larcker, D. F. (1981). Evaluating structural equation models with unobservable variables and measurement error. *JMR, Journal of Marketing Research*, *18*(1), 39–50. doi:10.2307/3151312

Fox, S. (2011). *The social life of health information 2011*. Washington, DC: Pew Internet & American Life Project.

Free, C., Phillips, G., Watson, L., Galli, L., Felix, L., Edwards, P., & Haines, A. (2013). The effectiveness of mobile-health technologies to improve health care service delivery processes: A systematic review and meta-analysis. *PLoS Medicine*, *10*(1), e1001363. doi:10.1371/journal.pmed.1001363 PMID:23458994

Gagnon, M. P., Ngangue, P., Payne-Gagnon, J., & Desmartis, M. (2015). m-Health Adoption by Healthcare Professionals: A Systematic Review. *Journal of the American Medical Informatics Association.* PMID:26078410

Guo, X., Sun, Y., Wang, N., Peng, Z., & Yan, Z. (2013). The dark side of elderly acceptance of preventive mobile health services in China. *Electronic Markets*, *23*(1), 49–61. doi:10.1007/s12525-012-0112-4

Guo, X., Zhang, X., & Sun, Y. (2016). The privacy–personalization paradox in mHealth services acceptance of different age groups. *Electronic Commerce Research and Applications*, *16*, 55–65. doi:10.1016/j.elerap.2015.11.001

Hasanain, R. A., Vallmuur, K., & Clark, M. (2015). Electronic Medical Record Systems in Saudi Arabia: Knowledge and Preferences of Healthcare Professionals. *Journal of Health Informatics in Developing Countries*, *9*(1).

Holden, R. J., & Karsh, B. T. (2010). The technology acceptance model: Its past and its future in health care. *Journal of Biomedical Informatics*, *43*(1), 159–172. doi:10.1016/j.jbi.2009.07.002 PMID:19615467

Holtz, B., & Lauckner, C. (2012). Diabetes management via mobile phones: A systematic review. *Telemedicine Journal and e-Health*, *18*(3), 175–184. doi:10.1089/tmj.2011.0119 PMID:22356525

Hoque, M. R., Karim, M. R., & Amin, M. B. (2015). Factors Affecting the Adoption of mHealth Services among Young Citizen: A Structural Equation Modeling (SEM) Approach. *Asian Business Review*, *5*(2), 60–65. doi:10.18034/abr.v5i2.416

Hoque, M. R., & Sorwar, G. (2015). Factors Influencing mHealth Acceptance among Elderly People in Bangladesh. *Australasian Conference on Information Systems*.

Huang, E. Y., Lin, S. W., & Fan, Y. C. (2015). MS-QUAL: Mobile service quality measurement. *Electronic Commerce Research and Applications*, *14*(2), 126–142. doi:10.1016/j.elerap.2015.01.003

Hubert, M., Blut, M., Brock, C., Backhaus, C., & Eberhardt, T. (2017). Acceptance of Smartphone-Based Mobile Shopping: Mobile Benefits, Customer Characteristics, Perceived Risks, and the Impact of Application Context. *Psychology and Marketing*, *34*(2), 175–194. doi:10.1002/mar.20982

Huili, Y. A. O., & Zhong, C. (2011). The analysis of influencing factors and promotion strategy for the use of mobile banking. *Canadian Social Science*, *7*(2), 60–63.

Idrish, S., Rifat, A., Iqbal, M., & Nisha, N. (2017). Mobile health technology evaluation: Innovativeness and efficacy vs. cost effectiveness. *International Journal of Technology and Human Interaction*, *13*(2), 1–21. doi:10.4018/IJTHI.2017040101

Jackson, J. D., Mun, Y. Y., & Park, J. S. (2013). An empirical test of three mediation models for the relationship between personal innovativeness and user acceptance of technology. *Information & Management*, *50*(4), 154–161. doi:10.1016/j.im.2013.02.006

James, D. C., Harville, C., Whitehead, N., Stellefson, M., Dodani, S., & Sears, C. (2015). Willingness of African American women to participate in e-Health/m-Health research. *Telemedicine Journal and e-Health*. PMID:26313323

Jimison, H. B., & Sher, P. P. (2008). Consumer health informatics: Health information technology for consumers. *Journal of the American Society for Information Science*, *46*(10), 783–790. doi:10.1002/(SICI)1097-4571(199512)46:10<783::AID-ASI11>3.0.CO;2-L

Jung, M. (2008). *From health to e-Health: Understanding citizens' acceptance of online health care* (Doctoral thesis). Luleå University of Technology. Retrieved from http://epubl.ltu.se/1402-1544/2008/68/LTU-DT-0868-SE.pdf

Kahn, J. G., Yang, J. S., & Kahn, J. S. (2010). Mobile health needs and opportunities in developing countries. *Health Affairs*, *29*(2), 252–258. doi:10.1377/hlthaff.2009.0965 PMID:20348069

Khalilzadeh, J., Ozturk, A. B., & Bilgihan, A. (2017). Security-related factors in extended UTAUT model for NFC based Mobile Payment in the Restaurant Industry. *Computers in Human Behavior*, *70*, 460–474. doi:10.1016/j.chb.2017.01.001

Kumar, S., Nilsen, W., Pavel, M., & Srivastava, M. (2013). Mobile health: Revolutionizing healthcare through trans-disciplinary research. *Computer*, *1*(1), 28–35. doi:10.1109/MC.2012.392

Lallmahamood, M. (2007). An examination of individual's perceived security and privacy of the Internet in Malaysia and the influence of this on their intention to use e-Commerce: Using an extension of the Technology Acceptance Model. *Journal of Internet Banking and Commerce*, *12*(3), 1–26.

Lau, M. M., Cheung, R., Lam, A. Y. C., & Chu, Y. T. (2013). Measuring service quality in the banking industry: A Hong Kong based study. *Contemporary Management Research*, *9*(3), 263–282. doi:10.7903/cmr.11060

Lee, J., & Rho, M. J. (2013). Perception of influencing factors on acceptance of mobile health monitoring service: A comparison between users and non-users. *Healthcare Informatics Research*, *19*(3), 167–176. doi:10.4258/hir.2013.19.3.167 PMID:24175115

Lee, K. C., & Chung, N. (2009). Understanding factors affecting trust in and satisfaction with mobile banking in Korea: A modified DeLone and McLean's model perspective. *Interacting with Computers*, *21*(5), 385–392. doi:10.1016/j.intcom.2009.06.004

Lin, H. (2011a). An empirical investigation of mobile banking adoption: The effect of innovation attributes and knowledge-based trust. *International Journal of Information Management, 31*(3), 252–260. doi:10.1016/j.ijinfomgt.2010.07.006

Lin, H. (2011b). The effect of multi-channel service quality on mobile customer loyalty in an online-and-mobile retail context. *Service Industries Journal, 32*(11), 1865–1882. doi:10.1080/02642069.2011.559541

Maddison, R., Pfaeffli, L., Stewart, R., Kerr, A., Jiang, Y., Rawstorn, J., ... Whittaker, R. (2014). The HEART mobile phone trial: The partial mediating effects of self-efficacy on physical activity among cardiac patients. *Frontiers in Public Health, 2.* PMID:24904918

Masrek, M. N., Uzir, N. A., & Khairuddin, I. I. (2012). Trust in mobile banking adoption in Malaysia: A conceptual framework. *Journal of Mobile Technologies, Knowledge & Society,* 1-12.

Moores, T. T. (2012). Towards an integrated model of IT acceptance in healthcare. *Decision Support Systems, 53*(3), 507–516. doi:10.1016/j.dss.2012.04.014

Nambisan, P. (2011). Information seeking and social support in online health communities: Impact on patients' perceived empathy. *Journal of the American Medical Informatics Association, 18*(3), 298–304. doi:10.1136/amiajnl-2010-000058 PMID:21486888

Nelson, R. R., Todd, P. A., & Wixom, B. H. (2005). Antecedents of information and system quality: An empirical examination within the context of data warehousing. *Journal of Management Information Systems, 21*(4), 199–235. doi:10.1080/07421222.2005.11045823

Nisha, N. (2016). Exploring the dimensions of mobile banking service quality: Implications for the banking sector. *International Journal of Business Analytics, 3*(3), 60–76. doi:10.4018/IJBAN.2016070104

Nisha, N., Iqbal, M., Rifat, A., & Idrish, S. (2015). Mobile health services: A new paradigm for health care systems. *International Journal of Asian Business and Information Management, 6*(1), 1–18. doi:10.4018/IJABIM.2015010101

Nisha, N., Iqbal, M., Rifat, A., & Idrish, S. (2016a). Exploring the role of service quality and knowledge for mobile health services. *International Journal of E-Business Research, 12*(2), 45–64. doi:10.4018/IJEBR.2016040104

Nisha, N., Iqbal, M., Rifat, A., & Idrish, S. (2016b). Mobile health services: A new paradigm for health care systems. In *E-Health and Telemedicine: Concepts, Methodologies, Tools, and Applications* (pp. 1551–1567). Hershey, PA: IGI Global. doi:10.4018/978-1-4666-8756-1.ch078

Nunnally, J. C., & Bernstein, I. H. (1994). *Psychometric Theory.* New York: McGraw-Hill.

Parasuraman, A., Zeithaml, V. A., & Malhotra, A. (2005). E-S-QUAL: A multiple-item scale for assessing electronic service quality. *Journal of Service Research, 7*(3), 213–233. doi:10.1177/1094670504271156

Park, J. K., Yang, S. J., & Lehto, X. (2007). Adoption of mobile technologies for Chinese consumers. *Journal of Electronic Commerce Research, 8*(3), 196–206.

Park, S., & Tussyadiah, I. P. (2016). Multidimensional facets of perceived risk in mobile travel booking. *Journal of Travel Research.*

Phichitchaisopa, N., & Naenna, T. (2013). Factors affecting the adoption of healthcare information technology. *EXCLI Journal, 12*, 413–436. PMID:26417235

Putzer, G. J., & Park, Y. (2012). Are physicians likely to adopt emerging mobile technologies? Attitudes and innovation factors affecting smartphone use in the Southeastern United States. American Health Information Management Association.

Rashidee, A. H. (2013). Emerging mobile health in Bangladesh. *The Daily Star*. Retrieved from http://archive.thedailystar.net/beta2/news/emerging-mobile-Health-in-bangladesh/

Ren, Y., Pazzi, R. W. N., & Boukerche, A. (2010). Monitoring patients via a secure and mobile healthcare system. *Wireless Communications, IEEE, 17*(1), 59–65. doi:10.1109/MWC.2010.5416351

Reza, P. R. (2012). Bangladesh: Mobile health service for expecting and new mothers. *Global Voice*. Retrieved from http://globalvoicesonline.org/2012/12/26/bangladesh-mobile-Health-service-for-expecting-and-new-mothers/

Sieverdes, J. C., Treiber, F., Jenkins, C., & Hermayer, K. (2013). Improving diabetes management with mobile health technology. *The American Journal of the Medical Sciences, 345*(4), 289–295. doi:10.1097/MAJ.0b013e3182896cee PMID:23531961

Stofega, W., & Llamas, R. T. (2009). *Worldwide Mobile Phone 2009-2013 Forecast Update. IDC Document Number 217209*. Framingham, MA: IDC.

Sultana, S. (2014). Taking care of health through mobile phones. *The Financial Express*. Retrieved from http://www.thefinancialexpress-bd.com/2014/02/15/18873

Sun, Y., Wang, N., Guo, X., & Peng, Z. (2013). Understanding the acceptance of mobile health services: A comparison and integration of alternative models. *Journal of Electronic Commerce Research, 14*(2), 183–200.

Sunyaev, A., Dehling, T., Taylor, P. L., & Mandl, K. D. (2014). Availability and quality of mobile health app privacy policies. *Journal of the American Medical Informatics Association*. doi:10.1136/amiajnl-2013-002605 PMID:25147247

Tamrat, T., & Kachnowski, S. (2012). Special delivery: An analysis of mHealth in maternal and newborn health programs and their outcomes around the world. *Maternal and Child Health Journal, 16*(5), 1092–1101. doi:10.1007/s10995-011-0836-3 PMID:21688111

Townsend, A., Leese, J., Adam, P., McDonald, M., Li, L. C., Kerr, S., & Backman, C. L. (2015). eHealth, Participatory Medicine, and Ethical Care: A Focus Group Study of Patients' and Health Care Providers' Use of Health-Related Internet Information. *Journal of Medical Internet Research, 17*(6), e155. doi:10.2196/jmir.3792 PMID:26099267

Vedder, A., Cuijpers, C., Vantsiouri, P., & Ferrari, M. Z. (2014). The law as a 'catalyst and facilitator' for trust in e-health: Challenges and opportunities. *Law. Innovation and Technology, 6*(2), 305–325. doi:10.5235/17579961.6.2.305

Venkatesh, V. (1999). Creating favourable user perceptions: Exploring the role of intrinsic motivation. *Management Information Systems Quarterly, 23*(2), 239–260. doi:10.2307/249753

Venkatesh, V., & Davis, F. D. (2000). A theoretical extension of the technology acceptance model: Four longitudinal field studies. *Management Science, 46*(2), 186–204. doi:10.1287/mnsc.46.2.186.11926

Venkatesh, V., Morris, M. G., Davis, G. B., & Davis, F. D. (2003). User acceptance of information technology: Toward a unified view. *Management Information Systems Quarterly, 27*(3), 425–478.

Venkatesh, V., Thong, J. Y. L., & Xin, X. (2012). Consumer acceptance and use of information technology: Extending the Unified Theory of Acceptance and Use of Technology. *Management Information Systems Quarterly, 36*(1), 157–178.

Venkatesh, V., & Zhang, X. (2010). Unified theory of acceptance and use of technology: U.S. vs. China. *Journal of Global Information Technology Management, 13*(1), 5–27. doi:10.1080/109719 8X.2010.10856507

Washington, G., Ward, J., & Kameka, M. (2015). Spare Me: Towards an Empathetic Tool for Helping Adolescents & Teenagers Cope with Sickle Cell. In *Healthcare Informatics (ICHI), 2015 International Conference on* (pp. 555-561). IEEE.

West, D. (2012). How mobile devices are transforming healthcare. *Issues in Technology Innovation, 18*(1), 1–11.

Wilson, E. V., & Lankton, N. K. (2004). Modeling patients' acceptance of provider-delivered E-health. *Journal of the American Medical Informatics Association, 11*(4), 241–248. doi:10.1197/jamia.M1475 PMID:15064290

Wu, J., Wang, S., & Lin, L. (2007). Mobile computing acceptance factors in the healthcare industry: A structural equation model. *International Journal of Medical Informatics, 76*(1), 66–77. doi:10.1016/j. ijmedinf.2006.06.006 PMID:16901749

Xue, L., Yen, C.C., Chang, L., Tai, B.C., Chan, H.C., Duh, H.B.L. & Choolani, M. (2012). Journeying Toward Female-focused m-Health Applications. *Advances in Affective and Pleasurable Design*, 295.

Yin, S. Y., Huang, K. K., Shieh, J. I., Liu, Y. H., & Wu, H. H. (2015). Tele-health services evaluation: A combination of SERVQUAL model and importance-performance analysis. *Quality & Quantity*, 1–16.

Yu, C. (2012). Factors affecting individuals to adopt mobile banking: Empirical evidence from the UTAUT model. *Journal of Electronic Commerce Research, 13*(2), 104–121.

ADDITIONAL READING

Dwivedi, Y. K., Shareef, M. A., Simintiras, A. C., Lal, B., & Weerakkody, V. (2016). A generalised adoption model for services: A cross-country comparison of mobile health (m-health). *Government Information Quarterly, 33*(1), 174–187. doi:10.1016/j.giq.2015.06.003

Guo, X., Han, X., Zhang, X., Dang, Y., & Chen, C. (2015). Investigating m-health acceptance from a protection motivation theory perspective: Gender and age differences. *Telemedicine Journal and e-Health, 21*(8), 661–669. doi:10.1089/tmj.2014.0166 PMID:25919800

Saad, N. M., Alias, R. A., & Ismail, Z. (2013). Initial framework on identifying factors influencing individuals' usage of telehealth. In *Research and Innovation in Information Systems (ICRIIS), 2013 International Conference on* (pp. 174-179). IEEE.

Shareef, M. A., Kumar, V., & Kumar, U. (2014). Predicting mobile health adoption behaviour: A demand side perspective. *Journal of Customer Behaviour, 13*(3), 187–205. doi:10.1362/14753921 4X14103453768697

Shin, D. H., Lee, S., & Hwang, Y. (2017). How do credibility and utility play in the user experience of health informatics services? *Computers in Human Behavior, 67,* 292–302. doi:10.1016/j.chb.2016.11.007

KEY TERMS AND DEFINITIONS

Behavioral Intention: Individual intention to use a particular technology that directly affects actual usage.

E-Health: Healthcare services delivered via the electronic platform with the help of desktops or laptops in order to help people obtain immediate medical services, and useful information or guidance to manage their health better.

Healthcare Knowledge: Defined as the users' extent of knowledge and understanding of personal health problems that determines their need for healthcare services.

M-Health: Healthcare services provided to people over a mobile platform that aims to remove locational and temporal constraints while increasing both coverage and the quality of healthcare.

Perceived Risk: Level of uncertainty with which users approach a particular technology.

Service Quality: Defined as the evaluation of a user's expectation of a service with the performance of that service.

Chapter 9
Connecting and Sharing Tacit Knowledge:
Do Social Media Help or Hinder?

Kimiz Dalkir
McGill University, Canada

ABSTRACT

Collaboration has become a part of our everyday life – including our everyday work life. In addition, our work colleagues are often not in close physical proximity, making face-to-face interactions rare. As a result, we have come to rely on information and communication technologies to connect – in particular, social networking technologies or social media. While traditional technologies are well suited for sharing explicit knowledge that has been articulated and documented as text or other media, tacit knowledge is more challenging. Tacit knowledge is typically experiential knowledge that is very difficult to put into words or document in any way. This chapter investigates the benefits and barriers to using social media with respect to professional communication and collaboration. Recommendations are proposed to help select the best knowledge sharing medium for tacit knowledge.

INTRODUCTION

The two major types of knowledge is defined by the Business Dictionary (http://www.businessdictionary.com/definition/explicit-knowledge.html) as:

Explicit knowledge: Articulated knowledge, expressed and recorded as words, numbers, codes, mathematical and scientific formulae, and musical notations. Explicit knowledge is easy to communicate, store, and distribute and is the knowledge found in books, on the web, and other visual and oral means. Opposite of tacit knowledge.

Tacit knowledge: Unwritten, unspoken, and hidden vast storehouse of knowledge held by practically every human being, based on his or her emotions, experiences, insights, intuition, observations and internal-

DOI: 10.4018/978-1-5225-5014-3.ch009

ized information. Tacit knowledge is integral to the entirety of a person's consciousness, is acquired largely through association with other people, and requires joint or shared activities to be imparted from on to another. Like the submerged part of an iceberg it constitutes the bulk of what one knows, and forms the underlying framework that makes explicit knowledge possible. Concept of tacit knowledge was introduced by the Hungarian philosopher-chemist Michael Polanyi (1891-1976) in his 1966 book 'The Tacit Dimension.' Also called informal knowledge.

Explicit knowledge has been documented in some way, usually as text but it can also be an audio or video recording. Tacit knowledge, on the other hand, exists only in the minds of people. It is very difficult to articulate (verbalize, explain) let alone document. The challenge stems from the fact that tacit knowledge usually results from years of experience, involves judgment, can be very subjective and prescriptive and is usually quite complex (Nonaka, 2008). Social media are therefore expected to be better suited to the sharing of tacit knowledge as they are based on social networks (relationships) that connect people to people. As people interact with one another, they are more likely to have the time and motivation to contextualize their tacit knowledge to share with others. Similarly, they will be more open to doing so if they are reciprocating or returning a favor to others who have helped them in the past.

Knowledge sharing refers to "the ability of employees to share their work-related experience, expertise, know-how, and contextual information with other employees through informal and formal interactions within or across teams or work units. This knowledge-sharing capability "…also refers to employees' ability to acquire knowledge that is held by other divisions with the organization" (Kim and Lee, 2006, p. 371).

Van Den Hooff and De Ridder"s (2004) conceptualize knowledge sharing as a "process where individuals mutually exchange their implicit (tacit) and explicit knowledge to create new knowledge" (p.119). Taylor (2017) studied knowledge sharing between entrepreneurs and their senior managers and noted that over the past 20 years, entrepreneurs have had an increasingly participative role in decision making, their autonomy increased and norms were established. In addition, ""senior managers who interacted more frequently with the entrepreneur learned increasingly to think like the entrepreneur…" (p. 119). Increased interaction led to more tacit knowledge sharing and the senior manager learned how the entrepreneur works and thinks. For example, initial perceptions that the entrepreneur made decisions too quickly without having sufficient facts was eliminated.

Tacit knowledge is very challenging to access and communicate to others as it requires extensive interaction in order to ensure that knowledge is effectively transferred, received and understood. This chapter explores the effectiveness of using traditional and emerging social media to foster the sharing of tacit knowledge in organizations.

TYPES OF TECHNOLOGIES USED FOR KNOWLEDGE SHARING

A variety of technologies can and have been used in organizational knowledge sharing. Any form of interaction that does not occur face-to-face in real time in the same physical space will necessarily have some type of technology mediating the connection between two or more people. Historically, this took place as a form of computer-mediated communication: "communication that takes place between human beings via the instrumentality of computers" (Herring, 1996, p. 1). Today, it is more common to refer to information and communication technologies (ICTs) that can be used to mediate communication, conversation and knowledge sharing as there are more diverse devices available in addition to computers.

Technology has become a fundamental component of the way information and knowledge is shared within organizations. Employees and people in general are also much more technologically savvy. In parallel, most work is done in teams so collaboration and knowledge sharing is necessary in order to successfully complete our work (Keyes, 2012). A recent survey by Dimensional Research (2015) of 753 business professionals found that 98% collaborated, 65% collaborated multiple times a day and 83% reported they depended on technology to collaborate.

The different types of technologies that can be used to share knowledge can be categorized in a number of different ways. Table 1 highlights one approach, the Global Health Collaborative categories (https://www.globalhealthknowledge.org/resources/useful-technology-km-practitioners). Young (2010) provides a list of similar categories.

More recently, idea crowdsourcing networks have emerged in the social media category. Pugh (2011) describes a "knowledge jam" where social and collaboration technologies are used to identify where pockets of insight may reside in a given organization. Weisz et al (2006) first described a similar approach used at IBM called FreeJam. Web-conferencing or online discussion tools are then used to draw out the insights of these people (in a synchronous or asynchronous fashion with or without a moderator). All participants end up sharing knowledge (contributing and/or using) and as a result everyone learns. The interactions are captured (e.g. minutes of the meeting or via an online threaded discussion) so that people can refer back to the ideas that were generated.

Table 1. Categories of knowledge sharing technologies

Category	Description	Examples
Remote meetings	Meeting participants are not collocated and may be in different time zones	Adobe Connect, Skype, Google Hangout
File sharing	Centralized storage space to store content	DropBox, Google Drive
Online collaboration	Allows people to work together (converse, coordinate tasks)	BaseCamp, Open Atrium, Huddle
Website/blog hosting	Content management tools to create and maintain website, blogs	Drupal, WordPress, Tumblr
Mailing lists/newsletters	Tools to help manage distribution lists and mailing e.g. email lists, marketing campaigns	MailChimp, iContact, Constant Contact
Social media	Allows posting of profiles, connecting with others online privately and/or publicly to share news, other content	Facebook, LinkedIn, Twitter
Photography	Sharing images, can "like" and annotate them	Flickr, Picasa, PhotoShare
Audio/video capture and hosting	Sharing videos	YouTube, Vimeo,
Webcasting/live broadcasting	Sharing webcasts (e.g. recording classroom lectures)	Mediasite, CoveritLive
Content curation	Collect, store and organize content for later reuse based on explicit criteria (e.g. social bookmarking)	Delicious, Scoop It
Screen capture	Capture and store computer screen images for later use	Camtasia, SnagIt
Discussions	Discussion forums (usually text-based)	Google Groups, Facebook Groups

BENEFITS AND BARRIES TO TACIT KNOWLEDGE SHARING

Field (2004) uses the term "social capital" to denote the value that is produced through social media. This value can be simply knowing who knows what or who you can turn to for assistance on a specific topic. As Thurlow et al (2004) stated: "…it's all about the transformation of our patterns of social interaction" p. 2. There are a number of benefits that can be gained from sharing tacit knowledge such as breaking down silos so people know who is who and are therefore more likely to work together. The more people interact, the more synergy will be created which can in turn foster more creativity and innovation. The more tacit knowledge has been shared, the less likely it will be lost to the organization when knowledgeable people leave. Tacit knowledge sharing can create a sense of belonging, a common identity with like-minded peers which, in turn, can lead to greater loyalty and less turnover for the organization. Knowing who knows what means knowing who you can turn to for help and for answers which will in turn contribute to increased efficiency, solving problems faster and avoiding duplication of work. Nonaka (2008) noted that networks promote a shared understanding which in turn helps the development of new ideas. Innovation and creativity are promoted as members of the network react to, clarify and help develop the new idea.

However, most organizations find it difficult to foster sustained and effective knowledge sharing (Riege, 2005). It is even more challenging to get employees to share their tacit knowledge. While technology can connect and provide an infrastructure for sharing, it is often not enough. Technology is not a one-size-fits-all solution. There has to be strong compatibility between the specific tool and the intended end-users – beyond user friendliness and technological competency. A number of studies noted that the ICT must be easy and intuitive to use. If there is a learning curve, chances are the organizational ICT (e.g. the official portal) will be quickly discarded in favor of an easier to use tool (such as social media). Choo et al (2000) identifies a steep learning curve as the major reason why people discard official knowledge sharing ICTs in favor of easier to use tools.

Riege (2005) identified some of the potential barriers to include not integrating ICTs seamlessly into work processes; lack of support; mismatch between users' needs and IT functionalities; lack of training to use ICTs; and not clearly communicating and demonstrating how ICTs can help employees not only share knowledge but get their work done. ICT constraints range from technical issues to human factors. Technical issues include connectivity, access, language and time zone barriers as well as difficulties in maintaining a trace of tacit knowledge that was shared.

Human factors also play a significant role in which ICTs are used to share tacit knowledge. In general, tacit knowledge sharing requires a great deal of trust which in turn tends to be built up on a solid track record of reciprocity as well as personal and professional credibility (Evans et al, 2015). Individual trust also interacts with the overall organizational culture as each organization will contain a set of values, norms, ways of behaving and incentives that underlie the behavior of individuals and groups. The motivation to share knowledge often stems from individual trust and organizational values. This is especially true for knowledge that is complex and more tacit in nature. The social constructivist view of knowledge sharing is a good theoretical model for tacit knowledge sharing as the sharing of knowledge is viewed as two or more individuals actively creating meaning from their experience of interacting with one another rather than a passive transmission of "stuff" (Hislop, 2002). The more the individuals involved have in common, the easier it will be to share tacit knowledge such as similar professional backgrounds, similar experiences and a shared culture.

Other researchers have demonstrated ways in which some of these obstacles to tacit knowledge sharing can be overcome. Kim and Lee (2006) found that social networks and user-friendly IT systems were positively significantly associated with high levels of employee knowledge-sharing capabilities. Garcia-Perez and Ayres (2010) studied the limitations of a wiki for knowledge sharing by researchers in diverse disciplines. All participants made use of the wiki and a significant number contributed content but only initially. Usage decreased over time until it was hardly being used at all one year after it was implemented. Most people said they did not have time but there was also a lack of critical mass of valuable content as only a small portion were contributing to the wiki. Balubaid (2013) looked at Web 2.0 technology to share knowledge with students in an academic unit in a university. Users tend to find Web 2.0 technologies such as social networks "easy to use and familiar, allowing learners to share and generate knowledge within the small group environment" (p. 406). 70% of students surveyed chose Facebook as their preferred platform for more tacit and informal knowledge. They preferred the official unit website for formal explicit knowledge sharing (e.g. exam times, lecture cancellations, events). The author noted a similar outcome for a wiki for graduate students in a university. In the latter case, the major reason for the "demise" of the wiki was that students had set up a Facebook page and they much preferred using that for informal interactions. This means that a definite preference exists for easy-to-use social networks to share tacit knowledge.

THE ROLE OF TRUST

Holste and Fields (2010) investigated the role of trust in knowledge sharing and found it to be absolutely critical for tacit knowledge: "Tacit knowledge is not readily captured or stored by information technology systems" (p. 135). They define two types of trust: cognition-based trust is a fairly rational assessment of the other as credible, dependable and knowledgeable. Affect-based trust is much more emotional, subjective and based on the specific track record with the other (e.g. reciprocity). The authors found that affect-based trust promoted the sharing their tacit knowledge with someone else whereas cognition-based trust was a greater factor in decided whether or not to use tacit knowledge from someone else. Traditional technologies were found to be better suited for sharing explicit knowledge and cognition-based trust. Tacit knowledge requires more affect-based trust which will take longer to develop through social networks and social media. Employees will tend to share valuable tacit knowledge they have gained through personal experience with those they have a strong relationship or tie with (Granovetter, 1973). There is also always concern about how their shared knowledge will be used: will they be correctly attributed? Correctly quoted? Or, in the very worst-case scenario where their knowledge has been incorrectly revised and yet correctly attributed to them). Finally, the more the provider of tacit knowledge is perceived to have a good professional reputation, then the more likely their knowledge will be used by others. This implies that some form of vouching or voting system may be helpful – the number of endorsements someone has garnered in LinkedIn for example or the number of likes that a specific post elicited.

Trust is therefore difficult to develop when using any form of technology-mediated communication but social media are so far the best candidates (Dalkir, 2017). This is mostly because social media have greater levels of media richness and social presence. The Media Richness Model was proposed by Daft and Lengel in 1984 and looked at the speed with which feedback can be provided, whether multimedia content is possible, and whether it can be informal, impersonal and can support different types of languages (natural, numeric, other). Vickery et al (2004) note that tacit knowledge requires media rich technologies to be shared effectively. Social presence was first described by Thurlow et al (2004) and it refers to how much people think they are interacting with other people rather than with a technological interface. The more tacit the knowledge to be shared, the higher the social presence should be (Chua, 2001). The more tacit the knowledge to be shared is, the harder it will be to share through traditional ICTs with low social presence and media richness.

The best we may be able to do with social media and other networking technologies is to facilitate finding people and keep some type of profile information on their expertise that includes information on how many people have positive things to say about knowledge they used from them. In this way, we give people the opportunity to demonstrate their competencies and provide the means for some type of peer-to-peer evaluation and endorsement. The concept of a "social intranet" was proposed by Mergel (2016) who describes as a central wiki where employees can go to find knowledge they need such as specific information or specific people who can help them out. People quickly find out who is knowledgeable about what topic as they read the various discussion threads

A feature in LinkedIn provides an example. Not only do people read up on the individual's profile but they can easily see if they share connections in common. This would allow them to contact the other people and have them "vouch" or recommend the person they are considering sharing knowledge with. In this way, additional information can be gathered which can help decide whether or not to trust the other person and to share knowledge with them (either provide them with knowledge and/or make use of their knowledge).

EMERGING TECHNOLOGIES

Most knowledge sharing in today's organizations mirrors what is happening in everyday life: people are using online communities as their preferred technology to connect and to share information and knowledge. Online communities, which are woven together by social media, are definitely the predominant emerging technology. Sometimes referred to as Web 2.0 technologies, they are characterized by community building and aiding collaboration. Faraj et al (2016) note that the value of online communities stems from the collective flow of knowledge among participants. Online communities consist of geographically dispersed individuals who share a common interest, activity or profession often producing innovative products, services or processes. Digital social technologies have become a seamless part of many peoples' working and living days. The boundary between face-to-face and technology-mediated has blurred as newer technologies have much greater media richness and social presence. It is increasingly easy to connect to "groupings of similarly relevant others...on a global scale" (Faraj et al, 2016, p. 5).

While social media can support online community interactions, the main focus of social networks is on individual networks and relationships. For example, each individual can decide to no longer interact with another (e.g. "unfriend" on Facebook or "unfollow" on Twitter) whereas this is not the case in an online community. Asking someone to leave would be a collective decision as communities are governed by a different set of rules. Similarly all communities have a digital platform that allows connectivity which can also shape the interactions of participants.

All knowledge has some tacit knowledge component and the same challenges remain in trying to share tacit knowledge within online communities. A major challenge in sharing tacit is when people have different backgrounds, experiences, and communication preferences. However, linguistic and other communication means tend to evolve in an online community such that participants soon come to share a common jargon and at times, an official glossary of terms. This is often a specialized language with acronyms and terms that denote ways of doing. Once this shared language has emerged, tacit knowledge sharing becomes easier. "First, the exchange of tacit knowledge can only occur via intense engagement in the social process" (Faraj et al, 2016, p. 9). Repeated interactions create increased context for the conversational exchanges which in turn leads to greater mutual comprehension. Repeated interactions also unveil who has expertise in what area. Last but not least, repeated interactions increase reciprocity thus helping to build trust which will lead to more tacit knowledge sharing.

While online communities may not be appropriate to share tacit knowledge that requires deep embodied knowledge of a task (e.g. how to learn how to skate or ride a bicycle or even judge when the best time to invest in a particular fund would be), they can be used to share fairly rich and complex knowledge. Storytelling (Dalkir, 2016) has been shown to be very effective at encapsulating and sharing tacit knowledge. There is the added benefit that stories are preserved so that future users can also access and learn from the stories. Luttrell (2016) also notes that time is needed to develop trusted social relationships – the stability and continuity of the social connection in a network must solidify. As there is more social interaction, then the strength of the relationship increases and more knowledge – particularly tacit knowledge in the form of stories – will eventually be shared.

Emerging technologies such as collaborative platforms, (wikis, blogs), digital content repositories (GoogleDocs, DropBox), academic sites (ResearchGate, Academia.edu) and platforms (SharePoint) are being increasingly used by academics and researchers to generate, document, store and share their tacit knowledge. Rambe and Mbeo (2017) studied the transfer of knowledge from senior university researchers to novices and found that they effectively interacted using an online platform (SharePoint) to transfer their tacit knowledge. Research knowledge is highly personal, hard to formalize as it consists of insights, hunches, and intuitions. Some examples include: critical review of more junior researchers' working papers; coaching, mentoring, storytelling, co-authoring and critical reading groups. Tacit knowledge sharing requires mutual trust and open communication to foster strong personal relationships and at least partial externalization (rendering tangible) of tacit knowledge so that it can be shared digitally.

Finally, knowledge sharing is occurring more and more via mobile devices including the sharing of tacit knowledge. For example, Bullock (2013) looked at knowledge-sharing practices of physicians who used mobile devices and Web 2.0 technologies. Doctors need to access critical information in a timely manner in order to make decisions. Mobile devices can provide "just-in-time" access to this vital content. The study looked at not only the acquisition of explicit information but also tacit knowledge. Contextual knowledge was easier to share using social media (although mobile devices can also be used to access social media sites). Web 2.0 tools proved better at sharing tacit knowledge as they promote more informal interaction and collaboration ("off-the-record"). Tacit knowledge sharing requires more discussion, participation and reflection enabling virtual communities of doctors to form. Mobile ICTs provide the means to maintain sustained connectivity to build up a history of trusted interactions that is a requirement for the sharing of valuable tacit knowledge.

RECOMMENDED TACIT KNOWLEDGE SHARING TECHNOLOGIES

ICTs generally favor the sharing of knowledge that can be codified i.e. rendered explicit or tangible (e.g. know-how or procedural knowledge). Tacit knowledge on the other hand usually consists of know-how (and even know-why and know-who) acquired through informal on-the-job learning. "Tacit knowledge, though, often requires considerable time to acquire....gained during an apprenticeship or a period of "learning by doing"..." (Roberts, 2000, p. 433). Some elements of tacit knowledge can only be shared through showing how (e.g. a demonstration) which means face-to-face interaction is the best knowledge sharing "technology." Tacit knowledge sharing ideally also requires close physical proximity during the interaction(s). Technologies with high media richness and social presence are the next best choice. "In a sense, the transfer of know-how requires a process of show-how" (Roberts, 2000, p.439). For example, the ability to see the other people in real-time such as a Skype call or a videoconference is better for tacit knowledge sharing than, say, email text. Tacit knowledge is embedded in the background and experience of a given person which means that it tends to be highly idiosyncratic. ICTs can partly support the exchange of tacit knowledge but not fully – e.g. can send an image but interpreting what the image means will require more "input" from the person who sent it. ICTs must therefore be combined with a high degree of trust, shared social and cultural contexts in order transfer a significant amount of tacit knowledge effectively.

The ability to use ICTs to share tacit knowledge is limited by the need to first develop a strong relationship based on trust and a shared context with those you will be sharing with. This normally requires face-to-face interactions, ideally at an early stage of sharing. The media richness and social presence of in-person face-to-face interactions cannot be replicated by ICTs. The longer a group of people have worked together with high continuity (i.e. the same members were present throughout the collaboration or duration of a project), then the easier it is for them to use ICTs to share knowledge instead of face-to-face interactions. Coaches or facilitators have also proven to be effective as they actively ensure that the ICT tools are easy to use by everyone.

However, this situation may change (may already be changing) as social media becomes a seamless part of everyday lives. The line between face-to-face contact and technology-mediated contact may eventually disappear. Emerging technologies that make use of augmented or virtual reality will likely become components in cost-effective social media and these will have even higher media richness and social presence. These new virtual environments may approximate face-to-face contact and enable the effective sharing of tacit knowledge.

Virtual teams use ICTs to do their work and share knowledge with one another. Griffith et al (2003) noted that the dimensions of physical distance, percentage of time apart on a task and the level of ICT support can be used to select the most appropriate ICT. The two extremes are teams that only meet face-to-face and those who never meet face-to-face. Most organizations will fall somewhere in between – hybrid teams. Virtual teams are more likely to be formed when expertise is harder to find – thus tending to be more heterogeneous with respect to membership. Members are less likely to have worked together before thus having only very weak social ties (Granovetter, 1973). Teams who spend less time together on task, are located further apart, and who make greater use of ICTs will be more likely to transfer explicit knowledge than tacit knowledge. They will need to transform more tacit knowledge in order to share with the others. The added benefit is that knowledge becomes visible (tangible) and therefore leaves a trace that can preserved and reused in the future. The remaining tacit knowledge will then have to be shared using different less traceable tools such as Skype. More tacit knowledge can be shared if a conscious effort is made to clearly state rules, terminology etc. The more ICTs are used, the harder it will be to establish a shared context. However, higher media richness of ICTs will moderate this effect somewhat.

The recommendation is to therefore kick-off tacit knowledge sharing via face-to-face interactions (ideally) for as long as is feasible and cost-effective. If this is not possible, then the ICTs with the highest media richness and social presence should be used for these initial meetings. With time, more traditional

ICTs can be used to sustain the tacit knowledge sharing. In parallel, social networks should be harnessed to support tacit knowledge sharing. The more successful ones will be pre-existing and may not be limited to boundaries of the organization (e.g. a professional online community). Official organizational networks should be compatible with the overall culture of the workplace.

Tacit knowledge is sharing content that is "specific to the organization (or groups) and that involves subjective insights, intuitions, hunches, and know-how" (Lee-Endres et al, 2007, p.93). Person-to-person transfer will always be best for tacit knowledge. People find it easier to share tacit knowledge in informal networks (voluntary participation, no hierarchy) than traditional work units. Organizational context and culture therefore will have large influence on how successfully knowledge is shared regardless of the ICTs used. Social networks that exist outside of organizational boundaries tent to involve more tacit knowledge-sharing activities. Organizations that see knowledge as an object independent of people ("knowers") will make use of information repositories for explicit knowledge. Organizations that see knowledge as arising from the experiences of people, will tend to use ICTs that provide greater contact between knowledgeable people to share tacit knowledge (Hansen and Avital, 2005).

In order to improve knowledge sharing, Huysman and Woolf (2006) advocate that IT tools need to be embedded in the social networks of which it is part – socially embedded IT. In this way, IT tools can help create social capital. The growth of virtual organizations, teleworkers, and geographically dispersed teams have increased the difficulty of sharing knowledge. Most knowledge sharing tools do not become institutionalized in organizations – top-down, authority-imposed tools tend not to be adopted by employees. Technology push, in other words, tends to fail. Informal sharing appears to be much more effective. Most formal IT tools have been designed to support the acquisition and retrieval of explicit knowledge. Little research has been done on how IT can support emergent knowledge sharing within communities or networks.

Social capital theory is widely accepted as having three critical components: a shared frame of reference, a shared purpose or motivation to share knowledge, and some type of structure such as a shared space. "It is not the technology itself but the way people use it that determines the role of IT in supporting knowledge sharing" (Huysman and Wulf, 2006, p.2). In the case of tacit knowledge, knowledge resides in peoples' heads and knowledge is shared between different people. One of the major reasons documented knowledge content is not reused to any great extent is that knowledge loses meaning when it is separated from the people who either created it or want to use it. When sharing tacit knowledge such as experiences people prefer to talk to other peers not download a document from a knowledge repository. This is because they want meta-knowledge as well as knowledge: what really happened, what is different today, why did this person do x, y and z…It therefore seems more fruitful to have IT support the social connections needed to share tacit knowledge rather than convert tacit into explicit knowledge.

New emerging social media tools hold the promise of providing the necessary interactive and collaborative technologies to be able to share tacit knowledge. This is increasingly important as the more traditional methods of tacit knowledge sharing, such as apprenticeship/mentoring, face-to-face meetings, direct observation, "show and tell" among others, are no longer cost effective. Most existing knowledge management systems tend to be centralized repositories that are much better suited to sharing and preserving explicit knowledge. Social media should allow for more experiential knowledge sharing e.g. online discussion forums, and social networking sites where experts (or at least knowledgeable people) can informally share, critique and validate their collective knowledge. Panahi et al (2012) list five major characteristics of social media that enable tacit knowledge sharing:

1.   User-generated content;
2.   Peer-to-peer communication;
3.   Networking;
4.   Multimedia oriented;
5.   User-friendly.

User-generated content means that all participants are both consumers and creators of content. They can create, annotate, edit, evaluate and redistribute content created by the community. Peer-to-peer communication means all connections are many-to-many as opposed to traditional broadcast technologies were one-to-many connections. Networking means that people with similar interests can share a common online space to talk about their interests. Multimedia oriented means that more than text can be shared: images, videos, audio. User-friendly means that social media are all very easy to use (and to learn how to use). The combination of these five features means that social media help people to connect, to identify who has expertise in which area, build trusted relationships and share their knowledge – both explicit and tacit. ICTs can certainly help share knowledge that has a low to moderate degree of tacitness.

Another group of researchers looked at the concept of "group tacit knowledge" (Erden et al, 2008). Innovation is often not the product of a single person's mind but a collective work of a group of people. Other researchers sometimes refer to this as "collective intelligence" (e.g. O'Reilly, 2009) or, even earlier, as a world or global brain (e.g. Wells, 1938). Group tacit knowledge has six key characteristics:

1.   Socially constructed;
2.   Deeply rooted in action;
3.   Depends on requisite variety and is more than the simple sum of all its parts –synergy;
4.   Embedded in group culture, norms, routines and commitment, ideals, values, senses and emotions;
5.   Group has the capability to agree on the best action for "common goodness" and to find the means to achieve this;
6.   Not only reduces uncertainty but also allows the group to deal with uncertainty.

Group tacit knowledge represents the capacity of the group to act as a collective, use a collective mind and make decisions and act without a central directive authority. Group tacit knowledge is a highly valuable resource that can be relied on to deal with uncertainty, unanticipated situations which often require intuition and spontaneous collective action. One of the major challenges is to identify knowledge sources and make them available to the group. ICTs can help with this by overcoming any time and space constraints. ICTs can help combine, organize, classify, and distribute explicit knowledge. ICTs can also help with tacit knowledge sharing but to a lesser extent. ICTs can serve as a group or project memory allowing group members to access past experiences, written reflections on past events etc. This could be a database of stories, best practices or lessons learned as well as pointers to knowledgeable people ("Expertise Locator Systems"). Information systems such as email, chat rooms, collaboration platforms, and bulletin boards can help create weak ties (Granovetter, 1973) that have the potential to develop into stronger ties for tacit knowledge sharing. The ICTs can also contribute to creating trust and a shared identity among members which in turn will help promote explicit and tacit knowledge sharing.

Huysman and Woolf (2006) note that there is also a bias towards one (expert) individual sharing their knowledge with one other (less expert) individual. However, most knowledge sharing is not one-to-one but many-to-many resulting in collective community-based learning. It is still essential, however, that knowledge sharing be supported by technologies. A socio-technological approach is needed for the design of IT tools which focuses on the continuous interactions between IT, people and the organizational context. Social aspects must be taken into account so that electronic networks such as intranets co-exist and converge with the corresponding social networks. Electronic networks cannot continue to be designed based only an analysis of the physical infrastructure as they have been in the past. In addition, a cultural analysis should take place to identify how people share knowledge, how trust develops and how the value of social capital increases.

Social capital is one of the three major types of intellectual capital (physical capital and human capital being the other two). Human capital refers to human expertise while physical capital refers to the physical inventory of goods owned by a company. Social capital refers to the value of the social network (knowing who knows what, knowing who you can ask for help, the relationships formed with constituents, customers, partners, as well as the value of the "brand" or reputation of the organization). The focus is on communities (the group and not the individual level). Community members are more likely to use IT to share knowledge with other members if they are motivated and enabled (have the opportunity and know how to use the IT).Some good IT tools are member-only communication spaces as they foster social ties. These can be topic-centered such as news feeds. There are also virtual spaces that allow more than communication to take place – members can work contribute content, annotate existing content. Recommender systems can help connect people who appear to share common interests based on content they contributed. Other sites allow collaborative content rating and recommendations. Simple things like keeping a visible history of past interactions can help foster more connections and social ties. Newcomers can easily browse through historical content to become more familiar with the topic, to learn and eventually to contribute to the community. Last but not least, attribution and recognition features are important components of IT tools to support tacit knowledge sharing. There should be a way to recognize and praise good contributions, acknowledge expertise of members and public rewards of some kind (good be ratings similar to Facebook "likes").

As discussed so far, at a minimum, we must make a distinction between ICTs that best suited for explicit knowledge (most ICTs) and those better suited for the sharing of tacit knowledge (Bolisani and Scarso, 2000). ICTs with very high media richness and social presence are better suited to tacit knowledge. This would include multimedia and synchronous ICTs such as FaceTime, Skype, video/web conferencing, collaborative work spaces, virtual communities, wikis and expert locator systems. The general guideline is that there will never be the "best" ICT for tacit knowledge. It is therefore important to select several as studies show that multiple channels tend to reinforce knowledge sharing rather than provide competing choices (Boase et al, 2006, Lee et al, 2009, Leonardi et al, 2011). Today's world is very interconnected and most people will browse a website, only to then download an app on their phone and maybe even text a colleague to alert them to the valuable resource they just found. Multiple media channels thus play complementary and cooperative roles to create synergy in a much more interlinked environment.

CONCLUSION

A wide range of ICTs are currently being used to share knowledge, interact and collaborate with others in a workplace setting. Each ICT, like any technology, will have its set of strengths and drawbacks. The first key criterion to consider is to what extent is the knowledge to be shared explicit and/or tacit. The more explicit or the better documented the knowledge, then most ICTs can be used effectively to share and preserve this content. The next criterion to consider would the characteristics of the ICT. The ICTs that are well-suited to sharing tacit knowledge, however, represent a much smaller subset of ICTs as they must provide for a very high degree of media richness, social presence and co-exist with social networks. The latter is a co-requisite for effective tacit knowledge sharing: technology alone will rarely be sufficient. Whenever possible, participants should have the opportunity for face-to-face interactions. This is particularly critical in cases where they have not worked together before. Once socialization has taken place, trust has been established, then it is more effective to continue communicating, connecting and sharing tacit knowledge using ICTs.

Another important recommendation is that it is rare to find one single ICT that will be the "best," In most organizations, there will be multiple ICTs being used by employees. Some will be organizational tools and others personal tools (e.g. mobile telephones). However, this distinction has become quite blurred with the advent of social media. It is therefore the best practice to make use of multiple channels as they most users today do so already in a very seamless manner. Dalkir (2016) noted that:

Key attributes to take into account when choosing an ICT - or a combination of ICTs includes the purpose of the knowledge sharing interaction, how tacit the knowledge is, and the urgency involved. The approach to use is that of a portfolio of effective tools that can be used together (either at the same time or one after the other) in order to ensure that the message is conveyed not just in an intact fashion but in a way that it is understood as it was intended to by the other person (p. 51).

Finally, tried and true best practices should not be neglected. Users need to know how to use the ICTs and the ICTs need to be designed so that they are not only user-friendly but compatible with the cultural norms of knowledge sharing in the organization. The ultimate goal is to have social media ICTs fully integrated in all the social networks employees are part of in order to create and continuously increase the value of their social capital.

REFERENCES

Balubaid, M. A. (2013). Using Web 2.0 technology to enhance knowledge sharing in an academic department. *Procedia: Social and Behavioral Sciences*, *102*, 406–420. doi:10.1016/j.sbspro.2013.10.756

Boase, J., Horrigan, J. B., Wellman, B., & Rainie, L. (2006). The strength of internet ties. The Internet and email aid users in maintaining their social networks and provide pathways to help when people face big decisions. *PEW Internet and American Life Proejct Report Report Number 202-419-4500*. Available online at: http://www.pewinternet/org

Bolisani, E., & Scarso, E. (2000). Electronic communication and knowledge transfer. *International Journal of Technology Management*, *20*(1-2), 116–133. doi:10.1504/IJTM.2000.002855

Bullock, A. (2013). Does technology help doctors to access, use and share knowledge? *Medical Education*, *48*(1), 28–33. doi:10.1111/medu.12378 PMID:24330114

Choo, C., Detlor, B., & Turnbull, D. (2000). *Web work: information seeking and knowledge work on the World Wide Web*. Springer. doi:10.1007/978-94-015-9405-9

Chua, A. (2001). Relationship between the types of knowledge shared and types of communication channels used. *Journal of Knowledge Management Practice*. Retrieved from http://www.tlainc.com/articl26.htm

Daft, R., & Lengel, R. (1984). Information richness: A new approach to managerial behaviour and organizational design. *Research in Organizational Behavior, 6*, 191–233.

Dalkir, K. (2016). The Role of Stories and Simulations in the Lessons Learned Process. *International Journal of Organizational and Collective Intelligence, 6*(3), 21–32. doi:10.4018/IJOCI.2016070102

Dalkir, K. (2017in press). Complexity in online collaboration: the role of shared vision, trust and leadership style. Chapter. In K. Ditte (Ed.), *Online collaboration and communication in contemporary organizations*. Hershey, PA: IGI Global.

Dimensional Research. (2015). *Collaboration trends and technology. A survey of knowledge workers.* Retrieved June 5, 2017 from: https://www.alfresco.com/sites/www.alfresco.com/files/dimesional-research-collab-survey-findings-report-082415.pdf

Erden, Z., Von Krogh, G., & Nonaka, I. (2008). The quality of group tacit knowledge. *The Journal of Strategic Information Systems, 17*(1), 4–18. doi:10.1016/j.jsis.2008.02.002

Evans, M. M., Wensley, A. K. P., & Frissen, I. (2015). The mediating effects of trustworthiness on social-cognitive factors and knowledge sharing in a large professional service firm. *Electronic Journal of Knowledge Management, 13*(3), 240–254.

Faraj, S., Lakani, K., Monteiro, E., & von Krogh, G. (2016). Online Community as space for knowledge flows. *Information Systems Research, 27*(4), 668–684. doi:10.1287/isre.2016.0682

Field, J. (2004). *Social capital*. London, UK: Routledge.

Garcia-Perez, A., & Ayres, R. (2010). Wikifailure: The limitations of technology for knowledge sharing. *Electronic Journal of Knowledge Management, 8*(1), 43–52.

Granovetter, M. (1973). The strength of weak ties. *American Journal of Sociology, 78*(6), 1360–1380. doi:10.1086/225469

Griffith, T. L., Sawyer, J. E., & Neale, M. A. (2003). Virtualness and knowledge in teams: Managing the love triangle of organizations, individuals, and information technology. *Management Information Systems Quarterly, 27*(2), 265–287.

Hansen, S., & Avital, M. (2005). Share and share alike: The social and technological influences on knowledge sharing behavior. *Sprouts: Working Papers on Information Environments, Systems and Organizations, 5*(1), 1-19.

Herring, S. (1996). *Computer-mediated communication: Linguistic, social and cross-cultural perspectives*. Amsterdam: Benjamins. doi:10.1075/pbns.39

Hislop, D. (2002). Mission impossible? Communicating and sharing knowledge via information technology. *Journal of Information Technology, 17*(3), 165–177. doi:10.1080/02683960210161230

Holste, J. S., & Fields, D. (2010). Trust and tacit knowledge sharing and use. *Journal of Knowledge Management, 14*(1), 128–140. doi:10.1108/13673271011015615

Huysman, M., & Wulf, V. (2006). IT to support knowledge sharing in communities, towards a social capital analysis. *Journal of Information Technology, 21*(1), 40–51. doi:10.1057/palgrave.jit.2000053

Keyes, J. (2012). *Enterprise 2.0: social networking tools to transform your organization.* Boca Raton, FL: CRC Press. doi:10.1201/b12532

Kim, S., & Lee, H. (2006). The impact of organizational context and information technology on employee knowledge-sharing capabilities. *Public Administration Review, 66*(3), 370–385. doi:10.1111/j.1540-6210.2006.00595.x

Lee, C. S., Watson-Manheim, M., & Ramaprasad, A. (2009). Communication portfolios usage in the distributed work environments. *First Monday, 14*(8). doi:10.5210/fm.v14i8.2595

Lee Endres, M., Endres, S. P., Chowdhury, S. K., & Alam, I. (2007). Tacit knowledge sharing, self-efficacy theory, and application to the Open Source community. *Journal of Knowledge Management, 11*(3), 92–103. doi:10.1108/13673270710752135

Leonardi, P., Neeley, T., Hall, M., & Gerber, E. (2011). How managers use multiple media: Discrepant events, power, and timing in redundant communication. *Organization Science, 23*(1), 98–117. doi:10.1287/orsc.1110.0638

Luttrell, R. (2016). *Social media: How to engage, share, and connect.* Lanham, MD: Rowman & Littlefield.

Mergel, I. (2016). *The Social Intranet: Insights on Managing and Sharing Knowledge Internally.* IBM Center for the Business of Government Report. Retrieved June 1, 2017 from: http://www.businessof-government.org/report/social-intranet-insights-managing-and-sharing-knowledge-internally

Nonaka, I. (2008). *The knowledge-creating company.* Boston, MA: Harvard Business Review Press.

O'Reilly, T. (2009). *What is web 2.0.* Sebastopol, CA: O'Reilly Media, Inc.

Panahi, S., Watson, J., & Partridge, H. (2012). Social media and tacit knowledge sharing: Developing a conceptual model. *World Academy of Science, Engineering and Technology,* (64): 1095–1102.

Polanyi, M. (1966). *The tacit dimension.* Chicago, IL: University of Chicago press.

Pugh, K. (2011). *Sharing hidden know-how: How managers solve thorny problems with the knowledge jam.* New York, NY: John Wiley & Sons.

Rambe, P., & Mbeo, M. A. (2017). Technology-Enhanced Knowledge Management Framework for Retaining Research Knowledge among University Academics. *Technology, 9*(1), 189–206.

Riege, A. (2005). Three-dozen knowledge-sharing barriers managers must consider. *Journal of Knowledge Management, 9*(3), 18–35. doi:10.1108/13673270510602746

Roberts, J. (2000). From know-how to show-how? Questioning the role of information and communication technologies in knowledge transfer. *Technology Analysis and Strategic Management, 12*(4), 429–443. doi:10.1080/713698499

Schwemmer, R., & Havrilla, R. (2011). *Dynamic collaboration: How to share information, solve Problems, and increase productivity without compromising security.* Third Bridge Press.

Taylor, L. (2017). Experience, Knowledge Transfer and Entrepreneurial Learning. In *The Entrepreneurial Paradox* (pp. 109–134). Basingstoke, UK: Palgrave Macmillan. doi:10.1057/978-1-137-56949-3_5

Thurlow, C., Engel, L., & Tomic, A. (2004). *Computer-mediated communication: Social interaction and the Internet.* London, UK: Sage Publications.

Van Den Hooff, B., & De Ridder, J. A. (2004). Knowledge sharing in context: The influence of organizational commitment, communication climate and CMC use on knowledge sharing. *Journal of Knowledge Management, 8*(6), 117–130. doi:10.1108/13673270410567675

Vickery, S., Droge, C., Stank, T., Goldsby, T., & Markland, R. (2004). The performance implications of media richness in a business-to-business service environment: Direct and indirect effects. *Management Science, 50*(8), 1106–1119. doi:10.1287/mnsc.1040.0248

Wells, H. G. (1938). *World Brain.* Garden City, NY: Doubleday, Doran & Co., Inc.

Wiesz, J. D., Erickson, T., & Kellog, W. A. (2006). Synchronous broadcast messaging: the use of ICT. In Proceedings, Computer-Mediated Communication, CHI2006. Montreal, Canada: ACM. doi:10.1145/1124772.1124967

Young, R. (Ed.). (2010). Knowledge management tools and techniques manual. Tokyo, Japan: APO (Asian Productivity Centre).

KEY TERMS AND DEFINITIONS

Collaboration: Working with one or more colleagues to solve a problem or accomplish a common task. Collaboration involves more than dividing up the parts but really working together in a synergistic fashion.

Explicit Knowledge: Knowledge that exists in a physical form. For example, a document, a slide deck, an audio recording, an image, or a video.

Knowledge Sharing: The communication of either explicit or tacit knowledge to someone else (or to a group of others) in such a way that the recipients not only understand the content but they are able to make use of it (e.g., to solve a problem or make a decision).

Media Richness: The ability of a given channel to accommodate more than just text (e.g., also images, videos, sound).

Reciprocity: The act of returning a "favor." Within the context of knowledge sharing, individuals are much more likely to share their knowledge with people who have already shared theirs with them.

Social Capital: The value that is produced through the social connections that are created. An example is the value of knowing who to ask for help, to answer a question or solve a problem in a specific area as compared to the value of knowing the answer.

Social Presence: The extent to which someone feels like they are interacting with another human being as opposed to using a technological tool. The degree to which a technology "disappears" during connection.

Tacit Knowledge: Knowledge that exists only in the mind(s) of people and that has not been documented in any physical way.

Traceability: When an interaction leaves behind a record of what was communicated. A trace persists over time and can be consulted again in the future. An example would be a recording or minutes of meeting.

Virtual Team/Meeting: When a group's members are not physically co-located in the same geographical location.

Chapter 10

Attracting the Right Employees?
The Effects of Social Media as an Innovative E–Entrepreneurship Recruitment Method for Enterprises

Anthony Lewis
University of South Wales, UK

Brychan Celfyn Thomas
University of South Wales, UK

Gwenllian Marged Sanders
University of South Wales, UK

ABSTRACT

This chapter investigates effects and issues associated with social media and recruitment and whether it is effective as an innovative e-entrepreneurship method of attracting the right employees for enterprises from a multi stakeholder perspective. Human resources management professionals have been using different methods of social media in their recruitment strategies with varying degrees of success. By examining social media and its effect, this can support the development of a more effective human resources recruitment strategy. Additionally, increased communication channels might enable the development of a more positive internal enterprise culture. The study was conducted using both primary and secondary data. Professionals, recruiters, and employees have been questioned on their views of Social Media from a personal and a professional perspective through a variety of methods including focus groups and questionnaires. This chapter provides a framework that can be used by enterprises in order to create their own social media recruitment cycle.

INTRODUCTION

This chapter is a further investigation, to previous studies of e-recruitment (Lewis et al, 2010; Lewis et al, 2013), with an aim to critically explore whether social media and online recruitment are effective innovative e-entrepreneurship methods in attracting appropriate employees for enterprises.

DOI: 10.4018/978-1-5225-5014-3.ch010

An innovative e-entrepreneurship method is an effective new method used by enterprises involving electronic processes. Further dimensions, not covered in this study, are recruiting for new ventures and new ventures for recruiting, which are interesting avenues for future research. Social media enables enterprises to provide a dedicated service (vehicle) to attract appropriate employees to augment their talent management strategy (Eduardo, 2006). Social media is used by many enterprises and individuals in order to market their corporate brands and can give the enterprise a new identity to compete in a competitive market (Doherty, 2010). Social Media can be an excellent starting point for recruitment as "key metrics" such as cost and time to hire are measurable and it is possible to substantiate improvement (Doherty, 2010). Social Media allows individuals to create their online profile and have a network of friends and colleagues (Henderson and Bowley 2010). Individuals can then upload pictures and personal details enabling users to create an online profile and a visible, virtual network of their friends (Henderson and Bowley 2010).

Online recruitment has dramatically grown since the mid 1990's when the economic climate resulted in a considerable demand for employees with a strong academic background and relevant experience (Lee, 2005:175). Recruitment methods have consequently changed in enterprises, and by individuals when looking for their next opportunity, and also looking at the ways in which individuals are applying for roles. Online recruitment has consistently shown itself to be one of the most substantial shifts in recruitment practice in the last ten years (Lee, 2005:175).

The literature review in this chapter details previous research and media coverage regarding social media and online recruitment. Much of the research is focused on the importance of having a clear social media strategy and how the subsequent changes implemented by these enterprises might impact on individuals who use these sites. Although existing research indicates that recruitment websites are used, it does not fully cover industry specific recruitment agencies. This chapter considers Social Media and online recruitment from the perspective of Employers, Recruitment Agencies and Individuals in an attempt to ascertain the relevance to enterprises and individuals.

This research will carefully consider social media in recruitment and how it can be used by enterprises. Several areas such as intellectual property law, good Human Resources practice and how practical these methods are in recruitment are explored further in the Literature review, and discussed throughout the chapter. Social Media is a relatively new area of interest and yet something which adapts very quickly and could be instrumental in selecting and retaining the best possible people for the enterprise.

With almost two billion internet users Worldwide in 2010, up from approximately 360 million at the end of 2000, there has been dramatic growth in internet usage over the last decade (www.internetworld-stats.com). A growing number of enterprises are using Social Media in order to communicate with their staff and customers. Some social media tools may be viewed as being more suited to different individuals; however the number of users grows rapidly over time.

Mobile internet usage has also had a huge impact on the way the tools are used. Twitter, (a social networking and micro-blogging service) asks "what are you doing?" (www.twitter.com). This type of service is used as a way of instantly letting people know exactly what is happening to an individual at any given time, it can also be an excellent way for enterprises to communicate with their customers who may be reading tweets on the train on their way to work.

The sociological impact of social media is likely to be extensive, it is changing the way individuals view others as there is simply a huge amount of information available at the click of a mouse. Facebook (www.facebook.com) holds a huge amount of information about individuals and this may be viewed by hundreds, or thousands of people who are "friends" with the user. This could have implications on privacy, and the law has had to adapt to deal with the rise in internet crime.

Twitter (www.twitter.com a) and Facebook (www.facebook.com) have proved to be a time efficient and cost effective way in which information can be shared amongst a large number of people. Facebook was used at one college in the United States when snow prevented students travelling to University (www.washingtonpost.com) – the lecturer posted the topic and the students worked together to complete the lesson. With the advent of websites such as Wikileaks (http://www.guardian.co.uk/media/wikileaks) information about enterprises is freely available to many people and so enterprises must decide how transparent they wish to be and whether they would like to control any public relations situations which may arise from the information being leaked in an untimely manner. Confidential documents may be stored on hard drives or using cloud computing (a network of remote servers hosted on the Internet to store, manage, and process data, rather than a local server or personal computer), and more people are now able to work remotely, which means that Social Media is also useful for networking throughout enterprises. Members of staff in a specific function may be able to speak to colleagues in different locations about how they dealt with a situation well, and to share their expertise.

Some enterprises even have "Facebook Fridays" (Gittlen, 2008) where employees are given the opportunity to update their profiles and to share their experiences. An excellent example of using Facebook is with Graduate Recruitment for Klijnveld Peat Marwick Gordeler (KPMG), (www.facebook.com c) where employees who have been recruited to the programmes share their experiences and talk through the methods for potential new recruits.

The goals of this chapter are to critically explore the effects of Social Media as an innovative e-entrepreneurship method of recruitment; whether it is an effective method of attracting appropriate employees for an enterprise, and what the associated problems may be in using this method of recruitment. With regard to this the following research questions have been formulated and are investigated:

- What are the advantages and disadvantage of Social Media (SM) from the perspectives of Human Resources (HR) professionals, recruitment professionals, and potential job seekers?
- What factors are likely to drive/reduce the effectiveness of recruitment via SM?
- What are the legal considerations associated with recruitment via SM?

LITERATURE REVIEW

The following sections of the literature review are organized beginning with an overview of social media, broad limitations of using social media, social media and enterprises, impact of social media on enterprises and finally company's and employee's search strategies.

Overview of Social Media

Due to there being a range of social media services there are some major challenges of definition. There are, however, some common features for social media and these include Web 2.0 internet based applications, user generated content, user created services with specific profiles for web sites or apps, and the facilitation of the development of online social networks (Obar and Wildman, 2015; Kaplan and Haenlein, 2010; Boyd and Ellison, 2007). In fact, social media enables communication between individuals, communities, organisations, businesses and enterprises (Kietzmann and Hermkens, 2011).

A survey reported that in America eighty four per cent of young people had a Facebook account (O'Keefe, 2011), with over sixty per cent having at least one social media profile with many on social networking sites for more than 2 hours a day (Hajirnis, 2015). Moreover, the time spent on social media sites in the United States increased from 66 billion minutes in July 2011 to 121 billion minutes in July 2012 (Social Media Report, 2012). Benefits such as monetary income, career opportunities and social sharing arise from participating in social media (Tang, Gu and Whinston, 2012). Differences between paper based media/traditional electronic media and social media include permanence, immediacy, usability, frequency and quality (Agichtein et al., 2008). The way of operation for social media is through many sources to many receivers which is a dialogic transmission system (Pavlik and MacIntoch, 2015). In particular, social media is an effective marketing and communication tool for businesses and enterprises.

A recent definition of social media is "forms of electronic communication (such as web sites) through which people create online communities to share information, ideas, personal messages, etc." (Merriam-Webster, 2016). Social networking sites include Facebook (online social networking site), Twitter (internet service enabling the posting of "tweets") and LinkedIn (networking web site for the business community) (Christensson, 2013). Many forms of social media technologies are apparent which include social networks, forums, enterprise social networks, business networks and blogs (Aichner and Jacob, 2015).

Table 1 lists the leading social networks based on active user accounts in April 2017 (Statista, 2017).

Table 1. Leading social networks based on active user accounts

No	Social network	Users
1	Facebook	1,968,000,000
2	WhatsApp	1,200,000,000
3	YouTube	1,000,000,000
4	Facebook Messenger	1,000,000,000
5	WeChat	889,000,000
6	QQ	868,000,000
7	Instagram	600,000,000
8	QZone	595,000,000
9	Tumblr	550,000,000
10	Twitter	319,000,000
11	Sina Weibo	313,000,000
12	Baidu Tieba	300,000,000
13	Snapchat	300,000,000
14	Skype	300,000,000
15	Viber	260,000,000
16	Line	220,000,000
17	Pinterest	150,000,000

Source: Statista (2012)

Mulgan et al (2007:4) state that the "results of Social Innovation – new ideas that meet unmet needs are all around us." The Young Foundation, which has developed and promoted ideas from the Open University to Which? and Wikipedia (Mulgan et al., 2007) has become a leader in the idea of Social Innovation, and has an infrastructure in place to help innovators develop existing ideas. "New methods for advancing social innovation are relevant in every sector, but are likely to offer most... in fields where new possibilities (such as mobile technologies and open source methods) are not being adequately exploited" (Mulgan et al., 2007). Since April 2007, active users of Facebook have multiplied more than 25 times, from 20 million, to 500 million in 2010 (www.facebook.com a), with 12 million users of LinkedIn in July 2007 (Sundar, 2007) to their present 100 million. These are examples of Social innovation in technology, fulfilling a need by consistently developing their software to meet the needs of the users (www.facebook.com a).

Social media is helping shape news stories, where content may be very limited, such as in Iran during the unrest in 2009, where news networks were not allowed to comment on what was happening, people were able to use mobile telephones to use social media platforms, for example Twitter in order to communicate events to the outside World (Addley, 2009).

In terms of the scope of social media services that provide a medium for recruitment there are many different Web sites that provide such services. These involve four different types of social media including blogs and microblogs (Twitter), content communities (YouTube), social networking sites (Facebook, MySpace), and professional networks (LinkedIn). Since these four types of social media are the most appropriate for recruitment the most common forms of these have been investigated.

Facebook

Facebook allows people to bring together their ideas and thoughts before expressing them (Moody, 2010). Users registered on Facebook vary by five percent between household income brackets, nine percent between rural, suburban and urban users, and thirteen percent according to different levels of education (PRC, 2012). There is also a large gap between age brackets with only thirty five percent of sixty and above year old users compared to eighty six percent of eighteen to twenty nine year olds as registered users (PRC, 2012).

Globally, there are more than 500 million individuals who check their Facebook account on at least a monthly basis; of these 250 million access Facebook on any given day (www.facebook.com). The average user has 130 "friends" – these could be colleagues or friends, and Facebook users spend 700 billion minutes a month on Facebook. Facebook is used by companies as a way of integrating information from their website to a profile or fan page.

It may be possible to encourage high level of communication with staff members, Human Resources and IT Departments and Internal communications (Ingham, 2010). As the information is available in the public domain, it is very important that there is a straightforward social media policy for employees to ensure that the brand has a certain level of protection as AXA UK (Ingham 2010). Facebook is commonly used in recruiting for graduate level and entry level employees (Adams, b 2009).

Twitter

Communication building and critical thinking can be enhanced by Twitter (Domizi, 2013). Twitter contributes to social media in many ways and enables people to be connected with their peers and to keep up-to-date with social events (Ghosh, 2011). Posts that are popular will be tweeted many times and become viral (Ghosh, 2011). Users of Twitter will be notified of events, posts and trends through retweeting (Yang, 2010).

Twitter was launched on 14th March 2006, today there are an estimated 195 million users (Rushe, 2010) with 20 million of these users accessing their accounts on a regular basis. Twitter users "tweet" 140 million times a day (Smith, 2011). A tweet is 140 characters long, so information can be posted, including links to other sites to include "additional information, deeper context and embedded media" (www.twitter.com). Enterprises may use Twitter in order to communicate with their followers to share information about new products or services and to build relationships with these individuals (www. twitter.com). Twitter estimate that 460,000 new users are setting up Twitter accounts every day (www. twitter.com), though Schofield (2009) cites a Nielsen Survey which showed that only 40% of new Twitter users will remain active users.

LinkedIn

LinkedIn links together professionals to help them become more successful and productive (LinkdIn, 2015a). Users maintain information and content in a career focused and professional way (MLM, 2015). The fastest growing membership on the site are recent college graduates and students with over thirty nine million (LinkedIn, 2015b) who are encouraged to develop their profiles for credibility through professionals sharing knowledge and connecting with them (eLI, 2015).

LinkedIn is viewed by many as the Professional Social Media site. On 22nd March 2011, LinkedIn reported that they had reached 100 million users Worldwide, with 44% of these being based in the US (www.linkedin.com). LinkedIn has information available to users including CV and contact details.

In order to make contacts on LinkedIn, a user must send an invitation to the person they wish to Link to. There are several suggestions of people that an individual may know, colleagues from former enterprises, or people that are in the same industry, or friends of friends. LinkedIn warn against adding people that an individual does not know, as this person would be able to get in contact with an individual's contacts (www.linkedin.com c).

"Almost all banks are at least dipping their toes in the water by posting ads on....LinkedIn...Generally preferred over Facebook as a Recruitment tool" (Adams, b 2009:23). Adams (a 2009) cites Union Bank's recruiting efforts for a new Senior Manager; the potential employee contacted the bank directly, speeding up the recruitment process, and saving Union Bank a recruitment fee. Union Bank now conduct approximately 20% of their recruitment efforts online.

YouTube

YouTube is the second most visited web site in the World (Moran et al., 2012). It has been claimed that YouTube increases productivity, customisation, personalisation and participation (Sherer and Shea, 2011). It also provides opportunities for improving digital skills.

Created in 2005, YouTube had 490 million active users as of February 2011 (Elliot, 2011). YouTube is a Social Networking site where users can upload videos and share them with other users globally (www.youtube.com). It is possible to share links to the site from Facebook and embed links on Twitter and LinkedIn (www.youtube.com a). Some enterprises use YouTube in order to post links of their employees, explaining certain aspects of the enterprise, and recruitment process.

Broad Limitations in Using Social Media

The negative effects of social media include Internet fraud, information overload and privacy issues (Lundblad, 2017; Postman, 2017). Negative social effects have been shown by studies to have an effect on the self esteem of people and it is found that individuals with a low social comparison orientation appear to use social media less than those with a higher social comparison orientation (Vogel et al., 2015). Further to these negative effects broad limitations in using social media include legal implications and the impact of social media on individuals, which are described below.

Legal Implications

It is suggested (Everett, 2010) that employers who wish their employees to use Social Media must guide the employees regarding what is expected from them, and outlining usage policies, as well as ensuring that there is someone within the enterprise who takes responsibility for the policy, monitoring and updating the information as necessary.

In some enterprises, such as FSAugusta, the company has separate "corporate identities" for its' staff members on Twitter and Facebook, where content is monitored and specifically uploaded to ensure that the information is in keeping with the "Brand" by employees (www.facebook.com e).

Impact of Social Media on Individuals

Cober et al. (2000) suggest that the individuals who are most likely to benefit from online applications are those individuals who already have jobs, but are interested to see which other opportunities may be available to them. Using Social Media may allow the individual to search for enterprises related to their industry, e.g. Accountancy, and search for information using Social Media, which can then be targeted at specific groups, such as with KPMG's general page (www.facebook.com g, www.twitter.com b) and the graduate recruitment page (www.facebook.com h). It is also possible to have separate pages for specific geographic areas (www.twitter.com c), and alumni pages in order to keep in contact with ex employees (www.facebook.com i).

Most of the Social Media recruitment pages have links to the large amount of content available about corporate enterprises through the websites. There is a far greater amount than could previously be communicated through traditional methods, such as print advertisements, journals, and corporate literature, such as brochures (Cober et al., 2000; Cober et al., 2004). McKeown (2003) also explains that additional paperwork, such as application forms may also be available online.

Smith (1999, cited in McKeown 2003:23) suggests that one of the best features of using online recruitment is that an individual is able to ascertain what the work is, what skills they need to do it, salary expectations, and location before applying for the role. Hoffman et al. (1995) and Lee (2005) remind us that this information is available 24 hours a day. Cober et al. (2000) adds that the relevant information relating to the role can be found (at least in theory) speedily and easily using online recruitment methods.

Cober et al. (2000) warns there is a correlation between the image the applicant has of the enterprise, and the likelihood of that individual applying for a role within the enterprise. An enterprise's e-recruitment section of their website will give potential employees the opportunity to gather information about the enterprise, including its "mission, diversity, benefits, career development and corporate culture" so that individuals are better prepared to make decisions about any potential career with the enterprise (Lee,

2005). There had been complaints about enterprises failing to "sell themselves" and as such, giving the candidate little incentive to, or desire to, work within the enterprise (Hilpern, 2001). Rebecca Baker, head of recruitment at network 3 said that the company redesigned its recruitment website to make it simpler in order to give candidates a good experience which will reflect well on the company (Chubb, 2008). A personalised service also offers consumers a positive experience when using a recruitment website; it makes it easier for consumers to find job opportunities (Marketing Week, 2006).

Cober et al. (2000:493) propose that additional information will allow candidates to make an informed decision as to how well they will fit within an enterprise. However, candidates must be aware that it is possible that the enterprises will "project only what they desire others to see" (Miller and Arnold, 2000:337).

An article in Personnel Today (2004) suggests that individuals who use e-recruitment are also more confident that their application will meet equality expectations as it is the applicant's skills and experience that will be looked at by potential employers, not their ethnicity. The number of people who are online grows daily; therefore data about internet users is quickly out of date. The majority of internet users are "white, well-educated and affluent" (Odell et al, 2000:855). Smethurst (2004:38) suggests that the group of people who are most unlikely to have access to the internet are "young black men". This could mean that applicants with suitable skills and qualifications may not have the opportunity to hear about, or the means to apply for positions. This is clearly a loss for both employers and potential applicants.

Czerny (2004) reported that female applicants were not applying for as many graduate positions online, due to the nature of the application and the feelings of the individual that the entire recruitment process is being "dehumanised". Smethurst (2004) reports findings by the Disability Rights Commission that 80% of e-recruitment websites may be inaccessible to people with disabilities such as vision impairment or dyslexia, although changes can be made to these sites to minimize this type of discrimination. The Chartered Institute of Personnel and Development (CIPD) e-recruitment factsheet (2009) indicated that using e-recruitment made the process more flexible and easier for candidates to use successfully.

Social Media and Enterprises

Berry (2005:43) cites the CIPD report showing that the job pages of an enterprise make it the "fourth most popular recruitment method" (Goldberg and Allen, 2008) and suggests that websites differ from other recruitment methods; they are a more vivid and varied method of communicating, and it is here that social media allows enterprises to interact with potential candidates. In order for any enterprise to use social media and online recruitment to its best advantage, Human Resources professions must include it as part of their recruitment strategy (King, 2004).

Accountancy giant KPMG were the leaders in moving recruitment online, this was perceived as a somewhat risky move in that candidates may not have been secure in their applications for the roles (Personnel Today, 2008:8). Using social media, and online recruitment, the time taken to recruit new employees has fallen, it is a fast way to attract a huge number of candidates globally, as long as they are able to access the technology (Taylor, 2001; Hall, 2004; Lee, 2005; Crail, 2007; Smethurst, 2004; People Management, 2008). Tulip (2003) states that 44% of internet users have searched online for jobs and 28% of the working population expect to find their next role online. Generation Y candidates can juggle more than one task at a time, and are more flexible than previous generations, they are eager to move to a new role, or even a new country with very little notice (The Economist 2009). Cober et al.

(2000) suggest that enterprises should design the recruitment pages on the website so that the needs of the enterprise are explicitly met.

Lee (2005) and Taylor (2001) suggest benefits of using online recruitment include increased efficiency and convenience for both potential employees and enterprises, however, where the systems are not designed correctly, it can create increased difficulties for the enterprise in communicating with potential employees. Berry (2005) suggests that a significant problem could be the high number of candidates applying for positions through online recruitment websites, who may not have the qualifications and skills required for the position for which they are applying (HR Focus Hiring survey, 2004:S2). Sorting inappropriate, irrelevant applicants could result in increased administration costs, outweighing any potential savings in reduction of recruiting cost (Manufacturers' Monthly, 2004).

Harvey Sinclair (Tulip, 2003) argues that employers have been slower to adapt to online recruitment, where potential employees have been looking for an online presence for a longer period of time. Mannion (2008) also warns that the process of filtering the applications is challenging as people may seem highly qualified but may often lack the necessary practical experience. An enterprise with recruitment pages which are unable to discern appropriate candidates of the right calibre in a resourceful and time efficient manner may struggle to survive in the current economic climate (Long, 2009).

The HR Focus 2004 Survey (S2) suggests that using online recruitment is only successful where an "industry specific website is used". Subsequently Spence (2009) has suggested a 7 step process to successfully filter applications: Develop clear job descriptions, use targeted advertising, consider the application method, consider automated selection, profile the candidate as well as the role, ensure interviewers know what they are looking for and monitor the process carefully. In using social media for recruitment, employers may have the opportunity to "fine tune" their applications appropriately to ensure that recruiting for the enterprise remains manageable.

Impact of Social Media on Enterprises

Pitcher (2008) reported that many high street retailers were not focusing on the recruitment areas of their websites. In certain cases, stores received applications from only 2% of the individuals who had visited the website in order to apply online. Reasons for this could be the time taken to investigate the availability of applying for appropriate positions and the time incurred in filling out the form itself.

Cober et al. (2000: 481) state that "through a corporate Web page, information can be presented that highlights unique aspects of the corporate culture that may attract individuals whom would fit especially/particularly well within the enterprise".

Enterprises such as Signet have included screening methods throughout their recruitment process, so that candidates who do not fit the "corporate culture" of the enterprise are eliminated through use of a questionnaire (Weekes, 2004). In 2008, River Island restricted applications for temporary Christmas positions so that the process had to be completed online. Although 100,000 people applied for roles, 46,000 failed to complete the applications, effectively screening themselves out (People Management, 2008).

Cober et al. (2000: 481) suggest that it is the enterprises' recruitment pages which provide the first impression to potential employees. Enterprises have the opportunity to strengthen their corporate identity (Hall, 2004:21; Smethurst, 2004:38). And by using Social Media as a tool to assist in this, they may well be successful.

Enterprises ought to be aware of how the information available on the website may influence a potential employees' perspective of them (Wilmott, 2003). Curry (2000) suggests that although negative information about an enterprise may also be available online, it is not necessarily damaging, as it could serve to shape an individual's perception of the enterprise. Problems will occur where information could be construed as out of date. It will give a negative impression to how potential applicants may view the webpage. Cober et al. (2000) advise that the attitude of the individual towards the recruitment site will influence the intention of the individual to apply for a position.

The current generation of University graduates appear to use the internet more extensively and effectively than ever before (Curry, 2000) for all aspects of their day to day lives from social networking to shopping, and they expect speedy response times (Weekes, 2004). In their online graduate programme, KPMG ensure that they respond to applications with feedback within 24 hours. They (KPMG) feel that they are able to do this through using available technology to the best of its capabilities (Personnel Today, 2008:1).

KPMG have attempted to minimize difficulties in recruiting within its Graduate Programme by using Social Media sites used frequently by their target market (Personnel Today, 2008). Minton-Eversole (2007a) and Schramm (2007) argue that enterprises can use Social Media sites to uncover information about candidates that would not be available on the application form. Indeed, Peacock (2009) warns that 12% of enterprises in the United Kingdom (UK) are looking at a potential candidate's social networking profile before making the decision to interview them.

Company's and Employee's Search Strategies

Human Resources personnel and recruiters are under pressure to attract suitably qualified applicants when there are lower levels of unemployment which means that the enterprise's recruitment search strategies must be innovative in order to retain sustainable competitive advantage (Cober et al., 2000; Lee, 2005).

Cober et al. (2000:484) suggest three stages that need to be considered when a company is designing a recruitment search strategy. Initially, they must have the ability to attract potential candidates to the website, then they must successfully engage with the candidates in order to pass on the information posted on the site. Finally, the enterprise needs to ensure that the candidate actually applies for the position from the web site. Figure 1 shows these steps clearly illustrating each component.

Figure 1. Conceptual model of the online recruitment cycle
Source: Cober et al. (2000)

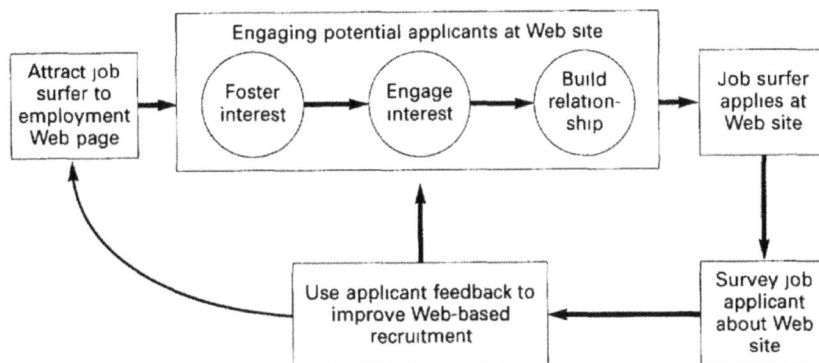

The CIPD e-recruitment factsheet (2009:5) states that there are "no fundamental philosophical differences" between using traditional methods, such as print media and using e-recruitment. It suggests a mix of old and new media to meet their target applicants in the most efficient manner.

The literature suggests that problems with social media and online recruitment stem from poor information that is not kept up to date, and where there is no clear social media strategy implemented throughout the enterprise. Online recruitment has been used to effectively select candidates based on selection criteria, and potential candidates will have an idea of what the corporate culture of an enterprise is before they apply, so that effectively, the potential candidate can select whether or not they feel they would fit in with the enterprise or not. It is also more possible than ever to access wide amounts of information, including using a Smartphone to keep totally up to date with new roles so that individuals can be first in line to apply for their desired role within the enterprise.

METHODOLOGY

This research has elements of both positivist and interpretivist research methods. A theoretical framework has been used for the questionnaires and the majority of the remainder of the study has a more emergent approach to the way the information has been gathered.

The primary data was collected exclusively for this piece of research (Zikmund, 2003) by the researchers from an "original source" (Collis and Hussey, 2009:73). This type of research may be useful in that new "insights" may come to light, and that the researchers may feel more confident in the validity of the data gathered (Easterby-Smith et al, 2008:11).

Primary data may take the form of "questionnaire survey, interviews or focus groups" (Collis and Hussey, 2009:73). In this research, all three data collection methods were used in order to look at information from different perspectives. This is where more than one method of research is used in order to examine the same phenomenon (Collis and Hussey, 2009). Bryman and Bell (2007) describe this type of investigatory research as methodological triangulation, the implication being that the results from each type of investigation will be cross checked. These techniques can be used in order to provide rich data and provide the opportunity to recognize anomalies in data analysis. Webb et al. (1998) conceptualised this concept as a way of developing how information was collated and reviewed, which would mean that there would be a greater level of confidence in the findings (Bryman and Bell, 2007). With regard to this triangulation is a way of "cross-checking findings derived from both qualitative and quantitative research" (Bryman and Bell, 2007:413). Triangulation was a key concept for this research and the initial personal interviews were what the questionnaires were based on, and from that subsequent focus groups and follow up personal interviews. The research tools were both qualitative and quantitative.

The research was therefore conducted through (i) an employees/prospective employees' questionnaire survey, (ii) an employers' questionnaire survey, (iii) a focus group and (iv) personal interviews.

1. The employees/prospective employees' questionnaire survey had a sample size of 100 and the respondents were mainly from the Channel Islands and the UK, focusing more on the British employment market. The questionnaires were conducted using the online survey website www. surveymonkey.com. Using this method, the researchers were able to conduct the survey in a timely manner, using Facebook, Twitter, LinkedIn and e-mail to ask people to complete the survey online. It took less than 72 hours for the 100 responses to be received. The research population was made

up of contacts of the researchers; this was limited to around 1,000 contacts giving a 10% response rate (Bryman and Bell, 2007). Respondents were represented from a variety of sectors including students, unemployed, banking/finance, IT, healthcare, beauty/fitness, factory, call centre, agriculture, tradesperson, hospitality and other sectors. Major questions asked concerned age, location, industry, gender, how often social media was used, would social media be used when looking for their next job, their online presence, how social media is accessed, and whether they would use social media to help get an introduction to an employer.

2. The employers' questionnaire survey had a sample size of 25 and again the respondents were mainly from the Channel Islands and the UK. Employers were represented from banking/finance, trades people, hospitality, and other sectors. Major questions asked concerned location, industry, whether they would use social media when advertising their upcoming vacancies, their online presence, how social media is accessed, and whether they thought social media was effective when looking for potential employees.

3. The size of the focus group was 22 participants who were all Human Resources professionals working in Guernsey. They were selected through an invitation to attend the focus group and were representative of HR professionals working in the various sectors. This method was used in order to find out the key methods that HR practitioners would use in order to find suitable employees. Major questions asked in the focus group concerned how social media could be used in their organizations, understanding of terminology, how to use groups, how to add contacts, technological understanding and timing issues. The interviewees for the focus groups were members of the researchers' CIPD group and the results were filmed so that notes could be made.

4. The personal interviews were undertaken with the selection of 2 recruitment agents who agreed to be interviewed following contact by the researchers, and were representative of recruitment agents in Guernsey. The personal interviews were carried out initially in person, and later over the telephone. The major questions asked concerned users of recruitment websites, what practices were in place, competition from other recruitment agencies on the island of Guernsey, whether the agency was affected by increasing numbers of organizations having more advanced Social Media and online recruitment sites, the impact of the global economic downturn on the organization and how the offshore economy had been affected by such measures. For the purpose of the initial interview the researchers felt that it would be appropriate for this type of interview not to have a prescribed structure and to see which subjects were emergent from the subsequent conversation.

This research project used cross-sectional methodologies due to financial resources and time constraints (Bryman and Bell, 2007). Furthermore, the research objectives meant that existing perceptions of individual's opinions of Social Media were explored. Therefore, obtaining and analysing information over a short cross-sectional period of time is crucial in enhancing the contextual validity of results (Saunders et al., 2007). Nevertheless, cross-sectional studies are associated with static positivistic epistemological considerations. Furthermore, the complexities in research which are associated with cross-sectional time horizons involve selecting "a large enough sample to be representative of the total population" (Collis and Hussey, 2009:346).

FINDINGS, ANALYSIS AND DISCUSSION

Employee/Prospective Employee and Employer Questionnaires

The key research findings for i) the employee/prospective employee questionnaire survey and ii) the employer questionnaire survey are presented at iii) the aggregate level with statistical information involving percentages.

1. The 100 respondents to the employee/prospective employee questionnaire survey, was limited by using the free version of survey monkey. There were a further 28 respondents in the time that the survey remained open, but these had to be disregarded as they were inaccessible. Of the collected responses, 64% were female and 34% male with the remaining 2% not wishing to answer. Although the responses were predominately from women, it is useful to see female perceptions.

    There were more respondents under forty than of any other age group, particularly those aged 25-35. This may be related to the fact that the respondents were all acquaintances of the researchers. It may also be related to theory that it is predominately "Generation Y", where the request to complete questionnaires was sent. "Generation Y" is more likely to be on social networking sites with 89% of that generation having an online presence, rather than the "baby boomers" which only 72% have an online presence (Heller-Baird and Parasnis, 2011),

    Almost half of the respondents were from Guernsey, with the remainder being mainly resident in the UK. The employment status of respondents was varied, with 75% of the respondents being employed, 6% being unemployed, and a further 4% being homemakers. Some 15% of the respondents were students. The researchers had thought it likely that most of the respondents would use social media, as the majority of requests to fill out the questionnaire were sent using Facebook and Twitter, this was confirmed with 96% of the respondents using Facebook (the most used social media platform by the respondents.

    Collis and Hussey (2009:194) describe "two major problems in using questionnaires...*Questionnaire fatigue*" where individuals are reluctant to respond to questionnaires as they are "inundated with requests by post, e-mail, telephone and in the street" (Collis and Hussey, 2009:145) and *"non response bias"* where not all of the questionnaires are returned, which could have an impact on validity and reliability of findings (Collis and Hussey, 2009:145).

    The responses to this questionnaire were also affected by "non response" (Collis and Hussey, 2009:204) as certain aspects of questions were left unanswered. This could be related to the design of the questionnaire, as some respondents early on in the questionnaire stated that they did not use certain social media platforms and so could not have responded to further questions about the platforms along the survey.

2. The employer questionnaire survey again involved using the free version of survey monkey which was undertaken at about the same time as the employee/prospective employee questionnaire survey. None of the respondents from the employer's survey said that their decision regarding employing an individual would be affected by pictures of an employee or potential employee drinking. The important factor (Lauby 2010) is what a candidate is capable of, "their ability to perform the ap-

propriate tasks in relation to the position". Employers need to look at postings to determine how they wish to proceed with applications. The respondents from the employer's survey concur, by stating that the things that would most likely affect their opinion of a candidate to be photographs of the potential employee being perceived as unsocial.

There is a great deal of variation in the number of people who use Social Media and how they use it, with Twitter and LinkedIn being less used than Facebook, and even less using MySpace and YouTube, amongst the participants in the questionnaire surveys. This has an impact on the results gathered, as those platforms will tend not to be considered as first choice methods of looking for work.

3.   The results of the questionnaire surveys for employees/potential employees, as to whether they used social media when looking for their next job, and employers when advertising upcoming vacancies, are shown in Tables 2 and 3.

Table 2. Employees/Potential Employees - Would you use Social Media when looking for your next job?

Would You Use Social Media when looking for your next job?	%
	Facebook
My friend's post	22
A recruitment Agency post	17
A promoted advert from an employer	11
An organisation looking directly	5
None	12
I would not use this platform	25
No reply	8
	Twitter
My friend's post	6
A recruitment Agency post	2
A promoted advert from an employer	3
An organisation looking directly	7
None	8
I would not use this platform	54
No reply	20
	Linked in
My friend's post	2
A recruitment Agency post	9

continued in next column

Table 2. Continued

Would You Use Social Media when looking for your next job?	%
A promoted advert from an employer	5
An organisation looking directly	5
None	9
I would not use this platform	52
No reply	18
	My Space
My friend's post	0
A recruitment Agency post	2
A promoted advert from an employer	0
An organisation looking directly	3
None	13
I would not use this platform	62
No reply	20
	You Tube
My friend's post	2
A recruitment Agency post	0
A promoted advert from an employer	2
An organisation looking directly	2
None	10
I would not use this platform	64
No reply	20

n= 100

Table 3. Employers - Would you use Social Media when advertising your upcoming vacancies?

Would You Use Social Media when advertising your upcoming vacancies?	%
	Facebook
Yes	56
No	20
I would not use this platform	20
No reply	4
	Twitter
Yes	28
No	20
I would not use this platform	40
No reply	12
	LinkedIn
Yes	28
No	32
I would not use this platform	28
No reply	12
	MySpace
Yes	4
No	36
I would not use this platform	48
No reply	12
	YouTube
Yes	8
No	32
I would not use this platform	48
No reply	12

n=25

The results in Table 2 show that 55% of employees/potential employees would use Facebook, 18% Twitter, 21% LinkedIn, 5% MySpace and 6% You Tube, when looking for their next job. The results show that Facebook is the platform that the highest percentage of participants would choose in order to look for work, but the results are indicative that using Social Media is not one of the main ways that respondents would choose to look for work.

Table 3 shows that 56% of employers would use Facebook, 28% Twitter, 28% LinkedIn, 4% My Space and 8% You Tube, to advertise upcoming vacancies. The results therefore show that employers appear to be more likely to advertise roles on Social Media, particularly on Facebook.

Focus Group

The key research findings from the focus groups included i) issues relating to Social Media, ii) social media platforms and strategy for recruitment, iii) Twinterns, and iv) internet policy and online recruitment strategies.

1. "The consequences of social exchange relationships have received significant research attention" (Dulac et al., 2008:1082). All of the respondents were currently working in HR or Senior Management in Guernsey, they were aged between 20 and 60, with the majority being women aged 45-60. There were 4 men present, aged between 35 and 60. The results of the findings were mainly focused on the issues relating to using Social Media efficiently as part of a small island community. The key trends which came out as a result of these findings were issues with advertising roles so that suitable candidates would be informed of the vacancies in a timely manner and who would be finding candidates who could meet the skills requirements of the enterprise's needs and would be able to work in part of the World with strict housing laws, (Economist, 2009). There were also issues with how it could be done, the potential for time-wasting and sifting through applicants without the correct skills and qualifications for the role.

2. There is a great deal of information available on social media platforms, and it is important that the enterprise remains vigilant in the amount of time spent on updating Social Media platforms to ensure the brand stays on message. Many of the respondents struggled with the basics of social media, with two of the participants not having a Facebook account. In these cases, in order to establish an effective social media strategy for recruitment, it might be more cost effective to bring in a Social Media Consultant. In Guernsey, one of the most well respected individuals is Jo Porrit, at Crowd Media, the team there offer training, from the most basic to higher level, and can also evolve a strategy that best fits the enterprise, and the industry in which they are working (www.facebook.com i). By using an external company, costs can be kept to a set level, and time taken to run the site by the enterprise can be minimized, whilst still ensuring the enterprise has an online presence, this will go some way to alleviating concerns.

3. Twinterns or "twittering interns" are typically interns taken on by large enterprises in order to keep communication channels open on day to day activities, such as at Pizza Hut, who launched a campaign where potential Twinterns had to apply for a role working for the company by posting a YouTube video of themselves online (Clifford, 2009). Indvick (2011) reported on the case at Marc Jacobs where the Twittern launched a tirade against his manager, calling him a "tyrant" before leaving the enterprise. @MarcJacobsIntl's response was "All well here at MJ. Twitter is a crazy place. Protect your Passwords" (www.twitter.com a). This is a clear example of the importance of keeping a watchful eye on the content that is posted by employees.

4. One of the topics considered was internet policy "We changed our Internet Policy at work recently, so people can't use Social Media in the office" – The implementation of a new internet policy, or social media policy is crucial for the enterprise. A response was "I don't think we'll use any of them, I want to employ people like me" may stem from the idea that "generally, the adoption of a technology does not take place uniformly across the entire economy or the entire population...If a person's family, friends and *broader* community are users... there would be increased incentive..."

(Agarwal et al., 2009:277). Though the same is true the other way round, it may be seen as a negative impact on the enterprise not to have an effective social media and online recruitment strategy in place.

Personal Interviews

Several issues were discussed by the researchers with the agencies as the key topics became emergent through the literature. The recruitment agencies operating in Guernsey are operating in a very competitive market, and have had to diversify to continue trading in the current economic climate, including developing their offshore payroll services, and providing HR consultancy to small businesses. This should not have an impact on their ability to remain specialised in their field and grow as the market picks up once more.

The key research findings from the personal interviews included i) current legislation, ii) tools available to update social media platforms, iii) topics concerning information about a candidate, iv) candidates online, v) content uploaded to Social Media sites, vi) effective communication with candidates, and vii) an effective Social Media strategy.

1. It is important that agencies keep up with current legislation, as Employment legislation is different from UK and European Union (EU) legislation and there are professional bodies active on LinkedIn, Facebook and Twitter, such as the CIPD who strive to keep people who are interested and up to date with current changes in the legislation.

2. There are several tools available to update all of the Social Media platforms that the agencies choose to use such as www.twitterfeed.com, which can convert an RSS feed of the information which has been uploaded into the content management system that keeps the website up to date into Tweets, and then there are several applications which allow Tweets to be "fed" into Facebook (www.facebook.com c) and LinkedIn (http://learn.linkedin.com/twitter/). After these applications have been set up, they need to be checked periodically to ensure that they are functioning correctly.

3. Several issues were raised as the researchers found new topics through the critical literature review, and were discussed at length with the agencies to see how they would respond and what their thoughts were on certain things. Guernsey is a very close knit community and so it is relatively simple to "Google" a candidate on Google (www.google.com) and see what comes up about what an individual may have done by a relatively simple search. There is also a website from the local newspaper (www.thisisguernsey.com) where it may also be possible to gather information about a candidate. This is a standard policy for some recruitment agencies. Additionally, it is common for an agency to have a policy relating to Criminal Convictions which have not been "spent" under the Rehabilitation of Offenders Act (Bailiwick of Guernsey Act 2002) and whether the agency decides to take on the individual to help them find work. Some agencies on the Island will not deal with candidates who have unspent convictions.

4. With the development of Social Media Strategies which include checking available information about candidates online, more information can be gathered. As a recruitment agent, it can be common for candidates to "like" the agency on Facebook and to "follow" them on Twitter, so it can be very easy to access information about the candidates which they may not otherwise wish to divulge, it is

then up to the agent to decide how they use the information. It is suggested (Lauby, 2010) that any enterprise that is going to conduct a background check on an individual on any social media sites which are available in the public domain ought to "provide notice" before conducting searches.

5. The content that Recruitment Agencies upload to Social Media sites can vary from staff events, corporate events which the enterprise may have sponsored or participated in, to charity work in which the enterprise participates, and local enterprises that staff participate in. A good example of this is Guernsey Recruitment agency "Situations Recruitment" and their Facebook page (www. facebook.com).

6. In order to have effective communication with employees of the enterprise and candidates of the agency, the personal interviews also highlighted the need for "fake" corporate accounts that can be monitored centrally. This could be as simple as employees setting up accounts for use at work. It only takes a few minutes to set up a basic Facebook Profile, where all of the contact details and work history can be set up with details of the recruitment agency, corporate images can be used, so that there is continuity between images that appear on the enterprise's website, and other social media platforms. This is a different way of communicating with candidates, and another way it is possible to keep candidates updated "on the go". This information can be monitored by a central person, who would be "friends" with the individuals, and would also have access to the passwords and usernames of the employees.

7. Decisions must also be made so that an effective Social Media strategy also includes information about what to do when an employee leaves. If there are "corporate" Facebook and Twitter accounts, contacts of these should remain with the company. This could be more difficult using a LinkedIn account, where individuals may have built up a rapport with clients and colleagues, and wish to retain the contacts, or could easily do so again. However, it is stated that "The formation and maintenance of relationships is predicated on the reciprocation of valued resources" (Dulac et al., 2008:1079).

FUTURE RESEARCH

Although the research obtained responses from people working in Recruitment Agencies it would perhaps be a learning point to conduct semi-structured interviews with recruitment agencies in different geographical locations globally, and in different industries as the recruitment agencies in Guernsey primarily deal with financial recruitment, with just a couple concentrating on the hospitality market. This is a very different way of recruiting since commission is far less, and people tend not to stay in jobs for a period of more than a few months in the hospitality industry.

CONCLUSION AND RECOMMENDATIONS

The unique contribution of the research to the literature is that information systems, tools and strategies are vital to an effective Social Media Recruitment Strategy. Enterprises must make available as much information as they possibly can, so that employees can make better informed decisions about whether or not they will fit with the enterprise. Ultimately the more information that is available, the more informed the decisions are likely to be. Enterprises must make the best possible use of the latest software available to them for online recruitment advances, and should ensure that all relevant staff are trained to use it. The more information that is available from both the employer, and the candidate the more likely that the potential candidate should "fit in" to their new position with minimal issue. This is of particular importance during times of economic difficulty, as it could be that a candidate who is not really suited to a place of work, or the role itself may not be able to find alternative employment easily. In addition, recruitment is an expensive ("Contracting a recruiter to find an executive who earns $150,000 annually can cost $15,000 in fees" (Koeppel, 2009)) and often is a time consuming process. By using "social media tools are mostly free and offer added value: Candidates bring their own online networks... and references which speeds up the recruitment process" (Koeppel, 2009). Therefore, it is vital for the employer to ensure they get it right the first time to avoid further cost implications.

The social media strategy must be planned to be inclusive to all potential employees, and also to customers – after all they could be the employees of the future. It is apparent that social media policies ought to be inclusive, so that an employer cannot be accused of discriminating against employees because of race, age, sex, sexual orientation or act in contravention of the Equality Act 2010 (www.acas.org. uk). This could leave the enterprise open to possible litigation if an employee feels that they have been discriminated against. It is important that an employee looks at the industry they are based in, in order to make informed choices about the best way to recruit for the role.

It may be possible to come up with a simple strategy for social media and recruitment within the enterprise. Once planned, the social media strategy must be made available to all employees and relevant training given (this must also be included in costings, time taken for staff training, operational costs of training).

If a social media strategy is to be effective, it is important that the employees are clearly informed of changes in procedures, and understand why these changes have come about. Clear guidelines must be set in order for employees to understand what they can and cannot say regarding the enterprise, their work, and their customers so as to minimize potential litigation.

Employees are very likely to be using Social Media in their own lives and will have an understanding of what effects social media have on their lives and understanding of brands, and this could help shape the social media strategy for recruitment within the enterprise.

If the enterprise has chosen to implement its social media and recruitment strategy through an external enterprise the next step would be to bring the implementation of the social media strategy back "in house" over a period of time, and only if the budget allows. This Organic Development Strategy known as "knowledge and capability development" (Johnson et al., 2008:357) within the social media and recruitment strategy will continue to grow, as employee's have "greater market knowledge and therefore competitive advantage over other rivals more distant from their customers".

Through the literature review and subsequent analysis of the primary data it is evident that quality of information is a key factor. Therefore it is essential that any enterprise attempting to recruit staff ensure that they provide as much information as possible in order to allow the candidate to make a more informed decision about their potential decision to apply and or accept a position. If this information is in place, it should reduce the time taken to process the application for all parties involved. In order to do this, it is important that all parties keep their information up-to-date at all times. For agencies and enterprises, this is perhaps more important, for the initial impression the candidate has of the enterprise may have an impact on whether or not they will choose to apply for the position (Cober et al., 2000).

Although LinkedIn profiles may seem to take longer to complete than Facebook (a few minutes) or Twitter (a couple of minutes) as an individual has to upload a certain amount of information, such as a

CV, write a summary, as well as asking people to recommend their work, it would be possible to display many of the key skills above in about 30 minutes, and the information stored on the LinkedIn profile can be quickly kept up to date.

Facebook was by far the preferred social media platform for the majority of respondents from the focus group and the questionnaire respondents, as well as being firm favourites with the Recruitment consultants in conjunction with other Social Media platforms.

It was not clear from the questionnaires and focus group whether LinkedIn, Twitter, YouTube are not well used due to lack of interest? Or a lack of training? From the results from all three stakeholders, however, in the case of MySpace, it is now viewed as a platform to share music on, not a social network anymore, so there would be little point building a social media strategy including MySpace, unless of course the enterprise was working in the Music, or Arts industries. It is also very important to ensure that other sorts of information on roles, and what is going on within the enterprise is kept up to date, and information is readily available for all applicants. A member of staff can explain the recruitment process, and have that available from YouTube, with links from Facebook and Twitter.

Approximate costs to keep company x's website, and social media platforms updated throughout one calendar year in terms of time are around £5,000 per annum. This includes an hour of administrative time on the website and social media platforms per day to ensure that the information available is as comprehensive as possible. There is also two hours Senior Administrator monitoring time per week to ensure other sorts of data are kept up to date, as well as time to make videos and other items for YouTube, to keep the content fresh. This keeps the website available and relevant to as many people as possible.

In terms of cost, each individual company would need to be costed according to its needs and to fit in with the social media strategy that had been worked out. Using outside companies such as web developers and Social media experts may add significant costs to the strategy. However, Ochman (2009:4) warns that "Many people claim to be "social media gurus" but hype doesn't compare to experience". It is important to investigate consultants or firms, to look at other work they have done, and to seek testimonials before spending money on a campaign.

It would be advisable for the researchers to make changes so that there were more responses to the questionnaire. Bryman and Bell (2008) suggest that where there have been more than 1,000 respondents to the survey, there is far less of a margin for error. It would have been more beneficial to have focused the data on specific geographical locations, tailor the questionnaires so that they would apply in different countries, so that questions could be asked without causing sensitivity to individuals. That information could be used at a later stage to provide analysis by sectors. In further studies the researchers would seek ways in which there could be a more balanced age and race demographic so that further research could be carried out. This could then result in correlations between older users and those users from an ethnic background. Further investigation should also be carried out to find what characteristics make a web page more accessible to users with disabilities and to determine if there are changes which can be implemented by recruitment agencies with ease and in a cost efficient manner.

The participants in the focus group were not frequent users of Social Media, so the topics were more on "how to use" Social Media, rather than how they were using it as part of their social media and recruitment strategy. It would be advisable to repeat the focus group with a group of individuals who were using Social Media more frequently in order to gain higher levels of validity to the research (Collis and Hussey, 2009:204). With the responses that were collected from the focus group, it would not be fair to say that the "research findings accurately represent what is happening in the situation" (Collis and Hussey, 2011:204).

In response to the first research question concerning the advantages/disadvantages of Social Media (SM) from the perspectives of HR professionals, recruitment professionals, and potential job seekers, the research found the advantages of using SM for online recruitment include increased efficiency and convenience for both potential employees and enterprises, whereas where the systems are not designed correctly, it can create increased difficulties for the enterprise in communicating with potential employees. Furthermore, it was found that the disadvantages with SM for online recruitment stem from poor information that is not kept up to date, and where there is no clear social media strategy implemented throughout the enterprise.

With regard to the second research question as to the factors likely to drive/reduce the effectiveness of recruitment via SM it was found that these included the rapid changes in technology, recruitment management, the current global economic climate and the impact this has on the way in which individuals are now seeking employment.

Regarding the third research question concerning legal considerations associated with recruitment via SM it was found that employers who wish their employees to use Social Media must guide the employees regarding what is expected from them, and outlining usage policies, as well as ensuring that there is someone within the enterprise who takes responsibility for the policy, monitoring and updating the information as necessary.

REFERENCES

Adams, J. (2009a). A new way to find 'Union' workers. *Bank Technology News*, *22*(5), 23.

Adams, J. (2009b). The Strongest Link. *Bank Technology News*, *22*(5), 23.

Addley, E. (2009). *The Twitter crisis: how site became voice of resistance in Iran*. Retrieved from http://www.guardian.co.uk/world/2009/jun/16/twitter-social-networking-iran-opposition

Agarwal, R., Animesh, A., & Prasad, K. (2009). Social interactions and the "Digital Divide": Explaining Variations in Internet Use. *Information Systems Research*, *20*(2), 277–294. doi:10.1287/isre.1080.0194

Agichtein, E., Castillo, C., Donato, D., Gionis, A., & Mishne, G. (2008) Finding high-quality content in social media. *WISDOM – Proceedings of the 2008 International Conference on Web Search and Data Mining*, 183-193.

Aichner, T., & Jacob, F. (2015). Measuring the Degree of Corporate Social Media Use. *International Journal of Market Research*, *57*(2), 257–275.

Berry, M. (2005, May). Online recruitment grows in popularity. *Personnel Today*, 43.

Boyd, D. M., & Ellison, N. B. (2007). Social Network Sites: Definition, History and Scholarship. *Journal of Computer-Mediated Communication*, *13*(1), 210–230. doi:10.1111/j.1083-6101.2007.00393.x

Bryman, A., & Bell, E. (2007). *Business Research Methods* (2nd ed.). Oxford University Press.

Christensson, P. (2013). Social Media Definition. *Tech Terms*. Retrieved June 18, 2017, from http://techterms.com/definition/social_media

Chubb, L. (2008). Stripped-down jobsite is a good call for 3. *People Management*, *14*(2), 14.

CIPD. (2009). E-Recruitment Fact sheet. *CIPD Publication*. Retrieved March 17, 2011, from http://www.cipd.co.uk/subjects/recruitmen/onlnrcruit/onlrec.htm

Clifford, S. (2009). Tweeting Becomes a Summer Job Opportunity. *NY Times*. Retrieved April 27, 2011, from http://www.nytimes.com/2009/04/20/business/media/20twitter.html

Cober, R. T., Brown, D. J., Blumental, A. J., Doverspike, D., & Levy, P. E. (2000). The Quest for the qualified job surfer: It's Time the Public Sector Catches the Wave. *Public Personnel Management*, *29*(4), 479–496. doi:10.1177/009102600002900406

Cober, R. T., Brown, D. J., Keeping, L. M., & Levy, P. E. (2004). Recruitment on the Net:How Do Enterpriseal Web Site Characteristics Influence Applicant Attraction? *Journal of Management*, *30*(5), 623–646. doi:10.1016/j.jm.2004.03.001

Collis, J., & Hussey, R. (2009). *Business Research: A Practical Guide for Undergraduate and Postgraduate Students* (3rd ed.). Palgrave Macmillan.

Crail, M. (2007). Online Recruitment delivers more applicants and wins vote of most Employers. *Personnel Today*. Retrieved March 17, 2011 from http://www.personneltoday.com /articles/2007/11/20/43298/online-recruitment- delivers-more-applicants-and-wins-vote-of-most-employers.html

Curry, P. (2000). Log on for Recruits. *Industry Week*, *249*(17), 46.

Czerny, A. (2004). Log on Turn off for women. *People Management*, *10*(15), 10.

Doherty, R. (2010). Getting social with recruitment. *Strategic HR Review, 9*(6).

Domizi, D. P. (2013). Microblogging To Foster Connections And Community in a Weekly Graduate Seminar Course. *TechTrends*, *57*(1), 43–51. doi:10.1007/s11528-012-0630-0

Dulac, T., Coyle-Shapiro, J. A.-M., Henderson, D. J., & Wayne, S. J. (2008). Not all Responses to Breach are the Same: The Interconnection of Social Exchange and Psychological Contract Processes in Enterpriseations. *Academy of Management Journal*, *51*(6), 1079–1098. doi:10.5465/AMJ.2008.35732596

Easterby-Smith, M., Thorpe, R., & Jackson, P. R. (2008). *Management Research* (3rd ed.). Sage.

Economist. (2009). Generation Y goes to work. *Economist, 390*(8612), 47-48.

Eduardo, M. (2006). E-Entrepreneurship. *Munich Personal RePEc Archive*. Retrieved April 24, 2011, from http://mpra.ub-muenchen.de/2237/

eLearning Industry (eLI). (2015). *5 Steps To Use LinkedIn For Social Learning – eLearning Industry*. Retrieved June 18, 2017, from http://elearningindustry.com/5-steps-use-linkedin-for-social-learning

Elliott, A.-M. (2011). *10 Fascinating YouTube Facts that May Surprise You*. Retrieved April 24, 2011, from http://mashable.com/2011/02/19/youtube-facts/

Everett, C. (2010). *Social media still feared by graduate recruiters*. Retrieved April 20, 2011, from http://www.hrzone.co.uk/topic/recruitment/social-media-still-feared-graduate- recruiters/105572

Facebook. (2010a). Retrieved April 20, 2011, from http://www.facebook.com/press/ info.php

Facebook. (2010b). *Statistics.* Retrieved March 3, 2011, from http://www.facebook.com/homephp#!/press/info.php?statistics

Facebook. (2010c). *Twitter App for Facebook.* Retrieved April 25, 2011, from http://www.facebook.com/apps/application.php?id=2231777543

Facebook. (2010d). *University of Glamorgan Facebook Enterprise.* Retrieved December 1, 2010, from http://www.facebook.com/?ref=home#!/uniglamlife

Facebook. (2010e). *Situations Recruitment.* Retrieved April 26, 2011, from http://www.facebook.com/situationsgnsy?ref=ts

Facebook. (2011a). *Zinzi Coetzee.* Retrieved April 25, 2011, from http://www.facebook.com/zinzi.coetzee?ref=ts#!/zinzi.coetzee

Facebook. (2011b). *Facebook KPMG Recruitment Page.* Retrieved April 25, 2011, from http://www.facebook.com/profile.php?id=100001464093443&ref=ts#!/pages/KPMG/108372102518243

Facebook. (2011c). *Facebook KPMG Graduate Page.* Retrieved April 25, 2011, from http://www.facebook.com/kpmg.graduates?ref=ts

Facebook. (2011d). *Facebook Crowd Media Page.* Retrieved April 27, 2011, from http://www.facebook.com/wearecrowd?sk=info

Facebook. (2011e). *Facebook KPMG Channel Islands Allumni page.* Retrieved April 25, 2011, from http://www.facebook.com/kpmg.graduates?ref=ts#!/pages/KPMG-Channel-Islands-Limited-Alumni/47271650921

Ghosh, R. (2011). *Entropy-based Classification of 'Retweeting' Activity on Twitter.* Retrieved June 18, 2017, from https://arxic.org

Gittlen, S. (2008). Web 2.0: Just Say Yes. *New World (New Orleans, La.), 25*(9), 32–34.

Goldberg, C. B., & Allen, D. G. (2008). Black and white and read all over: Race differences in reactions to recruitment web sites. *Human Resource Management, 47*(2), 217–236. doi:10.1002/hrm.20209

Hajirnis, A. (2015). Social media networking: Parent guidance required. *The Brown University Child and Adolescent Behavior Letter, 31*(12), 1–7. doi:10.1002/cbl.30086

Hall, S. (2004, February). See Website Recruitment through for best results. *Personnel Today,* 21.

Heller-Baird, C., & Parasnis, G. (2011). *From Social Media to Social CRM: What customers want.* IBM Institute for Business Value Study. Retrieved April 26, 2011, from http://www-935.ibm.com/services/us/gbs/thoughtleadership/ibv- social-crm-whitepaper.html? cntxt=a1005261

Henderson, A., & Bowley, R. (2010). Authentic dialogue? The role of "friendship" in a social media recruitment campaign. *Journal of Communication Management, 14*(3), 237–257. doi:10.1108/13632541011064517

Hilpern, K. (2001). Reading between the Lines. *Guardian Newspaper.* Retrieved October 10, 2008, from: http://www.guardian.co.uk/money/2001/jul/16/careers.jobsadvice5

Hoffman, D., Novak, T., & Chatterjee, P. (1995). Commercial scenarios for the web: opportunities and challenges. *Journal of Computer-Mediated Communication, 5*(1).

Indvick, L. (2011). *Marc Jacobs Intern Calls CEO a "Tyrant" in Twitter Meltdown.* Retrieved March 30, 2011, from http://mashable.com/2011/03/28/marc-jacobs-twitter- intern-meltdown/

Ingham, I. (2010). Social media at work: Breaking down barriers to communication. *Personnel Today.* Retrieved April 21, 2010, from http://www.personneltoday.com/articles/2010/03/18/54886/social-media-at-work-breaking-down-barriers-to- communication.html

Inter World Stats. (2011). *Number of Internet users worldwide.* Retrieved January 19, 2011, from http://www.internetworldstats.com/stats.htm

Johnson, G., Scholes, K., & Whittington, R. (2008). *Exploring Corporate Strategy* (8th ed.). Pearson Education.

Kaplan, A. M., & Haenlein, M. (2010). Users of the world unite! The challenges and opportunities of social media. *Business Horizons, 53*(1), 61. doi:10.1016/j.bushor.2009.09.003

Kietzmann, J. H., Hermkens, K., McCarthy, I. P., & Silvestre, B. S. (2011). Social media? Get serious! Understanding the functional building blocks of social media. *Business Horizons, 54*(3), 241–251. doi:10.1016/j.bushor.2011.01.005

King, J. (2004, January). The web habit is HR's manna from heaven. *Personnel Today*, 2.

Koeppel, D. (2009). HR by Twitter. *Fortune Small Business, 19*(7), 57.

Lauby, S. (2010). *Should you Search Social Media Sites for Job Candidate Information?* Retrieved September 6, 2010 from http://mashable.com/2010/09/05/social-media-job-recruiting/

Lee, I. (2005). Evaluation of Fortune 100 companies' career web sites. *Human Systems Management, 24*(2), 175–182.

Lewis, A., Daunton, L., Thomas, B., & Sanders, G. (2010). A Critical Exploration into whether E-Recruitment is an Effective E-Entrepreneurship Method in Attracting Appropriate Employees for Enterprises. *International Journal of E-Entrepreneurship and Innovation, 1*(2), 30–44. doi:10.4018/jeei.2010040103

Lewis, A., Thomas, B., & Sanders, G. (2013). Pushing the Right Buttons? A Critical Exploration into the Effects of Social Media as an Innovative E-Entrepreneurship Method of Recruitment for Enterprises. *International Journal of E-Entrepreneurship and Innovation, 4*(3), 16–37. doi:10.4018/ijeei.2013070102

LinkedIn. (2015a). *About Us – LinkedIn.* Retrieved June 18, 2017, from http://www.linkedin.com/about-us

LinkedIn. (2015b). *About Us – LinkedIn Newsroom.* Retrieved June 18, 2017, from http://press.linkedin.com/about-linkedin

Long, D. (2009, January 15). Monster invests $130m in face of falling vacancies. *New Media Age*, 4.

Lundblad, N. (2017). *Privacy in a Noisy Society.* Retrieved June 18, 2017, from http://www.citeserx.ist.psu.edu

Management, P. (2008). *Fatface appetite for e-recruitment*. Retrieved March 17, 2009, from http://www. peoplemanagement.co.uk/pm/articles/2008/ 01/fatfaceappetiteforerecruitment.htm

Mannion, M. (2008). Consider differences in culture in Virgin territory. *People Management, 14*(5), 15.

Manufacturers' Monthly. (2004, December). Internet job ads a turn off for industry. *Manufacturers' Monthly*, 16.

McKeown, C. (2003). Applied Management: Nurse Internet Recruitment. *Nursing Management – UK, 10*(4), 23-27.

Merriam-Webster. (2016). *Dictionary and Thesaurus*. Retrieved June 18, 2017, from http://www. merriam-webster.com

Miller, H., & Arnold, J. (2000). Gender and home pages. *Computers & Education, 34*(3-4), 335–339. doi:10.1016/S0360-1315(99)00054-8

Miller Littlejohn Media (MLM). (2015). *7 Ways Students Should Use LinkedIn*. Retrieved June 18, 2017, from http://www.millerlittlejohnmedia.com

Minton-Eversole, T. (2007a). E-Recruitment Comes of Age, Survey Says. *HRMagazine, 52*(8), 34.

Moody, M. (2010). Teaching Twitter and Beyond: Tip for Incorporating Social Media in Traditional Courses. *Journal of Magazine & New Media Research, 11*(2), 1–9.

Moran, M., Seaman, J., & Tiniti-Kane, H. (2012). *How today's higher education faculty use social media*. Retrieved June 18, 2017, from http://pearsonlearningsolutions.com

Mulgan, G., Tucker, S., Rushanara, A., & Sanders, B. (2007). *Social Innovation, What it is, Why it Matters and How it can be Accelerated*. Skoll Centre for Social Entrepreneurship, Oxford Said Business School. Retrieved February 2, 2011, from http://www.youngfoundation.org/publications/reports/social-innovation-what-it-why-it-matters-how-it-can-be-accelerated-march-2007

O'Keefe, G. S. (2011). The Impact of Social Media on Children, Adolescents and Families. *Paediatrics, 127*(4), 801–805.

Obar, J. A., & Wildman, S. (2015). Social media definition and the governance challenge: An introduction to the special issue. *Telecommunications Policy, 39*(9), 745–750. doi:10.1016/j.telpol.2015.07.014

Ochman, B. L. (2009, April). It is no longer possible to resist social media. *Public Relations Tactics Magazine*.

Odell, P. M., Korgen, K. O., Schumacher, P., & Delucchi, M. (2000). Internet Use Among Female and Male College Students. *Cyberpsychology & Behavior, 3*(5), 855–862. doi:10.1089/10949310050191836

Ozemir, V. E., & Hewett, K. (2010). The Effect of Collectivism on the Importance of Relationship Quality and Service Quality for Behavioural Intentions: A Cross-National and Cross-Contextual Analysis. *Journal of International Marketing, 18*(1), 41–62. doi:10.1509/jimk.18.1.41

Pavlik, J., & MacIntoch, S. (2015). *Converging Media* (4th ed.). New York, NY: Oxford University Press.

Peacock, L. (2009). *Social networking sites used to check out job applicants*. Retrieved December 4, 2009, from: http://www.personneltoday.com/articles/2009/03/17/ 49844/social-networking-sites-used-to-check-out-job-applicants.html

Pew Research Centre (PRC). (2012) *The Demographics of Social Media Users – 2012*. Pew Research Centre: Internet, Science & Tech. Retrieved June 18, 2017, from http://printabletemplates.com/pew-report-social-networking-site-users

Pitcher, G. (2008, March). Unfriendly job websites lose retailers top talent. *Personnel Today*, 3.

Postman, N. (2017). *Informing ourselves to death*. Retrieved June 18, 2017, from http://w2.eff.org

Raynes-Goldie, K. (2010). Aliases, creeping, and wall cleaning: Understanding privacy in the age of Facebook. *First Monday*, *15*(2).

Report, S. M. (2012). *State of the media: The social media report 2012. Featured Insights, Global, Media and Entertainment*. Nielsen.

Rushe, D. (2010). *Twitter 'in early talks with potential buyers Facebook and Google. Approximate Number of Twitter users 2010*. Retrieved April 14, 2011, from http://www.guardian.co.uk/technology/2011/feb/10/twitter-talks-buyers-facebook-google

Saunders, M., Lewis, P., & Thornhill, A. (2007). *Research Methods for Business Students* (4th ed.). Harlow: FT Prentice Hall.

Schofield, J. (2009). Twitter users are quick quitters. *Guardian Online*. Retrieved April 17, 2011, from http://www.guardian.co.uk/technology/blog/2009/apr/29/twitter-quitters-nielsen1?INTCMP=SRCH

Schramm, J. (2007). Internet Connections. *HRMagazine*, *52*(9), 176.

Sherer, P., & Shea, T. (2011). Using Online Video to Support Student Learning and Engagement. *College Teaching*, *59*(2), 56–59. doi:10.1080/87567555.2010.511313

Smethurst, S. (2004). The allure of online. *People Management*, *10*(15), 38.

Smith, C. (2011). Twitter User Statistics Show Stunning Growth. *Huffington Post*. Retrieved April 14, 2011, from http://www.huffingtonpost.com/2011/03/14/ twitter-user-statistics_n_835581.html

Spence, B. (2009). How to…filter job applications. *People Management*, 45. Retrieved March 19, 2009, from: http://www.peoplemanagement.co.uk/pm/articles/2009/03/how-to-filter-job-applications.htm

Statista. (2017). *Leading global social networks 2016 Statistics*. Retrieved June 18, 2017, from http://www.statista.com/statistics

Sundar, M. (2007). This week on LinkedIn July 9th 2007. *LinkedIn Blog*. Retrieved April 25, 2010, from http://blog.linkedin.com/2007/07/14/this-week-in-li/

Tang, Q., Gu, B., & Whinston, A. B. (2012). Content Contribution for Revenue Sharing and Reputation in Social Media: A Dynamic Structural Model. *Journal of Management Information Systems*, *29*(2), 41–45. doi:10.2753/MIS0742-1222290203

Taylor, C. (2001). E-recruitment is powerful weapon in war for talent. *People Management*. Retrieved December 5, 2009, from: http://www.peoplemanagement.co.uk/pm/articles/2001/05/856.htm

Personnel Today. (2004, April). Online Jobseekers more confident about equality. *Personnel Today*, 2.

Personnel Today. (2008, August). How I made a difference...? online recruitment burning career issues? closed-rank committee. *Personnel Today*, 8.

Tulip, S. (2003, August). A flying start. *People Management Magazine*, 38. Retrieved February 5, 2010, from http://www.peoplemanagement.co.uk/pm/articles/2003/08/ 9256.htm

Twitter. (2011a). *MarcJacobsInt*. Retrieved May 26, 2011, from http://twitter.com/#!/MarcJacobsIntl

Twitter. (2011b). *Twitter KPMG Recruitment Page*. Retrieved April 25, 2011, from http://twitter.com/#!/ KPMGRecruitment

Twitter. (2011c). *Twitter KPMG UK page*. Retrieved April 25, 2011, from http://twitter.com/#!/KPMG_ UK_LLP

Vogel, E. A., Rose, J. P., Okdie, B. M., Eckles, K., & Franz, B. (2015). Who compares and despairs? The effect of social comparison orientation on social media and its outcomes. *Personality and Individual Differences*, *86*, 249–256. doi:10.1016/j.paid.2015.06.026

Webb, T. J. (1998). *Researching for Business: Avoiding the 'Nice to know' Trap* (1st ed.). London: Aslib.

Week, M. (2006). E-recruitment in Web 2.0 boost. *Marketing Week*, *29*(43), 32.

Weekes, S. (2004, June). Unearthing diamonds in a tough recruitment market. *Personnel Today*, 10.

Willmott, B. (2003). Firms tackle skills and diversity crisis online. *Personnel Today*, *7*(1), 4.

Yang, Z. (2010). Understanding retweeting behaviours in social networks. *Proceedings of the 19th ACM international conference on information and knowledge management*. Retrieved June 18, 2017, from https://www.cs.cmu.edu

Zikmund, W. G. (2003). *Business Research Methods* (7th ed.). Thomson South Western.

Chapter 11
Knowledge Sharing in Distributed Teams:
Influence of National and Organizational Culture

Kerstin Viola Siakas
Alexander Technological Educational Institute of Thessaloniki, Greece

Elli Georgiadou
Middlesex University, UK

Dimitrios Siakas
Citec Oy Ab, Finland

ABSTRACT

Recent trends in the world economy, including globalization and advances in ICTs and social media, have enabled networking as a business model. As a result, distributed teams have emerged. This chapter provides a basis for discussion and analysis of knowledge sharing between distributed team members working in a global context in different organizational and national cultures. Cultural dynamics influencing knowledge sharing in different cultural settings is examined by investigating the different cultural values and perceptions related to knowledge sharing. The aims are to make the human and cultural dynamics that bear on knowledge sharing and knowledge management success more explicit. The use of the cultural and organizational diversity evaluation (CODE) model is proposed for assessing the fit between national and organizational culture. The objective of using the CODE model is to raise awareness of the cultural values and attitudes in distributed teams and to help ensure an effective quality management process, and foster a knowledge sharing culture within distributed teams.

DOI: 10.4018/978-1-5225-5014-3.ch011

INTRODUCTION

In today's competitive global business environment there is a push for organizations to produce innovative products and services for survival, growth, and sustainability. At the same time processes need to be innovative and to promote knowledge sharing in order to keep costs down and to improve productivity. Increasingly large numbers of organizations use distributed teams in their international operations.

Knowledge is an important competitive factor and one of the most valuable strategic assets of businesses. If knowledge is considered a critical resource and an important tool for competition in the global market, then it demands a good process for acquiring, sharing and managing knowledge. Many organizations are struggling to comprehend the Knowledge Management (KM) concept and do not perform any KM activity (Holsapple & Joshi, 2002). In a global context the problem is intensified due to the distance and the fact that people rarely meet. Metaxiotis et al. (2005) assert that the primary objectives of KM are to identify and leverage the collective knowledge in an organization in order to achieve the overriding goal of supporting the organization to compete and survive.

In order to increase competitiveness in the global market place distributed teams, such as dispersed knowledge workers of multinational organizations, service providers and clients in outsourcing partnerships, and partners of joint ventures, need to improve their knowledge in order to gain competitive advantage. Although the field is under-researched, scholars have started to pay attention to global and cultural dynamics influencing the KM process (Holden, 2001; Bhagat et al., 2002; Siakas & Georgiadou, 2006; Ang & Massingham, 2007; Ai-Alawi et. al, 2007; Siakas & Siakas, 2008; Siakas, et al., 2010; Melon et al., 2016; Al-Busaidi & Ohlman, 2017; Paliszkiewicz et al, 2017).

The aim of this paper is to unfold the human and cultural challenges that can help understand and address cultural disparities, and help in creating added competitive value for distributed and networked organizations and teams. The main contribution is the analysis of the cultural dynamics influencing knowledge sharing in different cultural settings. The CODE model and associated tool is proposed to be used for assessing the fit between national and organizational culture in order to raise awareness of the cultural values and potential conflicts arising from differences.

BACKGROUND

In today's highly competitive and rapidly changing global environment an increasing amount of distributed teams are formed in order to gain access to world class capabilities, reduce costs and integrate diverse perspectives (Siakas & Balstrup, 2006). Distributed teams, by their very nature, imply the presence of a group of geographically dispersed individuals often from different cultural, educational and professional backgrounds. They work within a specific time frame on a joint project or common task originating from collaboration between subsidiaries in multinational organization, between customers and service providers in outsourcing relationships, between members of joint ventures or other types of global partnerships. The distributed team is comprised of experts and staff usually situated in different locations, organizations, countries and time zones. Distributed teams consist of goal oriented team members / knowledge workers, who collaborate towards a shared goal (Lipnack & Stamps, 1997; Handy, 2000; Mansour-Cole, 2001), more apart than in same location. Distributed team members are dispersed geographically and collaborate supported by a web of ICTs. The main characteristics of distributed teamwork include goal orientation, joint decision making, co-ordination, interrelation of activities and mutual accountability for team results (Bal & Teo, 2000).

Our arguments derive from the literature reviews and reports on the state-of-the-art in KM and cross-cultural research. The results of field-studies related to knowledge sharing between members of distributed teams carried out in both academia and industry in several countries are reported. We also reflect on our own experience from different European countries and various transnational projects with partners of different work values.

KNOWLEDGE MANAGEMENT

The Need for a KM System

KM is an emerging set of principles, processes, organizational structures, and technology applications that help people share and leverage their knowledge to meet their business objectives (Gurteen, 1999). This focuses the individual, and places responsibility on the individual knowledge worker. At the same time KM programs emphasize the holistic nature of creating, sharing and managing knowledge.

Knowledge is formally captured, managed and stored explicitly with the help of ICTs, which seem to enhance the KM capabilities (Alavi & Leidner, 2001; Tanriverdi, 2005; Shahabi, et al., 2012). On the lowest hierarchical level routine decisions are based on information from Transaction Processing Systems (TPS), in which the lowest level of data is entered. On the middle hierarchical level tactical decisions are taken based on information captured through processing data in Management Information Systems (MIS) and Decision Support Systems (DSS). On the highest hierarchical level strategic decisions are taken based on information drawn from Executive Support Systems (ESS). All the information received from these systems is based on the data entered in the TPS. Nevertheless, technology by itself usually does not solve inherent problems relating to intellectual capital, knowledge and information management. Davis et al. (2005) argue that KM is based on implemented systems only by 30% while the rest 70% are based on people. The fact is that the view of knowledge is changing and today it is seen as human capital that *'walks out the door at the end of the day'* (Spiegler, 2000).

Organizations are facing today a new challenging environment, characterized by globalization, dynamism and increasing levels of complexity due to rapid changes in technology and its connected intricate knowledge. Internet-based distributed tools have created new opportunities for rapid access to business information world-wide. Identifying potential business partners and developing business links with organizations in other countries has become easier for organizations that are experienced in monitoring web-based information sources, and are able to combine tacit knowledge with new knowledge sources that are enabled by ICTs, such as internet, intranet, social media, groupware and Computer Supported Co-operated Work (CSCW) systems. Explicit knowledge is transferable through formal and systematic languages. Tacit or implicit knowledge is context-specific, personal and subjective including cognitive elements and thus difficult to formalize and communicate (Davis et. al, 2005, Siakas & Georgiadou, 2006).

Views on KM and ICTs are wide ranging between two poles - one considering the relationships between KM and ICTS minor – the other considering ICTs being the core of KM (Holsapple, 2007). This paper considers KM being a social and human phenomenon which by using ICTs as a communication and collaboration tool can improve the efficiency of knowledge creation, visualization, transfer and preservation. ICTs facilitate the amplification, augmentation and leverage of innate human knowledge handling capabilities. The advances in ICTs provide organizations with increased flexibility and responsiveness, permitting them to rapidly form dispersed and disparate experts and employees into a distributed team that can work on an urgent project. ICTs support faster, cheaper and more reliable knowledge work of large scale and the existence of efficient ICTs is inevitably an imperative requirement for the existence of distributed collaboration.

Knowledge sharing (transfer) is the process where individuals mutually exchange both tacit and explicit knowledge, and jointly create new knowledge. This process is essential in transferring individual knowledge into organizational knowledge. The capability of an organization to create, recognize, widely disseminate and embed knowledge in new products and technologies is critical when faced with turbulent markets, high competition and financial instability (Nonaka, 1991). Continuous knowledge creation requires voluntary actions including openness, scrutiny, trust and tolerance towards different views and interpretations. Organizations expect employees to keep professionally up-to-date by continuously obtaining internal and external information relating to their profession. Knowledge evolves continuously as the individual and the organization adapt to influences from the external and the internal environment.

Communities of Practice Wenger (1999) asserts that strong identity within Communities of Practice (CoP) contributes towards better collaboration, learning and innovation. CoPs are defined by Lave & Wenger (1991) as "*an aggregate of people who come together around mutual engagement in an endeavor*" and by Bettoni et al. (2006) as "*the participative cultivation of knowledge in a voluntary informal social group*". The highlight in both definitions is on a type social construction or community leading to a kind of culture including common practices that emerge in the course of the mutual endeavor. A CoP is usually born around a shared profession and its topics of discussion outside of the traditional structural boundaries. However, both experience and research show that our knowledge for designing online CoPs is limited (Barab et al., 2004). Some researchers even claim that enthusiasm about CoPs is well beyond empirical evidence (Schwen & Hara, 2003). In fact, many communities lack sustainability by falling apart soon after their initial launch due to lack of enough energy and synergies or by adopting a short-term opportunity driven behavior, which in turn leads to both uncertainty and mistrust between the members and consequently to low quality of shared work results (Bettoni et. al, 2006). The benefits of CoP seem to include the facilitation of greater variety in the knowledge domains of the members (De Carolis & Corvello, 2006).

A sense of identity is important because identity shapes what one pays attention to and constitutes a primary factor in learning and sharing of personal experiences (knowledge transfer) (Wenger, 1999). A potential conflict arises when the team members belonging to different organizational and cultural units, do not know where to place their loyalty (Balstrup, 2004). In distributed environments this is exacerbated, because informal communication is reduced, due to the fact that members rarely meet face-to-face. Distributed teams act in a similar way as CoP for maximizing value of the mutual engagement and common goals. A sense of identity is central because it determines how the team member focuses their attention.

Social Media as Tool for CoP

Today social media is increasingly used in CoP for creating and maintaining mutual social connections among individuals through social networking (Kwai Fun IP & Wagner, 2007). These new forms of business intelligence provide the individual with control content generated by the team. Individuals may maximize personal utility, but for various, mainly cultural reasons they also tend to hoard knowledge. They constitute learning communities in the sense that they evolve through collective building and transfer of knowledge (Lave & Wenger, 1991). This kind of social networking is an important source for building trust, creating reciprocal respect, as well as for developing a feeling of identity and group-belonging (Siakas & Balstrup, 2006; Siakas & Siakas, 2008). If the relationships and social rules are based more on professional rather than on personal or affective factors the social networking can constitute an important, yet often unrecognized, supplement to the value that individual members of a community obtain in the form of enriched learning and a higher motivation to transfer what they learn and in this sense even substitute formal teaching programs (De Carolis & Corvello, 2006). There is also evidence asserting that CoP create organizational / institutional value (Storck & Hill, 2000; Wenger & Snyder, 2000). Social networks contribute to a high degree to tacit knowledge sharing. CoPs are usually governed by mutual benefit perceptions in which the community welfare takes priority over individual interests. Individual members of distributed teams and communities of dispersed workers show difficulties in interacting with colleagues and keeping themselves up to date (Balstrup, 2004). There is a lack of informal communication when team members are dispersed. Harorimana (2006) argued that it is impossible to transfer knowledge that is not embedded in local cultural practices and settings because reciprocity norms dominate successful knowledge transfer.

KM in Distributed Teams

Knowledge sharing, in distributed teams in a global context is considerably much more difficult due to communication difficulties originating from differences in language, culture, time and distance. In this paper we argue that poor knowledge sharing due to distance can mainly be addressed by raising cultural awareness in order to create team identity and increased mutual understanding and reciprocal support between team members for reaching project goals.

The distributed team members mainly communicate by electronic means (e-mails, teleconferencing and social media). Knowledge sharing, however, with bad communication is difficult to achieve. Bad communication can either be technical (common in distributed teams) or cultural (language, communication style and comprehension). Elron & Vigoda-Gadot (2006) found that when ICTs are used as the main communication channel between team members the limitations of the communication increase, as technology cannot provide the same richness as face-to-face interactions, and potentially they hinder the effectiveness of knowledge sharing. In ICT based communication a lot of informal communication is omitted or constrained, such as influence tactics and political maneuvers. Teams lacking adequate communication and knowledge sharing will easily turn into detached groups of uninvolved strangers out of leadership and cooperation. The individuals of the distributed team and the leader must build a unified team committed to the common goal and through interdependent interaction generate team identity and create a feeling of belonging to the team (Balstrup, 2004).

Despite the many technologies that support collaboration among distributed work groups, organizations still face difficulties building online work environments. What is lacking in most distributed teams is a proven methodology for identifying and converting individual expertise, skills, and experience into organizational and team knowledge and to strategically align organizational knowledge transfer and learning investment with expected value outcomes. Developing such a methodology and then applying it to everyday processes will ensure that the output of every team adheres to the overall strategy of the involved companies. The responsibility of the management of the distributed team is to provide the necessary structure and to create systematic ways to identify and convert individual expertise, skills, and experience into organizational team knowledge and to strategically align organizational knowledge transfer and learning investment with organizational desired value outcome taking into account both current and future organizational tasks of the distributed team.

By sharing information across the organization, distributed teams naturally build their own knowledge bases that are consistent with the company they belong to. The ideal environment and working practices will be to change the mindset and behavior of team members so that instead of perceiving knowledge sharing as an extra task for the team members, isolated from the knowledge of other team members, it (knowledge sharing) becomes the natural way to work for everyone. The result will be a well-integrated, highly responsive team whose employees can quickly take action regardless of location.

CULTURAL DYNAMICS AND KM

Culture has been identified as the biggest impediment to knowledge transfer (Ruggles, 1998) and an utmost complex and simultaneously important factor affecting knowledge transfer at all levels, especially at the transnational level (Duan et al., 2006). Culture influences and moulds beliefs about the value of knowledge for the individual, the team and the organization. De Long & Fahey (2000) identified four issues influenced by culture central to knowledge creation, sharing and use, namely:

- Culture shapes assumptions about what knowledge is and which knowledge is worth managing;
- Culture defines the relationship between individual, team and organizational knowledge, determining who can utilize it, share it, control it and how it can be used in a certain situation;
- Culture creates the context for social interaction;
- Culture shapes the processes by which new knowledge is created, legitimated and distributed.

Research over the last twenty years regarding knowledge creation, capture, storage and distribution, as well as regarding organizational learning indicates that communication, knowledge sharing and learning are profoundly influenced by cultural values of individual stakeholders (Hambrick et al., 1998; Pfeffer & Sutton, 2000; Hofstede, 2001; Siakas & Georgiadou, 2003; Hutchings & Michailova, 2004; Siakas & Georgiadou, 2006). Many scholars and practitioners also claim that a supportive culture can enable the successful implementation of KM (De Long et al., 2000; Lopez et al. 2004; Park et al., 2004; Ardichvili et al., 2006; Siakas & Georgiadou, 2006). Since culture seems to be an issue of utmost importance, but also a multifaceted issue involving many different viewpoints and many different research disciplines, we consider that a deeper presentation, drawn from the literature, is needed for a better comprehension of cultures and their importance in KM. In particular, the impact of national culture on KM has been neglected in the literature.

Culture

Culture is a very elusive concept hence the many attempts by researchers to understand and define it. In 1952 Kroeger & Kluckholm (1952) found 164 different definitions, with different meanings for the concept of culture. Culture has different often overlapping layers. Hofstede (2001) argues that culture is a collection of characteristics possessed by people who have been conditioned by similar socialization practices, educational procedures and life experiences. There is cultural variation within and among cultures and there are different levels and forms of cultures. National culture is relatively stable and cannot easily be changed. Organizational culture is principally created by the founder of the organization. In distributed team work different national and organizational cultures co-exist. Awareness of the characteristics of these cultures will ease international operations and knowledge sharing.

National Culture

Hofstede distinguished six elements, or dimensions, of culture (Hofstede 1994; 2001) as follows:

- Power Distance (PD), which describes the extent to which hierarchies and unequal distribution of power is accepted;
- Uncertainty Avoidance (UA), which indicates the extent to which a society feels threatened by ambiguous situations and tries to avoid them by providing rules, believing in absolute truths, and refusing to tolerate deviance;
- Masculinity versus Femininity (Mas/Fem), which describes the relationship between the masculine assertiveness, competitiveness and materialism opposed to the feminine concern for quality of relationships, nurturing and social well-being;
- Individualism versus Collectivism (Ind/Col), which describes the relationship between the individual independence and the collective interdependence of a group;
- Long-term versus Short-term Orientation (influenced by Confucius) was introduced later, and describes the relationship between persistence and thrift opposed to personal stability and respect for tradition. This dimension has not been well received, because it appears confusing both to western readers and to Chinese minds (Fang, 2003);
- Indulgence versus Restraint is the most recent dimension specified by Hofstede. It deals with the level of satisfaction of basic and natural human drives related to enjoying life and having fun (Hofstede, 2016).

All these dimensions are measured on a continuum between two extremes (0 and 100) and only very few national cultures, if any, lie wholly at one or the other extreme. Hofstede's work has both been praised (Goodstein, 1981; Redding, 1994; Sondergaard, 1994; Williamson, 2002) and criticized (Hunt 1981; Tayeb 1988; Dorfman & Howell, 1988; McSweeney, 2002; Fang 2003; Jabri, 2005; Fang, 2006). Most of the criticism of Hofstede's work has involved methodological issues. The fact, that each dimensional index in Hofstede's model is constructed from three items or questions and that all the data comes from the same company is considered to be a sampling problem (Cray & Mallory, 1998). We believe that precisely because of the fact that Hofstede carried out his study in one single corporate organization (IBM) across many countries; any variability could be reasonably attributed to differences in national culture.

Hofstede's model is also considered to be static in the sense that it reflects the anthropological view, which considers that culture is static and the fundamental values are inherited from generation to generation and only slowly change. The sociological view on the contrary considers that different values in society interact with changing economic and political conditions, and thus culture is believed to be dynamic despite the fact that underlying basic values remain unchanged (Cray & Mallory, 1998).

Westwood and Everett (1987) were in a dilemma regarding to use or not use Hofstede's model due to the criticisms of the model. They concluded that to ignore his model is like ignoring the Indian Ocean. They carried out a replication study in Southeast Asia. Furthermore they argued that despite some shortcomings of Hofstede's model fruitful advances can be obtained from its use particularly in management and organizational contexts. McSweeny (2002) on the contrary totally rejected Hofstede's model by considering national culture implausible as a systematic causal factor of behaviour. However, Williamson (2002) responds to this criticism by asserting that, for scientists working within the functionalist paradigm, quantification of national culture opens up what is otherwise a black box of cultural factors. He concludes that McSweeney's critique raises warnings for researchers following Hofstede's model regarding assumptions, such as *'members of a culture homogeneously have the same cultural attributes'* and *'individuals' values or behavior are wholly determined by their cultural background'*. Hofstede & McCrae (2004) acted in response to these discussions by affirming that personality traits are biologically based dispositions and the question seems to be how personality traits (comparison of individuals - psychology) and culture (comparison of societies - anthropology) interact to shape the behavior of individuals and social groups. They stress that culture is a collective attribute (common to most of the people in a social group) manifested in behavior. Individuals are to societies as trees are to forest. The metaphor of flowers, bouquets and gardens was also used by Hofstede (1995) in comparing studies of individuals, organizational cultures and national cultures. Cultures, as a whole, cannot be understood only in terms of personality dynamics of individuals (Hofstede & McCrae, 2004).

Redding (1994) considered that research in organizational cultural issues and comparative organizational theory suffer from theoretical poverty and lack of clear direction in general. In order to provide adequate perspectives in the multiple and complex field inputs from other disciplines are required. These inputs improve understanding not only of facts, but also of the underlying meaning. Hofstede's work contains references to various theoretical approaches, especially to psychology, and can, according to Cray & Mallory (1998), be considered more theoretically sophisticated than the majority of the comparative work in the field. Hofstede recognizes that there is cultural variation within and among cultures and there are different levels and forms of cultures. This complexity makes it difficult to allow for systematic comparisons between cultures. In order to solve this problem, it is widely accepted that countries possess distinct and relatively stable cultures (Rodrigues & Blumberg, 2000). The strength of Hofstede's paradigm lies in its clarity and consistency in identifying cultural dimensions and thus facilitating cross-cultural comparisons (Fang, 2006).

Some important advances have been made in developing a dynamic view of culture, such as culture negotiation/formation through intercultural interactions (Brannen & Salk 2000), multiple cultures perspective (Sackmann & Phillips, 2004), and multilevel cultural dynamics (Leung et al., 2005).

Harris & Morgan (1991) suggest that when global organizations are aware of cultural strengths and biases in terms of national and organizational characteristics, they can build upon such foundations. International managers can take advantage of both differences and similarities, such as commonalities, through mutual cross-cultural synergy, for growth and development.

Organizational Culture

The concept of organizational culture has been popular since the early 1980s. The organizational culture is the internal environment of an organization that influences decision making, strategy, approach to markets and the behavior of stakeholders, such as management, employees, customers and supplies.

Researchers and practitioners have identified and discussed the importance of culture for organizations and business operations (Schein, 1985; Hofstede, 1994; Trompenaars & Hampden-Turner, 1997; Brown, 1998, Hofstede, 2001) and related differences between cultures to different approaches to solving common human problems. An example of the importance of culture in business operations can be demonstrated by the experience of Strang et al. (2010), who assert that local team members dealing with new product development and coming from diverse cultures with different languages may not be able to objectively express the voice of the customer regarding high-priority local market needs. Similarly engineers and senior management may have different and inaccurate perceptions of localized market needs.

Hofstede (1985, 1994; 2001; Hofstede et al., 1990) provided strong evidence that national cultural differences shape organizational behavior (organizational culture) at a local level and that difference in national and regional cultures affect work values. Hatch (1993) in her literature review reported *"the main focus seems to be on organizational culture and the organizational cultural changes imposed by globalization and the unprecedented development of ICTs"*. Changes in strategy with subsequent changes in structure and operations create new organizational cultures with different team settings (Brannen & Salk, 2000; Sackmann & Phillips, 2004).

Hofstede (1994; 2001) depicts different layers of organizational culture as an onion, indicating that values represent the deepest and symbols the most superficial manifestation of cultures. In between there are Heroes and Rituals. Symbols are characteristics of a cultural group, such as words, objects, conditions, acts or characteristics of persons that have a deeper meaning for an individual or a group. Superficial symbols and can easily be changed and copied by other cultural groups. Heroes consist of persons, who possess characteristics highly priced in a culture - the person everyone will count on when things get tough. Rituals are collective activities, considered as socially important, and carried out for their own sake. Ways of greeting are examples of rituals. Symbols, heroes and rituals are visible to outsiders and are collectively called practices. Their cultural meaning is invisible and lies in the way these practices are interpreted by the insiders.

Many business and political meetings have ritual purposes in addition to rational purposes. At the core lie the basic assumptions, values, and beliefs that guide human behaviors. Values are tendencies to prefer certain states of affairs over others. Their qualities, principles or behaviors are taken for granted and considered morally or intrinsically valuable or desirable and they remain usually unconscious to those who hold them.

Others have used the structure of the organization to explain corporate culture (Lofland & Lofland, 1995). Sahni & Rastogi (1995) suggest that organizational culture is defined as the integrated pattern of human behavior in a corporation, which includes the way employees think, speak and act. It is a rigid tacit infrastructure of ideas that shape not only our thinking but also our behavior and perception of our business environment (Gurteen, 1999).

Fang (2006) considers that culture can be compared to an ocean with visible wave patterns on the surface of the ocean in a given context at a given time (compared to visible cultural artefacts) but also numerous ebbs and flows underneath the surface (comparable to deeply rooted cultural values and behaviors). Similarly Siakas & Georgiadou (1999) describe the societal iceberg, where the visible part of the iceberg shows the formal aspects of an organization (goals, strategy, structure, standards and procedures) while the informal aspects of an organization hide under water (values, attitudes, beliefs, leadership style, norms of behavior, power, politics, conflicts and informal groupings). The informal part is the larger part of the organizational iceberg and will act to help or hinder an organizational process of change. It often leads to resistance to the change process (Siakas & Georgiadou, 1999).

However, Fang (2006) points to a neglected issue in cross-cultural management literature, namely that values and beliefs can be changed and manipulated by behavior. He argues that when cultures interact with each other, a behavioral change process begins which, in turn, eventually initiates a value change process among the interacting cultures.

The more members of the distributed team who accept, use and talk the language of the culture the stronger it will be (Sheriff et al., 2013). In doing so this forcefully influences the attitudes and actions of the distributed team as a whole.

Assessing the Fit Between National and Organizational Culture

The basic assertion in cross-cultural studies is that national culture, expressed in terms of values and beliefs, has a direct impact on organizational culture and individual behavior (Schein, 1985; Hofstede 1994; 2001). The economic, political and legal environment imposed by governmental rules, the technical environment, such as communication networks, and the socio-cultural environment in which the organization exists, directly affect organizational culture and the functioning of organizations.

Organizational culture in turn directly affects individual behavior by placing expectations on the members of the organization. Values of other stakeholders, such as employees / shareholders, also create impact on the organizational culture. One of the key issues for managers dealing with global transactions is shared commitment and collaboration which entail sharing of information, knowledge and viewpoints with team members and other stakeholders. Collaboration requires communication, which in turn builds trust.

The organizational structures and structural elements of distributed teams can formally indicate and facilitate connections and communications between individuals and thus influence the collaboration and sharing of knowledge within organizations (O'Dell & Grayson, 1998) and distributed teams, as well as they may place limitations on communications or create intentional or unintentional obstacles both within and across organizational boundaries and thus hinder collaboration and knowledge sharing (Gold et al., 2001). In distributed teams many different organizations may be involved and the team needs to be seen as a separate entity with its own overriding culture. Similarly Goh (2002) stresses that a co-operative and collaborative organizational culture (and team culture) can lead individuals or teams to have higher propensity to share knowledge. In distribute teams a strong team culture needs to be cultivated so that team members feel convenient with knowledge sharing.

Clarke (1994) argued that the essence of sustainable change is to understand the culture of the organization (and distributed teams). He stressed that if planned changes contradict cultural traditions and biases, resistance to the change and difficulties in its implementing are likely to occur. This entails global organizations and distributed teams to recognize the importance of different national cultures and organizational cultures involved in the set-up of distributed teams when planning a radical change. The more committed the members of an organization are to the current frame the more resistance is likely to occur when introducing a new system, particularly if this is likely to bring a major cultural change. People who have been steeped in the traditions and values of an organization will experience considerable uncertainty, anxiety and pain in the process of change.

The CODE Model

For assessment of the fit between national and organizational culture the Cultural and Organizational Diversity Evaluation (CODE) was developed (Siakas and Georgiadou, 2000; Siakas, 2002; Siakas & Georgiaodu, 2008; Siakas & Siakas, 2015), comprised of the C.HI.D.DI. (Clan, HIerarchical, Democratic, DIsciplined) typology (assessment of national culture) and the Authoritarian-Participative model (assessment of individual's, team and organizational culture) (Siakas, 2002). the classification in dimensions defines the national culture. The authoritarian-participative sub-model defines the organizational culture considering organizational characteristics, such as organizational structure, degree of formalization, management style, leader's role, handling of rules and degree of control. these are visible artefacts in shein's levels of cultures and their interaction. Two of Hofstede's dimensions, particularly visible in organizational cultures, are used in CODE, namely Power Distance (artefacts expressed in organizational culture as structure, power distribution, control, centralization management style etc.) and Uncertainty Avoidance (expressed in organizational culture as degree of rules and regulations, security, degree of bonding etc). The CODE model can schematically be expressed on the C.HI.D.DI typology (figure 1), which classifies organizations into four categories and was named after the four quadrants Clan, HIerarchical, Democratic, DIsciplined that are created by two axis of Power Distance and Uncertainty Avoidance. On the horizontal axis Uncertainty Avoidance (UA) starting from weak UA and ending in strong UA is pictured, while on the vertical axis Power Distance (PD) starting from weak PD and ending in Strong PD is pictured. The four quadrants form a specific typology where Hofstedes values for national culture and equivalently the values from the organizational, team or personal culture. These four cognitive types of culture should be considered as ideal types.

The CODE tool can be used for an individual, a team, an organizational or a national assessment and will give an indication of contradictions or conformity of values. The tool is needed for assessing the cultural fit of potential global partners in their search, selection and collaboration process, thus CODE is useful for distributed teams. According to our knowledge there does not exist another similar tool. The underlying results of the assessment are to proactively address potential problems, and by raising cultural awareness to diminish risks of potential conflicts. A cultural fit in global transactions is significant for obtaining commitment and avoiding resistance.

The most obvious clients for CODE are organizations involved in global partnerships, international and multi-national organizations, as well as consulting companies that deal with strategic, change or human resource matters of global organizations. The current process comprises a pilot study and after refining the tool it will be available on the market.

Figure 1. The C.HI.D.DI. typology of Organizational Cultures

	Clan	Hierarchical
Strong PD	Clan	Hierarchical
Weak PD	Democratic	Disciplined
	Weak UA	Strong UA

Global organizations would benefit from using the CODE assessment in their subsidiaries. The organizational culture in the mother organization might not be suitable in other countries. The mother organization has to be aware of the differences in cultures and be flexible enough to take into consideration differences between the organizational and the national culture.

Similarly organizations which aim to delegate part of their business activities to external service providers and/or to establish business partnerships beyond geographical boundaries would save a lot of effort and money on practices which do not have the cultural foundation to be successful without a lot of dynamism and hard work. Assessment of the cultural fit between the contractor (the global organization) and the business partner (service provider) will be beneficial for both parts. In outsourcing relationships and joint ventures it is of utmost importance to have an awareness of the differences in national cultures and in organizational cultures of the involved stakeholders.

The CODE tool can be used in the following cases:

- Internationalization of a company and identification of the fundamental changes required in the organizational culture to capitalize on the development of internationalization.
- Company mergers and acquisitions. Taking into account cultural gaps between the new partners following an acquisition, merger or alliance is crucial for integrating practices into common praxis. The identification of potential areas of culture conflicts between partners need to be assessed as soon as possible for motivation and dedication of staff. Understanding of requirements of existing staff for reaching the goals of the new company is important in order to build suitable integration programs.
- Establishment of a company or a subsidiary on the foreign market including setting up production, sales office, office of representatives etc. This process often happens slowly because of lack of cross-cultural knowledge and mutual understanding of the targets and contents of plans.
- Recruitment of suitable personnel for the company. CODE assesses the cultural suitability for potential new staff. Legal issues of recruitment are usually defined differently in diverse countries. Negotiation with cross-cultural and local human resource experts may also be necessary. The understanding of the cultural fit of potential personnel is an added value in recruitments.
- The increase of the effectiveness of international managers and distributed teams can only be achieved if the different parts understand the cultural traits and propositions of the diverse workforce. The CODE tool assists multinational management/project teams to agree on goals, have effective meetings, delegate, motivate and build and implement project plans. Cultural constraints determine which strategies are feasible and which are not.

Distributed team may consist of many different organizations influenced by different national organizational cultures. An assessment with CODE will help in mapping the cultural similarities and differences. The aims are to raise understanding of divergent cultural values in order to ease communication and collaboration, as well as to facilitate knowledge sharing.

Cultural diversity can be a competitive advantage for the company and the distributed team. Measuring the development of organizational cultures and the culture of the distributed teams over time will show whether attempted culture changes have materialized the cultural effects of external changes which may have occurred after previous assessments.

Several drivers in the business environment scheme show business opportunities for business tools like CODE. More and more companies already have extended or want to extend their business globally by using distributed teams through subsidiaries, mergers, acquisitions, joint ventures and outsourcing. The CODE is not yet a business concept due to the fact that it still is piloted among targeted client groups. The CODE concept is ready for the market, but needs to be registered and branded. This will be the future work of the CODE development process.

A Knowledge-Oriented Organizational and Team Culture

A knowledge-oriented organizational and team culture is clearly one of the most influential factors for successful KM and knowledge transfer (Davenport & Prusak, 1998), because a culture that promotes innovative behavior and change encourages active exchange of ideas and increased knowledge sharing. A business orientation promoting information and knowledge transfer is reflected in a general atmosphere of inventiveness, creativity, and willingness to make changes (Menon & Varadarajan, 1992).

While ICTs are enablers of knowledge-sharing processes, technology alone is not enough to ensure that people share and use each other's knowledge. A team's ability to use knowledge depends on how enthusiastic people are about sharing it. Leveraging knowledge is possible only when people value building on each other's ideas and sharing their own insights. Much of this is shaped by the culture of the team. Culture is critical to KM, but is equally critical to related processes such as learning, entrepreneurship, innovation and achieving high performance for competitive advantage. The same type of open, responsive and trusting environment is needed to support all these processes.

Team cohesion, trust and effective knowledge sharing are facilitated in organizations with high process maturity which in turn results in high knowledge sharing. There are many definitions of trust but none can claim a universal application. In this paper we view trust as institutional trust tied to formal societal rules, depending on individual or firm-specific attributes or on intermediary mechanisms, such as a common goal of a distributed team. Anderson et al., 2010 argue that trust is a necessary condition of an effective virtual network; hence trust between distributed team members reduce uncertainty, breeds transparency, openness, ease of communication and knowledge sharing. For multinational and distributed project teams a preliminary assessment is useful particularly in the case of acquisitions and mergers. The highest level of both process maturity and knowledge sharing is the innovative level which is characterized by optimizability and continuous improvement. Knowledge sharing is institutionalized and quantitative. Improvements are achieved from continuous feedback, across teams, within and across projects and across the whole organization. All employees understand, embraced and practice the philosophy of knowledge sharing. Processes are continuously improving and innovative ideas of all employees find fertile ground.

In Table 1 Hofstede's dimensions are related to KM, trust and knowledge sharing.

Table 1 shows that in low Power Distance (PD) countries, low Uncertainty Avoidance countries (UA), Feminine countries and countries with high Indulgence trust is high and knowledge sharing is an expected natural process, one of the basic values of the culture. In Individualistic cultures, voluntary knowledge sharing is relatively hard to achieve and other supplementary activities, such as incentive systems are recommended. In collectivistic cultures, knowledge sharing can be enhanced if knowledge sharing is rewarded and made prominent with higher reputation and status (Handzic & Lagumdzija, 2006).

Evidence from a two months field study and observations in a global Danish organization, with subsidiaries in the USA and Germany confirm the correctness of the theoretical judgment derived from the literature review. In total 56 interviews with employees in software development on different levels was conducted in Denmark, USA and Germany (Siakas, 2002).

Table 1. Trust and Knowledge Sharing potential in different cultural settings (adapted from Siakas & Georgiadou, 2008)

Dimension	Level	KM Characteristic	Trust	Knowledge Sharing Practices
Power Distance	**High**	Authoritative leadership, Centralized decision structures, Inequality between higher ups and lower downs	Low	Only if required by superiors
	Low	Participative leadership, Decentralized decision structures	High	A natural process
Uncertainty Avoidance	**High**	Suspiciousness to innovations and new knowledge, Uncertainty for ambiguous situations	Low	Has to be enforced by regulations and instructions
	Low	Problem solving tasks preferred	High	Expected
Masculinity / Femininity	**Mas.**	Assertiveness, Sympathy for strong	Low	Hiding of knowledge for competition reasons
	Fem.	Co-operation important Sympathy for weak	High	A basic value
Individualism / Collectivism	**Ind.**	'I' consciousness	Low	If personal advantage can be identified
	Coll.	In-groups Out-groups	High Low	Trust has to be established before any knowledge sharing can take place between in- and out- groups. Can be enhanced by intrinsic motives (e.g. higher reputation and status)
Orientation	**Long Term**	Societal links with past Societal change seen with suspicion	High	Trust in change has to be established before any knowledge sharing can take place
	Short Term	Time is money	Low	If effectiveness can be identified
Indulgence / Restraint	**Ind.**	Loose social norms with emphasis on pleasure and having fun.	High	If delight is noticed
	Res.	Strict social norms	Low	If norms require. Relevant and timely knowledge is shared in a cost effective manner.

Hofstede (1994) articulated that Power Distance and Uncertainty Avoidance apply for organizational culture due to the fact that these two dimensions are more work-related than the other dimensions. Our observations from the field study confirmed that both Power Distance and Uncertainty Avoidance are clearly identifiable in organizational culture. They translate to organizational hierarchy and degree of formalization through rules and regulations.

The results of the field study are depicted in figure 2.

The field study was the validation stage of a larger survey study encompassing 306 questionnaire respondents from other countries as well. The evidence showed that a knowledge sharing culture is almost occurring naturally in an environment with low Power Distance and low Uncertainty Avoidance values, whilst in cultures with a higher Power Distance and Uncertainty Avoidance a more serious cultural change will be needed for embracing knowledge sharing as a natural process (Siakas and Georgiadou, 2008).

Figure 2 shows the fit between national and organizational culture, such as in the Danish company (DK), the two Finnish companies (FI2 and FI3) and the Greek company GR2, with a dotted circle around

Figure 2. CODE scores plotted in the C.HI.D.DI typology

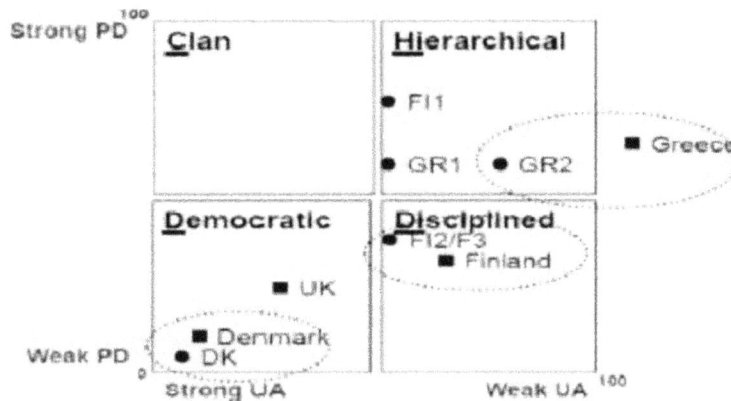

the company values and the country values and the Power Distance and Uncertainty Avoidance scales. In these companies the operations run smoothly and the workforce was satisfied with the company. In the Finnish company FI1 and the Greek company GR1 there was a considerable mismatch between the national and the organizational culture and as a result the operations seemed to be problematic and the workforce was exceptionally dissatisfied with the company.

SOLUTIONS AND RECOMMENDATIONS

Global organizations and organizations which aim to delegate part of their business activities to external service providers and/or to establish business partnerships beyond geographical boundaries with the use of distributed teams need to take cultural divergent values into consideration for their operations.

All the above business partnerships would benefit from using the CODE tool for assessing the cultural fit and for mapping eventual cultural mismatches of potential global partners in their search, selection and collaboration process. The CODE tool can be used for an individual, a team, an organizational or a national assessment and will give an indication of contradictions or conformity of values. The underlying results of the assessment are to proactively address potential problems, and by raising cultural awareness to diminish risks of potential conflicts. A cultural fit in global transactions is significant for obtaining commitment and avoiding resistance.

FUTURE RESEARCH DIRECTIONS

Future work will extend the CODE tool to enable multinational management / project teams to agree on goals, have effective meetings, delegate, motivate and build and implement project plans. Cultural constraints determine which strategies are feasible and which are not.

CODE could also be extended to cover assessments for conscious or unconscious bias which is detrimental to organizations. By allowing any form of bias, it can be harmful to an organization because bias of any sort restricts the range of views and experiences. Bias, conscious or unconscious, could relate to many issues such as ethnicity, color, gender, religion, disability whether physical or otherwise, or age whether too young or too old. Bias can affect the profitability and the quality of the product of organizations, by potentially preventing new or different ideas being developed (McKinsey 2015).

CONCLUSION

The focus in this paper was to provide a basis for discussion and analysis of knowledge sharing and the learning process in distributed and networked organizations in different organizational and national cultures. Different KM concepts were analyzed and the role of ICTs was discussed. The potential role of new forms of business intelligence, such as CoP and social computing, which enable a bottom-up approach for supporting knowledge activities and provide the individual with control of their own generated content, were discussed. The main contribution of this paper is the analysis of the human and cultural dynamics that bear on knowledge sharing and KM success. These dynamics were unfolded by extensively analyzing cultural issues (national and organizational) on knowledge sharing and learning in organizations in order to promote an effective knowledge sharing culture within distributed teams existing in a global context. Finally cultural characteristics revealed in a field study conducted in Danish global organization with subsidiaries in the USA and Germany were mapped to Hofstede's dimensions and conclusions were presented. The use of Cultural and Organizational Diversity Evaluation (CODE) was proposed for assessing the fit between national and organizational culture for raising cultural awareness of divergent values among distributed team members. Future work will introduce and monitor KM programs in selected organizations in different countries spanning cultural diversity in order to collect further qualitative and quantitative empirical data.

ACKNOWLEDGMENT

This research received no specific grant from any funding agency in the public, commercial, or not-for-profit sectors.

REFERENCES

Ai-Alawi, A. I., Al-Marzooqi, N. Y., & Mohammed, Y. F. (2007). Organizational Culture and Knowledge Sharing: Critical Success Factors. *Journal of Knowledge Management, 11*(2), 22–42. doi:10.1108/13673270710738898

Al-Busaidi, K., & Ohlman, L. (2017). Knowledge sharing through inter-organizational knowledge sharing systems. *VINE Journal of Information and Knowledge Management Systems, 47*(1), 110–136. doi:10.1108/VJIKMS-05-2016-0019

Alavi, M., & Leidner, D. E. (2001). Review: Knowledge Management and Knowledge Management Systems: Conceptual Foundations and Research Issues. *Management Information Systems Quarterly, 25*(1), 107–136. doi:10.2307/3250961

Anderson, A. R., Steinerte, E., & Russell, E. O. (2010). The Nature of Trust in Virtual Entrepreneurial Networks. *International Journal of E-Entrepreneurship and Innovation, 1*(1), 1–21. doi:10.4018/jeei.2010010101

Ang, Z., & Massingham, P. (2007). National Culture and Standardization versus Adaption of knowledge Management. *Journal of Knowledge Management, 11*(2), 5–21. doi:10.1108/13673270710738889

Ardichvili, A., Mauner, M., Li, W., Wenting, T., & Stuedemann, R. (2006). Cultural influences on knowledge sharing through online communities of practice. *Journal of Knowledge Management, 10*(1), 94–107. doi:10.1108/13673270610650139

Bal, J., & Teo, P. K. (2000). Implementing distributed teamworking. Part 1: A literature review of best practice. *Logistics Information Management, 13*(6), 346–352. doi:10.1108/09576050010355644

Bo, B. (2004). *Leading by Detached Involvement – Success factors enabling leadership of distributed teams* (MBA Dissertation). Henley Management College, UK.

Bhagat, R. S., Kedia, B. L., Harveston, P. D., & Triandis, H. C. (2002). Cultural variations in the cross-border transfer of organizational knowledge: An integrative framework. *Academy of Management Review, 27*(2), 204–221.

Barab, S. A., Kling, R., & Gray, J. H. (2004). *Designing for Distributed Communities in the Service of Learning*. Camebridge, UK: Cambridge University Press. doi:10.1017/CBO9780511805080

Bettoni, M., Andenmatten, S., & Mathieu, R. (2006). Knowledge Cooperation in Online Communities: A Duality of Participation and Cultivation. In *Proceedings of 7th European Conference of Knowledge Management (ECKM06)*. Public Academic Conferences Ltd.

Brannen, M. Y., & Salk, J. (2000). Partnering Across Borders. *Human Relations, 53*(4), 451–487. doi:10.1177/0018726700534001

Brown, A. D. (1998). *Organizational Culture*. London, UK: Financial Times Management, Pitman Publishing.

Clarke, L. (1994). *The Essence of Change*. London, UK: Prentice-Hall.

Cray, D., & Mallory, G. R. (1998). *Making Sense of Managing Culture*. London, UK: International Thomson Business Press.

Davenport, T. H., & Prusak, L. (1998). *Working Knowledge: How Organizations Manage What They Know*. Boston: Harvard Business School Press.

De Carolis, M., & Corvello, V. (2006). Multiple Competences in Distributed Communities of Practice: The Case of a Community of Financial Advisors. In *Proceedings of 7th European Conference of Knowledge Management (ECKM06)*. Public Academic Conferences Ltd.

De Long, D. W., & Fahey, L. (2000). Diagnosing cultural barriers to knowledge management. *The Academy of Management Executive, 14*(4), 113–127.

Davis, J. G., Subrahmanian E. & Westerberg, W. (2005). The "global" and the "local" in knowledge management. *Journal of Knowledge Management, 1*(1), 101-112.

Dorfman, P. W., & Howell, J. P. (1988). Dimensions of national culture and effective leadership patterns: Hofstede revisited. *Advances in International Comparative Management, 3,* 127–150.

Duan, Y., Xu, X., & Fu, Z. (2006). Understanding Transnational Knowledge Transfer. In *Proceedings of 7th European Conference of Knowledge Management (ECKM06).* Public Academic Conferences Ltd.

Elron, E., & Vigoda-Gadot, E. (2006). Influence and Political Processes in Cyberspace: The Case of Global Distributed Teams. *International Journal of Cross Cultural Management, 6*(3), 295–317. doi:10.1177/1470595806070636

Fang, T. (2006). From "Onion" to "Ocean", Paradox and Change in National Cultures. *International Studies of Management & Organization, 35*(4), 71–90.

Fang, T. (2003). A Critique of Hofstede's Fifth National Culture Dimension. *International Journal of Cross Cultural Management, 3*(3), 347–368. doi:10.1177/1470595803003003006

Goh, S. C. (2002). Managing effective knowledge transfer: An integrative framework and some practice implications. *Journal of Knowledge Management, 6*(6), 23–30. doi:10.1108/13673270210417664

Gold, A. H., Malhotra, A., & Segars, A. H. (2001). Knowledge Management: An Organizational Capabilities Perspective. *Journal of Management Information Systems, 18*(1), 185–214. doi:10.1080/07421 222.2001.11045669

Goodstein, L. D. (1981). American Business Values and Cultural Imperialism. *Organizational Dynamics, 10*(1), 49–54. doi:10.1016/0090-2616(81)90011-5

Gurteen, D. (1999). Creating a Knowledge Sharing Culture. *Knowledge Management Magazine, 2*(5). Available on-line at http://www.gurteen.com/gurteen/gurteen.nsf/0/FD35AF9606901C42802567C70068CBF5/

Hambrick, D., Davison, S., Snell, S., & Snow, C. (1998). When groups consist of multiple nationalities: Toward a new understanding of implications. *Organization Studies, 12*(2), 181–205. doi:10.1177/017084069801900202

Handy, C. (2000). *Trust and the Distributed Organization* (HBR OnPoint Enhanced Edition). HBR On Point.

Handzic, M., & Lagumdzija, A. (2006). Motivational Influences On Knowledge Sharing. In *Proceedings of 7th European Conference of Knowledge Management (ECKM06).* Public Academic Conferences Ltd.

Harorimana, D. (2006). Knowledge Networks: A Mechanism of Creation and Transfer of Knowledge in Organizations? In *Proceedings of 7th European Conference of Knowledge Management (ECKM06).* Public Academic Conferences Ltd.

Harris, P. R., & Morgan, R. T. (1991). *Managing Cultural Differences* (3rd ed.). Houston, TX: Gulf Publishing Company.

Hatch, M. J. (1993). The Dynamics of Organizational Culture. *Academy of Management Review, 18*(4), 657–693.

Hofstede, G. (1985). The interaction between national and organizational value system. *Journal of Management Studies, 22*(4), 347–357. doi:10.1111/j.1467-6486.1985.tb00001.x

Hofstede, G. (1994). *Cultures and Organizations, Intercultural co-operation and its importance for survival, Software of the mind.* McGraw-Hill.

Hofstede, G. (1995). Multilevel research of human systems: Flowers, Bouquets and Gardens. *Human Systems Management, 14,* 207–217.

Hofstede, G. (2001). *Culture's consequences: Comparing values, behaviors, institutions, and organizations.* Thousand Oaks, CA: Sage Publications.

Hofstede, G. (2016). *Geert Hofstede National culture.* Retrieved from https://geert-hofstede.com/national-culture.html

Hofstede, G., & McCrae, R. R. (2004). Personality and Culture Revisited: Linking Traits and Dimensions of Culture. *Cross-Cultural Research, 38*(1), 52–85. doi:10.1177/1069397103259443

Hofstede, G., Neuijen, B., Ohayv, D., & Sanders, G. (1990). Measuring Organizational Cultures, A Qualitative Study Across Twenty Cases. *Administrative Science Quarterly, 35*(2), 286–316. doi:10.2307/2393392

Holden, N. (2001). Knowledge management: Raising the specter of the cross-cultural dimension. *Knowledge and Process Management, 8*(3), 155–163. doi:10.1002/kpm.117

Holsapple, C. W., Joshi, K. D. (2002). Knowledge Management: A Threefold Framework. *The Information Society, 18,* 47-64.

Hunt, J. W. (1981). Applying American Behavioral Science: Some Cross-Cultural Problems. *Organizational Dynamics, 10*(1), 55–62. doi:10.1016/0090-2616(81)90012-7

Hutchings, K., & Michailova, S. (2004). Facilitating knowledge sharing in Russian and Chinese subsidiaries: The role of personal networks and group membership. *Journal of Knowledge Management, 8*(2), 84–94. doi:10.1108/13673270410529136

Jabri, M. M. (2005). Commentaries and Critical Articles: Text–context Relationships and Their Implications for Cross Cultural Management. *International Journal of Cross Cultural Management, 5*(3), 349–360. doi:10.1177/1470595805058415

Kroeger, A., & Kluckhohn, F. (1952). *Culture: A Critical Review of Concepts and Definitions.* Cambridge, MA: Harvard Business Review.

Kwai Fun, I. P. R., & Wagner, C. (2007). Weblogging: A study of social computing and its impact on organizations. ScienceDirect – Decision Support Systems, Elsevier B. V.

Lave, J., & Wenger, E. (1991). *Situated learning: Legitimate peripheral participation.* Cambridge, UK: Cambridge University Press. doi:10.1017/CBO9780511815355

Leung, K., Bhagat, R. S., Buchan, N. R., Erez, M., & Gibson, C. B. (2005). Culture and International Business: Recent Advances and Their Implications for Future Research. *Journal of International Business Studies, 36*(4), 357–378. doi:10.1057/palgrave.jibs.8400150

Lipnack, J., & Stamps, J. (1997). *Distributed Teams: Reaching across space, time and organizations with technology.* New York: Wiley.

Lofland, J., & Lofland, L. H. (1995). *Analytic Social Settings, A guide of qualitative observation and analysis*. Wadsworth Publishing Company.

Mansour-Cole, D. (2001). Team Identity Formation in Distributed Teams. In S. Beyerlein, M. Beyerlein, & D. Johnson (Eds.), *Distributed Teams, Advances in interdisciplinary studies of work teams* (Vol. 8). Oxford, UK: Elsevier Science.

McKinsey. (2015). *Diversity Matters*. Retrieved 1 June 2017, from http://www.mckinsey.com/business-functions/organization/our- insights/why-diversity-matters

McSweeney, B. (2002). Model of National Cultural Differences and Their Consequences: A Triumph of Faith—A Failure of Analysis. *Human Relations, 55*(1), 89–118. doi:10.1177/0018726702551004

Melon, E., Levy, Y., & Dringus, L. P. (2016). study on the success of group formation and cohesiveness in virtual teams using computer-mediated communications. *Online Journal of Applied Knowledge Management, 4*(1), 61–81.

Menon, A., & Varadarajan, P. R. (1992). A model of Marketing Knowledge Use Within Firms. *Journal of Marketing, 56*(4), 53–71. doi:10.2307/1251986

Metaxiotis, K., Ergazakis, K., & Psarras, J. (2005). Exploring the world of knowledge management: Agreements and disagreements in the academic/practitioner community. *Journal of Knowledge Management, 9*(2), 6–18. doi:10.1108/13673270510590182

Nonaka, I. (1991). The knowledge-creating company. *Harvard Business Review, 69*(6), 96–104.

O'Dell, I., & Grayson, C. J. (1998). If only we knew what we know: Identification and transfer of internal best practices. *California Management Review, 40*(3), 154–174. doi:10.2307/41165948

Paliszkiewicz, J., Svanadxe, S., & Jikia, M. (2017). The role of knowledge management processes on organizational culture. *Online Journal of Applied Knowledge Management, 5*(2), 28–44.

Park, H., Ribiere, V., & Schulte, W. D. Jr. (2004). Critical attributes of organizational culture that culture that promote knowledge management technology implementation success. *Journal of Knowledge Management, 8*(3), 106–117. doi:10.1108/13673270410541079

Pfeffer, J., & Sutton, R. (2000). *The Knowing Doing Gap: How Smart Companies Turn Knowledge into Action*. Boston, MA: Harvard Business School Press.

Redding, S. G. (1994). Comparative Management Theory: Jungle, Zoo or Fossil Bed? *Organization Studies, 15*(3), 323–359. doi:10.1177/017084069401500302

Rodrigues, C. A., & Blumberg, H. (2000). Do Feminine Cultures Really Behave More Feminine than Masculine Cultures? A Comparison of 48 Countries' Femininity-Masculinity Ranking to Their Human Development Rankings. *Cross Cultural Management, 7*(3), 25–34. doi:10.1108/13527600010797110

Ruggles, R. (1998). The state of notion: Knowledge management in practices. *California Management Review, 40*(3), 80–89. doi:10.2307/41165944

Sackmann, S. A., & Phillips, M. E. (2004). One's Many Cultures: A Multiple Cultures Perspective. In Crossing Cultures: Insights from Master Teachers (pp. 38–47). New York: Routledge.

Sahni, A. K., & Rastogi, A. K. (1995). Transforming Corporate Culture through Total Quality Commitment. *5th world congress on Total Quality*, 42 – 45.

Shahabi, A., Faez, A., & Fazli, D. (2012). Organizational intelligence dismounting barriers prioritization: A real-world case study. MSL Journal, 2(8).

Schein, E. H. (1985). How Culture Forms, Develops and Changes in R. H. Kilmann & M. J. Saxton. In R. Serpa (Ed.), *Gaining control of the Corporate Culture*. San Francisco, CA: Jossey Bass.

Schwen, T. M., & Hara, N. (2003). Community of Practice. A Metaphor for Online Design? *The Information Society*, *19*(3), 257–270. doi:10.1080/01972240309462

Sheriff, M., Georgiadou, E., Abeysinghe, G., & Siakas, K. (2013). INCUVA: A meta-framework for sustaining the value of innovation in multi-cultural settings. In F. McCaffery, R.V. O'Connor, & R. Messnarz (Eds.), EuroSPI 2013. Springer.

Siakas, K., & Siakas, D. (2015). Cultural and Organizational Diversity Evaluation (CODE): A Tool for Improving Global Transactions. *Strategic Outsourcing*, *8*(2/3), 206–228. doi:10.1108/SO-04-2015-0012

Siakas, K., Georgiadou, E., & Balstrup, B. (2010). Cultural Impacts on Knowledge Sharing: Empirical Data from EU Project Collaboration. *VINE: The Journal of Information and Knowledge Management Systems*, *40*(3/4), 376–389. doi:10.1108/03055721011071476

Siakas, K., & Georgiadou, E. (2008). Knowledge Sharing in Virtual and Networked Organizations in Different Organizational and National Cultures. In Building the Knowledge Society on the Internet. Idea Publishing.

Siakas, K., & Siakas, E. (2008). The need for trust relationships to enable successful distributed team collaboration and software outsourcing. *The International Journal of Technology, Policy and Management*, *8*(1), 59–75.

Siakas, K. V., & Georgiadou, E. (2006). Knowledge Sharing: Cultural Dynamics. In *Proceedings of 7th European Conference of Knowledge Management (ECKM06)*. Public Academic Conferences Ltd.

Siakas, K. V., & Balstrup, B. (2006). Software Outsourcing Quality Achieved by Global Distributed Collaboration. *Software Process: Improvement and Practice (SPIP) Journal, 11*(3), 319–328.

Siakas, K. V., & Georgiadou, E. (2003). Learning in a Changing Society and the Importance of Cultural Awareness. *IADIS 2003 (International Association for development of the Information Society) International Conference*, 696-702.

Siakas, K. V. (2002). *SQM-CODE: Software Quality Management – Cultural and Organizational Diversity Evaluation* (PhD Thesis). London Metropolitan University, London, UK.

Siakas, K. V., & Georgidaou, E. (2000). A New Typology of National and Organizational Cultures to Facilitate Software Quality Management. In E. Georgiadou, G. King, P. Pouyioutas, M. Ross, & G. Staples (Eds.), *Quality and Software Development: Teaching and Training Issues, The fifth International conference on Software Process Improvement - Research into Education and Training (INSPIRE 2000)*. The British Computer Society.

Siakas, K. V., & Georgiadou, E. (1999). Process Improvement: The Societal Iceberg. *European Software Process Improvement Conference, EuroSPI '99*, 25-37.

Sondergaard, M. (1994). Research Note: Hofstede's Consequences: a Study of reviews, Citations and Replications. *Organization Studies, 15*(3), 447–456. doi:10.1177/017084069401500307

Spiegler, I. (2000). Knowledge Management: A New Idea or a recycled Concept? *Communications of the Association for Information Systems, 3*(14), 1-23.

Strang, K. D., & Chan, C. E. L. (2010). Simulating E-Business Innovation Process Improvement with Virtual Teams Across Europe and Asia. *International Journal of E-Entrepreneurship and Innovation, 1*(1), 22–41. doi:10.4018/jeei.2010010102

Storck, J., & Hill, P. (2000). Knowledge Diffusion through 'Strategic Communities'. *Sloan Management Review, 41*(2), 63–74.

Tanriverdi, H. (2005). Information Technology Relatedness, Knowledge Management Capability and Performance of Multi-business Firms. *MIS Quarterly, 29*(2), 311-334.

Tayeb, M. (1988). *Organizations and National Culture: A Comparative Analysis*. London, UK: Sage Publishers.

Trompenaars, F., & Hampden-Turner, C. (1997). *Riding the waves of Culture*. Nicholas Brealey.

Wenger, E. (1999). *Communities of Practice: Learning, Meaning and Identity*. Cambridge University Press.

Williamson, D. (2002). Forward from a critique of Hofstede's model of national culture. *Human Relations, 55*(11), 1373–1395. doi:10.1177/00187267025511006

Wenger, E., & Snyder, W. (2000, January). Communities of practice: The organizational frontier. *Harvard Business Review*, 139–145.

Chapter 12

Entrepreneurship Education in Engineering Curriculum:
Some Insights Into Students' Viewpoints

Mukta Mani
Jaypee Institute of Information Technology, India

ABSTRACT

Entrepreneurship education programs are commonly offered in business schools, but recently, the educationists have started recognizing the need for such programs in engineering education. This chapter is targeted to empirically explore the suitability of entrepreneurship education in engineering curriculum from the perspective of students. The study attempts to unearth the levels of willingness of engineering students to take entrepreneurial activities and investigate the factors that motivate them and the factors that deter them to go for entrepreneurship. The analysis revealed that the students are highly interested in taking entrepreneurship as a career option because of some intrinsic motivating factors such as being their own boss, chasing their dreams. They consider decision-making skills, risk-taking capacity, creativity, communication skills, and ability to prepare business plan are the most important skills. However, lack of experience and funds deter them. The right kind of entrepreneurship education programs can promote more entrepreneurial activities among the engineering students.

INTRODUCTION

It is well understood that entrepreneurship has a significant impact on economic growth (Carree et al., 2002). Some early researchers argued that entrepreneurs are born not bred. It is beyond the capabilities of business schools or universities to teach individuals to become more enterprising (Johannison, 1991). In general, individuals are reluctant to take entrepreneurial career, since they consider it to be highly uncertain and risky (Petridou et al., 2009). However, recent studies show that entrepreneurship can be promoted through entrepreneurship education and training (Petridou and Glaveli, 2008). The entrepreneurship education has been defined as a collection of formalized teachings that educate anyone interested in business creation (Bechard and Toulouse, 1998). The entrepreneurship education can trig-

DOI: 10.4018/978-1-5225-5014-3.ch012

ger the entrepreneurial initiatives by enhancing entrepreneurial mindset among the students (Petridou et al., 2009; Lubis, 2014). A study conducted on college students in China conclude that entrepreneurship education should be included in colleges and universities' reform and development plan, personnel training system, and teaching evaluation index system (Zou, 2015). Considering the growing interest towards entrepreneurship in passing out students, many higher education institutes have started entrepreneurship education courses in their degree programs. Many higher education institutes in India such as Indian Institutes of Technology (IITs) have started Master's degree programs where the curriculum includes Engineering and Management subjects [Goel, 2013].

The need of entrepreneurship education has been well recognized by the higher education institutes. However, there is a debate on how the education should be provided, what are the students' expectations out of these entrepreneurship education programs. There is a debate about the role of universities and business schools in their contribution to entrepreneurship education (Kirby, 2004). It is argued that the traditional education system does not promote the attributes and skills that are required to produce entrepreneurs. The traditional education system teaches students how to become a good employee instead of a successful entrepreneur (Solomon, 1989). Considerable changes are required in the process of teaching and learning. Entrepreneurship should not be equated with new venture creation but with creativity and change (Kirby, 2004). There is a need to carry out more research on the way of providing the entrepreneurship education. The students are one of main stakeholders in the entrepreneurship education process. The current study is aimed to study the view point of the students: what students understand about the entrepreneurship education; what is their level of awareness and what are their concerns about the entrepreneurship education.

REVIEW OF LITERATURE

Entrepreneurship Education Programs

The entrepreneurship programs run by business schools equate entrepreneurship with new venture creation and educate "about" entrepreneurship rather than educating "for" entrepreneurship (Kirby, 2004). A review carried out in 123 HEIs of United Kingdom in 2006 found that the entrepreneurship education was offered at post graduate level mostly and on part-time basis. The delivery methods were traditional with little action learning or technology (Timmons, 1989). The studies conducted on effectiveness of such programs found that these programs were ineffective in creating entrepreneurial intentions. The goal of entrepreneurship education is the development of behavioral and attitudinal competencies to enable the students to see opportunities and bring them into execution (Kirby, 2007).The skill set needed to become entrepreneur include; persuasion skills, creativity, critical thinking, leadership skills, negotiation skills, problem solving skills, social networking and time management (Rae, 1997). To activate creativity and innovation, right brain thinking is required. The right brain thinking deals with uncertainties, open-ended questions, decision making with incomplete information, lateral thinking, intuitive thinking (Lewis, 1987). The entrepreneurship education programs should be designed in such a way to activate the right brain thinking of the students. Nowadays, entrepreneurship education programs use different teaching methods including lectures, guest speakers, case studies and role models (Solomon, 2007; Wilson et al., 2007). While designing the education program for entrepreneurs, the following points should be kept in mind- Student specific requirements should be understood; the teaching should be more specific to student requirements; didactic methods such as lectures, readings, text books and seminar should be used for providing new information; active case studies, group discussions, brainstorming etc. should be used for skills building; problem solving in real-world situation, consultancy with small firms should be taken to provide hands-on experience. The output should be assessed on behavioral and skill outcomes, product development, prototypes etc. (Hynes, 1996). It has also been found that there are gender differences in the motivational factors for participating in entrepreneurship program. There is a need to customize education programs to serve the need of female and male students. The entrepreneurship programs should be designed to train the students about how to solve the real world problems and presenting the ways in which the complexities can be overcome (Petridou et al., 2009).

In a research conducted in United Kingdom in 2007, business schools are found to be the main higher education institutions to provide entrepreneurship education. Nevertheless other disciplines also have a significant role to play in entrepreneurship education. Faculty of engineering follows business schools in providing Entrepreneurship education (Matlay and Carey, 2007; Mc Keown et al., 2006). At university level, entrepreneurship courses need to be taught in all faculties whether it is business or non-business (Hynes, 1996). The reason being many product ideas emerge in science and technology disciplines, but are not developed as business ideas because of lack of sufficient knowledge for business start-ups in the students (Pittaway et.al., 2009). In terms of number of startups created by the students it is found that science, technology, engineering, art and design faculties create more start-ups as compared to business disciplines (Mc Keown et al., 2006). Researchers have highlighted that interdisciplinary project between business and non-business faculties in entrepreneurship education are very rewarding (Bechard and Crregoire, 2005).

Students' Expectations

One can find a large number of studies on entrepreneurship education programs but not many studies have been conducted to find out students' expectations about entrepreneurship education. Few studies which delve into the students' view point have been discussed here. A study conducted on Post graduation students in United Kingdom found that gaining skills and knowledge to help them start a business, developing confidence, developing capabilities to start a business were the main expectations of students from the entrepreneurship education. The students responded that their skills about new venture planning, recognizing and developing opportunities have developed due to participation in entrepreneurship module. The students perceived financial planning to be least valuable and market research as significantly valuable while creative thinking is considered to be highly valuable (Rae and Woodier-Harris, 2012). Another study conducted on university students in Malaysia concluded that the students' attitude in terms of innovation, self-control, tolerance for ambiguity and risk control is low. The students also display low capabilities for environmental analysis, idea generation and market sensitivity. The study also highlights the students' perception about the readiness of universities to provide entrepreneurship education. According to them, universities lack to provide entrepreneurial environment in terms of campus conditions, lecturers, curriculum, and support to carryout entrepreneurial activities on campus (Norasmah, Norashidah and Hariyaty, 2012). There are gaps in the entrepreneurship education provided in the universities and colleges and the expectations of the students. The right sets of skills that are required for becoming a successful entrepreneur are need to be developed through a well drafted curriculum. Students widely differ in their expectations from the entrepreneurship education programs and thus there is a need for providing customized programs.

Prompted by these considerations, the aim of this study is to understand the engineering students' expectations from entrepreneurship education; to identify the factors that motivate them and to find out the factors which deter them to take entrepreneurial activities; their opinion about need and importance of entrepreneurship education subjects in their curriculum; to find out the skill sets required to become a successful entrepreneur.

RESEARCH METHODOLOGY

The discussion in the previous section draws attention to the fact that the entrepreneurship education should focus on developing the right skill sets for entrepreneurs. The programs should be customized according to the students' needs. And the entrepreneurship education should be promoted in non-business disciplines. In this research paper, we have attempted to comprehend these issues from students' point of view. The following six research questions have been framed:

RQ1: What percentages of students wish to pursue entrepreneurship in engineering discipline?
RQ2: What do students perceive about the need of entrepreneurship as a subject in engineering curriculum?
RQ3: What do students perceive about the importance of entrepreneurship as a subject?
RQ4: What skills are important to become an entrepreneur?
RQ5: What motivates the students to take entrepreneurship as a career option?
RQ6: What deters the students to take entrepreneurship as a career option?

The above research questions have been addressed through primary data collected from students. Since the study is focused on the entrepreneurship education in non-business disciplines, engineering students have been considered for data collection. A well structured, close-ended questionnaire is developed to collect the data from students. The questionnaire includes questions about their desire to become entrepreneur, the motivating and deterring factors, and their perception about the importance of entrepreneurship education (See Annexure). Before administering the questionnaire to respondents, a pilot study is carried out to check the reliability and validity of the instrument. Validity of the questionnaire is tested through detailed discussion with experts and faculty members of entrepreneurship education. The pilot study is conducted on 45 students. Reliability of the questionnaire is tested by calculating Cronbach's alpha coefficient as in Table 1. The Cronbach's alpha is a measure of internal consistency of the research instrument (Christmann & S, 2006). A Cronbach's alpha value, greater than 0.7 is considered to be acceptable. It indicates that the instrument is fit for the study (Peterson, 1994). The Cronbach's alpha of our questionnaire was found to be 0.801, which is clearly higher than 0.7. Thus the questionnaire is found to be fit for the study. The final questionnaire was administered to around 200 students of two engineering colleges located in National capital Region of India. The colleges are all private colleges and students are in the final year of their engineering degree. Finally, 168 completely filled questionnaires have been used for further study.

Table 1. Reliability Statistics

Number of Cases	Cronbach's Alpha	Number of Items
45	0.801	9

DATA ANALYSIS AND DISCUSSION

The data collected through the questionnaire has been analyzed using SPSS 16.0 software. The questions in the questionnaire were focused towards the research questions so data analysis has been done question-wise in the following subsections.

RQ1: What Percentages of Students Wish to Pursue Entrepreneurship?

The students were asked whether they plan to start their own business in future. They were asked to choose one of the five options given to them. The responses in Table 2 show that 87 percent of the students wish to start their own business sooner or later; only 13 percent of students feel that they will never start their own business. Out of total 87 percent students who wish to start their own business, only 2 percent of the students wish to start their business immediately after graduation and the largest number of students (42 percent) wishes to start business after 1 to 5 years of college. Subsequently 32 percent of students wish to start their business after 5 to 10 years of college. Despite this high level of interest in entrepreneurship few are equipped for entrepreneurship. According to Employability report, 2016, out of the total students passed out of engineering institutes in 2015, 8 percent aspire to work in start-ups nevertheless only 3.84 percent are found to be employable for start-up job (Employability Report, 2016). Many students seek to take entrepreneurship but the support required at the grassroots level in terms of mentorship, guidance and investors is largely missing (Fernandes, 2017 and Mani, 2015).

Further, to check the significance of the results, t-test has been conducted on the data. The results of t-test shown in Table 3 indicate that the t-value is significant at 95 percent confidence interval. The mean (=2.13) is significantly different from zero. It may be interpreted that the students wish to start their own business mainly after 5 to 10 years of college or 1 to 5 years after college. Students wish to enter into business but not immediately after college. The reason behind this may be their lack of knowledge, confidence and funds due to which they wish to gain some experience before entering into entrepreneurship or they may wish to save some money for starting their business.

RQ2: What do Students Perceive about the Need of Entrepreneurship as a Subject in Engineering Curriculum?

The students were asked to give their opinion about the need of entrepreneurship education in engineering colleges. The data analysis in Table 4 shows that 84 percent of the students perceive that

Table 2. Descriptive Statistics

Question: Do you plan to start your own business in future? (Variable 1)		
Options	**No. of respondents**	**Percentage**
Never	22	13%
Immediately after college	4	2%
1 to 5 years after college	70	42%
5 to 10 years after college	54	32%
After 10 years	18	11%

Table 3. One Sample t-test of Variable 1

| | | | | | 95% Confidence Interval of the Difference | |
| | Test Value = 0 | | | | | |
Mean	t	df	Sig. (2-tailed)	Mean Difference	Lower	Upper
2.13	18.135	167	0.000	2.127	1.89	2.36

entrepreneurship education should be provided in engineering colleges and 34 percent of the students strongly agree with the fact. Only 4 percent students believe that entrepreneurship should not be taught in engineering colleges. To check the significance of results obtained, one-sample t-test has been conducted on the data in Table 5. The results show that the t-value is significant at 95 percent level of confidence interval. It indicates that the results we obtained are not by chance. The mean value (=1.14) is significantly different from zero. Thus we may interpret that the students perceive that entrepreneurship should be taught in engineering curriculum.

The findings match with many earlier studies where researchers have established that entrepreneurship should be taught in engineering colleges. However entrepreneurship education is not yet common in engineering institutions. There is no dearth of entrepreneurship aptitude in the students, but engineering institutions have played a passive role (Nelson and Byers, 2010; Kanduja and Kaushik, 2009). Recently some Indian Institutes of Technology (IITs) have started incubation centers and e-cells etc. to promote entrepreneurship but still there is a need to change the scenario across the country. Taking cognizance of the fact, in India, All India Council for Technical Education (AICTE) has included the objective of inculcating entrepreneurship in its mission statement. National Skill Development Centre is working with Universities, University Grants Commission and AICTE to integrate skill based trainings into the academic cycle of the Universities.

Table 4. Descriptive Statistics

Statement: Entrepreneurship should be taught in engineering colleges. (Variable 2)		
Options	No. of respondents	Percentage
Strongly Agree	57	34%
Agree	85	50%
Neutral	20	12%
Disagree	6	4%
Strongly Disagree	0	0%

Table 5. One-sample t-test of Variable 2

| | | | | | 95% Confidence Interval of the Difference | |
| | Test Value = 0 | | | | | |
Mean	t	df	Sig. (2-tailed)	Mean Difference	Lower	Upper
1.14	12.980	167	0.000	1.139	0.96	1.31

RQ3: What do Students Perceive about the Importance of Entrepreneurship as a Subject?

To answer the above question two statements were put up to the students for their opinion. Firstly, the entrepreneurship education is useful for students even if they never plan to start their own business and second, entrepreneurs are born, entrepreneurship can't be taught in classroom.

From the data analysis in Table 6, it is found that 74 percent of the students consider entrepreneurship education to be useful for students even if they never plan to start their business, while only 8 percent students disagree with the statement. The data in Table 7 shows that 53 percent of the students disagree with the statement thus they believe that entrepreneurship can be taught in classroom, 21 percent of students agree with the statement. 26 percent of the students are neutral to this statement.

The responses are further tested to check whether the mean values obtained are significantly different from zero, where the zero means neutral. One-sample t-tests are conducted on the data and the results are shown in Table 8 and Table 9. The results show that the means values are significantly different from zero. Although the mean values are small, 0.46 for Variable 3 and 0.78 for Variable 4. Thus it may

Table 6. Descriptive Statistics

Statement: The Entrepreneurship education is useful for students even if they never plan to start their own business. (Variable 3)		
Options	No. of respondents	Percentage
Strongly Agree	26	16%
Agree	98	58%
Neutral	30	18%
Disagree	14	8%
Strongly Disagree	0	0%

Table 7. Descriptive Statistics

Statement: Entrepreneurs are born. Entrepreneurship can't be taught in classroom. (Variable 4)		
Options	No. of respondents	Percentage
Strongly Agree	7	4%
Agree	29	17%
Neutral	44	26%
Disagree	70	42%
Strongly Disagree	18	11%

Table 8. One sample t-test of Variable 3

Mean	Test Value = 0					
	t	df	Sig. (2-tailed)	Mean Difference	95% Confidence Interval of the Difference	
					Lower	Upper
0.46	4.228	167	0.000	0.456	0.24	0.67

Table 9. One sample t-test of Variable 4

Mean	Test Value = 0					
	t	df	Sig. (2-tailed)	Mean Difference	95% Confidence Interval of the Difference	
					Lower	Upper
0.78	9.149	167	0.000	0.785	0.61	0.96

be interpreted that the students believe entrepreneurship education to be important but they don't attach too much importance to the same.

From the above analysis, we may interpret that, students understand the importance of entrepreneurship education although they themselves have never studied entrepreneurship. They feel that the entrepreneurship education is valuable and the entrepreneurs can be prepared by teaching entrepreneurship. In India, entrepreneurship education is completely missing at school level education. The debate at large is about the promotion of entrepreneurship education at higher education level. However, our argument is that entrepreneurship education is important from the basic levels of learning. The entrepreneurship education should be provided to the students even if they never plan to start their own business. Entrepreneurship education has an effect on the overall personal characteristics of a person. The persons involved in start-up phase of entrepreneurship have demonstrated a decrease in external locus of control attributes and increase in internal locus attributes (Littunen, 2000). According to theory of locus of control (Rotter, 1966), internal control means control over one's own life where the individual considers that the results of his/her actions are dependent on his/her own behaviour and permanent characteristics. Thus internal locus is responsible for active learning and motivates for continuous striving. On the other hand external locus refers to the attitude where the results are considered to be the function of others' actions or fate or chance. External locus impedes learning and encourages passivity. By going through the start-up stage of entrepreneurship, individuals become more independent and open for new ideas and learning. Entrepreneurship education is viewed as a process of changing the mindsets of people towards applying creative thinking and innovative approaches to solving problems (Eze, 2011). It is an important factor in increasing the employability skills of graduates and motivating them for self-employment. Entrepreneurship education get to change people's beliefs and approaches and to prepare them with the ability necessary to plan, launch and successfully manage their own business enterprises (Akhuemonkhan, 2005). Not just starting their own enterprise but thinking and acting creatively in all situations and problems of their employment and life.

The following lines of John Dearborn (Dearborn, 2012) emphasize the same thoughts:

While entrepreneurship classes are designed to give budding entrepreneurs the tools to turn a new idea into reality, their value may be even greater than that: I think it gives all students the ability to view their careers and opportunities in a different light. It's so important that the benefits of an entrepreneurial-focused education are available to all students and not just those planning on entering the start-up world.

RQ4: What Skills are Important To Become an Entrepreneur?

The students are given a closed-ended question to rate the given set of skills according to the importance of those skills to become a successful entrepreneur. The results are shown in Table 10. Decision making skills and risk taking capacity are the top rated skills as they have got 92 percent and 90 percent score respectively. Communication skill is the next most important skill at 87 percent score. Creativity and ability to prepare business plan have got 86 percent score each. Sales techniques and knowledge of finance have been given least importance by the students as their scores are 78 percent and 77 percent respectively.

The mean values of the score vary from 3.61 to 2.81. So we need to know whether the mean values differ significantly from each other. An Analysis of Variance has been carried out to test the following hypothesis:

H_0: All the skills are equally important i.e. $\mu1=\mu2=\mu3=\mu4=\mu5=\mu6=\mu7=\mu8$
H_1: At least two means are different

The results in Table 11 show that the p-value is 1.86936E-14, which is less than $\alpha = 0.05$, the assumed level of significance. Therefore, there is enough evidence to reject the null hypothesis. This means that the difference in the importance of various skills cannot be attributed to chance. At least one of the skills is significantly more important than the other skills. Therefore, it is important to examine, that the mean of which skill is significantly higher than the other. The results of descriptive analysis give rise to following hypothesis:

Table 10. Descriptive Statistics

	Question: Which of the following skills are important to be a successful entrepreneur? Give ratings. (Variable 5)			
S.No.	Skills	Importance (percentage)	Average	Variance
1	Decision making skills	92%	3.61	0.29
2	Risk taking capacity	90%	3.49	0.25
3	Communication skills	87%	3.29	0.59
4	Creativity	86%	3.28	0.41
5	Ability to prepare business plan	86%	3.27	0.61
6	Negotiation skills	84%	3.15	0.59
7	Sales techniques	78%	2.84	0.73
8	Knowledge of finance	77%	2.81	0.69

Table 11. Analysis of Variance for Variable 5

Source of Variation	SS	df	MS	F	P-value	F crit
Between Groups	43.93513	7	6.276447	12.03718	1.86936E-14	2.024238
Within Groups	325.3671	1336	0.521422			
Total	369.3022	1343				

Set I H$_0$: Risk taking capacity and Creativity are equally important μ1=μ2

H$_1$: Risk taking capacity is more important than Creativity μ2>μ1

Set II H$_0$: Decision making skill and Risk taking capacity are equally important μ2=μ7

H$_1$: Decision making skill are more important than Risk taking capacity μ7>μ2

Set III H$_0$: Creativity and Communication skills are equally important μ1=μ6

H$_1$: Communication skills are more important than Creativity μ6>μ1

Set IV H$_0$: Sales techniques and Knowledge of Finance are equally important μ4=μ5

H$_1$: Sales techniques are more important than Knowledge of Finance μ4>μ5

Set V H$_0$: Creativity and Negotiation skills are equally important μ1=μ8

H$_1$: Creativity is more important than Negotiation skills μ1>μ8

The hypothesis presented in the above five sets have been examined using five independent sample t-test. The results are presented in Table 12.

The results of the t-tests as presented in Table 12 indicate the following results:

The null hypothesis of Set I is rejected. This is because the p-value is equal to 0.0100. Since the p value is less than 0.05, assumed level of significance, the hypothesis of equality of mean of two skills is rejected in favor of the alternate hypothesis. Therefore it can be concluded that Risk taking capacity is more important than Creativity.

The null hypothesis of Set II is rejected. This is because the p-value is equal to 0.0008. Since the p value is less than 0.05, assumed level of significance, the hypothesis of equality of mean of two skills is rejected in favor of the alternate hypothesis. Therefore it can be concluded that Decision making skills are more important than Risk taking capacity.

The null hypothesis of Set III is accepted. This is because the p-value is equal to 0.4553. Since the p value greater than 0.05, assumed level of significance, the hypothesis of equality of mean of two skills is accepted. Therefore it can be concluded that Communication skills and Creativity are equally important.

The null hypothesis of Set IV is accepted. This is because the p-value is equal to 0.4253. Since the p value is greater than 0.05, assumed level of significance, the hypothesis of equality of mean of two

Table 12. Independent sample t-tests for hypothesis given in Set I to Set V

	Skills	Mean	Variance	df	t Stat	P(T<=t) one-tail	t Critical one-tail
Set I	Creativity	3.2785	0.4086	334	-2.3511	0.0100	1.6547
	Risk Taking capacity	3.4937	0.2532				
Set II	Decision making skills	3.6076	0.2928	334	3.2008	0.0008	1.6547
	Risk taking capacity	3.2658	0.6079				
Set III	Communication skills	3.2911	0.5936	334	0.1124	0.4553	1.6547
	Creativity	3.2785	0.4086				
Set IV	Sales techniques	2.8354	0.7290	334	0.1886	0.4253	1.6547
	Knowledge of Finance	2.8101	0.6943				
Set V	Creativity	3.2785	0.4086	334	1.1247	0.1312	1.6547
	Negotiation Skills	3.1519	0.5920				

skills is accepted. Therefore it can be concluded that Sales techniques and Knowledge of finance are equally important.

The null hypothesis of Set V is accepted. This is because the p-value is equal to 0.1312. Since the p value is greater than 0.05, assumed level of significance, the hypothesis of equality of mean of two skills is accepted. Therefore it can be concluded that Creativity and Negotiation skills are equally important.

From the above analysis it can be concluded that decision making skills are statistically most important. Risk taking capacity is the second most significantly important skill, and then Creativity, Communication skills and Negotiation skills are statistically equally important followed by Sales techniques and Knowledge of Finance which are statistically equally important. These findings confirm other researches where objectives of curriculum building were determined on the basis of required skill sets. These objectives include- Personal development and Enterprise development. Personal development objectives include networking, negotiating and deal-making skills, and creativity and innovation skills, entrepreneurial and ethical self assessment. The Enterprise development objectives include identifying and evaluating business opportunities, commercialising a concept, constructing a business plan, finding capital and growing the business (Vesper and Gartner, 2001).

Development of these skills requires development of right brain thinking. In neuropsychology it is recognized that human brain is divided into two hemispheres- Left and Right. The left and right hemispheres of brain are responsible for different ways of thinking and doing things (Ornstein, 1977 and Sperry, 1968). Left brain supports logical, step by step, analytical and systematic thinking where the answers to the problems are found on the basis of facts and figures in a structured fashion. The right brain is responsible for emotional, intuitive and lateral thinking where the decisions are made in uncertainty, ambiguity, and spontaneity by looking at the problems from a wider perspective. Conventional formal education system trains students for left brain thinking. The classroom teaching and examinations test the abilities of a student on the basis of his/her left brain skills. Time management, punctuality, keeping notes, ability to control emotions, ability to follow instructions and meet others' expectations, all demand left brain capabilities (Kirby, 2007). Although the two brain hemispheres complement each other in most of the situations. Early research studies on entrepreneurial brain preferences profile confirmed that successful entrepreneurs demonstrate a preference for right brain thinking. It may well clarify the fact that many of the successful entrepreneurs failed in formal education system (Nieuwenhuizen and Groenwald, 2004). The two hemispheres of brain are clearly complimentary and it is evident that to be a successful entrepreneur, both creative and critical thinking are necessary. Right brain thinking can be enhanced by many techniques. The most important thing is to ask 'why' along with 'what' and 'how'. The key to success lies in keeping an open and enquiring mind.

RQ5: What Motivates the Students to Take Entrepreneurship as a Career Option?

The students were asked to choose among the factors that motivate them to take entrepreneurship as a career option. They were free to choose more than one option as well. The responses have been shown in Table 13. It is seen that the largest number of respondents i.e. 64 percent have chosen 'Being your own boss', as the most motivating factor. It is followed by 'chasing your dreams' and 'independent decision making' as these factors have been chosen by 50 percent and 52 percent of the respondents respectively. 'High returns' and 'your own confidence and knowledge' are next important motivating factors as 43 percent and 42 percent respondents have chosen respectively. 'To do something differently', 'to do something for society' and 'family support' are the least chosen factors by the students.

Table 13. Descriptive Statistics

Question: What motivates you to become an Entrepreneur?		
Options	No. of respondents	Percentage
Being your own boss	108	64%
Independent decision making	88	52%
Chasing your dreams	84	50%
High returns	72	43%
Your own confidence and knowledge	70	42%
To do things differently	52	31%
To do something for society	40	24%
Family support	12	7%
Other	2	1%

It indicates that intrinsic factors like being one's own boss, chasing dreams and independence in decision making are the main motivating factors for the students. Similar, findings have been observed in a study conducted on entrepreneurs in India, where following one's dreams, being one's own boss and earning lots of money are found to be the main motivating factors for entrepreneurs (Mani, 2013). Nowadays many fresh graduates go for entrepreneurship because of lack of suitable job opportunities. The Information Technology companies are witnessing a sharp decline in their hiring numbers mainly because of automation of their processes. In the coming years also about 80 percent of off-shore IT jobs and about 30-40 percent of jobs in finance and accounting will be eliminated (Fernandes, 2017).

RQ6: What Deters the students to Take Entrepreneurship?

The students were asked to choose among the factors that deter them to take entrepreneurship as a career option immediately after their college education. They were free to choose more than one option. The responses have been presented in Table 14. The data shows that lack of experience is the most deterring factor among the students for taking entrepreneurship as 70 percent of the students have chosen this factor. The next important factor is lack of funds as 58 percent of the students have chosen this factor. The third important factor is lack of knowledge, 44 percent of the students have chosen this factor. Subsequently, too much of risk, family responsibilities and other objectives have been chosen by 29 percent, 19 percent and 17 percent students respectively. Only 7 percent of the students have chosen 'not interested' as their reason for not going for entrepreneurship.

It can be interpreted that students consider lack of experience and lack of funds as the most deterring factors for entering into business immediately after college. This finding is validated by the findings in Table 2, where 74 percent of the students wish to start their business either after 5 to 10 years or after 1 to 5 years after college. The students feel that they should first gain some experience and collect some funds before venturing into business.

Higher Education Institutes can play an important role in the development of entrepreneurship skills in graduates. Formal education system is found to have a strong influence on entrepreneurial initiatives

Table 14. Descriptive Statistics

Question: What stops you to take Entrepreneurship as your career option immediately after college?		
Options	**No. of respondents**	**Percentage**
Lack of experience	118	70%
Lack of funds	98	58%
Lack of knowledge	74	44%
Too much of risk	48	29%
Family responsibilities	32	19%
Other objectives in life	28	17%
Lucrative job offers	14	8%
Not interested	12	7%
Parent's don't want	10	6%
Other	2	1%

in many countries. A study on entrepreneurial culture in different countries established that conformist and anti-entrepreneurial educational conditioning has resulted in ambivalent approach towards entrepreneurship in Kenya, South Africa and Singapore. Promotion of entrepreneurial culture through direct intervention in formal education system has resulted in greater entrepreneurship in North America, Scotland and Mexico (Morrison, 2000).

CONCLUSION

This paper is focused to examine different aspects of students' expectations of entrepreneurship education in engineering discipline. The study has been conducted on engineering students who have never taken any formal entrepreneurship education. Primary data from students has been collected through a well designed questionnaire. The data has been analyzed using descriptive statistics and t-tests.

From the data analysis it is found that students are highly interested in starting their own business and they consider that entrepreneurship is a very important subject and should be taught in engineering curriculum. They consider that decision making skills, risk taking capacity, creativity, communication skills and ability to prepare business plan are the most important skills for a successful entrepreneur. They feel motivated to start their own business because of intrinsic factors like being their own boss, chasing their dreams and independent decision making. However, they get deterred to immediately enter into entrepreneurship because they don't feel confident enough. Lack of experience and lack of funds are the most deterring factors. Since the respondents in this case are the students who have never taken any formal entrepreneurship education, we may suggest that formal entrepreneurship education can instill confidence in the students to start venture into business. The findings of this study may be highly useful for policymakers, academicians, teachers of entrepreneurship in shaping the entrepreneurship education in higher education system. A major limitation of the study is the geographies of primary data collection. The data has been collected from National Capital Region of India, thus the findings of the study may not be generalized without further research.

REFERENCES

Akhuemonkhan, I. A. (2005). *Modalities of teaching entrepreneurship in technical institution.* Paper presented at the National workshop on Capacity building for lecturers of Polytechnics and monotechnics in Nigeria, at the Federal Polytechnic, Uwana, Afikpo, Nigeria.

Aspiring Mind's National Employability Report-Engineers Annual Report. (2016). Aspiring Minds Assessment Pvt. Ltd. Available: http://www.aspiringminds.com/sites/default/files/National%20Employability%20Report%2020Engineers%20Annual%20Report%2020 16.pdf

Bechard, J. P., & Gregoire, D. (2005). Entrepreneurship education research re-visited: The case of higher education. *Academy of Management Learning & Education, 4*(1), 22–43. doi:10.5465/AMLE.2005.16132536

Bechard, J. P., & Toulouse, J. M. (1998). Validation of a didactic model for the analysis of training objectives in entrepreneurship. *Journal of Business Venturing, 13*(4), 317–332. doi:10.1016/S0883-9026(98)80006-2

Carree, M. A., van Stel, A. J., Thurik, A. R., & Wennekers, A. P. M. (2002). Economic development and business ownership: An analysis using data of 23 OECD countries in the period 1976-1996. *Small Business Economics, 19*(3), 271–290. doi:10.1023/A:1019604426387

Christmann, A., & Van Aelst, S. (2006). Robust estimation of cronbach's alpha. *Journal of Multivariate Analysis, 97*(7), 1660–1674. doi:10.1016/j.jmva.2005.05.012

Dearborn, J. (2012), The Unexpected Value of Teaching Entrepreneurship. *Huffington Post.* Retrieved on January 12, 2015, from http://www.huffingtonpost.com/john-dearborn/entrepreneurship b_1881096.html

Eze, J. F. (2011). *Entrepreneurship education for self-reliance and implications for the Millennium Development Goals.* Paper presented at the sixth international conference on development studies at Benue State University, Makurdi, Nigeria.

Fernandes, N. (2017). *Recruitment in Infosys falls to a Record Low since its Inception 33 Years Ago.* Dazeinfo.

Goel, S. (2013). *MTech (Information Technology and Entrepreneurship).* Available: https://goelsan.wordpress.com/2013/11/30/aninterdisciplinary-mtech-in-information-technology-and entrepreneurship/%20-%20comments

Hills, G. E. (1986). Entrepreneurship behavioural intentions and student independence, characteristics and experience. In *Frontiers of Entrepreneurship Research, Sixth Annual Babson College Entrepreneurship Research Conference.* Babson College.

Hynes, B. (1996). Entrepreneurship education and training # introducing entrepreneurship into non business disciplines. *Journal of European Industrial Training, 20*(8), 10–17. doi:10.1108/03090599610128836

Johannison, B. (1991). University training for entrepreneurship: Swedish approaches. *Entrepreneurship and Regional Development, 3*(1), 67–82. doi:10.1080/08985629100000005

Khanduja, D., & Kaushik, P. (2009). Exploring education driven entrepreneurship in engineering graduates in India. *International Journal of Continuing Engineering Education and Life-Long Learning, 19*(2/3), 256–270.

Kirby, D. (2007). Changing the entrepreneurship education paradigm. In *Handbook of Research in Entrepreneurship Education: A general perspective* (Vol. 1). Edward Elgar Publishing. doi:10.4337/9781847205377.00010

Kirby, D. A. (2004). Entrepreneurship education: Can business schools meet the challenge? *Education + Training, 46*(8/9), 510–519. doi:10.1108/00400910410569632

Lewis, D. (1987). *Mind Skills: Giving Your Child a Brighter Future*. London: Souvenir Press.

Littunen, H. (2000). Entrepreneurship and the characteristics of the entrepreneurial personality. *International Journal of Entrepreneurial Behaviour & Research, 6*(6), 295–309. doi:10.1108/13552550010362741

Lubis, R.L. (2014). Students' Entrepreneurial Strategy: Connecting Minds? *International Journal of Arts & Sciences, 7*(3), 545–568.

Mani, M. (2013). Motivation, Challenges and Success Factors of Entrepreneurs: An Empirical Analysis. *Pertanika Journal of Social Sciences & Humanities, 21*(2), 679 – 688.

Mani, M. (2015). Entrepreneurship Education: A Students' Perspective. *International Journal of E-Entrepreneurship and Innovation, 5*(1), 1-14.

Matlay, H., & Carey, C. (2007). Entrepreneurship education in the UK: A longitudinal perspective. *Journal of Small Business and Enterprise Development, 14*(2), 252–263. doi:10.1108/14626000710746682

McKeown, J., Millman, C., Sursani, S. R., Smith, K., & Martin, L. M. (2006). Graduate entrepreneurship education in the United Kingdom. *Education + Training, 48*(8/9), 597–613. doi:10.1108/00400910610710038

Morrison, A. (2000). Entrepreneurship: What triggers it? *International Journal of Entrepreneurial Behaviour & Research, 6*(2), 59–7. doi:10.1108/13552550010335976

Nelson, A.J., & Byers, T. (2010). *Challenges in University Technology Transfer and the Promising Role of Entrepreneurship Education*. Kauffman.

Nieuwenhuizen, C., & Groenwald, D. (2004). *Entrepreneurship training and education needs as determined by the brain preference profiles of successful established entrepreneurs*. Paper presented at the Internationalizing Entrepreneurship education and Training Conference, Naples, Italy.

Norasmah, O., Norashidah, H., & Hariyaty, A. W. (2012). Readiness towards entrepreneurship education. *Education + Training, 54*(8/9), 697–708. doi:10.1108/00400911211274837

Ornstein, R. (1977). *The Psychology of Consciousness*. New York: Harcourt Brace.

Peterson, R. A. (1994). A meta-analysis of Cronbach's coefficient alpha. *The Journal of Consumer Research, 21*(2), 381. doi:10.1086/209405

Petridou, E., & Glaveli, N. (2008). Rural women entrepreneurship within co-operatives: Training support. *Gender in Management, 23*(4), 262–277. doi:10.1108/17542410810878077

Petridou, E., Sarri, A., & Kyrgidou, L. P. (2009). Entrepreneurship education in higher educational institutions: The gender dimension. *Gender in Management, 24*(4), 286–309. doi:10.1108/17542410910961569

Pittaway, L., Hannon, P., Gibb, A., & Thompson, J. (2009). Assessment practice in enterprise education. *International Journal of Entrepreneurial Behaviour & Research, 15*(1), 71–93. doi:10.1108/13552550910934468

Rae, D., & Woodier-Harris, N. (2012). International entrepreneurship education. *Education + Training, 54*(8/9), 639–656. doi:10.1108/00400911211274800

Rae, D. M. (1997). Teaching entrepreneurship in Asia: Impact of a pedagogical innovation. *Entrepreneurship, Innovation, and Change, 6*(3), 193–227.

Rotter, J. B. (1966). Generalized expectations for internal versus external control of reinforcement. *Psychological Monographs, 80*(1), 1–27. doi:10.1037/h0092976 PMID:5340840

Scott, M. G., & Twomey, D. F. (1988). The long-term supply of entrepreneurs: Students' career aspirations in relation to entrepreneurship. *Journal of Small Business Management, 26*(4), 5–13.

Solomon, G. (1989). Youth: Tomorrow's entrepreneurs. *ICSB Bulletin, 26*(5), 1–2.

Solomon, G. (2007). An examination of entrepreneurship education in the United States. *Journal of Small Business and Enterprise Development, 14*(2), 168–182. doi:10.1108/14626000710746637

Sperry, R. W. (1968). Hemisphere disconnection and unity in conscious awareness. *The American Psychologist, 23*(10), 723–733. doi:10.1037/h0026839 PMID:5682831

Timmons, J. A. (1989). *The Entrepreneurial Mind.* Andover, MA: Brick House Publishing.

Vesper, K. H., & Gartner, W. B. (2001). *University Entrepreneurship Programs.* Los Angeles, CA: Lloyd Greif Center for Entrepreneurial Studies, Marshall School of Business, University of Southern California.

Wilson, F., Kickul, J., & Marlino, D. (2007). Gender, entrepreneurial self-efficacy, and entrepreneurial career intentions: Implications for entrepreneurship education. *Entrepreneurship Theory and Practice, 31*(3), 387–406. doi:10.1111/j.1540-6520.2007.00179.x

Zou, Li. (2015). Study on College Students Entrepreneurial Intentions Factors. *International Conference on Social Science and Technology Education (ICSSTE 2015).* Chongqing University of Science & Technology.

KEY TERMS AND DEFINITIONS

Behavioral Competencies: An attribute related to behavior such as knowledge, skillset, etc. that contributes to the development of an individual for a particular role.

Budding Entrepreneurs: The individuals who are in the early stages of development as entrepreneurs.

Entrepreneurship Education: Education to develop individuals as successful entrepreneurs.

Entrepreneurial Intentions: Intentions to take up entrepreneurship.

Lateral Thinking: Solving problems through an indirect and creative approach, using reasoning that is not immediately obvious and involving ideas that may not be obtainable by using only traditional step-by-step logic.

Locus of Control: Refers to the extent to which people feel that they have control over the events that influence their lives.

Neuropsychology: Study of structure and function of brain as it relates to specific psychological processes and behaviors.

Reliability: The ability of a research instrument to give similar answers if the questionnaire were administered to the same respondents soon after the first one.

Right Brain Thinking: Relating to the thought processes involved in creativity and imagination which are generally considered to be associated with the right hemisphere of the brain.

APPENDIX

ENTREPRENEURSHIP EDUCATION SURVEY

1. Do you plan to start your own business in future?
    ◦ Never
    ◦ Immediately after college
    ◦ 1 to 5 years after college
    ◦ 5 to 10 years after college
    ◦ After 10 years
    ◦ Entrepreneurship should be taught in engineering colleges.
    ◦ Strongly Agree
    ◦ Agree
    ◦ Neutral
    ◦ Disagree
    ◦ Strongly Disagree
2. The Entrepreneurship education is useful for students even if they never plan to start their own business.
    ◦ Strongly Agree
    ◦ Agree
    ◦ Neutral
    ◦ Disagree
    ◦ Strongly Disagree
3. Entrepreneurs are born. Entrepreneurship can't be taught in classroom.
    ◦ Strongly Agree
    ◦ Agree
    ◦ Neutral
    ◦ Disagree
    ◦ Strongly Disagree
4. What stops you to take Entrepreneurship as your career option immediately after college? (You can choose multiple options)
    ◦ Too much of risk
    ◦ Lack of experience
    ◦ Parent's don't want
    ◦ Lucrative job offers
    ◦ Lack of funds
    ◦ Lack of knowledge
    ◦ Family responsibilities
    ◦ Other objectives in life
    ◦ Not interested

Table 17.

	Highly important	Important	Neutral	Not important	Not required at all
Creativity	○	○	○	○	⊙
Risk taking capacity	⊙	○	○	○	○
Ability to prepare business plan	○	○	○	○	○
Sales techniques	○	○	○	○	○
Knowledge of finance	○	○	○	○	○
Communication skills	○	○	○	○	○
Decision making skills	○	○	○	○	○
Negotiation skills	○	○	○	○	○

5. What motivates you to become an Entrepreneur? (You can choose multiple options)
   ○ Chasing your dreams
   ○ Being your own boss
   ○ Independent decision making
   ○ High returns
   ○ Your own confidence and knowledge
   ○ To do things differently
   ○ Family support
   ○ To do something for society
6. Which of the following skills are important to be a successful entrepreneur?

Chapter 13
Multidisciplinary Group Case-Based Learning Environment:
An Education Paradigm to Cultivate Entrepreneurial Thinking

Despo Ktoridou
University of Nicosia, Cyprus

Epaminondas Epaminonda
University of Nicosia, Cyprus

Achilleas Karayiannis
Kes College, Cyprus

ABSTRACT

Technological, economic, and social developments represent dynamic changes for businesses across industries, creating opportunities for young entrepreneurs to build profitable companies. A key consideration relates to the need to recognize market opportunities and understand when and how to capitalize on them, whether starting a new type of business or growing on existing ideas; entrepreneurial thinking is a central attribute in cultivating an answer to this consideration. This chapter examines the impact of case-based learning introduced in a multidisciplinary undergraduate course, "Management of Innovation and Technology," at the University of Nicosia. A core element in this process are the students' and lecturers' experiences, benefits, and challenges of cultivating entrepreneurial thinking. The findings can be useful for academics teaching entrepreneurship-related topics and seeking ways to incorporate innovative approaches in their teaching and learning processes in order to motivate students towards the development of entrepreneurial thinking in their professional engagements.

INTRODUCTION

Living in a world of continuous scientific and technological change, university students need to be more prepared to effectively integrate themselves into the competitive working environments of the 21st century. A general observation is that teaching entrepreneurship through other courses besides business and management, generates important considerations such as: if any real world cases could be

DOI: 10.4018/978-1-5225-5014-3.ch013

Copyright © 2018, IGI Global. Copying or distributing in print or electronic forms without written permission of IGI Global is prohibited.

explained and if practical problems can be solved within a classroom environment; if all the knowledge generated within the classroom can meet students' ambitions and aspirations; if it is really motivating to tell students that they will someday need certain knowledge and skills in order to become successful in their professional engagements (Prince and Felder, 2006).

These considerations become more important when an educator has to teach entrepreneurial thinking to a multidisciplinary class with students coming from different specializations. Questions that are common include: How possible is it to convince such a diverse audience that a course that cultivates entrepreneurial thinking and acting skills will be useful for their professional careers? Which pedagogical approaches should be implemented to engage and motivate students towards entrepreneurial learning? Are there specific skills that students can learn in order to start thinking and acting as an entrepreneur? Some of these skills may be the following: be creative, come-up with innovative solutions, use problem-solving skills, work in teams, gather and evaluate data and finally take risks. These skills can be acquired through the use of a range of innovative teaching and learning methods such as student-centered methods that impose more responsibility on students for their own learning than more traditional teacher-centered methods.

In order to meet the demands of 21st century employment, educators and practitioners should prepare students in order to work in different environments with many complex requirements, by introducing theory in combination with real-world cases/applications for analysis. A student-centered approach where the student is responsible for his/her own learning by building his/her own version of reality is an alternative approach to learning. More specifically, in a student-centered approach students are primarily presented to a precise challenge, through complex, open-ended, real-world situations/problems/issues to analyze and seek solutions through interpretation and experimental data. While dealing with these challenges, students realize that they lack skills, knowledge, facts and conceptual understanding and they request the help of the lecturer, who plays the role of the facilitator. Ramsden (2003), Norman and Schmidt (1992) and Felder and Brent (2004) demonstrate that student-entered methods can potentially encourage students to adopt a deeper approach to learning that can lead to further intellectual development.

The urge for students to build and use their own version of reality in learning, blends well with Brecht's Epic Theatre and the Theory of Alienation, one of the most well-known theatrical approaches to what can potentially lead to good performance by actors, when on stage. Brecht characterized his approach to theatre as 'theatre for the scientific age' (Gordon, 2002: 226), looking for a theatre which 'might induce in its spectators an attitude of active engagement with the world and the possibilities for changing it' (Gordon, 2002: 226). Reflecting on the multidisciplinary approach to learning induced in this chapter, it can be argued that theatre, in its scientific sense, is a potential source of learning that can be transferred to a classroom environment and act as an important motivator towards students' active engagement in their own process of learning, through their own version of reality and understanding. In fact, the lecturer-trainer within such a multidisciplinary classroom learning environment, can be 'demonstrating the story' (Gordon, 2002: 226) while reminding the spectator (student) that was he or she is watching is "not in itself reality but the playwright's and actors' view of it" (Gordon, 2002: 233).

The work presented in this chapter, examines the impact of Case-based learning (CBL) introduced in the 'Management of Innovation and Technology', an undergraduate elective course at the University of Nicosia. It examines the students' and lecturer's experiences, benefits and challenges of implementing CBL, and gives recommendations to lecturers for designing a CBL based curriculum which aims at the development of entrepreneurial thinking and acting.

BACKGROUND

Case-Based Learning

Educators are continuously seeking ways to increasingly involve their students in classroom discussion, on the understanding that presenting real-life pragmatic cases can provide a good starting point for developing the students' problem-solving and decision-making skills. For many years the business, medical and law curricula of university courses, have been based on the analysis of realistic cases with professors providing evidence that case study utilization can help students to develop abilities and skills in analytical thinking and reflective judgment. Cases teach students about realistic decision-making situations involving one or more challenges, such as diagnosing technical problems and formulating solution strategies, making business management decisions by taking into account technical, economic, and possibly social and psychological considerations, and confronting ethical dilemmas (Prince and Felder, 2006). The cases should be real-life situations based on professional practice and coming from magazines, newspapers or interviews from those involved in the case.

Just as an in every effective case-based learning, the need to determine the specific goals expected to be accomplished is imperative. Generally, through cases, students can evaluate the application of concepts to complex real-life situations, thus developing analytical and decision making skills. In addition, communication and collaboration within the group can help students to develop interpersonal and collaboration skills that are highly rated and evaluated by educators. The idea of using real-world cases in the multidisciplinary elective course of Management of Innovation and Technology at the University of Nicosia, was based on the aim of developing the students' entrepreneurial thinking abilities and skills. More specifically, by dealing with real world cases, future entrepreneurs develop skills such as:

- Complex real-world case awareness and analysis
- Theoretical and practical knowledge acquisition
- Critical thinking and reasoning
- Creativity in proposing innovative solutions
- Data gathering for informal solutions
- Formation of positive attitudes toward the subject and level of confidence in knowledge or skills accrued
- Modifications in current prejudices, beliefs and patterns in order to accommodate the realities of the cases

This work presents the outcome of the implementation of Case-based Learning (CBL) in the curriculum of the Management of Innovation and Technology (MGT372) - an undergraduate, elective, multidisciplinary course. The main aim of implementing CBL to the specific course, is to immerse students in activities and expose them to entrepreneurial thinking not only through an in-depth understanding of course material but also through the development of abilities and skills such as the following: critical thinking, creativity in proposing innovative solutions, data gathering for informal solutions, formation of positive attitudes toward the subject and general level of confidence in the acquisition of relative knowledge and skills (Gates et al., 2011; Ktoridou, 2010). In addition, students struggle with these challenges/problems and recognize the need for facts, skills, and theoretical knowledge. Ktoridou and Eteokleous (2010), noted that group work learning is a valuable resource and an important part of an efficient teaching and learning process and consequently they argue that a productive group-work approach can be determined by how well students work together to share their individual findings and achieve a common goal. The lecturer who plays the role of the facilitator provides guidance and initiates students to be responsible for their own learning. In class, students are actively involved in discussing questions and solving problems (active learning), while in and out of class the work is done in groups (collaborative learning).

Lohman (2001) claims that similarities of case-based and problem-based learning are obvious; however, in problem-based learning students are confronted with poorly structured problems driving to the acquisition of new content knowledge while in case-based learning students analyze hypothetical situations which are well-structured, context-rich, involving solutions to problems and/or decision making. Katsikitis et al. (2002) found no significant difference between the two methods as far as performance or knowledge acquisition after comparing case studies to problem based learning. In the work presented in this chapter, the implementation CBL provided students with the opportunity to actively develop skills that enabled them to search, gather, analyze, evaluate and apply information on topics related to the management of technology and innovation.

The rest of this section, summarizes definitions and applications of CBL that have been implemented in this work while there is also a 'Key Terms & Definitions' section available at the end of the chapter.

Multidisciplinary Learning

Multidisciplinary learning can be defined as students of different disciplines (specializations) learning together. However, the deployment of multidisciplinary learning in education also offers students hands-on experiences with real-world complex situations that require knowledge of various subjects. In addition, students are encouraged to apply and share their diverse knowledge in a more practical way. Ktoridou and Doukanari (2016) provide evidence that through multidisciplinary group collaboration, students can develop deeper knowledge, share their diverse experiences and reach a consensus agreement on a professional solution. In the current study, the CBL method was applied in a multidisciplinary class of the Management of Innovation and Technology course in order to cultivate the students' entrepreneurial thinking and skills.

Entrepreneurship in University Curricula

Nowadays, it is argued that driving growth through innovation is key to business success. For this reason, entrepreneurship is a trendy present and future career choice for many undergraduate and postgraduate students. In addition, society has been very clear in its desire to include post-secondary entrepreneurship education in curriculum. Singh and Magee (2002) indicated that demand is driving education and the demand in this case is coming from corporations in need of cross functional thinkers with entrepreneurial skills (Harfst, 2010). During the 1950s and 1960s, Jeffrey Timmons, a trailblazing professor of entrepreneurship, played a significant role in developing entrepreneurship in the curricula of business schools within the context of higher education. More specifically, Timmons formulated entrepreneurship as:

- Entrepreneurship = Creativity *(how to create new ideas)* + Innovation *(how to implement new ideas successfully)*

The key elements in the Timmons model are the entrepreneur/founding team, the opportunity and the resources that are gathered in order to start the new business. The entrepreneur, as the key starting ingredient will deliberately search for an opportunity, and while finding it, form it so that is has the potential to be what Timmons calls a "high-potential venture". The entrepreneur then gathers the resources that are necessary to start a business to capitalize on his or her opportunity while often needs to take various risks: career, personal cash-flow, as well as net worth. In the last ten years, universities have been aiming to integrate entrepreneurship successfully into core curricula outside of the faculties of business and management. Entrepreneurship skills development now takes place also in the curriculum of areas such as engineering, science and MIS. A key consideration is how to do this successfully. The impact of Student-centered learning (SCL) in a new multidisciplinary undergraduate course is analyzed below. The paper addresses the organizational, pedagogic and practical challenges associated with immersing students in SCL activities that expose them to entrepreneurial thinking. It also outlines an approach on how lecturers of other, than business, specializations integrate entrepreneurship into their curriculum.

Management of Innovation and Technology Course (MGT-372)

Course Description

The Management of Innovation and Technology (MGT372), is an elective undergraduate course offered to students in Management, Business Administration and Management Information Systems (MIS) programs. Eight sections of MGT372 were offered from the Fall 2010 semester to the Fall 2016 semester, with 200 students attending (approximately 25 in each class). The students met once a week in sessions of 150 minutes each, broken down as follows: for the first 50 minutes the lecturer delivers the theoretical part of the course, then the students have a 20 minutes break and then the following 80 minutes are dedicated to group work, discussions and presentations based on SCL and used as the organizing principle of teaching and assessment practice, including both lectures and discussions.

The course focuses on how a manager or an entrepreneur can use a technology innovation strategy to enhance business performance. It emphasizes how technology innovation strategy can help businesses perform better by understanding (a) the process of technology evolution, (b) the ways that firms come up with innovations, (c) the strategies that firms use to benefit from innovation and (d) the process of implementing a technology innovation strategy (Shane, 2014). More specifically, the main objectives of the course are to:

- Introduce the important role of technology innovation in management strategy.
- Assist students to understand the theoretical knowledge underlying the technological change and the ways firms come up with innovations.
- Present an overview of the strategies that firms use to benefit from innovation.
- Enhance the understanding of the importance of formulating technology strategy.
- Provide the tools to design, develop and integrate a strategy of management of innovation and technology.

Assessment

The course has the following assessment methods: Project-25%, Homework-15%, Discussion/Participation/Attendance-20%, Final Exam-40%. Student active participation and contribution to class discussions through the following means: the presentation of their ideas and arguments especially in the light of answers of other students' questions and considerations; within and between group-work behavior (communication, collaboration and knowledge sharing).

TEACHING METHODOLOGY

A Case-based learning methodology was implemented in the Management of Innovation and Technology (MGT372) undergraduate multidisciplinary course. The aim of this implementation was to engage students, coming from diverse disciplines, in an intense group working environment in order to analyze cases that would continuously enhance/develop their entrepreneurial skills throughout the course. The students were given pragmatic cases that encompass all of the targeted teaching points conveyed through the specific course; they were specifically challenged to explore their existing preconceptions and modify them to accommodate the realities of the cases (Lundeberg, Levin and Harrington, 1999). It is worth mentioning that a basis for the direction followed in the methodology applied in MGT372, has its roots in one another academic institution/university in Nicosia that two of the three authors have worked together at, in the recent past. In that period and for different courses, the authors asked their students to use any movie they wanted and apply theoretical principles learned during the course, in the story outlined in the movie. The scope there was to make the students realize that knowledge can be transferred from one domain to another, whether that domain is an incident that takes place in everyday life (Goffman, 1959), within a professional working environment or within a classroom environment.

Eight sections of the MGT372 course were offered from the Fall 2010 semester to the Fall 2016 semester, with 200 students attending (approximately 25 in each class). The students met one a week in a 3-hour session each. Groups of 4-5 students from diverse disciplines (Management Information Systems, Management, Business Administration, Marketing, Finance and Economics) were formulated thus creating a supportive, challenging and conducive to risk-taking environment providing opportunities for individual and collective learning.

Students were given instructions on their responsibilities in order to prepare themselves to discuss a case within their group. In addition, there was a need for supplementary research and the educators who played the role of the facilitator, made suggestions for sources. In some cases, supportive questions were given to students as a basis for the main issues for discussion and the main ideas students should rely on. This way, the educator could monitor the directions of their discussion and their ability to apply knowledge and principles to real cases and experiences. The students' overall learning process and outcomes were evaluated mainly based on the level of discussion involvement that derived from the students' entrepreneurial-related abilities and skills in risk-taking, creative thinking, problem solving and leadership.

RESEARCH METHODOLOGY

For the purpose of this study, the data were elicited through students' focus groups and the lecturer's notes on CBL based on her in-class observations. The data were examined by employing a content analysis, a qualitative research approach which was considered ideal for this study especially since the research objectives were aligned with the collection of rich data based on the students' perceptions and perspectives on SCL in the course (Hatch, 2002). More specifically, in order to address the research objectives of the study, a case study design was employed (Rose et. al., 2015), a method of research that focuses on discovery, insight and understanding from the perspectives of those being studied, thus making significant contributions to the knowledge base and practice of education (Merriam, 1998).

A practical problem from a holistic perspective, is to gain an in-depth understanding of the situation and its meaning for higher education. According to Ktoridou (2010), the attention was focused on teaching/learning processes rather than on learning outcomes, in the general course context rather than in a particular variable and in the process of discovery rather than in confirmation. It was expected to gather a range of rich data from students' responses on their learning through the CBL approach, with the data collection mainly focused on investigating the relationships of the participants (student-to-student, student-to-lecturer) during the process of implementing a CBL approach in classes. The study also focused on exploring the roles of students coming from different specializations in an inductive learning environment: performance, collaboration, exchange of ideas and context learning. The data collection process took place through ongoing classroom observations and focus groups at the end of each semester.

- **Lecturer's In-Class Observations:** The lecturer's written notes based on her in-class observations and experiences were analyzed. The purpose was to elicit information about her views on the design, development, implementation, observations and experiences on CBL practices for achieving the educational goals and developing entrepreneurial mindsets.
- **Focus Groups:** Three focus groups took place upon the completion of the course at the end of each semester. The participants for each focus group were chosen based on specialization and educational background. Overall, 30 students participated in the focus groups (10 students in each one). On average, the duration of each focus group was from one to one and a half hours. During the focus groups, mainly open-ended questions were asked in an attempt to provide students with the opportunity to freely and openly express themselves on the subject under investigation. The focus groups were conducted in order to get insights and to analyze in-depth the concepts under investigation from the students' point of view (Kvale, 1996). More specifically, the focus groups aimed at investigating and exploring the students' views, experiences, and perceptions regarding the implementation of CBL. The following were investigated: learning experiences in the current and previous CBL environments; possible opportunities for discovery, innovation and creativity; collaborative team work; any comments students had while working in a SCL environment in order to become entrepreneurial thinkers; recommendations for improvements and/or changes.

The qualitative data collected from the observations, the focus groups and the lecturer's informal comments were analyzed with the method of continuous comparison of data (Morehouse and Maykut, 1994), thoroughly explained in the following section.

DATA ANALYSIS

Case Discussion Analysis: Student Involvement

Content analysis of the data reveals that the employment of CBL educational practice in a multidisciplinary class is beneficial in terms of meeting the students' educational goals and developing entrepreneurial mindsets. The analysis below, first presents the students' impressions of CBL; in general, they indicate that this environment is highly supportive, challenging and conducive to risk-taking for group interaction and collaboration. Students mentioned that sharing with their group even the simplest comment provided them with the opportunity for individual and collective learning. Overall, the students believe that they have learned a lot through real-life cases, thus consolidating the use and importance of the theoretical part of the course and recommended further implementation of CBL in other courses. Then, analysis of the lecturer's notes based on her in-class observations and experiences followed, which also revealed that CBL is a challenging and beneficial experience that can prepare students to become future entrepreneurs.

Students' Comments

Each comment made by students on an individual and a focus group basis, was placed under one of the following 4 sections:

1. **CBL:** A highly supportive, challenging and conducive to risk-taking environment for a multidisciplinary class.
2. Through multidisciplinary group discussion students were provided with opportunities for individual and collective learning.
3. **Real-Life Cases:** A way to justify the theoretical lecture providing a sound link between theory and practice.
4. Recommendations for further implementation of CBL in other courses.

The case-based approach in learning engages students in discussion of specific situations, typically real-life examples. This approach involves intense interaction between students. Case-based learning concentrates on knowledge building as the basis to examine a case. The lecturer plays the role of the facilitator and the resource provider for students to collaboratively address problems/controversies from an analytical perspective. Most of the cases involved students getting engaged with questions that had multiple correct answers. By bringing real-life authentic situations related to a topic into the classroom, case based learning is a promising approach by ensuring active participation and training students in proposing innovative solutions. In their effort to find solutions and reach decisions through discussion, students sorted out factual data, applied analytical tools, articulated issues, reflected on their relevant experiences, and drew conclusions that they could relate to in other cases. In the process, they acquired substantive knowledge and developed analytical, collaborative and communication skills that exposed them to entrepreneurial thinking and acting.

Focus Groups

Focus groups were also conducted to add to the richness of the data collected and enhance understanding of the learning process. The discussion focused mainly on:

- Learning experiences in a CBL environment.
- Opportunities for discovery, innovation and creativity and collaborative team work.
- Students' comments on whether working in a CBL environment helped them to cultivate their entrepreneurial thinking.
- Recommendations for improvements and/or change.

Overall, students seemed to enjoy the new learning environment and although they seemed to have experience in team work, most of them expressed the need for further training in gaining entrepreneurial skills, especially in decision making. Most students stated that they felt comfortable in exchanging ideas and sharing resources by practicing their team skills and helping one another to succeed, which they considered a major skill for their future careers as entrepreneurs.

- **Group 1 - CBL:** A highly supportive, challenging and conducive to risk-taking environment for a multidisciplinary class.
- I do prefer more guided learning, it takes me more time to study alone.
- Until now we have been taught that business issues are not purely based on technical solutions, this course taught us how to use entrepreneurial skills to deal with such issues.
- **Group 2:** Through multidisciplinary group discussion students were provided with opportunities for individual and collective learning.
- I never thought I could collaborate with students from other disciplines, share findings and, most importantly, come up with a solution.
- Since we needed to come up with our own solutions it was difficult to decide alone which solution was the most appropriate.
- **Group 3 - Real-Life Cases:** A way to justify the theoretical lecture providing a sound link between theory and practice.
- Using case studies helped me to develop my thinking in a more creative way, analyzing situations better and coming-up with innovative solutions.
- Through the analysis and group discussion of real-life cases and problems we feel more prepared to face our future work place.
- **Group 4:** Recommendations for further implementation of CBL in other courses.
- We need to analyze more real situations and in other courses, more case-studies and real problems, this way we connect theory and practice.

Lecturer's Comments

- It needs time to prepare for such method. It took me days to look for authentic cases and problems that are relevant to each chapter and of course prepare the questions.
- This is expected to be a challenge for any lecturer or practitioner who wishes to implement such a method in his/her curriculum.

- Previous experiences influence students' views of learning and the way they approach their learning.
- Some students didn't find individual learning as motivating.
- It was quite important to get to know my students' aspirations at the beginning of the semester so as to tap into their motivation.
- In my course syllabus the learning outcomes are written in a way that describe what students will be able to do, and know, as a result of their experiences thus enabling their learning to be assessed.
- From comments that I had from students the development of entrepreneurial skills objectives in the course syllabus was quite intriguing for them and influenced their decision to choose this course.
- The curriculum evaluation that I have used and I strongly recommend was based on: group work, collaboration, communication and context learning for the three inductive methods that I have implemented; these parameters matched perfectly with the entrepreneurship thinking and acting abilities students needed to develop.

CONCLUSION

The work presented in this chapter, underlines that the implementation of innovative approaches to teaching and learning should not only concentrate on content learning, but also on immersing students in activities that develop their entrepreneurial skills. The innovative approach used for this study in an undergraduate Management of Innovation and Technology course at the University of Nicosia has its basis on SCL elements. The participation and involvement of the lecturer and the students in learning through SCL, proved to be beneficial and it is significant to note that students effectively adopted the approach even though it was quite challenging for 2 reasons: a. they were used to learning in a lecturer-centered environment and b. CBL took place in a new, multidisciplinary course. Even though students were initially hesitant with this approach, after a few classes they started acquiring benefits of the SCL in the course since they were exposed to activities and problems that required entrepreneurial thinking and acting.

The inductive method used for this study incorporated inquiry learning, problem-based learning, and case-based teaching. Inquiry learning was the first experience students had with SCL and proved to be the approach that required a lot of effort from the lecturer in designing the context (finding questions and problems related to the topic), thus encouraging students to be self-directed – a critical skill students need to acquire for their future careers as entrepreneurs. With this method as the basis and as part of their effort to search and gather data so as to make informed decisions, students developed research skills that could be used throughout their educational experiences. Problem-based learning incorporated complex, open-ended, authentic problems whose solution requires knowledge and skills specified in the course aims and objectives. A variety of interpersonal problems had been raised during this method due to the multidisciplinary educational background presented during group-work. The lecturer had to interfere as a facilitator to help student groups become effective teams, thus tapping into the development of the students' professional skills such as problem-solving and self-directed or lifelong learning.

The use of case studies proved to be a great promise as a pedagogical practice for teaching the multidisciplinary undergraduate course on Management of Technology Innovations. The selection of cases must address the learning aims and objectives with a wide variety of scenarios, such as identifying technical problems, developing solution strategies and making entrepreneurial management decisions. With CBL in the curriculum, students were involved with real-life situations, saw theory in practice and had the opportunity to become decision makers. Real-life authentic situations exposed students to evaluate options from different perspectives, usually leading to differing outcomes that can be potentially explained by their multi-disciplinary orientation.

Moreover, students needed to analyze the cases, choosing appropriate analytical techniques, in order to arrive at a conclusion. Based on the lecturer's observations with case-based learning, students were more engaged, interested and involved in the class than with inquiry-based and problem-based learning. The adoption of inductive methods cannot guarantee better learning and satisfaction for both the lecturer and the student. Any new teaching method should be very well-planned, organized and implemented to meet the needs of the curriculum and the students. It is important for students exposed to such methods to know that they will have increased responsibility of their own learning with the lecturer playing the role of the facilitator.

This work encourages lecturers to seek ways to expose students to entrepreneurial thinking and educate them to become high-quality graduates flexible to work in a wide range of working environments. Lecturers deciding to implement inductive methods in their curriculum must consider that it will take them time to prepare (search for cases, problems, complex situations that are based on real life scenarios) in order to offer students opportunities to exchange ideas, beliefs, knowledge, experiences and come up with professional solutions. In other words, effective CBL learning is a two-way process where the students and the lecturers can potentially benefit as it provides for a great learning environment and opportunities for both groups to expand their knowledge and widen their horizons.

An indispensable part of this two-way process should be students' and lecturers' previous experiences in learning and the way they approach their learning. It can be very useful for lecturers to get to know the students' aspirations so as to motivate them towards learning the courses' main objectives. Based on the logic and scope behind the development of entrepreneurial abilities for students within a course, such objectives must be written in a way that describes what the students will be able to do and know, as a result of using their experiences within a classroom environment, thus enabling their learning to be effectively assessed and then applied in different learning and professional environments.

REFERENCES

Bateman, W. (1990). *Open to Question: The Art of Teaching and Learning by Inquiry*. San Francisco: Jossey-Bass.

Cannon, R. (2000). *Guide to support the implementation of the Learning and Teaching Plan Year 2000*. The University of Adelaide.

Collins, J. W. III, & O'Brien, N. P. (Eds.). (2003). *Greenwood Dictionary of Education*. Westport, CT: Greenwood.

Duch, B. J. (2001). Models for Problem-Based Instruction in Undergraduate Courses. Academic Press.

Felder, R. M., & Brent, R. (2004). The intellectual development of science and students. Pt. 1: Models and challenges; Pt. 2: Teaching to promote growth. *Journal of Education*, *93*(4), 269–277.

Froyd, J., & Simpson, N. (2010). *Student-Centered Learning Addressing Faculty Questions about Student centered Learning*. Texas A&M University. Retrieved Aug 28, 2016 from http://ccliconference.org/files/2010/03/Froyd_Stu-CenteredLearning.pdf

Gates, A. Q., Romero, R., Alonso, M., Klett, F., Fernando, N., & Requena, D. (2011). Cultivating Entrepreneurial Thinking through IEEE-CS Student Chapters. *IEEE Computer Magazine*, *44*(4), 48–55. doi:10.1109/MC.2011.69

Gijselaers, W. H. (1996). Connecting problem-based practices with educational theory. In L. Wilkerson & W. H. Gijselaers (Eds.), *Bring problem-based learning to higher education: Theory and practice* (pp. 13–21). San Francisco: Jossey-Bass.

Glaser, B. G., & Strauss, A. L. (1967). *The discovery of grounded theory, Strategies for qualitative research*. New York: Aldine.

Glister, P. (1997). A new digital literacy: A conversation with Paul Glister. *Educational Leadership*, *55*(3), 6–11.

Goffman, E. (1959). *The presentation of self in everyday life*. London: Penguin Books Ltd.

Gordon, P., Rogers, A., & Comfort, M. (2001). A taste of problem-based learning increases achievement of urban minority middle-school students. *Educational Horizons*, *79*(4), 171–175.

Gordon, R. (2006). *The Purpose of Playing*. The University of Michigan Press. doi:10.3998/mpub.93221

Guba, E. G., & Lincoln, Y. S. (1994). Competing paradigms in qualitative research. In N. K. Denzin & Y. S. Lincoln (Eds.), *Handbook of Qualitative Research*. Sage.

Harfst, K. L. (2010). *The Evolution and Implications of Entrepreneurship Curriculum at Universities*. Southern Illinois University Carbondale. Retrieved June 10, 2011 from http://opensiuc.lib.siu.edu/cgi/viewcontent.cgi?article=1020&context=ojwed&sei-redir=1#search=%22Entrepreneurship%20University%20Curricula%22

Hatch, J. A. (2002). *Doing qualitative research in education settings*. New York: State University of New York Press.

Huba, M. E., & Freed, J. E. (2000). *Learner-Centered Assessment on College Campuses: Shifting the Focus from Teaching to Learning*. Needham Heights, MA: Allyn & Bacon.

Ingleton, C., Kiley, M., Cannon, R., & Rogers, T. (2000). *Leap into Student-Centered Learning*. University of Adelaide ACUE. Retrieved Aug 02, 2011 from http://www.adelaide.edu.au/clpd/resources/leap/leapinto/ProblemBasedLearning.pdf

Kardash, C., & Wallace, M. (2001). The perceptions of science classes' survey: What undergraduate science reform efforts really need to address. *Journal of Educational Psychology*, *93*(1), 199–210. doi:10.1037/0022-0663.93.1.199

Katsikitis, M., Hay, P. J., Barrett, R. J., & Wade, T. (2002). Problem- Versus Case-based Approaches inTeaching Medical Students about Eating Disorders: A Controlled Comparison. *Ed. Psychology*, *222*(3), 277–283. doi:10.1080/01443410220138511

Ktoridou, D. (2010). *Applying an Inductive Method to a New, Multidisciplinary, Management of Innovation & Technology Course: Evidence from the University of Nicosia. In EDUCON* (pp. 452–460). Madrid, Spain: IEEE.

Ktoridou, D., & Doukanai, E. (2016). Teaching with Team Projects in Higher Education. Santa Rosa, CA: Informing Science Press.

Kvale, S. (1996). *Interviews: an introduction to qualitative research interviewing*. Thousand Oaks, CA: Sage.

Lee, V. S. (Ed.). (2004). *Teaching and Learning through Inquiry*. Stylus Publishing.

Lohman, M. (2001). Cultivating Problem-Solving Skills through Problem-Based Approaches to Professional Development. *Human Resource Development Quarterly, 13*(3), 243–261. doi:10.1002/hrdq.1029

Lundeberg, M., Levin, B., & Harrington, H. (1999). *Who learns what from cases and how? The research base for teaching and learning with cases*. Mahwah, NJ: Lawrence Erlbaum Associates.

Maykut, P., & Morehouse, R. (1994). *Beginning Qualitative Research, A Philosophic and Practical Guide*. London: The Falmer Press.

Merriam, S. B. (1998). *Qualitative research and case study applications in education*. San Francisco: Jossey-Bass.

Newble, D., & Cannon, R. (1995). *A handbook for teachers in universities and colleges: A guide to improving teaching methods* (3rd ed.). London: Kogan and Page.

Norman, G. R., & Schmidt, H. G. (1992). The psychological basis of problem-based learning: A review of the evidence. *Academic Medicine, 67*(9), 557–565. doi:10.1097/00001888-199209000-00002 PMID:1520409

Prince, M., & Felder, R. (2006). Inductive teaching and learning methods: Definitions, comparisons and research bases. *Journal of Education, 95*(2), 123–138.

Prince, M., & Felder, R. (2007). Many faces of inductive teaching and learning. *Journal of College Science Teaching*. Retrieved June 20, 2011 From: http://www4.ncsu.edu/unity/lockers/users/f/felder/public/Papers/Inductive(JCST).pdf

Ramsden, P. (2003). Learning to teaching higher Education (2nd ed.). London: Taylor and Francis.

Rose, S., Spinks, N., & Canhoto, A. I. (2015). *Management Research: Applying the Principles: Case study research: Design and methods* (2nd ed.). Thousand Oaks, CA: Sage.

Shane, Sc. (2014). *Technology Strategy for Managers and Entrepreneurs: Pearson New* (International Edition). Upper Saddle River, NJ: Prentice Hall.

Singh, R. P., & Magee, B. (2002). *Entrepreneurship Education: Is there a growing crisis?* (Unpublished paper). Retrieved May 20, 2011 from http://www.celcee.edu/publications/edinfo/ED02-10.html

ADDITIONAL READING

Biggs, J. B. (1990). Teaching: Design for Learning. In B. Ross (Ed.), *Teaching for Effective Learning*. Sydney: HERDSA.

Biggs, J. B. (1999). *Teaching for quality learning at university*. Buckingham: OUP.

Bransford, J. D., Brown, A. L., & Cocking, R. R. (Eds.). (2000). *How People Learn: Brain, Mind, Experience, and School*, Washington, D.C.: National Academy Press. Retrieved March 20, 2011. From http://www.nap.edu/ books/0309070368/html/

Brimble, R., & Davis, D. (2005). The power of the group: Foundations for lifelong experiment. *Annals of Community-Oriented Education, 5*, 193–198.

Danh Duc Nguyen, D. D. (2009). *A Study of the Implementation of a Problem-Based Learning Approach*. Vietnam: University Classes.

Dionysiou, I., & Ktoridou, D. (2011), Inductive Methods: Developing Teaching/Learning Strategies for an Information Security Undergaduate Course. *ICICTE-International Conference on ICT in Education,* (pp. 140-149). Rhodes, Greece.

Eteokleous, N., & Ktoridou, D. (2011), Higher Education: A Web 2.0 World of communication, collaboration, participation and sharing. *ICICTE-International Conference on ICT in Education:* (pp. 1-10). Rhodes, Greece.

Felder, R. M., & Brent, R. (1996). Navigating the bumpy road to student- centered instruction.[[From]. *College Teaching, 44*(2), 43–47. www.ncsu.edu/felderpublic/NPapers/Resist.html RetrievedJune122011. doi:10.1080/87567555.1996.9933425

Felder, R. M., & Brent, R. (2003). Designing and Teaching Courses to Satisfy the ABET MIS Criteria. *Journal. Engr. Education, 92*(1), 7–25. doi:10.1002/j.2168-9830.2003.tb00734.x

Felder, R. M., & Brent, R. (2004). The intellectual development of science and engineering students. Pt. 1: Models and challenges; Pt. 2: Teaching to promote growth. Journal of Engineering Education 93 (4): 269–77; 93 (4): 279–91. Pt. 1. Retrieved June 15, 2011. from www.ncsu.edu/felder-public/Papers/IntDev-I.pdfPt. 2 Retrieved June 15, 2011. From www.ncsu.edu/felder-public/Papers/IntDev-II.pdf

Hoang, T. (2008). *Requests for reforming education and urgent innovations*. conventional education: A review of the University of Limburg medical education

Hyman, M., & Luginbuhl, G. (2004) Inquiry-guided learning and the undergraduate major in the department of microbiology. *In Teaching and learning through inquiry: A guidebook for institutions and instructors*, ed. V.S. Lee, 129–41. Sterling, VA: Stylus. *Just-in-Time Teaching*. Retrieved March 2011. From http://webphysics.iupui.edu/jitt/jitt.html

Knight, P. (2002). Learning Contracts. In Assessment for Learning in Higher Education. Birmingham: SEDA series

Ktoridou, D. (2010). Applying an Inductive Method to a New, Multidisciplinary, Management of Innovation & Technology Course: Evidence from the University of Nicosia. EDUCON, IEEE MIS Education – The Future of Global Learning in Engineering Education: (pp. 452 – 460) Madrid, Spain. learning.

Ktoridou, D., & Dionysiou, I. (2011). *A Case-Based Learning: An Instructional Model to Incorporate Information Security Topics in Multidisciplinary Courses at the University of Nicosia* (pp. 46–469). Amman, Jordan: EDUCON, IEEE MIS Education – Learning Environments and Ecosystems in MIS Education.

Ktoridou, D., & Eteokleous, N. (2010). Computer Literacy for Socially Excluded Unemployed Women: Evidence from Cyprus. *ICICTE-International Conference on ICT in Education:* (pp. 20 -210). Corfu, Greece.

Lea, S. J., Stephenson, D., & Troy, J. (2003). Higher Education Students' Attitudes to Student Centred Learning: Beyond 'educational bulimia'. *Studies in Higher Education, 28*(3), 321–334. doi:10.1080/03075070309293

Mayer, R. (2002). Invited Reaction: Cultivating Problem-Solving Skills through Problem-Based Retrieved June 2, 2011 from http://www.tuanvietnam.net/vn/thongtindachieu/5928/index.aspx

Newble, D., & Cannon, R. (1995). *A handbook for teachers in universities and colleges: A guide to improving teaching methods* (3rd ed.). London: Kogan and Page.

Nicolau, N., Shane, S. A., Hunkin, J., Cherkas, L., & Spector, T. (2008). *Is the tendancy to engage in entrepreneurship genetic?* ((1st ed., Vol. 54, pp. 167–179). Hanover, MD: Management Science.

Schilling, M. A. (2008). *Strategic Management of Technological Innovation* (2nd ed.). Boston: McGraw Hill.

Schilling, M. A., & Phelps, C. (2007). Interfirm collaboration networks: The impact of network structure on rates of innovation. In E. Sheshinki, R. J. Strom, & W. J. Baumol (Eds.), *Entrepreneurship, Innovation and the Growth Mechanism of the Free- Market Economies* (pp. 100–134). Princeton, NJ: Princeton University Press.

Schmidt, H. G., Henry, P. A., & de Varies, M. (1992). Comparing problem-based with Classroom-Based Practices. *Journal of Engr. Education, 94*(1), 87–101.

Schunk, H. D. (2008). *Learning theories: an education perspective* (5th ed.). Ohio: Pearson Merrill Prentice Hall.

Shane, S. A. (2008). *Illusions of Entrepreneurship: The Costly Myths that Entrepreneurs, Investors, and Policy Makers Live By.* New Haven, CT: Yale University Press.

Shuell, T. J. (1986). Cognitive conceptions of Learning. *Review of Educational Research, 56*(4), 411–436. doi:10.3102/00346543056004411

Smith, K. A., Sheppard, S. D., Johnson, D. W., & Johnson, R. T. (2005). Pedagogies of Engagement: Approaches to Professional Development. *Human Resource Development Quarterly, 13*(3), 263.

KEY TERMS AND DEFINITIONS

Case-Based Instruction: Students analyze real-life case studies that involve solving problems and/or making decisions.

Entrepreneurship: Is a management style that involves undertaking innovations, finance, and business activities in an effort to come up with an innovation strategy to enhance business.

Inquiry-Based Learning: Students are actively involved in learning and possess skills and attitudes that permit them to seek resolutions to questions and issues while they construct new knowledge.

Problem-Based Learning: Students tackle an open-ended, real-world problem and work in groups to identify learning needs and develop a feasible solution, with instructors acting as facilitators.

Student-Centered Teaching Methods: Teaching methods that shift the focus of activity from the teacher to the learners.

Chapter 14
The Advantages and Disadvantages of Internet Commerce in China

James G. S. Yang
Montclair State University, USA

ABSTRACT

This chapter further considers the tax aspect of the internet commerce transaction, which found that the Chinese government imposes a value-added tax at a rate of 17%. The system to impose value-added is extremely complicated. The first buyer pays tax. The tax is transferred to the second buyer, so on and so forth until the last buyer. It requires detailed records. It makes the tax administration highly burdensome. On the contrary, in the United States, the sales tax rate is only 7% and is imposed only on the final consumer. There are no sales between the first buyer and the last buyer. The taxing system is much simpler than its counterpart in China.

1. INTRODUCTION

E-business was not introduced in China until four years ago, but since then its growth was unusually spectacular. Coupled with its vast consumer market and tremendous production capacity, China looks like a gold mine. Is it really encouraging to join the gold rush? This article develops some insights by investigating its E-business volume, consumer commodities, market competition, taxation problems and commerce potential in the future. Analysis of massive data supports the conclusion. This article further offers some planning strategies for those contemplating an exploration into the E-business market in China.

2. E-BUSINESS VOLUME IN THE PAST

In the U.S., the E-business started to emerge in 2001. At that time, the E-business volume was a meager $35 billion a year according to the data from the U.S. Department of Commerce (U.S. Department of

DOI: 10.4018/978-1-5225-5014-3.ch014

Commerce, 2013). However, it immediately took off at a growth rate of 25% a year. In 2008, the nation was hit by a financial crisis. The E-business was a victim too. In 2010, the E-business market resumed its growth. In 2016, the E-business volume had reached $391 billion (U.S. Department of Commerce, 2017). The growth rate was maintained at a steady 16% a year. This fact may indicate that the E-business market in the U.S. is now matured and stabilized in the near future. This observation is quite interesting in planning the E-business strategies for the future.

Another point of investigation is whether the E-business plays an important role in the whole retail market. The yard stick can be measured by its market share. In 2001, the market share was only 1.1% in the U.S. (U.S. Department of Commerce, 2013). In 2008, the market share was 3.6%. By 2012, the market share had reached 5.2%. This fact shows that the E-business market share was never slowing down in history. Instead, it grows rather steadily, though slowly. This observation is also interesting in planning the E-business strategies too. The growth rate provides a clue as to what volume of E-business can be expected as long as the whole retail sales size can be estimated.

As compared to the U.S. side, the Chinese E-business market was not started until 2008. At that time, the E-business sales volume was as little as $17 billion (China E-commerce Research Center, 2013). By 2012, the sales volume had exploded to $202 billion. This volume has almost caught up with the U.S. side. The growth rate is as high as 55% a year. This level has far surpassed the U.S. side. In the year of 2014, the E-business volume on the Chinese side has reached $387 billion, as compared to $299 billion on the U.S. This level has surpassed the U.S. side. By 2016, the Chinese side is almost twice as much as the U.S. counterpart, i.e., $752 billion versus $391 billion. This fact clearly shows that the E-business market on the Chinese side has much greater potential than the U.S. side. This aspect certainly serves as guidance in planning the future E-business strategies.

With respect to the aspect of degree of importance of the E-business relative to the whole retail sales, the market share in China has also been steadily increasing from 1.3% in 2008 to 15.3% in 2016 (China E-commerce Research Center, 2016.) In any viewpoint, the Chinese side is higher than the U.S. side. This fact clearly demonstrates again that the volume of the Chinese E-business will, beyond any reasonable doubt, surpass the U.S. side in the immediate future. This- observation serves again to formulate E-business planning strategies in China. The data are summarized in Table 1.

3. E-BUSINESS POTENTIAL IN THE FUTURE

In projecting the future market potential in the U.S. versus China, consider the size of population. According to the Internet Retailer Report, in 2016 the U.S. population was 323.1 million, and 1.379 billion in China. China is four times the size of the U.S. The Internet users are 287 million in the U.S. which accounts for as much as 88.5% of its population, while 731 million in China which accounts for only 38.4% (Internet Retailer, 2017). The Internet users in the U.S. are only one-half of China, while the percentage of users in the U.S. is two times as large as China.

These facts imply that the Internet users in the U.S. is almost saturated; whereas, there is still room for growth in China. In 2016, the E-business volume in the U.S. was $391 billion, and $752 billion in China. Had China been developed to its full potential, the E-business volume would have been $1,669 billion in 2016. This is an indication of the future E-business market potential in China. This observation definitely plays an important role in planning the E-business strategies.

Table 1. E-Business sales and market share in retail sales in the U.S. and China

	United States		China	
	E-Business Sales (in Billion)	**Market Share in Retail Sales**	**E-Business Sales (in Billion)**	**Market Share in Retail Sales**
2016	391	8.2%	752	15.3%
2015	342	7.2%	677	14.9%
2014	299	6.5%	387	14.7%
2013	261	5.7%	260	11.6%
2012	225	5.2%	202	6.3%
2011	193	4.6%	132	4.4%
2010	166	4.3%	85	3.5%
2009	144	4.0%	43	2.1%
2008	143	3.6%	17	1.3%
2007	138	3.4%	n/a	n/a
2006	114	2.9%	n/a	n/a
2005	93	2.5%	n/a	n/a
2004	74	2.1%	n/a	n/a
2003	58	1.7%	n/a	n/a
2002	45	1.4%	n/a	n/a
2001	35	1.1%	n/a	n/a

Sources: (A) The United States Department of Commerce; (B) China e-Commerce Research Center

4. E-BUSINESS COMPETITION IN THE MARKETPLACE

In planning the E-business strategies, competition in the marketplace is one of the most important factors. In the U.S., Amazon is the most dominant E-business giant. According to the Portal Statistics Report (Portal, 2016), Amazon accounted for 46.7% of the entire E-business in 2016. The second most dominant is Walmart which accounted for 12.7%. There are eight more competitors, but they all are insignificant. The data show that the E-business market is quite concentrated in a couple of operators.

On the other hand, the competition in China is far more daunting. The most prominent E-business icon is Tmall. According to the EU SME Report (EU SME, 2016), Tmall accounted for 56.6% of the entire E-business market in 2016. The next competitor is JD, but it accounts for only 24.7%. JD is trailing far behind Tmall. There are eight more competitors, but they all are insignificant. The data show that the E-business in China is far more concentrated than that of the U.S. The contrast is 4.7% for Amazon versus 56.6% for Tmall. The difference is 31.9% (56.6% - 24.7%) between these two giants, and it is quite significant. The situation may become even worse in the near future.

The above analysis shows that the E-business market in China is almost completely dominated by Taobo. This phenomenon is highly unhealthy to the nation's economy in general, and detrimental to the development of the E-business market in particular. This environment might be one of the most serious perils for a foreign E-business operator to enter into the Chinese market. It is almost impossible to break up the monopoly. All data are summarized in Table 2.

Table 2. Competitors in e-business market in China and the U.S. in 2016

China		United States	
Competitors	**Market Share**	**Competitors**	**Market Share**
Tmall	56.6%	Amazon	46.7%
JD	24.7%	Walmart	12.7%
Suning	6.7%	Apple	6.1%
Vip	4.3%	Home Depot	5.4%
Com	3.5%	Liberty Interactive	4.9%
Yihaodian	1.2%	Best Buy	4.0%
Amazon	1.1%	Macy's	3.7%
Dangdang	0.8%	CostCo	3.4%
Jumei	0.7%	Target	3.3%
Others	0.4%	Denali	3.2%
TOTAL	100.0%	TOTAL	100.0%

Source: Portal Statistics Report (2016); EU SME Report (2016).

5. E-BUSINESS MERCHANDISE AND CONSUMER BEHAVIOR

Another important factor in planning the E-business strategies is the E-business merchandise. What do consumers buy from E-businesses? Is there any difference between the consumers in China versus their counterparts in the U.S.? According to the McKinsey Report, the E-business merchandise can be classified into seven categories. The details of the merchandise are listed in Table 3.

On the Chinese side, the most popular items are computer and consumer electronic products which account for 35% of the entire E-business market. The second most popular is apparel and clothing which

Table 3.

	Merchandise	**China**	**U.S.**
1	Computer, consumer electronics, education, books, CDs, Recreation, music, video	35%	19%
2	Apparel, clothing. footwear, clothing accessory	24%	18%
3	Health care and personal products, drug	11%	7%
4	Housing, utilities, construction and home improvement materials	10%	9%
5	Household products, home appliance, furniture	7%	10%
6	Transportation, communication equipment, telephone service, car fuel, vehicle, office	6%	3%
7	Food, wine, beer	6%	3%
8	Sporting goods	0%	4%
9	Toys	0%	4%
10	Others	1%	23%
	TOTAL	100%	100%

Sources: (A) International Trade Center (2016); (B) The United States Department of Commerce (2016).

take up the market share for 24% (International Trade Center, 2016). The rest of the products are actually trailing far behind. The data indicate that the E-business pre really concentrated only on a few consumer products. A foreign E-business operator in China must be aware of what most popular products to offer in order to compete in the market.

With respect to the E-business products in the U.S., the products are as concentrated as that in China. According to the U.S. Department of Commerce survey, the most popular E-business products are computers and consumer electronics. It accounts for as much as 19% of the entire E-business market. The second place is apparel and clothing that takes up the market share for 18% (U.S. Department of Commerce, 2017). The rest of the products all are trailing far behind. They are not significant at all. These facts show that consumer behavior is far more concentrated in China that the U.S., though the product preference remain the same. A foreign E-business operator going to China must be aware of what products to offer in China. This observation definitely affects the E-business planning strategies. The above analyses can be summarized in Table 3.

6. TAX CONSEQUENCES OF E-BUSINESS

There is still another important aspect affecting the planning of the E-business strategies. This time it involves tax consequences on the sales of a product on E-business. Any purchase of merchandise or services in the main street store or online website is subject to sales tax (or use tax). In the U.S. the taxing authority and tax beneficiary exclusively belong to the state and local governments. The federal government has no jurisdiction over the sales tax.

The U.S. system has a problem. Sales tax is borne by the buyer but collected by the seller. The state governments collect the tax and use it. However, a state government has no control over an out-of-state seller. If a sale transaction involves an in-state buyer and an out-of-state seller, can the state government require the seller to collect the tax and remit it to the buyer's state government? The question is controversial. According to the United States Constitution the answer is negative, but it is subject to challenge. In fact, many cases have gone to the U.S. Supreme Court. A pending bill in the U.S. Congress, "Marketplace Fairness Act of 2013," may require all out-of-state sellers to collect sales tax (U.S. Congress, 2013).

As compared to the U.S., the Chinese tax system is quite different and more complicated. An international online retailer must be aware of the differences. The following sections elaborate some details.

Sales Tax vs. Value-Added Tax

Unlike the U.S., China has no sales tax. Instead, China has value-added tax. Sales tax in the U.S. is borne by the final buyer at the time of sales; whereas, value-added tax in China is imposed on the buyer at the time of purchase. In this process, sales tax in the U.S. is paid only once at the time of consumption; nevertheless, value-added tax in China is collected at each succeeding stage of production. The value-added tax law is governed by the "Provisional Regulation of the People's Republic of China on Value-added Tax" (China Tax Law, 1994).

The value-added tax in China is intended to finance the provincial governments. The provincial government has the taxing authority and is required to collect the tax, but tax revenue is given to the central government which in turn allocates only 25% of the tax revenue back to the provincial governments. In other words, taxing authority is the provincial government, while the tax beneficiary is the central government. Thus, the taxing authority and the tax beneficiary are inconsistent. As a consequence, there is no incentive for a provincial government to collect the value-added tax.

The flaw in the taxing system leads to a widespread tax evasion in China today. Every taxpayer would make every effort to avoid paying value-added tax. Only when the tax-evading act is caught by the tax authority does a taxpayer pay the tax. As a result, a great amount of value-added tax revenue has been lost. If that is the situation, how the value-added tax is collected? An international E-business marketer must be aware of this awkward tax environment. The problem will be explained in the following section.

Tax Rates

What is taxable and at what rate? The value-added tax has three different rates on three different products:

1. 17% for selling or importing goods, or rendering a taxable service.
2. 13% for grains, edible vegetable oil, tap water, heating, air conditioning, hot water, coal gas, natural gas, books, newspapers, magazines, feeds, chemical fertilizer, agricultural machinery.
3. Zero percent for exporting goods, self-produced and sold agricultural products, contraceptive medicine, antique books, imported instruments and equipment for scientific experimental research and education (China Tax Law, 1994, articles 2 and 16).

There are two kinds of taxpayers: regular taxpayers and small-scale taxpayers. By small-scale taxpayer it means those taxpayers with less than $1 million RMB (US$1 = RMB 6.10), and the regular taxpayers otherwise. The above rates are for the regular taxpayers. For the small-scale taxpayers, the regular tax rate is reduced to 6% (China Tax Law, 1994, Article 12).

Compared to the Chinese value-added tax rate, the U.S. sales tax rate is as low as 8% in New York, 7.5% in California, 7% in New Jersey plus other states. All these rates are even less than one-half of the 17% rate in China. This fact shows that it is more difficult to sell a product in China than in the U.S. This observation may discourage an international online retailer from entering into the Chinese E-business market.

Taxable Base

How much is taxable? The amount to be taxed can be termed "sales amount." According to the law, "The sales amount shall be the total costs plus all other charges received from the purchasers by taxpayer selling goods or taxable services, not including the sales tax amount received" [China Tax Law, 1994, article 6]. Thus, the sales amount multiplied by the tax rate leads to the sales tax amount, i.e.,

Sales Tax Amount = Sales Amount x Tax Rate

With the same token, the value-added tax paid at the time of purchase can be termed "purchase tax amount," i.e.,

Purchase Tax Amount = Purchase Amount x Tax Rate

Sales Tax Amount vs. Purchase Tax Amount

Value-added tax is assessed and paid at each succeeding stage of transfer of goods. Hence, the value-added tax paid at the preceding stage can be claimed as a credit against the tax liability of the next stage. The value-added tax that is paid at the time of purchase in the first stage can be termed "purchase tax amount," while the tax collected at the time of sales in the second stage can be called "sales tax amount." After claiming the credit for the "purchase tax amount," the net amount of the "value-added tax" to be paid to the government tax bureau is the difference, i.e.,

Value-added Tax = Sales Tax Amount - Purchase Tax Amount

The definition of "sales amount" indicated above is ambiguous. In addition to the selling price, does the "sales amount" also include commission and delivery expense? The definition does exclude "sales tax amount" only, but it does not exclude commission and delivery expense. This law can lead to a difference in interpretation. By accounting principles, the "sales amount" should include commission, but not delivery expense. Commission may be subject to a tax, but not the delivery expense. E-business transaction is also subject to value-added tax which faces the same problem as any transaction in a main street store. The following is an example to demonstrate how the value-added tax is actually carried out.

Example for Value-Added Tax

AA sold fabric to BB for a price of $10,000 plus $500 commission. BB then spent an additional $3,000 in labor cost to further process the fabric to become shirts and sold the shirts to CC for a price of $20,000. How much value-added tax should AA collect from BB and turn it over to the government? How much value-added tax should BB collect from CC and turn it over to the government?

The "sales amount" in the first stage between AA and BB is $10,500 ($10,000 + $500), not just $10,000. The "purchase tax amount" is $1,785 ($10,500 x 17%). The "value-added tax" is also $1,785. AA should collect $12,285 ($10,500 + $1,785) from BB but turn over only $1,785 value-added tax to the government.

The "sales amount" in the second stage between BB and CC is $20,000. The additional $3,000 labor cost was already included in the $20,000 selling price. The "sales tax amount" is $3,400 ($20,000 x 17%). However, since BB has already paid the $1,785 "purchase tax amount" to AA, BB can now claim this amount as a credit against the now $3,400 "sales tax amount." Hence, the net amount of "value-added tax" to be collected by BB from CC is the difference, i.e., $1,615 ($3,400 - $1,785). In fact, the additional value that BB has added to the fabric is $9,500 ($20,000 - $10,500) which leads to an additional "value-added tax" of $1,615 ($9,500 x 17% = $1,615). BB now should collect $21,615 ($20,000 + $1,615) from CC, but turn over only $1,615 to the government.

In the case of sales tax in the U.S., AA would collect no sales tax from BB because fabric is an input to produce shirts as the output. Input is not subject to sales tax at the time of purchase in the U.S. As a result, AA would have nothing to be turned over to the government. Not until the time when the shirts are sold to CC as an output, did BB collect the entire $3,400 ($20,000 x 17%) sales tax from CC and turn over the whole amount of $3,400 to the government.

This example demonstrates that the value-added tax in the preceding stage is excluded from the computation of value-added tax in the next stage. This value-added tax procedure in China is much harder to carry out than the sales tax in the U.S. Further, the value-added tax in China is also paid much earlier than the sales tax in the U.S. The time value of money matters. An international online marketer must be familiar with this rather complicated tax structure.

Tax on Production vs. Tax on Consumption

There is a rather intriguing point to observe in the Chinese value-added tax system. Should the cost of a machine be subject to value-added tax? In the U.S., the answer is negative, because the purchase of a machine is not consumption. Machine is an input, rather than an output. The cost of machinery will not become the cost of an output until it is depreciated. Depreciation expense is a part of production cost. Only when the product is sold can the cost of machinery be taxed. Therefore, the sales tax in the U.S. is a "consumption tax." The sales tax system discourages consumption, but not production.

On the contrary, under the value-added system in China the cost of machinery is taxed at the time of purchase. When the machinery is depreciated, the depreciation expense may be added to the cost of an output. The seller would charge value-added tax to the buyer. At that time, how should the seller now claim credit for value-added tax that was paid a long-time ago? This procedure would become an administrative nightmare. Most likely, the seller would just forego claiming the tax credit. As a result, the tax credit would be lost forever. This is the consequence of the value-added tax system.

Moreover, the cost of machinery was taxed at the beginning when the machinery was purchased. The machinery will be employed for production purposes. Hence, the value-added tax in China is a "production tax." As a consequence, the value-added tax system in China discourages production [Yang and Ma, 2004].

This observation points to the deficiency of the value-added tax system in China. This system is detrimental to economic development. As compared to the sales tax system in the U.S., an international E-business marketer should give it a second thought in planning the strategies.

7. MASSIVE COUNTERFEITED PRODUCTS IN CHINA

According to the U.S. Chamber of Commerce, the counterfeited and pirated products account for $250 billion in losses in international trade annually (Frohlich, etal 2014).[1]

Worse yet, 86% of the counterfeited products come from China. Any Chinese Internet commerce website offers two kinds of product: genuine and counterfeit. The prices are quite different.

The ten most counterfeited products sold in the U.S. and their losses are listed in Table 4. In the U.S., the most popular item is handbags, the second is watches, and the third is consumer electronics (Frohlich, Hess and Calio, 2014). In China, the most popular item is Gucci handbags, the second is MP3 players, and the third is jeans (Weigley, 2013).

Because the Internet commerce market is so flooded with counterfeited products from China, China has developed a system to minimize the losses. The system separates the purchase of an E-business product from the payment of the price. The former is called "trade platform," while the latter is called "payment platform." It is similar to the "PayPal" system in the U.S., but the Chinese system is more secure. The customer purchases the product online from "trade platform," but makes a deposit with the "payment platform." The "payment platform" is not authorized to pay the "trade platform" until the product is

Table 4. The ten most counterfeited products sold in the U.S. and China in 2014

	United States		China
	Products	**Losses in Sales (in Million)**	**Products**
1	Handbags, wallets	$700.2	Gucci handbag
2	Watches, jewelry	502.8	MP3 player
3	Consumer electronics, parts	145.9	Electric cords
4	Wearing apparel, accessories	116.2	Jeans
5	Pharmaceuticals, personal care	79.6	Diabetic strips
6	Footwear	54.9	Sneakers
7	Computers, accessories	47.7	
8	Labels, tags	41.8	
9	Optical media	26.8	Sunglasses
10	Toys	13.6	
	TOTAL	1,729.5	

Sources: (A) Frohlich, Hess and Calio, 2014; (B) Weighley, 2013.

received and inspected to the customer's satisfaction. In this way, the buyer takes no risk in purchasing merchandise from the E-business seller. The system of "payment platform" in China is more superior to the "PayPal" system in the U.S. in the sense that the buyer still has full control over the payment. An international E-business retailer must invariably deal with this time-delayed payment system.

The counterfeit market is truly tremendous and proliferating. There is no end in sight.

Actually, it may get worse before it gets better. When an international E-business retailer decides to join the market in China, should it also offer to sell counterfeited products? If the customers are willing to purchase counterfeited products at a much lower price, there is really no choice. This is the reality of the market. Table 4 shows what products to sell. However, there is always a balancing point between the quality and the price. The best strategy depends on whether this retailer is running a higher-end firm or a lower-end one. The former may not offer counterfeited products, while the latter may do so. An international Internet commerce marketer should take this business environment into account in planning the strategies.

8. INFRINGEMENT OF INTELLECTUAL PROPERTY RIGHTS IN CHINA

Besides the counterfeited products, there is one property that suffers the most monumental losses, and that is the infringement of intellectual property rights. According to a study by the U.S. International Trade Commission in 2011, the total global losses amount to $48.2 billion annually (Hammer and Linton, 2011). This amount represents about 15% of the total global trade losses to the counterfeited products. The number is truly astronomical. Table 5 shows the kinds of properties and their losses. The most serious infringement is copyright, the second is trademark, and the third is patent.

In today's computer age, the infringement of intellectual property rights has become even more rampant in scope and in volume. Many products now can be digitized, such as e-book, e-music, e-game,

Table 5. Losses on infringement of intellectual property rights in the U.S. in 2011

	Kinds of Losses	Amount of Losses (in Billion)
	Total Reported Global Losses	$48.2
	Losses By Intellectual Property Rights:	
1	Copyright infringement	23.7
2	Trademark infringement	6.1
3	Patent infringement	1.3
4	Misappropriation of trade secrets	1.1
5	Unspecified	16.0
	Losses By Sector:	
1	Information and other services	$26.7
2	High-tech and heavy manufacturing	18.5
3	Chemical manufacturing	2.0
4	Consumer goods manufacturing	0.8
5	Transportation manufacturing	0.2

Source: U.S. International Trade Commission

e-newspaper, e-magazine, etc. Most administrative work can be programmed by means of software such as Microsoft Office, Quickbooks, Peachtree Accounting, Turbotax, TaxAct, etc.

These products can be transferred easily from one computer to the other, and the E-business provides the vehicle to do it. This phenomenon happens on a worldwide scale, not only in China but anywhere in the world. In each country, it is just a matter of degree of tolerance on the infringement of intellectual property rights. China probably stands out to be the most notorious violator. When an international E-business retailer enters into the market in China, should it join the ranks? The decision calls for judgment on the value of business ethics. Nevertheless, this aspect serves to formulate more sustainable planning strategies.

9. PLANNING STRATEGIES FOR E-BUSINESS IN CHINA

In the last decade, there was a big rush to China for manufacturing. Its 1.35 billion of population turned into a production force. China became a world factory. Everything was made in China. China was a production market. Today, the same size of population has turned into a consumption force. There is now a gold rush to China to sell. China is currently becoming a consumption market. What potential can China offer and what are the perils? The rush requires strategic planning.

The market environment is now dominated by the E-business. Merchandise is sold through Internet commerce. The online business was initiated only nine years ago in China; nevertheless, it exploded immediately thereafter. The business volume has reached $752 billion in 2016. This size accounts for 15.3% of the entire retail business. The volume is growing at a spectacular rate of 55% a year. In any measure, this size has exceeded the level in the U.S. These facts clearly imply that there is now a burning desire to rush back to China again. This is the direction of strategic planning for the immediate future.

However, there are many perils in doing business in China. The most serious obstacle is competition. The E-business market is highly monopolized in China. The top marketer is Taobao that accounts for as much as 81.2% of the entire E-business market. Its website offers just about any kind of merchandise. Consumers need to go to only one place, and there is a great deal of choices on the website. The stores on the main street are now becoming obsolete. Taobao can out-beat and defeat any newcomers. Unlike the market in the U.S., this business environment in China is extremely undesirable, unhealthy and detrimental to the nation's economic development. Any international E-business marketers who plan to enter into the Chinese market will definitely face such an insurmountable obstacle.

If a foreign online retailer is unable to break up the Chinese monopoly the best strategy is to make alliance with the competitor. Accept the fact and surrender. A foreign seller can offer foreign merchandise. In complement to the Chinese merchandise, it would make a foreigner more acceptable and compatible with the Chinese side. In strategic terms, it is characterized as expansion through merger.

If a foreign online marketer refuses to compromise, the alternative surviving strategy might be to engage in a strategy of product differentiation. A great many of the Chinese consumers prefer foreign goods over indigent merchandise. An online store specializing in foreign merchandise may attract a certain segment of the Chinese consumers.

Another peril is the merchandise pricing. An online store can operate without paying overhead rent for space and wages for employees. It indeed enjoys a great deal of advantages over a brick-and-mortar store. As a dividend, an online store can offer as much as 40% discount over its counterpart on the main street. The brick-and-mortar stores will definitely demise soon. Can a foreign online retailer meet such a stiff competition in pricing? It is almost an impossible obstacle to overcome. Nevertheless, the strategic planning must take this difficulty into account.

Still yet, another peril is the taxation on Internet transactions. China imposes value-added tax on the merchandise sold at a rate of 17% as opposed to sales tax at 7% in the U.S. The difference is as high as 10% (17% - 7%) which is quite substantial. Moreover, the Chinese value-added tax is collected at each stage of transfer of merchandise, rather than at the last stage of the sale. These aspects put the Chinese market at a disadvantageous position as compared to the tax burden in the U.S. Obviously, it would be more difficult to sell merchandise in China than that in the U.S. Can a foreign Internet commerce marketer absorb such a shock? The answer is affirmative. It is feasible by means of improvement of quality of a foreign product over the Chinese counterpart. However, it requires elaborate planning strategies.

Worse yet, there is still another peril in China in operating an E-business. This time it involves the counterfeited products and infringement of intellectual property rights. This problem is pervasive in China today and getting worse. A fake product is almost synonymous to products "made in China." Every online store offers two lines of products for the same kind of merchandise. A shopper can choose either genuine or counterfeit at different prices. Can a foreign online seller follow the same business practice? The answer is negative. The shoppers are so sophisticated that they pay a higher price for a better quality product. Nonetheless, a foreign Internet commerce operator will invariably face this kind of business competition. The planning strategies must also take this aspect into consideration.

Despite these obstacles, the Chinese E-business market offers such a great potential that it is worthy of taking the risk. However, it requires a set of comprehensive planning strategies.

10. CONCLUSION

In the past four years, the Internet commerce in China has suddenly exploded. There is a big rush to China currently underway to join the market. This article discussed the potentials and perils of doing so. The paper points out that the E-business in China reached $752 billion in 2016 which accounts for 15.3% of its whole retail sales. It surpassed the level in the U.S. The growth rate has consistently been maintaining at 55% a year. There is indeed a great potential.

However, there are also many perils. The E-business competition in China is much tougher than that in the U.S. The most prominent market dominator in the U.S. is Amazon which accounted for 27.1% of the entire Internet commerce market in 2012. On the China side, the largest counterpart is Taobao which occupies as much as 81.2% of the E-business market. This article points out that there is almost no chance to break up the monopoly in China.

This paper further investigates the commodities that are sold through the Internet commerce. This article indicates that the most popular product is apparel in China that accounts for 35% of the E-business market, while in the U.S. it is electronics that take up the market share of 34%. This paper reveals that the consumer behaviors are quite different between China and the U.S.

This article points out another peril. In lieu of sales tax at 7% in the U.S., China imposes value-added tax at 17% and the tax is collected at each stage of sales. This paper demonstrates an example. The difference in tax rates is so substantial that it may discourage a foreign E-business retailer from entering into the Chinese market. This paper offers cautionary advice.

This article further reveals that the counterfeited products and infringement of intellectual property rights are rampant in China. The losses in sales on a worldwide scale are $360 billion annually. Eighty percent of them were originated in China. The most popular item is handbags that accounts for $511.2 million. This fact has tarnished the Chinese image.

This paper also investigates the commodities that are sold through the Internet commerce. This article indicates that the most popular product is apparel in China that accounts for 35% of the E-business market, while in the U.S. it is electronics that take up the market share of 34%. This paper reveals that the consumer behaviors are quite different between China and the U.S.

This paper further offers many planning strategies to those who are contemplating the operation of an E-business in China. This article cautions the international online retailer in considering the dominant competition, commodity pricing, tax burdens, and fake products in China. Notwithstanding these perils, this paper concludes that the potential still outweighs the risks.

REFERENCES

China E-Commerce Research Center. (2013). *Statistical Data on China's Internet Commerce Market.* China E-Commerce Research Center. Retrieved from http://100ec.cn

EU SME. (2016). *E-Commerce in China.* Available online at https://www.eas.ee/wp-content/uploads/2017/06/Rafael-Jimenez_-e-commerce- seminar_Tallinn.pdf

Frohlich, T. C., Hess, A. E. M., & Calio, V. (2014). Counterfeit Products May Cost the Global Economy Up to $250 billion a Year. *USA Today.* Available online at https://www.usatoday.com/story/money/business/2014/03/29/24-7-wall-st-counterfeited-products/7023233/

Hammer, A., & Linton, K. (2011). *China: Effects of Intellectual Property Infringement and Indigenous Innovation Policies on the U.S. Economy.* U.S. International Trade Commission. Investigation No. 332-519. Retrieved from http://www.usitc.gov/research and_analysis/commission_publication_4226.htm

International Trade Center. (2016). *E-Commerce in China: Opportunity for Asian Firms.* Available online at http://www.intracen.org/uploadedFiles/intracenorg/Content/Publications/E-COMMERCE%20 IN%20CHINA%20Low-res.pdf

Law, C. T. (1994). *Provisional Regulation of the People's Republic of China on Value-Added Tax.* Promulgated by Decree No.134 of the State Council of the People's Republic of China on December 13, 1993, and effective on January 1, 1994. Beijing: People's Republic of China. Retrieved from http://english.ccpit.org/contents/channel_101/2006/0525/847/content_847.htm

Portal. (2016). *Portal Statics Report.* Available online at https://www.statista.com/statistics/293089/leading-e-retailers-ranked-by-annual-web-e-commerce-sales/

U.S. Chamber of Commerce. (2013). *Counterfeited and Pirated Products Account for $360 billion in trade losses.* Retrieved from http://www.theglobalipcenter.com/counterfeit-pirated-products-360-billion/

U.S. Congress (2013). *Marketplace Fairness Act of 2013.* S-743 and House of Representatives, H.R. 684, May 6, 2013.

U.S. Department of Commerce. (2016). *New Insights on Retail E-commerce.* Available online at http://www.esa.doc.gov/sites/default/files/new-insights-retail-e-commerce.pdf

U.S. Department of Commerce. (2017). *E-Commerce Survey.* Retrieved from http://www.census.gov/retail/mrts/www/data/pdf/ec_current.pdf

Weigley, S. (2013). *Yahoo Finance.* Retrieved from http://finance.yahoo.com/news/the-10-most-counterfeited-products-in-america-180942491

Chapter 15
The Divergence of Entrepreneurial Landscapes in the European Union

Mark Potts
Central Michigan University, USA

George M. Puia
Saginaw Valley State University, USA

ABSTRACT

Understanding the importance of innovation and entrepreneurship to economic growth and stability, the European Union has implemented policies and programs to create a more uniform context for cross-border business activities within the EU. While initial efforts led to a more unified European region, they did not lead to a more uniform one. Over the past five years, dramatic changes in Europe resulting from the financial crisis, the Eurosceptic movement, and the Syrian refuge crisis have incented nations to create their own national innovation and entrepreneurship efforts. This chapter explores the results of those diverging national programs on entrepreneurial outcomes. Specifically, the research explores national landscapes created as a result of differing endowments, regulatory regimes, tax systems, and venture funding levels. Results indicate that differences in these factors create significantly different entrepreneurial outcomes as measured by patent applications and new business registrations.

INTRODUCTION

It is widely accepted that successful innovation and entrepreneurship provide a potentially sustainable strategy for national economic development. To that end, there has been considerable research conducted to identify and understand the factors that differentiate nations on their ability to foster innovation and entrepreneurship (Kogut, 1991; Nelson, 1993; Porter, 2000; Porter and Stern, 2004). Scholars continue to explore constructs that could influence the national innovation landscape, including: political frameworks (Lenway & Murtha, 1994; Spencer, Murtha & Lenway, 2005), economic frameworks (Bosma, 2013), and level and quality of regulation (Kaufmann et. al. 2008; Puia & Minnis, 2007). International business

DOI: 10.4018/978-1-5225-5014-3.ch015

scholars have added to this body of knowledge by exploring links between culture, cultural diversity and innovation and entrepreneurship at the nation level (Puia and Ofori-Dankwa, 2013; Shane, 1992).

Intuitively one would expect e-entrepreneurship to be borderless; this has proven to not be the case. E-entrepreneurs still face the issues of cultural differences, liability of foreignness, and complicated tax collection and remittance procedures (Gomez-Herrera et. al. 2014). An entirely new form of e-business, the ibusiness firm attempts to create value through user co-creation of content. Brouthers et. al (2016) theorize ibusiness firms suffer liability from foreignness greater than e-business firms due to the cultural challenges of coordinating cross border user networks. Convergence in European policies and practices favor e-business whereas divergence constrains e-business growth.

There are several common threads that emerge from this voluminous literature: a nation's contextual landscape influences innovative and entrepreneurial capacity; national competition is intensely dynamic and market economies of scale matter. With these elements in mind, EU leaders have been attempting to design and implement contextual elements that would position member countries for smart, sustainable, and inclusive economic growth in the context of European stability (Stabryła-Chudzio 2016). By minimizing trade barriers, reducing transaction costs and exchange rate risk through the use of a common currency, increasing cross-border flow of capital and more recently the flow of labor, the EU has attempted to create a contextual playing-field for member states that would provide advantages relative to non-member countries. During the past decade, the EU has focused policy decisions and resources specifically toward building an entrepreneurial knowledge economy through programs such as highly funded inter European educational exchange (Union, 2014).

Concurrent with the European Union's march toward a uniform policy framework has been the growth of a Eurosceptic movement (Peterson, 2016). While Eurosceptics were always present, the need to fund the costs of recovery from the Greek financial crisis, the rise of new nationalistic movements, the Syrian migrant crisis, and more recently Brexit have strained the European project to its limits.

This paper uses empirical data to explore the ways in which entrepreneurial policy and outcomes are diverging from a common European framework and shows unique national approaches to building an entrepreneurial knowledge economy. The paper contributes to the body of literature by identifying the factors that most greatly influence innovation and entrepreneurial growth. Further, this research shows how areas of convergence and divergence between European nations are shaping the entrepreneurial landscape more in the vein of national interests than supranational regional objectives.

This chapter has four specific goals: (1) Provide the conceptual background necessary to understand the current status of entrepreneurship development; (2) Identify the key actionable factors that appear to influence the growth of entrepreneurial economies; (3) Use empirical data to show areas of convergence and divergence in EU member approaches to fostering innovation and entrepreneurship; and (4) Provide recommendations for researchers, policy makers, and e-entrepreneurs operating in this arena.

BACKGROUND

The idea and making of a unified Europe has been a long and dynamic process. In the 1990s, new states in Central and Eastern Europe began the transition to market economies. These countries faced special challenges in redeveloping their economies because their endowments were underutilized or even diminished under both communism and the following transition. (Ganev & Venilin, 2007; Kayak & Dana, 2013). After political and economic upheaval to democratic governments and free markets, these countries moved into a second phase where they sought EU membership by conforming to European Union political, regulatory, and fiscal standards.

A third period focused on growth through the Lisbon Strategy (2000 to 2010) and the subsequent Europe 2020 Strategy. The Europe 2020 Strategy, set out achieve (1) Smart growth: developing an economy based on knowledge and innovation; (2) Sustainable growth: promoting a more resource efficient, greener and more competitive economy; and (3) Inclusive growth: fostering a high-employment economy delivering social and territorial cohesion, with the first and third being most important for social cohesion (Stabryła-Chudzio 2016).

The authors' previous study found the quest for unity did not bring uniformity (Potts & Puia 2012). The paper looked at the US as an analog to Europe having autonomous states with differing endowments, regulation, and taxation. Thus it provided a basis for comparison between states in the US and members of the European Union. (In this paper, the authors chose not to continue our comparison of US states to European nations, but focus on Europe as it has experienced profound landscape changes that may now only be reaching the US).

The research studied intellectual property, features of uniform systems, sources of regional differentiation, endowment, regulation of entry, and institutional support for entrepreneurship in the US and Europe. The study was prefaced on the literature positing employment growth is driven by high potential new firms. (Acs, et al., 2008), wealth creation (Venkataraman, 1997), and economic development (EC, 1999). The Lisbon Strategy (EC 2000),

... sought to usher in an era of full employment sought to usher in an era of full employment by investing in European human resource development, strengthening the link between research institutes, universities, and businesses; reducing red tape and other local business entry regulations, and developing green technologies to reduce the impact of economic growth. In essence, the Lisbon Strategy posited that innovation was a central ingredient in European economic growth and that entrepreneurs were agents of innovation. (Potts & Puia, 2012, pp. 121-122)

Potts & Puia (2012) indicated major variations in technical innovation was a result of policy differences (Kogut, 1991; Porter, 1990; Porter & Stern, 2004). National factors, national institutional configurations, and governance structures were offered as potential explanation for variations in wealth and investment levels (Bartholomew, 1997; Lenway & Murtha, 1994; Porter, 1990; Spencer, Murtha & Lenway, 2005; Teece, 1992; Van den Bosch & Van Prooijen, 1992).

Potts & Puia (2012) also found that endowment as measured by education was not significant for European countries in the 2000 to 2007 time frame. This may have been in part the result of the authors' use of higher education attainment as the metric for endowment due the proposed link to patents and high potential entrepreneurship. Entrepreneurship may contain a less formal education structure as it is driven by knowledge, skills, and mindset. Indeed, EU planning and programs reflect this literature.

The 2012 study, did show significance related to taxation. EU countries with more favorable tax environments had significantly higher levels of patent production. This patent production may also be explained by higher entrepreneurial activity and the fact large businesses may locate research and development in countries with a better tax position.

The authors' prior study also discussed institutional support for entrepreneurship. Carree & Thurik (2003) discuss the literature that supports the fact that countries with higher levels of institutional support for entrepreneurship will see greater entrepreneurial vitality. Institutional support comes in a variety of forms to support the entrepreneur as innovator, opportunity finder, and/or risk taker. (Hebert & Link, 1989; Schumpeter, 1934). The entrepreneur as innovator generates intellectual property in the form of patents or proprietary knowledge. Institutional support for these entrepreneurs may take the form of incubators or accelerators that support the transfer of knowledge from academic institutions to start ups. (Feller 2005; Shane 2005). In our current research, we attempt to evaluate the institutional support at the European as opposed to national level.

Potts & Puia (2012) also observed the EU regulatory environment as significantly associated with patent creation. Less strict regulatory regimes saw higher levels of patent production; it was these uncommon policies such as regulatory environment that enacted at the EU member state level that had a significant and differentiated effect on entrepreneurial vitality. The literature also observes that while the less competitive countries are increasing their competitiveness more dramatically, there are still huge disparities in competitiveness among EU member states (Balcarová 2016).

Between 2012 and 2017, the European entrepreneurial landscape has been significantly challenged. The authors' prior study was conducted at the time of the European debt crisis and before the current migrant crisis, Brexit, as well as other populist and nationalist gains.

The authors posit that the European Union is in a new phase marked by Euroscepticism. The term "Eurosceptic" dates back to the 1980s and has gone from the margins to the mainstream; now being embedded in EU member states. (Brack & Startin 2015). European populist and nationalist movements have manifested in the following, but not limited to, the UK's Brexit, the French National Front, the Austrian Freedom Party, the Dutch Party for Freedom, as well as various forces in Hungary, Greece, Germany, Italy, and Spain (Mudde 2007). Politicians and parties criticize the elites for supporting immigrants and refugees, multiculturalism, and advocating for minorities rather than the majority (Lesinska 2014). European populist movements, like those in the US, are associated with skepticism of the elite and xenophobia; this manifests through conversations about "us" and "them" in the xenophobic immigrant context. Likewise, between the "elite" or those "on top" and the ordinary people (Brubaker 2017). In the European context, the skepticism of the elite manifests nationalist preferences of EU interests.

National and European identity are highly complex (Wodak & Boukala 2015). However, to summarize the most popular way of explaining Brexit and similar populist and nationalist events is that "people consider themselves losers from globalization and turn against both the foreigners who steal their jobs and their own cosmopolitan establishment, which is selling them out." (Nodia 2017, p. 16). Some scholars indeed believe democracy itself is threatened in its home of Western Europe and North America (Nodia 2017). It would be premature to assess what effect an event as large as Brexit will have on the business context of the UK or the EU (Coulter and Hancké, 2017).

The migrant crisis brought questions of European identity and validity of the EU itself to a fore. Recently, we have seen the crumbling of carefully crafted and established structures of EU border policy and migration Schengen, Dublin, and Frontex and the establishment of a short-term national policies of whoever builds the highest fence wins (Borg-Barthet & Lyons 2016). EU members have refused to partake in meaningful burden sharing with regards to the refugee crisis. (Borg-Barthet & Lyons 2016). There is a constitutional conflict regarding the migrant crisis as the Union can only be as principled as its most selfish member state. (Borg-Barthet & Lyons 2016).

The lack of preparedness and ability to deal with the refugee crisis led to a loss of faith and credibility in the EU by its citizens (Popescu 2016). The EU has responded to the immigration and migrant crisis by earmarking over 50 billion Euros to address various needs over the 2014 to 2020 period (Stabryła-Chudzio 2016). The inference EU citizens can make is that these monies are not being spent on them in the context of "us" versus "them" populism. Some argue that the EU must find solutions to rebuild its structures in order to obtain socio-economic development for its member states (Ionescu 2016).

Other suggest that the quest for uniformity may be a fallacy. While the goal may be full uniformity and integration across the European Union the reality has been very different with opt-outs on the single currency, Schengen travel, and justice and home affairs in the cases of Ireland and the UK (Winzen & Schimmelfennig 2016). The diversity and divisiveness within the European Union has given rise to the notion of differentiated integration (that is allowing different members to cooperate and different levels based on abilities and preferences) as a proposed solution (Winzen & Schimmelfennig 2016). This may be in effect the de facto solution that is occurring in innovation and entrepreneurship.

Moreover, today the convergence of EU countries is unlikely even with the most optimistic of forecasts (Galperina 2016). It is to the current period and challenges to growth that this research is addressed. Eastern and Central European countries need to be more than simply manufacturing subsidiaries for Western companies; the solution being for member states to propel local entrepreneurs to create high growth businesses. Home gown entrepreneurs are necessary to preserve national identity. Fear of loss of identity is a driver for Euroscepticism.

When considering issues of international trade the European concept still prevails. The larger population of the European Union makes markets for good, services, and capital more attractive to outsiders. On the issue of entrepreneurship, policy makers leaned much more toward autonomy; within nation entrepreneurs are seen as symbols of national identity and progress. To that end, national policy makers are likely to seek ways to create local contexts that are more conducive to indigenous entrepreneurs as a means of securing national results that are superior to European results.

The focus of this paper is on the differential initiatives and outcomes. Given that countries are choosing unique innovation and entrepreneurship pathways and that they are generating different results, there is a naturally occurring experiment that will help scholars and policy-makers identify superior alternatives. This study shows which contextual elements lead to more positive entrepreneurial outcomes.

The elements this paper addressed were endowment as measured by educational attainment, government policy toward entrepreneurship as measured by regulatory quality, tax rates, and the availability of early stage capital as measured by venture capital measured by GDP. The paper posits these elements create an environment for entrepreneurs with far less risk and potential for greater reward.

RESEARCH FRAMEWORK

In analyzing the current EU innovation and entrepreneurship environment, the author wished to assess three questions. First, since the later members of the Union have had more time to adapt to the EU governance framework, the research sought to assess whether there as a convergence of environmental factors. Put more simply, has the EU converged to the point where entrepreneurs face the same contexts in each of the 28 countries?

Second, the authors were interested in potentially differential outcomes in entrepreneurship and innovation among the member nations. If the EU had transitioned from being unified to uniform, than one would expect similar or even identical entrepreneurship outcomes in terms of new business startup rates or patent applications per capita. To what extent do European nations share common entrepreneurial outcomes?

Lastly, if there were differences in entrepreneurial outcomes, can they be explained by nation-level factors? European nations began with different endowments, but it is possible that there has been convergence in the level and nature of entrepreneurial talent resources? While member states have adopted the mandatory EU policies, there is still significant discretion in member nations as to the regulation of entrepreneurial entry and the level of taxes levied on new businesses. Additionally, while there is capital mobility across EU nations, there are still local venture capital markets in each country. To what extent do these discretionary policy areas contribute to variation in innovation and entrepreneurship among EU members?

Measuring Entrepreneurship and Innovation

And a societal context, entrepreneurs play important roles as innovative opportunity finders and risk takers (Hebert & Link, 1989). Given that entrepreneurial roles are multidimensional, it is not surprising that there are significant differences in research approaches to entrepreneurial outcomes making it difficult to establish comparability between studies; scholars routinely employ different metrics for national levels of entrepreneurship. This is somewhat understandable given that there is great variability in research questions. In their prior work, Potts & Puia (2012) explored total entrepreneurial activity, a metric that include part-time entrepreneurs, and self-employment entrepreneurs. For this study the authors have chosen to use the World Bank data on 'new business entry density', which is defined as the number of newly registered corporations per 1,000 working-age people (those ages 15–64). When a business incorporates, they have or are moving in the direction of multiple employees. National policy makers have a much greater interest in this type of entrepreneur rather than self-employment or necessity entrepreneurs. New business entry density is based on the widely available OECD data on newly registered corporations and is collected annually.

In the innovation literature, it is somewhat more common to look at patents applications as an innovation metric. There is some debate as whether scholars should use patent applications or patents granted. Those favoring patents granted posit that applications may not necessarily result in patents and therefore should not be considered as a reliable innovation metric. Conversely, scholars and practitioners are keenly aware of the limitations of using granted patents. It is well known that there is a significant and non-linear delay between when a patent is requested and when it is granted. Further, these differences can accrue from either firm or industry characteristics. Given these serious limitations, it is difficult to link granted patents to policy or governance changes in a specific year. For this reason, the authors have chosen to explore patent applications as a measure of national innovation.

Model

This paper tested a general model that innovation and entrepreneurial growth result from a common set of factors. Specifically, the paper tests two discrete models: (1) patent applications as a function of endowments, regulatory quality, tax rates, and venture funding and (2) new business density as a function of endowments, regulatory quality, tax rates, and venture funding.

Dependent Variables

The paper uses patent applications as a metric for innovation. There is a well-established literature that intellectual property is an essential component of high expectation entrepreneurship. Since policy makers are keenly interested in employment growth, it is natural that they would seek policies that would enhance the creation of intellectual property. The cost of registering intellectual property in the form of a patent can be prohibitive. As a result, entrepreneurs are discouraged in investing in patents unless they believe strongly in the future economic viability of their offering. The combination of these characteristics makes patent applications a nearly ideal metric for capturing the growth of intellectual property within a nation (Jaffe & Trajtenberg 2002).

Similarly, policy makers are interested in directly capturing the growth in entrepreneurial ventures. Capturing this data can be challenging. When there is an absence of other opportunities, individuals may create self-employment opportunities to compensate for the lack of job opportunity. While this form of necessity entrepreneurship reduces a nation's welfare burden, it does not substantially increase its employment base. Equally challenging is the task of partialing out the effect of lifestyle entrepreneurs, individuals who form businesses primarily to manage a personal lifestyle rather than create a growing business that employs additional workers (Acs et. al. 2016 and Acs et. al. 2014). Since there are significant costs associated with incorporation, few necessity entrepreneurs and a limited number of lifestyle entrepreneurs incorporate; the clear majority of incorporations are form entrepreneurs with the expectation of employing more workers. On this basis, the authors have chosen new business density as one of the performance metrics.

Independent Variables

The paper empirically tests whether changes in the dependent variable result from changes in specific independent factors. The following paragraphs describe the literature and metrics seen in the innovation and entrepreneurship literature and develops the hypothetical relationships between them and their dependent counterparts.

Endowments

Each nation possesses a unique set of endowments, resources that have accumulated over long periods of time the provide benefit to present and future generations. These endowments include natural resources, human resources, and financial resources. Endowments can have positive and negative effects. Landlocked countries for example are endowed with higher transportation costs; ocean facing nations were often advantaged in terms of international trade.

The authors compared state endowments in the United States to European nations, noting unique attributes such as freshwater Michigan, natural beauty in Hawaii, coal in West Virginia, or oil in Texas. Perhaps more significant are human resource endowments; California's investment in engineering education created the human foundation for the early computer companies in Silicon Valley.

"Eastern and Central Europe faces a special challenge in that there is substantial evidence that their endowments were underutilized or even diminished under both communism and the rugged transition to open markets (Ganev & Venilin, 2007; Kayak & Dana, 2013). The residual corpus often needed substantial capital in order to regain competitive stature, capital that was scare during the transition from a command economy." (Potts & Puia, 2012, p. 124).

It is noteworthy that membership in the EU may moderate certain endowment effects. For example, the EU has made generous investments in infrastructure improvements to facility trade and factor mobility across borders. They have also challenged member states to higher standards of educational attainment.

At the same time, there is a significant debate as to whether European education standards infringe on national cultural values (Ertl, 2006). As in other areas, the strain between European and national interests results in European and national policy.

Hypothesis 1a: Nations with better endowments will have higher entrepreneurial outcomes as evidenced by greater entrepreneurial density

Hypothesis 1b: Nations with better endowments will generate higher levels of innovation as evidenced by higher levels of patent applications

Regulatory Quality

Membership in the European Union requires nations to adhere to a common set of policies based originally on a series of negotiated treaties and later supplemented by the European Parliament (Pinder, 2001). The larger portion of these laws and regulations refer to the relationships between countries rather than governance within countries. While there are policies to harmonize fiscal and monetary frameworks across nations, there is less law concerning the ways in which business is regulated.

There are certain regulations that particularly salient to entrepreneurs. One such set of regulations is the way in which nations encourage or restrict the entry of new businesses (Djankov et al. 2002). Regulating a business offers has significant market validity. Official registration can reduce counterfeiting, reduce a new firms liability of newness, offer legitimacy to prospective consumers, and in some cases help businesses become generally more reputable to the public (SRI 1999). Good regulation benefits businesses and consumers alike.

On the opposite end, regulations can be designed to empower incumbents with political connections over entrants with fewer resources but often better ideas. One category of dysfunctional regulation is referred to as a toll booth model (Desoto, 1990), where regulations is crafted largely to benefit government bureaucracies, political parties, or special constituencies (Djankov et al. 2002; McChesney 1987). At the darkest end of the scale, an ineffective regulation comes in the form of official bribery requiring firms to pay substantial fees or contribute unofficial fees (bribes or grease payments) to receive operating permits (Shleifer & Vishny 1993).

World Bank research (2004) clearly demonstrated that lower regulation levels significantly improve the rates of successful entrepreneurial entry. In a significant contribution to the field, Kaufmann & Kraay (2002) were able to assess whether measures were more or less harmful to the business environment. This paper has incorporated Kaufmann's regulatory quality measure, which indicates the extent to which regulatory matters support rather than inhibit business. Kaufmann's metric is multidimensional including sub-indices for voice and accountability, political stability in the absence of violence, rule of law, government effectiveness, and control of corruption. These sub- indices are aggregated to create an omnibus of regulatory effectiveness (Kaufmann et al., 2008).

Hypothesis 2a: Nations with higher regulatory quality will experience higher entrepreneurial outcomes as evidenced by greater entrepreneurial density.

Hypothesis 2b: Nations with higher regulatory quality will generate higher levels of innovation as evidenced by higher levels of patent applications.

Tax Rates

Countries differ greatly in their approaches to taxation with some governments choosing to place higher levels of taxes on individuals while others select businesses to bear a heavier tax burden. Tax rates are directly linked to government spending. To maintain the fiscal and monetary targets required for EU membership, nations must limit their budget deficits by either reducing or spending or raising tax revenues.

Taxes affect entrepreneurs in multiple ways. Higher taxes make it more difficult to generate profits commensurate with entrepreneurial risk, potentially reducing the perceived viability of some ventures. Investors in early stage companies demand higher rewards for the risks they undertake; high corporate tax rates effectively transfer dividends from investors to the government making investment less attractive. Taxes may also signal entrepreneurs as to whether government will be truly supportive of their efforts.

Measuring tax rates is fraught with research complications. Most countries employ different marginal tax rates for different earning levels. Some countries tax on total income, others base tax on the value added by the company. Given that we cannot determine the tax rate faced by an individual entrepreneur, we have chosen to employ a measure of average business tax rates.

Hypothesis 3a: Nations with higher tax rates will experience lower entrepreneurial outcomes as evidenced by greater entrepreneurial density.

Hypothesis 3b: Nations with higher tax rates will generate lower levels of innovation as evidenced by higher levels of applications

Venture Funding

As noted by Carree and Thurik (2003), nations that support entrepreneurship observe stronger entrepreneurial outcomes. While there are often state-supported forms to accelerate early-stage companies such as incubators, accelerators, and knowledge transfer systems, these systems seldom provide any substantial investment to entrepreneurs (Feller, 2005; Shane, 2005).

Investors in an individual new venture faces extraordinary risk. Since entrepreneurs are offering products or services that are new from a provider that is essentially unknown, risks are multiplied. It is well established in finance that rewards must be commensurate with risk. If entrepreneurs had to compensate investors for the full risks of the venture, they would be unlikely to receive support from anyone outside the circle of friends, family, and fools. One way for individual investors to meet this challenge is to diversify, essentially pooling their risks by simultaneously investing in multiple ventures, often in the same industry. To facilitate investing multiple ventures, investors pool their resources forming angel funds and venture capital firms. Angel investment and venture capital firms take concurrent positions in multiple firms. Since the rate of return is high for a venture that succeeds, investors can then absorb the losses from firms that fail to successfully launch.

Since European law allows for capital to flow across borders, one might expect there to be a centralized approach to venture capital. This is seldom the case. There are substantial differences between a large publicly traded firm and a new venture. In the publicly traded firm, any investor can examine the financial statements and observe comments from executives and industry analysts. To this end, the literature describes large markets as efficient in that the price of a share already includes all available information and any changes in information are immediately reflected in share price adjustments. (Fama et. al. 1969).

Entrepreneurial ventures operate in inefficient markets. Management is not transparent, often purposefully keeping secret ideas and technology as to make competitive responses more difficult. Further, investors are often not placing bets on new ventures, but on the management team that operates them. Therefore, local investors have a distinct advantage in their knowledge of the local firm. Not surprisingly then, there are national differences in the number and type of early stage investors.

Hypothesis 4a: Nations with higher levels of venture capital will experience higher entrepreneurial outcomes as evidenced by greater entrepreneurial density.

Hypothesis 4b: Nations with higher levels of venture capital will generate higher levels of innovation as evidenced by higher levels of patent applications

Methods

Data collection was restricted to member countries of the European Union and all data was collected from publicly available data sites. Given that there are a limited number of EU countries, the authors needed to limit the number of variables under study. While one would expect that other factors might influence these dependent variables, it was valuable to test this particular set of metrics.

Data for the study was drawn from the most currently available year for which there was complete data. Not all countries report data annually; given a small sample countries, the authors looked for years were data was available from all member nations. Recent data (2014-2015) gave the opportunity to see Europe after it had largely emerged from Greek debt crisis, but prior to the full effects of the migration crisis. The prior research described the years immediately preceding the financial crisis. Because the 2008-2009 crisis affected smaller economies more intensely then larger ones, and because newer members were harder hurt, it resulted in confounded annual comparisons. This research employs the same dimensions as the Potts and Puia (2012) paper, making direct comparisons to policy and context changes possible.

After compiling data, the authors completed a series of statistical tests, first developing a descriptive profile of the data. The descriptive data (See Table 1), since it compared with the prior study, was surprisingly informative; it provided indication as to whether nations were converging or diverging on entrepreneurial contexts and outcomes.

The initial data brought to our attention several key factors. First, there was a dramatic increase in patent applications with much higher national variation. There was also an increase in business registrations, which led directly to higher new venture density. These changes suggest that nations still have a non-uniform approach to entrepreneurship. Additionally, when exploring tertial educational attainment, there was an 8% increase over the study period but also a marked decrease in variation. It appears the EU policies have results in more uniform educational achievement (still with significant differences between countries). Over the same period, there was a large increase in the availability of venture capital

Table 1. Descriptive statistics

Descriptive Statistics	N	Mean	Std. Deviation
Tertial Educational attainment 2015	29	41.617	8.6241
Education endowment, 2004	29	33.262	10.9317
Venture capital Fin 2006% GDP	26	.03315	.049715
Venture capital Fin 2015% GDP	29	.14359	.275004
2004 regulatory quality	29	84.9224	10.04284
2014 regulatory quality	29	83.8697	10.10334
Changes in business registration (NBD) 2006-2007	29	-0.2486	3.74674
Changes in business registration (NBD) 2013-2014	29	2.0514	3.55689
Patent Application per million inhabitants in 2004	29	77.93	96.573
Patent applications per m inhabitants 2015	29	113.28	121.293
Valid N (listwise)	29		

and significantly, a much higher variation between countries. Since venture capital is not part of the mandatory EU policy framework, it is not surprising that there are large national differences. There were essentially no changes in the regulatory environment over time (but there are still differences in the quality of regulation across European nations).

Following the initial analysis of descriptive statistics, the paper used regression techniques to explore the effect these metrics on entrepreneurial outcomes. Since there was no precise apriori theoretical linkage between new business startup rates and patent applications, the regressions were conducted separately. Model A tested the variables associated with new business entry density while Model B tested the same variables on the dependent variable of patent applications.

Model A (For hypotheses 1a through 4a) tested whether the factors in our model had a significant impact on New Business Entry Density. The model was significant with an F value of 4.068 and p=0.012 and an adjusted R-square of .305.

Table 2 displays the regression coefficients for model A.

Table 2. Regression coefficients for model A

Coefficients[a]					
Model	Unstandardized Coefficients		Standardized Coefficients	t	Sig.
	B	Std. Error	Beta		
1 (Constant)	9.315	6.145		1.516	.143
Venture capital Fin 2015% GDP	-.381	2.330	-.026	-.164	.871
Tax rate 2014	-.379	.108	-.559	-3.491	.002
2014 regulatory quality	.140	.065	.352	2.167	.040
Education endowment	-.061	.058	-.166	-1.045	.306

a. Dependent Variable: New Business Density

Of note, the model provided support for hypothesis 2a and Hypothesis 3a. Taxes were significant at 0.002 and in the correct direction (higher taxes resulted in lower new business density). Similarly, countries with high quality business regulation were significantly associated with new business density at .04.

Model 2 tested whether the factors in our model had a significant impact on innovations levels as measured by patent applications. The model findings were very robust with and adjusted R-Square of .464. The regression equation was significant with an F value of 7.068, significant at 0.001.

While educational levels were not significant to the number of new ventures, there were highly associated with patent applications with significance of 0.016. The direction of the variable was the reverse of our hypothesis. One possible interpretation is that the data does not indicate the type of education, only the level. It may be that nations with lower overall educational attainment levels may have a higher percentage of graduates in fields other than science, technology, engineering, and math.

The model provided support for hypotheses 1b, 2b, and 4b: Tertial education, the availability of venture capital and regularity quality were positively and significantly associated with patent applications (P=0.026, P=0.025 and P=0.000 respectively)

FUTURE RESEARCH DIRECTIONS

As discussed in this paper's opening, Europe is once again going through a time of great transition. Two forces in particular could reshape the entrepreneurial context in Europe for the next ten years or more. First, the Eurosceptic movement has had major victories, most significantly, Brexit. Euroscepticism combined with rising nationalism suggest that there will be greater emphasis on national identity and politic. One could reasonably posit that this movement will result in greater variation in the entrepreneurial contexts and outcomes. The field would benefit from assessing the change in entrepreneurial context and outcomes relative to Euroscepticism or other measures of increased nationalism.

Similarly, the migrant crisis has opened old wounds and fostered new ones. Immigration raises complex research questions. First, there is great variation among EU members as to how many immigrants they will accept. The cost of the immigration crisis is being partially absorbed by the EU, but that means the Union will have fewer Euros to invest in infrastructure and technology, two investments that help entrepreneurs and particularly e-entrepreneurs. Second, the effects of immigration as reported in the literature vary greatly. There is substantial evidence the expatriate entrepreneurs have great success at

Table 3. The coefficients for Model B

Coefficients[a]					
Model	**Unstandardized Coefficients**		**Standardized Coefficients**	**t**	**Sig.**
	B	**Std. Error**	**Beta**		
(Constant)	-627.984	161.105		-3.898	.001
Tertial Educational attainment 2015	-6.610	2.561	-.470	-2.581	.016
1 Venture capital Fin 2015% GDP	148.720	62.370	.337	2.384	.025
Tax rate 2014	3.649	2.873	.178	1.270	.216
2014 regulatory quality	10.388	2.219	.865	4.681	.000

a. Dependent Variable: Patent applications per m inhabitants 2015

generating intellectual property. Conversely, there is research that suggests that forced migrants are more likely to pursue necessity entrepreneurship.

The combination of the Eurosceptic movement and migrant crisis have resulted in higher nationalistic aspirations and a deeper sense of national identity. This new national identity movement may restrict e-entrepreneurship, especially in the form of ibusiness which requires the coordination of collaborating groups across national boundaries. There is also a realistic concern that national taxation systems might influence the nature of e-business transactions across borders, adding to the otherwise low transaction costs faced by electronic entrepreneurs. At the same time, economic integration in Europe has created larger markets and lower transaction costs for cross border activities. Further, technology available in one European country is essentially available to all European firms. The combination of these new factors render it difficult to predict e-commerce outcomes and therefore requires fresh perspectives European e-commerce research.

The immigration crisis also has the potential to challenge the Schengen model of worker mobility. One could argue that a decline in labor mobility with everything else remaining constant would favor e-entrepreneurs. It is difficult to imagine ceterus paribus; the migrant crisis will differentially effect national budgets and national politics. Research is needed to model these differences that could clearly moderate entrepreneurial outcomes.

In addition to assessing policy outcomes, research is needed to help entrepreneurs assess the challenges of differing entrepreneurship landscapes. At this stage of industry evolution, it is difficult to determine whether variations in entrepreneurial entry strategies will generate different outcomes. Research that is accessible to practitioners is an important next-step in this field.

This paper explored entrepreneurial ventures that were likely to result in employment growth, but did not specifically look at technology based entrepreneurship. There may be value in replicating this study by looking at the same independent factors and their influence on new high-technology startups. Since technology is highly dependent on educational endowment and financial resources, national differences in high technology start up rates may be more exaggerated than for general entrepreneurs.

CONCLUSION

At the outset of this research, a series of major changes were re-shaping the European innovation and entrepreneurship landscape. Champions of the European idea were working to shape a new Europe in the face of increasing challenges from Eurosceptics resulting from the financial crisis, rise of a European nationalism, and migrant crisis. While the EU has worked to create a common legal and policy framework for member nations, the results have not resulted in uniform markets. In many cases, the opposite has occurred. Member nations have used their discretionary legislative and policy functions to shape unique national innovation and entrepreneurship landscapes and these new contexts have generated vastly different entrepreneurial outcomes.

This research contributes to the literature by identifying four constructs that significantly influence entrepreneurial outcomes in Europe. These constructs of endowment, regulatory quality, differential tax rates, and the availability of new venture financing vary greatly across nations. The results of this study demonstrate significant and meaningful relationships between entrepreneurial outcomes in Europe. Context matters; national difference in entrepreneurial landscapes result in uniquely different national entrepreneurial outcomes as measured by national patent applications and new business registrations.

REFERENCES

Acs, Z. J., Audretsch, D. B., Lehmann, E. E., & Licht, G. (2016). National systems of entrepreneurship. *Small Business Economics*, *46*(4), 527–535. doi:10.1007/s11187-016-9705-1

Acs, Z. J., Autio, E., & Szerb, L. (2014). National systems of entrepreneurship: Measurement issues and policy implications. *Research Policy*, *43*(3), 476–494. doi:10.1016/j.respol.2013.08.016

Acs, Z. J., Desai, S., & Klapper, L. F. (2008). What does "entrepreneurship" data really show? *Small Business Economics*, *31*(3), 265–281. doi:10.1007/s11187-008-9137-7

Balcarová, P. (2016). Is competitiveness in the European Union converging? *Acta Universitatis Agriculturae et Silviculturae Mendelianae Brunensis*, *64*(6), 1835–1842. doi:10.11118/actaun201664061835

Bartholomew, S. (1997). National systems of biotechnology innovation: Complex interdependence in the global system. *Journal of International Business Studies*, *28*(2), 241–266. doi:10.1057/palgrave.jibs.8490100

Borg-Barthet, J., & Lyons, C. (2016). The European Union Migration Crisis. *Edinburgh Law Review*, *20*(2), 230–235. doi:10.3366/elr.2016.0346

Bosma, N. (2013). The Global Entrepreneurship Monitor (GEM) and Its Impact on Entrepreneurship Research. Foundations and Trends in Entrepreneurship, 9(2).

Brack, N., & Startin, N. (2015). Introduction: Euroscepticism, from the margins to the mainstream. *International Political Science Review*, *36*(3), 239–249. doi:10.1177/0192512115577231

Brouthers, K. D., Geisser, K. D., & Rothlauf, F. (2016). Explaining the internationalization of ibusiness firms. *Journal of International Business Studies*, *47*(5), 513–534. doi:10.1057/jibs.2015.20

Brubaker, R. (2017). Between nationalism and civilizationism: The European populist moment in comparative perspective. *Ethnic and Racial Studies*, *40*(8), 1191–1226. doi:10.1080/01419870.2017.1294700

Carree, M. A., & Thurik, A. R. (2003). The impact of entrepreneurship on economic growth. In Handbook of entrepreneurship research (pp. 437-471). Springer US.

Coulter, S., & Hancké, B. (2016). A bonfire of the regulations, or business as usual? The UK labour market and the political economy of Brexit. *The Political Quarterly*, *87*(2), 148–156. doi:10.1111/1467-923X.12245

DeSoto, H. (1990). *The Other Path*. New York: Harper & Row.

Djankov, S., La Porta, R., Lopez-de-Silanes, F., & Shleifer, A. (2002). The regulation of entry. *The Quarterly Journal of Economics*, *117*(1), 1–37. doi:10.1162/003355302753399436

Ertl, H. (2006). Educational standards and the changing discourse on education: The reception and consequences of the PISA study in Germany. *Oxford Review of Education*, *32*(5), 619–634. doi:10.1080/03054980600976320

European Commission. (1999). *Action Plan to Promote Entrepreneurship and Competitiveness*. Brussels: Directorate-General for Enterprise.

European Commission. (2010). [*A strategy for smart, sustainable and inclusive growth*. Brussels: EC.]. *Europe*, 2020.

European Council. (2000). *Presidency Conclusions of the Lisbon European Council*. SN 100/00, 23-24 March. EC.

Fama, E. F., Fisher, L., Jensen, M. C., & Roll, R. (1969). The adjustment of stock prices to new information. *International Economic Review*, *10*(1), 1–21. doi:10.2307/2525569

Feller, I. (2005). *A historical perspective on government-university partnerships to enhance entrepreneurship and economic development. In Economic development through entrepreneurship: Government, university and business linkages* (pp. 6–28). Cheltenham, UK: Edward Elgar.

Galperina, L. (2016). Regional Diversity and Smart Growth of the European Union. *Evropejskij Issledovatel*, *113*(12), 584–591.

Ganev & Venilin. (2007). Preying on the state: The transformation of Bulgaria after 1989. London, UK: Cornell University Press.

Gomez-Herrera, E., Martens, B., & Turlea, G. (2014). The drivers and impediments for cross-border e-commerce in the EU. *Information Economics and Policy*, *28*, 83–96. doi:10.1016/j.infoecopol.2014.05.002

Hébert, R. F., & Link, A. N. (1989). In search of the meaning of entrepreneurship. *Small Business Economics*, *1*(1), 39–49. doi:10.1007/BF00389915

International, S. R. I. (1999). *International practices and experiences in business start-up procedures*. Arlington, VA: SRI.

Ionescu, R. (2016). European Union of the Regional Disparities. *Acta Universitatis Danubius: Oeconomica*, *12*(6), 168–178.

Jaffe, A. B., & Trajtenberg, M. (2002). *Patents, citations, and innovations: A window on the knoweledge economy*. MIT Press.

Kaufmann, D., & Kraay, A. (2002). *Governance Indicators, Aid Allocation, and the Millennium Challenge Account*. World Bank.

Kaufmann, D., Kraay, A., & Mastruzzi, M. (2008). *Governance matters VII: Aggregate and individual governace indicators 1996-2007*. Washington, DC: World Bank. doi:10.1596/1813-9450-4654

Kaynak, E., & Dana, L. P. (2013). *When economies change hands: A survey of entrepreneurship in the emerging markets of Europe from the Balkans to the Baltic States*. Routledge.

Kogut, B. (1991). Country capabilities and the permeability of borders. *Strategic Management Journal*, *12*, 33-47.

Lenway, S. A., & Murtha, T. P. (1994). The state as strategist in international business research. *Journal of International Business Studies*, *25*(3), 513–536. doi:10.1057/palgrave.jibs.8490210

Lesinska, M. (2014). The European backlash against immigration and multiculturalism. *Journal of Sociology (Melbourne, Vic.)*, *50*(1), 37–50. doi:10.1177/1440783314522189

McChesney, F. S. (1987). Rent extraction and rent creation in the economic theory of regulation. *The Journal of Legal Studies*, *16*(1), 101–118. doi:10.1086/467825

Mudde, C. (2007). *Populist Radical Right Parties in Europe*. Cambridge, UK: Cambridge University Press. doi:10.1017/CBO9780511492037

Nelson, R. R. (Ed.). (1993). *National innovation systems: a comparative analysis*. Oxford University Press.

Nodia, G. (2017). The End of the Postnational Illusion. *Journal of Democracy*, *28*(2), 5–19. doi:10.1353/jod.2017.0019

Peterson, J. (2016). All Roads Don't Lead to Brussels (But Most Do): European Integration and Transatlantic Relations. In The West and the Global Power Shift (pp. 101-125). Palgrave Macmillan UK.

Pinder, J. (2001). *The European Union: A very short introduction* (Vol. 36). Oxford University Press.

Popescu, A. (2016). The EU "costs" of the refugee crisis. *Europolity. Continuity and Change in European Governance*, *10*(1), 105–120.

Porter, M. E. (1990). The competitive advantage of nations. *Harvard Business Review*, *68*(4), 73–93.

Porter, M. E. (2000). *Attitudes, values, beliefs, and the microeconomics of prosperity. In Culture Matters* (pp. 14–28). New York: Basic Books.

Porter, M. E., & Stern, S. (2004). Ranking National Innovative Capacity: Findings from the National Innovative Capacity Index. In *The global competitiveness report*. New York, NY: Oxford University Press.

Potts, M., & Puia, G. M. (2012). Entrepreneurship in the European Union: Unified is not uniform. *Regional development: Concepts, methodologies, tools, and applications*, 121-132.

Puia, G. M., & Minnis, W. (2007). The Effects of Policy Frameworks and Culture on the Regulation of Entrepreneurial Entry. *The Journal of Applied Management and Entrepreneurship*, *12*(4), 36–50.

Puia, G. M., & Ofori-Dankwa, J. (2013). The effects of national culture and ethnolinguistic diversity on innovativeness. *Baltic Journal of Management*, *8*(3), 349–371. doi:10.1108/BJOM-Jan-2012-0002

Schumpeter, J. (1934). *Capitalism, socialism, and democracy*. Academic Press.

Shane, S. (1992). Why do some societies invent more than others? *Journal of Business Venturing*, *7*(1), 29–46. doi:10.1016/0883-9026(92)90033-N

Shane, S. (2005). Government policies to encourage economic development through entrepreneurship: The case of technology transfer. *Economic development through entrepreneurship: Government, university, and business linkages*, 33-46.

Shleifer, A., & Vishny, R. W. (1997). A survey of corporate governance. *The Journal of Finance*, *52*(2), 737–783. doi:10.1111/j.1540-6261.1997.tb04820.x

Spencer, J. W., Murtha, T. P., & Lenway, S. A. (2005). How Governments Matter to New Industry Creation. *Academy of Management Review*, *30*(2), 321–337. doi:10.5465/AMR.2005.16387889

Stabryła-Chudzio, K. (2016). Contribution of the EU Budget to the Implementation of the Social Cohesion Policy of the European Union. *Journal of Management and Business Administration, 24*(2), 89–106.

Teece, D. J. (1992). Foreign investment and technological development in silicon. *California Management Review, 34*(2), 88–106. doi:10.2307/41166695

Union, I. (2014). *Communication from the Commission to the European Parliament, the Council, the European Economic and Social Committee and the Committee of the Regions*. Brussels.

Van den Bosch, F. A. J., & van Prooijen, A. A. (1992). The competitive advantage of European nations: The impact of national culture, a missing element in Porter's analysis? *European Management Journal, 10*(2), 173–178. doi:10.1016/0263-2373(92)90066-D

Venkataraman, S. (1997). The distinctive domain of entrepreneurship research. In J. Katz & R. Brockhaus (Eds.), *Advances in Entrepreneurship, firm emergence and growth* (Vol. 3, pp. 119–138). Greenwich, CT: JAI Press.

Winzen, T., & Schimmelfennig, F. (2016). Explaining differentiation in European Union treaties. *European Union Politics, 17*(4), 616-637.

Wodak, R., & Boukala, S. (2015). European identities and the revival of nationalism in the European Union: A discourse historical approach. *Journal of Language and Politics, 14*(1), 87–109. doi:10.1075/jlp.14.1.05wod

World Bank. (2004). *Doing Business in 2004: Understanding regulation*. Oxford, UK: Oxford University Press.

Compilation of References

Aaker, D. (1996). *Building Strong Brands*. New York, NY: Free Press Business.

Abadi, M., Burrows, M., Kaufman, C., & Lampson, B. (1993). Authentication and delegation with smart-cards'. *Science of Computer Programming*, *21*(2), 93–113. doi:10.1016/0167-6423(93)90002-7

Aberdeen Group. (2008). *Social media monitoring and analysis: Generating consumer insights from online conversation*. Retrieved September 1, 2013 from: http://robertoigarza.files.wordpress.com/2008/10/rep-social-media-monitoring-and-analysis-aberdeen-group-2008.pdf

Acs, Z. J., Audretsch, D. B., Lehmann, E. E., & Licht, G. (2016). National systems of entrepreneurship. *Small Business Economics*, *46*(4), 527–535. doi:10.1007/s11187-016-9705-1

Acs, Z. J., Autio, E., & Szerb, L. (2014). National systems of entrepreneurship: Measurement issues and policy implications. *Research Policy*, *43*(3), 476–494. doi:10.1016/j.respol.2013.08.016

Acs, Z. J., Desai, S., & Klapper, L. F. (2008). What does "entrepreneurship" data really show? *Small Business Economics*, *31*(3), 265–281. doi:10.1007/s11187-008-9137-7

Adams, J. (2009a). A new way to find 'Union' workers. *Bank Technology News*, *22*(5), 23.

Adams, J. (2009b). The Strongest Link. *Bank Technology News*, *22*(5), 23.

Addley, E. (2009). *The Twitter crisis: how site became voice of resistance in Iran*. Retrieved from http://www.guardian.co.uk/world/2009/jun/16/twitter-social-networking-iran-opposition

Agarwal, R. (2000). Individual acceptance of information technologies. In *Framing the Domains of IT Management: Projecting the Future through the Past* (pp. 85–104). Academic Press. Retrieved July 2015 from http://www.c4ads.seas.gwu.edu/classes/CSci285_Fall_2004/readings/9/required/Agarwal_02.pdf

Agarwal, J., & Wu, T. (2015). Factors influencing growth potential of e-commerce in emerging economies: An institution based N-OLI framework and research propositions. *Thunderbird International Business Review*, *57*(3), 197–215. doi:10.1002/tie.21694

Agarwal, R., Animesh, A., & Prasad, K. (2009). Social interactions and the "Digital Divide": Explaining Variations in Internet Use. *Information Systems Research*, *20*(2), 277–294. doi:10.1287/isre.1080.0194

Agarwal, R., & Prasad, J. (1997). The role of innovation characteristics and perceived voluntariness in the acceptance of information technologies. *Decision Sciences*, *28*(3), 557–582. doi:10.1111/j.1540-5915.1997.tb01322.x

Agarwal, R., & Prasad, J. (1999). Are individual differences germane to the acceptance of new information technologies? *Decision Sciences*, *30*(2), 361–391. doi:10.1111/j.1540-5915.1999.tb01614.x

Agarwal, R., Sambamurthy, V., & Stair, R. M. (2000). Research report: The evolving relationship between general and specific computer self-efficacy - An empirical assessment. *Information Systems Research, 11*(4), 418–430. doi:10.1287/isre.11.4.418.11876

Agarwal, R., & Venkatesh, V. (2002). Assessing a firm's web presence: A heuristic evaluation procedure for the measurement of usability. *Information Systems Research, 13*(2), 168–186. doi:10.1287/isre.13.2.168.84

Agarwal, S., Perry, H. B., Long, L. A., & Labrique, A. B. (2015). Evidence on feasibility and effective use of mHealth strategies by frontline health workers in developing countries: Systematic review. *Tropical Medicine & International Health, 20*(8), 1003–1014. doi:10.1111/tmi.12525 PMID:25881735

Agichtein, E., Castillo, C., Donato, D., Gionis, A., & Mishne, G. (2008) Finding high-quality content in social media. *WISDOM – Proceedings of the 2008 International Conference on Web Search and Data Mining*, 183-193.

Ahn, T., Ryu, S., & Han, I. (2004). The impact of the online and offline features on the user acceptance of internet shopping malls. *Electronic Commerce Research and Applications, 3*(4), 405–420. doi:10.1016/j.elerap.2004.05.001

Ahn, T., Ryu, S., & Han, I. (2007). The impact of web quality and playfulness on user acceptance of online retailing. *Information & Management, 44*(3), 263–275. doi:10.1016/j.im.2006.12.008

Ahuja, M., & Carley, K. (1999). Network Structure in Virtual Organization. *Organization Science, 10*(6), 741–757. doi:10.1287/orsc.10.6.741

Ai-Alawi, A. I., Al-Marzooqi, N. Y., & Mohammed, Y. F. (2007). Organizational Culture and Knowledge Sharing: Critical Success Factors. *Journal of Knowledge Management, 11*(2), 22–42. doi:10.1108/13673270710738898

Aichner, T., & Jacob, F. (2015). Measuring the Degree of Corporate Social Media Use. *International Journal of Market Research, 57*(2), 257–275.

Ajzen, I. (1985). *From intentions to actions: A theory of planned behavior. In Action Control* (pp. 11–39). Berlin: Springer Berlin Heidelberg; doi:10.1007/978-3-642-69746-3

Ajzen, I. (1991). The theory of planned behavior. *Organizational Behavior and Human Decision Processes, 50*(2), 179–211. doi:10.1016/0749-5978(91)90020-T

Ajzen, I., & Fishbein, M. (1980). *Understanding attitudes and predicting social behavior.* Englewood Cliffs, NJ: Prentice Hall.

Akhuemonkhan, I. A. (2005). *Modalities of teaching entrepreneurship in technical institution.* Paper presented at the National workshop on Capacity building for lecturers of Polytechnics and monotechnics in Nigeria, at the Federal Polytechnic, Uwana, Afikpo, Nigeria.

Akter, S., D'Ambra, J., & Ray, P. (2010). *18th European Conference on Information Systems: conference proceedings.* University of Pretoria. Retrieved from http://ro.uow.edu.au/cgi/viewcontent.cgi?article=4188&context=commpapers

Akter, S., D'Ambra, J., & Ray, P. (2013). Development and validation of an instrument to measure user perceived service quality of mHealth. *Information & Management, 50*(4), 181–195. doi:10.1016/j.im.2013.03.001

Aladwani, A. M., & Palvia, P. C. (2002). Developing and validating an instrument for measuring user perceived web quality. *Information & Management, 39*(6), 467–476. doi:10.1016/S0378-7206(01)00113-6

Alavi, M., & Leidner, D. E. (2001). Review: Knowledge Management and Knowledge Management Systems: Conceptual Foundations and Research Issues. *Management Information Systems Quarterly, 25*(1), 107–136. doi:10.2307/3250961

Al-Busaidi, K., & Ohlman, L. (2017). Knowledge sharing through inter-organizational knowledge sharing systems. *VINE Journal of Information and Knowledge Management Systems*, *47*(1), 110–136. doi:10.1108/VJIKMS-05-2016-0019

Aldrich, H. (1999). *Organizations evolving*. Beverly Hills, CA: Sage Publications Limited.

Alfonso, R. M. (2011). *The American express OPEN state of women-owned business report: A summary of important trends 1997-2011*. Fort Lauderdale, FL: The American Express OPEN.

Algesheimer, R., Dholakia, U. M., & Herrmann, A. (2005). The social influence of brand community: Evidence from European car clubs. *Journal of Marketing*, *69*(3), 19–34. doi:10.1509/jmkg.69.3.19.66363

Allcorn, S. (1997). Parallel Enterprise Social Systems: Managing and working in the virtual workplace. *Administration & Society*, *29*(4), 412–439. doi:10.1177/009539979702900402

Al-Qeisi, K., Dennis, C., Alamanos, E., & Jayawardhena, C. (2014). Website design quality and usage behavior: Unified theory of acceptance and use of technology. *Journal of Business Research*, *67*(11), 2282–2290. doi:10.1016/j.jbusres.2014.06.016

Amoroso, D. L., & Ogawa, M. (2013). Comparing mobile and internet adoption factors of loyalty and satisfaction with online shopping consumers. *International Journal of E-Business Research*, *9*(2), 24–45. doi:10.4018/jebr.2013040103

Anderson, A. R., Steinerte, E., & Russell, E. O. (2010). The Nature of Trust in Virtual Entrepreneurial Networks. *International Journal of E-Entrepreneurship and Innovation*, *1*(1), 1–21. doi:10.4018/jeei.2010010101

Angst, M. C., & Agarwal, R. (2009). Adoption of electronic health records in the presence of privacy concerns: The Elaborate Likelihood Model and individual persuasion. *Management Information Systems Quarterly*, *33*(2), 339–370.

Ang, Z., & Massingham, P. (2007). National Culture and Standardization versus Adaption of knowledge Management. *Journal of Knowledge Management*, *11*(2), 5–21. doi:10.1108/13673270710738889

Antorini, Y. M., Muniz, A. M., & Askildsen, T. (2012). Collaborating With Customer Communities: Lessons from the Lego Group. *MIT Sloan Management Review*, *53*(3), 73.

Aoki, M. (1986). Horizontal vs. vertical information structure of the firm. *The American Economic Review*, 971–983.

Ardichvili, A., Mauner, M., Li, W., Wenting, T., & Stuedemann, R. (2006). Cultural influences on knowledge sharing through online communities of practice. *Journal of Knowledge Management*, *10*(1), 94–107. doi:10.1108/13673270610650139

Armando, A. (2005). The AVISPA Tool for the Automated Validation of Internet Security Protocols and Applications. In Lecture Notes in Computer Science: Vol. 3576. Proceedings of Computer Aided Verification'05 (pp. 281-285). Springer. doi:10.1007/11513988_27

Armbrust, M., Fox, A., Griffith, R., Joseph, A. D., Katz, R., Konwinski, A., ... Zaharia, M. (2010). A View of Cloud Computing. *Communications of the ACM*, *53*(4), 50–58. doi:10.1145/1721654.1721672

Aspiring Mind's National Employability Report-Engineers Annual Report. (2016). Aspiring Minds Assessment Pvt. Ltd. Available: http://www.aspiringminds.com/sites/default/files/National%20Employability%20Report%2020Engineers%20Annual%20Report%2020 16.pdf

Bagozzi, R. P. (1982). A field investigation of causal relations among cognitions, affect, intentions, and behavior. *JMR, Journal of Marketing Research*, *19*(4), 562–583. doi:10.2307/3151727

Bailey, D. E., Barley, S. R., & Leonardi, P. M. (2012). The Lure of the Virtual. *Organization Science*, *23*(5), 1485–1504. doi:10.1287/orsc.1110.0703

Bajaj, A., & Nidumolu, S. R. (1998). A feedback model to understand information system usage. *Information & Management, 33*(4), 213–224. doi:10.1016/S0378-7206(98)00026-3

Balcarová, P. (2016). Is competitiveness in the European Union converging? *Acta Universitatis Agriculturae et Silviculturae Mendelianae Brunensis, 64*(6), 1835–1842. doi:10.11118/actaun201664061835

Baldwin, C., & von Hippel, E. (2010). *Modeling a paradigm shift: From producer innovation to user and open collaborative innovation.* Working Paper No. 4764-09. MIT Sloan School of Management.

Bal, J., & Teo, P. K. (2000). Implementing distributed teamworking. Part 1: A literature review of best practice. *Logistics Information Management, 13*(6), 346–352. doi:10.1108/09576050010355644

Balogun, J., Bartunek, J. M., & Do, B. (2015). Senior Managers' Sensemaking and Responses to Strategic Change. *Organization Science, 26*(4), 960–979. doi:10.1287/orsc.2015.0985

Balubaid, M. A. (2013). Using Web 2.0 technology to enhance knowledge sharing in an academic department. *Procedia: Social and Behavioral Sciences, 102*, 406–420. doi:10.1016/j.sbspro.2013.10.756

Barab, S. A., Kling, R., & Gray, J. H. (2004). *Designing for Distributed Communities in the Service of Learning.* Camebridge, UK: Cambridge University Press. doi:10.1017/CBO9780511805080

Barkhi, R., Belanger, F., & Hicks, J. (2008). A model of the determinants of purchasing from virtual stores. *Journal of Organizational Computing and Electronic Commerce, 18*(3), 177–196. doi:10.1080/10919390802198840

Barkhi, R., & Wallace, L. (2007). The impact of personality type on purchasing decisions in virtual stores. *Information Technology Management, 8*(4), 313–330. doi:10.1007/s10799-007-0021-y

Barley, S., & Tolbert, P. (1997). Institutionalization and Structuration: Studying the Links between Action and Institution. *Organization Studies*, 18.

Baron, R. A., & Nambisan, S. (2010). Different Roles, Different Strokes: Organizing Virtual Customer Environments to Promote Two Types of Customer Contributions. *Organization Science, 21*(2), 554–572. doi:10.1287/orsc.1090.0460

Bartel, C. A., Wiesenfeld, B. M., & Wrzesniewski, A. (2012). Knowing Where You Stand: Physical Isolation, Perceived Respect, and Organizational Identification Among Virtual Employees. *Organization Science, 23*(3), 743–757. doi:10.1287/orsc.1110.0661

Bartholomew, S. (1997). National systems of biotechnology innovation: Complex interdependence in the global system. *Journal of International Business Studies, 28*(2), 241–266. doi:10.1057/palgrave.jibs.8490100

Basdeo, D., Smith, K. G., Grimm, C., Rindova, V. P., & Derfus, P. (2006). The impact of market actions on firm reputation. *Strategic Management Journal, 27*(12), 1183–1204. doi:10.1002/smj.556

Bastone, J. (2010). Evaluate social media by listening, leveraging and engaging. *Direct: Magazine of Direct Marketing.* Retrieved February 12, 2014 from http://www.chiefmarketer.com/web-marketing/evaluate-social-media-by-listening-leveraging-and-engaging-17082010

Bateman, W. (1990). *Open to Question: The Art of Teaching and Learning by Inquiry.* San Francisco: Jossey-Bass.

Bechard, J. P., & Gregoire, D. (2005). Entrepreneurship education research re-visited: The case of higher education. *Academy of Management Learning & Education, 4*(1), 22–43. doi:10.5465/AMLE.2005.16132536

Bechard, J. P., & Toulouse, J. M. (1998). Validation of a didactic model for the analysis of training objectives in entrepreneurship. *Journal of Business Venturing, 13*(4), 317–332. doi:10.1016/S0883-9026(98)80006-2

Beer, S. (1984). The viable system model: Its prvenance, development, methodology and pathology. *The Journal of the Operational Research Society, 35*(1), 7–25. doi:10.1057/jors.1984.2

Ben-Shabat, H., Nilforoushan, P., Yuen, C., & Moriarty, M. (2015). *Global retail e-commerce keeps on clicking: The 2015 global retail e-commerce index*. Retrieved on July, 2015, from https://www.atkearney.com/consumer-products-retail/e-commerce-index/full-report/-/asset_publisher/87xbENNHPZ3D/content/global-retail-e-commerce-keeps-on-clicking/10192?_101_INSTANCE_87xbENNHPZ3D_redirect=%2Fconsumer-products-retail%2Fe-commerce-index

Berglann, H., Moen, E. R., Røed, K., & Skogstrøm, J. F. (2011). Entrepreneurship: Origins and returns. *Labour Economics, 18*(2), 180–193. doi:10.1016/j.labeco.2010.10.002

Berry, M. (2005, May). Online recruitment grows in popularity. *Personnel Today*, 43.

Bettoni, M., Andenmatten, S., & Mathieu, R. (2006). Knowledge Cooperation in Online Communities: A Duality of Participation and Cultivation. In *Proceedings of 7th European Conference of Knowledge Management (ECKM06)*. Public Academic Conferences Ltd.

Bhagat, R. S., Kedia, B. L., Harveston, P. D., & Triandis, H. C. (2002). Cultural variations in the cross-border transfer of organizational knowledge: An integrative framework. *Academy of Management Review, 27*(2), 204–221.

Bird, B. J. (1989). *Entrepreneurial behavior*. Glenview, IL: Scott Foresman and Co.

Bisdee, D. (2007). *Consumer attitudes review*. Office of Fair Trading. Retrieved on June 2015 from http://citeseerx.ist.psu.edu/viewdoc/download?doi=10.1.1.106.2145&rep=rep1&type=pdf

Blom, R., Carpenter, S., Bowe, B. J., & Lange, R. (2014). Frequent contributors within U.S. newspaper comment forums: An examination of their civility and information value. *The American Behavioral Scientist, 58*(10), 1314–1328. doi:10.1177/0002764214527094

Bo, B. (2004). *Leading by Detached Involvement – Success factors enabling leadership of distributed teams* (MBA Dissertation). Henley Management College, UK.

Boase, J., Horrigan, J. B., Wellman, B., & Rainie, L. (2006). The strength of internet ties. The Internet and email aid users in maintaining their social networks and provide pathways to help when people face big decisions. *PEW Internet and American Life Proejct Report Report Number 202-419-4500*. Available online at: http://www.pewinternet/org

Bolisani, E., & Scarso, E. (2000). Electronic communication and knowledge transfer. *International Journal of Technology Management, 20*(1-2), 116–133. doi:10.1504/IJTM.2000.002855

Boontarig, W., Chutimaskul, W., Chongsuphajaisiddhi, W., & Papasratorn, B. (2012). Factors influencing the Thai elderly intention to use smartphone for e-Health services. *IEEE Symposium on Humanities, Science and Engineering Research*, p242-246. doi:10.1109/SHUSER.2012.6268881

Booth, N., & Matic, J. A. (2011). Mapping and leveraging influencers in social media to shape corporate brand perceptions. *Corporate Communications, 16*(3), 184–191. doi:10.1108/13563281111156853

Borg-Barthet, J., & Lyons, C. (2016). The European Union Migration Crisis. *Edinburgh Law Review, 20*(2), 230–235. doi:10.3366/elr.2016.0346

Bosma, N. (2013). The Global Entrepreneurship Monitor (GEM) and Its Impact on Entrepreneurship Research. Foundations and Trends in Entrepreneurship, 9(2).

Boudreaux, E. D., Waring, M. E., Hayes, R. B., Sadasivam, R. S., Mullen, S., & Pagoto, S. (2014). Evaluating and selecting mobile health apps: Strategies for healthcare providers and healthcare organizations. *Translational Behavioral Medicine*, *4*(4), 363–371. doi:10.1007/s13142-014-0293-9 PMID:25584085

Boukhedouma, S., Alimazighi, Z., & Oussalah, M. (2017). Adaptation and Evolution Frameworks for Service Based Inter-Organizational Workflows. *International Journal of E-Business Research*, *13*(2), 28–57. doi:10.4018/IJEBR.2017040103

Boyd, D. M., & Ellison, N. B. (2007). Social Network Sites: Definition, History and Scholarship. *Journal of Computer-Mediated Communication*, *13*(1), 210–230. doi:10.1111/j.1083-6101.2007.00393.x

Brack, N., & Startin, N. (2015). Introduction: Euroscepticism, from the margins to the mainstream. *International Political Science Review*, *36*(3), 239–249. doi:10.1177/0192512115577231

Brancheau, J. C., & Wetherbe, J. C. (1990). The adoption of spreadsheet software: Testing innovation diffusion theory in the context of end-user computing. *Information Systems Research*, *1*(1), 115–143. Retrieved onJuly2015. doi:10.1287/isre.1.2.115

Brannen, M. Y., & Salk, J. (2000). Partnering Across Borders. *Human Relations*, *53*(4), 451–487. doi:10.1177/0018726700534001

Breu, K., & Hemingway, C. (2004). Making organisations virtual: The hidden cost of distributed teams. *Journal of Information Technology*, *19*(3), 191–202. doi:10.1057/palgrave.jit.2000018

Brian, R. M., & Ben-Zeev, D. (2014). Mobile health (mHealth) for mental health in Asia: Objectives, strategies, and limitations. *Asian Journal of Psychiatry*, *10*, 96–100. doi:10.1016/j.ajp.2014.04.006 PMID:25042960

Brinberg, D. (1979). An examination of the determinants of intention and behavior: A comparison of two models. *Journal of Applied Social Psychology*, *9*(6), 560–575. doi:10.1111/j.1559-1816.1979.tb00816.x

Brogan, C., & Bastone, J. (2014). Acting on customer intelligence from social media. *AMA Marketing Effectiveness Online Seminar Series*. Retrieved February 12, 2014 from https://www.sas.com/offices/NA/canada/en/resources/whitepaper/wp_21122.pdf

Brouthers, K. D., Geisser, K. D., & Rothlauf, F. (2016). Explaining the internationalization of ibusiness firms. *Journal of International Business Studies*, *47*(5), 513–534. doi:10.1057/jibs.2015.20

Brown, A. D. (1998). *Organizational Culture*. London, UK: Financial Times Management, Pitman Publishing.

Brown, J. S., & Duguid, P. (1991). Organizational Learning and Communities of Practice: Toward a Unified View of Working, Learning, and Innovation. *Organization Science*, *2*(1), 40-57.

Brown, S., Kozinets, R. V., & Sherry, J. F. Jr. (2003). Teaching old brands new tricks: Retro branding and the revival of brand meaning. *Journal of Marketing*, *67*(3), 19–33. doi:10.1509/jmkg.67.3.19.18657

Brown, W., Rahman, M., & Hacker, T. (2006). Home page usability and credibility. *Information Management & Computer Security*, *14*(3), 252–269. doi:10.1108/09685220610670404

Brubaker, R. (2017). Between nationalism and civilizationism: The European populist moment in comparative perspective. *Ethnic and Racial Studies*, *40*(8), 1191–1226. doi:10.1080/01419870.2017.1294700

Bruner, G. C. II, & Kumar, A. (2005). Explaining consumer acceptance of handheld Internet devices. *Journal of Business Research*, *58*(5), 553–558. doi:10.1016/j.jbusres.2003.08.002

Brush, C., Carter, N., Gatewood, E., Greene, P., & Hart, M. (2001). *The Diana project: Women business owners and equity capital: The myths dispelled*. Kansas City, MO: Kauffman Center for Entrepreneurial Leadership.

Bryant, J., & Zillmann, D. (2002). Media influences on marketing communications. In *Media Effects: Advances in Theory and Research* (pp. 353–396). Taylor & Francis. Retrieved on June 2015 from https://books.google.com/books?hl=en&lr=&id=KnQXQOP5uoMC&pgis=1

Bryman, A., & Bell, E. (2007). *Business Research Methods* (2nd ed.). Oxford University Press.

Bullock, A. (2013). Does technology help doctors to access, use and share knowledge? *Medical Education*, *48*(1), 28–33. doi:10.1111/medu.12378 PMID:24330114

Burgess, L., & Sargent, J. (2007). Enhancing user acceptance of mandated mobile health information systems: The ePOC (electronic point-of-care project) experience. *Studies in Health Technology and Informatics*, *129*(2), 1088–1092. PMID:17911883

Burner, E., Menchine, M., Taylor, E., & Arora, S. (2013). Gender differences in diabetes self-management: A mixed-methods analysis of a mobile health intervention for inner-city Latino patients. *Journal of Diabetes Science and Technology*, *7*(1), 111–118. doi:10.1177/193229681300700113 PMID:23439166

Burrows, M., Abadi, M., & Needham, R. (1990). A logic of authentication. *ACM Transactions on Computer Systems*, *8*(1), 18–36. doi:10.1145/77648.77649

Burton-Jones, A., & Hubona, G. S. (2005). Individual differences and usage behavior. *ACM SIGMIS Database*, *36*(2), 58–77. doi:10.1145/1066149.1066155

Buttner, E. H., & Moore, D. P. (1997). Women's Organizational Exodus to Entrepreneurship: Self-Reported Motivations and Correlates with Success. *Journal of Small Business Management*, *35*(1), 34–46.

Cairney, J., Veldhuizen, S., Vigod, S., Streiner, D. L., Wade, T. J., & Kurdyak, P. (2013). Exploring the social determinants of mental health service use using intersectionality theory and CART analysis. *Journal of Epidemiology and Community Health*, *68*(2), 145–150. doi:10.1136/jech-2013-203120 PMID:24098046

Campbell, R., Muhtadi-Al, J., Naldurg, P., Sampemane, G., & Mickunas, M. D. (2003). Towards security and privacy for pervasive computing. In M. Okada, B. C. Pierce, A. Scedrov, H. Tokuda, & A. Yonezawa (Eds.), *Software Security - Theories and Systems* (Vol. 2609, pp. 1–15). Berlin: Springer Berlin Heidelberg. doi:10.1007/3-540-36532-X_1

Cannon, R. (2000). *Guide to support the implementation of the Learning and Teaching Plan Year 2000*. The University of Adelaide.

Carland, J. W., Boulton, F. H. W., & Carland, J. C. (1984). Differentiating entrepreneurs from small busi- ness owners: A conceptualization. *Academy of Management Review*, *9*(2), 354–359.

Carree, M. A., & Thurik, A. R. (2003). The impact of entrepreneurship on economic growth. In Handbook of entrepreneurship research (pp. 437-471). Springer US.

Carree, M. A., van Stel, A. J., Thurik, A. R., & Wennekers, A. P. M. (2002). Economic development and business ownership: An analysis using data of 23 OECD countries in the period 1976-1996. *Small Business Economics*, *19*(3), 271–290. doi:10.1023/A:1019604426387

Carter, N. M., Brush, C. G., Greene, P. G., Gatewood, E., & Hart, M. M. (2003). Women entrepreneurs who break through to equity financing: The influence of human, social and financial capital. *Venture Capital*, *5*(1), 1–28. doi:10.1080/1369106032000082586

Casaló, L. V., Flavián, C., & Guinalíu, M. (2007). The role of security, privacy, usability and reputation in the development of online banking. *Online Information Review*, *31*(5), 583–603. doi:10.1108/14684520710832315

Cases, A.-S., Fournier, C., Dubois, P.-L., & Tanner, J. F. Jr. (2010). Web Site spill over to email campaigns: The role of privacy, trust and shoppers' attitudes. *Journal of Business Research, 63*(9-10), 993–999. doi:10.1016/j.jbusres.2009.02.028

Cebi, S. (2013). Determining importance degrees of website design parameters based on interactions and types of websites. *Decision Support Systems, 54*(2), 1030–1043. doi:10.1016/j.dss.2012.10.036

Center for Women's Business Research. (2009). *The economic impact of women-owned businesses in the United States (Report No. 1)*. McLean, VA: Author.

Chang, Y., Chang, C., & Huang, H. (2005). Digital signature with message recovery using self-certified public keys without trustworthy system authority. *Applied Mathematics and Computation, 161*(1), 211–227. doi:10.1016/j.amc.2003.12.020

Charmaz, K. (2000). Grounded Theory: Objectivist and Constructivist Methods. In *Handbook of qualitative research*. Sage Publications.

Chen, L.-D., & Tan, J. (2004). Technology adaptation in e-commerce: Key determinants of virtual stores acceptance. *European Management Journal, 22*(1), 74–86. doi:10.1016/j.emj.2003.11.014

Chen, Q. (1999). Attitude toward the site. *Journal of Advertising Research, 39*(5), 27–37. Retrieved from http://dialnet.unirioja.es/servlet/articulo?codigo=474770

Chen, S.-C., Li, S.-H., & Li, C.-Y. (2011). Recent related research in technology acceptance model: A literature review. *Australian Journal of Business and Management Research, 1*(9), 124–127. Retrieved from http://search.proquest.com/openview/3b8f1978447af91117b06bf44adf319b/1?pq-origsite=gscholar

Chen, Y., & Barnes, S. (2007). Initial trust and online buyer behaviour. *Industrial Management & Data Systems, 107*(1), 21–36. doi:10.1108/02635570710719034

Childers, T. L., Carr, C. L., Peck, J., & Carson, S. (2001). Hedonic and utilitarian motivations for online retail shopping behavior. *Journal of Retailing, 77*(4), 511–535. doi:10.1016/S0022-4359(01)00056-2

Child, J., Ihrig, M., & Merali, Y. (2014). Organization as Information – a Space Odyssey. *Organization Studies, 35*(6), 801–824. doi:10.1177/0170840613515472

China E-Commerce Research Center. (2013). *Statistical Data on China's Internet Commerce Market*. China E-Commerce Research Center. Retrieved from http://100ec.cn

Chin, W. W., Marcolin, B. L., & Newsted, P. R. (2003). A partial least squares latent variable modeling approach for measuring interaction effects: Results from a Monte Carlo Simulation study and an Electronic-Mail Emotion/Adoption study. *Information Systems Research, 14*(2), 189–217. doi:10.1287/isre.14.2.189.16018

Cho, E. C., & Youn-Kyung, K. (2012). The effects of website designs, self-congruity, and flow on behavioral intention. *International Journal of Design, 6*(2), 31–39.

Choo, C., Detlor, B., & Turnbull, D. (2000). *Web work: information seeking and knowledge work on the World Wide Web*. Springer. doi:10.1007/978-94-015-9405-9

Chou, C. (2014). Social media characteristics, customer relationship and brand equity. *The Journal of Applied Business and Economics, 16*(1), 128–139.

Christensen, L. T. (2002). Corporate communication: The challenge of transparency. *Corporate Communications, 7*(3), 162–168. doi:10.1108/13563280210436772

Christensson, P. (2013). Social Media Definition. *Tech Terms*. Retrieved June 18, 2017, from http://techterms.com/definition/social_media

Christmann, A., & Van Aelst, S. (2006). Robust estimation of cronbach's alpha. *Journal of Multivariate Analysis, 97*(7), 1660–1674. doi:10.1016/j.jmva.2005.05.012

Christodoulides, G., Jevons, C., & Bonhomme, J. (2012). Memo to marketers: Quantitative evidence for change. How user-generated content really affects brands. *Journal of Advertising Research, 52*(1), 53–64. doi:10.2501/JAR-52-1-053-064

Chua, A. (2001). Relationship between the types of knowledge shared and types of communication channels used. *Journal of Knowledge Management Practice*. Retrieved from http://www.tlainc.com/articl26.htm

Chubb, L. (2008). Stripped-down jobsite is a good call for 3. *People Management, 14*(2), 14.

Chudoba, K. M., & Maznevski, M. L. (2000). Bridging Space Over Time: Global Virtual Team Dynamics And Effectiveness. *Organization Science, 11*(5), 473–492. doi:10.1287/orsc.11.5.473.15200

CIPD. (2009). E-Recruitment Fact sheet. *CIPD Publication*. Retrieved March 17, 2011, from http://www.cipd.co.uk/subjects/recruitmen/onlnrcruit/onlrec.htm

Clarke, L. (1994). *The Essence of Change*. London, UK: Prentice-Hall.

Clark, W. R., Ezell, J., Clark, J., & Sheffield, D. N. (2009). Stay or leave: Applying approach-avoidance theory to virtual environments. *Journal of Database Marketing & Customer Strategy Management, 16*(4), 231–240. doi:10.1057/dbm.2009.25

Clifford, S. (2009). Tweeting Becomes a Summer Job Opportunity. *NY Times*. Retrieved April 27, 2011, from http://www.nytimes.com/2009/04/20/business/media/20twitter.html

Cober, R. T., Brown, D. J., Blumental, A. J., Doverspike, D., & Levy, P. E. (2000). The Quest for the qualified job surfer: It's Time the Public Sector Catches the Wave. *Public Personnel Management, 29*(4), 479–496. doi:10.1177/009102600002900406

Cober, R. T., Brown, D. J., Keeping, L. M., & Levy, P. E. (2004). Recruitment on the Net:How Do Enterpriseal Web Site Characteristics Influence Applicant Attraction? *Journal of Management, 30*(5), 623–646. doi:10.1016/j.jm.2004.03.001

Cohen, S. G., Gibbs, J. L., Gibson, C. B., Stanko, T. L., & Tesluk, P. (2011). Including the "I" in Virtuality and Modern Job Design: Extending the Job Characteristics Model to Include the Moderating Effect of Individual Experiences of Electronic Dependence and Copresence. *Organization Science, 22*(6), 1481–1499. doi:10.1287/orsc.1100.0586

Colky, D. L., Colky, M., & Young, W. H. (2006). Mentoring in the virtual organization: Keys to building successful schools and businesses. *Mentoring & Tutoring, 14*(4), 433–447. doi:10.1080/13611260500493683

J. W. Collins III, & N. P. O'Brien (Eds.). (2003). *Greenwood Dictionary of Education*. Westport, CT: Greenwood.

Collins, R. (1981). On the Microfoundations of Macrosociology. *American Journal of Sociology, 86*(5), 984–1014. doi:10.1086/227351

Collis, J., & Hussey, R. (2009). *Business Research: A Practical Guide for Undergraduate and Postgraduate Students* (3rd ed.). Palgrave Macmillan.

Cook, S. G. (2012). Women Lead in Adopting New Technologies. *Women in Higher Education, 21*(2), 24–25. doi:10.1002/whe.10296

Costello, A. B., & Osborne, J. W. (2005). Best practices in exploratory factor analysis: Four recommendations for getting the most from your analysis. *Practical Assessment, Research & Evaluation, 10*(7). Retrieved from http://pareonline.net/pdf/v10n7a.pdf

Coulter, S., & Hancké, B. (2016). A bonfire of the regulations, or business as usual? The UK labour market and the political economy of Brexit. *The Political Quarterly, 87*(2), 148–156. doi:10.1111/1467-923X.12245

Coursaris, C., & Kripintris, K. (2012). Web Aesthetics and Usability: An Empirical Study of the effects of white space. *International Journal of E-Business Research, 8*(1), 35–53. doi:10.4018/jebr.2012010103

Crail, M. (2007). Online Recruitment delivers more applicants and wins vote of most Employers. *Personnel Today.* Retrieved March 17, 2011 from http://www.personneltoday.com/articles/2007/11/20/43298/online-recruitment-delivers-more-applicants-and-wins-vote-of-most-employers.html

Cray, D., & Mallory, G. R. (1998). *Making Sense of Managing Culture.* London, UK: International Thomson Business Press.

Creed, A., & Zutshi, A. (2008). The wellhouse of knowledge globalization: IT and virtual communities. *Journal of Knowledge Globalization, 1*(1), 29–42.

Cremers, C. J. F. (2006). *Scyther-Semantics and Verification of Security Protocols* (Ph.D. Thesis). Eindhoven University of Technology.

Crisp, C. B., Mortensen, M., & Wilson, J. (2013). Extending Construal-Level Theory to Distributed Groups: Understanding the Effects of Virtuality. *Organization Science, 24*(2), 629–644. doi:10.1287/orsc.1120.0750

Curran, J. M., & Lennon, R. (2013). Comparing younger and older social network users: An examination of attitudes and intentions. *The Journal of American Academy of Business, Cambridge, 19*(1), 28–37.

Curry, P. (2000). Log on for Recruits. *Industry Week, 249*(17), 46.

Cyert, R. M., & March, J. G. (1963). *A Behavioral Theory of the Firm.* Englewood Cliffs, NJ: Prentice-Hall.

Cyert, R. M., & March, J. G. (1992). *Behavioral Theory of the Firm.* Blackwell Publishing.

Cyr, D., Hassanein, K., Head, M., & Ivanov, A. (2007). The role of social presence in establishing loyalty in e-Service environments. *Interacting with Computers, 19*(1), 43–56. doi:10.1016/j.intcom.2006.07.010

Czaja, S. J., Fisk, A. D., Hertzog, C., Rogers, W. A., Charness, N., Nair, S. N., & Sharit, J. (2006). Fac- tors Predicting the Use of Technology: Findings From the Center for Research and Education on Aging and Technology Enhancement (CREATE). *Psychology and Aging, 21*(2), 333–353. doi:10.1037/0882-7974.21.2.333 PMID:16768579

Czerny, A. (2004). Log on Turn off for women. *People Management, 10*(15), 10.

Daft, R., & Lengel, R. (1984). Information richness: A new approach to managerial behaviour and organizational design. *Research in Organizational Behavior, 6*, 191–233.

Dahlberg, T., Mallat, N., & Öörni, A. (2003). Trust enhanced technology acceptable model: Consumer acceptance of mobile payment solutions. In *Stockholm Mobility Roundtable* (pp. 22–23). Academic Press.

Dai, X., Ayoade, O., & Grundy, J. (2006). Off-line micro-payment protocol for multiple vendors in mobile commerce. *Proc. 7th Int. Conf. Parallel Distrib. Comput. Appl. Technol. (PDCAT)*, 197–202. doi:10.1109/PDCAT.2006.83

Dalkir, K. (2016). The Role of Stories and Simulations in the Lessons Learned Process. *International Journal of Organizational and Collective Intelligence, 6*(3), 21–32. doi:10.4018/IJOCI.2016070102

Dalkir, K. (2016). The Role of Technology and Social Media in Tacit Knowledge Sharing. *International Journal of E-Entrepreneurship and Innovation, 6*(2), 40–56. doi:10.4018/IJEEI.2016070103

Dalkir, K. (2017in press). Complexity in online collaboration: the role of shared vision, trust and leadership style. Chapter. In K. Ditte (Ed.), *Online collaboration and communication in contemporary organizations*. Hershey, PA: IGI Global.

Davenport, T. H., & Prusak, L. (1998). *Working Knowledge: How Organizations Manage What They Know*. Boston: Harvard Business School Press.

Davis, F. D. (1985). *A technology acceptance model for empirically testing new end-user information systems: Theory and results* (Doctoral dissertation).

Davis, J. G., Subrahmanian E. & Westerberg, W. (2005). The "global" and the "local" in knowledge management. *Journal of Knowledge Management, 1*(1), 101-112.

Davis, F. D. (1989). Perceived usefulness, perceived ease of use, and user acceptance of information tech- nology. *Management Information Systems Quarterly, 13*(3), 319–339. doi:10.2307/249008

Davis, F. D., Bagozzi, R. P., & Warshaw, P. R. (1989). User acceptance of computer technology: A comparison of two theoretical models. *Management Science, 35*(8), 982–1003. doi:10.1287/mnsc.35.8.982

Davis, F. D., Bagozzi, R. P., & Warshaw, P. R. (1992). Extrinsic and intrinsic motivation to use computers in the work-place. *Journal of Applied Social Psychology, 22*(14), 1111–1132. doi:10.1111/j.1559-1816.1992.tb00945.x

Davis, F. D., & Venkatesh, V. (1996). A critical assessment of potential measurement biases in the technology acceptance model: Three experiments. *International Journal of Human-Computer Studies, 45*(1), 19–45. doi:10.1006/ijhc.1996.0040

De Carolis, M., & Corvello, V. (2006). Multiple Competences in Distributed Communities of Practice: The Case of a Community of Financial Advisors. In *Proceedings of 7th European Conference of Knowledge Management (ECKM06)*. Public Academic Conferences Ltd.

de la Torre-Diez, I., López-Coronado, M., Vaca, C., Aguado, J. S., & de Castro, C. (2015). Cost-utility and cost-effec-tiveness studies of telemedicine, electronic and mobile health systems in the literature: A systematic review. *Telemedicine Journal and e-Health, 21*(2), 81–85. doi:10.1089/tmj.2014.0053 PMID:25474190

De Long, D. W., & Fahey, L. (2000). Diagnosing cultural barriers to knowledge management. *The Academy of Manage-ment Executive, 14*(4), 113–127.

de Vries, L., Gensler, S., & Leeflang, P. S. H. (2012). Popularity of brand posts on brand fan pages: An investigation of the effects of social media. *Journal of Interactive Marketing, 26*(2), 83–91. doi:10.1016/j.intmar.2012.01.003

De Vries, N., & Carlson, J. (2014). Examining the drivers and brand performance implications of customer engagement with brands in the social media environment. *Journal of Brand Management, 21*(6), 495–515. doi:10.1057/bm.2014.18

Dearborn, J. (2012), The Unexpected Value of Teaching Entrepreneurship. *Huffington Post*. Retrieved on January 12, 2015, from http://www.huffingtonpost.com/john-dearborn/entrepreneurship b_1881096.html

Dede, C. (1996). Emerging technologies and distributed learning. *American Journal of Distance Education, 10*(2), 4–36. doi:10.1080/08923649609526919

Deephouse, D. L., & Carter, S. M. (2005). An examination of differences between organizational legitimacy and orga-nizational reputation. *Journal of Management Studies, 42*(2), 329–360. doi:10.1111/j.1467-6486.2005.00499.x

Deglise, C., Suggs, L. S., & Odermatt, P. (2012). SMS for disease control in developing countries: A systematic review of mobile health applications. *Journal of Telemedicine and Telecare, 18*(5), 273–281. doi:10.1258/jtt.2012.110810 PMID:22826375

Delmar, F., & Holmquist, C. (2004). *Promoting entrepreneurship and innovative smes in a global economy: Towards a more responsible and inclusive globalization.* Istanbul, Turkey: Organisation for Economic Co-operation and Development.

Deng, Z., Mo, X., & Liu, S. (2014). Comparison of the middle-aged and older users adoption of mobile health services in China. *International Journal of Medical Informatics, 83*(3), 210–224. doi:10.1016/j.ijmedinf.2013.12.002 PMID:24388129

DeSoto, H. (1990). *The Other Path.* New York: Harper & Row.

Devaraj, S., Fan, M., & Kohli, R. (2002). Antecedents of B2C channel satisfaction and preference: Validating e-commerce metrics. *Information Systems Research, 13*(3), 316–333. doi:10.1287/isre.13.3.316.77

Dew, N., Read, S., Sarasvathy, S. D., & Wiltbank, R. (2008). Outlines of a behavioral theory of the entrepreneurial firm. *Journal of Economic Behavior & Organization, 66*(1), 37–59. doi:10.1016/j.jebo.2006.10.008

DiMaggio, P. J. (1995). Comments on "What Theory is Not". *Administrative Science Quarterly, 40*(3), 391–397. doi:10.2307/2393790

Dimensional Research. (2015). *Collaboration trends and technology. A survey of knowledge workers.* Retrieved June 5, 2017 from: https://www.alfresco.com/sites/www.alfresco.com/files/dimesional-research-collab-survey-findings-report-082415.pdf

Directorate General of Health Services (DGHS). (2014). *Health information system & e-Health.* Retrieved from http://www.dghs.gov.bd/index.php/en/ehealth/our-ehealth-eservices/84-englishroot/ehealth-eservice/97-telimedicine-services-in-comunity-clinics

Djankov, S., La Porta, R., Lopez-de-Silanes, F., & Shleifer, A. (2002). The regulation of entry. *The Quarterly Journal of Economics, 117*(1), 1–37. doi:10.1162/003355302753399436

Dodgson, M., Gann, D. M., & Phillips, N. (2013). Organizational Learning and the Technology of Foolishness: The Case of Virtual Worlds at IBM. *Organization Science, 24*(5), 1358–1376. doi:10.1287/orsc.1120.0807

Doganova, L., & Eyquem-Renault, M. (2009). What do business models do? Innovation devices in technology entrepreneurship. *Research Policy, 38*(10), 1559–1570. doi:10.1016/j.respol.2009.08.002

Doherty, R. (2010). Getting social with recruitment. *Strategic HR Review, 9*(6).

Domínguez-Mayo, F. J., Escalona, M. J., Mejías, M., Aragón, G., García-García, J. A., Torres, J., & Enríquez, J. G. (2015). A Strategic Study about Quality Characteristics in e-Health Systems Based on a Systematic Literature Review. *The Scientific World Journal, 2015*, 1–11. doi:10.1155/2015/863591 PMID:26146656

Domizi, D. P. (2013). Microblogging To Foster Connections And Community in a Weekly Graduate Seminar Course. *TechTrends, 57*(1), 43–51. doi:10.1007/s11528-012-0630-0

Dorfman, P. W., & Howell, J. P. (1988). Dimensions of national culture and effective leadership patterns: Hofstede revisited. *Advances in International Comparative Management, 3*, 127–150.

Duan, Y., Xu, X., & Fu, Z. (2006). Understanding Transnational Knowledge Transfer. In *Proceedings of 7th European Conference of Knowledge Management (ECKM06).* Public Academic Conferences Ltd.

Duch, B. J. (2001). Models for Problem-Based Instruction in Undergraduate Courses. Academic Press.

Dulac, T., Coyle-Shapiro, J. A.-M., Henderson, D. J., & Wayne, S. J. (2008). Not all Responses to Breach are the Same: The Interconnection of Social Exchange and Psychological Contract Processes in Enterpriseations. *Academy of Management Journal, 51*(6), 1079–1098. doi:10.5465/AMJ.2008.35732596

Dutton, J. E., & Dürkerich, J. M. (1991). Keeping an Eye in the Mirror: Image and Identity in Organizational Adaption. *Academy of Management Journal, 34*(3), 517–554. doi:10.2307/256405

Easterby-Smith, M., Thorpe, R., & Jackson, P. R. (2008). *Management Research* (3rd ed.). Sage.

Eastin, M. S. (2002). Diffusion of e-commerce: An analysis of the adoption of four emerging activities. *Telematics and Informatics, 19*(3), 251–267. doi:10.1016/S0736-5853(01)00005-3

Economist. (2009). Generation Y goes to work. *Economist, 390*(8612), 47-48.

Eduardo, M. (2006). E-Entrepreneurship. *Munich Personal RePEc Archive*. Retrieved April 24, 2011, from http://mpra.ub-muenchen.de/2237/

Eisenhardt, K. M. (1989). Making Fast Strategic Decisions In High-Velocity Environments. *Academy of Management Journal, 32*(3), 543–576. doi:10.2307/256434

Eisenhardt, K. M., & Graebner, M. E. (2007). Theory building from cases: Opportunities and challenges. *Academy of Management Journal, 50*(1), 25–32. doi:10.5465/AMJ.2007.24160888

eLearning Industry (eLI). (2015). *5 Steps To Use LinkedIn For Social Learning – eLearning Industry*. Retrieved June 18, 2017, from http://elearningindustry.com/5-steps-use-linkedin-for-social-learning

Elliott, A.-M. (2011). *10 Fascinating YouTube Facts that May Surprise You*. Retrieved April 24, 2011, from http://mashable.com/2011/02/19/youtube-facts/

Elron, E., & Vigoda-Gadot, E. (2006). Influence and Political Processes in Cyberspace: The Case of Global Distributed Teams. *International Journal of Cross Cultural Management, 6*(3), 295–317. doi:10.1177/1470595806070636

Erden, Z., Von Krogh, G., & Nonaka, I. (2008). The quality of group tacit knowledge. *The Journal of Strategic Information Systems, 17*(1), 4–18. doi:10.1016/j.jsis.2008.02.002

Ertl, H. (2006). Educational standards and the changing discourse on education: The reception and consequences of the PISA study in Germany. *Oxford Review of Education, 32*(5), 619–634. doi:10.1080/03054980600976320

EU SME. (2016). *E-Commerce in China*. Available online at https://www.eas.ee/wp-content/uploads/2017/06/Rafael-Jimenez_-e-commerce- seminar_Tallinn.pdf

European Commission. (1999). *Action Plan to Promote Entrepreneurship and Competitiveness*. Brussels: Directorate-General for Enterprise.

European Commission. (2010). [*A strategy for smart, sustainable and inclusive growth*. Brussels: EC.]. *Europe*, 2020.

European Council. (2000). *Presidency Conclusions of the Lisbon European Council*. SN 100/00, 23-24 March. EC.

Evans, M. M., Wensley, A. K. P., & Frissen, I. (2015). The mediating effects of trustworthiness on social-cognitive factors and knowledge sharing in a large professional service firm. *Electronic Journal of Knowledge Management, 13*(3), 240–254.

Evans, W. D., Abroms, L. C., Poropatich, R., Nielsen, P. E., & Wallace, J. L. (2012). Mobile health evaluation methods: The Text4baby case study. *Journal of Health Communication, 17*(1), 22–29. doi:10.1080/10810730.2011.649157 PMID:22548595

Everett, C. (2010). *Social media still feared by graduate recruiters*. Retrieved April 20, 2011, from http://www.hrzone.co.uk/topic/recruitment/social-media-still-feared-graduate- recruiters/105572

Expert Choice, Inc. (2000). Retrieved from http://www.expertchoice.com

Eze, J. F. (2011). *Entrepreneurship education for self-reliance and implications for the Millennium Development Goals*. Paper presented at the sixth international conference on development studies at Benue State University, Makurdi, Nigeria.

Facebook. (2010a). Retrieved April 20, 2011, from http://www.facebook.com/press/ info.php

Facebook. (2010b). *Statistics*. Retrieved March 3, 2011, from http://www.facebook.com/homephp#!/press/info.php?statistics

Facebook. (2010c). *Twitter App for Facebook*. Retrieved April 25, 2011, from http://www.facebook.com/apps/application.php?id=2231777543

Facebook. (2010d). *University of Glamorgan Facebook Enterprise*. Retrieved December 1, 2010, from http://www.facebook.com/?ref=home#!/uniglamlife

Facebook. (2010e). *Situations Recruitment*. Retrieved April 26, 2011, from http://www.facebook.com/situationsgnsy?ref=ts

Facebook. (2011a). *Zinzi Coetzee*. Retrieved April 25, 2011, from http://www.facebook.com/zinzi.coetzee?ref=ts#!/zinzi.coetzee

Facebook. (2011b). *Facebook KPMG Recruitment Page*. Retrieved April 25, 2011, from http://www.facebook.com/profile.php?id=100001464093443&ref=ts#!/pages/KPMG/108372102518243

Facebook. (2011c). *Facebook KPMG Graduate Page*. Retrieved April 25, 2011, from http://www.facebook.com/kpmg.graduates?ref=ts

Facebook. (2011d). *Facebook Crowd Media Page*. Retrieved April 27, 2011, from http://www.facebook.com/wearecrowd?sk=info

Facebook. (2011e). *Facebook KPMG Channel Islands Allumni page*. Retrieved April 25, 2011, from http://www.facebook.com/kpmg.graduates?ref=ts#!/pages/KPMG-Channel-Islands-Limited-Alumni/47271650921

Fama, E. F., Fisher, L., Jensen, M. C., & Roll, R. (1969). The adjustment of stock prices to new information. *International Economic Review*, *10*(1), 1–21. doi:10.2307/2525569

Fang, T. (2006). From "Onion" to "Ocean", Paradox and Change in National Cultures. *International Studies of Management & Organization*, *35*(4), 71–90.

Fang, T. (2003). A Critique of Hofstede's Fifth National Culture Dimension. *International Journal of Cross Cultural Management*, *3*(3), 347–368. doi:10.1177/1470595803003003006

Fan, W.-S., & Tsai, M.-C. (2010). Factors driving website success: The key role of internet customization and the influence of website design quality and internet marketing strategy. *Total Quality Management & Business Excellence*, *21*(11), 1141–1159. doi:10.1080/14783363.2010.529335

Faraj, S., Lakani, K., Monteiro, E., & von Krogh, G. (2016). Online Community as space for knowledge flows. *Information Systems Research*, *27*(4), 668–684. doi:10.1287/isre.2016.0682

Farber, H. S. (1999). Alternative and part-time employment arrangements as a response to job loss. *Journal of Labor Economics*, *17*(4), 1–12.

Farny, S., Hannibal, M., Frederiksen, S., & Jones, S. (2016). A CULTure of Entrepreneurship Education. *Entrepreneurship and Regional Development*, *28*(7-8), 514–535. doi:10.1080/08985626.2016.1221228

Featherman, M. S., & Pavlou, P. A. (2003). Predicting e-services adoption: A perceived risk facets perspective. *International Journal of Human-Computer Studies*, *59*(4), 451–474. doi:10.1016/S1071-5819(03)00111-3

Felder, R. M., & Brent, R. (2004). The intellectual development of science and students. Pt. 1: Models and challenges; Pt. 2: Teaching to promote growth. *Journal of Education, 93*(4), 269–277.

Feller, I. (2005). *A historical perspective on government-university partnerships to enhance entrepreneurship and economic development. In Economic development through entrepreneurship: Government, university and business linkages* (pp. 6–28). Cheltenham, UK: Edward Elgar.

Fernandes, N. (2017). *Recruitment in Infosys falls to a Record Low since its Inception 33 Years Ago.* Dazeinfo.

Field, J. (2004). *Social capital.* London, UK: Routledge.

File, T., & Ryan, C. (2014). *Computer and Internet Use in the United States: 2013. American Community Survey Reports.* U.S. Department of Commerce. Retrieved from https://www.census.gov/history/ pdf/2013computeruse.pdf

Fiol, C. M., & O'Connor, E. J. (2005). Identification In Face-to-Face, Hybrid, And Pure Virtual Teams: Untangling The Contradictions. *Organization Science, 16*(1), 19–32. doi:10.1287/orsc.1040.0101

Fishbein, M., & Ajzen, I. (1975). *Belief, attitude, intention, and behavior: An introduction to theory and research.* Reading, MA: Addison-Wesley Pub. Co.

Flake, G. W., Pennock, D. M., & Fain, D. C. (2003, July). *The self-organized web: the Yin to the semantic web's Yang. IEEE Intelligent Systems,* 72–86.

Flavián, C., & Guinalíu, M. (2006). Consumer trust, perceived security and privacy policy. *Industrial Management & Data Systems, 106*(5), 601–620. doi:10.1108/02635570610666403

Flick, U. (2009). *An introduction to qualitative research.* Sage Pubns Ltd.

Forman, E., Saaty, T., Selly, M., & Waldron, R. (1983). *Expert Choice.* McLean, VA: Decision Support Software, Inc.

Fornell, C., & Larcker, D. F. (1981). Evaluating structural equation models with unobservable variables and measurement error. *JMR, Journal of Marketing Research, 18*(1), 39–50. doi:10.2307/3151312

Forouhandeh, B., Nejatian, H., & Ramanathan, K. (2011). The online shopping adoption: Barriers and advantages. In *2nd International Conference on Business and Economic Research (2nd ICBER 2011) Proceeding* (pp. 2149–2171). Academic Press. Retrieved on June 2015 from http://www.internationalconference.com.my/proceeding/icber2011_proceeding/390-2nd ICBER 2011 PG 2149-2171 Online Shopping Adption.pdf

Forrester Research, Inc. (2011). *Listening and engaging in the digital marketing age.* Retrieved August 31, 2013 from: http://i.dell.com/sites/content/corporate/secure/en/Documents/listening-and-engaging-in-the-digital-marketing-age.pdf

Fouladgar, M., Yazdani-Chamzini, A., Lashgari, A., Zavadskas, E., & Turskis, Z. (2012). Maintenance strategy selection using AHP and COPRAS under fuzzy environment. *International Journal of Strategic Property, 16*(1), 85–104. doi:10.3846/1648715X.2012.666657

Fournier, S., & Lee, L. (2009, April). Getting brand communities right. Harvard Business Review, 1-10.

Fournier, S., & Avery, J. (2011). The uninvited brand. *Business Horizons, 54*(3), 193–207. doi:10.1016/j.bushor.2011.01.001

Fox, S. (2011). *The social life of health information 2011.* Washington, DC: Pew Internet & American Life Project.

Frederick, D., Mohler, J., Vorvoreanu, M., & Clotzbach, R. (2015). The Effects of parallax scrolling on User Experience on Web Design. *Journal of Usability Studies, 10*(2), 87–95.

Free, C., Phillips, G., Watson, L., Galli, L., Felix, L., Edwards, P., & Haines, A. (2013). The effectiveness of mobile-health technologies to improve health care service delivery processes: A systematic review and meta-analysis. *PLoS Medicine*, *10*(1), e1001363. doi:10.1371/journal.pmed.1001363 PMID:23458994

Frohlich, T. C., Hess, A. E. M., & Calio, V. (2014). Counterfeit Products May Cost the Global Economy Up to $250 billion a Year. *USA Today*. Available online at https://www.usatoday.com/story/money/business/2014/03/29/24-7-wall-st-counterfeited-products/7023233/

Frolick, M. N., & Chen, L.-D. (2004). Assessing M-Commerce Opportunities. *Information Systems Management*, *21*(2), 53–61. doi:10.1201/1078/44118.21.2.20040301/80422.8

Froyd, J., & Simpson, N. (2010). *Student-Centered Learning Addressing Faculty Questions about Student centered Learning*. Texas A&M University. Retrieved Aug 28, 2016 from http://ccliconference.org/files/2010/03/Froyd_Stu-CenteredLearning.pdf

Fry, A. (2014). Helping the public see the value of social research using social media. *International Journal of Market Research*, *56*(4), 421–423. doi:10.2501/IJMR-2014-030

Gabrielli, V., & Balboni, B. (2010). SME practice towards integrated marketing communications. *Marketing Intelligence & Planning*, *28*(3), 275–290. doi:10.1108/02634501011041426

Gagnon, M. P., Ngangue, P., Payne-Gagnon, J., & Desmartis, M. (2015). m-Health Adoption by Healthcare Professionals: A Systematic Review. *Journal of the American Medical Informatics Association.* PMID:26078410

Galperina, L. (2016). Regional Diversity and Smart Growth of the European Union. *Evropejskij Issledovatel*, *113*(12), 584–591.

Ganev & Venilin. (2007). Preying on the state: The transformation of Bulgaria after 1989. London, UK: Cornell University Press.

Gans, J. S., & Stern, S. (2003). The product market and the market for "ideas": Commercialization strategies for technology entrepreneurs. *Research Policy*, *32*(2), 333–350. doi:10.1016/S0048-7333(02)00103-8

Garcia-Perez, A., & Ayres, R. (2010). Wikifailure: The limitations of technology for knowledge sharing. *Electronic Journal of Knowledge Management*, *8*(1), 43–52.

Gates, A. Q., Romero, R., Alonso, M., Klett, F., Fernando, N., & Requena, D. (2011). Cultivating Entrepreneurial Thinking through IEEE-CS Student Chapters. *IEEE Computer Magazine*, *44*(4), 48–55. doi:10.1109/MC.2011.69

Gefen, D., Karahanna, E., & Straub, D. W. (2003). Trust and TAM in online shopping: An integrated model. *Management Information Systems Quarterly*, *27*(1), 51–90. Retrieved from http://dl.acm.org/citation.cfm?id=2017181.2017185

Gefen, D., & Straub, D. W. (1997). Gender differences in the perception and use of e-mail: An extension to the technology acceptance model. *Management Information Systems Quarterly*, *21*(4), 389–400. doi:10.2307/249720

Gefen, D., & Straub, D. W. (2003). Managing user trust in B2C e-services. *e-Service Journal*, *2*(2), 7–24. doi:10.2979/esj.2003.2.2.7

George, D., & Mallery, P. (2003). *SPSS for windows step by step: A simple guide and reference. 11.0 update* (4th ed.). Boston: Allyn & Bacon.

Ghosh, R. (2011). *Entropy-based Classification of 'Retweeting' Activity on Twitter.* Retrieved June 18, 2017, from https://arxic.org

Giddens, A. (1984). *The Constitution of Society*. Berkeley, CA: University of California Press.

Giddens, A. (1990). *The Consequences of Modernity*. Stanford, CA: Stanford University Press.

Gijselaers, W. H. (1996). Connecting problem-based practices with educational theory. In L. Wilkerson & W. H. Gijselaers (Eds.), *Bring problem-based learning to higher education: Theory and practice* (pp. 13–21). San Francisco: Jossey-Bass.

Gilbert, B. A., Audretsch, D. B., & McDougall, P. P. (2004). The emergence of entrepreneurship policy. *Small Business Economics*, *22*(3), 313–323. doi:10.1023/B:SBEJ.0000022235.10739.a8

Gittlen, S. (2008). Web 2.0: Just Say Yes. *New World (New Orleans, La.)*, *25*(9), 32–34.

Glaser, B. G. (1978). *Theoretic Sensitivity*. Mill Valley, CA: The Sociology Press.

Glaser, B. G. (1992). *Basics of Grounded Theory Analysis*. Mill Valley, CA: Sociology Press.

Glaser, B. G., & Strauss, A. (1967). *The Discovery of Grounded Theory*. Chicago: Aldine.

Glaser, B. G., & Strauss, A. L. (1967). *The discovery of grounded theory, Strategies for qualitative research*. New York: Aldine.

Glaser, B. G., & Strauss, A. L. (1967). *The discovery of grounded theory: strategies for qualitative research*. New York, NY: Aldine Publishing Company.

Glister, P. (1997). A new digital literacy: A conversation with Paul Glister. *Educational Leadership*, *55*(3), 6–11.

Godin, S. (2002). *The big red fez: How to make any web site better*. Simon & Schuster.

Goel, S. (2013). *MTech (Information Technology and Entrepreneurship)*. Available: https://goelsan.wordpress.com/2013/11/30/aninterdisciplinary-mtech-in-information-technology-and entrepreneurship/%20-%20comments

Goffman, E. (1959). *The presentation of self in everyday life*. London: Penguin Books Ltd.

Goh, S. C. (2002). Managing effective knowledge transfer: An integrative framework and some practice implications. *Journal of Knowledge Management*, *6*(6), 23–30. doi:10.1108/13673270210417664

Gold, A. H., Malhotra, A., & Segars, A. H. (2001). Knowledge Management: An Organizational Capabilities Perspective. *Journal of Management Information Systems*, *18*(1), 185–214. doi:10.1080/07421222.2001.11045669

Goldberg, C. B., & Allen, D. G. (2008). Black and white and read all over: Race differences in reactions to recruitment web sites. *Human Resource Management*, *47*(2), 217–236. doi:10.1002/hrm.20209

Gomez-Herrera, E., Martens, B., & Turlea, G. (2014). The drivers and impediments for cross-border e-commerce in the EU. *Information Economics and Policy*, *28*, 83–96. doi:10.1016/j.infoecopol.2014.05.002

Goodall, K., & Roberts, J. (2003). Repairing Managerial Knowledge-Ability Over Distance. *Organization Studies*, *24*(7), 1153–1175. doi:10.1177/01708406030247007

Goodstein, L. D. (1981). American Business Values and Cultural Imperialism. *Organizational Dynamics*, *10*(1), 49–54. doi:10.1016/0090-2616(81)90011-5

Gordon, P., Rogers, A., & Comfort, M. (2001). A taste of problem-based learning increases achievement of urban minority middle-school students. *Educational Horizons*, *79*(4), 171–175.

Gordon, R. (2006). *The Purpose of Playing*. The University of Michigan Press. doi:10.3998/mpub.93221

Grabner-Kräuter, S., & Kaluscha, E. A. (2003). Empirical research in on-line trust: A review and critical assessment. *International Journal of Human-Computer Studies*, *58*(6), 783–812. doi:10.1016/S1071-5819(03)00043-0

Granovetter, M. (1973). The strength of weak ties. *American Journal of Sociology*, *78*(6), 1360–1380. doi:10.1086/225469

Greene, P. G., Hart, M., Gatewood, E., Brush, C., & Carter, N. (2003). *Women Entrepreneurs: Moving Front and Center: An Overview of Research and Theory* (white paper).

Gregg, D. G., & Walczak, S. (2010). The relationship between website quality, trust and price premiums at online auctions. *Electronic Commerce Research*, *10*(1), 1–25. doi:10.1007/s10660-010-9044-2

Grewal, D., Lindsey-Mullikin, J., & Munger, J. (2004). Loyalty in e-Tailing. *Journal of Relationship Marketing*, *2*(3-4), 31–49. doi:10.1300/J366v02n03_03

Griffith, T. L., Sawyer, J. E., & Neale, M. A. (2003). Virtualness and knowledge in teams: Managing the love triangle of organizations, individuals, and information technology. *Management Information Systems Quarterly*, *27*(2), 265–287.

Guadagnoli, E., & Velicer, W. F. (1988). Relation to sample size to the stability of component patterns. *Psychological Bulletin*, *103*(2), 265–275. doi:10.1037/0033-2909.103.2.265 PMID:3363047

Guba, E. G., & Lincoln, Y. S. (1994). Competing paradigms in qualitative research. In N. K. Denzin & Y. S. Lincoln (Eds.), *Handbook of Qualitative Research*. Sage.

Guedria, W. (2014). A Conceptual Framework for Enterprise Interoperability. *International Journal of E-Business Research*, *10*(3), 54–64. doi:10.4018/ijebr.2014070104

Guo, X., Sun, Y., Wang, N., Peng, Z., & Yan, Z. (2013). The dark side of elderly acceptance of preventive mobile health services in China. *Electronic Markets*, *23*(1), 49–61. doi:10.1007/s12525-012-0112-4

Guo, X., Zhang, X., & Sun, Y. (2016). The privacy–personalization paradox in mHealth services acceptance of different age groups. *Electronic Commerce Research and Applications*, *16*, 55–65. doi:10.1016/j.elerap.2015.11.001

Gurteen, D. (1999). Creating a Knowledge Sharing Culture. *Knowledge Management Magazine*, *2*(5). Available on-line at http://www.gurteen.com/gurteen/gurteen.nsf/0/FD35AF9606901C42802567C70068CBF5/

Habibi, M. R., Laroche, M., & Richard, M. (2014). The roles of brand community and community engagement in building brand trust on social media. *Computers in Human Behavior*, *37*, 152–161. doi:10.1016/j.chb.2014.04.016

Hair, J. F., Ringle, C. M., & Sarstedt, M. (2011). PLS-SEM: Indeed a silver bullet. *Journal of Marketing Theory and Practice*, *19*(2), 139–152. doi:10.2753/MTP1069-6679190202

Hajirnis, A. (2015). Social media networking: Parent guidance required. *The Brown University Child and Adolescent Behavior Letter*, *31*(12), 1–7. doi:10.1002/cbl.30086

Hajli, N., Shanmugam, M., Papagiannidis, S., Zahay, D., & Richard, M. (2016). Branding co- creation with members of online communities. *Journal of Business Research*, *70*, 136–144. doi:10.1016/j.jbusres.2016.08.026

Hall, S. (2004, February). See Website Recruitment through for best results. *Personnel Today*, 21.

Hambrick, D., Davison, S., Snell, S., & Snow, C. (1998). When groups consist of multiple nationalities: Toward a new understanding of implications. *Organization Studies*, *12*(2), 181–205. doi:10.1177/017084069801900202

Hammer, A., & Linton, K. (2011). *China: Effects of Intellectual Property Infringement and Indigenous Innovation Policies on the U.S. Economy*. U.S. International Trade Commission. Investigation No. 332-519. Retrieved from http://www.usitc.gov/research and_analysis/commission_publication_4226.htm

Hampton, K. N., Goulet, L. S., Rainie, L., & Purcell, K. (2010). *Social networking sites and our lives*. Washington, DC: Pew Research Centre.

Handy, C. (2000). *Trust and the Distributed Organization* (HBR OnPoint Enhanced Edition). HBR On Point.

Handzic, M., & Lagumdzija, A. (2006). Motivational Influences On Knowledge Sharing. In *Proceedings of 7th European Conference of Knowledge Management (ECKM06)*. Public Academic Conferences Ltd.

Hansen, S., & Avital, M. (2005). Share and share alike: The social and technological influences on knowledge sharing behavior. *Sprouts: Working Papers on Information Environments, Systems and Organizations, 5*(1), 1-19.

Harfst, K. L. (2010). *The Evolution and Implications of Entrepreneurship Curriculum at Universities*. Southern Illinois University Carbondale. Retrieved June 10, 2011 from http://opensiuc.lib.siu.edu/cgi/viewcontent.cgi?article=1020&context=ojwed&sei-redir=1#search=%22Entrepreneurship%20University%20Curricula%22

Harker, P., & Vargas, L. (1987). The theory of ratio scale estimation: Saaty's analytic hierarchy process. *Management Science, 33*(11), 1383–1403. doi:10.1287/mnsc.33.11.1383

Harorimana, D. (2006). Knowledge Networks: A Mechanism of Creation and Transfer of Knowledge in Organizations? In *Proceedings of 7th European Conference of Knowledge Management (ECKM06)*. Public Academic Conferences Ltd.

Harrington, J. (1991). *Organizational structure and information technology*. Hertfordshire, UK: Prentice Hall International.

Harris, P. R., & Morgan, R. T. (1991). *Managing Cultural Differences* (3rd ed.). Houston, TX: Gulf Publishing Company.

Ha, S., & Stoel, L. (2009). Consumer e-shopping acceptance: Antecedents in a technology acceptance model. *Journal of Business Research, 62*(5), 565–571. doi:10.1016/j.jbusres.2008.06.016

Hasanain, R. A., Vallmuur, K., & Clark, M. (2015). Electronic Medical Record Systems in Saudi Arabia: Knowledge and Preferences of Healthcare Professionals. *Journal of Health Informatics in Developing Countries, 9*(1).

Hatch, J. A. (2002). *Doing qualitative research in education settings*. New York: State University of New York Press.

Hatch, M. J. (1993). The Dynamics of Organizational Culture. *Academy of Management Review, 18*(4), 657–693.

Hatch, M. J., & Schultz, M. (1997). Relations between organizational culture, identity and image. *European Journal of Marketing, 31*(5/6), 356–365. doi:10.1108/eb060636

Hébert, R. F., & Link, A. N. (1989). In search of the meaning of entrepreneurship. *Small Business Economics, 1*(1), 39–49. doi:10.1007/BF00389915

Heller-Baird, C., & Parasnis, G. (2011). *From Social Media to Social CRM: What customers want*. IBM Institute for Business Value Study. Retrieved April 26, 2011, from http://www-935.ibm.com/services/us/gbs/thoughtleadership/ibv-social-crm-whitepaper.html? cntxt=a1005261

Henderson, A., & Bowley, R. (2010). Authentic dialogue? The role of "friendship" in a social media recruitment campaign. *Journal of Communication Management, 14*(3), 237–257. doi:10.1108/13632541011064517

Hennig-Thurau, T., Malthouse, E., Friege, C., Gensler, S., Lobschat, L., Rangaswamy, A., & Skiera, B. (2010). The impact of new media on customer relationships. *Journal of Service Research, 13*(3), 311–330. doi:10.1177/1094670510375460

Herring, S. (1996). *Computer-mediated communication: Linguistic, social and cross-cultural perspectives*. Amsterdam: Benjamins. doi:10.1075/pbns.39

Herring, S. C. (2001). *Gender and Power in Online Communication*. Bloomington, IN: Center for Social Informatics, Indiana University.

Hills, G. E. (1986). Entrepreneurship behavioural intentions and student independence, characteristics and experience. In *Frontiers of Entrepreneurship Research, Sixth Annual Babson College Entrepreneurship Research Conference*. Babson College.

Hilpern, K. (2001). Reading between the Lines. *Guardian Newspaper*. Retrieved October 10, 2008, from: http://www.guardian.co.uk/money/2001/jul/16/careers.jobsadvice5

Hinchcliffe, D. (2007). The state of Enterprise 2.0. *ZDNet*. Retrieved from http://www.zdnet.com/blog/hinchcliffe/the-state-of-enterprise-2-0/143

Hislop, D. (2002). Mission impossible? Communicating and sharing knowledge via information technology. *Journal of Information Technology*, *17*(3), 165–177. doi:10.1080/02683960210161230

Hisrich, R. D. (1990). Entrepreneurship/intrapreneurship. *The American Psychologist*, *45*(2), 209–222. doi:10.1037/0003-066X.45.2.209

Hoffman, D., Novak, T., & Chatterjee, P. (1995). Commercial scenarios for the web: opportunities and challenges. *Journal of Computer-Mediated Communication*, *5*(1).

Hoffman, D. L., & Fodor, M. (2010). Can you measure the ROI of your social media marketing? *MIT Sloan Management Review*, *52*(1), 41–49.

Hoffman, D. L., Novak, T. P., & Peralta, M. (1999). Building consumer trust online. *Communications of the ACM*, *42*(4), 80–85. doi:10.1145/299157.299175

Hofstede, G. (2016). *Geert Hofstede National culture*. Retrieved from https://geert-hofstede.com/national-culture.html

Hofstede, G. (1985). The interaction between national and organizational value system. *Journal of Management Studies*, *22*(4), 347–357. doi:10.1111/j.1467-6486.1985.tb00001.x

Hofstede, G. (1994). *Cultures and Organizations, Intercultural co-operation and its importance for survival, Software of the mind*. McGraw-Hill.

Hofstede, G. (1995). Multilevel research of human systems: Flowers, Bouquets and Gardens. *Human Systems Management*, *14*, 207–217.

Hofstede, G. (2001). *Culture's consequences: Comparing values, behaviors, institutions, and organizations*. Thousand Oaks, CA: Sage Publications.

Hofstede, G., & McCrae, R. R. (2004). Personality and Culture Revisited: Linking Traits and Dimensions of Culture. *Cross-Cultural Research*, *38*(1), 52–85. doi:10.1177/1069397103259443

Hofstede, G., Neuijen, B., Ohayv, D., & Sanders, G. (1990). Measuring Organizational Cultures, A Qualitative Study Across Twenty Cases. *Administrative Science Quarterly*, *35*(2), 286–316. doi:10.2307/2393392

Holden, N. (2001). Knowledge management: Raising the specter of the cross-cultural dimension. *Knowledge and Process Management*, *8*(3), 155–163. doi:10.1002/kpm.117

Holden, R. J., & Karsh, B. T. (2010). The technology acceptance model: Its past and its future in health care. *Journal of Biomedical Informatics*, *43*(1), 159–172. doi:10.1016/j.jbi.2009.07.002 PMID:19615467

Holsapple, C. W., Joshi, K. D. (2002). Knowledge Management: A Threefold Framework. *The Information Society*, *18*, 47-64.

Holste, J. S., & Fields, D. (2010). Trust and tacit knowledge sharing and use. *Journal of Knowledge Management, 14*(1), 128–140. doi:10.1108/13673271011015615

Holtz, B., & Lauckner, C. (2012). Diabetes management via mobile phones: A systematic review. *Telemedicine Journal and e-Health, 18*(3), 175–184. doi:10.1089/tmj.2011.0119 PMID:22356525

Holtz-Eakin, D., & Kao, C. (2003). *Entrepreneurship and Economic Growth: the Proof is in the Productivity (February 1, 2003).* Syracuse University Center for Policy Research Working Paper No. 50. Available at SSRN: https://ssrn.com/abstract=1809885

Hoque, M. R., Karim, M. R., & Amin, M. B. (2015). Factors Affecting the Adoption of mHealth Services among Young Citizen: A Structural Equation Modeling (SEM) Approach. *Asian Business Review, 5*(2), 60–65. doi:10.18034/abr.v5i2.416

Hoque, M. R., & Sorwar, G. (2015). Factors Influencing mHealth Acceptance among Elderly People in Bangladesh. *Australasian Conference on Information Systems.*

Hosseini, S., Ezazi, M., Heshmati, M., Moghadam, S., & Moghadam, H. (2013). Top companies ranking based on financial ratio with AHP-TOPSIS combined approach and indices of Tehran stock exchange. *International Journal of Economics and Finance, 5*(3), 126–133. doi:10.5539/ijef.v5n3p126

Hsu, C., Chen, Y., Yang, T., & Lin, W. (2017). Do website features matter in an online gamification context? Focusing on the mediating roles of user experience and attitude. *Telematics and Informatics, 34*(4), 196–205. doi:10.1016/j.tele.2017.01.009

Huang, E. Y., Lin, S. W., & Fan, Y. C. (2015). MS-QUAL: Mobile service quality measurement. *Electronic Commerce Research and Applications, 14*(2), 126–142. doi:10.1016/j.elerap.2015.01.003

Huba, M. E., & Freed, J. E. (2000). *Learner-Centered Assessment on College Campuses: Shifting the Focus from Teaching to Learning.* Needham Heights, MA: Allyn & Bacon.

Hubert, M., Blut, M., Brock, C., Backhaus, C., & Eberhardt, T. (2017). Acceptance of Smartphone-Based Mobile Shopping: Mobile Benefits, Customer Characteristics, Perceived Risks, and the Impact of Application Context. *Psychology and Marketing, 34*(2), 175–194. doi:10.1002/mar.20982

Huili, Y. A. O., & Zhong, C. (2011). The analysis of influencing factors and promotion strategy for the use of mobile banking. *Canadian Social Science, 7*(2), 60–63.

Hunt, J. W. (1981). Applying American Behavioral Science: Some Cross-Cultural Problems. *Organizational Dynamics, 10*(1), 55–62. doi:10.1016/0090-2616(81)90012-7

Hu, P. J., Chau, P. Y. K., Sheng, O. R. L., & Tam, K. Y. (1999). Examining the Technology Acceptance Model using physician acceptance of telemedicine technology. *Journal of Management Information Systems, 16*(2), 91–112. doi:10.1080/07421222.1999.11518247

Hutchings, K., & Michailova, S. (2004). Facilitating knowledge sharing in Russian and Chinese subsidiaries: The role of personal networks and group membership. *Journal of Knowledge Management, 8*(2), 84–94. doi:10.1108/13673270410529136

Huysman, M., & Wulf, V. (2006). IT to support knowledge sharing in communities, towards a social capital analysis. *Journal of Information Technology, 21*(1), 40–51. doi:10.1057/palgrave.jit.2000053

Hynes, B. (1996). Entrepreneurship education and training # introducing entrepreneurship into non business disciplines. *Journal of European Industrial Training, 20*(8), 10–17. doi:10.1108/03090599610128836

Ibarra, H. (1999). Provisional Selves: Experimenting with Image and Identity in Professional Adaptation. *Administrative Science Quarterly*, *44*(4), 764–791. doi:10.2307/2667055

IBM Smart Business. (2010). *Dispelling the vapor around cloud computing*. Thought Leadership White Paper. Retrieved from ftp://public.dhe.ibm.com/common/ssi/ecm/en/ciw03062usen/CIW03062USEN.PDF

Idrish, S., Rifat, A., Iqbal, M., & Nisha, N. (2017). Mobile health technology evaluation: Innovativeness and efficacy vs. cost effectiveness. *International Journal of Technology and Human Interaction*, *13*(2), 1–21. doi:10.4018/IJTHI.2017040101

Igbaria, M., Guimaraes, T., & Davis, G. B. (1995). Testing the determinants of microcomputer usage via a structural equation model. *Journal of Management Information Systems*, *11*(4), 87–114. doi:10.1080/07421222.1995.11518061

Indvick, L. (2011). *Marc Jacobs Intern Calls CEO a "Tyrant" in Twitter Meltdown*. Retrieved March 30, 2011, from http://mashable.com/2011/03/28/marc-jacobs-twitter- intern-meltdown/

Ingham, I. (2010). Social media at work: Breaking down barriers to communication. *Personnel Today*. Retrieved April 21, 2010, from http://www.personneltoday.com/articles/2010/03/18/54886/social-media-at-work-breaking-down-barriers-to- communication.html

Ingleton, C., Kiley, M., Cannon, R., & Rogers, T. (2000). *Leap into Student-Centered Learning*. University of Adelaide ACUE. Retrieved Aug 02, 2011 from http://www.adelaide.edu.au/clpd/resources/leap/leapinto/ProblemBasedLearning.pdf

Inter World Stats. (2011). *Number of Internet users worldwide*. Retrieved January 19, 2011, from http://www.internet-worldstats.com/stats.htm

International Trade Center. (2016). *E-Commerce in China: Opportunity for Asian Firms*. Available online at http://www.intracen.org/uploadedFiles/intracenorg/Content/Publications/E- COMMERCE%20IN%20CHINA%20Low-res.pdf

International, S. R. I. (1999). *International practices and experiences in business start-up procedures*. Arlington, VA: SRI.

Ionescu, R. (2016). European Union of the Regional Disparities. *Acta Universitatis Danubius: Oeconomica*, *12*(6), 168–178.

Ito, M., Davidson, C., Jenkins, H., Lee, C., Eisenberg, M., & Weiss, J. (2008). Youth online authorship. In D. Buckingham (Ed.), *Youth, identity, and digital media. The John D. and Catherine T. MacArthur Foundation Series on Digital Media and Learning (pp. vii-ix)*. Cambridge, MA: The MIT Press.

Jabri, M. M. (2005). Commentaries and Critical Articles: Text–context Relationships and Their Implications for Cross Cultural Management. *International Journal of Cross Cultural Management*, *5*(3), 349–360. doi:10.1177/1470595805058415

Jackson, J. D., Mun, Y. Y., & Park, J. S. (2013). An empirical test of three mediation models for the relationship between personal innovativeness and user acceptance of technology. *Information & Management*, *50*(4), 154–161. doi:10.1016/j.im.2013.02.006

Jaffe, A. B., & Trajtenberg, M. (2002). *Patents, citations, and innovations: A window on the knoweledge economy*. MIT Press.

James, D. C., Harville, C., Whitehead, N., Stellefson, M., Dodani, S., & Sears, C. (2015). Willingness of African American women to participate in e-Health/m-Health research. *Telemedicine Journal and e-Health*. PMID:26313323

Jaruwachirathanakul, B., & Fink, D. (2005). Internet banking adoption strategies for a developing country: The case of Thailand. *Internet Research*, *15*(3), 295–311. doi:10.1108/10662240510602708

Jett, Q. R., Metiu, A., O'Leary, M. B., & Wilson, J. M. (2008). Perceived Proximity in Virtual Work: Explaining the Paradox of Far-but-Close. *Organization Studies*, *29*(7), 979–1002. doi:10.1177/0170840607083105

Jimison, H. B., & Sher, P. P. (2008). Consumer health informatics: Health information technology for consumers. *Journal of the American Society for Information Science*, *46*(10), 783–790. doi:10.1002/(SICI)1097-4571(199512)46:10<783::AID-ASI11>3.0.CO;2-L

Johannison, B. (1991). University training for entrepreneurship: Swedish approaches. *Entrepreneurship and Regional Development*, *3*(1), 67–82. doi:10.1080/08985629100000005

Johnson, G., Scholes, K., & Whittington, R. (2008). *Exploring Corporate Strategy* (8th ed.). Pearson Education.

Jome, L. M., Donahue, M. P., & Siegel, L. A. (2006). Working in the uncharted technology frontier: Char- acteristics of women web entrepreneurs. *Journal of Business and Psychology*, *21*(1), 127–147. doi:10.1007/s10869-005-9019-9

Jones, G., & Wadhwani, R. D. (2006). *Entrepreneurship and Business History: Renewing the Research Agenda* (working paper, No 07-007). Harvard Business School.

Joshi, P., & Upadhyay, H. (2014, January). e-Retailing in India: Despite issues, customers satisfied with top retailers. *Consumer Voice*, 35–40. Retrieved on May 2015 from http://consumeraffairs.nic.in/consumer/writereaddata/e-Retailingindia.pdf

Jung, M. (2008). *From health to e-Health: Understanding citizens' acceptance of online health care* (Doctoral thesis). Luleå University of Technology. Retrieved from http://epubl.ltu.se/1402-1544/2008/68/LTU-DT-0868-SE.pdf

Kahn, J. G., Yang, J. S., & Kahn, J. S. (2010). Mobile health needs and opportunities in developing countries. *Health Affairs*, *29*(2), 252–258. doi:10.1377/hlthaff.2009.0965 PMID:20348069

Kaiser, H. F., & Rice, J. (1974). Little Jiffy, Mark IV. *Educational and Psychological Measurement*, *34*(1), 111–117. doi:10.1177/001316447403400115

Kamoche, K., Kannan, S., & Siebers, L. Q. (2014). Knowledge-Sharing, Control, Compliance and Symbolic Violence. *Organization Studies*, *35*(7), 989–1012. doi:10.1177/0170840614525325

Kaplan, A. M., & Haenlein, M. (2010). Users of the world unite! The challenges and opportunities of social media. *Business Horizons*, *53*(1), 61. doi:10.1016/j.bushor.2009.09.003

Karahanna, E., Straub, D. W., & Chervany, N. L. (1999). Information technology adoption across time: A cross-sectional comparison of pre-adoption and post-adoption beliefs. *Management Information Systems Quarterly*, *23*(2), 183–213. doi:10.2307/249751

Kardash, C., & Wallace, M. (2001). The perceptions of science classes' survey: What undergraduate science reform efforts really need to address. *Journal of Educational Psychology*, *93*(1), 199–210. doi:10.1037/0022-0663.93.1.199

Katsikitis, M., Hay, P. J., Barrett, R. J., & Wade, T. (2002). Problem- Versus Case-based Approaches in Teaching Medical Students about Eating Disorders: A Controlled Comparison. *Ed. Psychology*, *222*(3), 277–283. doi:10.1080/01443410220138511

Kaufmann, D., & Kraay, A. (2002). *Governance Indicators, Aid Allocation, and the Millennium Challenge Account*. World Bank.

Kaufmann, D., Kraay, A., & Mastruzzi, M. (2008). *Governance matters VII: Aggregate and individual governace indicators 1996-2007*. Washington, DC: World Bank. doi:10.1596/1813-9450-4654

Kaynak, E., & Dana, L. P. (2013). *When economies change hands: A survey of entrepreneurship in the emerging markets of Europe from the Balkans to the Baltic States*. Routledge.

Keller, K. L. (1993). Conceptualizing, measuring, and managing customer-based brand equity. *Journal of Marketing*, *57*(1), 1–22. doi:10.2307/1252054

Keller, K. L. (2009). Building strong brands in a modern marketing communications environment. *Journal of Marketing Communications*, *15*(2), 139–155. doi:10.1080/13527260902757530

Kelley, D., Singer, S., & Herrington, M. (2016). *2015/16 global report.* Global Entrepreneurship Monitor. Retrieved from http://www.gemconsortium.org/

Kelley, D. J., Brush, C. G., Greene, P. G., & Litovsky, Y. (2013). *Global Entrepreneurship monitor: 2012 Women's Report.* Boston, MA: Global Entrepreneurship Monitor. Retrieved from www.gemconsortium.org

Keyes, J. (2012). *Enterprise 2.0: social networking tools to transform your organization.* Boca Raton, FL: CRC Press. doi:10.1201/b12532

Khalilzadeh, J., Ozturk, A. B., & Bilgihan, A. (2017). Security-related factors in extended UTAUT model for NFC based Mobile Payment in the Restaurant Industry. *Computers in Human Behavior*, *70*, 460–474. doi:10.1016/j.chb.2017.01.001

Khanduja, D., & Kaushik, P. (2009). Exploring education driven entrepreneurship in engineering graduates in India. *International Journal of Continuing Engineering Education and Life-Long Learning*, *19*(2/3), 256–270.

Kiesler, S., & Sproull, L. (1992). Group decision making and communication technology. *Organizational Behavior and Human Decision Processes*, *52*(1), 96–123. doi:10.1016/0749-5978(92)90047-B

Kietzmann, J. H., Hermkens, K., McCarthy, I. P., & Silvestre, B. S. (2011). Social media? Get serious! Understanding the functional building blocks of social media. *Business Horizons*, *54*(3), 241–251. doi:10.1016/j.bushor.2011.01.005

Kim, J. B. (2012). An empirical study on consumer first purchase intention in online shopping: Integrating initial trust and TAM. *Electronic Commerce Research*, *12*(2), 125–150. doi:10.1007/s10660-012-9089-5

Kim, J., & Forsythe, S. (2007). Hedonic usage of product virtualization technologies in online apparel shopping. *International Journal of Retail & Distribution Management*, *35*(6), 502–514. doi:10.1108/09590550710750368

Kim, J., & Forsythe, S. (2010). Factors affecting adoption of product virtualization technology for online consumer electronics shopping. *International Journal of Retail & Distribution Management*, *38*(3), 190–204. doi:10.1108/09590551011027122

Kim, J., & Yu, E. (2016). The holistic brand experience of branded mobile applications affects brand loyalty. *Social Behavior and Personality*, *44*(1), 77–87. doi:10.2224/sbp.2016.44.1.77

Kim, S., & Lee, H. (2006). The impact of organizational context and information technology on employee knowledge-sharing capabilities. *Public Administration Review*, *66*(3), 370–385. doi:10.1111/j.1540-6210.2006.00595.x

King, J. (2004, January). The web habit is HR's manna from heaven. *Personnel Today*, 2.

Kirby, D. (2007). Changing the entrepreneurship education paradigm. In *Handbook of Research in Entrepreneurship Education: A general perspective* (Vol. 1). Edward Elgar Publishing. doi:10.4337/9781847205377.00010

Kirby, D. A. (2004). Entrepreneurship education: Can business schools meet the challenge? *Education + Training*, *46*(8/9), 510–519. doi:10.1108/00400910410569632

Klopping, I. M., & Eark, M. (2004). Extending the Technology Acceptance Model and the task-technology fit model to consumer e-commerce. *Information Technology, Learning and Performance Journal*, *22*(1), 35–48.

Knights, D., Noble, F., Vurdubakis, T., & Willmott, H. (2001). Chasing Shadows: Control, Virtuality and the Production of Trust. *Organization Studies*, *22*(2), 311–336. doi:10.1177/0170840601222006

Koeppel, D. (2009). HR by Twitter. *Fortune Small Business*, *19*(7), 57.

Kogut, B. (1991). Country capabilities and the permeability of borders. *Strategic Management Journal*, *12*, 33-47.

Kolb, D. G. (2008). Exploring the Metaphor of Connectivity: Attributes, Dimensions and Duality. *Organization Studies*, *29*(1), 127–144. doi:10.1177/0170840607084574

Koufaris, M., & Hampton-Sosa, W. (2004). The development of initial trust in an online company by new customers. *Information & Management*, *41*(3), 377–397. doi:10.1016/j.im.2003.08.004

Kouyoumjian, V. (2010). The New Age of Cloud Computing and GIS, ArchWatch. *ESRI*. Retrieved from http://www.esri.com/news/arcwatch/0110/feature.html

Kowalczyk, R., Ulieru, M., & Unland, R. (2003). *Integrating mobile and intelligent agents in advanced e-commerce: A survey*. South Clayton, Australia: CSIRO Mathematical and Information Sciences. doi:10.1007/3-540-36559-1_22

Kracher, B., Corritore, C. L., & Wiedenbeck, S. (2005). A foundation for understanding online trust in electronic commerce. *Journal of Information. Communication and Ethics in Society*, *3*(3), 131–141. doi:10.1108/14779960580000267

Kraft, C. (2012). *User Experience Innovation, User Centered Design That Works*. New York: Apress Media.

Kritikos, A. S. (2014). *Entrepreneurs and their impact on jobs and economic growth*. IZA World of Labor. Retrieved http://wol.iza.org/articles/entrepreneurs-and-their-impact-on-jobs-and-economic-growth/long

Kroeger, A., & Kluckhohn, F. (1952). *Culture: A Critical Review of Concepts and Definitions*. Cambridge, MA: Harvard Business Review.

Krug, S. (2014). *Don't make me think, revisited: A common sense approach to web usability* (3rd ed.). New Riders.

Ktoridou, D., & Doukanai, E. (2016). Teaching with Team Projects in Higher Education. Santa Rosa, CA: Informing Science Press.

Ktoridou, D. (2010). *Applying an Inductive Method to a New, Multidisciplinary, Management of Innovation & Technology Course: Evidence from the University of Nicosia. In EDUCON* (pp. 452–460). Madrid, Spain: IEEE.

Kuek, T., & Lai, M. (2006). An exploratory study on online banking in Malaysia. *The Journal of Business*, *6*(2), 65–84.

Kumar, S., Nilsen, W., Pavel, M., & Srivastava, M. (2013). Mobile health: Revolutionizing healthcare through transdisciplinary research. *Computer*, *1*(1), 28–35. doi:10.1109/MC.2012.392

Kungpisdan, S., Srinivasan, B., & Le, P. D. (2003). *Lightweight Mobile Credit-Card Payment Protocol. In LNCS 2904* (pp. 295–308). INDOCRYPT.

Kvale, S. (1996). *Interviews: an introduction to qualitative research interviewing*. Thousand Oaks, CA: Sage.

Kwai Fun, I. P. R., & Wagner, C. (2007). Weblogging: A study of social computing and its impact on organizations. ScienceDirect – Decision Support Systems, Elsevier B. V.

Lai, L. S. L., & Turban, E. (2008). Groups Formation and Operations in the Web 2.0 Environment and Social Networks. *Group Decision and Negotiation*, *17*(5), 387–402. doi:10.1007/s10726-008-9113-2

Lakhani, K. R., & von Hippel, E. (2003). How open source software works: "Free" user-to-user assistance. *Research Policy*, *32*(6), 923–943. doi:10.1016/S0048-7333(02)00095-1

Lakoff, G., & Johnson, M. (1980). *Metaphors we live by*. Chicago, IL: University of Chicago Press.

Lallmahamood, M. (2007). An examination of individual's perceived security and privacy of the Internet in Malaysia and the influence of this on their intention to use e-Commerce: Using an extension of the Technology Acceptance Model. *Journal of Internet Banking and Commerce*, *12*(3), 1–26.

Lamoreaux, N. R. (2010). Entrepreneurship in the United States, 1865-1920. In *D.S. Landes, J. Mokyr, & W. J. Baumol (Eds.), The invention of enterprise: Entrepreneurship from ancient Mesopotamia to modern times* (pp. 367–399). Princeton, NJ: Princeton University Press. doi:10.1515/9781400833580-017

Lauby, S. (2010). *Should you Search Social Media Sites for Job Candidate Information?* Retrieved September 6, 2010 from http://mashable.com/2010/09/05/social-media-job-recruiting/

Lau, H. C. W., Lee, C. K. M., Ho, G. T. S., Ip, W. H., Chan, F. T. S., & Ip, R. W. L. (2006). M-commerce to support the implementation of a responsive supply chain network. *Supply Chain Management, 11*(2), 169–178. doi:10.1108/13598540610652564

Lau, M. M., Cheung, R., Lam, A. Y. C., & Chu, Y. T. (2013). Measuring service quality in the banking industry: A Hong Kong based study. *Contemporary Management Research, 9*(3), 263–282. doi:10.7903/cmr.11060

Lave, J., & Wenger, E. (1991). *Situated learning: Legitimate peripheral participation.* Cambridge, UK: Cambridge University Press. doi:10.1017/CBO9780511815355

Law, C. T. (1994). *Provisional Regulation of the People's Republic of China on Value-Added Tax.* Promulgated by Decree No.134 of the State Council of the People's Republic of China on December 13, 1993, and effective on January 1, 1994. Beijing: People's Republic of China. Retrieved from http://english.ccpit.org/contents/channel_101/2006/0525/847/content_847.htm

Lederer, A. L., Maupin, D. J., Sena, M. P., & Zhuang, Y. (2000). The technology acceptance model and the World Wide Web. *Decision Support Systems, 29*(3), 269–282. doi:10.1016/S0167-9236(00)00076-2

Lee Endres, M., Endres, S. P., Chowdhury, S. K., & Alam, I. (2007). Tacit knowledge sharing, self-efficacy theory, and application to the Open Source community. *Journal of Knowledge Management, 11*(3), 92–103. doi:10.1108/13673270710752135

Lee, C. S., Watson-Manheim, M., & Ramaprasad, A. (2009). Communication portfolios usage in the distributed work environments. *First Monday, 14*(8). doi:10.5210/fm.v14i8.2595

Lee, H., Fiore, A. M., & Kim, J. (2006). The role of the technology acceptance model in explaining effects of image interactivity technology on consumer responses. *International Journal of Retail & Distribution Management, 34*(8), 621–644. doi:10.1108/09590550610675949

Lee, H.-H., & Chang, E. (2011). Consumer attitudes toward online mass customization: An application of extended technology acceptance model. *Journal of Computer-Mediated Communication, 16*(2), 171–200. doi:10.1111/j.1083-6101.2010.01530.x

Lee, I. (2005). Evaluation of Fortune 100 companies' career web sites. *Human Systems Management, 24*(2), 175–182.

Lee, I. (2011). Overview of emrging web 2.0-based business models and web 2.0 applications in business: An ecological perspective. *International Journal of E-Business Research, 7*(4), 1–16. doi:10.4018/jebr.2011100101

Lee, J., & Rho, M. J. (2013). Perception of influencing factors on acceptance of mobile health monitoring service: A comparison between users and non-users. *Healthcare Informatics Research, 19*(3), 167–176. doi:10.4258/hir.2013.19.3.167 PMID:24175115

Lee, K. C., & Chung, N. (2009). Understanding factors affecting trust in and satisfaction with mobile banking in Korea: A modified DeLone and McLean's model perspective. *Interacting with Computers, 21*(5), 385–392. doi:10.1016/j.intcom.2009.06.004

Lee, K. O. M., & Turban, E. (2001). A trust model for consumer internet shopping. *International Journal of Electronic Commerce, 6*(1), 75–91. doi:10.1080/10864415.2001.11044227

Lee, M.-C. (2009). Predicting and explaining the adoption of online trading: An empirical study in Taiwan. *Decision Support Systems*, *47*(2), 133–142. doi:10.1016/j.dss.2009.02.003

V. S. Lee (Ed.). (2004). *Teaching and Learning through Inquiry*. Stylus Publishing.

Legris, P., Ingham, J., & Collerette, P. (2003). Why do people use information technology? A critical review of the technology acceptance model. *Information & Management*, *40*(3), 191–204. doi:10.1016/S0378-7206(01)00143-4

Lenway, S. A., & Murtha, T. P. (1994). The state as strategist in international business research. *Journal of International Business Studies*, *25*(3), 513–536. doi:10.1057/palgrave.jibs.8490210

Leonardi, P., Neeley, T., Hall, M., & Gerber, E. (2011). How managers use multiple media: Discrepant events, power, and timing in redundant communication. *Organization Science*, *23*(1), 98–117. doi:10.1287/orsc.1110.0638

Lesinska, M. (2014). The European backlash against immigration and multiculturalism. *Journal of Sociology (Melbourne, Vic.)*, *50*(1), 37–50. doi:10.1177/1440783314522189

Leung, K., Bhagat, R. S., Buchan, N. R., Erez, M., & Gibson, C. B. (2005). Culture and International Business: Recent Advances and Their Implications for Future Research. *Journal of International Business Studies*, *36*(4), 357–378. doi:10.1057/palgrave.jibs.8400150

Levina, N., & Orlikowski, W. J. (2009). Understanding Shifting Power Relations within and across Organizations: A Critical Genre Analysis. *Academy of Management Journal*, *52*(4), 672–703. doi:10.5465/AMJ.2009.43669902

Lewis, A., Daunton, L., Thomas, B., & Sanders, G. (2010). A Critical Exploration into whether E-Recruitment is an Effective E-Entrepreneurship Method in Attracting Appropriate Employees for Enterprises. *International Journal of E-Entrepreneurship and Innovation*, *1*(2), 30–44. doi:10.4018/jeei.2010040103

Lewis, A., Thomas, B., & Sanders, G. (2013). Pushing the Right Buttons? A Critical Exploration into the Effects of Social Media as an Innovative E-Entrepreneurship Method of Recruitment for Enterprises. *International Journal of E-Entrepreneurship and Innovation*, *4*(3), 16–37. doi:10.4018/ijeei.2013070102

Lewis, D. (1987). *Mind Skills: Giving Your Child a Brighter Future*. London: Souvenir Press.

Lewis, K., Kaufman, J., Gonzalez, M., Wimmer, A., & Christakis, N. (2008). Tastes, ties, and time: A new social network dataset using Facebook.com. *Social Networks*, *30*(4), 330–342. doi:10.1016/j.socnet.2008.07.002

Li, C. (2009). *The world's most valuable brands. Who's most engaged? ENGAGEMENTdb: Ranking the top 100 global brands*. Retrieved February 9, 2014 from: http://www.altimetergroup.com/2009/07/engagementdb.html

Liaw, S.-S., & Huang, H.-M. (2003). An investigation of user attitudes toward search engines as an information retrieval tool. *Computers in Human Behavior*, *19*(6), 751–765. doi:10.1016/S0747-5632(03)00009-8

Liberatore, M., & Miller, T. (1998). A framework for integrating activity-based costing and the balanced scorecard into the logistics strategy development and monitoring process. *Journal of Business Logistics*, *19*(2), 131–155.

Lim, W. M., & Ting, D. H. (2012). E-shopping: An analysis of the Technology Acceptance Model. *Modern Applied Science*, *6*(4), 49. doi:10.5539/mas.v6n4p49

Lin, H. (2011a). An empirical investigation of mobile banking adoption: The effect of innovation attributes and knowledge-based trust. *International Journal of Information Management*, *31*(3), 252–260. doi:10.1016/j.ijinfomgt.2010.07.006

Lin, H. (2011b). The effect of multi-channel service quality on mobile customer loyalty in an online-and-mobile retail context. *Service Industries Journal*, *32*(11), 1865–1882. doi:10.1080/02642069.2011.559541

LinkedIn. (2015a). *About Us – LinkedIn*. Retrieved June 18, 2017, from http://www.linkedin.com/about-us

LinkedIn. (2015b). *About Us – LinkedIn Newsroom*. Retrieved June 18, 2017, from http://press.linkedin.com/about-linkedin

Linstead, S., & Thanem, T. (2007). Multiplicity, Virtuality and Organization: The Contribution of Gilles Deleuze. *Organization Studies*, *28*(10), 1483–1501. doi:10.1177/0170840607075675

Lipnack, J., & Stamps, J. (1997). *Distributed Teams: Reaching across space, time and organizations with technology*. New York: Wiley.

Lipsman, A., Mudd, G., Rich, M., & Bruich, S. (2012). The power of "like": How brands reach (and influence) fans through social media. *Journal of Advertising Research*, *52*, 40–52. doi:10.2501/JAR-52-1-040-052

Lipson, H., & Kurman, M. (2013). *Fabricated: The new world of 3D printing*. John Wiley & Sons.

Littunen, H. (2000). Entrepreneurship and the characteristics of the entrepreneurial personality. *International Journal of Entrepreneurial Behaviour & Research*, *6*(6), 295–309. doi:10.1108/13552550010362741

Liu, S., Tucker, D., Koh, C. E., & Kappelman, L. (2003). Standard user interface in e-commerce sites. *Industrial Management & Data Systems*, *103*(8), 600–610. doi:10.1108/02635570310497648

Li, W., Wen, Q., Su, Q., & Jin, Z. (2012). An efficient and secure mobile payment protocol for restricted connectivity scenarios in vehicular ad hoc network. *Computer Communications*, *35*(2), 188–195. doi:10.1016/j.comcom.2011.09.003

Li, X., Rong, G., & Thatcher, J. B. (2009). Swift trust in web vendors: The role of appearance and functionality. *Journal of Organizational and End User Computing*, *21*(1), 88–108. doi:10.4018/joeuc.2009092205

Lofland, J., & Lofland, L. H. (1995). *Analytic Social Settings, A guide of qualitative observation and analysis*. Wadsworth Publishing Company.

Lohman, M. (2001). Cultivating Problem-Solving Skills through Problem-Based Approaches to Professional Development. *Human Resource Development Quarterly*, *13*(3), 243–261. doi:10.1002/hrdq.1029

Long, D. (2009, January 15). Monster invests $130m in face of falling vacancies. *New Media Age*, 4.

Louis, M. R. (1980). Surprise and Sense Making: What Newcomers Experience in Entering Unfamiliar Organizational Settings. *Administrative Science Quarterly*, *25*(2), 226–251. doi:10.2307/2392453 PMID:10247029

Lubis, R.L. (2014). Students' Entrepreneurial Strategy: Connecting Minds? *International Journal of Arts & Sciences*, *7*(3), 545–568.

Luhmann, N. (1982). Trust and power. *Studies in Soviet Thought*, *23*(3), 266–270. Retrieved from http://philpapers.org/rec/LUHTAP-2

Lumpkin, G. T., & Dess, G. G. (1996). Clarifying the entrepreneurial orientation construct and linking it to performance. *Academy of Management Review*, *21*(1), 135–172. doi:10.2307/258632

Lundblad, N. (2017). *Privacy in a Noisy Society*. Retrieved June 18, 2017, from http://www.citeserx.ist.psu.edu

Lundeberg, M., Levin, B., & Harrington, H. (1999). *Who learns what from cases and how? The research base for teaching and learning with cases*. Mahwah, NJ: Lawrence Erlbaum Associates.

Luo, X., Zhang, J., & Duan, W. (2013). Social media and firm equity value. *Information Systems Research*, *24*(1), 146–VI. doi:10.1287/isre.1120.0462

Luttrell, R. (2016). *Social media: How to engage, share, and connect*. Lanham, MD: Rowman & Littlefield.

Lyon, D. W., Lumpkin, G. T., & Dess, G. G. (2000). Enhancing Entrepreneurial Orientation Research: Operationalizing and Measuring a Key Strategic Decision Making Process. *Journal of Management*, *26*(5), 1055–1085. doi:10.1177/014920630002600503

Lyytinen, K., & Newman, M. (2008). Explaining information systems change: a punctuated socio-technical change model. *European Journal of Information Systems*, *17*, 589-613. Retrieved from www.palgrave-journals.com/ejis/

Maddison, R., Pfaeffli, L., Stewart, R., Kerr, A., Jiang, Y., Rawstorn, J., ... Whittaker, R. (2014). The HEART mobile phone trial: The partial mediating effects of self-efficacy on physical activity among cardiac patients. *Frontiers in Public Health*, *2*. PMID:24904918

Management, P. (2008). *Fatface appetite for e-recruitment*. Retrieved March 17, 2009, from http://www.peoplemanagement.co.uk/pm/articles/2008/ 01/fatfaceappetiteforerecruitment.htm

Mani, M. (2013). Motivation, Challenges and Success Factors of Entrepreneurs: An Empirical Analysis. *Pertanika Journal of Social Sciences & Humanities*, *21*(2), 679 – 688.

Mani, M. (2015). Entrepreneurship Education: A Students' Perspective. *International Journal of E-Entrepreneurship and Innovation*, *5*(1), 1-14.

Mannion, M. (2008). Consider differences in culture in Virgin territory. *People Management*, *14*(5), 15.

Mansour-Cole, D. (2001). Team Identity Formation in Distributed Teams. In S. Beyerlein, M. Beyerlein, & D. Johnson (Eds.), *Distributed Teams, Advances in interdisciplinary studies of work teams* (Vol. 8). Oxford, UK: Elsevier Science.

Manufacturers' Monthly. (2004, December). Internet job ads a turn off for industry. *Manufacturers' Monthly*, 16.

March, J. G. (1995). The Future, Disposable Organizations and the Rigidities of Imagination. *Organization*, *2*(3-4), 427–440. doi:10.1177/135050849523009

March, J. G. (2006). Rationality, foolishness, and adaptive intelligence. *Strategic Management Journal*, *27*(3), 201–214. doi:10.1002/smj.515

Masrek, M. N., Uzir, N. A., & Khairuddin, I. I. (2012). Trust in mobile banking adoption in Malaysia: A conceptual framework. *Journal of Mobile Technologies, Knowledge & Society*, 1-12.

Mathieson, K. (1991). Predicting user intentions: Comparing the technology acceptance model with the theory of planned behavior. *Information Systems Research*, *2*(3), 173–191. doi:10.1287/isre.2.3.173

Matlay, H., & Carey, C. (2007). Entrepreneurship education in the UK: A longitudinal perspective. *Journal of Small Business and Enterprise Development*, *14*(2), 252–263. doi:10.1108/14626000710746682

Mattis, M. C. (2004). Women entrepreneurs: Out from under the glass ceiling. *Women in Management Review*, *19*(3), 154–163. doi:10.1108/09649420410529861

Maykut, P., & Morehouse, R. (1994). *Beginning Qualitative Research, A Philosophic and Practical Guide*. London: The Falmer Press.

McAfee, A. P. (2006). Enterprise 2.0: The Dawn of Emergent Collaboration. *MIT Sloan Management Review*, *47*(3), 21–28.

McChesney, F. S. (1987). Rent extraction and rent creation in the economic theory of regulation. *The Journal of Legal Studies*, *16*(1), 101–118. doi:10.1086/467825

McCloskey, D. (2004). Evaluating electronic commerce acceptance with the technology acceptance model. *Journal of Computer Information Systems*, *44*(22), 49–57.

McKechnie, S., Winklhofer, H., & Ennew, C. (2013). Applying the technology acceptance model to the online retailing of financial services. *International Journal of Retail & Distribution Management, 34*(4), 388–410. doi:10.1108/09590550610660297

McKeown, C. (2003). Applied Management: Nurse Internet Recruitment. *Nursing Management – UK, 10*(4), 23-27.

McKeown, J., Millman, C., Sursani, S. R., Smith, K., & Martin, L. M. (2006). Graduate entrepreneurship education in the United Kingdom. *Education + Training, 48*(8/9), 597–613. doi:10.1108/00400910610710038

McKinney, V. R., & Whiteside, M. M. (2006). Maintaining Distributed Relationships. *Communications of the ACM, 49*(3), 82–86. doi:10.1145/1118178.1118180

McKinsey. (2015). *Diversity Matters*. Retrieved 1 June 2017, from http://www.mckinsey.com/business-functions/organization/our- insights/why-diversity-matters

McKnight, D. H., & Chervany, N. L. (2001). What trust means in e-commerce customer relationships: An interdisciplinary conceptual typology. *International Journal of Electronic Commerce, 6*(2), 35–59. doi:10.1080/10864415.2001.11044235

McSweeney, B. (2002). Model of National Cultural Differences and Their Consequences: A Triumph of Faith—A Failure of Analysis. *Human Relations, 55*(1), 89–118. doi:10.1177/0018726702551004

Melon, E., Levy, Y., & Dringus, L. P. (2016). study on the success of group formation and cohesiveness in virtual teams using computer-mediated communications. *Online Journal of Applied Knowledge Management, 4*(1), 61–81.

Menachem, D., Sujata, J., Padman, A., Bishnoi, K., & Upadhye, R. (2016). Online Brand Communities and Their Impact on Brand Equity of Indian Telecommunication Industry. *International Conference on Qualitative and Quantitative Economics Research. Global Science and Technology Forum*, 16–24.

Menezes, A., & Van Oorschot, P. S. (1997). *Handbook of Applied Cryptography*. CRC Press.

Menon, A., & Varadarajan, P. R. (1992). A model of Marketing Knowledge Use Within Firms. *Journal of Marketing, 56*(4), 53–71. doi:10.2307/1251986

Mergel, I. (2016). *The Social Intranet: Insights on Managing and Sharing Knowledge Internally*. IBM Center for the Business of Government Report. Retrieved June 1, 2017 from: http://www.businessofgovernment.org/report/social-intranet-insights-managing-and-sharing-knowledge-internally

Merriam, S. B. (1998). *Qualitative research and case study applications in education*. San Francisco: Jossey-Bass.

Merriam-Webster. (2016). *Dictionary and Thesaurus*. Retrieved June 18, 2017, from http://www.merriam-webster.com

Merton, R. K. (1968). *Social theory and social structure*. Free press.

Metaxiotis, K., Ergazakis, K., & Psarras, J. (2005). Exploring the world of knowledge management: Agreements and disagreements in the academic/practitioner community. *Journal of Knowledge Management, 9*(2), 6–18. doi:10.1108/13673270510590182

Miller Littlejohn Media (MLM). (2015). *7 Ways Students Should Use LinkedIn*. Retrieved June 18, 2017, from http://www.millerlittlejohnmedia.com

Miller, R. (2007). Enterprise 2.0 Definition and Solutions. *CIO*. Retrieved from http://www.cio.com/article/print/123550

Miller, D., & Garnsey, E. (2000). Entrepreneurs and technology diffusion: How diffusion research can benefit from a greater understanding of entrepreneurship. *Technology in Society, 22*(4), 445–465. doi:10.1016/S0160-791X(00)00021-X

Miller, H., & Arnold, J. (2000). Gender and home pages. *Computers & Education, 34*(3-4), 335–339. doi:10.1016/S0360-1315(99)00054-8

Minniti, M., & Arenius, P. (2003, April). *Women in Entrepreneurship.* Paper presented at the Entrepreneurial Advantage of Nations: First Annual Global Entrepreneurship Symposium, New York, NY.

Minton-Eversole, T. (2007a). E-Recruitment Comes of Age, Survey Says. *HRMagazine, 52*(8), 34.

Mitchel, L. (2011). *Overcoming the gender gap: women entrepreneurs as economic drivers.* Ewing Marion Kauffman Foundation.

Moody, M. (2010). Teaching Twitter and Beyond: Tip for Incorporating Social Media in Traditional Courses. *Journal of Magazine & New Media Research, 11*(2), 1–9.

Moon, J.-W., & Kim, Y.-G. (2001). Extending the TAM for a World-Wide-Web context. *Information & Management, 38*(4), 217–230. doi:10.1016/S0378-7206(00)00061-6

Moores, T. T. (2012). Towards an integrated model of IT acceptance in healthcare. *Decision Support Systems, 53*(3), 507–516. doi:10.1016/j.dss.2012.04.014

Moran, M., Seaman, J., & Tiniti-Kane, H. (2012). *How today's higher education faculty use social media.* Retrieved June 18, 2017, from http://pearsonlearningsolutions.com

Morgan, G. (2006). *Images of organization.* Sage.

Morning Consult. (n.d.). Frequency of Facebook use in the United States as of October 2017. *Statista - The Statistics Portal.* Retrieved October 22, 2017, from https://www.statista.com/statistics/199266/frequency-of-use-among-facebook-users-in the-united-states/

Morris, M. H., Miyasaki, N. N., Watters, C. E., & Coombes, S. M. (2006). The dilemma of growth: Un- derstanding venture size choices of women entrepreneurs. *Journal of Small Business Management, 44*(2), 221–244. doi:10.1111/j.1540-627X.2006.00165.x

Morrison, A. (2000). Entrepreneurship: What triggers it? *International Journal of Entrepreneurial Behaviour & Research, 6*(2), 59–7. doi:10.1108/13552550010335976

Mudde, C. (2007). *Populist Radical Right Parties in Europe.* Cambridge, UK: Cambridge University Press. doi:10.1017/CBO9780511492037

Muhammad, S., Furqan, Z., & Guha, R. K. (2006). Understanding the intruder through attacks on cryptographic protocols. *Proceedings of the 44th ACM Southeast Conference ACMSE,* 667–672. doi:10.1145/1185448.1185594

Muhammad, S., Furqan, Z., & Guha, R. K. (2007). A logic-based verification framework for authentication protocols. *Int. J. Internet Technology and Secured Transactions, 1*(1/2), 49–80. doi:10.1504/IJITST.2007.014834

Mulgan, G., Tucker, S., Rushanara, A., & Sanders, B. (2007). *Social Innovation, What it is, Why it Matters and How it can be Accelerated.* Skoll Centre for Social Entrepreneurship, Oxford Said Business School. Retrieved February 2, 2011, from http://www.youngfoundation.org/publications/reports/social-innovation-what-it-why-it-matters-how-it-can-be-accelerated-march-2007

Nalin, V. (2004). *Multi-Protocol Attacks: A Survey of Current Research.* Academic Press.

Nambisan, P. (2011). Information seeking and social support in online health communities: Impact on patients' perceived empathy. *Journal of the American Medical Informatics Association, 18*(3), 298–304. doi:10.1136/amiajnl-2010-000058 PMID:21486888

Nasution, H. N., Mavondo, F. T., Matanda, M. J., & Ndubisi, N. O. (2011). Entrepreneurship: Its relation- ship with market orientation and learning orientation and as antecedents to innovation and customer value. *Industrial Marketing Management, 40*(3), 336–345. doi:10.1016/j.indmarman.2010.08.002

Nelson, A.J., & Byers, T. (2010). *Challenges in University Technology Transfer and the Promising Role of Entrepreneurship Education.* Kauffman.

R. R. Nelson (Ed.). (1993). *National innovation systems: a comparative analysis.* Oxford University Press.

Nelson, R. R., Todd, P. A., & Wixom, B. H. (2005). Antecedents of information and system quality: An empirical examination within the context of data warehousing. *Journal of Management Information Systems, 21*(4), 199–235. doi: 10.1080/07421222.2005.11045823

Nevo, S., Nevo, D., & Kim, H. (2012). From recreational applications to workplace technologies: An empirical study of cross-context IS continuance in the case of virtual worlds. *Journal of Information Technology, 27*(1), 74–86. doi:10.1057/jit.2011.18

Newbert, S. L., Gopalakrishnan, S., & Kirchhoff, B. A. (2008). Looking beyond resources: Exploring the importance of entrepreneurship to firm-level competitive advantage in technologically intensive industries. *Technovation, 28*(1-2), 6–19. doi:10.1016/j.technovation.2007.07.002

Newble, D., & Cannon, R. (1995). *A handbook for teachers in universities and colleges: A guide to improving teaching methods* (3rd ed.). London: Kogan and Page.

Newman, M., & Landay, J. (2000). *Sitemaps, storyboards, and specifications: A sketch of website design practice.* ACM. doi:10.1145/347642.347758

Nieuwenhuizen, C., & Groenwald, D. (2004). *Entrepreneurship training and education needs as determined by the brain preference profiles of successful established entrepreners.* Paper presented at the Internationalizing Entrepreneurship education and Training Conference, Naples, Italy.

Nisha, N. (2016). Exploring the dimensions of mobile banking service quality: Implications for the banking sector. *International Journal of Business Analytics, 3*(3), 60–76. doi:10.4018/IJBAN.2016070104

Nisha, N., Iqbal, M., Rifat, A., & Idrish, S. (2015). Mobile health services: A new paradigm for health care systems. *International Journal of Asian Business and Information Management, 6*(1), 1–18. doi:10.4018/IJABIM.2015010101

Nisha, N., Iqbal, M., Rifat, A., & Idrish, S. (2016a). Exploring the role of service quality and knowledge for mobile health services. *International Journal of E-Business Research, 12*(2), 45–64. doi:10.4018/IJEBR.2016040104

Nisha, N., Iqbal, M., Rifat, A., & Idrish, S. (2016b). Mobile health services: A new paradigm for health care systems. In *E-Health and Telemedicine: Concepts, Methodologies, Tools, and Applications* (pp. 1551–1567). Hershey, PA: IGI Global. doi:10.4018/978-1-4666-8756-1.ch078

Nodia, G. (2017). The End of the Postnational Illusion. *Journal of Democracy, 28*(2), 5–19. doi:10.1353/jod.2017.0019

Nonaka, I. (1991). The knowledge-creating company. *Harvard Business Review, 69*(6), 96–104.

Nonaka, I. (2008). *The knowledge-creating company.* Boston, MA: Harvard Business Review Press.

Norasmah, O., Norashidah, H., & Hariyaty, A. W. (2012). Readiness towards entrepreneurship education. *Education + Training, 54*(8/9), 697–708. doi:10.1108/00400911211274837

Norman, G. R., & Schmidt, H. G. (1992). The psychological basis of problem-based learning: A review of the evidence. *Academic Medicine, 67*(9), 557–565. doi:10.1097/00001888-199209000-00002 PMID:1520409

Novak, T. P., Hoffman, D. L., & Yung, Y.-F. (2000). Measuring the customer experience in online environments: A structural modeling approach. *Marketing Science, 19*(1), 22–42. doi:10.1287/mksc.19.1.22.15184

Nunnally, J. C., & Bernstein, I. H. (1978). *Psychometric Theory* (3rd ed.). New York: McGraw Hill.

O'Cass, A., & Fenech, T. (2003). Web retailing adoption: Exploring the nature of internet users Web retailing behaviour. *Journal of Retailing and Consumer Services, 10*(2), 81–94. doi:10.1016/S0969-6989(02)00004-8

O'Dell, I., & Grayson, C. J. (1998). If only we knew what we know: Identification and transfer of internal best practices. *California Management Review, 40*(3), 154–174. doi:10.2307/41165948

O'Keefe, G. S. (2011). The Impact of Social Media on Children, Adolescents and Families. *Paediatrics, 127*(4), 801–805.

O'Leary-Kelly, S. W., & Vokurka, R. J. (1998). The empirical assessment of construct validity. *Journal of Operations Management, 16*(4), 387–405. doi:10.1016/S0272-6963(98)00020-5

O'Reilly, T. (2005). *What is Web 2.0.* Retrieved from http://oreilly.com/lpt/a/6228

O'Reilly, T. (2005). *What is web 2.0: design patterns and business models for the next generation of software.* Retrieved from http://www.oreillynet.com/lpt/a/6228

O'Reilly, K., & Lancendorfer, K. M. (2013). Consumers as "integrators" of marketing communications: When "like" is as good as "buy". *International Journal of E-Business Research, 9*(4), 1–15. doi:10.4018/ijebr.2013100101

O'Reilly, T. (2009). *What is web 2.0.* Sebastopol, CA: O'Reilly Media, Inc.

Obar, J. A., & Wildman, S. (2015). Social media definition and the governance challenge: An introduction to the special issue. *Telecommunications Policy, 39*(9), 745–750. doi:10.1016/j.telpol.2015.07.014

Ochman, B. L. (2009, April). It is no longer possible to resist social media. *Public Relations Tactics Magazine.*

Odell, P. M., Korgen, K. O., Schumacher, P., & Delucchi, M. (2000). Internet Use Among Female and Male College Students. *Cyberpsychology & Behavior, 3*(5), 855–862. doi:10.1089/10949310050191836

Olins, W. (2003). *On B®and.* London: Thames & Hudson Ltd.

Orlikowski, W. (1996). Improvising organizational transformation over time: A situated change perspective. *Information Systems Research, 7*(1), 63–92. doi:10.1287/isre.7.1.63

Orlikowski, W. (2002). Knowing in Practice: Enacting a Collective Capability in Distributed Organizing. *Organization Science, 13*(3), 249–273. doi:10.1287/orsc.13.3.249.2776

Orlikowski, W. J. (1992). The duality of technology: Rethinking the concept of technology in organizations. *Organization Science, 3*(3), 398–427. doi:10.1287/orsc.3.3.398

Orlikowski, W. J. (2000). Using technology and constituting structures: A practice lens for studying technology in organizations. *Organization Science, 11*(4), 404–428. doi:10.1287/orsc.11.4.404.14600

Orlikowski, W. J., & Robey, D. (1991). Information technology and the structuring of organizations. *Information Systems Research, 2*(2), 143–169. doi:10.1287/isre.2.2.143

Orlikowski, W., & Yates, J. (2002). It's About Time: Temporal Structuring in Organizations. *Organization Science, 13*(6), 684–700. doi:10.1287/orsc.13.6.684.501

Ornstein, R. (1977). *The Psychology of Consciousness.* New York: Harcourt Brace.

Ortega Egea, J. M., & Román González, M. V. (2011). Explaining physicians' acceptance of EHCR systems: An extension of TAM with trust and risk factors. *Computers in Human Behavior*, *27*(1), 319–332. doi:10.1016/j.chb.2010.08.010

Overby, E. (2008). Process Virtualization Theory and the Impact of Information Technology. *Organization Science*, *19*(2), 277–291. doi:10.1287/orsc.1070.0316

Owyang, J. (2009). *The future of the social web: In five eras*. Retrieved April 24, 2012 from: http://www.web-strategist.com/blog/2009/04/27/future-of-the-social-web/

Ozemir, V. E., & Hewett, K. (2010). The Effect of Collectivism on the Importance of Relationship Quality and Service Quality for Behavioural Intentions: A Cross-National and Cross-Contextual Analysis. *Journal of International Marketing*, *18*(1), 41–62. doi:10.1509/jimk.18.1.41

Paliszkiewicz, J., Svanadxe, S., & Jikia, M. (2017). The role of knowledge management processes on organizational culture. *Online Journal of Applied Knowledge Management*, *5*(2), 28–44.

Pallud, J., & Straub, D. (2014). Effective website design for experience-influenced environments: The case of high culture museums. *Information & Management*, *51*(3), 359–373. doi:10.1016/j.im.2014.02.010

Palmer, J. W., & Speier, C. (1997). *A Typology of Enterprise Social Systems: An Empirical Study*. Retrieved from http://hsb.baylor.edu/ramsower/ais.ac.97/papers/palm_spe.htm

Panahi, S., Watson, J., & Partridge, H. (2012). Social media and tacit knowledge sharing: Developing a conceptual model. *World Academy of Science, Engineering and Technology*, (64): 1095–1102.

Pantano, E., & Di Pietro, L. (2012). Understanding consumer's acceptance of technology-based innovations in retailing. *Journal of Technology Management & Innovation*, *7*(4), 1–19. doi:10.4067/S0718-27242012000400001

Parasuraman, A., Zeithaml, V. A., & Malhotra, A. (2005). E-S-QUAL: A multiple-item scale for assessing electronic service quality. *Journal of Service Research*, *7*(3), 213–233. doi:10.1177/1094670504271156

Park, H., Ribiere, V., & Schulte, W. D. Jr. (2004). Critical attributes of organizational culture that culture that promote knowledge management technology implementation success. *Journal of Knowledge Management*, *8*(3), 106–117. doi:10.1108/13673270410541079

Park, J. K., Yang, S. J., & Lehto, X. (2007). Adoption of mobile technologies for Chinese consumers. *Journal of Electronic Commerce Research*, *8*(3), 196–206.

Park, S., & Tussyadiah, I. P. (2016). Multidimensional facets of perceived risk in mobile travel booking. *Journal of Travel Research*.

Pascall, N. (2010). Women and ICT status report 2009: Women in ICT. Lisbon: European Commission Information Society and Media.

Pastore, M. (2000). *Young consumers shy away from e-commerce*. Retrieved on July 2015, from http://www.clickz.com/clickz/news/1708147/young-consumers-shy-away-e-commerce

Patil, V., & Shyamasundar, R. K. (2004). An efficient, secure and delegable micro-payment system. *Proc. IEEE Int. Conf. e-Technol. e-Commerce e-Service (EEE)*, 394–404.

Pavlik, J., & MacIntoch, S. (2015). *Converging Media* (4th ed.). New York, NY: Oxford University Press.

Pavlou, P. (2001). Integrating trust in electronic commerce with the technology acceptance model: Model development and validation. In *Americas Conference on Information Systems (AMCIS) Proceedings* (pp. 816–822). Academic Press. Retrieved on May 2015 from http://aisel.aisnet.org/cgi/viewcontent.cgi?article=1598&context=amcis2001

Pavlou, P. A. (2003). Consumer acceptance of electronic commerce: Integrating trust and risk with the Technology Acceptance Model. *International Journal of Electronic Commerce*, *7*(3), 101–134. doi:10.1080/10864415.2003.11044275

Peacock, L. (2009). *Social networking sites used to check out job applicants*. Retrieved December 4, 2009, from: http://www.personneltoday.com/articles/2009/03/17/ 49844/social-networking-sites-used-to-check-out-job-applicants.html

Perrin, A., & Duggan, M. (2015). *Americans' Internet Access: 2000-2015*. Pew Research Center. Retrieved from http://www.pewinternet.org/2015/06/26/americans-internet-access-2000-2015/

Personnel Today. (2004, April). Online Jobseekers more confident about equality. *Personnel Today*, 2.

Personnel Today. (2008, August). How I made a difference...? online recruitment burning career issues? closed-rank committee. *Personnel Today*, 8.

Peterson, J. (2016). All Roads Don't Lead to Brussels (But Most Do): European Integration and Transatlantic Relations. In The West and the Global Power Shift (pp. 101-125). Palgrave Macmillan UK.

Peterson, R. A. (1994). A meta-analysis of Cronbach's coefficient alpha. *The Journal of Consumer Research*, *21*(2), 381. doi:10.1086/209405

Petridou, E., & Glaveli, N. (2008). Rural women entrepreneurship within co-operatives: Training support. *Gender in Management*, *23*(4), 262–277. doi:10.1108/17542410810878077

Petridou, E., Sarri, A., & Kyrgidou, L. P. (2009). Entrepreneurship education in higher educational institutions: The gender dimension. *Gender in Management*, *24*(4), 286–309. doi:10.1108/17542410910961569

Pew Internet. (2011). Why Americans use social media. *Pew Research Center*. Retrieved October 25, 2017, from http://www.pewinternet.org/2011/11/15/why-americans-use-social-media/

Pew Research Centre (PRC). (2012) *The Demographics of Social Media Users – 2012*. Pew Research Centre: Internet, Science & Tech. Retrieved June 18, 2017, from http://printabletemplates.com/pew-report-social-networking-site-users

PewResearchCenter. (2015). *Demographics of Key Social Networking Platforms*. Retrieved from http://www.pewinternet.org/files/2015/01/PI_SocialMediaUpdate20144.pdf

Pfeffer, J., & Sutton, R. (2000). *The Knowing Doing Gap: How Smart Companies Turn Knowledge into Action*. Boston, MA: Harvard Business School Press.

Phichitchaisopa, N., & Naenna, T. (2013). Factors affecting the adoption of healthcare information technology. *EXCLI Journal*, *12*, 413–436. PMID:26417235

Pinder, J. (2001). *The European Union: A very short introduction* (Vol. 36). Oxford University Press.

Pitcher, G. (2008, March). Unfriendly job websites lose retailers top talent. *Personnel Today*, 3.

Pittaway, L., Hannon, P., Gibb, A., & Thompson, J. (2009). Assessment practice in enterprise education. *International Journal of Entrepreneurial Behaviour & Research*, *15*(1), 71–93. doi:10.1108/13552550910934468

Polanyi, M. (1966). *The tacit dimension*. Chicago, IL: University of Chicago press.

Popescu, A. (2016). The EU "costs" of the refugee crisis. *Europolity. Continuity and Change in European Governance*, *10*(1), 105–120.

Portal. (2016). *Portal Statics Report*. Available online at https://www.statista.com/statistics/293089/leading-e-retailers-ranked-by-annual-web-e-commerce-sales/

Porter, M. E., & Stern, S. (2004). Ranking National Innovative Capacity: Findings from the National Innovative Capacity Index. In *The global competitiveness report*. New York, NY: Oxford University Press.

Porter, C. E., & Donthu, N. (2008). Cultivating trust and harvesting value in virtual communities. *Management Science*, *54*(1), 113–128. doi:10.1287/mnsc.1070.0765

Porter, C. E., Donthu, N., MacElroy, W. H., & Wydra, D. (2011). How to foster and sustain engagement in virtual communities. *California Management Review*, *53*(4), 59–73. doi:10.1525/cmr.2011.53.4.80

Porter, M. (1998). *Competitive Advantage: Creating and Sustaining Superior Performance* (1st ed.). Free Press. doi:10.1007/978-1-349-14865-3

Porter, M. (2001). Strategy and the internet. *Harvard Business Review*, *89*(3), 63–78. PMID:11246925

Porter, M. E. (1990). The competitive advantage of nations. *Harvard Business Review*, *68*(4), 73–93.

Porter, M. E. (2000). *Attitudes, values, beliefs, and the microeconomics of prosperity. In Culture Matters* (pp. 14–28). New York: Basic Books.

Postman, N. (2017). *Informing ourselves to death*. Retrieved June 18, 2017, from http://w2.eff.org

Potts, M., & Puia, G. M. (2012). Entrepreneurship in the European Union: Unified is not uniform. *Regional development: Concepts, methodologies, tools, and applications*, 121-132.

Prandelli, E., Sawhney, M., & Verona, G. (2006). Innovation and Virtual Environments: Towards Virtual Knowledge Brokers. *Organization Studies*, *27*(6), 765–788. doi:10.1177/0170840606061073

Pricewaterhouse Coopers (PwC) PLC. (2014). *Evolution of e-commerce in India: Creating the bricks behind the clicks*. Retrieved on July 2015 from http://www.pwc.in/assets/pdfs/publications/2014/evolution-of-e-commerce-in-india.pdf

Prince, M., & Felder, R. (2007). Many faces of inductive teaching and learning. *Journal of College Science Teaching*. Retrieved June 20, 2011 From: http://www4.ncsu.edu/unity/lockers/users/f/felder/public/Papers/Inductive(JCST).pdf

Prince, M., & Felder, R. (2006). Inductive teaching and learning methods: Definitions, comparisons and research bases. *Journal of Education*, *95*(2), 123–138.

Pugh, K. (2011). *Sharing hidden know-how: How managers solve thorny problems with the knowledge jam*. New York, NY: John Wiley & Sons.

Puia, G. M., & Minnis, W. (2007). The Effects of Policy Frameworks and Culture on the Regulation of Entrepreneurial Entry. *The Journal of Applied Management and Entrepreneurship*, *12*(4), 36–50.

Puia, G. M., & Ofori-Dankwa, J. (2013). The effects of national culture and ethnolinguistic diversity on innovativeness. *Baltic Journal of Management*, *8*(3), 349–371. doi:10.1108/BJOM-Jan-2012-0002

Putzer, G. J., & Park, Y. (2012). Are physicians likely to adopt emerging mobile technologies? Attitudes and innovation factors affecting smartphone use in the Southeastern United States. American Health Information Management Association.

Quadrini, V. (1999). The importance of entrepreneurship for wealth concentration and mobility. *Review of Income and Wealth*, *45*(1), 1–19. doi:10.1111/j.1475-4991.1999.tb00309.x

Rae, D. M. (1997). Teaching entrepreneurship in Asia: Impact of a pedagogical innovation. *Entrepreneurship, Innovation, and Change*, *6*(3), 193–227.

Rae, D., & Woodier-Harris, N. (2012). International entrepreneurship education. *Education + Training*, *54*(8/9), 639–656. doi:10.1108/00400911211274800

Ramayah, T., Rouibah, K., Gopi, M., & Rangel, G. J. (2009). A decomposed theory of reasoned action to explain intention to use Internet stock trading among Malaysian investors. *Computers in Human Behavior*, *25*(6), 1222–1230. doi:10.1016/j.chb.2009.06.007

Rambe, P., & Mbeo, M. A. (2017). Technology-Enhanced Knowledge Management Framework for Retaining Research Knowledge among University Academics. *Technology*, *9*(1), 189–206.

Ramcharran, H. (2013). E-commerce growth and the changing structure of the retail sales industry. *International Journal of E-Business Research*, *9*(2), 46–60. doi:10.4018/jebr.2013040104

Ramsden, P. (2003). Learning to teaching higher Education (2nd ed.). London: Taylor and Francis.

Ranganathan, C., & Ganapathy, S. (2002). Key dimensions of business-to-consumer websites. *Information & Management*, *39*(6), 457–465. doi:10.1016/S0378-7206(01)00112-4

Rao, P. M. (2001). The ICT revolution, internationalization of technological activity, and the emerging economies: Implications for global marketing. *International Business Review*, *10*(5), 571–596. doi:10.1016/S0969-5931(01)00033-6

Rapp, A., Beitelspacher, L. S., Grewal, D., & Hughes, D. E. (2013). Understanding social media effects across seller, retailer, and consumer interactions. *Academy of Marketing Science Journal*, *41*(5), 547–566. doi:10.1007/s11747-013-0326-9

Rashidee, A. H. (2013). Emerging mobile health in Bangladesh. *The Daily Star*. Retrieved from http://archive.thedailystar.net/beta2/news/emerging-mobile-Health-in-bangladesh/

Rayna, T., & Striukova, L. (2014). The Impact of 3D Printing Technologies on Business Model Innovation. In P. J. Benghozi, D. Krob, A. Lonjon, & H. Panetto (Eds.), *Digital Enterprise Design & Management* (Vol. 261, pp. 119–132). Springer International Publishing. doi:10.1007/978-3-319-04313-5_11

Raynes-Goldie, K. (2010). Aliases, creeping, and wall cleaning: Understanding privacy in the age of Facebook. *First Monday*, *15*(2).

Read, S., Dew, N., Sarasvathy, S. D., Song, M., & Wiltbank, R. (2009). Marketing Under Uncertainty: The Logic of an Effectual Approach. *Journal of Marketing*, *73*(3), 1–18. doi:10.1509/jmkg.73.3.1

Redding, S. G. (1994). Comparative Management Theory: Jungle, Zoo or Fossil Bed? *Organization Studies*, *15*(3), 323–359. doi:10.1177/017084069401500302

Reichheld, F. F., & Schefter, P. (2000). E-Loyalty. *Harvard Business Review*, *78*(4), 105–113. Retrieved from http://academy.clevelandclinic.org/Portals/40/SamsonParticipants/E-Loyalty.pdf

Ren, Y., Pazzi, R. W. N., & Boukerche, A. (2010). Monitoring patients via a secure and mobile healthcare system. *Wireless Communications, IEEE*, *17*(1), 59–65. doi:10.1109/MWC.2010.5416351

Renzulli, L., Aldrich, H., & Moody, J. (2000). Family matters: Gender, networks and entrepreneurial out- comes. *Social Forces*, *79*(2), 523–546. doi:10.1093/sf/79.2.523

Report, S. M. (2012). *State of the media: The social media report 2012. Featured Insights, Global, Media and Entertainment*. Nielsen.

Reza, P. R. (2012). Bangladesh: Mobile health service for expecting and new mothers. *Global Voice*. Retrieved from http://globalvoicesonline.org/2012/12/26/bangladesh-mobile-Health-service-for-expecting-and-new-mothers/

Riege, A. (2005). Three-dozen knowledge-sharing barriers managers must consider. *Journal of Knowledge Management*, *9*(3), 18–35. doi:10.1108/13673270510602746

Riemer, K., & Klein, S. (2008). Is the V-form the next generation organization? An analysis of challenges, pitfalls and remedies of ICT-enabled virtual organisations based on social capital theory. *Journal of Information Technology, 23*(3), 147–162. doi:10.1057/palgrave.jit.2000120

Roberts, J. (2000). From know-how to show-how? Questioning the role of information and communication technologies in knowledge transfer. *Technology Analysis and Strategic Management, 12*(4), 429–443. doi:10.1080/713698499

Robey, D., & Orlikowski, W. (1991). *Information Technology and the Structuring of Organizations*. The Institute of Management Sciences.

Rodrigues, C. A., & Blumberg, H. (2000). Do Feminine Cultures Really Behave More Feminine than Masculine Cultures? A Comparison of 48 Countries' Femininity-Masculinity Ranking to Their Human Development Rankings. *Cross Cultural Management, 7*(3), 25–34. doi:10.1108/13527600010797110

Rogers, E. M. (1995). *Diffusion of Innovations* (3rd ed.). New York: Free Press. Retrieved on May 2015 from http://www.nehudlit.ru/books/detail8765.html

Romao & da Silva. (2001). Secure mobile agent digital signatures with proxy certificates. *LANI, 2033*, 206–220.

Rose, S., Spinks, N., & Canhoto, A. I. (2015). *Management Research: Applying the Principles: Case study research: Design and methods* (2nd ed.). Thousand Oaks, CA: Sage.

Rotter, J. B. (1966). Generalized expectations for internal versus external control of reinforcement. *Psychological Monographs, 80*(1), 1–27. doi:10.1037/h0092976 PMID:5340840

Ruggles, R. (1998). The state of notion: Knowledge management in practices. *California Management Review, 40*(3), 80–89. doi:10.2307/41165944

Rungtusanatham, M. J. (1998). Let's not overlook content validity. *Decision Line, 29*(4), 10–13.

Rushe, D. (2010). *Twitter 'in early talks with potential buyers Facebook and Google. Approximate Number of Twitter users 2010*. Retrieved April 14, 2011, from http://www.guardian.co.uk/technology/2011/feb/10/twitter-talks-buyers-facebook-google

Saaty, T. L. (1980). *Analytic Hierarchy Process: Planning, Priority Setting, Resource Allocation*. New York: McGraw-Hill International Book Company.

Saaty, T. L. (1994). How to make a decision: The analytic hierarchy process. *Interfaces, 24*(6), 19–43. doi:10.1287/inte.24.6.19

Saaty, T. L. (1996). *The analytic hierarchy process*. Pittsburg, PA: RWS Publications.

Sachs, P. (1995). Transforming Work: Collaboration, Learning and Design. *Communications of the ACM, 38*(9), 36–45. doi:10.1145/223248.223258

Sackmann, S. A., & Phillips, M. E. (2004). One's Many Cultures: A Multiple Cultures Perspective. In Crossing Cultures: Insights from Master Teachers (pp. 38–47). New York: Routledge.

Sahni, A. K., & Rastogi, A. K. (1995). Transforming Corporate Culture through Total Quality Commitment. *5th world congress on Total Quality*, 42 – 45.

Salesforce.com. (2012). *Software as a Service*. Retrieved from http://www.salesforce.com/saas/

Salo, J., & Karjaluoto, H. (2007). A conceptual model of trust in the online environment. *Online Information Review, 31*(5), 604–621. doi:10.1108/14684520710832324

Sambamurthy, V., Bharadwaj, A., & Grover, V. (2003). Shaping Agility through Digital Options: Reconceptualizing the Role of Information Technology in Contemporary Firms. *Management Information Systems Quarterly, 27*(2), 237–263.

Sandberg, W. R. (1986). *New venture performance: The role of strategy and industry structure.* Lexington, MA: Lexington Books.

Sarasvathy, S. D. (2001). Causation and Effectuation: Toward a Theoretical Shift from Economic Inevitability to Entrepreneurial Contingency. *Academy of Management Review, 26*(2), 243–263. doi:10.2307/259121

Sarasvathy, S. D. (2003). Entrepreneurship as a science of the artificial. *Journal of Economic Psychology, 24*(2), 203–220. doi:10.1016/S0167-4870(02)00203-9

Sarasvathy, S. D. (2008). *Effectuation: elements of entrepreneurial expertise.* Cheltenham, UK: Edward Elgar Publishing. doi:10.4337/9781848440197

Sargeant, W., & Moutray, C. (2010). *The small business economy (SBR publication No. 375).* Washington, DC: Small Business Administration. Retrieved from http://www.sba.gov/sites/default/files/sb_econ2010.pdf

Saunders, M., Lewis, P., & Thornhill, A. (2007). *Research Methods for Business Students* (4th ed.). Harlow: FT Prentice Hall.

Schein, E. H. (1985). How Culture Forms, Develops and Changes in R. H. Kilmann & M. J. Saxton. In R. Serpa (Ed.), *Gaining control of the Corporate Culture.* San Francisco, CA: Jossey Bass.

Schein, E. H. (2010). *Organizational culture and leadership* (4th ed.). Jossey-Bass.

Schmidt, S. M. P., & Ralph, D. L. (2013). Marketing using your website. *The Business Review, Cambridge, 21*(1), 52–58.

Schneberger, S., Amoroso, D. L., & Durfee, A. (2007). Factors that influence the performance of computer-based assessments: an extension of the technology acceptance model. *The Journal of Computer Information Systems, 48*(2), 74–90. Retrieved on June 2015-from-http://search.proquest.com/openview/6db431e40f310a511b62e7c85b3c47f3/1?pq-origsite=gscholar

Schofield, J. (2009). Twitter users are quick quitters. *Guardian Online.* Retrieved April 17, 2011, from http://www.guardian.co.uk/technology/blog/2009/apr/29/twitter-quitters-nielsen1?INTCMP=SRCH

Schramm, J. (2007). Internet Connections. *HRMagazine, 52*(9), 176.

Schultz, D. E. (1999). Integrated marketing communications and how it relates to traditional media advertising. In J.P. Jones (Ed.), The Advertising Business: Operations, Creativity, Media Planning, Integrated Communications (pp. 325-338). London, UK: Sage. doi:10.4135/9781452231440.n34

Schultz, D. E., & Peltier, J. (2013). Social media's slippery slope: Challenges, opportunities and future research directions. *Journal of Research in Interactive Marketing, 7*(2), 86–99. doi:10.1108/JRIM-12-2012-0054

Schultze, U., & Orlikowski, W. (2001). Metaphors of Virtuality: Shaping and Emergent Reality. *Information and Organization, 11*(1), 45–77. doi:10.1016/S1471-7727(00)00003-8

Schumpeter, J. (1934). *Capitalism, socialism, and democracy.* Academic Press.

Schumpeter, J. A. (1954). *History of Economic Analysis.* New York, NY: Oxford University Press Inc.

Schwartz, E. (1976). Entrepreneurship: A new female frontier. *Journal of Contemporary Business, 5*(1), 47–76.

Schwemmer, R., & Havrilla, R. (2011). *Dynamic collaboration: How to share information, solve Problems, and increase productivity without compromising security.* Third Bridge Press.

Schwen, T. M., & Hara, N. (2003). Community of Practice. A Metaphor for Online Design? *The Information Society*, *19*(3), 257–270. doi:10.1080/01972240309462

Scott, M. G., & Twomey, D. F. (1988). The long-term supply of entrepreneurs: Students' career aspirations in relation to entrepreneurship. *Journal of Small Business Management*, *26*(4), 5–13.

Serarols-Tarrés, C., Padilla-Meléndez, A., & Aguila-Obra, A. R. (2006). The influence of entrepreneur characteristics on the success of pure dot.com firms. *International Journal of Technology Management*, *33*(4), 373–388. doi:10.1504/IJTM.2006.009250

Shahabi, A., Faez, A., & Fazli, D. (2012). Organizational intelligence dismounting barriers prioritization: A real-world case study. MSL Journal, 2(8).

Shah, S. K., & Tripsas, M. (2007). The accidental entrepreneur: The emergent and collective process of user entrepreneurship. *Strategic Entrepreneurship Journal*, *1*(1-2), 123–140. doi:10.1002/sej.15

Shane, S. (2005). Government policies to encourage economic development through entrepreneurship: The case of technology transfer. *Economic development through entrepreneurship: Government, university, and business linkages*, 33-46.

Shane, S. (1992). Why do some societies invent more than others? *Journal of Business Venturing*, *7*(1), 29–46. doi:10.1016/0883-9026(92)90033-N

Shane, S. (1996). Explaining variation in rates of entrepreneurship in the United States: 1899-1988. *Journal of Management*, *22*(5), 747–781.

Shane, Sc. (2014). *Technology Strategy for Managers and Entrepreneurs: Pearson New* (International Edition). Upper Saddle River, NJ: Prentice Hall.

Shang, R.-A., Chen, Y.-C., & Shen, L. (2005). Extrinsic versus intrinsic motivations for consumers to shop on-line. *Information & Management*, *42*(3), 401–413. doi:10.1016/j.im.2004.01.009

Shao, Z. (2004). Improvement of digital signature with message recovery and its variants based on elliptic curve discrete logarithm problem. *Computer Standards & Interfaces*, *27*(1), 61–69. doi:10.1016/j.csi.2004.03.011

Shepherd, D. A. (2003). Learning from Business Failure: Propositions of Grief Recovery for the Self-Employed. *Academy of Management Review*, *28*(2), 318–328. doi:10.2307/30040715

Shepherd, D. A. (2004). Educating entrepreneurship students about emotion and learning from failure. *Academy of Management Learning & Education*, *3*(3), 274–287. doi:10.5465/AMLE.2004.14242217

Sheppard, B. H., Hartwick, J., & Warshaw, P. R. (1988). The theory of reasoned action: A meta-analysis of past research with recommendation for modification and future research. *The Journal of Consumer Research*, *15*(3), 325–343. doi:10.1086/209170

Sherer, P., & Shea, T. (2011). Using Online Video to Support Student Learning and Engagement. *College Teaching*, *59*(2), 56–59. doi:10.1080/87567555.2010.511313

Sheriff, M., Georgiadou, E., Abeysinghe, G., & Siakas, K. (2013). INCUVA: A meta-framework for sustaining the value of innovation in multi-cultural settings. In F. McCaffery, R.V. O'Connor, & R. Messnarz (Eds.), EuroSPI 2013. Springer.

Shih, H.-P. (2004). An empirical study on predicting user acceptance of e-shopping on the Web. *Information & Management*, *41*(3), 351–368. doi:10.1016/S0378-7206(03)00079-X

Shim, S., Eastlick, M. A., Lotz, S. L., & Warrington, P. (2001). An online prepurchase intentions model: The role of intention to search: Best overall paper award - The sixth triennial AMS/ACRA retailing conference, 2000. *Journal of Retailing*, *77*(3), 397–416. doi:10.1016/S0022-4359(01)00051-3

Shleifer, A., & Vishny, R. W. (1997). A survey of corporate governance. *The Journal of Finance*, *52*(2), 737–783. doi:10.1111/j.1540-6261.1997.tb04820.x

Shobeiri, S., Mazaheri, E., & Laroche, M. (2014). Improving customer website involvement through experiential marketing. *Service Industries Journal*, *34*(11), 885–900. doi:10.1080/02642069.2014.915953

Shroff, R. H., Deneen, C. C., & Ng, E. M. W. (2011). Analysis of the technology acceptance model in examining students' behavioural intention to use an e-portfolio system. *Australasian Journal of Educational Technology*, *27*(4), 600–618. doi:10.14742/ajet.940

Siakas, K. V. (2002). *SQM-CODE: Software Quality Management – Cultural and Organizational Diversity Evaluation* (PhD Thesis). London Metropolitan University, London, UK.

Siakas, K. V., & Georgiadou, E. (2006). Knowledge Sharing: Cultural Dynamics. In *Proceedings of 7th European Conference of Knowledge Management (ECKM06)*. Public Academic Conferences Ltd.

Siakas, K. V., & Georgidaou, E. (2000). A New Typology of National and Organizational Cultures to Facilitate Software Quality Management. In E. Georgiadou, G. King, P. Pouyioutas, M. Ross, & G. Staples (Eds.), *Quality and Software Development: Teaching and Training Issues, The fifth International conference on Software Process Improvement - Research into Education and Training (INSPIRE 2000)*. The British Computer Society.

Siakas, K., & Georgiadou, E. (2008). Knowledge Sharing in Virtual and Networked Organizations in Different Organizational and National Cultures. In Building the Knowledge Society on the Internet. Idea Publishing.

Siakas, K. V., & Balstrup, B. (2006). Software Outsourcing Quality Achieved by Global Distributed Collaboration. *Software Process: Improvement and Practice (SPIP) Journal*, *11*(3), 319–328.

Siakas, K. V., & Georgiadou, E. (1999). Process Improvement: The Societal Iceberg. *European Software Process Improvement Conference, EuroSPI '99*, 25-37.

Siakas, K. V., & Georgiadou, E. (2003). Learning in a Changing Society and the Importance of Cultural Awareness. *IADIS 2003 (International Association for development of the Information Society) International Conference*, 696-702.

Siakas, K., Georgiadou, E., & Balstrup, B. (2010). Cultural Impacts on Knowledge Sharing: Empirical Data from EU Project Collaboration. *VINE: The Journal of Information and Knowledge Management Systems*, *40*(3/4), 376–389. doi:10.1108/03055721011071476

Siakas, K., & Siakas, D. (2015). Cultural and Organizational Diversity Evaluation (CODE): A Tool for Improving Global Transactions. *Strategic Outsourcing*, *8*(2/3), 206–228. doi:10.1108/SO-04-2015-0012

Siakas, K., & Siakas, E. (2008). The need for trust relationships to enable successful distributed team collaboration and software outsourcing. *The International Journal of Technology, Policy and Management*, *8*(1), 59–75.

Sieverdes, J. C., Treiber, F., Jenkins, C., & Hermayer, K. (2013). Improving diabetes management with mobile health technology. *The American Journal of the Medical Sciences*, *345*(4), 289–295. doi:10.1097/MAJ.0b013e3182896cee PMID:23531961

Simonson, I., & Emanuel, R. (2014). *Absolute value: What really influences customers in the age of (nearly) perfect information*. HarperCollins Publishers.

Singh, R. P., & Magee, B. (2002). *Entrepreneurship Education: Is there a growing crisis?* (Unpublished paper). Retrieved May 20, 2011 from http://www.celcee.edu/publications/edinfo/ED02-10.html

Smethurst, S. (2004). The allure of online. *People Management, 10*(15), 38.

Smith, C. (2011). Twitter User Statistics Show Stunning Growth. *Huffington Post*. Retrieved April 14, 2011, from http://www.huffingtonpost.com/2011/03/14/ twitter-user-statistics_n_835581.html

Smith, A. (2010). *Americans and their gadgets*. Washington, DC: Pew Research Center's Internet & American Life Project.

Smith, A. N., Fischer, E., & Yongjian, C. (2012). How does brand-related user-generated content differ across YouTube, Facebook, and Twitter? *Journal of Interactive Marketing, 26*(2), 102–113. doi:10.1016/j.intmar.2012.01.002

Social Media Examiner. (2013). Retrieved January 3, 2014 from: http://www.socialmediaexaminer.com/social-media-marketing-industry-report-2013/

Solomon, G. (1989). Youth: Tomorrow's entrepreneurs. *ICSB Bulletin, 26*(5), 1–2.

Solomon, G. (2007). An examination of entrepreneurship education in the United States. *Journal of Small Business and Enterprise Development, 14*(2), 168–182. doi:10.1108/14626000710746637

Solomon, G. T., Duffy, S., & Tarabishy, A. (2002). The state of entrepreneurship education in the United States: A nationwide survey and analysis. *International Journal of Entrepreneurship Education, 1*(1), 65–86.

Sondergaard, M. (1994). Research Note: Hofstede's Consequences: a Study of reviews, Citations and Replications. *Organization Studies, 15*(3), 447–456. doi:10.1177/017084069401500307

Spanos, Y. E., Prastacos, G. P., & Poulymenakou, A. (2002). The relationship between information and communication technologies adoption and management. *Information & Management, 39*(8), 659–675. doi:10.1016/S0378-7206(01)00141-0

Spence, B. (2009). How to…filter job applications. *People Management*, 45. Retrieved March 19, 2009, from: http://www.peoplemanagement.co.uk/pm/articles/2009/03/how-to-filter-job-applications.htm

Spencer, J. W., Murtha, T. P., & Lenway, S. A. (2005). How Governments Matter to New Industry Creation. *Academy of Management Review, 30*(2), 321–337. doi:10.5465/AMR.2005.16387889

Sperry, R. W. (1968). Hemisphere disconnection and unity in conscious awareness. *The American Psychologist, 23*(10), 723–733. doi:10.1037/h0026839 PMID:5682831

Spiegler, I. (2000). Knowledge Management: A New Idea or a recycled Concept? *Communications of the Association for Information Systems, 3*(14), 1-23.

Sproull, L., & Kiesler, S. (1992). *Connections: New ways of working in the networked organization*. MIT press.

Stabryła-Chudzio, K. (2016). Contribution of the EU Budget to the Implementation of the Social Cohesion Policy of the European Union. *Journal of Management and Business Administration, 24*(2), 89–106.

Statista. (2017). *Leading global social networks 2016 Statistics*. Retrieved June 18, 2017, from http://www.statista.com/statistics

Statista. (n.d.). Number of Facebook users in the United States from 2015 to 2022 (in millions). *Statista - The Statistics Portal*. Retrieved October 20, 2017, from https://www.statista.com/statistics/408971/number-of-us-facebook-users/

Sternberg, R., & Wennekers, S. (2005). Determinants and effects of new business creation using global entrepreneurship monitor data. *Small Business Economics, 24*(3), 193–203. doi:10.1007/s11187-005-1974-z

Stofega, W., & Llamas, R. T. (2009). *Worldwide Mobile Phone 2009-2013 Forecast Update. IDC Document Number 217209*. Framingham, MA: IDC.

Stone, M., & Woodcock, N. (2013). Social intelligence in customer engagement. *Journal of Strategic Marketing, 21*(5), 394–401. doi:10.1080/0965254X.2013.801613

Storck, J., & Hill, P. (2000). Knowledge Diffusion through 'Strategic Communities'. *Sloan Management Review, 41*(2), 63–74.

Strang, K. D., & Chan, C. E. L. (2010). Simulating E-Business Innovation Process Improvement with Virtual Teams Across Europe and Asia. *International Journal of E-Entrepreneurship and Innovation, 1*(1), 22–41. doi:10.4018/jeei.2010010102

Suh, B., & Han, I. (2002). Effect of trust on customer acceptance of internet banking. *Electronic Commerce Research and Applications, 1*(3-4), 247–263. doi:10.1016/S1567-4223(02)00017-0

Sultana, S. (2014). Taking care of health through mobile phones. *The Financial Express*. Retrieved from http://www.thefinancialexpress-bd.com/2014/02/15/18873

Sundar, M. (2007). This week on LinkedIn July 9th 2007. *LinkedIn Blog*. Retrieved April 25, 2010, from http://blog.linkedin.com/2007/07/14/this-week-in-li/

Sun, Y., Wang, N., Guo, X., & Peng, Z. (2013). Understanding the acceptance of mobile health services: A comparison and integration of alternative models. *Journal of Electronic Commerce Research, 14*(2), 183–200.

Sunyaev, A., Dehling, T., Taylor, P. L., & Mandl, K. D. (2014). Availability and quality of mobile health app privacy policies. *Journal of the American Medical Informatics Association*. doi:10.1136/amiajnl-2013-002605 PMID:25147247

Swanson, E. B. (1982). Measuring user attitudes in MIS research: A review. *Omega, 10*(2), 157–165. doi:10.1016/0305-0483(82)90050-0

Szajna, B. (1996). Empirical evaluation of the revised Technology Acceptance Model. *Management Science, 42*(1), 85–92. doi:10.1287/mnsc.42.1.85

Tamrat, T., & Kachnowski, S. (2012). Special delivery: An analysis of mHealth in maternal and newborn health programs and their outcomes around the world. *Maternal and Child Health Journal, 16*(5), 1092–1101. doi:10.1007/s10995-011-0836-3 PMID:21688111

Tang, L., & Jang, S. (2014). Information Value and Destination Image: Investigating the Moderating Role of Processing Fluency. *Journal of Hospitality Marketing & Management, 23*(7), 790–814. doi:10.1080/19368623.2014.883585

Tang, Q., Gu, B., & Whinston, A. B. (2012). Content Contribution for Revenue Sharing and Reputation in Social Media: A Dynamic Structural Model. *Journal of Management Information Systems, 29*(2), 41–45. doi:10.2753/MIS0742-1222290203

Tanriverdi, H. (2005). Information Technology Relatedness, Knowledge Management Capability and Performance of Multi-business Firms. *MIS Quarterly, 29*(2), 311-334.

Tao, D. (2009). Intention to use and actual use of electronic information resources: further exploring Technology Acceptance Model (TAM). In *AMIA Annual Symposium Proceedings* (Vol. 2009, pp. 629–633). AMIA. Retrieved on May 2015 from http://www.pubmedcentral.nih.gov/articlerender.fcgi?artid=2815463&tool=pmcentrez&rendertype=abstract

Tayeb, M. (1988). *Organizations and National Culture: A Comparative Analysis*. London, UK: Sage Publishers.

Taylor, C. (2001). E-recruitment is powerful weapon in war for talent. *People Management*. Retrieved December 5, 2009, from: http://www.peoplemanagement.co.uk/pm/articles/2001/05/856.htm

Taylor, L. (2017). Experience, Knowledge Transfer and Entrepreneurial Learning. In *The Entrepreneurial Paradox* (pp. 109–134). Basingstoke, UK: Palgrave Macmillan. doi:10.1057/978-1-137-56949-3_5

Taylor, S., & Todd, P. (1995a). Assessing IT usage: The role of prior experience. *Management Information Systems Quarterly*, *19*(4), 561–570. doi:10.2307/249633

Taylor, S., & Todd, P. A. (1995). Understanding information technology usage: A test of competing models. *Information Systems Research*, *6*(2), 144–176. doi:10.1287/isre.6.2.144

Teece, D. J., Pisano, G., & Shuen, A. (1997). Dynamic capabilities and strategic management. *Strategic Management Journal*, *18*(7), 509–533. doi:<509::AID-SMJ882>3.0.CO;2-Z10.1002/(SICI)1097-0266(199708)18:7

Teece, D. J. (1992). Foreign investment and technological development in silicon. *California Management Review*, *34*(2), 88–106. doi:10.2307/41166695

Teece, D. J. (1993). The dynamics of industrial capitalism: Perspectives on Alfred Chandler's Scale and Scope (1990). *Journal of Economic Literature*, *31*(1), 199–225.

Téllez, J., & Sierra, J. (2007). Anonymous payment in a client centric model for digital ecosystems. In IEEE international conference on digital ecosystems and technologies (IEEE-DEST 2007) (pp. 422–427). IEEE.

Téllez, J., & Sierra, J. (2007). *A secure payment protocol for restricted connectivity scenarios in M-commerce*. EC-Web.

Téllez, J., Sierra, J., Izquierdo, A., & Torres, J. (2006). Anonymous payment in a Kiosk centric model using digital signature scheme with message recovery and low computational power devices. *Journal of Theoretical and Applied Electronic Commerce Research*, *1*(2), 1–11.

Téllez, J., Sierra, J., Zeadally, S., & Torres, J. (2008). A secure vehicle-to-roadside communication payment protocol in vehicular ad hoc networks. *Computer Communications*, *31*(10), 2478–2484. doi:10.1016/j.comcom.2008.03.012

Teo, T. S. H., Lim, V. K. G., & Lai, R. Y. C. (1999). Intrinsic and extrinsic motivation in internet usage. *Omega*, *27*(1), 25–37. doi:10.1016/S0305-0483(98)00028-0

Thurlow, C., Engel, L., & Tomic, A. (2004). *Computer-mediated communication: Social interaction and the Internet*. London, UK: Sage Publications.

Timmons, J. A. (1989). *The Entrepreneurial Mind*. Andover, MA: Brick House Publishing.

Toma, S., Grigore, A., & Marinescu, P. (2014). Economic Development and Entrepreneurship. *Procedia Economics and Finance*, *8*, 436–443. doi:10.1016/S2212-5671(14)00111-7

Tomkins, C. (2001). Interdependencies, trust and information in relationships, alliances and networks. *Accounting, Organizations and Society*, *26*(2), 161–191. doi:10.1016/S0361-3682(00)00018-0

Townsend, A., Leese, J., Adam, P., McDonald, M., Li, L. C., Kerr, S., & Backman, C. L. (2015). eHealth, Participatory Medicine, and Ethical Care: A Focus Group Study of Patients' and Health Care Providers' Use of Health-Related Internet Information. *Journal of Medical Internet Research*, *17*(6), e155. doi:10.2196/jmir.3792 PMID:26099267

Triantaphyllou, E., & Mann, S. (1995). Using the analytic hierarchy process for decision making in engineering applications: Some challenges. *International Journal of Industrial Engineering: Applications and Practice*, *2*(1), 35–44.

Trompenaars, F., & Hampden-Turner, C. (1997). *Riding the waves of Culture*. Nicholas Brealey.

Tseng, Y.-C., Shen, C.-C., & Chen, W.-T. (2003, May). Integrating Mobile IP with Ad Hoc Networks. *Computer, Volume*, *36*(5), 48–55.

Tseng, Y., Jan, J., & Chien, H. (2003). Digital signature with message recovery using self-certified public keys and its variants. *Applied Mathematics and Computation, 136*(2–3), 203–214. doi:10.1016/S0096-3003(02)00010-3

Tsiaousis, A. S., & Giaglis, G. M. (2014). Mobile websites: Usability evaluation and design. *International Journal of Mobile Communications, 12*(1), 29–55. doi:10.1504/IJMC.2014.059241

Tsoukas, H. (1991). The missing link: A transformational view of metaphors in organizational science. *Academy of Management Review, 16*(3), 566–585.

Tulip, S. (2003, August). A flying start. *People Management Magazine*, 38. Retrieved February 5, 2010, from http://www.peoplemanagement.co.uk/pm/articles/2003/08/ 9256.htm

Tung, F.-C., Chang, S.-C., & Chou, C.-M. (2008). An extension of trust and TAM model with IDT in the adoption of the electronic logistics information system in HIS in the medical industry. *International Journal of Medical Informatics, 77*(5), 324–335. doi:10.1016/j.ijmedinf.2007.06.006 PMID:17644029

Turban, E., David, K., Lee, J., Warkentin, M., & Chung, M. H. (2008). *E-Commerce: A Managerial Perspective*. Prentice Hall Inc.

Twitter. (2011a). *MarcJacobsInt*. Retrieved May 26, 2011, from http://twitter.com/#!/MarcJacobsIntl

Twitter. (2011b). *Twitter KPMG Recruitment Page*. Retrieved April 25, 2011, from http://twitter.com/#!/KPMGRecruitment

Twitter. (2011c). *Twitter KPMG UK page*. Retrieved April 25, 2011, from http://twitter.com/#!/KPMG_UK_LLP

Tzenga & Hwang. (2004). Digital signature with message recovery and its variants based on elliptic curve discrete logarithm problem. *Computer Standards & Interfaces, 26*(2), 61–71. doi:10.1016/S0920-5489(03)00069-2

U.S. Chamber of Commerce. (2013). *Counterfeited and Pirated Products Account for $360 billion in trade losses*. Retrieved from http://www.theglobalipcenter.com/counterfeit-pirated-products-360-billion/

U.S. Congress (2013). *Marketplace Fairness Act of 2013*. S-743 and House of Representatives, H.R. 684, May 6, 2013.

U.S. Department of Commerce. (2016). *New Insights on Retail E-commerce*. Available online at http://www.esa.doc.gov/sites/default/files/new-insights-retail-e-commerce.pdf

U.S. Department of Commerce. (2017). *E-Commerce Survey*. Retrieved from http://www.census.gov/retail/mrts/www/data/pdf/ec_current.pdf

Union, I. (2014). *Communication from the Commission to the European Parliament, the Council, the European Economic and Social Committee and the Committee of the Regions*. Brussels.

Utkin, L. V., & Simanova, N. V. (2012). The DS/AHP method under partial information about criteria and alternatives by several levels of criteria. *International Journal of Information Technology & Decision Making, 11*(2), 307–326. doi:10.1142/S0219622012400044

Van den Bosch, F. A. J., & van Prooijen, A. A. (1992). The competitive advantage of European nations: The impact of national culture, a missing element in Porter's analysis? *European Management Journal, 10*(2), 173–178. doi:10.1016/0263-2373(92)90066-D

Van Den Hooff, B., & De Ridder, J. A. (2004). Knowledge sharing in context: The influence of organizational commitment, communication climate and CMC use on knowledge sharing. *Journal of Knowledge Management, 8*(6), 117–130. doi:10.1108/13673270410567675

Van der Heijden, H., & Verhagen, T. (2004). Online store image: Conceptual foundations and empirical measurement. *Information & Management*, *41*(5), 609–617. doi:10.1016/j.im.2003.07.001

Vedder, A., Cuijpers, C., Vantsiouri, P., & Ferrari, M. Z. (2014). The law as a 'catalyst and facilitator' for trust in e-health: Challenges and opportunities. *Law. Innovation and Technology*, *6*(2), 305–325. doi:10.5235/17579961.6.2.305

Ven, A. H. V. d., & Poole, M. S. (2002). Field research methods. In J. A. C. Baum (Ed.), *The Blackwell Companion to Organizations* (pp. 867–888). New York, NY: Oxford University Press.

Venaketsh, V., Morris, M., Davis, G., & Davis, F. (2003). User acceptance of information technology: Toward a unified view. *Management Information Systems Quarterly*, *27*(3), 425–478.

Venkataraman, S. (1997). The distinctive domain of entrepreneurship research. In J. Katz & R. Brockhaus (Eds.), *Advances in Entrepreneurship, firm emergence and growth* (Vol. 3, pp. 119–138). Greenwich, CT: JAI Press.

Venkatarman, S., & Das, R. (2013). The influence of corporate social media on firm level strategic decision making: A preliminary exploration. *International Journal of E-Business Research*, *9*(1), 1–20. doi:10.4018/jebr.2013010101

Venkatesh, V. (1999). Creating favourable user perceptions: Exploring the role of intrinsic motivation. *Management Information Systems Quarterly*, *23*(2), 239–260. doi:10.2307/249753

Venkatesh, V., & Davis, F. D. (2000). A theoretical extension of the Technology Acceptance Model: Four longitudinal field studies. *Management Science*, *46*(2), 186–204. doi:10.1287/mnsc.46.2.186.11926

Venkatesh, V., Morris, M. G., Davis, G. B., & Davis, F. D. (2003). User acceptance of information technology: Toward a unified view. *Management Information Systems Quarterly*, *27*(3), 425–478.

Venkatesh, V., Speier, C., & Morris, M. G. (2002). User acceptance enablers in individual decision making about technology: Toward an integrated model. *Decision Sciences*, *33*(2), 297–316. doi:10.1111/j.1540-5915.2002.tb01646.x

Venkatesh, V., Thong, J. Y. L., & Xin, X. (2012). Consumer acceptance and use of information technology: Extending the Unified Theory of Acceptance and Use of Technology. *Management Information Systems Quarterly*, *36*(1), 157–178.

Venkatesh, V., & Zhang, X. (2010). Unified theory of acceptance and use of technology: U.S. vs. China. *Journal of Global Information Technology Management*, *13*(1), 5–27. doi:10.1080/1097198X.2010.10856507

Venters, W., & Whitley, E. (2012). A critical review of cloud computing: Researching desires and realities. *Journal of Information Technology*, *27*(3), 179–197. doi:10.1057/jit.2012.17

Vesper, K. H., & Gartner, W. B. (2001). *University Entrepreneurship Programs*. Los Angeles, CA: Lloyd Greif Center for Entrepreneurial Studies, Marshall School of Business, University of Southern California.

Vickery, S., Droge, C., Stank, T., Goldsby, T., & Markland, R. (2004). The performance implications of media richness in a business-to-business service environment: Direct and indirect effects. *Management Science*, *50*(8), 1106–1119. doi:10.1287/mnsc.1040.0248

Vijayasarathy, L. R. (2004). Predicting consumer intentions to use on-line shopping: The case for an augmented technology acceptance model. *Information & Management*, *41*(6), 747–762. doi:10.1016/j.im.2003.08.011

Vivek, S. D., Beatty, S. E., & Morgan, R. M. (2012). Customer engagement: Exploring customer relationships beyond purchase. *Journal of Marketing Theory and Practice*, *20*(2), 127–145. doi:10.2753/MTP1069-6679200201

Vogel, E. A., Rose, J. P., Okdie, B. M., Eckles, K., & Franz, B. (2015). Who compares and despairs? The effect of social comparison orientation on social media and its outcomes. *Personality and Individual Differences*, *86*, 249–256. doi:10.1016/j.paid.2015.06.026

Von Krogh, G., & von Hippel, E. (2006). The promise of research on open source software. *Management Science, 52*(7), 975–983. doi:10.1287/mnsc.1060.0560

Wakefield, R. J., Stocks, M. H., & Wilder, W. M. (2004). The role of website characteristics in initial trust formation. *Journal of Computer Information Systems, 45*(1), 94–103.

Wales, W. J. (2016). Entrepreneurial orientation: A review and synthesis of promising research directions. *International Small Business Journal, 34*(1), 3–15. doi:10.1177/0266242615613840

Wang, J., Gu, L., & Aiken, M. (2010). A study of the impact of individual differences on online shopping. *International Journal of E-Business Research, 6*(1), 52–67. doi:10.4018/jebr.2010100904

Wang, Y., Ma, S., & Li, D. (2015). Customer participation in virtual brand communities: The self-construal perspective. *Information & Management, 52*(5), 577–587. doi:10.1016/j.im.2015.04.003

Wani, M., Raghavan, V., Abraham, D., & Kleist, V. (2017). Beyond utilitarian factors: User Experience and travel company website successes. *Information Systems Frontiers, 19*(4), 769–785. doi:10.1007/s10796-017-9747-1

Wareham, J., Busquets, X., & Austin, R. (2009). Creative, convergent, and social: Prospects for mobile computing. *Journal of Information Technology, 24*(2), 139–143. doi:10.1057/jit.2009.1

Washington, G., Ward, J., & Kameka, M. (2015). Spare Me: Towards an Empathetic Tool for Helping Adolescents & Teenagers Cope with Sickle Cell. In *Healthcare Informatics (ICHI), 2015 International Conference on* (pp. 555-561). IEEE.

Webb, T. J. (1998). *Researching for Business: Avoiding the 'Nice to know' Trap* (1st ed.). London: Aslib.

Web-HIPRE. (1998). Retrieved from http://www.hipre.hut.fi/

Weekes, S. (2004, June). Unearthing diamonds in a tough recruitment market. *Personnel Today*, 10.

Week, M. (2006). E-recruitment in Web 2.0 boost. *Marketing Week, 29*(43), 32.

Weick, K. E. (1979). *The Social Psychology of Organizing* (2nd ed.). Reading, MA: Addison-Wesley.

Weick, K. E. (1995). *Sensemaking in Organizations*. Thousand Oaks, CA: Sage.

Weick, K. E., Sutcliffe, K. M., & Obstfeld, D. (2005). Organizing and the Process of Sensemaking. *Organization Science, 16*(4), 409–421. doi:10.1287/orsc.1050.0133

Weigley, S. (2013). *Yahoo Finance*. Retrieved from http://finance.yahoo.com/news/the-10-most-counterfeited-products-in-america-180942491

Wells, H. G. (1938). *World Brain*. Garden City, NY: Doubleday, Doran & Co., Inc.

Wenger, E. (1999). *Communities of Practice: Learning, Meaning and Identity*. Cambridge University Press.

Wenger, E., & Snyder, W. (2000, January). Communities of practice: The organizational frontier. *Harvard Business Review*, 139–145.

West, D. (2012). How mobile devices are transforming healthcare. *Issues in Technology Innovation, 18*(1), 1–11.

Wiesz, J. D., Erickson, T., & Kellog, W. A. (2006). Synchronous broadcast messaging: the use of ICT. In Proceedings, Computer-Mediated Communication, CHI2006. Montreal, Canada: ACM. doi:10.1145/1124772.1124967

Wikipedia.org. (2009) Retrieved from https://en.wikipedia.org/wiki/User_experience

Williamson, D. (2002). Forward from a critique of Hofstede's model of national culture. *Human Relations, 55*(11), 1373–1395. doi:10.1177/00187267025511006

Willmott, B. (2003). Firms tackle skills and diversity crisis online. *Personnel Today, 7*(1), 4.

Wilson, E. V., & Lankton, N. K. (2004). Modeling patients' acceptance of provider-delivered E-health. *Journal of the American Medical Informatics Association, 11*(4), 241–248. doi:10.1197/jamia.M1475 PMID:15064290

Wilson, F., Kickul, J., & Marlino, D. (2007). Gender, entrepreneurial self-efficacy, and entrepreneurial career intentions: Implications for entrepreneurship education. *Entrepreneurship Theory and Practice, 31*(3), 387–406. doi:10.1111/j.1540-6520.2007.00179.x

Winter, S. J. M., Chudoba, K., & Gutek, B. A. (1998). Attitudes toward computers: When do they predict computer use? *Information & Management, 34*(5), 275–284. doi:10.1016/S0378-7206(98)00065-2

Winzen, T., & Schimmelfennig, F. (2016). Explaining differentiation in European Union treaties. *European Union Politics, 17*(4), 616-637.

Wodak, R., & Boukala, S. (2015). European identities and the revival of nationalism in the European Union: A discourse historical approach. *Journal of Language and Politics, 14*(1), 87–109. doi:10.1075/jlp.14.1.05wod

Womenable. (2015). *The Growth and Development of Women-Owned Enterprise in the United States, 2002– 2012. An Analysis of Trends From the U.S. Census Bureau's Survey of Business Owners.* Author. Retrieved from https://www.nwbc.gov/sites/default/files/Growth%20of%20WOBs%202002-2012%20 for%20NWBC%20FINAL.pdf

Womenable. (2016). *The state of women-owned businesses in 2016: summary of key trends.* Author. Retrieved from http://www.womenable.com/content/userfiles/2016_State_of_Women Owned_Businesses_Executive_Report.pdf

World Bank. (2004). *Doing Business in 2004: Understanding regulation.* Oxford, UK: Oxford University Press.

Wu, I. L., & Chen, J. L. (2005). An extension of Trust and TAM model with TPB in the initial adoption of on-line tax: An empirical study. *International Journal of Human-Computer Studies, 62*(6), 784–808. doi:10.1016/j.ijhcs.2005.03.003

Wu, J., Wang, S., & Lin, L. (2007). Mobile computing acceptance factors in the healthcare industry: A structural equation model. *International Journal of Medical Informatics, 76*(1), 66–77. doi:10.1016/j.ijmedinf.2006.06.006 PMID:16901749

Xue, L., Yen, C.C., Chang, L., Tai, B.C., Chan, H.C., Duh, H.B.L. & Choolani, M. (2012). Journeying Toward Female-focused m-Health Applications. *Advances in Affective and Pleasurable Design,* 295.

Yang, Z. (2010). Understanding retweeting behaviours in social networks. *Proceedings of the 19ᵗʰ ACM international conference on information and knowledge management.* Retrieved June 18, 2017, from https://www.cs.cmu.edu

Yao-Hua Tan, W. T. (2014). Toward a generic model of trust for electronic commerce. *International Journal of Electronic Commerce, 5*(2), 61–74. doi:10.1080/10864415.2000.11044201

Yin, R. K. (2013). *Case study research: Design and methods.* Sage Publications.

Yin, S. Y., Huang, K. K., Shieh, J. I., Liu, Y. H., & Wu, H. H. (2015). Tele-health services evaluation: A combination of SERVQUAL model and importance-performance analysis. *Quality & Quantity,* 1–16.

Young, R. (Ed.). (2010). Knowledge management tools and techniques manual. Tokyo, Japan: APO (Asian Productivity Centre).

Yu, C. (2012). Factors affecting individuals to adopt mobile banking: Empirical evidence from the UTAUT model. *Journal of Electronic Commerce Research, 13*(2), 104–121.

Yu, J., Ha, I., Choi, M., & Rho, J. (2005). Extending the TAM for a t-commerce. *Information & Management, 42*(7), 965–976. doi:10.1016/j.im.2004.11.001

Zander, U., & Kogut, B. (1995). Knowledge and Speed of the Transfer and Imitation of Organizational Capabilities: An Empirical Test. *Organization Science, 6*(1), 76–92. doi:10.1287/orsc.6.1.76

Zavyalova, A., Pfarrer, M., Reger, R., & Shapiro, D. (2012). The effects of firm actions and industry spillovers on media coverage following wrongdoing. *Academy of Management Journal, 55*(5), 1079–1101. doi:10.5465/amj.2010.0608

Zou, Li. (2015). Study on College Students Entrepreneurial Intentions Factors. *International Conference on Social Science and Technology Education (ICSSTE 2015)*. Chongqing University of Science & Technology.

About the Contributors

Mehdi Khosrow-Pour, D.B.A., received his Doctorate in Business Administration from the Nova Southeastern University (Florida, USA). Dr. Khosrow-Pour taught undergraduate and graduate information system courses at the Pennsylvania State University – Harrisburg for almost 20 years. He is currently Executive Editor at IGI Global (www.igi-global.com). He also serves as Executive Director of the Information Resources Management Association (IRMA) (www.irma-international.org), and Executive Director of the World Forgotten Children's Foundation (www.world-forgotten-children.org). He is the author/editor of more than 100 books in information technology management. He is also the Editor-in-Chief of the *International Journal of Open Source Software and Processes*, *International Journal of Green Computing*, *International Journal of Digital Library Systems*, *International Journal of E-Entrepreneurship and Innovation*, *International Journal of Art, Culture, and Design Technologies*, *International Journal of Signs and Semiotic Systems*, and *International Journal of Disease Control and Containment for Sustainability*, and has authored more than 50 articles published in various conference proceedings and scholarly journals.

* * *

Shaik Shakeel Ahamad is currently working as an Assistant Professor in CCIS, Majmaah University, Kingdom of Saudi Arabia. He was a Professor in the Department of CSE, KL University, Guntur, India (now on lien). He holds a PhD in Computer Science from the University of Hyderabad (a Central University which ranks second in India) and IDRBT (Institute For Development and Research in Banking Technology), Hyderabad, India in the realm of secure mobile payments protocols and formal verification. He has published more than 25 research papers in reputed International journals / Proceedings indexed by ISI, Scopus, ACM Digital Library, DBLP and IEEE Digital Library. He is serving as a Review Committee Member of the following journals Computer Methods and Programs in Biomedicine, Elsevier (Five year Impact Factor: 2.051), Mobile Networks and Applications Journal, Springer (Five year Impact Factor: 1.538), Computers & Electrical Engineering, Elsevier (Five year Impact Factor: 1.09), Digital Investigation Journal, Elsevier (Five year Impact Factor: 1.171) (since 02/2014), Information Security Journal: A Global Perspective Journals, Taylor & Francis publications, International Journal of E-Services and Mobile Applications (IJESMA), IGI Global, International Journal of Network Security (IJNS). He is supervising nine Ph.D. Scholars in India. His research interests include cloud-based mobile commerce, secure mobile healthcare frameworks and protocols, wireless public key infrastructure and digital forensics. He is a member of IEEE, Association for Computing Machinery (ACM) and OWASP (Open Web Application Security Project).

Md. Moddassir Alam is a Ph.D. Research Scholar from Birla Institute of Technology (Mesra), Ranchi, (India). His domain of research is marketing with a focus on pharmaceutical branding. Branding and Advertising are his specific areas of interest. Mr. Alam has corporate experience of working as a Brand Manager in a pharmaceutical major prior to joining doctoral program.

Colleen Carraher Wolverton, PhD is the Edith Winn Estate Endowed Assistant Professor at the University of Louisiana Lafayette. Her research interests include IT outsourcing, adoption of new technology, Distance Learning, and creativity with IT. Previous work by Dr. Colleen Carraher Wolverton has been published in top journals such as the Journal of Information Technology, European Journal of Information Systems, Information & Management, Communications of the AIS, Journal of Organizational and End User Computing, Journal of Information Technology Theory and Application, Journal of Management History, and Small Group Research. She has won awards for her research, including the Outstanding Researcher of the Year Award from the BI Moody College of Business Administration and the Research Excellence Award from the University of Louisiana Lafayette. She is a Senior Editor at The Data Base for ADVANCES IN INFORMATION SYSTEMS and an Associate Editor at Information & Management. Prior to her career in academia, Colleen was an IT professional, working as a project manager for an IT development firm, an IT analyst for a Fortune 50 oil and gas company, and organizational development in an IT department.

Ron Cheek is a former banker, real estate developer, and a life-long serial entrepreneur. The focus of his teaching and research is on Digital-Based Entrepreneurship.

Kimiz Dalkir is an Associate Professor and Director of the School of Information Studies at McGill University. She has a Ph.D. in Educational Technology, an MBA in Management Science and Management Information Systems and a B.Sc. in Human Genetics. Dr. Dalkir wrote Knowledge Management in Theory and Practice, soon to be released as a third edition, which has had an international impact on KM education and on KM practice. She recently published Intelligent Intelligent learner modeling in real-time and co-edited Utilizing Evidence-Based Lessons Learned for Enhanced Organizational Innovation and Change. Dr. Dalkir pursues research on the effectiveness of knowledge processing in both profit and non-profit organizations, learning in peer networks and measurement frameworks for assessing knowledge management success. Prior to joining McGill, Dr. Dalkir worked in the field of knowledge transfer for 17 years. She designed and developed KM systems for clients in Europe, Japan and North America.

Epaminondas Epaminonda is an Assistant Professor and Associate Head of the Management and MIS Department of the Business School of the University of Nicosia, Cyprus. He is the Coordinator of the Doctoral Programs of the School. Epaminondas has been teaching at University for more than 12 years and has also seven years of industry experience in the banking, tourism and marker research sectors. His research interests are in the areas of comparative management, socioeconomic change and job satisfaction, and he has presented and published papers in refereed conferences and journals in these fields. Dr. Epaminonda holds a BA and an MA from the University of Cambridge, an MBA from Imperial College and a PhD from Manchester Business School.

Elli Georgiadou is a Fellow of the BCS, a Quality Management consultant and a Visiting Academic & EU Projects Advisor (having managed several large European Research and Knowledge Transfer projects) at the Faculty of Engineering and Information Sciences, Middlesex University, London, UK. She has over 30 years of teaching in Higher Education as a Principal Lecturer and has published widely on Software Quality Engineering, and Education.

Martin Hannibal is associate professor in International Business & Entrepreneurship at University of Southern Denmark. He holds a master's degree in Philosophy and received the PhD degree in Entrepreneurship in 2012. Dr Hannibal has published in several journals such as Journal of International Marketing, International Journal of Innovation & Regional Development, and International Business & Economic Review. In addition to acting assistant Editor at the International Journal of Entrepreneurial Behaviour & Research, Dr Hannibal has considerable international experience in research and teaching in entrepreneurship. Since 2013 he has been associate researcher on the international PACE (Promoting a Culture of Entrepreneurship) project.

Jessica Hill is an assistant Professor of Economics at Holyoke Community College in Holyoke, Massachusetts, USA.

Jessica Ludescher Imanaka is an Associate Professor of Business Ethics in the Albers School of Business and Economics at Seattle University, holding a joint appointment in Management and Philosophy. Ludescher's research has focused on corporate social responsibility, theory of the firm, political economy, sustainability, globalization, virtuality, and spirituality in business.

Mehree Iqbal is a Senior Lecturer in the School of Business and Economics at North South University. She has been teaching here since 2012. Ms. Iqbal received her Bachelor's Degree from North South University, Bangladesh and Master's Degree in International Business and Entrepreneurship from University of Glasgow, UK. She usually teaches the courses of International Business, International Competitiveness, International Strategy, Entrepreneurship and International Marketing. In addition to teaching, Ms. Iqbal has a research interest in areas in consumer behaviour/perception, strategic internationalization, sustainability, green banking and Technology Acceptance Models. Ms. Iqbal has published papers on these areas as well. She is a regular writer on issues of current international affairs in Business Asia Magazine. She is the founder of Synergy: Personal Development and Counselling, which provides counselling to the people in need as a part of social responsibility and sustainability of the society.

Achilleas Karayiannis holds the position of the Coordinator of Business and Logistics Programs at KES College while he is also an External Collaborator at the University of Nicosia. Since 2005. Dr. Karayiannis held a number of academic positions in different academic institutions in Cyprus and the UK, teaching both in undergraduate and postgraduate programs of study. He successfully completed his university studies in the following academic institutions: BSc in Business and Psychology at the Oxford Brookes University (2004), MA in Organisation Studies at the University of Warwick (2005) and PhD in Management at the University of Essex (2009). As part of his research activities, he currently has in submission to the Organisation Studies Journal, an article titled 'Brecht and Stanislavski: a managerial approach'.

Brett M. Kelley is currently an undergraduate student at Western Michigan University. She was Haworth College of Business' 2016-2017 Marketing Student of the Year. She is planning to pursue graduate studies for a future career in academic research.

Despo Ktoridou is currently an Associate Professor and Head of Management & MIS Department at the University of Nicosia in Cyprus. Dr. Ktoridou holds a B.Sc. (1991), M.Sc. (1993) in Computer Engineering and a Ph.D. (2000) in the field of Expert Systems from Saint Petersburg State Electrotechnical University in Russia. Dr. Ktoridou has worked as a Senior Computer Engineer for different organizations in Cyprus (1992 – 1999), from 2000 – 2007 as an Assistant Professor of Educational Technology and currently as an Associate Professor of MIS at the University of Nicosia. Dr. Ktoridou's research focuses on areas of ICT-Information Communication Technologies application in education, Innovation and Technology Management in Education and Business and Innovative Teaching /Learning Pedagogies in Higher Education. Dr. Ktoridou has presented papers in numerous refereed international conferences and has published several papers in refereed journals. Dr. Ktoridou participated in EU and local funded programs and has been invited by foreign universities as a guest lecturer.

Amresh Kumar is an Assistant Professor of Marketing Research at Symbiosis Institute of Business Management (SIBM), Pune, Symbiosis International University. He holds an MBA and currently pursuing PhD (Thesis submitted) in the area of retail marketing from Birla Institute of Technology, Mesra, Ranchi (India). His areas of research interests include retailing, e commerce, and social media marketing. Mr. Kumar has also contributed articles to repute national and international journals such as International Journal of Bank Marketing, International Journal of Business and Economics, International Journal of Retail and Distribution Management, Management Research Review, etc.

Karen M. Lancendorfer (Ph.D., Michigan State University) is Associate Professor of Marketing in the Haworth College of Business at Western Michigan University. She is also Director of the Advertising & Promotion Program, where she is the 2011 recipient of the WMU Distinguished Teaching Award and the 2012 Haworth College of Business Service Award. Her current research interests focus on political advertising, crisis management, corporate image, and consumer behavior. Her work has been included in a number of publications including the Journal of Business Research, Harvard International Journal of Press/Politics, Journal of Information Technology, Journal of Internet Commerce, Asian Journal of Communication, International Journal of Nonprofit and Voluntary Sector Marketing, Corporate Reputation Review, International Journal of E-Business Research, Journal of Political Marketing, and Qualitative Market Research, as well as in conference proceedings. She is the former associate editor for the Journal of Interactive Advertising, and the 2015 President of the American Academy of Advertising.

James Lee is a Genevieve Albers Visiting Professor of Albers School of Business and Economics. He teaches primarily in the areas of Business Analytics, Internet Business Strategies, and Information Systems. His current research interests are IT-driven business value propositions, specialized in Big Data Analytics, Web Technologies & Strategies, and Service Oriented Architecture.

Anthony Lewis is a Senior Lecturer in Organisational Leadership, Learning and Management at the Business School, University of South Wales and is Programme Leader for the MSc Leadership and Management. He has an MBA from the University of Glamorgan involving a dissertation which investigated "Transnational Cultural Effects on Organisational Theories of Motivation". Previous industrial experience has included working for a blue-chip company in Organisational Psychology. He has published papers in international conference proceedings and journals and is currently undertaking a PhD in Talent Management.

Krisanna Machtmes is an Associate Professor in the Patton College of Education at Ohio University in Athens, Ohio, USA.

Ryan Machtmes is a Doctoral student of evaluation studies, within the College of Education and Human Development's Department of Organizational Leadership, Policy, and Development, at the University of Minnesota - Twin Cities. A professional research consultant and accredited statistician of the American Statistical Association.

Mukta Mani has about 16 years experience of teaching to undergraduate and postgraduate students of Management and Engineering. She has taught courses on Finance, Economics and Entrepreneurship. Her area of interest in teaching is Banking, Financial management, Indian financial system, financial markets and Entrepreneurship. She is actively involved in research work in the area of banking, finance, mutual funds and entrepreneurship. She has successfully supervised two Ph.D. and supervising many other scholars. She has written around 25 research papers in international and national journals.

Erastus Ndinguri is an Assistant Professor of Management and Entrepreneurship. His research and publications focus on Entrepreneurship, Organization Human Capital Development and Strategic Organizational Leadership.

Nabila Nisha is currently teaching as a Senior Lecturer at the Department of Accounting & Finance under School of Business and Economics of North South University. She completed her Bachelor's degree with dual concentration in Accounting & Finance and Marketing from North South University, Bangladesh. She received her Master's degree in Banking & Finance from University of Essex, UK. Besides teaching, she has been part of a research project on Green Banking financed by World Bank and Ministry of Education of Bangladesh. Her research interests include technology acceptance models, banking sector, accounting disclosures, empirical research methods in finance and business case studies. She has a number of international journal publications in USA, UK and India, along with local and international book chapters as part of her research work. She has authored two books as well, which has been published by Lambert Academic Publishing and is available in the international market.

Kelley O'Reilly (Ph.D., Utah State University) is Associate Professor of Sales and Business Marketing at Western Michigan University and the recipient of the 2013 Haworth College of Business Research Award, and the 2014 Haworth College of Business Teaching award. She has more than twenty years of executive level experience in franchise retail and service businesses and her research interests are qualitative research methods, customer relationship management (CRM), sales, and service quality. Her work has been included in publications of Organizational Research Methods, International Journal of Retail and Distribution Management, Journal of Research in Marketing and Entrepreneurship, Qualitative Market Research: An International Journal, International Journal of Electronic Business Research, and Journal of Relationship Marketing, among others.

Mark Potts is currently a member of the Teaching Faculty in the Department of Finance and Law at Central Michigan University. He was formerly the Assistant Dean of the College of Business and Management at Saginaw Valley State University. Potts's teaching experience and research interest relate to entrepreneurship, finance, international business, and law. He is a returned Peace Corps Volunteer (Bulgaria 2000-2002) and taught for a year as part of a Fulbright Program in Vienna, Austria. Potts is a licensed attorney and earned a bachelor's degree from the University of Michigan as well as a Juris Doctor, cum laude, from Western Michigan University Cooley Law School. Potts is professionally fluent in German and Bulgarian.

George Puia holds the Dow Chemical Company Centennial Chair in Global Business at Saginaw Valley State University. He earned a Ph.D. in Strategic Management from the University of Kansas. Before joining SVSU, Dr. Puia held faculty positions at Indiana State University and the University of Tampa. Puia was named a Distinguished Fellow by the Academy for Global Business Advancement and was selected for the inaugural Oxford Journal Global Top 50 Educators Award. He is widely published in journals and textbooks. He has extensive management and consulting experience, and is a founding member of the Mid-Michigan Innovation Team (MMIT), where he served as board chair.

Erik S. Rasmussen is employed at the department of Marketing and Management (University of Southern Denmark) as associate professor. He received his Ph.D. in 2001 from the University of Southern Denmark on the theme of Fast Internationalising, Danish Small and Medium sized firms. His research focuses especially on international entrepreneurship and Born Global firms. In later years he has particularly focused on the international entrepreneurs that are able to avoid domestic path dependence by establishing ventures, which already from the beginning develop routines for a multi-cultural workforce, coordinates resources across nations and targets customers in several geographic places simultaneously. He has published in international journals such as the International Small Business Journal, the Journal of Management & Governance, the Journal of Small Business and Enterprise Development, the International Journal of Innovation Management, and Corporate Communications plus published a large number of book chapters.

Afrin Rifat is a Senior Lecturer of Accounting and Finance department at the School of Business & Economics of North South University (NSU). Since Fall 2012, Ms. Rifat has been teaching courses of Accounting at NSU. Currently she is teaching major courses of Intermediate Accounting and Managerial Accounting at the undergraduate level. Ms. Rifat earned her Bachelor of Business Administration (BBA) degree with major in finance & accounting and minor in economics from North South University, Bangladesh and Masters Degree in Banking and Finance from University of Essex, UK in 2010 and 2011 respectively. Her current research interests include technology acceptance models, financial statement analysis and decision-making, banking strategies, capital market, and empirical research methods in finance and country specific studies.

Gwenllian Sanders completed her MSc in Human Resources Management at the Glamorgan Business School, University of Glamorgan in 2011. Her particular interests were in the area of e-recruitment and the title of her dissertation for her degree was "Pushing the right buttons? A critical exploration into whether e-recruitment is an effective method in attracting appropriate employees for organizations". Her dissertation supervisor was Anthony Lewis.

Dimitrios Siakas is a civil Engineer from Novia University of Applied Sciences, Finland. He has an extensive industrial experience in multi-discipline engineering, layout engineering and information management services to the Energy and Power industry. He also has experience from leading multicultural teams and following up global status of Industrial Area (IA) Key Performance Indicators (KPIs) regarding Quality of service and work process development. He is also involved in strategy creation for competence area, IA geographical allocation of competence availability and long-term competence development. His research interests are in the energy and power field. He has publications in global management and innovation management. He is interested in Situational Application Development as a potential to solve business challenges in a cost-effective way and to capture the part of IT that directly impacts end users and company priorities.

Kerstin Siakas is currently professor at the Department of Informatics, ATEI of Thessaloniki. She holds a BSc and MSc in Economics from Handelshögskolan vid Åbo Academy, Finland and a PhD in Software Quality Management from the department of Computing at the London Metropolitan University, UK. She also has an extensive industrial experience in developing Information Systems on different levels (programmer, analyst, IT manager) from mainly global organizations in different countries. She is engaged in research in Multidisciplinary Approaches of Software Engineering. She has a particular interest in the social, cultural and political approaches and their effect on society, as well as on the subsequent challenges for managers, educators and governments. She has published more than 100 scientific papers about her research in journals, book chapters and international refereed conferences. She has been very active in different EU sponsored Research and Knowledge Transfer projects.

Pallab Sikdar is an Assistant Professor of Finance and Banking at Bharatiya Vidya Bhavan's Usha and Lakshmi Mittal Institute of Management (BULMIM), New Delhi (India). He holds a Bachelor's Degree in commerce and an MBA, and has submitted his doctoral thesis in the area of commercial bank risk management. His research has been published in International Journal of Bank Marketing, Journal of Business and Economics, International Journal of Business Data Communications and Networking, and Computers in Human Behavior. Mr. Sikdar has presented his work at various international and national conferences. His research interests include bank risk management, e-banking adoption, brand promotion via social media and technology enabled service delivery.

Brychan Thomas is a Visiting Professor in Innovation Policy at the University of South Wales, a Doctoral Supervisor in Entrepreneurship and Innovation at the University of Gloucestershire, and an Examiner for the International Baccalaureate Business and Management Diploma. He has a Science degree and an MSc in the Social Aspects of Science and Technology from Aston University and a PhD in Science and Technology Policy, CNAA, London. Before retiring in October 2012, he was Reader in Innovation Policy at the University of Glamorgan Business School. He has over 390 publications in the areas of science communication, entrepreneurship and innovation and small business - including 134 refereed journal articles and 130 refereed conference papers. His books include 'Triple Entrepreneurial Connection: College, Government and Industry' (2000), 'E-Commerce Adoption and Small Business in the Global Marketplace: Tools for Optimization' (2010, co-editor), 'Innovation and Small Business', Volumes 1 and 2 (2011, co-editor), author of 'Technology-Based Entrepreneurship' (2013), and co-editor of 'Academic Working Lives: Experience, Practice and Change' (hardback 2014, paperback 2015).

James G. S. Yang, M.Ph., CPA, CMA, is a Professor of Accounting at Montclair State University in Montclair, Montclair, New Jersey. He specializes in international taxation and Internet commerce taxation, and has published 123 refereed journal articles.

Index

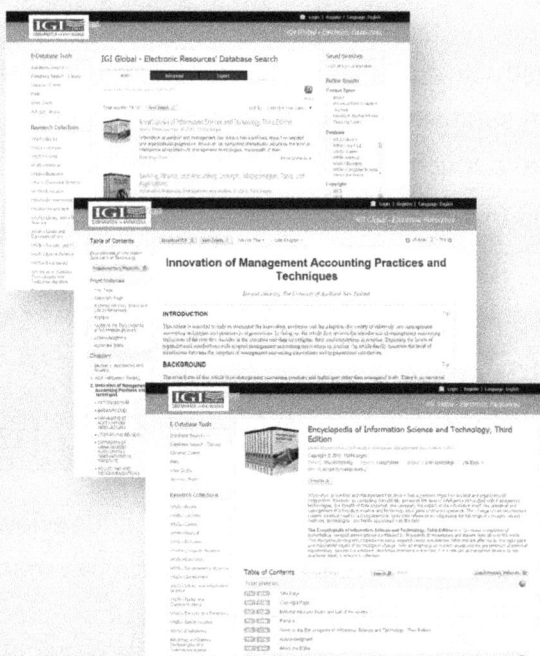

Lightning Source UK Ltd.
Milton Keynes UK
UKHW030632211218
334277UK00004B/80/P